General Securities Representative Exam

Series 7

11TH Edition

Securities License Exam Manual

SERIES 7 GENERAL SECURITIES REPRESENTATIVE EXAM
SECURITIES LICENSE EXAM MANUAL, 11TH EDITION
©2017 Kaplan, Inc.

Published in December 2017 by Kaplan Financial Education.

Printed in the United States of America.

ISBN: 978-1-4754-7073-4

Contents

2   Debt Securities   39

3   Municipal Securities   103

4   Options   163

14   Economics and Analysis   513

15   Ethics, Recommendations, and Taxation   557

16   U.S. Government and State Rules and Regulations   599

17   Other SEC and SRO Rules and Regulations   619

Introduction

INTRODUCTION

Thank you for choosing Kaplan for your educational needs, and welcome to the General Securities Representative Examination (Series 7) License Exam Manual (LEM). This manual applies adult learning principles to give you the tools you'll need to pass your exam on the first attempt.

Why Do I Need to Pass the Series 7 Exam?

The Financial Industry Regulatory Authority (FINRA) or another self-regulatory organization requires its members and employees of its members to pass a qualification exam to become registered as a General Securities Representative. You must pass the Series 7 exam to be qualified to sell all types of securities.

Are There Any Prerequisites?

There are no prerequisite exams to pass before sitting for the Series 7 exam.

What Is the Series 7 Exam Like?

The Series 7 is a 6-hour, 250-question exam administered by FINRA. It is offered as a computer-based exam at Prometric testing centers around the country.

What Score Must I Achieve to Pass?

You need a score of at least 72% on the Series 7 exam to pass and become eligible for registration as a General Securities Representative.

What Topics Will I See on the Exam?

The questions you will see on the Series 7 exam do not appear in any particular order. The computer is programmed to select a new, random set of questions for each exam taker, selecting questions according to the preset topic weighting of the exam.

Each Series 7 candidate will see the same number of questions on each topic, but a different mix of questions. The Series 7 exam is divided into five major job function areas:

Five Major Job Functions	No. of Questions	% of Exam
F1. Seeks Business for the Broker-Dealer through Customers and Potential Customers	68	27%
F2. Evaluates Customers' Other Security Holdings, Financial Situation and Needs, Financial Status, Tax Status, and Investment Objectives	27	11%
F3. Opens Accounts, Transfers Assets, and Maintains Appropriate Account Records	27	11%
F4. Provides Customers with Information on Investments and Makes Suitable Recommendations	70	28%
F5. Obtains and Verifies Customer's Purchase and Sales Instructions, Enters Orders, and Follows Up	58	23%

Test candidates should be aware that within each major job function, FINRA has identified tasks and knowledge statements that test questions are based on. The complete Series 7 General Securities Representative Qualification Examination Content Outline can be viewed on FINRA's website: *www.FINRA.org.*

When you complete your exam, you will receive a printout that identifies your performance in each of the five major job function areas.

PREPARING FOR THE EXAM

How Is the License Exam Manual Organized?

The License Exam Manual is organized in units. There is a glossary that can help clarify unfamiliar terms you come across, and an index makes it easy to locate content within the LEM. In addition to the regular text, each unit ends with a test. Look for unique features created to help you understand and comprehend the material. When additional emphasis is critical to your success, the following distinctions are made.

TAKE NOTE

Each Take Note provides special information designed to amplify important points.

TEST TOPIC ALERT

Each Test Topic Alert! highlights content that is likely to appear on the exam.

E X A M P L E   Examples provide practical applications that convert theory into understanding.

Q U I C K   Q U I Z   Quick Quizzes are a quick interactive review of what you just read. These ensure you understand and retain the material.

Additional Study Resources

To accompany and supplement your License Exam Manual your study package may contain additional study resources. Be sure to spend some time on your homepage, view the best practices video, and understand all that is available to help you study.

Securities Pro QBank

Coordinating with the LEM, the SecuritiesPro™ QBank includes a large number of questions that are similar in style and content to those you will encounter on the exam. You may use it to generate tests by a specific unit or combination of units. The QBank also allows you to create weighted mock exams that mimic your test. There is no limit on the number of QBank exams you can create.

Practice and Mastery Exams

Depending on the study package purchased, you may also have a fixed Practice Exam or a fixed Practice and Mastery Exam. These exams are designed to closely replicate the true exam experience, both in terms of the degree of difficulty and topical coverage. They provide scores and diagnostic feedback, but you will not be given access to, or be able to obtain from Kaplan, correct answers or question explanations. The Practice and Mastery Exams are sound indicators of potential actual exam scores—the better you do on these exams, the more likely you are to pass your actual exam. These may be taken just once each.

Video Library

You may also have access to various topics from our video library. These short, engaging videos cover key topics from your manual. If your package includes access to our video library, please review the topics as you complete your reading assignments in the study manual.

Exam Tips & Content Updates Link

Don't forget to monitor your Exam Tips & Content Updates. When rules and regulations change, or we want to share new information regarding your exam, it's posted there.

What Topics Are Covered in the Course?

The License Exam Manual consists of 17 Units, each devoted to a particular area of study that you will need to know to pass the Series 7. Each Unit is divided into study sections devoted to more specific areas with which you need to become familiar.

The Series 7 License Exam Manual addresses the following topics:

Unit	Topic	Unit	Topic
1	Equity Securities	10	Investment Company Products
2	Debt Securities	11	Retirement Plans
3	Municipal Securities	12	Variable Annuities
4	Options	13	Direct Participation Programs
5	Customer Accounts	14	Economics and Analysis
6	Margin Account	15	Ethics, Recommendations, and Taxation
7	Issuing Securities	16	U.S. Government and State Rules and Regulations
8	Trading Securities	17	Other SEC and SRO Rules and Regulations
9	Brokerage Support Services		

How Much Time Should I Spend Studying?

Plan to spend approximately 150–200 hours reading the material and carefully answering the questions. Spread your study time over the 6–8 weeks before the date on which you are scheduled to take the Series 7 exam. Your actual time may vary depending on your reading rate, comprehension, professional background, and study environment.

What Is the Best Way to Structure My Study Time?

The following schedule is suggested to help you obtain maximum retention from your study efforts. Remember, this is a guideline only, because each individual may require more or less time to complete the steps included.

Step 1. Read a Unit and complete the Unit Test. Review rationales for all questions whether you got them right or wrong (2–3 hours per Unit).

Step 2. Using the SecuritiesPro™ QBank, create and complete a test for each topic included under that Unit heading. For best results, select the maximum number of questions within each topic. Carefully review all rationales. Do an additional test on any topic on which you score under 65%. After completion of all topic tests, create a 125-question test comprising all Unit topics. Repeat this 125-question test until you score at least 70% (4–6 hours).

■ Do not become too overwhelmed or bogged down in any one unit. You don't want to lose sight of the finish line because you're having trouble with one hurdle. Keep moving forward. It's a steady pace that wins the race.

■ View rationales after each question initially, and spend time studying each rationale in order to learn the concepts. Later, you will want to create exam scenarios in which scores and rationales are viewed at the end of each exam.

■ Perfection is not the goal during the reading phase; scores in the mid- to high-60s are good initially.

Step 3. When you have completed all the Units in the License Exam Manual and their Unit Tests, using the SecuritiesPro™ QBank, create and complete as many 125-question tests as necessary to achieve scores of at least 80–90% consistently. Create and complete specific topic tests if necessary to correct problem areas. You should also utilize the mock weighted exam function that will generate tests weighted similar to the FINRA licensing exam (10–20 hours).

Step 4. The Online Practice Final and Mastery Exam present you with questions from the topics covered based on their weighting and emphasis on the actual exam. You will not receive rationales for the answers you select, nor will you receive immediate feedback as you take the exam. You should complete these exams while observing the time limits for the actual exam. Upon completing the exam, you will receive a diagnostic report that identifies topics for further review (3–4 hours per Exam).

Note: After completing Practice, Mastery, and Mock exams, be sure to review your Performance Tracker so you can identify areas of weakness. You can then create focused exams on topics as needed. Also, review your LEM and video library for additional help.

How Well Can I Expect to Do?

The exams administered by FINRA are not easy. You must display considerable understanding and knowledge of the topics presented in this course to pass the exam and qualify for registration.

Our practice questions were carefully crafted to simulate the actual exam. In addition, weighting was considered (i.e., the number of questions likely seen on each topic). The wording must be somewhat different, but if you understand the subject matter, you will be able to find the correct response when you sit for the test. We often add new questions to refresh our question bank, sometimes with no direct supporting information pertaining to a specific question's subject in our LEM. In that case, there will be a thorough rationale to help you capture and retain the information you need. Because complex questions require you to link different concepts together to arrive at a correct answer, dealing with questions not directly addressed in the LEM will help develop that skill.

If you study diligently, complete all sections of the course, and consistently score at least 85% on the tests, you should be well prepared to pass the exam. However, it is important for you to realize that merely knowing the answers to our questions will not enable you to pass unless you understand the essence of the information behind the question.

TEST-TAKING TIPS

Passing the exam depends not only on how well you learn the subject matter, but also on how well you take exams. You can develop your test-taking skills—and improve your score—by learning a few test-taking techniques:

- Read the full question
- Avoid jumping to conclusions—watch for hedge clauses
- Interpret the unfamiliar question
- Look for key words and phrases
- Identify the intent of the question
- Memorize key points
- Use a calculator

- Beware of changing answers
- Pace yourself

Each of these pointers is explained below, including examples that show how to use them to improve your performance on the exam.

Read the Full Question

You cannot expect to answer a question correctly if you do not know what it is asking. If you see a question that seems familiar and easy, you might anticipate the answer, mark it, and move on before you finish reading it. This is a serious mistake. Be sure to read the full question before answering it. Mistakes are often made when assuming too much (or too little).

Avoid Jumping to Conclusions—Watch for Hedge Clauses

The questions on FINRA exams are often embellished with deceptive distractors as choices. To avoid being misled by seemingly obvious answers, make it a practice to read each question and each answer twice before selecting your choice. Doing so will provide you with a much better chance of doing well on the exam.

Watch out for hedge clauses embedded in the question. (Examples of hedge clauses include the terms *if*, *not*, *all*, *none*, and *except*.) In the case of *if* statements, the question can be answered correctly only by taking into account the qualifier. If you ignore the qualifier, you will not answer correctly.

Qualifiers are sometimes combined in a question. Some that you will frequently see together are *all* with *except* and *none* with *except*. In general, when a question starts with *all* or *none* and ends with *except*, you are looking for an answer that is opposite to what the question appears to be asking.

Interpret the Unfamiliar Question

Do not be surprised if some questions on the exam seem unfamiliar at first. If you have studied your material, you will have the information to answer all the questions correctly. The challenge may be a matter of understanding what the question is asking.

Very often, questions present information indirectly. You may have to interpret the meaning of certain elements before you can answer the question. Be aware that the exam will approach a concept from different angles.

Look for Key Words and Phrases

Look for words that are tip-offs to the situation presented. For example, if you see the word *prospectus* in the question, you know the question is about a new issue. Sometimes a question will even supply you with the answer if you can recognize the key words it contains. Few questions provide blatant clues, but many do offer key words that can guide you to selecting the correct answer if you pay attention. Be sure to read all instructional phrases carefully. Take time to identify the key words to answer this type of question correctly.

Identify the Intent of the Question

Many questions on FINRA exams supply so much information that you lose track of what is being asked. This is often the case in story problems. Learn to separate the story from the question.

Take the time to identify what the question is asking. Of course, your ability to do so assumes you have studied sufficiently. There is no method for correctly answering questions if you don't know the material.

Memorize Key Points

Reasoning and logic will help you answer many questions, but you will have to memorize a good deal of information. Some memorization will be automatic as you go over the material and answer questions; some you will simply have to do systematically.

Use a Calculator

Most of the questions found on FINRA exams requiring calculations are written so that any math needed is simple in nature and function. However, using a calculator is recommended to ensure that common math errors do not lead you to incorrect answers. While test centers generally have calculators available for your use, you should have a simple function calculator with you if needed in case of test center shortages. Test center staff will advise you as to whether you may use your own calculator or not.

Avoid Changing Answers

If you are unsure of an answer, your first hunch is the one most likely to be correct. Do not change answers on the exam without good reason. In general, change an answer only if you:

- discover that you did not read the question correctly; or
- find new or additional helpful information in another question.

Pace Yourself

Some people will finish the exam early and some do not have time to finish all the questions. Watch the time carefully (your time remaining will be displayed on your computer screen) and pace yourself through the exam.

Do not waste time by dwelling on a question if you simply do not know the answer. Make the best guess you can, mark the question for *Record for Review*, and return to the question if time allows. Make sure that you have time to read all the questions so that you can record the answers you do know.

THE EXAM

How Do I Enroll in the Exam?

To obtain admission to a FINRA-adminstered exam, your firm must electronically apply for and pay a fee to FINRA through its Central Registration Depository, better known as the Web CRD®. To take the exam, you must make an appointment with a Prometric Testing Center as far in advance as possible to get the date you would like to sit for the exam.

■ Prometric secure website at **www.prometric.com**. 1-800-578-6273.

You must have your Central Registration Depository (CRD) number available when scheduling your exam. This unique personal identification number should be provided to you by your employing member firm. On a cautionary note, failure to show for an examination will be permanently recorded on your examination history on the Web CRD.

What Should I Take to the Exam?

Take one form of personal identification with your signature and photograph as issued by a government agency. No personal items, food, or drinks, including coffee and water, are permitted inside the testing room. Personal items include, but are not limited to: pens, pagers, cellular phones, watches, hats, nonmedical electronic devices, outerwear, purses, and wallets. Personal items must be kept in your assigned locker or returned to your car prior to the start of your exam. Because the testing vendor is not responsible for any personal items, the vendor encourages you to bring only your identification into the Center.

Erasable note boards and pens will be provided to you upon admittance to the testing room. If you need additional note boards or pens, please alert your proctor. The note boards and pens must be returned at the end of your exam or continuing education session.

If you need a calculator for your testing session, please see the Test Center Administrator. You will be provided with a nonprogrammable, nonprinting calculator.

Additional Trial Questions

During your exam, you may see extra (generally 10 for the Series 7 exam) trial questions. These are potential future exam-bank questions being tested during the course of the exam. These questions are not included in your final score.

Exam Results and Reports

At the end of the exam, your score will be displayed, indicating whether you passed. The next business day after your exam, your results will be mailed to your firm and to the self-regulatory organization and state securities commission specified on your application.

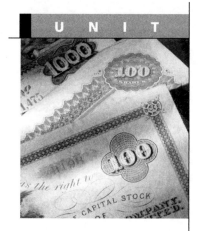

1

Equity Securities

B ecause equity is such an important capital market security, the
fundamentals that you learn in this Unit will lay the groundwork
for your success in future units. This Unit will cover common stock,
preferred stock, and related equity securities.

The investment world is divided between owners (stock or equity)
and lenders (bonds or debt). Owning equity in a company is perhaps the
most visible and accessible means by which wealth is created. Individual
investors become owners of a publicly traded company by buying stock in
that company. In so doing, they can participate in the company's growth
over time.

This Unit will cover information that will account for approximately
10–15 questions on the Series 7 exam. ■

When you have completed this Unit, you should be able to:

- **describe** the basic features of a security;

- **compare** and contrast the four classifications of common stock;

- **identify** and describe the three methods of common stock valuation;

- **list** rights, benefits, and risks of common stock ownership;

- **describe** six types of preferred stock and the unique features of each;

- **calculate** return on investment in common stock;

- **describe** the process of transferring stock ownership;

- **interpret** financial charts that report performance of equity securities;

- **compare** and contrast the features of rights and warrants; and

- **identify** and describe the features of ADRs and REITs.

1. 1 WHAT IS A SECURITY?

In the simplest terms, a **security** is an investment that represents either an ownership stake or a debt stake in a company. An investor becomes part owner in a company by buying shares of the company's stock. A **debt security** is usually acquired by buying a company's bonds. A **debt investment** is a loan to a company in exchange for interest income and the promise to repay the loan at a future maturity date. It does not confer ownership.

Stocks and bonds are normally purchased and sold on a stock exchange or in the **over-the-counter (OTC)** market. A stock exchange, such as the **New York Stock Exchange (NYSE)**, is an auction market where buyers and sellers are matched by a specialist (Designated Market Maker) who maintains a fair and orderly market for a particular set of stocks.

The OTC market is an interdealer market linked by computer terminals to **Financial Industry Regulatory Authority (FINRA)** member firms across the country. The OTC market has no physical location, and traders do not transact business face to face as they do on stock exchange floors.

1. 1. 1 EQUITY AND DEBT

Stock represents **equity** or ownership in a company, and **bonds** are a loan to a company (a debt). A company discloses the composition of its total capitalization—equity and debt—by publishing a balance sheet.

1. 1. 1. 1 The Balance Sheet

The **balance sheet** summarizes the company's:

- **assets**—what the company owns: cash in the bank, accounts receivable (money it is owed), investments, property, inventory, and so on;
- **liabilities**—what the company owes: accounts payable (current bills it must pay), short- and long-term debt, and other obligations; and
- **equity**—the excess of the value of assets over the value of liabilities (the company's net worth).

1. 1. 1. 2 Net Worth

A company's **net worth** is computed by subtracting all liabilities from the value of total assets. This computation is summarized by the basic balance sheet equation: **assets – liabilities = net worth**.

TAKE ✓ NOTE

Two ways to express this same equation are as follows:

Assets = liabilities + net worth

Assets – liabilities = net worth

1. 2 STOCK

A company issues stock as its primary means of raising business capital. Investors who buy the stock buy a share of ownership in the company's net worth. Whatever a business owns (its assets) less its creditors' claims (its liabilities) belongs to the businessowners (its stockholders).

Each share of stock entitles its owner to a portion of the company's profits and dividends and an equal vote on directors and other important matters. Most corporations are organized in such a way that their stockholders regularly vote for and elect candidates to a **board of directors (BOD)** to oversee the company's business. By electing a BOD, stockholders have some say in the company's management but are not involved with the day-to-day details of its operations.

TAKE NOTE An individual's stock ownership represents his proportionate interest in a company. If a company issues 100 shares of stock, each share represents an identical 1/100, or 1%, ownership position in the company. A person who owns 10 shares of stock owns 10% of the company; a person who owns 50 shares of stock owns 50% of the company.

1. 2. 1 COMMON STOCK

Corporations may issue two types of stock: common and preferred. When speaking of stocks, people generally refer to common stock. **Preferred stock** represents equity ownership in a corporation, but it usually does not have the same voting rights or appreciation potential as common stock. **Preferred stock** normally pays a fixed, semiannual dividend and has priority claims over common stock; that is, the preferred is paid first if a company declares bankruptcy.

Common stock can be classified as:

- authorized;
- issued;
- outstanding; and
- treasury.

1. 2. 1. 1 Authorized Stock

Authorized stock refers to a specific number of shares the company has authorization to issue or sell. This is laid out in the company's original charter. Often, a company sells only a portion of the authorized shares to raise enough capital for its foreseeable needs. The company may sell the remaining authorized shares in the future or use them for other purposes. Should the company decide to sell more shares than are authorized, the charter must be amended through a stockholder vote.

1. 2. 1. 2   Issued Stock

Issued stock has been authorized and distributed to investors. When a corporation issues, or sells, fewer shares than the total number authorized, it normally reserves the unissued shares for future needs, including:

- raising new capital for expansion;
- paying stock dividends;
- providing stock purchase plans for employees or stock options for corporate officers;
- exchanging common stock for outstanding convertible bonds or preferred stock; or
- satisfying the exercise of outstanding stock purchase warrants.

Authorized but unissued stock does not carry the rights and privileges of issued shares and is not considered in determining a company's total capitalization.

1. 2. 1. 3   Outstanding Stock

Outstanding stock includes any shares that a company has issued but has not repurchased—that is, stock that is investor owned.

1. 2. 1. 4   Treasury Stock

Treasury stock is stock a corporation has issued and subsequently repurchased from the public. The corporation can hold this stock indefinitely or can reissue or retire it. A corporation could reissue its treasury stock to fund employee bonus plans, distribute it to stockholders as a stock dividend, or under certain circumstances, redistribute it to the public in an additional offering. Treasury stock does not carry the rights of outstanding common shares, such as voting rights and the right to receive dividends.

By buying its own shares in the open market, the corporation reduces the number of shares outstanding. If fewer shares are outstanding and operating income remains the same, earnings per share increase. A corporation buys back its stock for a number of reasons, such as to:

- increase earnings per share;
- have an inventory of stock available to distribute as stock options, fund an employee pension plan, and so on; or
- use for future acquisitions.

TEST TOPIC ALERT   Expect to see a question on outstanding stock similar to the following.

ABC company has authorized 1 million shares of common stock. It issued 800,000 shares one year ago. It then purchased 200,000 shares for its treasury. How many shares of ABC stock are outstanding?

The solution requires that you know a basic formula:

Issued stock − treasury stock = outstanding stock

In applying this formula to our sample question, the solution is as follows:

800,000 − 200,000 = 600,000

Alternatively, treasury stock equals issued shares minus outstanding shares.

TAKE NOTE This question illustrates a point about FINRA exams. The question provided information about the number of shares of authorized stock, but that information was not necessary for you to solve the problem. Prepare for questions that give you more information than you need. The Series 7 exam expects you to know concepts so well that you can determine both what is and what is not essential to the solution of a problem.

1. 2. 2   COMMON STOCK VALUES

The laws of supply and demand (based largely on the perception of a company's profitability and business prospects) determine the company's stock price in the market. Although a stock's market price is the most meaningful measure of its value, other measures include par value and book value.

1. 2. 2. 1   Par Value

For investors, a common stock's **par value** is meaningless. It is an arbitrary value the company gives the stock in the company's articles of incorporation and has no effect on the stock's market price. If a stock has been assigned a par value for accounting purposes, it is usually printed on the face of the stock certificate.

When the corporation sells stock, the money received exceeding par value is recorded on the corporate balance sheet as **capital in excess of par**, also known as **paid-in surplus, capital surplus**, or **paid-in capital**.

1. 2. 2. 2   Book Value

A stock's **book value** per share is a measure of how much a common stockholder could expect to receive for each share if the corporation were liquidated. Most commonly used by analysts, the book value per share is the difference between the value of a corporation's tangible assets and its liabilities divided by the number of shares outstanding. The book value per share can—and usually does—differ substantially from a stock's market value.

1. 2. 2. 3   Market Value

Market price, the price investors must pay to buy the stock, is the most familiar measure of a stock's value. Market value is influenced by a company's business prospects and the consequent effect on **supply** (the number of shares available to investors) and **demand** (the number of shares investors want to buy).

TEST TOPIC ALERT The three methods of common stock valuation do not result in the same amount.

Par value = an arbitrary value
Book value = current liquidation value of a share
Market value = supply and demand value

The market value is most meaningful and familiar to the typical investor.

QUICK QUIZ 1.A   Match each of the following terms with the appropriate description below.

A.   Outstanding stock
B.   Authorized stock
C.   Book value
D.   Par value

_____   1.   Number of shares that a corporation is permitted to issue

_____   2.   Dollar amount assigned to a share of stock by its issuer

_____   3.   Liquidation value of each share of common stock

_____   4.   Issued stock – treasury stock

Quick Quiz answers can be found at the end of the Unit.

1. 2. 3   RIGHTS OF COMMON STOCK OWNERSHIP

Stockholders are owners of a company and therefore have certain rights that protect their ownership interests.

1. 2. 3. 1   Voting Rights

Common stockholders use their **voting rights** to exercise control of a corporation by electing a board of directors and by voting on important corporate policy matters at annual meetings, such as:

- issuance of convertible securities (dilutive to current stockholders) or additional common stock;
- substantial changes in the corporation's business, such as mergers or acquisitions; and
- declarations of stock splits (forward and reverse).

Stockholders have the right to vote on the issuance of convertible securities because they will dilute current stockholders' proportionate ownership when converted (changed into shares of common).

1. 2. 3. 1. 1   Calculating the Number of Votes

A stockholder can cast one vote for each share of stock owned. Depending on the company's bylaws and applicable state laws, a stockholder may have either a statutory or cumulative vote.

Statutory Voting. Statutory voting allows a stockholder to cast one vote per share owned for each item on a ballot, such as candidates for the BOD. A board candidate needs a simple majority to be elected.

Cumulative Voting. Cumulative voting allows stockholders to allocate their total votes in any manner they choose.

Statutory vs. Cumulative Voting

Example One: Mr. X owns 100 Shares

Statutory Voting	
Board of Directors Seat 1	100
Board of Directors Seat 2	100
Board of Directors Seat 3	100

Example Two: Mr. X owns 100 Shares

Cumulative Voting			Cumulative Voting	
Board of Directors Seat 1	175		Board of Directors Seat 1	300
Board of Directors Seat 2	50	**OR**	Board of Directors Seat 2	0
Board of Directors Seat 3	75		Board of Directors Seat 3	0

EXAMPLE   XYZ Corp. will be electing three directors at its annual meeting. Each XYZ shareholder has a number of votes equal to the number of shares owned times the number of directorships up for election. Assume a shareholder owns 100 shares. Under statutory voting, the shareholder may use a maximum of 100 votes for any one seat on the board.

Under cumulative voting, the shareholder may allocate all 300 votes to one director, giving the shareholder a greater impact.

TAKE NOTE   Cumulative voting benefits the smaller investor, whereas statutory voting benefits larger shareholders.

TEST TOPIC ALERT   Shareholders do not vote on dividend-related matters, such as when they are declared and how much they will be. They do vote on stock splits, board members, and issuance of additional equity-related securities like common stock, preferred stock, and convertible securities.

1.2.3.2   Proxies

Stockholders often find it difficult to attend the annual stockholders' meeting, so most vote on company matters by means of a **proxy,** a form of absentee ballot. After it has been returned to the company, a proxy can be automatically canceled if the stockholder attends the meeting, authorizes a subsequent proxy, or dies. When a company sends proxies to shareholders, usually for a specific meeting, it is known as a **proxy solicitation.**

Companies that solicit proxies must supply detailed and accurate information to the shareholders about the proposals to be voted on. Before making a proxy solicitation, companies must submit the information to the **Securities and Exchange Commission (SEC)** for review.

If a proxy vote could change control of a company (a **proxy contest**), all persons involved in the contest must register with the SEC as participants or face criminal penalties. This registration requirement includes anyone providing unsolicited advice to stockholders about how to vote. However, brokers who advise customers who request advice are not considered to be participants. A stockholder may revoke a proxy at any time before the company tabulates the final vote at its annual meeting.

1. 2. 3. 2. 1   Nonvoting Common Stock

Companies may issue both **voting** and **nonvoting** (or limited voting) common stock, normally differentiating the issues as Class A and Class B, respectively. Issuing nonvoting stock allows a company to raise additional capital while maintaining management control and continuity without diluting voting power.

1. 2. 3. 3   Preemptive Rights

When a corporation raises capital through the sale of additional common stock, it may be required by law or its corporate charter to offer the securities to its common stockholders before the general public. This is known as an **antidilution provision**. Stockholders then have a **preemptive right** to purchase enough newly issued shares to maintain their proportionate ownership in the corporation.

TAKE NOTE

Preemptive rights give investors the right to maintain a proportionate interest in a company's stock.

EXAMPLE

ABC has 1 million shares of common stock outstanding. Mr. X owns 100,000 shares of ABC common stock, or 10%. If ABC issues an additional 500,000 shares, Mr. X will have the opportunity to purchase 50,000 of those shares.

	Original		New		
ABC:	1,000,000 shares	+	500,000	=	1,500,000 shares
Mr. X:	100,000 shares	+	50,000	=	150,000 shares
	10%		10%		10%

1. 2. 3. 4   Limited Liability

Stockholders cannot lose more than the amount they have paid for a corporation's stock. **Limited liability** protects stockholders from having to pay a corporation's debts in bankruptcy.

1. 2. 3. 5   Inspection of Corporate Books

Stockholders have the right to receive annual financial statements and obtain lists of stockholders. Inspection rights do not include the right to examine detailed financial records or the minutes of BOD's meetings.

1. 2. 3. 6   Residual Claims to Assets

If a corporation is liquidated, the common stockholder (as owner) has a residual right to claim corporate assets after all debts and other security holders have been satisfied. The common stockholder is at the bottom of the liquidation priority list.

TAKE NOTE   Because common stock is last in line in a corporate liquidation, it is known as the most junior security.

1. 2. 4   STOCK SPLITS

Although investors and executives are generally delighted to see a company's stock price rise, a high market price may inhibit trading of the stock. To make the stock price attractive to a wider base of investors—that is, retail versus institutional investors—the company can declare a **stock split**.

1. 2. 4. 1   Forward Splits

A **forward stock split** increases the number of shares and reduces the price without affecting the total market value of shares outstanding; an investor will receive more shares, but the value of each share is reduced. The total market value of the ownership interest is the same before and after the split.

TAKE NOTE   More shares, less value = same total ownership interest before and after.

EXAMPLE   If an investor has 100 shares at $60 per share, the total value is $6,000 [100 × $60 = $6,000].

Assume a 2:1 split. To find the new number of shares, multiply the original number by 2 (the first number of the split) and then divide by 1 (the second number of the split) (100 × 2 = 200; 200 ÷ 1 = 200). Because the total value of the shares is the same before and after the split, determine the new per share value as follows:

200 × ? = 6,000 (6,000 ÷ 200 = 30). The new per share value is $30.

Assume a 5:4 split this time (original position is 100 shares at $60):

100 × 5 = 500; 500 ÷ 4 = 125. The new number of shares is 125.
125 × ? = 6,000 (6,000 ÷ 125 = 48). The new per share value is $48.

TAKE NOTE   In a forward stock split, the percentage decrease in price will always be less than the percentage increase in shares. In a 2:1 split, the number of shares doubles (a 100% increase), whereas the price of the stock is halved (a 50% decrease).

1. 2. 4. 2   Reverse Splits

A **reverse split** has the opposite effect on the number and price of shares. After a reverse split, investors own fewer shares worth more per share.

EXAMPLE   After a 1:2 reverse split, a stockholder who owned 100 shares with a market value of $5 per share will own 50 shares worth $10 per share. If operating income remains the same, earnings per share increase because fewer shares are outstanding. The rule for reverse splits is as follows:

Fewer shares, more value = same total interest before and after

Assume the original interest of 100 shares at $5:

$$100 \times \$5 = \$500$$

After a 1:4 reverse split, what is the new number and value of shares?

$100 \times \underline{1} = 100$; $100 \div \underline{4} = 25$. The new number of shares is 25.
$25 \times ? = 500$ $(500 \div 25 = 20)$. The new per share value is $20.

Not all questions on splits involve calculations. If you remember that there are more or fewer shares at lower or greater value as a result of the split, you might be able to answer the question without using math.

1. 2. 5   BENEFITS AND RISKS OF OWNING COMMON STOCK

Generally, and throughout this course, it is assumed an investor buys or owns shares of stock with the intent of selling them at a higher price in the future—buy low, sell high later. An investor who buys shares is considered **long** the stock.

An investor may also sell shares before he owns them, with the intent of buying them back at a lower price in the future—sell high, buy low later. Such a transaction, known as a **short sale**, involves borrowing shares to sell that the investor must eventually replace. An investor who sells borrowed shares is considered **short** the stock until he buys and returns the shares to the lender.

1. 2. 5. 1   Benefits of Owning Stock

People generally expect to receive financial growth, income, or both from common stock investments.

1. 2. 5. 1. 1   *Growth*

An increase in the market price of shares is known as **capital appreciation**. Historically, owning common stock has provided investors with high real returns.

1. 2. 5. 1. 2   *Income*

Many corporations pay regular quarterly **cash dividends** to stockholders. A company's dividends may increase over time as profitability increases. Dividends, which can be a significant source of income for investors, are a major reason many people invest in stocks. Issuers may also pay **stock dividends** (additional shares in the issuing company) or **property dividends** (shares in a subsidiary company or a product sample).

TEST TOPIC ALERT   Stock dividends, rather than cash dividends, are more likely to be paid by companies that wish to reinvest earnings for research and development. Technology companies, aggressive growth companies, and new companies are examples of companies likely to pay stock dividends. Property dividends are the least common form of dividend payment.

1. 2. 5. 2   Tax Effects of Selling and Owning Stock

Buying low and selling high is one of the main objectives of stock investors. When this is accomplished, investors experience **capital gains**. If the investor sells the stock at the higher price, the investor has a **realized gain** and will be responsible for taxes on the gain. If the investor does not sell the stock, the investor has an **unrealized gain**, which is not taxed. Stock gains are taxable only when they are realized.

Another reason people buy stock is to generate income from the dividends paid. Investors who receive dividends must generally pay income taxes on them. The IRS makes no exceptions for individuals. Corporations, however, receive a 70% exclusion on dividend income received from investments in other companies.

1. 2. 5. 3   Risks of Owning Stock

Regardless of their expectations, investors have no assurance of receiving the returns they expect from their investments.

1. 2. 5. 3. 1   *Market Risk*

The chance that a stock will decline in price at a time the investor needs his money is one risk of owning common stock. A stock's price fluctuates daily as perceptions of the company's business prospects change and affect the actions of buyers and sellers. Investors have no assurances that they will be able to recoup their investment in a stock at any time.

TAKE NOTE   A long investor's losses are limited to his total investment in a stock. A short seller's losses are theoretically unlimited because there is no limit to how high a stock's price may climb.

1. 2. 5. 3. 2   Decreased or No Income

Another risk of stock ownership is the possibility of dividend income decreasing or ceasing entirely if the company loses money.

1. 2. 5. 3. 3   Low Priority at Dissolution

If a company declares bankruptcy, the holders of its bonds and preferred stock have priority over common stockholders, making a company's debt and preferred shares considered to be **senior securities**. Common stockholders have only residual rights to corporate assets upon dissolution.

1. 2. 5. 4   Long and Short Positions

When a customer purchases stock to open a position, the customer is said to be long the stock. To close the position, the customer would sell the stock (a long sale). The risk of a long position is that the price of the stock falls. Maximum loss occurs if the stock becomes worthless.

When a customer sells short to open a position, the customer is selling stock he does not own. He does this by borrowing stock from a stock lender and selling the borrowed shares. The customer is taking the view that the stock will decline in price, enabling him to buy the shares back at a lower price for return to the stock lender. In this scenario, the customer profits by the difference between the short sale price and the price at which the shares are bought back. A customer who sells short is said to be short the stock. The risk to a short seller is that the price of the borrowed shares increases, forcing him to buy back at a higher price. Because there is no limit on how high a stock's price may rise, a short seller has unlimited loss potential.

QUICK QUIZ 1.B

1. Which of the following represent(s) ownership, or equity, in a company?

   I.   Corporate bonds
   II. Common stock
   III. Preferred stock
   IV. Mortgage bonds

   A. I and IV
   B. II only
   C. II and III
   D. I, II, III and IV

2. Treasury stock

   I.   has voting rights and is entitled to a dividend when declared
   II. has no voting rights and no dividend entitlement
   III. has been issued and repurchased by the company
   IV. is authorized but unissued stock

   A. I and III
   B. I and IV
   C. II and III
   D. II and IV

3. At the annual meeting of ABC Corporation, 5 directors are to be elected. Under the cumulative voting system, an investor with 100 shares of ABC would have a total of

   A. 100 votes to be cast among 5 directors
   B. 500 votes to be cast in any way the investor chooses for 5 directors
   C. 500 votes to be cast for each of 5 directors
   D. 100 votes to be cast for only 1 director

4. Cumulative voting rights

   A. benefit the large investor
   B. aid the corporation's best customers
   C. give preferred stockholders an advantage over common stockholders
   D. benefit the small investor

5. Stockholders must approve

   A. a declaration of a cash dividend
   B. a 3:1 stock split
   C. a repurchase of 100,000 shares for the treasury
   D. a declaration of a 15% stock dividend

6. If a stock undergoes a 1:5 reverse split, which of the following are TRUE?

   I. Market price per share increases.
   II. The number of shares outstanding increases.
   III. Earnings per share typically increase.

   A. I and II
   B. I and III
   C. II and III
   D. I, II and III

1. 3 PREFERRED STOCK

Preferred stock has features of both equity and debt securities. Preferred stock is an **equity security** because it represents ownership in the corporation. However, it does not normally offer the appreciation potential associated with common stock.

Like a bond, preferred stock is usually issued as a **fixed-income security** with a fixed dividend. Its price tends to fluctuate with changes in interest rates rather than with the issuing company's business prospects unless, of course, dramatic changes occur in the company's credit quality. Unlike common stock, most preferred stock is nonvoting.

Although preferred stock does not typically have the same growth potential as common stock, preferred stockholders generally have the following two advantages over common stockholders.

■ When the BOD declares dividends, owners of preferred stock receive their dividends before common stockholders.

■ If a corporation goes bankrupt, preferred stockholders have a priority claim over common stockholders on the assets remaining after creditors have been paid.

1. 3. 1   PREFERRED STOCK CHARACTERISTICS

1. 3. 1. 1   Fixed Rate of Return

A preferred stock's **fixed dividend** is a key attraction for income-oriented investors. Normally, a preferred stock is identified by its annual dividend payment stated as a percentage of its par value, usually $100. Always assume preferred par value is $100 unless stated differently.

EXAMPLE   A preferred stock with a par value of $100 that pays $6 in annual dividends is known as a 6% preferred.

The dividend of preferred stock with no par value is stated in a dollar amount, such as a $6 no-par preferred.

TAKE NOTE   Preferred stock dividends, like common stock dividends, are not guaranteed. While they are often paid semiannually, they can be paid on any schedule that is specified in each preferred class prospectus. Payment would have to be approved by the board of directors (BOD).

1. 3. 1. 2   Adjustable-Rate Preferred

Some preferred stocks are issued with **adjustable,** or **variable,** dividend rates. Such dividends are usually tied to the rates of other interest rate benchmarks, such as Treasury bill and money market rates, and can be adjusted as often as semiannually. The date of dividend adjustment is sometimes referred to as the **reset date.**

1. 3. 1. 3   Limited Ownership Privileges

Except for rare instances, preferred stock does not have voting or preemptive rights.

1. 3. 1. 4   No Maturity Date or Set Maturity Value

Although it is a fixed-income investment, preferred stock, unlike bonds, has no preset date at which it matures and no scheduled redemption date.

TAKE NOTE   Although preferred stock is an equity instrument, it fluctuates in price more like a debt instrument. The fixed rate of dividend payment causes preferred stock to trade like bonds.

EXAMPLE   Consider a 6% preferred. If interest rates are currently 8% and you want to sell your preferred, you will have to sell at a discounted price. Who would be willing to pay full value for an investment that is not paying a competitive market rate?

However, if interest rates fall to 5%, the 6% preferred will trade at a premium. Because it is offering a stream of income above the current market rate, it will command a higher price.

When interest rates rise, the preferred price falls. Conversely, when interest rates fall, the preferred stock's price rises. This exact relationship occurs in bonds and is known as the **inverse relationship** between price and interest rates.

1. 3. 2   CATEGORIES OF PREFERRED STOCK

Separate categories of preferred stock may differ in the dividend rate, in profit participation privileges, or in other ways. All, however, maintain a degree of preference over common stock. Preferred stock may have one or more of the following characteristics.

With two exceptions, preferred shareholders do not have voting rights. If a corporation defaults on its dividend payments for a certain number of payment dates or wishes to issue a new class of preferred stock equal to or senior to the existing preferred stock, shareholders will be given the right to vote.

1. 3. 2. 1   Straight Preferred

Straight preferred (noncumulative) has no special features beyond the stated dividend payment. Missed dividends are not paid to the holder.

1. 3. 2. 2   Cumulative Preferred

Buyers of preferred stock expect fixed semiannual dividend payments. The directors of a company in financial difficulty can reduce or suspend dividend payments to both common and preferred stockholders. Most likely, the corporation will never make up any dividends common stockholders miss. In contrast to this, all dividends due cumulative preferred stock accumulate on the company's books until the corporation can pay them.

When the company can resume full payment of dividends, **cumulative preferred stockholders** receive their current dividends plus the total accumulated dividends—dividends in arrears—before any dividends may be distributed to common stockholders. Therefore, cumulative preferred stock is safer than straight preferred stock.

EXAMPLE   RST Corporation has both common stock and cumulative preferred stock outstanding. Its preferred stock has a stated dividend rate of 5% (par value $100). Because of financial difficulties, no dividend was paid on the preferred stock in 2002 and 2003.

If RST wished to declare a common stock dividend in 2004, RST is required to first pay $15 in dividends to the cumulative preferred shareholders. This amount includes the dividends in arrears for 2002 ($5) and 2003 ($5), plus the $5 dividend for 2004.

1. 3. 2. 3   Convertible Preferred

A preferred stock is **convertible** if the owner can exchange each preferred share for shares of common stock.

The price at which the investor can convert is a preset amount and is noted on the stock certificate. Because the value of a convertible preferred stock is linked to the value of the issuer's common stock, the convertible preferred's price fluctuates in line with the common, provided the common stock's value is high enough to make conversion attractive.

Convertible preferred is often issued with a lower stated dividend rate than nonconvertible preferred because the investor may have the opportunity to convert to common shares and enjoy capital gains. In addition, the conversion of preferred stock into shares of common increases the total number of common shares outstanding, which decreases earnings per common share and may decrease the common stock's market value.

1. 3. 2. 4   Participating Preferred

In addition to fixed dividends, **participating preferred** stock offers its owners a share of corporate profits that remain after all dividends and interest due other securities are paid. The percentage to which participating preferred stock participates is noted on the stock certificate.

EXAMPLE   If a preferred stock is described as XYZ 6% preferred participating to 9%, the company pays its holders up to 3% in additional dividends in profitable years if the BOD declares so.

1. 3. 2. 5   Callable Preferred

Corporations often issue **callable**, or **redeemable**, preferred, which a company can buy back from investors at a stated price after a specified date. The right to call the stock allows the company to replace a relatively high fixed dividend obligation with a lower one.

When a corporation calls a preferred stock, dividend payments and conversion rights generally cease on the call date. In return for the call privilege, the corporation usually pays a premium exceeding the stock's par value at the call, such as $103 for a $100 par value stock.

TEST TOPIC ALERT   Which type of preferred stock typically has the highest stated rate of dividend, all other factors being equal?

Callable preferred; when the stock is called, dividend payments are no longer made. To compensate for that possibility, the issuer pays a higher dividend.

Of straight and cumulative preferred, which would you expect to have the higher stated rate?

Straight preferred; cumulative preferred is safer, and there is always a risk/reward trade-off. Because straight preferred has no special features, it will pay a higher stated rate of dividend.

1. 4 RETURN ON INVESTMENT

An investment's total return is a combination of the dividend income and price appreciation or decline over a given period.

1. 4. 1   DIVIDENDS

Dividends are distributions of a company's profits to its stockholders. Investors who buy stock are entitled to dividends only when the company's board of directors votes to make such distributions. Stockholders are automatically sent any dividends to which their shares entitle them.

1. 4. 1. 1   Cash Dividends

Cash dividends are normally distributed by check if an investor holds the stock certificate or are automatically deposited to a brokerage account if the shares are held in **street name** (held in a brokerage account in the firm's name to facilitate payments and delivery). Cash dividends are taxed in the year they are received.

1. 4. 1. 2   Stock Dividends

If a company uses its cash for business purposes rather than to pay cash dividends, its board of directors may declare a **stock dividend**. This is typical of many growth companies that invest their cash resources in research and development. Under these circumstances, the company issues shares of its common stock as a dividend to its current stockholders. A stock's market price declines after a stock dividend, as with a stock split, but the company's total market value remains the same.

TAKE NOTE   Stock dividends, like splits, are not taxable. The only tax effect of a stock dividend or a stock split is to reduce the investor's cost basis per share.

EXAMPLE   An investor buys 200 shares of XYZ at $60 per share for a total cost of $12,000. If XYZ were to declare and pay a 20% stock dividend, the investor would have 240 shares. Dividing $12,000 by 240 shares results in a cost basis per share of $50.

1. 4. 1. 3   Calculating Current Yield

The **current yield,** or **dividend yield**, is the annual dividend (normally four times the quarterly dividend) divided by the current market value of the stock.

You will probably be asked to calculate dividend yield on your exam.

$$\text{Dividend yield} = \frac{\text{annual dividend}}{\text{current market value of the stock}}$$

EXAMPLE

RST stock has a current market value of $50. Total dividends paid during the year were $5. What is the dividend yield?

The solution is found by dividing $5 by $50 (5 ÷ 50 = .10). The yield is 10%.

Be alert for a slightly tricky approach to this question. The question might state that RST has a current market value of $50. The most recent quarterly dividend paid was $1.25. What is the dividend yield?

The solution is found by annualizing the dividend (multiplying by 4) first. $1.25 × 4 = $5. $5 ÷ $50 = a 10% dividend yield. Remember to use annual dividends in calculating yield.

1. 5   TRANSFERABILITY OF OWNERSHIP

The ease with which stocks and other securities can be bought and sold contributes to the smooth operation of the securities markets. When an investor buys or sells a security, the exchange of money and ownership requires little or no additional action on his part.

1. 5. 1   FEATURES OF TRANSFERABLE SECURITIES

1. 5. 1. 1   The Stock Certificate

A **stock certificate** indicates the shares of a corporation a person owns. The vast majority of stock transactions are for round-lot numbers of shares—that is, share amounts evenly divisible by 100. Odd-lot transactions are share amounts of fewer than 100 shares, such as 4 or 99. Individual stock certificates may be issued for any number of shares.

TAKE NOTE

For over-the-counter (OTC) equity securities that trade at or above $175 per share, the unit of trade or round lot will be 1 share. For these securities, trades of less than 100 shares will no longer be considered odd-lot transactions and for last sale dissemination purposes will be treated as round lots.

Among other things, stock certificates identify the company's name, number of shares, and the investor's name. In addition, each certificate is printed with the security's CUSIP number.

1. 5. 1. 2 CUSIP Numbers

A **Committee on Uniform Securities Identification Procedures (CUSIP)** number is a universal security identification number. Each issue of common stock, preferred stock, corporate bond, and municipal bond has its own CUSIP number that helps identify and track the certificate if it is lost or stolen. The CUSIP number is also used in trade confirmations and correspondence regarding specific securities.

1. 5. 2 TRANSFER PROCEDURES

The **transfer** and **registration** of stock certificates are two distinct functions that, by law, cannot be performed by a single person or department operating within the same institution. Issuers typically use commercial banks and trust companies to handle these functions.

1. 5. 2. 1 Transfer Agent

The **transfer agent** for a corporation is responsible for:

- ensuring that its securities are issued in the correct owner's name;
- canceling old and issuing new certificates;
- maintaining records of ownership; and
- handling problems relating to lost, stolen, or destroyed certificates.

The transfer agent distributes additional shares in the event of a stock split or new certificates in the event of a reverse split. If a stock dividend or stock split results in fractional shares, under most circumstances the transfer agent sends the beneficial owner a check for a fractional share's value.

TAKE NOTE   In a stock split, par value changes, as does the market price of a stock. In the event of a stock split, the customer will receive the additional shares directly from the transfer agent. In addition, the investor will receive a sticker to put on his existing certificate to change its par value.

EXAMPLE   In a 2:1 split, the price of the shares and the par value of the stock are halved, whereas the number of shares outstanding doubles. It's like having two nickels instead of one dime. Unlike stock splits, with a stock dividend, par value does not change.

1. 5. 2. 2 Registrar

The registrar is a state entity. A state will generally employ the services of a bank or trust company to perform the functions of the registrar who, unlike the transfer agent, must be independent of the issuing corporation. Any stock or bond transaction requiring the registration and issuance of new certificates is routed through the state registrar as well as the transfer agent.

While the registrar does not keep a list of the names of the owners of the company's securities, the **registrar** ensures that a corporation does not have more shares outstanding than have been authorized and is also responsible for certifying that a bond represents a legal debt of the issuer. To perform these functions, the registrar will audit the issuer's transfer agent.

QUICK QUIZ 1.C

Match each of the following terms with the appropriate item below.

A. CUSIP number
B. Preemptive right
C. Current yield
D. Registrar
E. Transfer agent

_____ 1. Party responsible for recording security owners' names and holdings and delivering new securities

_____ 2. Assigned to each security for identification

_____ 3. Stockholders may maintain proportionate ownership by purchasing newly issued shares before they are offered to the public

_____ 4. Party responsible for accounting for all of an issuer's outstanding stock

_____ 5. Annualized dividend divided by current market price

1.6 TRACKING EQUITY SECURITIES

Common and preferred stock prices are listed in numerous places and formats, such as websites and daily newspapers. A stock's market price is quoted in whole dollars, also known as **points**, plus cents.

EXAMPLE

ABC stock is quoted at 83.13. How much does an investor pay for 100 shares? To determine the price of a round lot (100 shares), simply multiply by 100 (83.13 × 100 shares = $8,313.00). $8,313 is the cost for a round lot when the stock is priced at 83.13.

NYSE Composite Transactions

New York Stock Exchange Composite Prices

Tuesday, September 14, 2004

52 Weeks High	Low	Stock	Div	Yld %	PE Ratio	Sales 100s	High	Low	Last	Chg
80	40	ABCorp	.75	1	12	3329	78	71	73	- 1.50
8.38	6.50	ACM IncFd	1.01	12.4	...	178	8.25	8.13	8.13	- .13
42.63	26.88	ALFA	2.40	5.6	12	x 1265	42.63	41.25	42.63	+1.25
35	24.63	Anchor	1.48	4.9	36	1960	30	29.75	30	+ .25
27.25	25	ANR pf	2.67	10.3	...	6	26	26	26	...
6	1.88	ATT Cap wt	...	...	...	20	5.88	5.75	5.75	- .25
22.75	14	AVEMCO	.40	1.9	17	6	21.50	21.38	21.50	...
84.25	40	BrlNth	2.20	3.7	13	2701	59.38	58.25	58.75	+ .50
4.75	.50	Brooke rt	...	...	...	26	4.63	4.63	4.63	...
7	2.50	CV REIT	.25	4.0	...	10	6.38	6.25	6.25	...
3.13	2.25	CalifREIT	.40	13.9	...	3	2.88	2.88	2.88	...
39.38	17.88	Circus wi	...	...	...	14	39.25	38.88	39.25	+ .63
82.50	39.63	Dsny	.32	.6	17	6211	53.75	52	53.25	+1.25
38.38	19.50	Febar	.24	.9	13	z 1454	28	26.88	27.38	+ .25
8.75	3.63	Navistr	...	...	...	6484	4.50	4.13	4.25	...

EXPLANATORY NOTES

High-Low: High-low numbers are the highest and lowest prices for the stock in the last 52 weeks, not including yesterday's trading.

Stock: Stocks are listed alphabetically, by the company's full name (not by its abbreviation). Company names that are made up of initials appear at the beginning of the letter's list.

Div: Current annual dividend rate paid on stock, based on the latest quarterly or semiannual declaration, unless otherwise footnoted.

PE Ratio: Closing price of the stock divided by the company's earnings per share for the latest 12-month period reported. No PE shown for stocks with no profit or for preferred stocks.

Last: The price at which the stock was trading when the exchange closed for the day.

Chg: The loss or gain for the day, compared with previous session's closing price. No change at the close is indicated by ... mark.

pf: Preferred stock. Dividends paid to preferred shareholders take precedence over those on common stock. **rt:** Rights. **wi:** When- and if-issued. Stock may be authorized but not yet issued; it may be a new issue; or it may have been split. **wt:** Warrant. The right to buy a set number of shares at a specific price and until a certain date. **x:** Ex-dividend, meaning the seller of the stock, not the buyer, receives the latest declared dividend. **z:** Sales total is given in full, not in hundreds.

* This sample comprises formats, styles, and abbreviations from a variety of currently available sources and has been created for educational purposes.

1. 6. 1   EXCHANGE-LISTED STOCKS

The previous table is an example of an NYSE composite transactions listing as it might be printed in a financial publication. These consolidated stock tables present the most complete information available and report activity for the previous business day. Using the table, the stocks symbol is found in column 3.

1. 6. 1. 1   Range of Prices

Using the table, the range of prices is shown for the previous 52 weeks (columns 1 and 2) but does not include the latest trading day.

E X A M P L E   ALFA has had a 52-week high of $42.63 and a low of $26.88 per share.

1. 6. 1. 2   Stock Name and Dividend

The stock name and annual dividend follow the 52-week price range. The dividend is quoted as an annual dollar amount based on the most recent quarter. Using the table (column 4), ALFA is paying an annual dividend of $2.40 per share. The Yld column (column 5) reports the security's current yield. For ALFA, the yield is 5.6% ($2.40 ÷ 42.63 = 5.6%).

1. 6. 1. 3   PE Ratio

The **PE ratio (price-to-earnings ratio)** column (column 6) follows the Yld column (column 5). It gives the ratio of the stock's current price to its most recent 12 months earnings per share. ALFA's PE ratio is 12.

1. 6. 1. 4   Number of Shares

The Sales column (column 7) reports the number of shares traded during the day. Trading is reported in round lots of 100 shares. The entry for ALFA is 1265, which means that 126,500 shares of stock were traded.

1. 6. 1. 5   Ex-Dividend

The *x* before the sales volume entries indicates that the stock is selling **ex-dividend**, or **ex-rights**, meaning that a buyer will not receive the next dividend check.

1. 6. 1. 6   High and Low

The two columns after Sales list the daily range of prices—the stock's high and low prices for the day (columns 8 and 9). ALFA sold for a high of 42.63 and a low of 41.25. The column labeled Last (column 10) shows the final price for the day. ALFA closed at 42.63, at the top of its 52-week range.

1. 6. 1. 7   Net Change in Price

The final column (column 11) reports the **net change in price**. The net change is the difference between the closing price on the trading day reported and the previous day's closing price. ALFA closed up 1.25 points from the previous day's close.

1. 6. 2   OVER-THE-COUNTER STOCKS

Thousands of securities trade in the **over-the-counter (OTC)** market as opposed to being traded on an exchange. OTC stocks that have both national and global interest are listed on the **National Association of Securities Dealers Automated Quotation system (Nasdaq)**.

Over-the-counter stocks that do not qualify for a Nasdaq listing are referred to as non-Nasdaq stocks. These issues can be found listed on the Over-the-Counter Bulletin Board (OTCBB) or on the electronic OTC *Pink*. The electronic OTC *Pink* quotes are disseminated from the OTC Markets Group, Inc.

1. 6. 3   DIVIDEND DEPARTMENT

The **dividend department** collects and distributes cash dividends for stocks held in street name. In addition to processing cash dividends, the department handles interest payments, stock dividends, stock splits, rights offerings, warrants, and any special distributions to stockholders or bondholders.

1. 6. 3. 1   Dividend Disbursing Agent

Stockholders are sent cash, property or stock dividends, or new shares after a split. If the broker-dealer holds the securities in street name, the **dividend disbursing agent (DDA)** (in the case of dividends) or the **transfer agent** (in the case of stock splits) makes the appropriate distributions or transfers directly to the broker-dealer. The broker-dealer's dividend department then distributes the dividends or additional shares to the appropriate accounts. If a stockholder has possession of the shares, the DDA or the transfer agent contacts the stockholder directly.

1. 6. 3. 2   Dividend Disbursing Process

1. 6. 3. 2. 1   Declaration Date

When a company's board of directors approves a dividend payment, it also designates the payment date and the dividend record date. The SEC requires any corporation that intends to pay cash dividends or make other distributions to notify FINRA or the appropriate exchange at least 10 business days before the record date. This enables FINRA or exchange to establish the ex-date.

1. 6. 3. 2. 2   Ex-Dividend Date

On the basis of the dividend record date, FINRA or the exchange (if the stock is listed) posts an ex-date. The **ex-date** is one business day before the record date. Because most trades settle regular way—two business days after the trade date—a customer must purchase the stock two business days before the record date to qualify for the dividend.

TAKE NOTE

Customers are at risk for securities transactions when the trade is executed. However, for dividends only, the buyer is considered the owner as of the settlement date, not the trade date.

The word *ex* is Latin, and it means "without." If the investor wishes to purchase the stock with the dividend, they must purchase the stock before it is without the dividend—the ex-date.

On the ex-date, the stock's opening price is reduced by the amount of the dividend to compensate for the fact that customers who buy the stock that day do not qualify for the dividend. Trades executed regular way on or after the ex-date do not settle until after the record date.

Dividend Record Date. The stockholders of record on the record date receive the dividend distribution.

Payable Date. Three or four weeks after the record date, the dividend disbursing agent sends dividend checks to all stockholders whose names appear on the books as of the record date.

Cash Trades. Cash trades settle the same day, so they go ex-dividend on the day after the record date because no lag occurs between the trade date and the transaction settlement.

TAKE NOTE

DERP will help you remember the order in which the dates involving dividend distributions occur.

The order of dates is **D**eclaration, **E**x, **R**ecord, **P**ayable.

TEST TOPIC ALERT

Declaration, record, and payment are determined by the board of directors, and FINRA, or the exchange, determines ex-date.

EXAMPLE

If RST declares a cash dividend of $.75 to stockholders of record on Wednesday, June 21, the ex-date is Tuesday, June 20.

TEST TOPIC ALERT

Let's work through some scenarios involving the ex-date. The calendar below assumes a record date of June 21. Will an investor who purchases the stock on Friday, June 16, receive the dividend?

June

Sun	Mon	Tue	Wed	Thu	Fri	Sat
				1	2	3
4	5	6	7	8	9	10
11	12	13	14	15	16	17
18	19	20	21	22	23	24
25	26	27	28	29	30	

Record Date →

In this situation, the investor would receive the dividend because regular way settlement takes place two business days after the trade. Monday and Tuesday are the two business days that must be counted. The investor settles on Tuesday, June 20, which means he owns the stock before the record date and is entitled to the dividend. When is the ex-date? June 20.

But what if the transaction had taken place on Tuesday, June 20, instead? Counting the two business days required, regular way settlement would take place on Thursday, June 22. The investor would own the stock on the business day after the record date—too late to receive the dividend.

This example illustrates that June 20 is the first day the investor buys the stock without the dividend (the ex-date) when the record date is June 21. An investor must buy the stock before the ex-date to get the dividend. The seller receives the dividend if the transaction takes place on or after the ex-date.

The ex-date is one business day before the record date in transactions executed with regular way settlement.

Referring to the calendar again, assume the investor purchased the stock on Wednesday, June 21, in a cash settlement transaction. Because the settlement takes place the same day, the investor receives the dividend, and he owns the stock on the record date of June 21. The ex-date in this circumstance is the business day after the record date.

1. 6. 3. 3   Stock Dividends and Splits

Normal stock dividends are handled the same as cash dividends. A stock distribution of 25% or more of the shares outstanding is subject to **special handling**. The same is true of stock splits where total shares outstanding increase by 25% or more. The ex-date on stock dividends of 25% or more and stock splits of 5 for 4 or better is the first business day following the payable date.

1. 6. 3. 4   Due Bills

A **due bill** is a printed statement showing a buyer's right to a dividend. If securities are purchased before the ex-date but, for whatever reason, settle after the record date, the wrong party (the seller) will receive the dividend from the issuer. In this case the buyer's firm will send a due bill to the seller's firm demanding remittance of the dividend.

1. 7   RIGHTS AND WARRANTS

1. 7. 1   CHARACTERISTICS OF RIGHTS

1. 7. 1. 1   Issuance

Existing stockholders have **preemptive rights** that entitle them to maintain their proportionate ownership in a company by buying newly issued shares before the company offers them to the general public. A **rights offering** allows stockholders to purchase common stock below the current market price. The rights are valued separately from the stock and trade in the secondary market during the subscription period.

A stockholder who receives rights may:

- exercise the rights to buy stock by sending the rights certificates and a check for the required amount to the rights agent;
- sell the rights and profit from their market value (rights certificates are negotiable securities); or
- let the rights expire and lose their value.

1. 7. 1. 2   Subscription Right Certificate

A **subscription right** is a certificate representing a short-term (typically 30 to 45 days) privilege to buy additional shares of a corporation. One right is issued for each common stock share outstanding.

1. 7. 1. 3   Terms of the Offering

The **terms** of a rights offering are stipulated on the subscription right certificates mailed to stockholders. The terms describe how many new shares a stockholder may buy, the price, the date the new stock will be issued, and the final date for exercising the rights.

EXAMPLE   ABC Co. plans to raise capital by issuing additional stock and, on April 1, declares a rights offering. Common stockholders as of May 1, the record date, can subscribe to one new share, at a price of $30, for each 10 shares of stock they own. ABC stock trades in the open market for $41 per share. The rights will expire on June 18.

The corporation will issue rights to stockholders of record May 1. Stock is traded cum rights until the ex-date. An investor who buys stock **cum rights** receives the right. An investor who buys stock **ex-rights** does not.

The number of rights required to buy one new share is based on the number of shares outstanding and the number of new shares offered.

EXAMPLE   ABC has 10 million shares outstanding and will issue 1 million additional shares. Because each existing share is entitled to one right, the company will issue 10 million rights. Because 10 million rights entitle stockholders to buy 1 million shares, it will require 10 rights to buy one new share.

TEST TOPIC ALERT   Rights have a theoretical value based on the savings to investors, who then purchase stock below the market price.

Before the ex-date, when the stock is trading with rights, the value of a right is found using the cum rights formula. Consider the following: ABC's price per share is $41; the subscription per share is $30. Ten rights are needed to purchase one share of stock. The value of one right is found as follows:

$$\frac{\text{Market price} - \text{subscription price}}{\text{Number of rights to purchase 1 share} + 1}$$

$$\frac{41 - 30}{10 + 1} = \frac{11}{11} = \$1$$

On the morning of the ex-date, the market price typically drops by the value of the right. Use the ex-rights formula to determine the value of a right after the ex-date. The ex-rights formula is:

$$\frac{\text{Market price} - \text{subscription price}}{\text{Number of rights to purchase 1 share}}$$

If ABC had dropped after the ex-date to $40 (reduced by the $1 value of the right), the solution is:

$$\frac{40 - 30}{10} = \frac{10}{10} = \$1$$

TAKE NOTE   In dealing with any question on the value of a right, you will not have to adjust market price. The questions deal only with value, so your only decision is whether to divide MP-SP by N or N + 1. The easy way to remember is this: if you are asked the value of a right before the ex-date (cum rights), use the 1. If you are asked the value of a right on or after the ex-date, don't use the 1. Cum means "with" whereas ex means "without."

1. 7. 1. 4   Standby Underwriting

If the current stockholders do not subscribe to all the additional stock, the issuer may offer unsold rights to an investment banker in a standby underwriting. A **standby underwriting** is done on a firm commitment basis, meaning the underwriter buys all unsold shares from the issuer and then resells them to the general public.

1. 7. 2   CHARACTERISTICS OF WARRANTS

A **warrant** is a certificate granting its owner the right to purchase securities from the issuer at a specified price (normally higher than the current market price) as of the date of issue of the warrant. Warrants represent the right to purchase shares but, in and of themselves, do not represent ownership. Therefore, warrant holders do not have voting rights like shareholders do until they exercise the warrants and become shareholders. Unlike a right, a warrant is usually a long-term instrument, giving the investor the choice of buying shares at a later date at the exercise price.

TAKE NOTE
Warrants typically have a life of five years, but in the past, perpetual warrants have been issued, which do not expire.

1. 7. 2. 1   Origination of Warrants

Warrants are usually offered to the public as **sweeteners,** or inducements, in connection with other securities, such as bonds or preferred stock, to make those securities more attractive. Such offerings are often bundled as **units.**

After issuance, the warrants are detachable and trade separately from the bond or preferred stock. When first issued, a warrant's exercise price is set well above the stock's market price. If the stock's price increases above the exercise price, the owner can exercise the warrant and buy the stock below the market price or sell the warrant in the market.

Rights	Warrants
Short term	Long term
On issuance, exercise price below market price	On issuance, exercise price higher than market price
May trade with or separate from the common stock	May trade with or separate from the units
Offered to existing shareholders with preemptive rights	Offered as a sweetener for another security

TAKE NOTE
The long-term nature of warrants is said to be attractive to speculators because of the leverage it offers. Warrants also allow issuers to offer bonds or preferred stock at an interest or dividend rate lower than the market rate because the issuer is offering investors something extra: the long-term right to buy stock at a fixed price.

1. 8 AMERICAN DEPOSITARY RECEIPTS

American depositary receipts (ADRs) are U.S. securities that facilitate the trading of foreign stocks in U.S. markets. An ADR is a negotiable security that represents a receipt for shares of stock in a non-U.S. corporation, usually from 1 to 10 shares. ADRs are bought and sold in the U.S. securities markets like stock.

1. 8. 1   CHARACTERISTICS OF ADRs

1. 8. 1. 1   Custodian Bank

Foreign branches of large commercial U.S. banks issue ADRs. A custodian, typically a bank in the issuer's country, holds the shares of foreign stock that the ADRs represent. The stock must remain on deposit as long as the ADRs are outstanding because the ADRs are the depository bank's guarantee that it holds the stock.

1. 8. 1. 2   Rights of ADR Owners

ADR owners have most of the rights common stockholders normally hold. These include the right to receive dividends when declared. Generally, ADRs do not have voting rights, though some ADR issuers will pass on voting rights to the holders of ADRs. As for preemptive rights, the issuing bank sells off the rights and distributes the proceeds pro rata to holders.

1. 8. 1. 2. 1   Delivery of Foreign Security

ADR owners have the right to exchange their ADR certificates for the foreign shares they represent. They can do this by returning the ADRs to the depository banks, which cancel the ADRs and deliver the underlying stock.

1. 8. 1. 2. 2   Taxes on ADRs

In most countries a withholding tax on dividends is taken at the source. In the case of investors holding ADRs this would be a foreign income tax. The foreign income tax may be taken as a credit against any U.S. income taxes owed by the investor.

1. 8. 1. 3   Currency Risk

In addition to the normal risks associated with stock ownership, ADR investors are subject to **currency risk**, the possibility that an investment denominated in one currency could decline if the value of that currency declines in its exchange rate with the U.S. dollar. Currency exchange rates are an important consideration because ADRs represent shares of stock in companies located in foreign countries.

T A K E   N O T E   Dividends are declared in the foreign currency but are payable in U.S. dollars, lending to currency risk.

1. 8. 1. 4   Registered Owner

ADRs are registered on the books of the U.S. banks responsible for them. The individual investors in the ADRs are not considered the stock's registered owners. ADRs are registered on the books of U.S. banks, so dividends are sent to the custodian banks as registered owners. The banks collect the payments and convert them into U.S. dollars.

1. 8. 1. 5   Sponsored ADRs

All exchange-listed ADRs are sponsored—that is, the foreign company sponsors the issue to increase its ownership base. Issuers that sponsor ADRs provide holders with financial statements in English. Sponsored ADRs are sometimes referred to as American Depositary Shares (ADSs). Nonsponsored ADRs are issued by banks without the assistance and participation of the issuer.

1. 9   REAL ESTATE INVESTMENT TRUSTS (REITs)

A **REIT** is a company that manages a portfolio of real estate investments in order to earn profits for shareholders. REITs are normally traded publicly and serve as a source of long-term financing for real estate projects. A REIT pools capital in a manner similar to an investment company, and shareholders receive dividends from investment income or capital gains distributions.

REITs are organized as trusts where investors buy shares or certificates of beneficial interest either on stock exchanges or in the OTC market. Under the guidelines of Subchapter M of the Internal Revenue Code, a REIT can avoid being taxed as a corporation by having at least 75% of total investment assets in real estate, deriving at least 75% of gross income from rents or mortgage interest, and distributing 90% or more of its net investment income to its shareholders.

1. 9. 1   EQUITY, MORTGAGE, AND HYBRID REITS

REITs can be set up to have different portfolio structures. When the trusts own property, they are known as **equity REITs**. When the trusts own mortgages on property, they are known as **mortgage REITs**. Those that hold both are **hybrid REITs**.

Reasons that an investor might include REITs in their investment portfolio include the following:

- REITs allow investors the opportunity to invest in real estate without incurring the degree of liquidity risk historically associated with real estate because REITs trade on exchanges and OTC.

- REITs can provide some hedge to price movements in other equity markets. While it isn't always the case, real estate prices historically have had a negative correlation to stock prices.

- REITs provide a reasonable expectation of income from dividends and capital appreciation due to the appreciation of the assets the trust holds.

Risks generally associated with REITs include the following:

- The investor has no direct control over the portfolio and relies on professional management to make all purchase and sale decisions. While the expectation of having a professionally managed portfolio should be considered advantageous, the quality of the portfolio lies with the quality of the professional management.

- Problematic loans within mortgage REIT portfolios can cause decreases in income flow and diminish capital returns.

- Dividends paid by the trusts do not meet the requirements of qualified dividends and therefore are taxable at full ordinary income tax rates to the investor.

TEST TOPIC ALERT

ADRs:

■ No preemptive rights

■ Dividends in dollars

■ Currency risk

REITs:

■ Not a limited partnership

■ Not an investment company

■ Pass through income, not losses

■ 75% of total investment assets in real estate

■ 75% of gross income from rents or mortgage interest

■ Must distribute 90% or more of income to shareholders to avoid taxation as a corporation

■ Trade on exchanges or OTC

■ Dividends received from REITS are taxed as ordinary income

QUICK QUIZ 1.D

1. ADRs are used to facilitate

   A. the foreign trading of domestic securities
   B. the foreign trading of U.S. government securities
   C. the domestic trading of U.S. government securities
   D. the domestic trading of foreign securities

2. Which of the following are characteristics of a REIT?

   I.   It is traded on an exchange or over the counter.
   II. It is professionally managed.
   III. It passes through both gains and losses to investors.
   IV. It is a type of limited partnership.

   A. I and II
   B. I, II and III
   C. III and IV
   D. I, II, III and IV

3. All of the following characteristics are advantages of a REIT investment EXCEPT

   A. liquidity
   B. tax deferral
   C. diversification
   D. professional management

4. To avoid taxation at the corporate level, REITs must derive at least 75% of their income from real property and must distribute to shareholders

   A. 75% of net income
   B. 90% of net income
   C. 95% of net income
   D. 98% of net income

UNIT TEST

1. The board of directors is responsible for setting all of the following EXCEPT

    A. declaration date
    B. payable date
    C. ex-dividend date
    D. record date

2. ABC common stock is currently selling for $150 per share with a quarterly dividend of $1.50. The current yield for ABC common stock is

    A. 1%
    B. 4%
    C. 12.5%
    D. 25%

3. ABC Corporation has declared a record date of Thursday, May 17, for its next quarterly cash dividend. When is the last day the investor could purchase the stock regular way and receive the dividend?

    A. Monday, May 14
    B. Tuesday, May 15
    C. Wednesday, May 16
    D. Thursday, May 17

4. Which of the following statements regarding warrants is TRUE?

    A. Warrants give the holder a perpetual interest in the issuer's stock.
    B. The term of a warrant is generally shorter than the term of a right.
    C. Warrants are issued with other securities to make the offering more attractive.
    D. Warrants are safer than corporate bonds.

5. Which of the following have equity positions in a corporation?

    I. Common stockholders
    II. Preferred stockholders
    III. Convertible bondholders
    IV. Mortgage bondholders

    A. I and II
    B. I and III
    C. II and III
    D. III and IV

6. The following chart shows the capital transactions of ABC Corporation.

Date	Event	Amount
10-19-96	Initial offering	6 million shares
4-1-00	Treasury purchase	500,000 shares

ABC wants to raise additional capital by selling 2 million shares through a rights offering and engages an underwriter on a standby basis. By expiration date, ABC was able to sell only 1 million shares to existing shareholders. After expiration, how many shares does ABC have outstanding?

    A. 6.5 million
    B. 7.0 million
    C. 7.5 million
    D. 8.0 million

7. An ADR represents

    A. a U.S. security in a foreign market
    B. a foreign security in a domestic market
    C. a U.S. security in both a domestic and a foreign market
    D. a foreign security in both a domestic and a foreign market

8. If a corporation attaches warrants to a new issue of debt securities, which of the following would be a resulting benefit?

    A. Dilution of shareholders' equity
    B. Reduction of the debt securities' interest rate
    C. Reduction of the number of shares outstanding
    D. Increase in earnings per share

9. Treasury stock

 I. has voting rights and is entitled to a dividend when declared

 II. has no voting rights and no dividend entitlement

 III. has been issued and repurchased by the company

 IV. is authorized but unissued stock

 A. I and III

 B. I and IV

 C. II and III

 D. II and IV

10. REITs must

 I. invest all of their assets in real estate–related activities

 II. distribute at least 90% of their net investment income

 III. be organized as trusts

 IV. pass along losses to shareholders

 A. I and II

 B. II and III

 C. II and IV

 D. III and IV

11. In a portfolio containing common stock, preferred stock, convertible preferred stock, and guaranteed common stock, changes in interest rates would be most likely to affect the market price of the

 A. common

 B. preferred

 C. convertible preferred

 D. guaranteed

12. Holders of both XYZ preferred stock and common shares are paid an annual dividend of $5 per share and then share equally in further dividends up to $1 per share in any one year. In these circumstances, the preferred stock is known as

 A. cumulative

 B. adjustable

 C. participating

 D. convertible

13. ABC Corp. has outstanding a 10% noncumulative preferred stock. Two years ago, ABC omitted its preferred dividend. Last year, it paid a dividend of $5 per share. In order to pay a dividend to common shareholders, each preferred share must be paid a dividend of

 A. $5

 B. $10

 C. $15

 D. $25

14. Shareholder approval is required for all of the following corporate events EXCEPT

 A. stock splits

 B. the acceptance of a tender offer

 C. stock dividends

 D. the issuance of convertible bonds

15. Which of the following statements regarding dividend payments on common stock is TRUE?

 A. They must be paid if the corporation has earnings.

 B. Dividend payments are always in direct proportion to corporate earnings.

 C. Dividends are sometimes paid before preferred stockholders receive theirs.

 D. Dividends on common stock are paid at the discretion of the board of directors and may be paid whether there are earnings or not.

16. An investor owns 3,000 shares of a low-priced common stock. After a 1:6 reverse split, how many shares would he hold?

 A. 500

 B. 3,000

 C. 5,000

 D. 18,000

17. A corporation has a 2:1 stock split. Before the split, there were 1 million shares of $10 par common stock outstanding. Which of the following is(are) TRUE?

    I. The par value remains at $10 per share.
    II. The par value is now $5 per share.
    III. There are still 1 million shares outstanding.
    IV. There are now 2 million shares outstanding.

    A. I and III
    B. II and III
    C. II and IV
    D. III and IV

18. If your client wished to purchase a preferred stock that would offer him the highest likelihood of assured income plus the opportunity to take part in the growth of the company's common stock, which of these features might he consider?

    I. Callable
    II. Convertible
    III. Cumulative
    IV. Straight

    A. I and II
    B. I and III
    C. II and III
    D. II and IV

19. All of the following accurately describe a warrant EXCEPT

    A. it is a sweetener to bond issues
    B. it is a long-term option to buy stock at a set price
    C. no voting rights are involved
    D. each warrant allows the owner to purchase a fractional share of the stock

20. If ABC Corp. has a 6% participating preferred, the 6% represents the

    A. dividend payment
    B. maximum dividend payment
    C. maximum dividend, but not the minimum
    D. minimum dividend, but not the maximum

ANSWERS AND RATIONALES

1. **C.** The ex-date for a distribution is set by the appropriate self-regulatory organization. The issuer determines the other dates listed.

2. **B.** To calculate current yield, the quarterly dividend must be annualized ($1.50 × 4 = $6). The $6 annual dividend ÷ the $150 market price = 4%.

3. **B.** To receive a cash dividend, an investor must be owner of record as of the close of business on record date. Because regular way settlement is 2 business days, the customer must purchase the stock no later than Tuesday, May 15. If the investor waits until Wednesday, May 16, to purchase the stock, the investor will not receive the dividend because the trade will settle on Friday, May 18. Wednesday, May 16, is the ex-date, which is the first day the stock trades without the dividend. For regular way trades, the ex-date is 1 business day before the record date.

4. **C.** Warrants are generally issued with bond offerings as a sweetener. Warrants are long-term options to buy stock and, because they are equity securities, warrants are junior in safety to bonds.

5. **A.** Common and preferred stockholders have equity positions, or ownership positions. Bondholders (mortgage or otherwise) are creditors, not stockholders.

6. **C.** Before the rights offering, the company had 5.5 million shares outstanding (6 million issued − 500,000 treasury shares). In connection with the offering, ABC engages a standby underwriter, which commits to purchasing any unsold shares. Therefore, regardless of the number of shares initially subscribed to, all 2 million shares will be sold.

7. **B.** ADR stands for American depositary receipt. ADRs are receipts issued by U.S. banks. They represent ownership of a foreign security and are traded in U.S. securities markets.

8. **B.** Usually, a warrant is issued as a sweetener to make the debt instrument more marketable. This enhancement allows the issuer to pay a slightly lower rate of interest. A warrant may be issued together with an issue of bonds or preferred stock, entitling the owner to purchase a given number of common shares at a specific price for a certain number of years.

9. **C.** Treasury stock is stock a corporation has issued and subsequently repurchased from the public in the secondary market. It does not carry the rights of other common shares, such as voting rights, rights to dividends, or preemptive rights.

10. **B.** Real estate investment trusts (REITs) engage in real estate activities and can qualify for favorable tax treatment if they invest at least 75% of their assets in real estate–related activities (not all of their assets) and pass through at least 90% of their net investment income to their shareholders. Although they can pass through income, they cannot pass through any losses; they are not DPPs.

11. **B.** Preferred stock most closely resembles bonds; therefore, it would be the most sensitive to interest rates among the alternatives listed. Convertible preferred stock is influenced by the common stock because it is convertible into the underlying security. Guaranteed common stock is common stock whose dividends are guaranteed by another corporation.

12. **C.** Participating preferred stock allows for an increase in the stated dividend when the common dividend is increased. Cumulative preferred requires that dividends in arrears be paid before the current dividend can be paid. Adjustable refers to an adjustable dividend rate. Convertible preferred can be converted into the issuer's common shares.

13. **B.** The company must pay the full stated dividend of $10 per preferred share in order to pay any dividends to the common shares. Note that this is straight, or noncumulative, preferred.

14. **C.** Shareholder approval is not required for the payment of dividends. Shareholder approval is normally required for actions that increase or potentially increase the number of shares outstanding, such as stock splits and the issuance of convertible bonds. A corporation's acceptance of a tender offer requires shareholder approval.

15. **D.** Dividends on common stock are variable and are never paid ahead of preferred stockholders. The board decides how much of the earnings to pay out as a dividend and may, in fact, decide to keep all of the earnings (or a very high percentage of the earnings) if the money is needed for future expansion, new equipment, and so on.

16. **A.** In a reverse split, we have fewer shares than before. Therefore, a 1:6 reverse split would give us ⅙ of the previous 3,000 shares, or 500 shares.

17. **C.** When a stock splits, the par value is always reduced (unless it is a reverse split, in which case the par value is increased). We will have twice as many shares worth half as much each.

18. **C.** The callable feature does nothing to ensure an investor income, whereas a cumulative preferred means that the common stockholder will never receive a dividend until the cumulative stockholder receives all current and prior dividends due the preferred. The only way to take part in the growth of the company's common stock would be to have an opportunity to obtain that common stock (the convertible feature).

19. **D.** The usual terms of a warrant permit the investor to purchase 1 share of the common stock for each warrant held. One other point to remember about warrants is that warrant holders do not receive dividends.

20. **D.** If ABC Corp. has a 6% participating preferred, the 6% represents the minimum expected dividend payment. Although this dividend is not guaranteed, no dividends can be paid on common if any of the preferred is unpaid. The key to participating preferred is that it also shares in the common dividend to which, theoretically, there is no maximum.

QUICK QUIZ ANSWERS

Quick Quiz 1.A

1. **B.**

2. **D.**

3. **C.**

4. **A.**

Quick Quiz 1.B

1. **C.** Owning either common or preferred stocks represents ownership, or equity, in a corporation. The other two choices represent debt instruments. Clients purchasing corporate or mortgage bonds are considered lenders, not owners.

2. **C.** Treasury stock is stock a corporation has issued but subsequently repurchased from investors in the secondary market. The corporation can either reissue the stock at a later date or retire it. Stock that has been repurchased by the corporation has no voting rights and is not entitled to any declared dividends.

3. **B.** With cumulative voting rights, this investor may cast 500 votes for the 5 directors in any way the investor chooses.

4. **D.** The cumulative method of voting gives an investor 1 vote per share owned times the number of directorships to be elected. For example, if an investor owns 100 stock shares and there are 5 directorships to be elected, the investor will have a total of 500 votes. The stockholder may cast all of his votes for one candidate, thereby giving the small investor more voting power.

5. **B.** Shareholder approval is required to change the stated value of stock, which occurs with a stock split. Decisions regarding payment of dividends or repurchase of stock are made by the board of directors (management only) since these are considered operational decisions.

6. **B.** After a reverse split, there will be fewer shares outstanding. As a result, market price and earnings per share should increase.

Quick Quiz 1.C

1. **E.**

2. **A.**

3. **B.**

4. **D.**

5. **C.**

Quick Quiz 1.D

1. **D.** ADRs are tradable securities issued by banks, with the receipt's value based on the underlying foreign securities held by the bank.

2. **A.** REITs are traded on exchanges and OTC, and they are professionally managed. REITs share some features with a limited partnership, but they are a different type of business entity. Both REITs and limited partnerships provide pass-through of gains to investors, but REITs do not provide pass-through of losses.

3. **B.** A REIT is a professionally managed company that invests in a diversified portfolio of real estate holdings. Many REITs are actively traded on exchanges and OTC, thereby providing liquidity. REIT portfolio losses are not passed through to investors.

4. **B.** REITs must distribute at least 90% of their net investment income to shareholders to avoid corporate taxation.

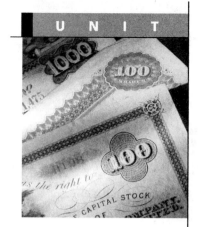

2

Debt Securities

This Unit reviews the process of issuers borrowing money from investors through the sale of bonds. When an investor loans money to the issuer, the issuer must make regular interest payments for the use of the funds. Because of the fixed interest payments that an investor receives, debt securities are also known as fixed-income securities.

Corporations, municipalities, and the U.S. government are issuers of debt securities. Each issuer has unique features, but overall they share many characteristics.

The Series 7 exam asks approximately 15–25 questions on the features of corporate and government debt, money market instruments, and interest rates. ■

When you have completed this Unit, you should be able to:

■ **list** and describe basic characteristics of all debt instruments;

■ **discuss** the inverse relationship between bond prices and yields;

■ **define** and explain the relationship between current yield, yield to maturity, and yield to call;

■ **identify** unique features of corporate debt instruments;

■ **calculate** conversion parity;

■ **compare** three different types of marketable government securities;

■ **name** and describe the most common agency issues;

■ **identify** the features and risks of CMOs;

■ **list** and describe money market instruments;

■ **name** the benchmark interest rates in our economy;

■ **describe** eurodollars and foreign exchange risk;

■ **interpret** debt instrument quotations from financial charts and tables; and

■ **calculate** accrued interest.

2. 1 CHARACTERISTICS OF BONDS

Unlike stockholders, **bondholders** have neither ownership interest in the issuing corporation nor voice in management. As creditors, bondholders receive preferential treatment over common and preferred stockholders if a corporation files for bankruptcy. Bonds are considered senior securities because creditor claims are settled before the claims of stockholders. Therefore, stockholders' interests are subordinate to those of bondholders.

2. 1. 1 ISSUERS

Corporations issue bonds to raise working capital or funds for capital expenditures such as plant construction or equipment and other major purchases. Corporate bonds with maturities of five years or more are commonly referred to as **funded debt**.

The federal government is the nation's largest borrower and the most secure credit risk. Treasury bills (less than one year), notes (2- to 10-year maturities), and bonds (maturities of more than 10 years) are backed by the full faith and credit of the government and its unlimited taxing powers.

Municipal securities are the debt obligations of state and local governments and their agencies. Most are issued to raise capital to finance public works or construction projects that benefit the general public.

2. 1. 2 INTEREST

Both the interest rate an issuer pays its bondholders and the timing of payments are set when a bond is issued. The interest rate, or **coupon**, is calculated from the bond's par value. **Par value**, also known as **face value**, is normally $1,000 per bond, meaning each bond will be redeemed for $1,000 when it matures. Interest on a bond accrues daily and is paid in semiannual installments over the life of the bond.

The final semiannual interest payment is made when the bond matures, and it is combined with repayment of the principal amount. If a bondholder has been receiving semiannual payments of $350 from 10 bonds, he will receive a check for $10,350 when the bonds mature.

TEST TOPIC ALERT

Be prepared to solve a question similar to the following:

An investor purchases 5M ABC J&J 15 8s of '21. What will the investor receive at maturity of the bond?

To solve the problem, decode the bond quote first.

5M: Five $1,000 bonds, or a total principal amount of $5,000

ABC: The issuer of the bond; it is a corporate bond because of its three-letter name (corporate stock and bond symbols are from one to five letters).

J&J 15: The bond pays interest on January 15 and July 15 each year. If there is no 15, assume interest is paid on the first of the month. The interest dates are six months apart. An M&S bond pays interest on March 1 and September 1.

8s: The bond pays a stated rate of interest of 8% annually. This is known as the coupon or nominal or stated rate of interest.

'21: The investor will receive the principal at the bond's maturity in 2021.

Now back to the original question. The investor will receive the full principal plus the last semiannual interest payment when the bond matures.

Bond principal:	$5,000	(Annual interest is $80 per thousand;
Semiannual interest:	+ 200	with $5,000 face value, the semiannual
Total at maturity:	$5,200	interest is $200.)

2. 1. 3 MATURITIES

On the **maturity date**, the loan principal is repaid to the investor. Each bond has its own maturity date. The most common maturities fall in the 5- to 30-year range. Three basic types of bond maturity structures are term, serial, and balloon.

2. 1. 3. 1 Term Maturity

A **term bond** is structured so that the principal of the whole issue matures at once. Because all of the principal is repaid at one time, issuers may establish a sinking fund account to accumulate money to retire the bonds at maturity.

2. 1. 3. 2 Serial Maturity

A **serial bond issue** schedules portions of the principal to mature at intervals over a period of years until the entire balance has been repaid.

2. 1. 3. 3 Balloon Maturity

An issuer sometimes schedules its bond's maturity using elements of both serial and term maturities. The issuer repays part of the bond's principal before the final maturity date, as with a serial maturity, but pays off the major portion of the bond at maturity. This bond has a **balloon**, or **serial and balloon**, maturity.

2. 1. 3. 4 Series Issues

Instead of placing all of its bonds in the hands of investors at one time, any bond issuer may spread out its borrowing over several years as its needs dictate by issuing the bonds in separate series.

2. 1. 4 BOND CERTIFICATE

Bonds were traditionally issued as **certificates**—physical evidence that designates the bond's ownership and characteristics: in essence, an IOU. All bond certificates contain basic information, including the:

- name of issuer;
- interest rate and payment date;
- maturity date;
- call features;

- principal amount;
- CUSIP number for identification;
- dated date—the date that interest starts accruing; and
- reference to the bond indenture.

2. 1. 4. 1   Registration of Bonds

Bonds are **registered**, in varying degrees, to record ownership should a certificate be lost or stolen. Tracking a bond's ownership through its registration has been common in the United States only since the early 1970s.

2. 1. 4. 2   Coupon (Bearer) Bonds

Though no longer issued, in past years most bonds were issued in coupon, or bearer, form. Issuers kept no records of purchasers, and securities were issued without an investor's name printed on the certificate. Coupon bonds are not registered, so whoever possesses them can collect interest on, sell, or redeem the bonds.

Interest coupons are attached to bearer bonds, and holders collect interest by clipping the coupons and delivering them to an issuer's paying agent. Individual coupons are payable to the bearer. When a bond matures, the bearer delivers it to the paying agent and receives the principal.

No proof of ownership is needed to sell a bearer bond. Even though bearer bonds are not issued today, the term *coupon* is still used to describe interest payments received by bondholders.

2. 1. 4. 3   Registered Bonds

A common form of bond issued today is the **registered bond**. When a registered bond is issued, the issuer's transfer agent records the bondholder's name. The buyer's name appears on the bond certificate's face.

2. 1. 4. 3. 1   Fully Registered

When bonds are registered as to both principal and interest, the transfer agent maintains a list of bondholders and updates this list as bond ownership changes. Interest payments are automatically sent to bondholders of record. The transfer agent transfers a registered bond whenever a bond is sold by canceling the seller's certificate and issuing a new one in the buyer's name. Most corporate bonds are issued in fully registered form.

2. 1. 4. 3. 2   Registered as to Principal Only

Principal-only registered bonds have the owner's name printed on the certificate, but the coupons are in **bearer form**. When bonds registered as to principal only are sold, the names of the new owners are recorded (in order) on the bond certificates and on the issuer's registration record. Like coupon bonds, bonds registered as to principal only are no longer issued.

2. 1. 4. 4 Book-Entry Bonds

Book-entry bond owners do not receive certificates. Rather, the transfer agent maintains the security's ownership records. Although the names of buyers of both registered and book-entry bonds are recorded (registered), the book-entry bond owner does not receive a certificate, but the registered bond owner does. The trade confirmation serves as evidence of book-entry bond ownership. Most U.S. government bonds are available only in book-entry form.

2. 1. 4. 5 Denominations

Bearer bonds were issued only in denominations of $1,000 and $5,000. Registered bonds are available in $1,000 denominations or multiples of $5,000 (e.g., $5,000, $10,000, or $20,000) up to $100,000 per certificate.

TEST TOPIC ALERT   The exam might ask which form a bond must be in for an investor to receive interest and principal payments by mail. Bonds must be fully registered or in book-entry form.

New bonds are issued only in fully registered and book-entry form. Even though bonds with coupons attached have not been issued since 1983, they are still available in the secondary market as are bonds registered to principal only.

2. 1. 5 PRICING

Once issued, bonds are bought and sold in the secondary market. Bond prices are determined primarily by interest rates. Additional influences may be unique to the issuer.

2. 1. 5. 1 Par, Premium, and Discount

Bonds are generally issued with a **face value**, or par value, of $1,000. **Par** represents the dollar amount of the investor's loan to the issuer, and it is the amount repaid when the bond matures. For Series 7 testing, always assume par value for bonds is $1,000 unless stated otherwise in the test question.

In the secondary market, bonds can sell for any price—**at par**, **below par** (at a **discount**), or **above par** (at a **premium**). The two primary factors affecting a bond's market price are the issuer's financial stability and overall trends in interest rates. If an issuer's credit rating remains constant, interest rates are the only factor that affect the market price.

Corporate bond quotes are commonly stated as percentages of par in increments of ⅛. A bid of 100 means 100% of par, or $1,000. A bond quote of 98⅛ means 98 and ⅛% (98.125%) of $1,000, or $981.25. Bond price changes are quoted in newspapers in points. One point is 1% of $1,000, or $10; ¼ point is $2.50. The minimum variation for most corporate bond quotes is ⅛ (.125%, or $1.25). In addition, there are 100 basis points in each point. Therefore, expressed in terms of percent, one basis point equals ¹⁄₁₀₀ of 1%.

EXAMPLE   If one point equals $10, one basis point equals $.10.

TEST TOPIC ALERT   Expect a question similar to the following.

How much is 80 basis points?

I. $8
II. $80
III. .8%
IV. 8%

A. I and III
B. I and IV
C. II and III
D. II and IV

Answer: A. We know that 100 basis points = $10 = 1% of a bond's face value. Therefore, 80 basis points = .8% and is worth $8.00 (80 × $.10).

2. 1. 6   RATING AND ANALYZING BONDS

Rating services, such as Standard & Poor's (S&P) and Moody's, evaluate the credit quality of bond issues and publish their ratings. Standard & Poor's and Moody's rate both corporate and municipal bonds. Both base their bond ratings primarily on an issuer's creditworthiness—that is, the issuer's ability to pay interest and principal as they come due.

A plus or minus sign in a Standard & Poor's rating indicates that the bond falls within the top (+) or bottom (–) of that particular category. Moody's uses A1 and Baa1 to indicate the highest quality bonds within those two categories. Moody's provides ratings for short-term municipal notes, designating MIG 1–4 (best–adequate) and SG (speculative grade).

The rating organizations rate those issues that either pay to be rated or have enough bonds outstanding to generate constant investor interest. The fact that a bond is not rated does not indicate its quality; many issues are too small to justify the expense of a bond rating.

2. 1. 6. 1   Basis for Bond Ratings

Bond ratings are based on an issuer's financial stability. The rating services apply a series of financial tests to assess a corporation's financial strength.

Specific criteria used to rate corporate and municipal bonds include:

■ the amount and composition of existing debt;

■ the stability of the issuer's cash flow;

■ the issuer's ability to meet scheduled payments of interest and principal on its debt obligations;

■ asset protection; and

■ management capability.

A bond's rating may change over time as the issuer's ability to make interest and principal payments changes.

TAKE NOTE

The SEC has recognized seven ratings firms under the Credit Rating Agency Reform Act of 2006 as being registered with the commission. They are A.M. Best Co., Inc. (historically associated with rating insurance companies' ability to pay claims and their debt issues); DBRS, Ltd.; Fitch, Inc.; Japan Credit Rating Agency, Ltd.; Moody's Investors Service, Inc.; Rating and Investment Information, Inc.; and Standard and Poor's Rating Service. Rating symbols used by Moody's and Standard & Poor's, are shown in the following chart. Note that Fitch uses rating symbols identical to those used by Standard & Poor's.

Bond Ratings

Standard & Poor's	Moody's	Interpretation
Bank-grade (investment-grade) bonds		
AAA	Aaa	Highest rating. Capacity to repay principal and interest judged high.
AA	Aa	Very strong. Only slightly less secure than the highest rating.
A	A	Judged to be slightly more susceptible to adverse economic conditions.
BBB	Baa	Adequate capacity to repay principal and interest. Slightly speculative.
Speculative (noninvestment-grade) bonds		
BB	Ba	Speculative. Significant chance that issuer could miss an interest payment.
B	B	Issuer has missed one or more interest or principal payments.
C	Caa	No interest is being paid on bond at this time.
D	D	Issuer is in default. Payment of interest or principal is in arrears.

2. 1. 6. 1. 1   Investment Grade

The Comptroller of the Currency, the Federal Deposit Insurance Corporation (FDIC), the Federal Reserve, and state banking authorities have established policies determining which securities banks can purchase. A municipal bond must be **investment grade** (a rating of BBB/Baa or higher) to be suitable for purchase by banks. Investment-grade bonds are also known as **bank-grade bonds**.

A plus or minus sign in a Standard & Poor's rating indicates that the bond falls within the top or bottom of a particular category (e.g., AA+ or A–). Moody's, however, adds numerical qualifiers such as 1, 2, 3, to their categories (e.g., Aa1 or Baa2). The lower the number the higher the rating within that category.

High-yield bonds that carry a speculative rating are suitable only for those with a high risk tolerance. They are characterized by greater returns coupled with greater credit risk.

TAKE NOTE
An easy way to distinguish between Moody's and S&P ratings is to remember that "Mood swings are Up and Down." This phrase reminds you that Moody's uses upper and lower case letters, while S&P uses only capital letters for its ratings. For Moody's, investment grade is Baa and above, whereas with S&P, investment grade is BBB and above.

2. 1. 6. 2 Relationship of Rating to Yield

Generally, the higher a bond's rating, the lower its yield. Investors will accept lower returns on their investments if their principal and interest payments are safe. Bonds with low ratings due to the issuer's instability pay higher rates because of the risks to principal and interest associated with such uncertainties.

2. 1. 6. 2. 1 Qualitative Analysis

In addition to financial statistics, qualitative factors, such as an industry's stability, the issuer's quality of management, and the regulatory climate, may be considered when bonds are rated.

2. 1. 6. 3 Comparative Safety of Debt Securities

Although there are exceptions to the rule, a hierarchy exists in the degree of safety associated with different categories of debt securities. Normally, the higher the degree of safety, the lower the yield relative to other investments at the same time.

2. 1. 6. 3. 1 U.S. Government Securities

The highest degree of safety is in securities backed by the full faith and credit of the U.S. government. These securities include U.S. Treasury bills, notes, and bonds and savings bonds like Series EE and HH bonds.

2. 1. 6. 3. 2 Government Agency Issues

The second highest degree of safety is in securities issued by government agencies and government-sponsored corporations, although the U.S. government does not back the securities; GNMA is the exception. These organizations include:

- Government National Mortgage Association (GNMA or **Ginnie Mae**);
- Federal Farm Credit Banks (FFCBs);
- Federal Home Loan Mortgage Corporation (FHLMC or **Freddie Mac**); and
- Federal National Mortgage Association (FNMA or **Fannie Mae**).

2. 1. 6. 3. 3 Municipal Issues

Generally, the next level of safety is in securities issued by municipalities. **General obligation bonds (GOs)**, backed by the taxing power of the issuer, are usually safer than revenue bonds. Revenue bonds are backed by revenues from the facility financed by the bond issue.

2. 1. 6. 3. 4   Corporate Debt

Corporate debt securities cover the safety spectrum, from very safe (AAA corporates) to very risky (**junk bonds**). Corporate bonds are backed, in varying degrees, by the issuing corporation. Usually, these securities are ranked from safe to risky, as follows:

- Secured bonds
- Debentures
- Subordinated debentures
- Income bonds

However, these rankings serve only as a rough guideline.

2. 1. 6. 4   Liquidity

Liquidity is the ease with which a bond or any other security can be sold. Many factors determine a bond's liquidity, including:

- size of the issue;
- quality;
- rating;
- maturity;
- call features;
- coupon rate and current market value;
- issuer; and
- existence of a sinking fund.

TAKE NOTE   The terms *liquidity* and *marketability* are synonymous. Either term refers to how quickly a security can be converted into cash.

2. 1. 7   DEBT RETIREMENT

The schedule of interest and principal payments due on a bond issue is known as the **debt service.**

2. 1. 7. 1   Redemption

When a bond's principal is repaid, the bond is **redeemed**. Redemption usually occurs on the maturity date.

In addition to maturity, other terms used in connection with redemption are:

- sinking fund;
- call;
- refunding; and
- pre-refunding.

2. 1. 7. 1. 1 Sinking Fund

To facilitate the retirement of its bonds, a corporate or municipal issuer may establish a **sinking fund** operated by the bonds' trustee. The trust indenture often requires a sinking fund, which can be used to call bonds, redeem bonds at maturity, or buy back bonds in the open market.

To establish a sinking fund, the issuer deposits cash in an account with the trustee. Because a sinking fund makes money available for redeeming bonds, it can aid the bonds' marketability.

TAKE NOTE   As a general rule, highly rated issuers do not establish sinking funds. Lower-rated issuers do so to make their issues more marketable.

2. 1. 7. 1. 2 Calling Bonds

Bonds are often issued with a call feature, or call option. A **call feature** allows the issuer to redeem a bond issue before its maturity date, either in whole or in part (in-whole or partial calls).

The issuer does this by notifying bondholders that it will call the bonds at a particular price on a certain date.

In a partial call, the issuer will call selected bonds, not the entire issue, at a particular call date and call price. The bonds called in a partial call are selected by lottery (i.e., randomly).

2. 1. 7. 1. 3 Call Premium

The right to call bonds for early redemption gives issuers flexibility in their financial management. In return, an issuer usually pays bondholders a premium, a price higher than par, known as a **call premium**. Various municipal bonds, corporate bonds, and preferred stocks are callable at some point over their terms.

TEST TOPIC ALERT   A call premium is the difference between the call price and par.

EXAMPLE   If a bond were callable at 102, the call premium would be two points, or $20 per bond.

2. 1. 7. 1. 4 Advantages of a Call to the Issuer

Callable bonds can benefit the issuer in many ways.

- If general interest rates decline, the issuer can redeem bonds with a high interest rate and replace them with bonds with a lower rate.
- The issuer can call bonds to reduce its debt any time after the initial call date.
- The issuer can replace short-term debt issues with long-term issues and vice versa.
- The issuer can call bonds as a means of forcing the conversion of convertible corporate bonds.

Term bonds are generally called by random drawing. **Serial bonds**, on the other hand, are usually called in inverse order of their maturities because longer maturities tend to have higher interest rates. Calling the long maturities lowers the issuer's interest expense by the largest amount.

If a bond issue's trust indenture does not include a call provision, the issuer normally can buy bonds in the open market, known as **tendering**, to retire a portion of its debt.

2. 1. 7. 1. 5   Call Protection

Bonds are called when general interest rates are lower than they were when the bonds were issued. Investors, therefore, are faced with having to replace a relatively high fixed-income investment with one that pays less; this is known as **call risk**. A newly issued bond normally has a noncallable period of five or 10 years to provide some protection to investors. During this period, the issuer cannot call any of its bonds.

When the call protection period expires, the issuer may call any or all of the bonds, usually at a premium. A **call protection feature** is an advantage to bondholders in periods of declining interest rates.

2. 1. 7. 1. 6   Effects of a Call on Trading

After a call notice is issued, but before the call date, called bonds continue to trade in the open market. When bonds are called, a bondholder can turn in the bonds to the issuer on the call date or sell them in the open market. The bonds will trade at a slight discount to the call price during this period. By selling at the small discount, the investor does not have to wait until the call date to get his money.

TEST TOPIC ALERT

Following are three test points pertaining to bond call features.

1.   Under what economic circumstances do issuers call bonds?

   Answer: Calls occur when interest rates are declining. Put yourself in the issuer's shoes. Would you want to pay more interest for the use of money than is necessary?

2.   Investors who purchase callable bonds face what types of investment risk?

   Answer: Call risk is the risk that the bonds will be called and the investor will lose the stream of income from the bond. Remember that bonds do not pay interest after they have been called. The call feature also causes reinvestment risk. If interest rates are down when the call takes place, what likelihood does the investor have of investing the principal received at a comparable rate?

   Both call risk and reinvestment risk also apply to callable preferred stock.

3.   Which of the following would an issuer most likely call?

   A.   High-interest bond, callable at a premium
   B.   High-interest bond, callable at par
   C.   Low-interest bond, callable at a premium
   D.   Low-interest bond, callable at par

Answer: B. Issuers want to call bonds that are costly to them at as low a price as possible. A high-interest bond with no call premium is the best combination. The issuer would be least likely to call a low-interest bond with a high call premium.

2. 1. 7. 2   Refunding Bonds

Refunding is the practice of raising money to call a bond. Specifically, the issuer sells a new bond issue to generate funds to retire an existing issue. Refunding, like a call, can occur in full or in part. Generally, an entire issue is refunded at once. Refunding is common for bonds approaching maturity. An issuer may not have enough cash to pay off the entire issue, or it may choose to use its cash for other needs.

TAKE NOTE

Refunding can be thought of as issuer refinancing. Homeowners know that when interest rates drop, it makes sense to replace a high interest mortgage with a new mortgage at a more competitive rate. An issuer can accomplish the same thing by refunding.

2. 1. 7. 3   Pre-refunding

When a bond issue is **pre-refunded**, also known as **advance refunding,** a new issue is sold at a lower coupon before the original bond issue can be called. An issuer pre-refunds a bond issue to lock in a favorable interest rate. The proceeds from the new issue are placed in an escrow account and invested in U.S. government securities. Interest received from the investment is used to pay interest on the original or pre-refunded bonds, called at the first call date using the escrowed funds.

Pre-refunded bonds are generally rated AAA or Aaa, the highest rating available. Advance refunding is a form of **defeasance**, or termination, of the issuer's obligation; pre-refunded bonds are considered defeased and no longer count as part of the issuer's debt.

2. 1. 7. 3. 1   Crossover Refunding

Crossover refunding is a method of advance refunding in which the revenue stream originally pledged to secure the refunded bonds continues to be used to pay debt service on those bonds until they mature or are called in by the issuer. At that time, the advance refunded (escrowed) dollars are used to pay off the original (refunded) bond issue, and the revenues pledged from the original issue "crossover" to now pay debt service on the new bonds.

TAKE NOTE

Pre-refunding often occurs where there is a call protection period. The issuer cannot legally call the bonds until a future date, but if interest rates are low, a low rate can be locked in by issuing the new bonds in advance of the call date.

Know the following facts about pre-refunded bonds.

- They are AAA rated (they cannot get any safer).
- They are considered defeased.
- The funds are escrowed in government securities.

- The marketability of the pre-refunded bond increases.
- Once pre-refunded, the issue is no longer considered part of the outstanding debt of the issuer.

With regard to noncallable bonds, issuers can lock in lower rates by pre-refunding in the same manner as above. Once the proceeds are placed in escrow, the bonds are said to be escrowed to maturity.

2. 1. 7. 4   Tender Offers

When general interest rates are down, companies may wish to redeem callable and non-callable bonds and replace them with bonds paying less interest. A bond issuer may make a **tender offer** for its outstanding bonds, most likely at a premium price as an inducement to bondholders to tender their securities.

2. 1. 7. 5   Putable Bonds (Bonds with Put Options)

Bonds issued with put options are known as **put**, or **putable**, bonds. In return for accepting a slightly lower interest rate, an investor receives the right to put, or sell, the bond to the issuer at full face value. Once the bond becomes putable, the investor has the right, generally once a year, to force the issuer to buy back the bonds at par.

TAKE NOTE   Put features are most commonly found in municipal bonds. Once putable, the investor is protected against market risk (interest rate risk) as the bonds, at that point, will not trade much below the put price, which is par.

2. 2   BOND YIELDS

A bond's **yield** expresses the cash interest payments in relation to the bond's value. Yield is determined by the issuer's credit quality, prevailing interest rates, time to maturity, and call features. Bonds can be quoted and traded in terms of their yield as well as a percentage of par dollar amount.

Comparing Yields

Bonds most frequently trade for prices other than par, so the price discount or premium from par is taken into consideration when calculating a bond's overall yield. You can look at a bond's yield in several ways.

2. 2. 7. 1   Nominal Yield

A bond's coupon yield is set at issuance and printed on the face of the bond. The **nominal yield,** or **coupon yield**, is a fixed percentage of the bond's par value.

EXAMPLE
A coupon of 6% indicates the bondholder is paid 6% of the face amount of $1,000 or $60 in interest annually until the bond matures.

2. 2. 7. 2   Current Yield

Current yield (CY) measures a bond's coupon payment relative to its market price, as shown in the following equation:

$$\text{Coupon payment} \div \text{market price} = \text{current yield}$$

Bond prices and yields move in opposite directions: as interest rates rise, bond prices fall and vice versa. When a bond trades at a discount, its current yield increases; when it trades at a premium, its current yield decreases.

TEST TOPIC ALERT

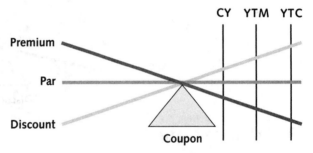

Current Yield, Yield to Maturity, and Yield to Call

CY = Current Yield   YTM = Yield to Maturity   YTC = Yield to Call

1. What is the current yield of a 6% bond trading for $800?

   Current yield = annual income ÷ current market price

   Find the solution as follows: $60 ÷ $800 = 7.5%. This bond is trading at a discount. When prices fall, yields rise. The current yield is greater than the nominal yield when bonds are trading at a discount.

2. What is the current yield of a 6% bond trading for $1,200?

   Find the solution as follows: $60 ÷ $1,200 = 5%. This bond is trading at a premium. The price is up so the yield is down. The current yield is less than the nominal yield when bonds are trading at a premium.

   It is critical to understand the inverse relationship between price and yield. An effective way to visualize it is through the chart. When bonds are at par, coupon and current yield are equal. When bonds are at a premium, the CY is less than the coupon. When bonds are at a discount, the CY is greater than the coupon.

Current market value (CMV) of bond with 10 years to maturity

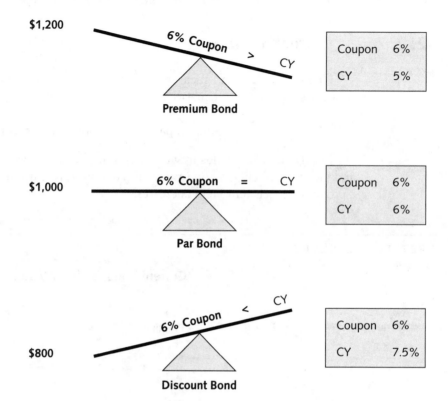

2. 2. 7. 3   Yield to Maturity

A bond's **yield to maturity (YTM)** reflects the annualized return of the bond if held to maturity. In calculating yield to maturity, the bondholder takes into account the difference between the price paid for a bond and par value. If the bond's price is less than par, the discount amount increases the return. If the bond's price is greater than par, the premium amount decreases the return.

EXAMPLE

An investor who buys a 10% coupon bond at 105 ($1,050 per bond) with 10 years remaining to maturity can expect $100 in interest per year. If he holds the bond to maturity, the bondholder loses $50, the amount of the premium. This loss is included in the YTM approximation.

The actual YTM calculation for this premium bond is shown below:

$$\frac{\text{Annual interest} - (\text{premium} \div \text{years to maturity})}{\text{Average price of the bond}}$$

A bond's average price is the price paid plus the amount received at maturity (par) divided by two. Alternatively, the average price is that price midway between the purchase price and par.

$$\frac{100 - (50 \div 10)}{1025} = \frac{95}{1025} = .093, \text{ or } 9.3\%$$

The YTM of a bond bought at a premium is always lower than both the coupon rate (nominal yield) and the current yield. In this example, the nominal yield is 10%, and the current yield is 9.52% (100 ÷ 1,050).

If an investor buys a 10-year bond with a 10% coupon for 95 ($950 per bond), he receives $100 per year in coupon interest payments and a gain of $50 (the amount of the discount) at maturity. This gain is included in the YTM approximation.

The actual YTM calculation for this discount bond is shown below:

$$\frac{\text{Annual interest} + (\text{discount} \div \text{years to maturity})}{\text{Average price of the bond}}$$

$$\frac{100 + (50 \div 10)}{975} = \frac{105}{975} = .1077, \text{ or } 10.77\%$$

The YTM of a bond bought at a discount is always higher than both the coupon rate (nominal yield) and the current yield. In this example, the nominal yield is 10%, and the current yield is 10.53% (100 ÷ 950).

If these calculations seem complicated, do not worry. You will have at most one question requiring a YTM calculation. Focus on the relationship between YTM and CY based on the price of the bond.

TAKE NOTE

Another term for yield to maturity is **basis**. A 4% bond trading on a 5% basis is trading at a price to yield 5% to maturity.

2. 2. 7. 4   Yield to Call

A bond with a call feature may be redeemed before maturity at the issuer's option. Unless the bond was bought at par and is callable at par, **yield to call (YTC)** calculations reflect the early redemption date and consequent acceleration of the discount gain or premium loss from the purchase price.

An investor who buys a callable bond at a premium loses the premium faster when the bond is called at par than if it were held to maturity. Because a bond sells for a premium when its coupon rate is higher than current market rates, premium bonds are likely to be called so the issuer can save on interest expenses. The sooner the bonds are called, the sooner the premium the investor paid is lost.

The YTC for a premium bond called at par, therefore, is always lower than the nominal yield, current yield, and YTM.

For a bond bought at a discount, YTC is always higher than the nominal yield, current yield, and YTM. If a discount bond is called at par, the gain is earned faster than if the bond were held to maturity.

EXAMPLE

Answer the following questions with **premium, par,** or **discount**.

1. If the bond has a YTC lower than its CY, it is trading at _____
2. If the bond has a YTM and CY that are equal, the bond is trading at _____
3. If the bond has a YTM less than its YTC, the bond is trading at _____
4. If a bond has a YTM greater than its coupon, the bond is trading at _____

The answers are: 1. premium; 2. par; 3. discount; 4. discount.

Memorize the following chart for the exam:

Ranking Yields from Highest to Lowest

Discounts	Premiums
YTC	Nominal
YTM	CY
CY	YTM
Nominal	YTC

Once you understand the yield ranking for discounts, the ranking for premium is easy—it is the exact opposite.

2.2.7.5   Yield Curve

Bond prices and yields have an **inverse relationship**: as interest rates rise, prices decline. In addition, under normal circumstances, the longer a bond's maturity, the greater its yield. The increased yield reflects the potential for credit quality or inflation risks over time.

The difference in yields between short-term and long-term bonds of the same quality is known as the **yield curve**. In a **normal yield curve**, the difference between short-term and long-term rates is about three percentage points (300 basis points) but may be much larger or smaller at any given time.

Normal (Positive) Yield Curve

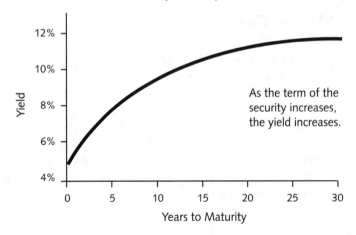

As the term of the security increases, the yield increases.

When interest rates are high and expected to begin declining, long-term bond yields can be lower than short-term yields as their market price anticipates the declining rates. When long-term interest rates are lower than short-term rates, the yield curve is considered **inverted**.

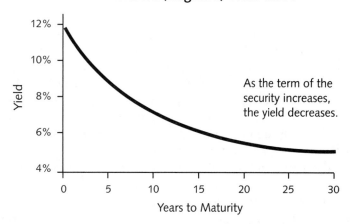

Inverted (Negative) Yield Curve

As the term of the security increases, the yield decreases.

When short-term and long-term rates are the same, the yield curve is flat.

TAKE NOTE

The shape of the yield curve varies with changes in the economic cycle.

■ A normal, or ascending, yield curve occurs during periods of economic expansion—it generally predicts that interest rates will rise in the future.

■ A flat yield curve occurs when the economy is peaking, and no change in interest rates is expected.

■ An inverted, or descending, yield curve occurs when the Federal Reserve Board has tightened credit in an overheating economy; it predicts that rates will fall in the future.

■ Yield curves for issuers with different risk levels can be compared to make economic predictions.

■ If the yield curve spread between corporate bonds and government bonds is widening, a **recession** is expected. Investors have chosen the safety of government bonds over higher corporate yields, which occurs when the economy slows down.

■ If the yield curve between corporate bonds and government bonds is narrowing, an economic **expansion** is expected and investors are willing to take risks. They will sell government bonds to buy higher-yielding corporates.

Corporate and Government Bonds

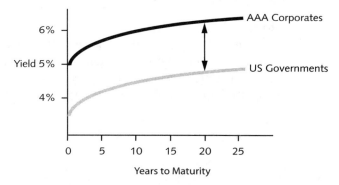

2. 2. 7. 6   Rate Changes and Bond Prices

There is an inverse relationship between interest rates and bond prices. As interest rates rise, bond prices fall; as interest rates fall, bond prices rise. Look at it this way: assume you have a 10-year bond with a 5% coupon trading at par. If rates rise, to 6% for comparable 10-year bonds, buyers in the secondary market will need more than a 5% yield to buy your bond. The only way you can provide buyers with a market yield is to sell the bond at a discount. The discount plus the 5% coupon will provide buyers with a market yield, which is now 6%.

Similarly, if rates for comparable 10-year bonds fall to 4%, buyers in the secondary market will pay a premium over par to buy a 5% bond. The loss of the premium over the life of the bond coupled with the 5% coupon will provide buyers with a market yield, which is now 4%.

As interest rates change, long-term bond prices move more in price than short-term bonds. As rates rise, long-term bond prices decline more than short-term bond prices. As rates fall, long-term bond prices appreciate more than short-term bond prices. If two bonds have the same time to maturity, the bond with the lower coupon will move more in price. In other words, given a change in interest rates, discounts tend to move more in price than premiums.

TEST TOPIC ALERT   If you are given two discount bonds and asked which will appreciate the most if rates fall, choose the bond trading at the deeper discount (i.e., the one with the lower coupon).

If you are given two callable bonds and asked which will appreciate the most if rates fall, choose the bond with the most distant call date.

2. 3   CORPORATE BONDS

Corporate bonds are issued to raise working capital or capital for expenditures such as plant construction and equipment purchases. The two primary types of corporate bonds are secured and unsecured.

2. 3. 1   SECURED BONDS

A bond is **secured** when the issuer has identified specific assets as collateral for interest and principal payments. A trustee holds the title to the assets that secure the bond. In a **default**, the bondholder can lay claim to the collateral.

2. 3. 1. 1   Mortgage Bonds

Mortgage bonds have the highest priority among all claims on assets pledged as collateral. Although mortgage bonds, in general, are considered relatively safe, individual bonds are only as secure as the assets that secure them and are rated accordingly.

When multiple classes of a mortgage bond exist, the first claim on the pledged property goes to first-mortgage bonds, second claim to second-mortgage bonds, and so on.

2. 3. 1. 1. 1   Open-End Indentures

An open-end trust indenture permits the corporation to issue more bonds of the same class later. Subsequent issues are secured by the same collateral backing the initial issue and have equal liens on the property.

2. 3. 1. 1. 2   Closed-End Indentures

A closed-end indenture does not permit the corporation to issue more bonds of the same class in the future. Any subsequent issue has a subordinated claim on the collateral.

2. 3. 1. 1. 3   Prior Lien Bonds

Companies in financial trouble sometimes attract capital by issuing mortgage bonds that take precedence over first-mortgage bonds. Before issuing prior lien bonds, however, a corporation must have the consent of first-mortgage bondholders (which is unlikely).

2. 3. 1. 2   Collateral Trust Bonds

Collateral trust bonds are issued by corporations that own securities of other companies as investments. A corporation issues bonds secured by a pledge of those securities as collateral. The trust indenture usually contains a covenant requiring that a trustee hold the pledged securities. Collateral trust bonds may be backed by:

- another company's stocks and bonds;
- stocks and bonds of partially or wholly owned subsidiaries;
- pledging company's prior lien long-term bonds that have been held in trust to secure short-term bonds; or
- installment payments or other obligations of the corporation's clients.

2. 3. 1. 3   Equipment Trust Certificates

Railroads, airlines, trucking companies, and oil companies use **equipment trust certificates (ETCs)**, or equipment notes and bonds, to finance the purchase of capital equipment. ETCs are issued serially so that the amount outstanding goes down year to year in line with the depreciating value of the collateral (e.g., aircraft or railroad cars).

Title to the newly acquired equipment is held in trust, usually by a bank, until all certificates have been paid in full. Because the certificates normally mature before the equipment wears out, the amount borrowed is generally less than the full value of the property securing the certificates.

2. 3. 2   UNSECURED BONDS

Unsecured bonds have no specific collateral backing and are classified as either debentures or subordinated debentures.

2. 3. 2. 1   Debentures

Debentures are backed by the general credit of the issuing corporation, and a debenture owner is considered a general creditor of the company. Debentures are below secured bonds and above subordinated debentures and preferred and common stock in the priority of claims on corporate assets.

2. 3. 2. 2   Subordinated Debentures

The claims of **subordinated debenture** owners are paid last of all debt obligations, including general creditors, in the case of liquidation. Subordinated debentures generally offer higher yields than either straight debentures or secured bonds because of their subordinate (thus riskier) status, and they often have conversion features.

2. 3. 2. 3   Liquidation

In the event a company goes bankrupt, the hierarchy of claims on the company's assets is:

- unpaid wages;
- IRS (taxes);
- secured debt (bonds and mortgages);
- unsecured liabilities (debentures) and general creditors;
- subordinated debt;
- preferred stockholders; and
- common stockholders.

TEST TOPIC ALERT   Be ready for a question on liquidation priority. Secured is safest, followed by unsecured or general creditors, then subordinated. Common stock is always last in line. Bonds are frequently called senior securities because of their priority in this hierarchy.

2. 3. 3   GUARANTEED BONDS

Guaranteed bonds are backed by a company other than the issuer, such as a parent company. This backing effectively increases the issue's safety.

2. 3. 4   INCOME BONDS

Income bonds, also known as **adjustment bonds**, are used when a company is reorganizing and coming out of bankruptcy. Income bonds pay interest only if the corporation has enough income to meet the interest payment and if the BOD declares a payment. Because missed interest payments do not accumulate for future payment, these bonds are not suitable investments for customers seeking income.

2. 3. 5   ZERO-COUPON BONDS

Bonds are normally issued as interest-paying securities. **Zero-coupon bonds (zeroes)** are an issuer's debt obligations that do not make regular interest payments. Instead, zeroes are issued, or sold, at a deep discount to their face value and mature at par. The difference between the discounted purchase price and the full face value at maturity is the return, or accreted interest, the investor receives.

The price of a zero-coupon bond reflects the general interest rate climate for similar maturities.

Zero-coupon bonds are issued by corporations, municipalities, and the U.S. Treasury and may be created by broker-dealers from other types of securities.

2. 3. 5. 1   Advantages and Disadvantages

A zero-coupon bond requires a relatively small investment, perhaps $300 to $400 per bond, and matures at $1,000. Zero-coupon bonds offer investors a way to speculate on interest rate moves. Because they sell at deep discounts and offer no cash interest payments to the holder, zeroes are substantially more volatile than traditional bonds; their prices fluctuate wildly with changes in market rates. Moreover, the longer the time to maturity, the greater the volatility. When interest rates change, a zero's price changes much more as a percentage of its market value than an ordinary bond's price.

TEST TOPIC ALERT   Zero-coupon bonds, which are purchased at a discount and mature at face value, are a suitable investment for future anticipated expenses such as college tuition.

2. 3. 5. 2   Taxation of Zero-Coupon Bonds

Although zeroes pay no regular interest income, investors in zeroes owe income tax each year on the amount by which the bonds have accreted, just as if the investor had received it in cash. The income tax is due regardless of the direction of the market price.

EXAMPLE   A customer buys a 10-year zero at a cost of $400. At maturity, the customer will realize $600 of interest income. Each year, however, the customer must accrete the discount and pay income tax on this phantom income.

Here is how it works: The IRS requires the customer to accrete the discount annually on a straight line basis. The total discount is $600. Because there are 10 years to maturity, the customer must accrete $60 annually ($600 ÷ 10 years). Each year, the customer pays income tax on $60 of interest income. The good news is that each year, the customer is permitted to adjust the cost basis of the zero upward by the amount of the annual accretion. After one year, the customer's cost basis is $460. After two years, the cost basis is $520. After three years, it is $580, and so on. At maturity, the cost basis will be adjusted to par. Therefore, if held to maturity, there is no capital gain (cost basis is par; redeemed at par).

However, if the customer sells the zero before maturity, there may be a capital gain or a capital loss, depending on the difference between sales proceeds and the cost basis (accreted value) at time of sale.

If the same 10-year zero bought at $400 is sold five years later for $720, the customer will realize a $20 per bond gain. At that point, the customer's cost basis is $700 ($400 plus five years of annual accretion of $60 per year).

TEST TOPIC ALERT   If the exam asks you to choose the security that has no reinvestment risk, the answer to look for is a zero because, with no interest payments to reinvest, the investor has no reinvestment risk. Furthermore, because there is no reinvestment risk, buying a zero is the only way to lock in a rate of return.

2. 4 THE TRUST INDENTURE

The **Trust Indenture Act of 1939** requires corporate bond issues of $50 million or more sold interstate to be issued under a trust indenture, a legal contract between the bond issuer and a trustee representing bondholders. Although the face of a bond certificate mentions the trust indenture, it is not automatically supplied to bondholders.

The trust indenture specifies the issuer's obligation and bondholders' rights, and it identifies the trustee.

2. 4. 5. 1 The Trustee

The Trust Indenture Act of 1939 requires a corporation to appoint a **trustee**, usually a commercial bank or trust company, for its bonds. The trustee monitors compliance with the covenants of the indenture and may act on behalf of the bondholders if the issuer defaults.

2. 4. 5. 2 Exemptions

Federal and municipal governments are exempt from the Trust Indenture Act provisions, although municipal revenue bonds are typically issued with a trust indenture to make them more marketable.

2. 4. 5. 3 Protective Covenants

In the trust indenture for a mortgage bond, the debtor corporation agrees to:
- pay the interest and principal of its bonds;
- specify where bonds can be presented for payment;
- defend the legal title to the property;
- maintain the property to ensure that business can be conducted;
- insure the mortgaged property against fire and other losses;
- pay all taxes and assessments (property, income, and franchise); and
- maintain its corporate structure and the right to do business.

Other covenants might include provisions for a sinking fund, a replacement fund, minimum working capital, or other requirements.

Mortgage bonds may be issued with either closed- or open-end covenants. Bonds issued with **closed-end covenants** have senior claim on the underlying assets, even if the corporation issues other bonds secured by the same assets. An **open-end covenant** permits subsequent issues to be secured by the same property and have equal liens on it.

TEST TOPIC ALERT   The test sometimes refers to closed-end indenture bonds as **senior lien bonds**. Remember that a trust indenture is a contract between the issuer and the trustee for the benefit of the bondholders. It is easy to mistakenly identify the contract as one between the issuer and the bondholders.

2. 5   TRADING CORPORATE BONDS

2. 5. 1   NYSE-LISTED BONDS

The **New York Stock Exchange (NYSE)** provides a central marketplace for trading corporate bonds. Most brokerage firms do not maintain regular floor brokers to execute bond orders; instead, they enlist bond brokers to execute the orders on their behalf. A bond broker charges a small fee (a give-up commission) for each order executed. In addition, a bond trading platform known as **NYSE Bonds** provides investors with cost-effective, real-time automatic order execution.

The SEC now permits exchange members and member organizations to trade some unlisted debt securities on the Exchange. NYSE Bonds has been expanded to trade the unlisted corporate debt issues of all NYSE-listed equity issuers.

TAKE NOTE   Most corporate bonds still trade in the OTC market.

2. 5. 2   CONVERTIBLE BONDS

Convertible bonds are corporate bonds that may be exchanged for a fixed number of shares of the issuing company's common stock. They are convertible into common stock, so convertible bonds pay lower interest rates than nonconvertible bonds and generally trade in line with the common stock. Convertible bonds have fixed interest payments and maturity dates, so they are less volatile than common stock.

2. 5. 2. 1   Advantages of Convertible Securities to the Issuer

A corporation adds a conversion feature to its bonds or preferred stock to make it more marketable. Other reasons corporations issue convertible securities include the following.

■ Convertibles can be sold with a lower coupon rate than nonconvertibles because of the conversion feature.

- A company can eliminate a fixed interest charge as conversion takes place, thus reducing debt.

- Because conversion normally occurs over time, it does not have an adverse effect on the stock price, which may occur after a subsequent primary offering.

- By issuing convertibles rather than common stock, a corporation avoids immediate dilution of primary earnings per share.

- At issuance, conversion price is higher than market price of the common stock.

2. 5. 2. 2   Disadvantages of Convertible Securities to the Issuer

On the other hand, convertibles have potential disadvantages for a corporation and its stockholders.

- When bonds are converted, shareholders' equity is diluted; that is, more shares are outstanding, so each share now represents a smaller fraction of ownership in the company.

- Common stockholders have a voice in the company's management, so a substantial conversion could cause a shift in the control of the company.

- Reducing corporate debt through conversion means a loss of leverage.

- The resulting decrease in deductible interest costs raises the corporation's taxable income. Therefore, the corporation pays increased taxes as conversion takes place.

2. 5. 2. 3   The Market for Convertible Securities

Convertible bonds offer the safety of the fixed-income market and the potential appreciation of the equity market, providing investors with the following advantages.

- As a debt security, a **convertible debenture** pays interest at a fixed rate and is redeemable for its face value at maturity, provided the debenture is not converted. As a rule, interest income is higher and surer than dividend income on the underlying common stock. Similarly, convertible preferred stock usually pays a higher dividend than does common stock.

- If a corporation experiences financial difficulties, convertible bondholders have priority over common stockholders in the event of a corporate liquidation.

- In theory, a convertible debenture's market price tends to be more stable during market declines than the underlying common stock's price. Current yields of other competitive debt securities support the debenture's value in the marketplace.

- Because convertibles can be exchanged for common stock, their market price tends to move upward if the stock price moves up.

- Conversion of a senior security into common stock is not considered a purchase and a sale for tax purposes. Thus, the investor incurs no tax liability on the conversion transaction.

- Stable interest rates tend to result in a stable bond market. When rates are stable, the most volatile bonds tend to be those with a conversion feature because of their link to the underlying common stock. Therefore, in a stable rate environment, a convertible bond can be volatile if the underlying stock is volatile.

2. 5. 2. 4   Conversion Price and Conversion Ratio

The **conversion price** is the stock price at which a convertible bond can be exchanged for shares of common stock. The **conversion ratio**, also called the **conversion rate**, expresses the number of shares of stock a bond may be converted into.

EXAMPLE   A bond with a conversion price of $40 has a conversion ratio of 25:1 ($1,000 ÷ $40 = 25).

Conversion terms are stated in the indenture agreement, either as a conversion ratio or as a conversion price.

TAKE NOTE   Although the conversion ratio of a bond is always stated on the bond certificate and the investor's confirmation, it is not stated directly in the number of shares, but in terms of the price at which a conversion can occur.

EXAMPLE   If a bond has a conversion price of $40 per share, you can determine that an investor is entitled to convert it into 25 shares. Always start with the par value of the instrument: par of $1,000 ÷ conversion price of $40 = conversion ratio of 25 shares.

The same concept applies to convertible preferred stock. An investor bought a share of preferred that converts at $20. By starting with an assumed par of $100, you can derive that the investor is entitled to five shares of common. $100 ÷ the conversion price of $20 = conversion ratio of 5 shares.

2. 5. 2. 4. 1   Stock Splits and Dividends

Conversion prices are adjusted if stock splits and stock dividends are declared on the underlying common stock during the life of the bond.

2. 5. 2. 4. 2   Mergers, Consolidations, and Dissolutions

If the corporation ceases to exist because of any of these situations, convertible bondholders may lose their conversion privileges.

2. 5. 2. 5   Calculating Conversion Parity

Parity means that two securities are of equal dollar value (in this case, a convertible bond and the common stock into which it can be converted).

EXAMPLE

If a corporation issues a bond convertible at $50, the conversion ratio is 20:1. If a bond selling for 104 ($1,040) is convertible into 20 shares of common, the common stock price would have to be $52 to be at parity with, or equal to, the convertible bond price ($1,040 ÷ 20 = 52). If the common stock is selling below 52, the convertible bond is worth more than the stock. If the stock is selling above 52, the investor can make more money by acquiring the bond, converting to common, and selling the shares.

The following formulas calculate the parity prices of convertible securities and their underlying common shares:

$$\frac{\text{Market price of the bond}}{\text{Conversion ratio (\# of shares)}} = \text{parity price of common stock}$$

Market price of common × conversion ratio = parity price of convertible

TEST TOPIC ALERT

On the Series 7 exam, there will most likely be questions on parity. Here are two methods to help you solve the problem.

RST bond is convertible to common at $50. If RST bond is currently trading for $1,200, what is the parity price of the common?

Method One: Parity means equal. Solve for the conversion ratio as follows:

Par value:	$1,000
Conversion price:	$ 50
Conversion ratio:	20

The parity stock price is found by dividing $1,200 by 20. The parity price of the common is $60.

Method Two: If you prefer to think in percentages, identify that the new bond price of $1,200 is 20% greater than the original $1,000 price. To be at equivalence, the stock price must also increase by 20%. So add 20% to 50 and the problem is solved. 20% of 50 is 10; 10 + 50 = parity price of $60.

Here is another style of parity question.

RST bond is convertible to common at $50. If the common is trading for $45, what is the parity price of the bond? Start by solving for the conversion ratio.

Par value:	$1,000
Conversion price:	$ 50
Conversion ratio:	20

The bond price is found by multiplying 20 × 45. The parity price of the bond is $900. Using the percentage method, you can determine that the market price of the common stock is 10% below that of the conversion price (5 ÷ 50 = 10%). Reducing the bond price of $1,000 by 10% results in a parity price of the bond of $900.

In a **rising** market, the convertible's value rises with the common stock's value. In a **declining** market, the convertible's market price tends to level off when its yield becomes competitive with the yield on nonconvertible bonds, and it may not decline in price as much as the common stock. Convertible bonds normally sell at a premium above parity, which is why they are not constantly exchanged for common stock when the stock price is rising.

2. 5. 2. 6 Antidilution Covenant

Dilution of an investor's ownership interest occurs when the percentage of ownership is lessened. Convertible bondholders are protected by an **antidilution covenant** found in the trust indenture. This covenant requires an adjustment to the conversion price for stock splits, stock dividends, and the issuance of new shares.

EXAMPLE   A convertible bond has a conversion price of $25. The investor is currently entitled to 40 shares. If the issuer declares a stock dividend of 25%, the convertible bondholder's 40 shares are adjusted to 50 shares (40 × 1.25 = 50). The conversion price is adjusted to $20 as a result (25 ÷ 1.25).

EXAMPLE   A convertible bond is issued with a conversion price of $40. If the issuer declares and pays a 10% stock dividend, what is the new conversion price? Before the stock dividend is declared and paid, the customer would receive 25 common shares ($1,000 ÷ $40). With the stock dividend paid, the customer would need to receive 10% more shares, or 27.5 shares to stay even; $1,000 ÷ 27.5 = 36.36, the new conversion price. Alternatively, divide the existing conversion price of $40 by 110%, which equals 36.36. To make sure this is correct, you can divide the new conversion price into $1,000 to see how many shares the customer will now receive if the bond is converted: $1,000 divided by 36.36 equals 27.5 shares.

2. 5. 2. 7 Forced Conversion

A **forced conversion** occurs when an issuer calls its convertible bonds and it is clearly in the best interest of bondholders to convert their bonds rather than let them be called away.

·25

40

EXAMPLE   XYZ Corp. has 7% callable convertible debentures outstanding currently trading at 113. The conversion price is $25, and the bonds are callable at 104. The price of XYZ common stock is $28. If XYZ announces a call, a bondholder has three options:

- ■ Tender bonds to the call, receiving $1,040
- ■ Sell the bonds in the open market, receiving $1,130
- ■ Convert the bonds and sell the stock, receiving $1,120

Given these choices, selling the bonds on the open market would appear to be the most advantageous choice. However, as soon as the call is announced, the price of the bond will move quickly to the conversion value of $1,120. As a result of announcing the call, the issuer has forced bondholders to either convert or sell the bonds.

1. A trust indenture spells out the covenants between

   A. trustee and underwriter
   B. issuer and underwriter
   C. issuer and bondholders
   D. issuer and a trustee for the benefit of a bondholder

2. ABC, Inc., has filed for bankruptcy. Interested parties will be paid off in which order?

   I. Holders of secured debt
   II. Holders of subordinated debentures
   III. General creditors
   IV. Preferred stockholders

   A. I, II, III, IV
   B. I, III, II, IV
   C. III, I, II, IV
   D. IV, I, II, III

3. Moody's bond page lists the following bonds: GMAC ZR '19 54¼, Ogden 5s '22 26½. The annual interest on 50 Ogden bonds is

   A. $93
   B. $500
   C. $930
   D. $2,500

4. Which of the following statements regarding convertible and callable bonds are TRUE?

   I. If called, the owners have the option of retaining the bonds and will continue to receive interest.
   II. After the date it is called, interest will cease to be paid.
   III. Upon conversion, there will be dilution.
   IV. The coupon rate would be lower than the rate for a nonconvertible bond.

   A. I and III
   B. I, III and IV
   C. II, III and IV
   D. II and IV

5. Which of the following statements regarding convertible bonds is NOT true?

   A. Coupon rates are usually higher than nonconvertible bond rates of the same issuer.
   B. Convertible bondholders are creditors of the corporation.
   C. Coupon rates are usually lower than nonconvertible bond rates of the same issuer.
   D. If the underlying common stock declines to the point where there is no advantage to convert the bonds into common stock, the bonds will sell at a price based on their inherent value as bonds, regardless of the convertible feature.

6. A bond is convertible to common stock at $20 per share. If the market value of the bond falls to $800, what is the new parity price of the stock?

   A. $12
   B. $16
   C. $25
   D. $40

7. A convertible bond is purchased at its face value and convertible at $125. What is the conversion ratio?

   A. 2
   B. 8
   C. 12
   D. 20

Quick Quiz answers can be found at the end of the Unit.

2. 6 U.S. GOVERNMENT AND AGENCY SECURITIES

The U.S. Treasury Department determines the quantity and types of government securities it must issue to meet federal budget needs. The marketplace determines the interest rates those securities will pay. In general, the interest government securities pay is exempt from state and municipal taxation but subject to federal taxation.

The federal government is the nation's largest borrower as well as the best credit risk. Securities issued by the U.S. government are backed by its full faith and credit, based on its power to tax.

Most government securities are issued in **book-entry form**, meaning that no physical certificates exist.

2. 6. 1 MARKETABLE GOVERNMENT SECURITIES

Treasury securities are classified as **bills**, **notes**, and **bonds** to distinguish an issue's term to maturity. Regular way settlement for these securities is next business day.

2. 6. 1. 1 Treasury Bills (T-Bills)

T-bills are short-term obligations issued at a discount from par. Rather than making regular cash interest payments, bills trade at a discount from par value; the return on a T-bill is the difference between the price the investor pays and the par value at which the bill matures.

2. 6. 1. 1. 1 Maturities and Denominations

Treasury bills are issued in denominations of $100 to $5 million, have original maturities of 4, 13, and 26 weeks and are auctioned weekly by the U.S. Treasury.

TAKE NOTE   Maximum T-bill maturities are subject to change.

2. 6. 1. 1. 2 Pricing for T-Bills

T-bills are quoted on a yield basis and sold at a discount from par. They are zero-coupon securities.

EXAMPLE

Issue	Bid	Ask
T-bills maturing 03/15/05	1.15	1.12

The bid reflects the yield buyers want to receive. The ask reflects the yield sellers are willing to accept.

TAKE NOTE The exam will not require you to calculate the bid and ask prices of T-bills.

Because T-bills are quoted in yield, a T-bill quote has a bid higher than its asked, which is the reverse of bid-ask relationships for other instruments. Higher yield on the bid side translates into a lower dollar price.

2. 6. 1. 2 Treasury Notes (T-Notes)

Unlike Treasury bills, **T-notes** pay interest every six months. They are sold at auction every four weeks.

2. 6. 1. 2. 1 Maturities and Denominations

Issued in denominations of $100 to $5 million, T-notes are intermediate-term bonds maturing in 2 to 10 years. T-notes mature at par, or they can be **refunded**. If a T-note is refunded, the government offers the investor a new security with a new interest rate and maturity date as an alternative to a cash payment for the maturing note.

2. 6. 1. 2. 2 Pricing for T-Notes

T-notes are issued, quoted, and traded as a percentage of par in $\frac{1}{32}$s.

EXAMPLE A quote of 98.24, which can also be expressed as 98-24 or 98:24, on a $1,000 note means that the note is selling for $98\frac{24}{32}$% of its $1,000 par value. In this instance, .24 designates $\frac{24}{32}$ of 1%, not a decimal. A quote of 98.24 equals 98.75% of $1,000, or $987.50.

Pricing of T-Notes

A bid of:	Means:	Or:
98.01	98$\frac{1}{32}$% of $1,000	$980.3125
98.02	98$\frac{2}{32}$% of $1,000	$980.6250
98.03	98$\frac{3}{32}$% of $1,000	$980.9375
98.10	98$\frac{10}{32}$% of $1,000	$983.1250
98.11	98$\frac{11}{32}$% of $1,000	$983.4375
98.12	98$\frac{12}{32}$% of $1,000	$983.7500

2. 6. 1. 3   Treasury Bonds (T-Bonds)

T-bonds are long-term securities (10 to 30 years in original maturity) that pay interest every six months.

2. 6. 1. 3. 1   Maturities and Denominations

Treasury bonds are issued in denominations of $100 to $5 million and mature in more than 10 years from the date of issue.

2. 6. 1. 3. 2   Pricing for T-Bonds

T-bonds are quoted exactly like T-notes.

Testable Features of Treasury Bills, Notes, and Bonds

Marketable Government Securities			
Type	**Maturity**	**Pricing**	**Form**
T-bills	Less than 1 year	Issued at a discount; priced on discount basis	Book entry
T-notes	2–10 years (intermediate-term)	Priced at percentage of par	Book entry
T-bonds	Greater than 10 years (long-term)	Priced at percentage of par	Book entry

2. 6. 1. 4   Treasury Receipts

Brokerage firms can create a type of zero-coupon bond known as **Treasury receipts** from U.S. Treasury notes and bonds. Broker-dealers buy Treasury securities, place them in trust at a bank and sell separate receipts against the principal and coupon payments. The Treasury securities held in trust collateralize the Treasury receipts. Unlike Treasury securities, Treasury receipts are not backed by the full faith and credit of the U.S. government.

To illustrate how Treasury receipts are created, think of a $1,000 10-year Treasury note with a 6% coupon as 21 separate payment obligations. The first 20 are the semiannual $30 interest payment obligations until maturity. The 21st is the obligation to repay the $1,000 principal at maturity. An investor may purchase a Treasury receipt for any of the 20 interest payments or the principal repayment.

Each Treasury receipt is priced at a discount from the payment amount, like a zero-coupon bond.

2. 6. 1. 4. 1 STRIPS

In 1984, the Treasury Department entered the zero-coupon bond market by designating certain Treasury issues as suitable for stripping into interest and principal components. These securities became known as **Separate Trading of Registered Interest and Principal of Securities (STRIPS)**. Although the securities underlying Treasury STRIPS are the U.S. government's direct obligation, major banks and dealers perform the actual separation and trading.

TEST TOPIC ALERT STRIPS are backed in full by the U.S. government. Receipts are not. Treasury receipts are sold under names like Certificates of Accrual on Treasury Securities (CATS) and Treasury Income Growth Receipts (TIGRS). Both are quoted in yield.

2. 6. 1. 5 Treasury Inflation Protection Securities (TIPS)

A type of Treasury issue, known as **Treasury Inflation Protection Securities (TIPS)**, helps protect investors against purchasing power risk. These notes are issued with a fixed interest rate, but the principal amount is adjusted semiannually by an amount equal to the change in the **Consumer Price Index (CPI)**, the standard measurement of inflation.

The interest payment the investor receives every six months is equal to the fixed interest rate times the newly adjusted principal. In times of inflation, the interest payments increase, while in times of deflation, the interest payments fall. These notes are sold at lower interest rates than conventional fixed-rate Treasury notes because of their adjustable nature.

Like other Treasury notes, TIPS are exempt from state and local income taxes on the interest income generated, but they are subject to federal taxation. However, in any year when the principal is adjusted for inflation, that increase is considered reportable income for that year even though the increase will not be received until the note matures.

TEST TOPIC ALERT The Series 7 exam may ask a question similar to the following.

A customer wishes to buy a security providing periodic interest payments, safety of principal, and protection from purchasing power risk. The customer should purchase

A. TIPS
B. TIGRS
C. CMOs
D. STRIPS

Answer: A. TIPS offer inflation protection and safety of principal because they are backed by the U.S. government.

2. 6. 2   AGENCY ISSUES

Congress authorizes the following agencies of the federal government to issue debt securities:

■ Farm Credit Administration
■ Government National Mortgage Association (GNMA or Ginnie Mae)

Other agency-like organizations operated by private corporations include the following:

■ Federal Home Loan Mortgage Corporation (FHLMC or Freddie Mac)
■ Federal National Mortgage Association (FNMA or Fannie Mae)
■ Student Loan Marketing Association (SLMA or Sallie Mae)

The term *agency* is sometimes used to refer to entities that are not technically government agencies but that do have ties to the government. Fannie Mae is privately owned but government sponsored.

TAKE NOTE   Settlement of agency securities is regular way (two business days).

2. 6. 2. 1   Yields and Maturities

Agency issues have higher yields than direct obligations of the federal government but lower yields than corporate debt securities. Their maturities range from short to long term. Agency issues are quoted as percentages of par and trade actively in the secondary market.

2. 6. 2. 2   Taxation for Agency Issues

Government agency issues that are backed by mortgages are taxed at the federal, state, and local levels. Other agency securities are generally taxed at the federal level only.

2. 6. 2. 3   Government National Mortgage Association (Ginnie Mae)

The **Government National Mortgage Association (GNMA)** is a government-owned corporation that supports the Department of Housing and Urban Development. Ginnie Maes are the only agency securities backed by the full faith and credit of the federal government.

2. 6. 2. 3. 1   Types of GNMA Issues

Ginnie Mae does not originate mortgage loans, nor does it purchase, sell, or issue securities. Instead, private lending institutions approved by GNMA originate eligible loans, pool them into securities, known as pass-through certificates, and sell the GNMA mortgage-backed securities (MBS) to investors. These lending institutions can include mortgage companies, commercial banks, and thrift institutions of all sizes, as well as state housing finance agencies.

Ginnie Mae guarantees only mortgage-backed securities backed by single and multifamily home loans insured by government agencies, primarily the Federal Housing Association (FHA) and the Department of Veteran Affairs (VA) as well as others. Like the principal on a single mortgage, the principal represented by a GNMA certificate constantly decreases as the mortgages are paid down. GNMA pass-throughs pay higher interest rates than comparable Treasury securities, yet are guaranteed by the federal government.

GNMA also guarantees timely payment of interest and principal. GNMAs are backed directly by the government, so risk of default is nearly zero. Prices, yields, and maturities fluctuate in line with general interest rate trends. If interest rates fall, homeowners tend to pay off their mortgages early, which accelerates the certificates' maturities. If interest rates rise, certificates may mature more slowly.

GNMAs are issued in $25,000 face value certificates but can be purchased in minimum denominations as low as $1,000. Because few mortgages last the full term, yield quotes are based on a 12-year prepayment assumption; that is, a mortgage balance should be prepaid in full after 12 years of normally scheduled payments.

In addition to interest rate risk (the risk that rates rise, causing the value of the underlying mortgages to fall), there are two other types of risk associated with mortgage-backed securities. The first is **prepayment risk**, the risk that the underlying mortgages will be paid off earlier than anticipated. This will occur if interest rates fall, causing homeowners to refinance their mortgages at lower rates.

The second is **extended maturity risk**, the risk that the underlying mortgages will remain outstanding longer than anticipated. This will occur if interest rates rise, virtually eliminating any refinancings.

2. 6. 2. 3. 2   Taxation for GNMA

Interest earned on GNMA certificates is taxable at the federal, state, and local levels.

TAKE NOTE

GNMAs are backed in full by the U.S. government. Other agency instruments discussed next are not; they are backed by their own issuing authority.

Know the following GNMA features:

- $1,000 minimums

- Monthly interest and principal payments

- Taxed at all levels

- Pass-through certificates

- Significant reinvestment risk

TEST TOPIC ALERT

The Series 7 exam expects you to know that mortgage-backed securities (MBS) are susceptible to reinvestment risk. The reasons are outlined below.

When interest rates fall, mortgage holders typically refinance at lower rates. This means that they pay off their mortgages early, which causes a prepayment of principal to holders of mortgage-backed securities. The early principal payments cannot be reinvested at a comparable return.

Sometimes the test asks which instruments are not subject to reinvestment risk. Of the ones listed, the best answer is typically a zero-coupon bond. No interest is paid on a current basis, so the investor has no reinvestment risk.

2. 6. 2. 4   Farm Credit System

The **Farm Credit System (FCS)** is a national network of lending institutions that provides agricultural financing and credit. The system is a privately owned, government-sponsored enterprise that raises loanable funds through the sale of Farm Credit Securities to investors. These funds are made available to farmers through a nationwide network of eight banks and 225 Farm Credit lending institutions. The Farm Credit Administration (FCA), a government agency, oversees the system.

The federal Farm Credit System issues discount notes, bonds, and master notes. The maturities range from one day to 30 years. The proceeds from the sale of securities are used to provide farmers with real estate loans, rural home mortgage loans, and crop insurance. Interest paid on these securities is exempt from state and local taxation.

2. 6. 2. 5   Federal Home Loan Mortgage Corporation (Freddie Mac)

The **Federal Home Loan Mortgage Corporation (FHLMC)** is a public corporation. It was created to promote the development of a nationwide secondary market in mortgages by buying residential mortgages from financial institutions and packaging them into mortgage-backed securities for sale to investors.

2. 6. 2. 5. 1   Pass-Through Certificates

A pass-through security is created by pooling a group of mortgages and selling certificates representing interests in the pool. The term **pass-through** refers to the mechanism of passing homebuyers' interest and principal payments from the mortgage holder to the investors. Fannie Mae, Ginnie Mae, and Freddie Mac function this way.

FHLMC sells two types of pass-through securities: **mortgage participation certificates (PCs)** and **guaranteed mortgage certificates (GMCs)**. PCs make principal and interest payments once a month; GMCs make interest payments twice a year and principal payments once a year.

2. 6. 2. 5. 2   Taxation for Freddie Mac

Income from FHLMC securities is subject to federal, state, and local income taxes.

2. 6. 2. 6   Federal National Mortgage Association (Fannie Mae)

The **Federal National Mortgage Association (FNMA)** is a publicly held corporation that provides mortgage capital. FNMA purchases conventional and insured mortgages from agencies such as the FHA and the VA. The securities it creates are backed by FNMA's general credit.

2. 6. 2. 6. 1   Types of FNMA Issues

FNMA issues debentures, short-term discount notes, and mortgage-backed securities. The notes are issued in denominations of $5,000, $25,000, $100,000, $500,000, and $1 million. Debentures with maturities from 3 to 25 years are issued in minimum denominations of $10,000 in increments of $5,000. Interest is paid semiannually. They are issued in book-entry form only.

2. 6. 2. 6. 2   Taxation for FNMA

Interest from FNMA securities is taxed at the federal, state, and local levels.

2. 6. 2. 7   Sallie Mae

The **Student Loan Marketing Association (Sallie Mae)** issues discount notes and short-term floating rate notes. The floaters have six-month maturities. The proceeds from the securities sales are used to provide student loans for higher education. Interest paid on Sallie Mae securities is taxable at the federal level and is exempt from taxation in most states. SLM stock is listed for trading.

QUICK QUIZ 2.B

1. Which of the following statements regarding T-bills are TRUE?

   I.   T-bills trade at a discount to par.
   II. T-bills mature in less than 1 year.
   III. Most T-bill issues are callable.
   IV. T-bills are a direct obligation of the U.S. government.

   A. I and II
   B. I, II and III
   C. I, II and IV
   D. I, II, III and IV

2. You buy ten 8% T-notes at 101–16. What is the dollar amount of this purchase?

   A. $1,001.50
   B. $1,011.60
   C. $10,150.00
   D. $10,812.00

3. Which of the following statements regarding U.S. government agency obligations are TRUE?

   I.   They are all direct obligations of the U.S. government.
   II. They generally have higher yields than yields of treasury securities.
   III. The FNMA is a publicly traded corporation.
   IV. Securities issued by GNMA trade on the NYSE floor.

   A. I and II
   B. I and III
   C. II and III
   D. II and IV

2. 6. 3   ISSUANCE OF GOVERNMENT SECURITIES

Like municipal securities, U.S. government securities are exempt securities, which means they are exempt from the registration provisions of the Act of 1933. Treasury bills and Treasury notes are sold through an auction conducted on behalf of the U.S. Treasury by the Federal Reserve.

In Treasury auctions, there are two types of bids that can be placed: competitive and noncompetitive. **Competitive bids** are those placed by primary dealers in U.S. government securities. The number of banks and broker-dealers designated as primary dealers by the Federal Reserve changes. Examples of primary dealers include HSBC, J.P. Morgan, Citigroup, and Bank of America Securities. These primary dealers are the largest banks and brokerage firms. Primary dealers are required to bid at Treasury auctions.

Noncompetitive bids are placed by other market participants: smaller banks and broker-dealers, insurance companies, and individuals. Noncompetitive bids are always filled, but the price these bidders pay is the lowest accepted competitive bid called the **stop out price**.

Competitive bids are made in yield, not dollar, price.

EXAMPLE

The Treasury is planning to auction $25 billion of 10-year notes. By noon on the day of the auction, the Fed has received $5 billion in noncompetitive bids. This leaves $20 billion to be auctioned to the primary dealers. By 1:00 pm, the Fed receives $30 billion in competitive bids as follows:

Dealer	Dollar Amount	Bid (Yield)
1	$4 billion	3.98
2	$5 billion	3.99
3	$3 billion	4.00
4	$5 billion	4.02
5	$3 billion	4.03
6	$4 billion	4.05
7	$6 billion	4.06

The highest bid (lowest yield) is accepted first and on down the line until $20 billion has been accepted. The lowest accepted bid (4.03) is the stop out price—the price that all bidders will pay, both competitive and noncompetitive. This type of auction is called a **Dutch auction**. Note that some bidders will pay less than they bid. Also note that the bids of Dealers 6 and 7 were not filled.

TAKE NOTE

Noncompetitive bids are always filled; competitive bids are not always filled.

Settlement of winning bids takes place on Thursday of that week for T-bills and the Thursday of the following week for T-notes. In some instances, T-notes can settle on other days as well.

U.S. government agency securities, on the other hand, are issued through underwriting groups who buy the securities directly from the agency, at par less a spread, and are sold to the public at par.

2. 7 ACCRUED INTEREST CALCULATIONS

Most bonds trade *and interest*, meaning a buyer pays a seller a bond's market price, plus any accrued interest since the last interest payment. The buyer receives the full amount of the next interest payment, including interest that accrued while the seller owned the bond.

Most bonds pay interest every six months on either the 1st or the 15th of the specified months. The payment dates are known as **coupon dates**. Accrued interest affects bond transactions when settlement occurs between coupon dates. Some examples of coupon dates follow.

If the interest dates are:	The bonds are known as:
January 1 and July 1	J&J bonds
February 15 and August 15	F&A 15 bonds
March 1 and September 1	M&S bonds
April 1 and October 1	A&O bonds
May 15 and November 15	M&N 15 bonds
June 15 and December 15	J&D 15 bonds

T A K E N O T E

When payment dates within the month are not specified, always assume the first of the month (e.g., J & J, assume January 1 and July 1).

2. 7. 1 ACCRUED INTEREST AND THE DATED DATE

For a new bond issue, the date from which interest accrual begins is called the **dated date**. Even if a bond is issued at a later date, the bond starts accruing interest on the date designated as the dated date.

T A K E N O T E

The accrued interest amount is calculated to add to the price that the buyer pays and the seller receives when the bond trades between its coupon payment dates. Consider a bond with interest payments on January 1 and July 1. If a trade is made in April, the seller is entitled to some of the July interest payment. Specifically, the seller will receive interest up to, but not including, the settlement date of the transaction as shown in the following graph.

2. 7. 2   CORPORATE AND MUNICIPAL BONDS

Unless a bond is trading flat (discussed later), the bond cost to the buyer and the proceeds to the seller include accrued interest. Accrued interest increases the bond cost to the buyer and the proceeds to the seller.

Accrued interest is calculated from the last interest payment date up to but not including the settlement date. The buyer owns the bond on the settlement date, which means that the interest for that day belongs to the buyer.

2. 7. 2. 1   Accrued Interest Calculations

Two methods are used to calculate accrued interest. The 30-day-month (360-day-year) method is used on all corporate and municipal bonds. The actual-calendar-days (365-day-year) method is used on all U.S. government bonds.

2. 7. 2. 1. 1   Accrued Interest Calculation: 360-Day Year

Accrued interest on corporate and municipal bonds is calculated for a 360-day year of 30-day months.

Principal × interest rate × elapsed days ÷ 360 days = accrued bond interest

---

EXAMPLE

If an F&A municipal bond is traded regular way on Monday, March 5, the number of days of accrued interest is calculated as follows:

February	30 days
March 5 trade	6 days (settles March 7)
Days of accrued interest	36 days

Because the trade settles on March 7, six days of interest accrue for March.

If an A&O corporate or municipal bond is bought or sold in a cash trade (same-day settlement) on August 16, the number of days of accrued interest is calculated as follows:

April	30 days
May	30 days
June	30 days
July	30 days
August	15 days
Days of accrued interest	135 days

2. 7. 2. 1. 2   Accrued Interest Calculation: 365-Day Year

For calculating time elapsed since the most recent interest payment on a government bond, an actual-days-elapsed method is used instead of the 30-day-month, 360-day-year method used for corporate and municipal bonds.

EXAMPLE   If an F&A government bond is traded regular way on Monday, March 5, the number of days of accrued interest would be calculated as follows:

February	28 days
March	5 days
Days of accrued interest	33 days (up to but not including the March 6 settlement date)

If an A&O government bond is traded for cash on August 16, the number of days of accrued interest would be calculated as follows:

April	30 days
May	31 days
June	30 days
July	31 days
August	15 days
Days of accrued interest	137 days (actual days elapsed)

Summary of Accrued Interest Calculations

	Corporate or Municipal Bonds	U.S. Government Bonds
Regular way settlement	Second business day (T+2) after trade date	Next business day (T+1) after trade date
Monthly interest days	30-day months (including February)	Actual calendar days per month
Accrued interest meter starts	Last interest payment date is day one for accrued interest purposes	Same
Accrued interest meter stops	Bond interest accrues up to, but does not include, settlement date	Same

TEST TOPIC ALERT   An ABC J&J 15 8s of '09 is purchased on Monday, April 15, in a regular way transaction. How many days of accrued interest are owed to the seller?

You must determine that ABC is a corporate bond (three-letter names are corporate instruments) that pays interest on January 15 and July 15. To set up the calculation, first determine the settlement date. Then count the number of days up to but not including the settlement date to determine the accrued interest owed to the seller.

The seller receives interest through April 16. The number of days are calculated on the basis of a corporate month of 30 days as follows:

- January: 16 days (You must *include* the 15th, which makes 16 days.)

- February: 30 days

- March: 30 days

- April: 16 days

The total is 92 days of accrued interest payable to the seller.

If you were asked to calculate the dollar amount of interest, take the number of days divided by 360 times the coupon amount: 92 ÷ 360 = .2555 × $80 = $20.44.

The Series 7 exam is probably more likely to ask the number of days than the dollar amount on accrued interest calculations.

Let's change the situation slightly. Assume a U.S. Treasury bond, J&J 15 8s of '09, is purchased on Monday, April 15, in a regular way transaction. How many days of accrued interest are owed to the seller?

This calculation involves the settlement rule of T+1 and actual-day months.

- January: 17 days (You must include the 15th, which makes 17 days.)

- February: 28 days (Always assume no leap years)

- March: 31 days

- April: 15 days

The total is 91 days of accrued interest payable to the seller.

Read the questions carefully so that all significant details are included in your accrued interest calculations. You are likely to see a concept and a calculation question about accrued interest.

Trading flat is a term used to describe a situation in which a bond trades without accrued interest. Zero-coupon bonds, as well as income bonds, trade flat. In addition, bonds in default also trade flat. Finally, if the settlement date of a bond transaction coincides with an interest payment date, there is no accrued interest. The seller will receive the entire six months' interest from the issuer.

TAKE NOTE

For agency securities, regular way settlement is two business days, and accrued interest is based on a 360-day year.

2. 8 COLLATERALIZED MORTGAGE OBLIGATIONS (CMOs)

CMOs are a type of **asset-backed security**. Asset-backed securities are ones whose value and income payments are derived from or backed by a specific pool of underlying assets. These pools of assets can include expected payments from different types of loans such as mortgages, as is the case with CMOs, auto loans, or other types of loans. In some instances, asset-backed securities can pool expected cash flow from credit cards, leases, or even royalty payments. Pooling the assets into financial instruments allows them to be sold to general investors more easily than selling them individually. This process is called securitization, and it allows the risk of investing in the underlying assets to be diversified because each security will now represent only a fraction of the total value of the diverse pool of underlying assets. CMOs pool a large number of mortgages, usually on single-family residences. A pool of mortgages is structured into maturity classes called **tranches**. CMOs are issued by private sector financing corporations and are often backed by Ginnie Mae, Fannie Mae, and Freddie Mac pass-through securities. As a result, CMOs backed by government agency securities have historically been rated high.

A CMO pays principal and interest from the mortgage pool monthly; however, it repays principal to only one tranche at a time. In addition to interest payments, investors in a short-term tranche must receive all of their principal before the next tranche begins to receive principal repayments. Principal payments are made in $1,000 increments to randomly selected bonds within a tranche. Changes in interest rates affect the rate of mortgage prepayments, and this, in turn, affects the flow of interest payment and principal repayment to the CMO investor.

TAKE NOTE

This type of CMO, also referred to as a **plain vanilla CMO**, pays interest on all tranches simultaneously. However, it pays principal to only one tranche at a time until it is retired. Subsequent principal payments are made to the next tranche in line until it is paid off, and so on.

A CMO's yield and maturity are estimates based on historical data or projections of mortgage prepayments from the **Public Securities Association (PSA)**. The particular tranche an investor owns determines the priority of his principal repayment. The time to maturity, amount of interest received, and amount of principal returned are not guaranteed. The model developed by the PSA compensates for the fact that prepayment assumptions will change during the life of an obligation and that this will affect the yield of the security.

Sample CMO Tranche Structure

Tranche	Interest Rate	Estimated Life in Years
1	5.125%	1.5
2	5.25%	3.5
3	5.5%	6.0
4	5.875%	8.5
5	6.125%	11.0

2. 8. 1   CLASSES OF CMOs

In addition to the standard CMOs discussed, some CMOs have been structured to suit specific needs of investors. Common CMO types include:

- principal only;
- interest only;
- planned amortization class; and
- targeted amortization class.

2. 8. 1. 1   Principal-Only CMOs (POs)

The flow of income from underlying mortgages is divided into principal and interest streams and directed to the owners of **principal-only CMOs (POs)** and **interest-only CMOs (IOs)**, respectively. For a PO, the income stream comes from principal payments on the underlying mortgages—both scheduled mortgage principal payments and prepayments. Thus, the security ultimately repays its entire face value to the investor.

A PO sells at a discount from par; the difference between the discounted price and the principal value is the investor's return. Its market value, like all deeply discounted securities, tends to be volatile. POs, in particular, are affected by fluctuations in prepayment rates. The value of a PO rises as interest rates drop and prepayments accelerate, and its value falls when interest rates rise and prepayments decline.

2. 8. 1. 2   Interest-Only CMOs (IOs)

IOs are by-products of POs. Whereas POs receive the principal stream from underlying mortgages, IOs receive the interest. An IO also sells at a discount, and its cash flow declines over time, just as the proportion of interest in a mortgage payment declines over time. Unlike POs, IOs increase in value when interest rates rise, and they decline in value when interest rates fall because the number of interest payments changes as prepayment rates change. Thus, they can be used to hedge a portfolio against interest rate risk.

When prepayment rates are high, the owner of an IO may receive fewer interest payments than anticipated. Because the entire CMO series receives more principal sooner and therefore less overall interest, the IO owner does not know how long the stream of interest payments will last.

2. 8. 1. 3   Planned Amortization Class CMOs (PACs)

PACs have targeted maturity dates; they are retired first and offer protection from **prepayment risk** and **extension risk** (the chance that principal payments will be slower than anticipated) because changes in prepayments are transferred to companion tranches, also called support tranches.

2. 8. 1. 4   Targeted Amortization Class CMOs (TACs)

A TAC structure transfers prepayment risk only to a companion tranche and does not offer protection from extension risk. TAC investors accept the extension risk and the resulting greater price risk in exchange for a slightly higher interest rate.

2. 8. 1. 5   Zero-Tranche CMO (Z-Tranche)

A Z-tranche receives no payment until all preceding CMO tranches are retired (the most volatile CMO tranches).

TEST TOPIC ALERT   Z-tranche CMOs would not be suitable for an investor needing funds in a specified amount of time, due to the unpredictable nature of when payment will be received.

2. 8. 2   CMO CHARACTERISTICS

Because mortgages back CMOs, they are considered relatively safe. However, their susceptibility to interest rate movements and the resulting changes in the mortgage repayment rate mean CMOs carry several risks.

- The rate of principal repayment varies.
- If interest rates fall and homeowner refinancing increases, principal is received sooner than anticipated (prepayment risk).
- If interest rates rise and refinancing declines, the CMO investor may have to hold his investment longer than anticipated (extended maturity risk).

2. 8. 2. 1   Yields

CMOs yield more than Treasury securities and normally pay investors interest and principal monthly. Principal repayments are made in $1,000 increments to investors in one tranche before any principal is repaid to the next tranche.

2. 8. 2. 2   Taxation

Interest from CMOs is subject to federal, state, and local taxes.

2. 8. 2. 3   Liquidity

There is an active secondary market for CMOs. However, the market for CMOs with more complex characteristics may be limited or nonexistent. Certain tranches of a given CMO may be riskier than others, and some CMOs in certain tranches carry the risk that repayment of principal may take longer than anticipated.

2. 8. 2. 4   Denominations

CMOs are issued in $1,000 denominations.

2. 8. 2. 5   Suitability

Some varieties of CMOs, such as PAC companion tranches, may be particularly unsuitable for small or unsophisticated investors because of their complexity and risks. The customer is required to sign a **suitability statement** before buying any CMO. Potential investors must understand that the rate of return on CMOs may vary because of early repayment. Also note that the performance of CMOs may not be compared to any other investment vehicle.

TEST TOPIC ALERT

It will be useful to know the following summary.

- CMOs are not backed by the U.S. government; they are corporate instruments.

- Interest paid is taxable at all levels.

- CMOs are backed by mortgage pools.

- CMOs yield more than U.S. Treasury securities.

- CMOs are subject to interest rate risk.

- CMOs are issued in $1,000 denominations and trade OTC.

- PACs have reduced prepayment and extension risk.

- TACs are protected against prepayment risk but not extension risk.

- PACs have lower yields than comparable TACs.

2. 8. 3 COLLATERALIZED DEBT OBLIGATIONS (CDOS)

CDOs are typically complex asset-backed securities. While CDOs do not specialize in any single type of debt, usually their portfolios consist of non-mortgage loans or bonds. The assets backing the CDOs can be a pool of bonds, auto loans, or other assets such as leases, credit card debt, a company's receivables, or even derivative products of any of the assets listed.

While the individual assets may be small and not very liquid, pooling the assets facilitates them being sold to individual investors in the secondary markets. This pooling or repackaging of assets is sometimes referred to as securitization. Securitization allows the risk of investing in the underlying assets to be diversified because each security will represent a fraction of the total value of the entire diverse pool of assets.

Similar in structure to collateralized mortgage obligations (CMOs), CDOs represent different types of debt and credit risk. Like CMOs, the different types of debt and risk categories are often referred to as *tranches* or *slices*. Each tranche has a different maturity and risk associated with it. The higher the risk, the more the CDO pays. In practice, the investor will choose a tranche with a risk and return combination that is suitable for them.

Cautions when investing with CDOs should include the following:

- Some CDOs are so complex that individual investors may not fully understand the product and, therefore, do not understand what they are purchasing. While the securitization of the assets easily enables their sale to individual investors, the product is recognized as being more suitable to institutional or sophisticated investors.

- The sale of the individual assets from the originators of the loans to those who are repackaging them allows the originators to avoid having to collect on them when they become due because they are now owned by someone else. In this case, the issuer of the CDO owns the assets. In turn, this may lead to originators of loans being less judicious and disciplined in adhering to sound lending practices when the loans are made.

2.9   NONMARKETABLE U.S. GOVERNMENT SECURITIES

The U.S. Treasury issues nonmarketable securities in the form of savings bonds. These bonds are nonmarketable because no secondary market exists. Buying and selling these bonds is effected directly between the investor and agents of the U.S. Treasury such as commercial banks, or sometimes directly from the U.S. Treasury Department through an account set up with Treasury Direct.

Examples of such savings bonds include Series EE bonds that return a fixed rate of return and Series I bonds designed to protect against inflation with interest linked to an inflation index.

QUICK QUIZ 2.C

1. CMOs are backed by

   A. mortgages
   B. real estate
   C. municipal taxes
   D. the full faith and credit of the U.S. government

2. The term *tranche* is associated with which of the following investments?

   A. FNMA
   B. CMO
   C. GNMA
   D. SLMA

3. Interest received from a CMO investment is taxable at which level(s)?

   I. Federal
   II. State
   III. Local

   A. I only
   B. II and III
   C. III only
   D. I, II and III

4. When selling a CMO to a customer, a registered representative must make which of the following disclosures?

   A. Repayment of principal is guaranteed by the federal government.
   B. The rate of return may vary owing to early repayment.
   C. The minimum investment is $15,000.
   D. A certificate is issued in the name of the beneficial owner.

5. Which of the following debt securities does NOT have a fixed maturity date?

   A. Collateralized mortgage obligation
   B. General obligation bond
   C. Treasury STRIPS
   D. Subordinated debenture

6. A registered representative may compare the performance of a CMO investment to the performance of a security issued by which of the following agencies?

   A. GNMA
   B. FDIC
   C. SLMA
   D. None of the above

2. 10   MONEY MARKET SECURITIES AND INTEREST RATES

In the financial marketplace, a distinction is made between the **capital market** and the **money market**. The capital market serves as a source of intermediate-term to long-term financing, usually in the form of equity or debt securities with maturities of more than one year.

The money market, on the other hand, provides very short-term funds to corporations, banks, broker-dealers, and the U.S. government. Money market securities are debt issues with maturities of one year or less.

2. 10. 1   THE MONEY MARKET

2. 10. 1. 1   Liquidity and Safety

Money market instruments are fixed-income securities with short-term maturities, typically one year or less. Money market securities are highly liquid because they are short-term instruments. Money market securities also provide a relatively high degree of safety because they are short term and have little chance of default.

Money market securities include:

- Treasury bills;
- repurchase agreements (repos);
- reverse repurchase agreements;
- banker's acceptances (time drafts);
- commercial paper (prime paper);
- negotiable certificates of deposit; and
- federal funds.

2. 10. 2   MONEY MARKET INSTRUMENTS

2. 10. 2. 1   Repurchase Agreements

In a **repurchase agreement (repo)**, a financial institution, such as a bank or broker-dealer, raises cash by temporarily selling some of the securities it holds with an agreement to buy back the securities at a later date. Thus, a repo is an agreement between a buyer and a seller to conduct a transaction (sale), and then to reverse that transaction (repurchase) in the future.

A repo contract includes both a **repurchase price** and a **maturity date**. If the agreement sets a specific date, the repo is considered a fixed agreement. If the maturity date is left to the initial buyer's discretion, the repo is known as an **open repo** and becomes a demand obligation callable at any time.

Though technically a sale of securities, a repo is similar to a fully collateralized loan. Instead of borrowing money and putting up securities as collateral for the loan, the dealer sells the securities and agrees to buy them back later at a higher price. The interest on the loan is the difference between the sale price and the repurchase price. The loan's interest rate (called the **repo rate**) is negotiated between the two parties and is generally lower than bank loan rates.

If the dealer defaults on the agreement to buy back the securities, the lender can sell the securities in the secondary market. If interest rates have risen sharply, causing bond prices to fall, the lender, in selling out, may experience a loss. Therefore, the major risk in a repo, assuming the underlying security has no credit risk (e.g., a U.S. government security), is interest rate risk.

2. 10. 2. 2   Reverse Repurchase Agreements

In a repo, a dealer agrees to sell its securities to a lender and buy them back at a higher price in the future. In a **reverse repurchase agreement, or reverse repo**, a dealer agrees to buy securities from an investor and sell them back later at a higher price.

2. 10. 2. 3   Banker's Acceptances

A **banker's acceptance (BA)** is a short-term time draft with a specified payment date drawn on a bank—essentially a postdated check or line of credit. The payment date of a banker's acceptance is normally between 1 and 270 days. American corporations use banker's acceptances extensively to finance international trade; that is, a banker's acceptance typically pays for goods and services in a foreign country.

A banker's acceptance is a secured money market instrument because the holder has a lien against the trade goods in the event the accepting bank fails. Banks frequently use banker's acceptances as collateral against **Federal Reserve Bank (FRB)** loans. Banker's acceptances are sold at a discount and mature at par. They are quoted in yield.

2. 10. 2. 4   Commercial Paper

Corporations issue short-term, unsecured **commercial paper**, or **promissory notes**, to raise cash to finance accounts receivable and seasonal inventory gluts. Commercial paper interest rates are lower than bank loan rates.

Commercial paper maturities range from 1 to 270 days, although most mature within 90 days, and they are normally issued in book-entry form. Typically, companies with excellent credit ratings issue commercial paper. The primary buyers of commercial paper are money market funds, commercial banks, pension funds, insurance companies, corporations, and nongovernmental agencies. Commercial paper is sold at a discount and matures at par. It is quoted in yield.

2. 10. 2. 4. 1 Direct Paper

Direct paper is commercial paper sold by finance companies directly to the public without the use of dealers. General Motors Acceptance Corporation (GMAC) is a well-known issuer. High-quality commercial paper is sometimes called prime paper.

2. 10. 2. 4. 2 Dealer Paper

Dealer paper is commercial paper sold by issuers through dealers rather than directly to the public.

2. 10. 2. 4. 3 Tax-Exempt Commercial Paper

Municipal commercial paper is similar to corporate paper, but the municipality usually has acquired a credit line or letter of credit for the issue.

2. 10. 2. 5 Certificates of Deposit (CDs)

Banks issue and guarantee **CDs** with fixed interest rates and minimum face values of $100,000, although face values of $1 million or more are more common. Some can be traded in the secondary market.

2. 10. 2. 5. 1 Nonnegotiable CDs

Most investors are familiar with the CD time deposits having set maturities and fixed interest rates and being offered by banks and savings and loans. Nonnegotiable CDs are not traded in the secondary market and are not money market securities.

2. 10. 2. 5. 2 Negotiable CDs

Negotiable CDs are time deposits that banks offer. They have minimum face values of $100,000, but most are issued for $1 million or more. A negotiable CD is an unsecured promissory note guaranteed by the issuing bank. Most negotiable CDs mature in one year or less, with the maturity date often set to suit a buyer's needs. CDs can be traded in the secondary market before their maturity because they are negotiable. Accrued interest is included in the price of a negotiable CD.

2. 10. 3 INTEREST RATES

The cost of doing business is closely linked to the cost of money; the cost of money is called **interest**. The money supply and inflation levels within the economy determine the level of general interest rates. The level of a specific interest rate can be tied to one or more benchmark rates, such as the federal funds rate, the prime rate, the discount rate, and the broker loan rate.

2. 10. 3. 1 Federal Funds Rate

The **federal funds rate** is the rate the commercial money center banks charge each other for overnight loans of $1 million or more. It is considered a barometer of the direction of short-term interest rates, which fluctuate constantly. The federal funds rate is listed in daily newspapers. It is the most volatile rate in the economy.

2. 10. 3. 2 Prime Rate

The **prime rate** is the interest rate that large U.S. money center commercial banks charge their most creditworthy corporate borrowers for unsecured loans. Each bank sets its own prime rate, with larger banks generally setting a rate other banks use. Banks lower their prime rates when the Federal Reserve Board (FRB or Fed) eases the money supply, and they raise rates when the Fed contracts the money supply.

2. 10. 3. 3 Discount Rate

The **discount rate** is the rate the Federal Reserve charges for short-term loans to member banks. The discount rate also indicates the direction of FRB monetary policy: a decreasing rate indicates an easing of FRB policy; an increasing rate indicates a tightening of FRB policy.

2. 10. 3. 4 Broker Loan Rate

The **broker loan rate** is the interest rate banks charge broker-dealers on money they borrow to lend to margin account customers. The broker loan rate is also known as the **call loan rate** or **call money rate**. The broker loan rate usually is a percentage point or so above other short-term rates. Broker call loans are callable on 24-hour notice.

2. 10. 3. 5 Interest Rate Summary

Interest rates reflect the cost of money and therefore the cost of doing business. The key interest rates people monitor is discussed below.

- **Federal Funds Rate—This rate is** the interest rate charged on reserves traded among member banks for overnight use in amounts of $1 million or more. The federal funds rate changes daily in response to the borrowing banks' needs and is considered the most volatile rate. The fed funds rate is a market rate of interest. Unlike the discount rate, it is not set by the Federal Reserve. The effective fed funds rate is the daily average of selected money center banks throughout the country.

- **CD Rate**—This rate is the bank rate offered on nonnegotiable CDs. It is considered the least volatile of the rates listed.

- **Prime Rate**—This is the base rate on corporate loans at large U.S. money center commercial banks. The prime rate changes when banks react to changes in FRB policy.

- **Discount Rate**—This is the charge on loans to depository institutions by the Federal Reserve. It is set by the Federal Reserve.

- **Call Money Rate**—This is the charge on loans to broker-dealers.

- **Commercial Paper**—This is the rate on commercial paper placed directly by finance companies or the rate on high-grade unsecured notes that major corporations sell through dealers.

TEST TOPIC ALERT   You will see several money market/interest rate questions. These are basically definition questions, so review the significant features of each instrument. Also note that of the four major rates—prime, discount, fed funds, and call loan—the prime rate is the highest and the fed funds rate is the lowest. From high to low, they are ranked as follows: prime rate, call loan rate, discount rate, and fed funds rate.

2. 10. 4 EURODOLLARS AND THE FOREIGN CURRENCY MARKETS

The cost of raising money and doing business is not restricted by national boundaries. International monetary factors, such as changes in foreign currency exchange rates, eurodollars, eurosecurities, and the interbank market, can also affect U.S. money markets and businesses.

2. 10. 4. 1 Eurodollars

Eurodollars are U.S. dollars deposited in banks outside the United States; that is, the deposits remain denominated in U.S. dollars rather than the local currency.

EXAMPLE

Euroyen are Japanese yen deposited in banks outside Japan. In other words, when a currency is preceded by the prefix *euro*, it refers to a bank deposit outside of the currency's home country.

Eurodollar time deposits tend to be short term, ranging from overnight to 180 days. European banks lend eurodollars to other banks in much the same way that U.S. banks lend federal funds. The interest rate is usually based on the **London Interbank Offered Rate (LIBOR)**.

2. 10. 4. 2 Eurobonds and Eurodollar Bonds

A **eurobond** is any long-term debt instrument issued and sold outside the country of the currency in which it is denominated. A U.S. dollar-denominated eurobond, or eurodollar bond, is a bond issued and sold outside the United States, but for which the principal and interest are stated and paid in U.S. dollars. Foreign corporations, foreign governments, domestic corporations, and domestic governments (including municipalities) can issue eurodollar bonds. The U.S. government does not issue eurodollar bonds.

TEST TOPIC ALERT

Test questions sometimes ask you to contrast eurobonds and eurodollar bonds. The name of the instrument tells you how principal and interest is paid. Eurodollar bonds pay in U.S. dollars; eurobonds pay in foreign currency. Note that these instruments must be issued outside of the United States. Also note that eurodollar bonds are issued in bearer form, interest is paid once a year, and holders are not subject to withholding tax.

2. 10. 4. 3 Interbank Market

The **interbank market** developed as a means of transacting business and trading, lending, and consolidating foreign currency deposits. It is an unregulated, decentralized international market that deals in the various major world currencies. The Federal Reserve buys and sells U.S. dollars in an attempt to influence the dollar's exchange rate in the interbank market.

If the Fed decides that the U.S. dollar is priced too high in the interbank market, it can sell U.S. dollars in the market. As the supply of dollars in the market increases, the price should decrease and the exchange rate should drop. Conversely, if the Fed decides that exchange rates for the U.S. dollar are too low, it can buy dollars in the market.

Prices quoted for immediate payment and delivery are known as spot prices or spot rates. This is in contrast to forward prices where contract terms are set now, but delivery and payment will occur at a future date.

TAKE NOTE
Spot trades in actively traded currencies settle in one business day, whereas trades of less actively traded currencies settle in two business days.

2. 10. 4. 4 Exchange Rates

An **exchange rate** is the rate at which one currency can be converted into another. Affected by many factors, exchange rates fluctuate daily. Exchange rates are usually quoted in terms of the currency of the country in which the quote is published.

A currency is **appreciating** if it is rising in value in comparison to other currencies on the foreign exchange market. A currency is **depreciating** when it falls in value on the foreign exchange market. In this case, it will buy fewer units of another country's currency. A declining U.S. dollar means that U.S. dollars are becoming cheaper for citizens of other countries, and American goods and services are becoming less expensive abroad.

2. 10. 4. 4. 1 Valuation

The exchange rate between currencies changes, or **floats**, constantly. The devaluation or revaluation in relationship to the currencies of other countries can result from market factors or central bank intervention.

2. 10. 4. 5 Speculating in Foreign Currencies

Foreign currencies provide speculative opportunities for sophisticated investors. Risks of foreign currency speculation include that the interbank market is unregulated and decentralized and that changes in a country's economic, governmental, or social policies could have immediate and dramatic impact on its currency's value.

2. 11 TRACKING DEBT SECURITIES

2. 11. 1 CORPORATE BONDS

Bonds are listed in daily newspapers and other financial publications. Dealers use numerous in-house systems to obtain and disseminate quotes on corporate bonds.

EXAMPLE

In the following graphic titled "Corporate Bond Quotations," refer to AlaP (Alabama Power).

The description of its 9s 2025 bond indicates that the bond pays 9% interest and matures in the year 2025. Current yield is given as 8.9%, indicating that the bond is selling at a premium.

The Vol (volume, or sales) column states how many bonds traded the previous day (day being reported). Eighteen bonds, or $18,000 par value, were traded in AlaP 9s of 2025. The next three columns explain the high, low, and closing prices for the day. For AlaP, the high was 100¾, the low was 100⅝, and the bonds closed at (last trade) 100¾.

Net change (last column) refers to how much the bond's closing price was up or down from the previous day's close. Alabama Power 9s of 2025 closed up ¼ of a point, or $2.50. AlaP closed yesterday at 100½ (100¾ – ¼). Note that the Allied Chemical (AlldC) zr bonds have "..." in the current yield column. This indicates that these are zero-coupon bonds that do not pay interest.

Corporate Bond Quotations

New York Exchange Bonds
Quotations as of 4 pm Eastern Time
Friday, March 16, 2011
Corporation Bonds
Volume $45,198,000

Bonds	Cur Yld	Vol	High	Low	Close	Net Chg
AForP 5s 32r	9.6	50	52 1/4	51 7/8	52	+3/4
rAbbtL 7 5/8s 23	7.6	21	99 3/4	99 3/4	99 3/4	...
Advst 9s 24	cv	72	103 1/2	103	103	...
AetnLf 8 1/8s 21	8.5	15	95 3/4	95 3/4	95 3/4	−1
AirbF 7 1/2s 21	cv	32	114	112	114	+1
AlaP 9s 2025	8.9	18	100 3/4	100 5/8	100 3/4	+1/4
AlaP 8 1/2s 23	8.6	13	98 3/8	98 3/8	98 3/8	−3/8
AlaP 8 7/8s 21	8.5	65	102 7/8	102 1/2	102 1/2	−3/8
AlldC zr 21	...	10	91 1/2	91 1/8	91 1/2	−1/8
viAmes 7 1/2s 24f	cv	79	15 1/2	14 3/4	15	+1
Ancp 13 7/8s 20f	cv	10	91	89 3/8	91	+2

EXPLANATORY NOTES

Yield is current yield. **cld:** Called. **cv:** Convertible bond. **dc:** Deep discount. **f:** Dealt in flat. **m:** Matured bonds, negotiability impaired by maturity. **na:** No accrual. **r:** Registered. **zr:** Zero coupon. **vi:** In bankruptcy or receivership or being reorganized.

*This sample comprises formats, styles, and abbreviations from a variety of currently available sources and has been created for educational purposes.

2. 11. 1. 1 Trade Reporting and Compliance Engine (TRACE)

The Trade Reporting and Compliance Engine (TRACE) is the FINRA-approved trade reporting system for corporate and government agency bonds trading in the OTC secondary market. Reporting to TRACE enables better market transparency as trade details are disseminated immediately to the investing public.

TRACE is a trade-reporting system only. It is not an execution system. It does not accept quotations, nor does it provide settlement and clearance functions. Following are the reporting rules for TRACE.

■ Both sides of the transaction must report.

■ Trades must be reported as soon as practicable and no later than 15 minutes of execution.

■ Execution date, time of trade, quantity, price, yield, and if price reflects a commission charged are all reportable and displayed.

While most corporate debt securities, asset-backed securities (ABS), Treasury securities, and collateralized mortgage obligations (CMOs) are TRACE eligible, there are exclusions. The following is a list of exclusions to know:

■ Debt of foreign governments

■ Money market instruments

■ Debt securities that are not Depository Trust eligible

2. 11. 2 TRACKING U.S. GOVERNMENT SECURITIES

Quotes for Treasury bonds, notes, and bills are listed in the graphic. Reading from left to right under "Govt. Bonds & Notes," you can determine the coupon rate, maturity date, bid and asked prices, bid change from the previous trading day, and the yield to maturity.

Treasury Securities Quotations

Treasury Bonds, Notes & Bills

Quotations as of mid-afternoon
Monday, March 5, 2011

Govt. Bonds & Notes

Rate	Maturity Mo/Yr		Bid	Asked	Chg	Ask Yld
7 1/2	Aug	15n	100:02	100:04	....	7.37
7 1/4	Aug	16	100:26	100:30	....	6.30
9 1/2	Oct	18	105:31	106:01	....	7.35
8 1/2	Apr	19	102:18	102:20	+1	7.92
9	May	20	104:24	104:26	....	8.07
3 1/2	Nov	20	94:05	95:05	– 1	4.28
13 3/8	Aug	23	134:26	135:02	....	8.19
10 3/4	Feb	25	117:27	118:03	– 1	8.28

U.S. Treasury STRIPS

Maturity	Type	Bid	Asked	Chg	Bid Yld
Nov 16	np	78:19	78:22	+1	7.46
Aug 17	ci	73:15	73:18	+1	7.78
Oct 17	ci	45:06	45:10	– 2	8.50
Nov 17	bp	32:19	32:23	....	8.62
Feb 19	ci	31:22	31:26	– 1	8.67
Nov 21	bp	20:19	20:22	....	8.83
May 27	ci	13:09	13:12	....	8.67
Aug 32	ci	9:11	9:14	....	8.33

EXPLANATORY NOTES

Colons in bid and asked quotes represent 1/32nds. 99:01 means 99 1/32. Net changes are in 1/32nds. **n:** Treasury note. Treasury bill quotes in hundredths, quoted on terms of a rate of discount. Yields are to maturity or to earliest call date.

U.S. Treasury STRIPS quotes are based on transactions of $1,000,000 or more. Colons represent 1/32nds. Abbreviations: **ci:** stripped coupon interest. **bp:** Treasury bond, stripped principal. **np:** Treasury note, stripped principal.

U.S. Treasury Bills

Maturity	Bid	Asked	Chg	Ask Yld
Aug 11	5.54	5.44	– 0.05	5.52
Oct 11	5.55	5.53	– 0.02	5.68
Dec 11	5.60	5.58	....	5.81
Jan 12	5.82	5.80	....	6.10
Feb 12	5.81	5.79	– 0.01	6.10

* This sample comprises formats, styles, and abbreviations from a variety of currently available sources and has been created for educational purposes.

2. 11. 2. 1 Treasury Bonds and Notes

T-bonds and notes are quoted at percentages of par. The first note shown pays a rate of 7½% and matures in August 2015. (An *n* after the year indicates that the security is a Treasury note; no letter after the year indicates a bond.) The bid and ask prices reflect the most recently reported OTC market prices; the bid change indicates how much the price has changed from the last report. At the current ask, this particular note would yield 7.37%.

Other government and agency issues are quoted in a similar fashion. In the second listing under "Govt. Bonds & Notes," the bonds have a 7¼% coupon rate and mature in August 2016. The bid was 100:26 (100²⁶⁄₃₂); the ask price was 100:30 (100³⁰⁄₃₂). The bonds have a YTM of 6.30%.

2. 11. 2. 2 Treasury Bills

Treasury bills are quoted at their annualized discount rates or yields. The maturity date is given in the first column of the Treasury bills quotation in the graphic. The second column shows the discount rate that results from the bid prices dealers will pay to buy the bills. The third column is the ask price. The number reflects the discount from par, and the discount on the ask side is smaller than that on the bid side.

The first bill in the table matures in August 2011. It is being offered for sale at par less a discount computed at a rate of 5.44%, to yield 5.52%. At maturity, the bill is redeemed at par.

2. 12   OTHER DEBT SECURITIES

2. 12. 1   EQUITY-LINKED NOTES (ELNs)

Equity-linked notes are debt instruments where the final payment at maturity is based on the return of a single stock, a basket of stocks, or an equity index. In the case where the note is based on the return of an index, the security would be known as an index-linked note (ILN). In the instances where the securities are traded on an exchange (most still are not), they are generally referred to as exchange-traded notes (ETNs). ELNs, exchange traded or not, are considered to be non-conventional structured products with unique risks, and therefore, not suitable for most investors.

2. 13   DEBT STRATEGIES AND SUITABILITY

Bonds are interest rate sensitive securities. One concern is that investors might not be fully aware of how their investments will react when interest rates move. We know that bond prices have an inverse relationship with interest rate movements. But investors purchasing fixed income securities as a safe haven when equities are either too volatile for their comfort levels or falling in value might not realize or consider this. As the interest rate environment changes and rates begin to creep upward for example, the prices of bonds held in portfolios or mutual funds will likely begin to fall, exposing investors to a risk they were unaware existed.

2. 13. 1   BOND LADDERING

Bond laddering is one example of a fixed income investment strategy. Like all strategies, there are desired goals and potential downsides to be aware of. Laddering involves purchasing several smaller bonds, each with a different maturity date spread over months or years rather than one larger bond maturing on a single date. In this way the investor holds both short and long-term bonds, and over time the strategy tends to decrease the overall risk of a fixed income portfolio via maturity diversification. The goal is threefold:

■ Reduce interest rate risk. As one bond matures the proceeds are reinvested into new bonds. Whether rates are rising or falling, the diversification of the maturity dates spreads the risk over a continuously moving interest rate curve.

■ Reduce reinvestment risk. As each bond matures the reinvested amount only represents a small portion of the entire portfolio. This becomes even more advantageous if prevailing rates are falling. In this way, only a small portion of the portfolio will be reinvested rather than a larger amount, at the current lower returns.

■ Maintain cash flow and increased liquidity. As bonds mature, cash is continually available to reinvest or withdraw if and when needed.

What might be the downsides?

■ Having bonds mature over set intervals is a way to increase liquidity of a portfolio. However, unexpected need for large cash amounts might cause an investor to liquidate bonds before they mature. Depending on the timing of the liquidation this can leave investors exposed to interest rate risk—bond prices being deflated because interest rates have been rising. In addition, liquidations before maturity could leave gaps of time in the maturities of bonds remaining in the portfolio, thus disrupting the strategy. Though laddering is generally associated with increased liquidity, it is recognized that the greater one's anticipated liquidity needs are, the closer the spacing of the maturities should be.

■ Because the strategy spreads risk over time, the potential for larger returns that might be had if selective timing for large purchases were employed, is given up.

Generally, only investors who place safety of principal and current income first as their investment objectives would find laddering a suitable strategy. In contrast, bond laddering would not align well with objectives such as portfolio growth.

UNIT TEST

1. A customer buys a 6% T-bond, maturing in 10 years, at a price of 91.07. The YTM is

   A. less than nominal yield
   B. greater than nominal yield
   C. less than current yield
   D. same as current yield

2. Identify the sequence that correctly orders the claim of the obligations below, from first to last, on the assets of a corporation in bankruptcy.

   I. Taxes
   II. Unpaid wages
   III. Preferred stock
   IV. Subordinated debt

   A. I, II, III, IV
   B. II, I, IV, III
   C. III, IV, I, II
   D. IV, III, II, I

3. Debt obligations of which of the following are directly guaranteed by the federal government?

   A. Federal Home Loan Banks
   B. Federal Housing Loan Guarantee Corporation
   C. Federal National Mortgage Association
   D. Government National Mortgage Association

4. Which of the following bonds trade flat?

   A. Revenue bonds
   B. Income bonds
   C. GO bonds
   D. Mortgage bonds

5. Which of the following regarding U.S. government agency obligations are TRUE?

   I. They are direct obligations of the U.S. government.
   II. They generally have higher yields than direct U.S. obligations.
   III. The Federal National Mortgage Association is a publicly traded corporation.
   IV. Securities issued by GNMA trade on the NYSE floor.

   A. I and II
   B. I and III
   C. II and III
   D. II and IV

6. In a new municipal bond transaction, the accrued interest is calculated

   I. from the trade date
   II. from the dated date
   III. up to the interest payment date
   IV. up to, but not including, the settlement date

   A. I and III
   B. I and IV
   C. II and III
   D. II and IV

7. Which of the following mortgage-backed securities would provide investors with the most predictable maturity date?

   A. PACs
   B. TACs
   C. GO bonds
   D. Revenue bonds

8. A corporate bond is quoted at 102⅝. A customer buying 10 bonds would pay

   A. $10,025.80
   B. $10,258.00
   C. $10,262.50
   D. $10,285.00

9. Interest rates have been rising for the past few days, which means that the price of bonds traded in the secondary market has

   A. increased
   B. decreased
   C. stayed the same
   D. Bond prices are not affected by interest rates.

10. A client acquires a newly issued $1,000 par, 5% convertible corporate bond convertible into common at $40 per share. The common stock increases 20% from initial parity as the result of a hopeful earnings projection. What is the parity price of the bond after the rise in the common stock's price?

    A. $800
    B. $1,000
    C. $1,200
    D. $1,250

11. A 10-year bond, callable in 5 years at par, is sold at a discount. Rank the following yields from lowest to highest.

    I. Nominal yield
    II. Current yield
    III. Yield to call
    IV. Yield to maturity

    A. I, II, III, IV
    B. I, II, IV, III
    C. II, I, IV, III
    D. IV, II, III, I

12. All of the following statements regarding convertible bonds are true EXCEPT

    A. holders may share in the growth of the common stock
    B. holders receive a higher rate of interest
    C. the issuer pays a lower rate of interest
    D. holders have a fixed rate of interest

13. All of the following statements regarding equity-linked notes (ELNs) are true EXCEPT

    A. they can be exchange-traded or traded OTC
    B. they have final payments at maturity linked to the return of an underlying stock or basket of stocks
    C. they are equity securities
    D. some ELNs offer principal protection

14. All of the following statements regarding eurodollar bonds are true EXCEPT

    A. U.S. investors are not subject to currency risk
    B. non-U.S. investors are not subject to currency risk
    C. they are issued outside of the United States
    D. interest and principal are paid in U.S. dollars

15. Of the following S&P ratings shown here, below which one of them would all other S&P ratings be considered speculative?

    A. A
    B. B
    C. BB
    D. BBB

16. Bonds

    I. represent a loan to the issuer
    II. give the bondholder ownership in the entity
    III. are issued to finance capital expenditures or to raise working capital
    IV. are junior securities

    A. I and II
    B. I and III
    C. II and III
    D. III and IV

17. All of the following would most likely be found in a money market fund's portfolio EXCEPT

    A. T-bills
    B. T-bonds with less than 1 year to maturity
    C. Negotiable CDs
    D. Common stock

18. The term *trading flat* means

    A. the bond is in default
    B. there is no accrued interest
    C. the price of the bond has remained level
    D. the bond is sold without markup or commission

19. During periods when the yield curve is normal, as market interest rates change, which of the following is TRUE?

    A. Both short-term and long-term bond prices move equally.
    B. Short-term bond prices move more sharply.
    C. Long-term bond prices move more sharply.
    D. There is no relationship between the relative price movements of short-term and long-term bonds.

20. Accrued interest on a bond confirmation is

    I. added to the buyer's contract price
    II. added to the seller's contract price
    III. subtracted from the buyer's contract price
    IV. subtracted from the seller's contract price

    A. I and II
    B. I and IV
    C. II and III
    D. III and IV

21. A convertible corporate bond has been issued with an antidilution covenant. If the issuer declares a 5% stock dividend, which of the following statements are TRUE as of the ex-date?

    I. The conversion ratio increases.
    II. The conversion ratio decreases.
    III. The conversion price increases.
    IV. The conversion price decreases.

    A. I and III
    B. I and IV
    C. II and III
    D. II and IV

22. Which of the following statements regarding Treasury bills are TRUE?

    I. They are sold in minimum denominations of $10,000.
    II. They mature in less than 1 year.
    III. Their interest is exempt from taxation at the state level.
    IV. They are callable by the U.S. Treasury at any time before maturity.

    A. I and II
    B. I and III
    C. II and III
    D. II and IV

23. A bond is selling at a premium over par value. Therefore, its

    A. current yield is less than its nominal yield
    B. nominal yield is less than its current yield
    C. yield to maturity is greater than its current yield
    D. none of the above

24. An investor buys a convertible bond at par with a conversion price of $25, and the current market value of the common stock is $23. Interest rates fall significantly, increasing the bond's price to 110; the stock market responds and the stock's price appreciates to $27 a share. Which of the following is the best option?

    A. Do not convert the bond at this time
    B. Convert on a plus tick
    C. Convert and sell the stock at a profit
    D. Convert and sell the stock short exempt

25. A type of zero-coupon bond issued by broker-dealers is referred to as a Treasury

    A. receipt
    B. certificate
    C. note
    D. series

ANSWERS AND RATIONALES

1. **B.** A bond whose price is below par or at a discount has a yield to maturity that is higher than current yield, which in turn is higher than the nominal yield.

2. **B.** When a corporation's assets are liquidated, all unpaid wages are paid first. Then, taxes must be paid, and then all other liabilities must be satisfied. Finally, shareholders are paid from what remains. Preferred shareholders have priority over common shareholders, and subordinated debenture holders have a lower claim than other debenture holders.

3. **D.** GNMA is the only agency whose securities are direct obligations of the U.S. government.

4. **B.** Bonds that trade flat do not trade with accrued interest. These include income bonds (also known as adjustment bonds), zeroes, bonds in default, and bonds that settle on an interest payment date.

5. **C.** U.S. government agency debt is an obligation of the issuing agency. This causes agency debt to trade at slightly higher yields, reflecting this greater risk. FNMA was created as a government agency but was spun off in 1968 and is now an NYSE-listed corporation. GNMA pass-through certificates trade OTC. GNMAs are the only agency whose securities are direct U.S. government obligations.

6. **D.** Interest accrues from the bond's dated date up to but not including the settlement date.

7. **A.** Of the four answer choices, only collateralized mortgage obligation PACs and TACs are mortgage-backed securities. PACs have established maturity dates because both prepayment and extension risks are transferred to support or companion tranches.

8. **C.** 102⅝% of par ($1,000 for bonds) = $1,026.25 (10 × $1,026.25 = $10,262.50). When quoting corporate bonds, ⅛ point = $1.25.

9. **B.** When interest rates rise, bond prices fall.

10. **C.** The answer is $1,000 × 120% = $1,200. At par, conversion price and market price are the same. Therefore, the common stock is in essence trading at parity ($40 per share). If the stock rises to $48 per share, on conversion, a holder receives 25 shares: 25 shares × $48 = $1,200.

11. **B.** The lowest of all yields for a discount bond is the nominal yield (coupon rate), which is a fixed percentage of par. The highest possible return to the owner of a bond purchased at a discount would occur if the bond were called before maturity, since less time needs to elapse for the investor to receive the discount.

12. **B.** Because of the possibility of participating in the growth of the common stock through an increase in the market price of the common, the convertible can be issued with a lower rate of interest.

13. **C.** Equity-linked notes (ELNs) are debt instruments, not equity instruments. They have a partial fixed return as well as a final payment linked to the performance of a single stock or equity index. Some are exchange-traded while others trade OTC and some ELNs, not all, are marketed as principal protected notes (PPNs).

14. **B.** Eurodollar bonds are issued outside the United States, but principal and interest are paid in U.S. dollars. Therefore, a U.S. investor bears no currency risk, although a foreign issuer or investor does.

15. **D.** A rating of BBB is the lowest investment-grade rating assigned by Standard & Poor's. Any rating beneath this is considered speculative.

16. **B.** Bonds are debt securities; as such, they represent loans to the issuer. As senior securities, they take precedence over common and preferred stock in claims against an issuer. They are issued to finance capital expenditures or to raise working capital.

17. **D.** Money market instruments are short-term, high-quality debt securities. This includes treasuries with less than 1 year to maturity and negotiable CDs. Because common stock is equity, it is not found in money market funds. Negotiable CDs (over $100,000) are considered money market securities. Treasuries due to mature in less than a year are money market securities, but common stock is not.

18. **B.** When a bond trades flat, the buyer does not owe accrued interest to the seller.

19. **C.** Long-term bond prices are more volatile than similar short-term prices, in large part because of the added risk of owning a longer-term debt security.

20. **A.** The accrued interest calculation is made to determine the seller's share of the upcoming interest payment. It is added to the buyer's contract price (the buyer pays), and it is added to the seller's contract price (the seller receives).

21. **B.** The bond will be convertible into an additional 5% more shares, so the conversion price will decrease in proportion. If the conversion price is lowered, the conversion ratio must increase.

22. **C.** Treasury bills are sold (can be purchased) in minimum denominations as low as $100 and are not callable before maturity. They mature in less than 1 year (from issuance) and are sold at a discount. Interest on Treasury bills is taxable at the federal level only.

23. **A.** Any bond selling at a premium will yield less than the coupon rate (nominal yield). Conversely, of course, a bond trading at a discount will yield more. Remember, there is an inverse relationship between bond prices and bond yields.

24. **A.** The bond's value is $1,100; the stock is worth $1,080 ($1,000 par ÷ conversion price of $25 = 40 shares; 40 shares × $27 per share = $1,080).

25. **A.** Treasury STRIPS and Treasury receipts both are types of zero-coupon bonds. Treasury STRIPS are backed in full by the U.S. government, but Treasury receipts, which are issued by broker-dealers, are not.

QUICK QUIZ ANSWERS

Quick Quiz 2.A

1. **D.** The trust indenture is a contract between the issuer and a trustee for the benefit of a bondholder. It spells out the covenants to be honored by the issuer and gives the trustee the power to monitor compliance with the covenants and the ability to take action on behalf of the bondholder(s) if a default of the covenants is found.

2. **B.** The order in a liquidation is as follows: IRS and other government agencies, secured debt holders, unsecured debt holders, general creditors (in most cases, unsecured debt holders are given a slight priority over all but the largest creditors), holders of subordinated debt, preferred stockholders, and common stockholders.

3. **D.** Ogden 5s means 5% bonds. Five percent of $1,000 par equals $50 interest per bond annually. For 50 bonds, the annual interest is $2,500.

4. **C.** When a bond is called and the owner does not redeem, the interest payments cease. Conversion causes dilution, and generally interest rates on convertible bonds are lower than straight debt issues.

5. **A.** Coupon rates are not higher; they are lower because of the value of the conversion feature. The bondholders are creditors, and if the stock price falls, the conversion feature will not influence the bond's price.

6. **B.** The calculations are: $1,000 ÷ $20 = 50 shares for one bond. $800 bond price ÷ 50 shares = $16 parity price.

7. **B.** $1,000 par ÷ $125 conversion price = 8 shares per bond.

Quick Quiz 2.B

1. **C.** T-bills trade at a discount to par, mature in less than 1 year, and are a direct obligation of the U.S. government. T-bills are noncallable.

2. **C.** Government notes and bonds are quoted in 32nds. Therefore, a quote of 101–16 means $101\frac{16}{32}$. To find the price of one of the bonds, multiply the price by 10 points: $101.5 \times 10 = \$1,015$; $\$1,015 \times 10$ bonds = $10,150.

3. **C.** U.S. government agency debt is an obligation of the issuing agency. This causes agency debt to trade at higher yields reflecting this greater risk. FNMA was created as a government agency but was spun off in 1968 and is now an NYSE-listed corporation. GNMA pass-through certificates trade OTC.

Quick Quiz 2.C

1. **A.** Collateralized mortgage obligations are collateralized by mortgages on real estate. They do not own the underlying real estate, so they are not considered to be backed by it.

2. **B.** CMOs are a type of mortgage-backed security. A CMO issue is divided into several tranches, which set priorities for payments of principal and interest.

3. **D.** Interest received from CMOs is fully taxable at federal, state, and local levels.

4. **B.** Prepayment risk is one of the important risks associated with CMOs and must be disclosed to prospective investors. All of the other statements are false.

5. **A.** Collateralized mortgage obligations (CMOs) are mortgage-backed securities. Because mortgages are often paid off ahead of the scheduled maturity, the maturity date of a CMO is not certain.

6. **D.** The performance of CMOs may not be compared to any other investment vehicle.

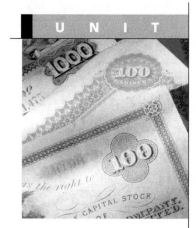

3

Municipal Securities

The municipal securities Unit is a critical section for success on the Series 7 exam. Learn the language of the municipal industry and pay attention to definitions and industry rules. There are very few calculations in this Unit—the primary emphasis is on knowing the industry.

Municipal securities offer investors a relatively safe means of investing for tax-free income. Because the interest municipal securities pay is not taxable by the federal government, the yield is lower than that of taxable corporate or government bonds. The two primary types of municipal securities are general obligation bonds (almost always issued in a competitive bid offering) and revenue bonds (normally issued in a negotiated offering).

The exam will ask approximately 30–40 questions on municipal securities and Municipal Securities Rulemaking Board (MSRB) rules—this may be the most heavily tested topic on the entire exam. ■

When you have completed this Unit, you should be able to:

■ **differentiate** municipal bonds from government and corporate bonds;

■ **compare** and contrast general obligation (GO) and revenue bonds;

■ **identify** documentation associated with a new issue of municipals;

■ **define** the steps involved in municipal securities underwriting;

■ **describe** the role of the syndicate and specific rules that apply to the syndicate manager;

■ **identify** unique features of municipal securities trading;

■ **discuss** available sources of municipal industry information;

■ **describe** the tax treatment of municipal securities; and

■ **identify** the role of the MSRB and list significant rules that affect the municipal securities industry.

3. 1 MUNICIPAL DEBT CHARACTERISTICS

Municipal bonds are securities issued either by state or local government or by U.S. territories, authorities, and special districts. Investors that buy such bonds are loaning money to the issuers for the purpose of public works and construction projects (e.g., roads, hospitals, civic centers, sewer systems, and airports). Municipal securities are considered second in safety of principal only to U.S. government and U.S. government agency securities. The safety of a particular issue is based on the issuing municipality's financial stability.

Municipal securities are exempt from the filing requirements of the Act of 1933. However, like all other securities, they are subject to the antifraud provisions of the **Securities Exchange Act of 1934**.

3. 1. 1. 1   Tax Benefits

Purchasers of municipal debt often benefit from favorable tax treatment on the interest payments. The federal government does not generally tax the interest payments. This tax treatment originated from the **Doctrine of Reciprocal Immunity (Doctrine of Mutual Reciprocity)**, established by a Supreme Court decision in 1895.

The doctrine specifies that a level of government can tax only the interest of its own issues. Interest on municipal securities may be taxed by the municipal level (state and local governments) but not by the federal government. Interest on issues of the federal government (Treasury bills, notes, and bonds) is taxed by the federal government but is exempt from taxation at the state and local levels. Interest on issues of U.S. territories is subject to a triple exemption (federal, state, and local).

TAKE NOTE

Two important municipal tax issues must be clarified.

- The interest on municipal debt is largely exempt from taxation, but not capital gains. Municipal bond investors who buy low and sell high will have capital gains to report.

- Investors that purchase municipal bonds issued by the state in which they live often receive a special tax exemption; they may not be required to pay taxes on interest to the federal *or* state government. For instance, if you live in Los Angeles, CA, and buy a State of California municipal bond, the interest will not be subject to taxation on your federal or State of California return. However, if you live in Tempe, AZ, and buy a California municipal bond, the interest will be exempt from taxation by the federal government but will be taxed by the State of Arizona.

As a result of the tax-advantaged status of municipal bond interest, municipalities generally pay lower interest rates than do corporate issuers. The amount of tax savings experienced by an investor will determine whether a municipal bond is a better investment choice than a corporate bond. Investors should be aware of the tax-equivalent yield when assessing the merits of a municipal bond investment. In general, tax-free municipal securities are more appropriate for investors in high tax brackets and are not suitable for investors in low tax brackets.

3. 1. 1. 2   Issuers

The following three entities are legally entitled to issue municipal debt securities:

- Territorial possessions of the United States (U.S. Virgin Islands, Puerto Rico, and Guam)
- State governments
- Legally constituted taxing authorities (county and city governments, agencies created by these governments, and authorities that supervise ports and mass transit systems, such as port authorities and special districts)

3. 1. 1. 3   Maturity Structures

Municipal notes and bonds are issued with maturities that range from less than one year to more than 30 years. There are three types of maturity schedules common to municipal and corporate debt issues.

3. 1. 1. 3. 1   Term Maturity

All principal matures at a single date in the future.

EXAMPLE $200 million Illinois GO 5% debentures due November 1, 2016.

Some issuers establish a **sinking fund account** to accumulate funds to pay off term bonds at or before the established maturity date. Term bonds are quoted by price (like corporate bonds) and are called **dollar bonds**.

3. 1. 1. 3. 2   Serial Maturity

Bonds within an issue mature on different dates according to a predetermined schedule. The sample serial maturity structure table below shows an example of a $100 million State of Illinois GO serial issue.

Sample Serial Maturity Structure

Amount	Coupon	Maturity	Price/Yield
$10,000,000	6%	11-1-14	5.80%
$10,000,000	6%	11-1-15	5.90%
$10,000,000	6%	11-1-16	100%
$10,000,000	6%	11-1-17	6.10%
$20,000,000	6%	11-1-18	6.20%
$20,000,000	6%	11-1-19	6.30%
$20,000,000	6%	11-1-20	6.40%

Serial bonds are quoted on the basis of their yield to maturity, called basis, to reflect the difference of maturity dates within one issue. A price/yield of 100% indicates the yield to maturity is equal to the coupon rate, which means the bond is being offered at par.

3. 1. 1. 3. 3 Balloon Maturity

An issuer pays part of a bond's maturity before the final maturity date, but the largest portion is paid off at maturity. The sample balloon maturity table below shows an example of a $100 million State of Illinois GO balloon maturity issue due November 1, 2017.

Sample Balloon Maturity

Amount	Coupon	Maturity	Price/Yield
$10,000,000	6%	11-1-14	5.80%
$10,000,000	6%	11-1-15	5.90%
$10,000,000	6%	11-1-16	100%
$70,000,000	6%	11-1-17	6.10%

TAKE NOTE   A balloon maturity is a type of serial maturity. Also note that most municipal bonds are issued serially.

3. 1. 2 TYPES OF MUNICIPAL ISSUES

Two categories of municipal securities exist: general obligation bonds (GOs), which are backed by the full faith, credit, and taxing powers of the municipality, and revenue bonds, which are backed by the revenues generated by the municipal facility the bond issue finances.

3. 1. 2. 1 General Obligation Issues (GOs)

General Obligation bonds (GOs) are municipal bonds issued for capital improvements that benefit the entire community. Typically, these projects do not produce revenues, so principal and interest must be paid by taxes collected by the municipal issuer. Because of this backing, general obligation bonds are known as **full faith and credit issues**.

3. 1. 2. 1. 1 Sources of Funds

GOs are backed by the issuing municipality's taxing power. Bonds issued by states are backed by income taxes, license fees, and sales taxes. Bonds issued by towns, cities, and counties are backed by property (**ad valorem**) taxes, license fees, fines, and all other sources of revenue to the municipality. School, road, and park districts may also issue municipal bonds backed by property taxes.

3. 1. 2. 1. 2 Statutory Debt Limits

The amount of debt that a municipal government may incur can be limited by state or local statutes to protect taxpayers from excessive taxes. Debt limits can also make a bond safer for investors. The lower the debt limit, the less risk of excessive borrowing and default by the municipality.

Voter Approval. If an issuer wishes to issue GO bonds that would put it above its statutory limit, a public referendum is required.

Tax Limits. Some states limit property taxes to a certain percentage of the assessed property value or to a certain percentage increase in any single year. The tax rate is expressed in mills; one mill equals $1 per $1,000, or $.001.

Limited Tax GO. A limited tax GO is a bond secured by a specific tax (e.g., income tax). In other words, the issuer is limited as to what tax or taxes can be used to service the debt. As a result, there is more risk with a limited tax GO than with a comparable GO backed by the full taxing authority of the issuer.

Overlapping Debt. Several taxing authorities that draw from the same taxpayers can issue debt. Bonds issued by different municipal authorities that tap the same taxpayer wallets are known as **coterminous debt**.

TEST TOPIC ALERT

In the context of municipal securities, the term *coterminous* refers to two or more taxing agencies that share the same geographic boundaries and are able to issue debt separately. Overlapping debt occurs when two or more issuers are taxing the same property to service their respective debt.

EXAMPLE

Take the town of Smithville, located in Jones County. If Smithville issues GO debt, it will tax property in Smithville to service that debt. If Jones County issues GO debt, it will tax property in the county, which includes Smithville, to service its debt. As a result, there are two issuers taxing the same property.

TAKE NOTE

Coterminous debt only occurs in property taxing situations. Because states do not generally tax real estate, state debt never overlaps.

Double-Barreled Bonds. **Double-barreled bonds** are revenue bonds that have characteristics of GO bonds. Interest and principal are paid from a specified facility's earnings. However, the bonds are also backed by the taxing power of the state or municipality and therefore have the backing of two sources of revenue. Although they are backed primarily by revenues from the facility, double-barreled bonds are rated and traded as GOs.

TEST TOPIC ALERT

You might see questions on GOs similar to the following.

A taxpayer's home is currently valued at $400,000. For property tax purposes, it is assessed a value equal to 50% of its market value. If the annual tax rate is 7 mills, what is the taxpayer's annual property tax liability?

Calculate the tax liability by multiplying the mill rate by the property's assessed value.

$200,000 (50% of $400,000) × .007 (a mill is $\frac{1}{1000}$) = $1,400.

To simplify the calculation, drop the last three zeroes off the property's assessed value (200) and multiply by the number of mill (7): 200 × 7 = $1,400.

1. Which of the following is NOT included in the definition of coterminous debt?

    A. County
    B. City
    C. School district
    D. State

    Answer: D. Coterminous, or overlapping, debt occurs when property taxes from one property are used in support of debt issued by various municipal issuers. For instance, property taxes on a home might support county, city, and school district debt obligations. Property taxes are not assessed by states, so states are not included in the definition of coterminous or overlapping debt.

2. All of the following are used to pay debt service on GOs EXCEPT

    A. sales taxes
    B. license fees
    C. tolls
    D. ad valorem taxes

    Answer: C. Generally, associate GOs with taxes. There will be some exceptions, but GOs are predominately backed by tax collections.

3. 1. 2. 2   Revenue Bonds

Revenue bonds can be used to finance any municipal facility that generates sufficient income. Revenue bonds are not subject to statutory debt limits and do not require voter approval. A particular revenue bond issue, however, may be subject to an additional bonds test before subsequent bond issues with equal liens on the project's revenue may be issued. The additional bonds test ensures the adequacy of the revenue stream to pay both the old and new debt.

3. 1. 2. 2. 1   Feasibility Study

Before issuing a revenue bond, an issuer will engage various consultants to prepare a report detailing the economic feasibility and the need for a particular project (e.g., a new bridge or airport). The study will include estimates of revenues that will be generated and details of the operating, economic, or engineering aspects of the proposed project.

3. 1. 2. 2. 2   Sources of Revenue

Revenue bonds' interest and principal payments are payable to bondholders only from the specific earnings and net lease payments of revenue-producing facilities, such as:

- utilities (water, sewer, and electric);
- housing;
- transportation (airports and toll roads);
- education (college dorms and student loans);
- health (hospitals and retirement centers);
- industrial (industrial development and pollution control); and
- sports.

Debt service payments do not come from general or real estate taxes and are not backed by the municipality's full faith and credit. Revenue bonds are considered self-supporting debt because principal and interest payments are made exclusively from revenues generated by the project for which the debt was issued.

3. 1. 2. 2. 3   Protective Covenants

The face of a revenue bond certificate may refer to a **trust indenture** (or **bond resolution**). This empowers the trustee to act on behalf of the bondholders.

In the trust indenture, the municipality agrees to abide by certain protective covenants, or promises, meant to protect bondholders. A trustee appointed in the indenture supervises the issuer's compliance with the bond covenants.

3. 1. 2. 2. 4   Bond Covenants

The trust indenture's provisions may vary, but a number of standard provisions are common to most bond issues, including the following:

- **Rate covenant**—a promise to maintain rates sufficient to pay expenses and debt service
- **Maintenance covenant**—a promise to maintain the equipment and facility(ies)
- **Insurance covenant**—a promise to insure any facility built so bondholders can be paid off if the facility is destroyed or becomes inoperable
- **Additional bonds test**—whether the indenture is **open-ended** (allowing further issuance of bonds with the same status and equal claims on assets or revenues if permitted under the provisions of the bond indenture) or **closed-ended** (allowing no further issuance of bonds with an equivalent lien on assets or revenues); with a closed-end provision, any additional bonds issued will be subordinated to the original issue unless the funds are specifically required to complete construction of the facility
- **Sinking fund**—money to pay off interest and principal obligations
- **Catastrophe clause**—a promise to use insurance proceeds to call bonds and repay bondholders if a facility is destroyed; a catastrophe call is also called a calamity call or an extraordinary mandatory call
- **Flow of funds**—the priority of disbursing the revenues collected
- **Books and records covenant**—requires outside audit of records and financial reports
- **Call features**

TAKE NOTE   Trust indentures are not required for municipal bonds by the Trust Indenture Act of 1939. Municipal issues are exempt from this act. The use of trust indentures is optional, but it greatly enhances the marketability of revenue issues. Revenue bonds have either a trust resolution or trust indentures, whereas GOs commonly have a bond resolution.

3. 1. 2. 2. 5   Types of Revenue Bonds

There are a number of categories of revenue bonds, depending on the type of facility the bond issue finances.

Industrial Development Revenue Bonds. A municipal development authority issues **industrial development revenue bonds (IDRs or IDBs)** to construct facilities or purchase equipment, which is then leased to a corporation. The municipality uses the money from lease payments to pay the principal and interest on the bonds. The ultimate responsibility for the payment of principal and interest rests with the corporation leasing the facility; therefore, the bonds carry the corporation's debt rating.

Technically, industrial revenue bonds are issued for a corporation's benefit. Under the **Tax Reform Act of 1986**, the interest on these nonpublic purpose bonds may be taxable because the act reserves tax exemption for public purposes. Because these bonds are used for a nonpublic purpose, the interest income may be subject to the alternative minimum tax (AMT) discussed later in this course.

Lease Rental Bonds. Under a typical lease-rental (or lease-back) bond arrangement, a municipality issues bonds to finance office construction for itself or its state or community.

EXAMPLE

An example of a lease-back arrangement follows.

A municipality might issue bonds to raise money to construct a school and lease the finished building to the school district. The lease payments provide backing for the bonds.

Lease payments come from funds raised through special taxes or appropriations, from the lessor's revenues, such as the school's tuition or fees, or from the municipality's general fund.

Certificates of Participation (COPs). These are a form of lease revenue bond that permits the investor to participate in a stream of revenue from lease, installment, or loan payments related to the acquisition of land or the acquisition or construction of specific equipment or facilities by the municipality. Like other revenue issues, they require no voter approval. COPs are not viewed legally as debt of a municipality because payment is tied to an annual appropriation that is made by the government body. One unique feature with these certificates, though this would be a rare occurrence, is that in theory the certificate holders themselves can foreclose on the equipment or facility that the certificates financed in the event of default.

Special Tax Bonds. These are bonds secured by one or more designated taxes other than ad valorem (property) taxes. For example, bonds for a particular purpose might be supported by sales, tobacco, fuel, or business license taxes. However, the designated tax does not have to be directly related to the project purpose. Such bonds are not considered self-supporting debt.

Special Assessment Bonds (or Special District Bonds). Special assessment bonds are issued to finance the construction of public improvements such as streets, sidewalks, or sewers. The issuer assesses a tax only on the property that benefits from the improvement and uses the funds to pay principal and interest.

New Housing Authority Bonds. Local housing authorities issue **New Housing Authority bonds (NHAs)** to develop and improve low-income housing. NHAs are backed by the full faith and credit of the U.S. government. NHAs are sometimes called **Public Housing Authority bonds (PHAs)**. Because of their federal backing, they are considered the most secure of all municipal bonds. PHAs are backed by the rental income from the housing. If the rental income is not sufficient to service the debt, the federal government makes up any shortfall. Note that these bonds are not considered to be double barreled. To be **double barreled**, a bond must be backed by more than one municipal revenue source. In this case, the second backing is the federal government.

PHAs (or NHAs) are the only municipal issues backed in full by the U.S. government. They are also called **Section 8** bonds.

Moral Obligation Bonds. A moral obligation bond is a state- or local-issued, or state or local agency-issued, bond. If revenues or tax collections backing the bond are not sufficient to pay the debt service, the state legislature has the authority to appropriate funds to make payments. The potential backing by state revenues tends to make the bond more marketable, but the state's obligation is not established by law; it is a moral obligation only.

TAKE NOTE   Moral obligation bonds are revenue bonds only. For instance, a state may take on the moral obligation to service debt on city-issued general obligation bonds when the city has surpassed its statutory debt limit. This situation occurred in New York City's financial crisis of 1975. Typically, moral obligation bonds are issued in times of financial distress and have increased credit risk.

Issuer Default. If a GO bond goes into default, bondholders have the right to sue to compel a tax levy to pay off the bonds. If a moral obligation bond goes into default, the only way bondholders can be repaid is through **legislative apportionment**. The issuer's legislature would have to apportion money to satisfy the debt but is not legally obligated to do so. Remember, the issuer has a moral but not legal obligation to service the debt.

TEST TOPIC ALERT   Be ready for five to seven questions that require you to differentiate between the features of GOs and revenue bonds. If you are not confident about the basic features of these instruments, review before continuing. It is important to be extremely familiar with these basics.

Following are typical questions on revenue bonds.

1. Which of the following is backed by the full faith and credit of the U.S. government?

   A. Moral obligation bonds
   B. PHAs
   C. IDRs
   D. Special tax bonds

   Answer: B. PHAs or NHAs are issued to construct, maintain, and improve low-income housing. The U.S. government guarantees the rent on these properties, and they are considered the most secure of all municipal revenue bonds.

2. All of the following are used to provide debt service for revenue bonds EXCEPT

   A. excise taxes
   B. business license taxes
   C. ad valorem taxes
   D. alcohol taxes

   Answer: C. Property taxes, or ad valorem taxes, are associated with GOs. Special taxes are used to back revenue bonds. Examples include hotel, tobacco, liquor, and gasoline taxes. These are the exceptions to the rule that taxes should be associated with GO issues.

3. 1. 2. 3   Municipal Notes

Municipal anticipation notes are short-term securities that generate funds for a municipality that expects other revenues soon. Usually, municipal notes have less than 12-month maturities, although maturities may range from three months to three years. They are repaid when the municipality receives the anticipated funds. Municipal notes fall into several categories.

- Municipalities issue **tax anticipation notes (TANs)** to finance current operations in anticipation of future tax receipts. This helps municipalities to even out cash flow between tax collection periods.

- **Revenue anticipation notes (RANs)** are offered periodically to finance current operations in anticipation of future revenues from revenue producing projects or facilities.

- **Tax and revenue anticipation notes (TRANs)** are a combination of the characteristics of both TANs and RANs.

- **Bond anticipation notes (BANs)** are sold as interim financing that will eventually be converted to long-term funding through a sale of bonds.

- **Tax-exempt commercial paper** is often used in place of BANs and TANs for up to 270 days, though maturities are most often 30, 60, and 90 days.

- **Construction loan notes (CLNs)** are issued to provide interim financing for the construction of housing projects.

- **Variable rate demand notes** have a fluctuating interest rate and are usually issued with a put option.

- **Grant anticipation notes (GANs)** are issued with the expectation of receiving grant money from the federal government.

3. 1. 2. 3. 1   Variable Rate Municipals (Variable Rate Demand Obligations—VR-DOs)

Some municipal bonds and notes are issued with **variable**, or **floating**, rates of interest. A **variable rate municipal bond** offers interest payments tied to the movements of another specified interest rate, much like an adjustable-rate mortgage. Because the coupon rate of the bond changes with the market, the price of these bonds remains relatively stable.

TAKE NOTE   Variable rate municipal bonds are sometimes called **reset bonds**. Their price remains near par at all times because their coupon is usually reset to the market rate of interest every six months.

3. 1. 2. 3. 2   Auction Rate Securities (ARS)

Typically issued by municipalities, nonprofit hospitals, utilities, housing finance agencies and universities, auction rate securities (ARS) are long-term variable rate bonds tied to short-term interest rates. With long-term maturities of 20 to 30 years, the interest rates are determined using a Dutch auction method at predetermined short-term intervals, typically 7, 28, or 35 days. This type of auction uses a competitive bid process where the lowest bid rate at which all of the bonds can be sold at par is used to establish the new or "reset" rate. This reset rate is referred to as the "clearing rate." Any customers that bid above the clearing rate receive no bonds and those that bid at or below the clearing rate receive the bonds at that rate. Interest paid in the current period is based on the interest rate reset in the prior auction.

Failed auctions are a hazard associated with ARSs. A failed auction can occur due to lack of demand and hence no bids received to reset the rate. To help ensure the success of an auction, underwriting BDs can submit a clearing rate bid but are not required to do so. This may change in the future as a result of numerous litigations. The failed auctions usually result in downgrades in the credit ratings of the securities and their issuers.

These securities trade at par and are callable at par on any interest payment date at the option of the issuer. They do not carry put features.

TAKE NOTE   Dealers for municipal auction rate securities (ARS) or variable rate demand obligations (VRDOs) are required to submit basic information to the MSRB through its Short-term Obligation Rate Transparency (SHORT) system about each auction remarketing, including the interest rate set for the next period.

3. 1. 2. 4   State and Local Government Securities Series (SLGS)

As noted in the previous Unit, bonds are often pre-refunded well before a call date if interest rates have fallen. With regard to municipal bonds, in order to comply with the complex arbitrage restrictions imposed by the IRS, the proceeds of a municipal pre-refunding are placed in an escrow account that immediately invests in **State and Local Government Securities Series (SLGS)**. These are U.S. government securities issued directly by the Treasury to municipal issuers only in connection with pre-refundings.

3. 1. 2. 5   Build America Bonds (BABs)

Build America Bonds (BABs) were created under the Economic Recovery and Reinvestment Act of 2009 to assist in reducing costs to issuing municipalities and stimulating the economy. While bonds to fund municipal projects have traditionally been sold in the tax-exempt arena, BABs are taxable obligations. Bondholders pay tax on interest received from BABs, but tax credits are provided in lieu of the tax-exempt status usually afforded the interest on municipal securities. These bonds attracted investors who would normally not buy tax-exempt municipal bonds and expanded the pool of investors to include those in lower income tax brackets, investors funding retirement accounts where tax-free securities would normally not be suitable, public pension funds, and foreign investors. There are two types of Build America Bonds issued: tax credit BABs and direct payment BABs.

3. 1. 2. 5. 1   Tax Credit BABs

These types of BABs provide the bondholder with a federal income tax credit equal to 35% of the interest paid on the bond in each tax year. If the bondholder lacks sufficient tax liability to fully use that year's credit, the excess credit may be carried forward.

3. 1. 2. 5. 2   Direct Payment BABs

Direct payment BABs provide no credit to the bondholder but instead provide the municipal issuer with payments from the U.S. Treasury equal to 35% of the interest paid by the issuer.

TAKE NOTE

The Build America Bonds (BABs) program expired on December 31, 2010, without being renewed. However, in the short time that municipalities were permitted to issue BABs, billions of dollars of capital had been raised to fund municipal projects throughout the United States, and many of these issues will remain outstanding for a number of years. Finally, it should be noted that the program could be reinstated at some time in the future, and the types of BABs offered and the credits they provide could be amended as well.

QUICK QUIZ 3.A

1. The main advantage of a variable rate municipal bond investment is that
   A. the bond is likely to increase in value
   B. the bond's price should remain relatively stable
   C. the bond is noncallable
   D. the bond's interest is exempt from all taxes

2. If a municipality wants to even out its cash flow, it is most likely to issue which of the following securities?
   A. TANs
   B. BANs
   C. RANs
   D. CLNs

3. All of the following are true of a municipality's debt limit EXCEPT
   A. the purpose of debt restriction is to protect taxpayers from excessive taxes
   B. revenue bonds are not affected by statutory limitations
   C. the debt limit is the maximum amount a municipality can redeem in a year
   D. a public referendum is required if an issuer wishes to issue GO debt that would put the issuer above its statutory debt limit

4. Which of the following is a double-barreled bond?
   A. New Housing Authority bond
   B. Project note
   C. Hospital bond backed by revenues and taxes
   D. GO bond to construct a new grade school

5. Your customer, a resident of Minnesota, is in the 28% federal tax bracket and the 14% state tax bracket. She must pay both federal and state taxes on which of the following investments?
   A. Minneapolis Housing Authority bonds
   B. Series HH bonds
   C. Ginnie Mae pass-throughs
   D. Treasury bills

Quick Quiz answers can be found at the end of the Unit.

3. 1. 3   MUNICIPAL SECURITY DOCUMENTS

3. 1. 3. 1   Bond Contract

A municipal issuer enters into a **bond contract** with the underwriters of, and prospective investors in, its securities. The bond contract is a collection of legal documents that includes a bond resolution or trust indenture, applicable state and federal law, and other legal documents pertaining to that particular issue and issuer. By issuing its securities, the issuer has agreed to abide by the terms and covenants in the documents that compose the bond contract.

3. 1. 3. 2   Authorizing Resolution

The municipality authorizes the issue and sale of its securities through the **bond resolution**. The authorizing resolution contains a description of the issue.

3. 1. 3. 3   Bond Resolution Indenture

On the face of most municipal revenue bond certificates is a reference to the bonds' **underlying trust indenture**, also known as a **protective covenant**. Although it is not required by law, most municipal issuers use indentures to make the issue more marketable. The indenture serves as a contract between the bond's issuer and a trustee appointed on behalf of the bond's investors.

Normally, the indenture includes a **flow of funds statement** establishing the priority of payments made from a facility's revenues. The indenture is too long to supply to all bondholders, although the issuer must make a complete copy available upon request. The official statement outlines the indenture's covenants.

3. 1. 3. 4   Official Statement (OS)

The **official statement,** which must be signed by an officer of the issuer, is the municipal securities industry's equivalent of the corporate prospectus. The official statement serves as a disclosure document and contains any material information an investor might need about an issue. Prepared by the issuer, the official statement identifies the issue's purpose, the source from which the interest and principal will be repaid, and the issuer's and community's financial and economic backgrounds. The official statement also has information relating to the issue's creditworthiness.

A typical official statement includes:

■ offering terms;

■ summary statement;

■ purpose of issue;

■ authorization of bonds;

■ security of bonds;

■ description of bonds;

■ description of issuer, including organization and management, area economy, and a financial summary;

■ construction program;

■ project feasibility statement;

■ regulatory matters;

■ specific provisions of the indenture or resolution, including funds and accounts, investment of funds, additional bonds, insurance, and events of default;

■ legal proceedings;

■ tax status;

■ appropriate appendixes, including consultant reports, the legal opinion, and financial statements; and

■ credit enhancements.

3. 1. 3. 4. 1   Preliminary Official Statement

Municipal issuers may also prepare preliminary official statements. The **preliminary official statement** discloses most of the same material information as the official statement, with the exception of the issue's interest rate(s) and offering price(s). Underwriters use a preliminary official statement to determine investors' and dealers' interest in the issue.

Any municipal securities dealer involved in the sale of a new issue must deliver a final **official statement** to every customer who has purchased the issue, at or before settlement date.

3. 1. 3. 5   Legal Opinion

Printed on the face of every bond certificate (unless the bond is specifically stamped *Ex-Legal*) is a legal opinion written and signed by the **bond counsel**, an attorney specializing in tax-exempt bond offerings. The legal opinion states that the issue is legally binding on the issuer and conforms with applicable laws. If interest from the bond is tax exempt, that too is stated in the legal opinion.

The legal opinion is issued either as a **qualified opinion** (there may be a legal uncertainty of which purchasers should be informed) or as an **unqualified opinion** (issued by the bond counsel unconditionally).

Some issuers, normally smaller municipalities, choose not to obtain a legal opinion. In such a case, the bond certificate must clearly state that the bonds are **ex-legal**. The ex-legal designation allows a bond to meet good delivery requirements without an attached legal opinion.

3. 1. 3. 5. 1   The Underwriter's Counsel

The managing underwriter may choose to employ another law firm as underwriter's counsel. This firm is not responsible for the legal opinion and is employed to represent the underwriter's interests.

TAKE NOTE   Issuers desire an unqualified legal opinion.

3. 2 ISSUING MUNICIPAL SECURITIES

A uniform sequence of events leads to a new municipal issue. The issuer must first obtain a **legal opinion**, which determines whether and how the bonds may be offered. Then, the terms of the municipal bond offering may be set by either **negotiation** or **competitive bidding**.

3. 2. 1   NEGOTIATED UNDERWRITING

In a **negotiated underwriting**, the municipality appoints an investment banker to underwrite the offering. The underwriter works with the issuer to establish the interest rate and the offering price in light of the issuer's financial needs and market conditions.

Negotiated underwritten issues can be distributed as either a public offering or via a private placement.

TAKE NOTE   Investment banks or bankers are financial institutions that assist corporations and municipal governments in raising capital by underwriting new securities and/or acting as the issuer's agent in the issuance of securities. Unlike traditional banks, investment banks do not take deposits or issue loans.

3. 2. 2   COMPETITIVE BIDDING

With competitive bid underwritings, a municipality publishes an invitation to bid. Investment bankers respond in writing to the issuer's attorney or other designated official requesting information on the offering. The bid representing the lowest net interest cost to the issuer is the winner in a competitive bid.

3. 2. 2. 1   Official Notice of Sale

The notice of bond sale to solicit bids for the bonds is usually published in *The Bond Buyer* and local newspapers and includes:

- date, time, and place of sale;
- name and description of issuer;
- type of bond;
- bidding restrictions (usually requiring a sealed bid);
- interest payment dates;
- dated date (interest accrual date) and first coupon payment date;
- maturity structure;
- call provisions (if any);
- denominations and registration provisions;
- expenses to be borne by purchaser or issuer;
- amount of good faith deposit that must accompany bid;
- paying agent or trustee;

- name of the firm (the bond counsel) providing the legal opinion;
- details of delivery;
- issuer's right of rejection of all bids;
- criteria for awarding the issue; and
- issuer's obligation to prepare the final official statement and deliver copies to the successful bidder.

The bond's rating and the underwriter's name are not included in a notice of sale because they have yet to be determined.

Investment bankers prepare bids for the securities based on information in the notice of sale, comparable new issue supply and demand, and general market conditions.

TAKE NOTE All new municipal debt is issued in fully registered form or in book-entry form.

---

3. 2. 3   SOURCES OF MUNICIPAL SECURITIES INFORMATION

A number of publications and services offer information on proposed new issues and secondary market activity for municipal issues. These include *The Bond Buyer* and Thomson Muni News, who publish the Thomson Muni Market Monitor (formerly known as *Munifacts*).

3. 2. 3. 1   The Bond Buyer

The Bond Buyer is published every business day and serves as an authoritative source of information on primary market municipal bonds. *The Bond Buyer* publishes the **30-day visible supply** (the total dollar volume of municipal offerings, not including short-term notes, expected to reach the market in the next 30 days) and the **placement, or acceptance, ratio indexes** (the percentage of the total dollar value of new issues sold, versus the total dollar value of new issues offered for sale the prior week).

TAKE NOTE If the visible supply is exceptionally large, interest rates are likely to rise to attract investors to the larger number of bonds available. A small visible supply is an indication that interest rates are likely to fall.

If the placement ratio is high, the market for municipal bonds is strong. If it is low, dealers will be likely to exhibit concern about bidding on new issues. A placement ratio of 90% means that market has absorbed 90% of the dollar volume of bonds issued for the week, with 10% left in the dealer's inventory.

The Bond Buyer also compiles the 40 Bond Index, 20 Bond Index, 11 Bond Index, and the Revdex 25.

Bond Buyer Compiled Indexes

40 Bond Index

Daily price index of 40 GO and revenue bonds with an average maturity of 20 years. A rise in the index indicates bond prices are rising and yields are falling.

20 Bond Index

Weekly index of 20 GO bonds with 20 years to maturity, rated A or better.

11 Bond Index

Weekly index of 11 of the 20 bonds from the 20 Bond Index, rated AA or better.

Revdex 25

Weekly index of 25 revenue bonds with 30 years to maturity, rated A or better.

TAKE NOTE   The yields on the Revdex are always higher than the yields on the GO 20 Bond Index because revenue bonds have higher risk. The yields on the 11 Bond Index are lower than the yields on the 20 Bond Index because the 11 Bond Index is more highly rated.

3. 2. 3. 2   Thomson Muni Market Monitor (formerly Munifacts)

Thomson has been offering wire services, such as Thomson Muni News and the Thomson Muni Market Monitor (formerly *Munifacts*), used by many municipal dealers for many years. Current news items pertaining to the secondary municipals market appear in these wire services throughout the day along with current municipal offerings. Comparatively, these wire services should be considered a source for bonds already trading in the municipal secondary markets, while the Daily Bond Buyer is a source for new issue municipal bonds (primary market).

TEST TOPIC ALERT   Test your knowledge of information sources on the municipal bond market.

1. Which municipal publication includes the 30-day visible supply index?

2. Which municipal publication provides the most up-to-the-minute information relevant to the secondary municipal bond market?

Answers: 1. *The Bond Buyer*; 2. *Thomson Muni Market Monitor*

3. 2. 3. 3   Real Time Transaction Reporting System (RTRS)

Up-to-the-minute pricing information regarding eligible municipal bond transactions is made available through an approved portal such as the National Securities Clearing Corporation (NSCC). The data is captured and made available to the marketplace within 15 minutes of a trade by the MSRB Real Time Transaction Reporting System (RTRS).

3. 2. 4 FORMATION OF THE UNDERWRITING SYNDICATE

Once an issuer's notice of sale has circulated, those investment bankers interested in placing competitive bids for an issue form **syndicates**. A syndicate is an account that helps spread the risk of underwriting an issue among a number of underwriters. Although the bidding process is competitive, successive offerings of a particular municipality are often handled by the same syndicate, which is composed of the same members.

TAKE NOTE

To acquire relevant details about a new issue, the syndicate manager typically orders the New Issue Worksheet from *The Bond Buyer*. This worksheet provides, in an organized format, all information presented in the Official Notice of Sale. It shows a schedule of year-by-year maturities and their corresponding dollar amounts and a computation of bond years. Bond years are the number of $1,000 bonds of a maturity multiplied by the number of years the bonds are outstanding. This computation is used to calculate the average life of an issue and its total interest cost.

Sample Computation of Bond Years and Average Life of a $3.5 Million Issue Dated 9/1/00

Maturity	Years to Maturity	Number of Bonds	Bond Years
9/1/10	10	1,000	10,000
9/1/11	11	1,000	11,000
9/1/12	12	1,000	12,000
9/1/13	13	500	6,500
		Total 3,500	**Total 39,500**

$$\text{Average life} = \frac{\text{total bond years}}{\text{total number of bonds}} = \frac{39,500}{3,500} = 11.286 \text{ years}$$

A firm makes the decision to participate as a syndicate member after it considers the:

- potential demand for the security;
- existence of presale orders;
- determination and extent of liability;
- scale and spread; and
- ability to sell the issue.

Participants formalize their relationship by signing a **syndicate letter** or **syndicate agreement** in a competitive bid or a **syndicate contract** or **agreement among underwriters** in a negotiated underwriting. About two weeks before the issue is awarded, the syndicate manager sends the syndicate letter or contract to each participating firm for an authorized signature. The member's signature indicates its agreement with the offering terms. Syndicate letters include:

- each member firm's level of participation or commitment;
- priority of order allocation;
- duration of the syndicate account;

- appointment of the manager(s) as agent(s) for the account;
- fee for the managing underwriter and breakdown of the spread; and
- other obligations, such as member expenses, good faith deposits, observance of offering terms, and liability for unsold bonds.

TAKE NOTE   Syndicate letters are not legally binding until the syndicate's submission of the bid. Firms may drop from the group until this point.

3. 2. 4. 1   Types of Syndicate Accounts

The financial liability to which each underwriter is exposed depends on the type of syndicate account. Underwriting syndicates use two arrangements: Western accounts and Eastern accounts.

3. 2. 4. 1. 1   Western Account

The **Western account** is a divided account. Each underwriter is responsible only for its own underwriting allocation.

3. 2. 4. 1. 2   Eastern Account

An **Eastern account** is an undivided account. Each underwriter is allocated a portion of the issue. After the issue has been substantially distributed, each underwriter is allocated additional bonds representing its proportionate share of any unsold bonds. Thus, an underwriter's financial liability might not end when it has distributed its initial allocation.

TAKE NOTE   When remembering the difference between Western and Eastern, divided and undivided accounts, try this phrase: "The continental *divide* is in the *west*." It helps remind you that Western accounts and divided accounts are the same, as are Eastern and undivided.

EXAMPLE   A syndicate is underwriting a $5 million municipal bond issue. There are five syndicate members, each with equal participation, including your firm. Your firm sells its entire allocation, but bonds worth $1 million remain unsold by the other syndicate members.

If this is a Western account, what is your firm's liability?

In a Western account, your firm would have no remaining liability because its entire share was sold. However, if your firm had sold only $700,000 of its $1 million allocation, it would have to purchase the remaining $300,000 for its own inventory.

If this is an Eastern account, what is your firm's liability?

In an Eastern account, the unsold amount is divided among all syndicate members based on their initial participation. In this example, your firm would be allocated 20% of the remaining amount, or $200,000. The responsibility for any unsold bonds continues until the entire bond issue is sold.

3. 2. 4. 2   Due Diligence

Municipal underwriters must investigate an issuer's financing proposals thoroughly. With revenue bonds, this due diligence investigation is conducted through a feasibility study, which focuses on the projected revenues and costs associated with the project and an analysis of competing facilities.

3. 2. 5   ESTABLISHING THE SYNDICATE BID

A syndicate arrives at its competitive bid over a series of meetings during which member dealers discuss the proposed reoffering scale and spread for the underwriters. Their goal is to arrive at the best price to the issuer while still making a profit. At a preliminary meeting, the manager seeks tentative agreement from members on the prices or yields of all maturities in the issue as well as the gross profit or underwriting spread.

A final bid price for the bond is set at a meeting conducted just before the bid is due. If the member dealers cannot all agree on a final bid, the syndicate can go ahead with its bid as long as the syndicate members agree to abide by the majority's decision.

TAKE NOTE   To win the bid, the syndicate must resolve this question: What is the lowest interest rate that can win the bid and provide a competitive investment to public buyers as well as provide a profit for the underwriter?

The process of establishing the reoffering yield (or price) for each maturity is called **writing the scale**. A scale is the list of the bond issue's different maturities. If the coupon rate has already been determined, each maturity listed is assigned a yield. If the rate has not been set, each maturity is assigned a coupon. A normal scale has higher yields for long-term bonds.

Once the underwriters have written a scale that allows them to resell the bonds, they prepare the final bid. Put another way, writing the scale is first determining what prices (yields) are necessary in order to be able to sell the various serial maturities and then backing off a little to arrive at a bid. Before they submit the bid, the underwriters ensure that they have met any unique specifications the issuer has set.

3. 2. 5. 0. 1   Firm Commitment

Competitive bids are submitted as firm commitments. Therefore, bids must be carefully written to be competitive yet profitable. Underwriters receive no profit guarantee. Note that syndicates bidding on the proposed issue must bid on the entire amount being offered for sale.

3. 2. 5. 0. 2   Disclosure of Fees

Fees to be paid to a clearing agency and the syndicate manager must be disclosed to syndicate members in advance. Normally, this disclosure is part of the syndicate letter or the agreement among underwriters. Management fees include any amount in the gross spread that is paid to the manager alone and not shared with syndicate members.

3. 2. 5. 1   Awarding the Issue

After the issuer meets with its attorneys and accountants to analyze each bid, it awards the municipal bond issue to the syndicate that offers to underwrite the bonds at the lowest net interest cost (NIC) or true interest cost (TIC) to the issuer.

Net interest cost is a common calculation used for comparing bids and awarding the bond issue. It combines the amount of proceeds the issuer receives with the total coupon interest it pays. **True interest cost** provides the same type of cost comparison adjusted for the time value of money.

In **split-rate bids** (bids with more than one interest rate), interest is determined by the lowest average interest cost to the issuer. If each bid calls for one rate for the whole issue, the award goes to the syndicate with the lowest rate.

TAKE NOTE   NIC is a straight mathematical interest rate calculation. The lowest net interest cost is the winner. TIC weights early interest payments more heavily to give greater value to dollars of today over dollars to be paid in the future, consistent with present value calculations.

When the issuer makes its choice, it announces the successful bidder and returns the good faith deposits to the remaining syndicates.

The successful syndicate has a firm commitment to purchase the bonds from the issuer and reoffer them to the public at the offering price the members agreed on. The issuer keeps the successful bidder's good faith deposit to ensure that the syndicate carries out its commitment.

TAKE NOTE   While the amount of the good faith deposit can differ from one issue to another, it is usually 1–2% of the total par value of the offering.

---

3. 2. 5. 2   Syndicate Account

The **syndicate account** is created when the issue is awarded. The **syndicate manager** is responsible for keeping the books and managing the account. All sale proceeds are deposited to the syndicate account, and all expenses are paid out of the account. Settlement of syndicate accounts is 30 calendar days after the issuer delivers the securities to the syndicate. Therefore, the maximum length of time for the syndicate to exist is 30 calendar days from the time the issuer delivers the securities to the syndicate.

3. 2. 6   BREAKDOWN OF THE SPREAD

The price at which the bonds are sold to the public is known as the **reoffering price** (or **reoffering yield**). The syndicate's compensation for underwriting the new issue is the **spread**, or the difference between the price the syndicate pays the issuer and the reoffering price. Each participant in the syndicate is entitled to a portion of the spread, depending on the role each member plays in the underwriting.

TAKE NOTE The term *production* refers to the total dollar sales earned from a municipal issue. The production less the amount bid for the issue results in the spread.

3. 2. 6. 1   Syndicate Management Fee

The syndicate manager receives a per-bond fee for its work in bringing the new issue to market.

EXAMPLE The manager might receive ⅛ point ($1.25) as a management fee from a total spread of 1 point ($10).

3. 2. 6. 2   Total Takedown

The portion of the spread that remains after subtracting the management fee is called the **total takedown**. Members buy the bonds from the syndicate manager at the takedown.

In the example, for a 1-point spread with a management fee of ⅛ point, the takedown is ⅞ point ($8.75). A member that has purchased bonds at the takedown can sell its bonds either to customers at the offering price or to a dealer in the selling group below the offering price.

Unlike syndicate members, firms that are part of the selling group do not assume financial risk. They are engaged to help the syndicate members sell the new issue. Their compensation for each bond sold is termed the **concession**.

3. 2. 6. 3   Selling Concession and Additional Takedown

A syndicate member can buy bonds from the manager for $991.25, sell them to the public for $1,000, and earn the takedown of ⅞ point ($8.75). If the firm chooses instead to sell bonds to a member of the selling group, it does so at a price less than $1,000, in this case $995.00. The discount the selling group receives from the syndicate member is called the **concession**—½ point ($5.00).

Selling group members buy bonds from syndicate members at the concession. The syndicate member keeps the remainder of the total takedown, called the **additional takedown**. The additional takedown in this example is ⅜ point ($3.75).

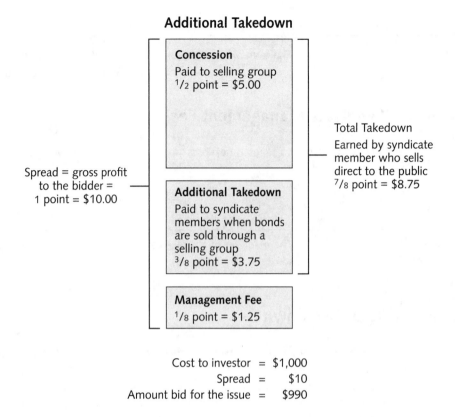

Additional Takedown

Concession
Paid to selling group
$^1/_2$ point = $5.00

Additional Takedown
Paid to syndicate members when bonds are sold through a selling group
$^3/_8$ point = $3.75

Management Fee
$^1/_8$ point = $1.25

Spread = gross profit to the bidder = 1 point = $10.00

Total Takedown
Earned by syndicate member who sells direct to the public
$^7/_8$ point = $8.75

Cost to investor =	$1,000
Spread =	$10
Amount bid for the issue =	$990

The syndicate manager may notify other firms who are not syndicate or selling group members of the new issue through *The Bond Buyer*. Interested firms may buy the bonds from the syndicate at a small discount from the reoffer price. This discount is termed a **reallowance,** which is generally one-half of the concession amount.

TEST TOPIC ALERT   Municipal spread questions are generally asked in terms of points, not dollars. One bond point equals $10.

Be ready for a question that asks you to rank parts of the spread in order of their size. Remember that the manager's fee is typically the smallest, and the total takedown is the largest. The additional takedown is actually a part of the total takedown amount, even though the name is a bit misleading.

You may see a question that asks under what circumstances a syndicate member can receive the full spread when a bond is sold. The answer is that the syndicate member receives the full spread if the member is also the syndicate manager. Also, be ready to define total takedown as the concession plus the additional takedown.

3. 2. 7   ORDER ALLOCATION

Municipal bond orders are allocated according to priorities the syndicate sets in advance. The **Municipal Securities Rulemaking Board (MSRB)** requires syndicates to establish **priority allocation provisions** for orders. The managing underwriter must submit these provisions to all syndicate members in writing. Normally, the manager includes allocation priorities and confirmation procedures in the syndicate agreement.

The syndicate must establish a definite sequence in which orders will be accepted and may not simply state that the order priority will be left to the manager's discretion.

Syndicate members must signify in writing their acceptance of the allocation priorities. In addition, the manager must notify the members in writing of any change to the set priorities.

3. 2. 7. 1   Order Period

The MSRB has established a timeline for municipal underwritings. The **order period** is the time set by the manager during which the syndicate solicits customers for the issue and all orders are allocated without regard to the sequence in which they were received. The order period usually runs for an hour on the day following the award of the bid.

3. 2. 7. 2   Allocation Priorities

A syndicate's **allocation priorities** become especially important when a bond issue is over-subscribed. The normal priority follows.

3. 2. 7. 2. 1   Presale Order

A **presale order** is entered before the date that the syndicate wins the bid, which means that a customer is willing to place an order without knowing the final price or whether the syndicate will even win the bid. A presale order takes priority over other types of orders, and individual syndicate members are not credited with any takedown on presale orders. The takedown is split among all syndicate members according to participation.

3. 2. 7. 2. 2   Group Net Order

A group order is placed after the bid is awarded. A syndicate member that wants a customer's order to receive priority enters the order as a **group net order**. The takedown on a group net order is deposited in the syndicate account, and upon completion of the underwriting, it is split among all syndicate members according to participation.

3. 2. 7. 2. 3   Designated Order

The next highest priority for orders received during the order period is assigned to **designated orders**. These orders are usually from institutions that wish to allocate the takedown to certain syndicate members.

3. 2. 7. 2. 4   Member Order and Member-Related Order

The lowest priority for orders goes to member and member-related orders. A member firm enters such an order for its own inventory or related accounts, such as for a dealer-sponsored **unit investment trust (UIT)**. The easiest way to remember the priority of the various types of orders is that the highest priority is given to those orders that benefit the most members. The lowest priority is given to orders that benefit a single member.

Under MSRB rules, a syndicate member placing an order for a related account must disclose this fact to the syndicate manager when the order is placed. Therefore, the manager knows to accord these orders the lowest priority.

Within two business days of the sale date, the syndicate manager must send a written summary of how orders were allocated to the other syndicate members.

TAKE NOTE

A simple way to remember the normal order allocation priority found is in the syndicate letter: "**P**ro **G**olfers **D**on't **M**iss." PGDM stands for **P**resale, **G**roup, **D**esignated, and **M**ember.

QUICK QUIZ 3.B

1. Your manager notifies you that a new municipal bond issue that you have been working on has been oversubscribed. How is the priority for acceptance of orders for this issue determined?

   A. On a first-come, first-served basis
   B. As outlined in the official statement
   C. As outlined in the official notice of sale
   D. As outlined in the syndicate agreement

2. Who signs the syndicate agreement for a municipal bond issue?

   A. Managing underwriter and the issuer
   B. Managing underwriter and the trustee
   C. Managing underwriter and the bond counsel
   D. All members of the underwriting syndicate

3. In a municipal underwriting, the scale is

   A. the first thing determined by the underwriting syndicate in calculating its bid
   B. the yield at which the syndicate plans to reoffer the bonds to the public
   C. both A and B
   D. neither A nor B

4. Your firm is bidding on a new municipal bond issue. As the issuer weighs and evaluates the competitive bids, what will be the most important factor in deciding who will be awarded the winning bid?

   A. Net interest cost
   B. Scale
   C. Takedown
   D. Concession

5. An order confirmed for the benefit of the entire underwriting syndicate placed after the bid is awarded is called

   A. a group net order
   B. a net designated order
   C. a presale order
   D. a member at the takedown order

6. A dealer should consider all of the following factors when determining the spread on a new issue EXCEPT

   A. prevailing interest rates in the marketplace
   B. amount bid on the issue
   C. type and size of the issue
   D. amount of the good faith check

7. An unqualified legal opinion means that

A. the issue is legal, but certain contingencies may limit the flow of funds in the future

B. the interest is not exempt from state or local taxes

C. the bond counsel has rendered an opinion without any qualifying limitations

D. the underwriter has failed to disclose sufficient information to qualify the issue

8. The reoffering yield on a new municipal bond issue is

A. the coupon rate on the new issue

B. the tax-equivalent yield of the new issue

C. the interest rate less any premiums that underwriters are willing to pay

D. the yield at which the bonds are offered to the public

3. 2. 8 PAYMENT AND DELIVERY

New municipal bond issues are usually sold on a **when-issued** basis, meaning the securities are authorized, but not yet issued. After awarding an issue to a syndicate, the issuer has the bond certificates printed and finalizes any other legal matters. If the bonds are to be eligible for automated comparison and clearing, the managing underwriter must register the securities with a registered clearing agency, providing the agency with notice of the securities' coupon rate and settlement date as soon as they are known.

When the bonds are ready, the syndicate manager gives notice of the **settlement date**. The syndicate members, in turn, give notice of the settlement date to the purchasers. On the settlement date, the newly issued bonds are delivered to the underwriters with a final legal opinion, and the underwriters pay for the bonds on delivery.

3. 2. 8. 1 Confirmations of Sales to Customers

On or before the completion of the transaction (settlement date), final confirmations must be sent to investors who purchased bonds from the underwriters. The investors' confirmations disclose the purchase price and settlement date for the transaction. The underwriters then deliver the bonds, accompanied by the legal opinion, to the investors.

The settlement date should not be confused with the **dated date** the issuer assigns to the bond issue. The dated date is the date on which interest begins to accrue. An investor must pay any interest that has accrued from the dated date up to, but not including, the settlement date. The investor starts receiving interest on the settlement date.

TAKE NOTE

When a bond is first issued, the first interest payment date may represent a **long coupon**. For example, assume a bond is issued on March 1 and the first interest payment date is the following January 1, with subsequent payments every six months (a J&J bond). The first payment date will include 10 months of interest—March 1 through January 1.

3. 3 ANALYSIS OF MUNICIPAL SECURITIES

Different criteria are used to evaluate the merits of general obligation and revenue bonds. When analyzing GOs, investors assess the municipality's ability to raise enough tax revenue to pay its debt. Revenue bond debt service depends on the income generated from a specific facility to cover its operating costs and pay its debt.

3. 3. 1 GENERAL OBLIGATION BONDS

3. 3. 1. 1 General Wealth of the Community

Because GOs are backed primarily by tax revenues, their safety is determined by the community's general wealth, which includes the following demographic data:

- Property values

- Retail sales per capita

- Local bank deposits and bank clearings

- Diversity of industry in its tax base

- Population growth or decline

A GO issuer's taxing power enables it to make principal and interest payments through all but the most unusual economic circumstances.

3. 3. 1. 2 Characteristics of the Issuer

A **quantitative analysis** focuses on objective information regarding a municipality's population, property values, and per capita income. A **qualitative analysis** focuses on subjective factors that affect a municipality's securities. The community's attitude toward debt and taxation, population trends, property value trends, and plans and projects being undertaken in the area are all relevant considerations.

3. 3. 1. 3 Debt Limits

To protect taxpayers from excessive taxes, statutory limits may be placed on the overall amount of debt a municipality can have. If a city's total debt is limited to 5% of the estimated market value of all taxable property within the city limits, this is the city's statutory debt limit. A bond's official statement discloses how close total outstanding debt, including newly issued debt, comes to its statutory debt limit.

A state constitution or city charter can also limit the purposes for which a city may issue bonds. Often, a city may issue bonds to finance capital improvements only if those bonds mature within the expected lifetimes of the improvements. This provision ensures that the city will not owe money on a facility when it becomes obsolete.

3. 3. 1. 4   Income of the Municipality

The primary sources of municipal income are discussed below.

■ Income and sales taxes are major sources of state income.

■ Real property taxes are the principal income source of counties and school districts; real property taxes are the largest source of city income.

■ City income can include fines, license fees, assessments, sales taxes, hotel taxes, city income taxes, utility taxes, and any city personal property tax.

3. 3. 1. 5   Ad Valorem Taxes

Property taxes are based on a property's assessed valuation, a percentage of the estimated market value. That percentage is established by each state or county and varies substantially. The market value of each piece of property in a county is determined by the county assessor, who relies on recent sale prices of similar properties, income streams, replacement costs, and other information.

Because the real property tax is based on the property's value, it is said to be an **ad valorem**, or per value, tax. The tax is a lien on the property, which means the property can be seized if the tax is not paid. GOs, backed by the power to tax and seize property, are considered safer than revenue bonds of the same issuer and therefore can be issued with a lower interest rate.

3. 3. 1. 6   Analyzing the Official Statement

Analysts study the documents included in the official statement to determine the issuer's financial condition at the present and in the foreseeable future.

3. 3. 1. 6. 1   Future Financial Needs

The municipality's financial statements should be scrutinized for signs of future debt requirements. The municipality might need to issue more debt if:

■ its annual income is not sufficient to make the payments on its short-term (or floating) debt;

■ principal repayments are scheduled too close together;

■ sinking funds for outstanding term bonds are inadequate;

■ pension liabilities are unfunded; or

■ it plans to make more capital improvements soon.

Issuing more debt in the near future could damage an issuer's credit rating, which would cause the current issue to trade at a lower price.

3. 3. 1. 6. 2   The Debt Statement

The **debt statement** is used in the analysis of GO debt. It includes the estimated full valuation of taxable property, the estimated assessed value of property, and the assessment percentage.

To evaluate the municipality's debt structure, an analyst calculates **total debt**, the sum of all bonds issued by the municipality, and subtracts **self-supporting debt** from this figure.

Although revenue bond debt is included in total debt, it is backed by revenues from the facility it financed and is not a burden on the municipality's taxpayers.

The result is the municipality's **net direct debt**, which includes GOs and short-term notes issued in anticipation of taxes or for interim financing. To net direct debt, the analyst adds overlapping debt.

Overlapping debt disclosed on the debt statement is the city's proportionate share of the county's, school district's, park district's, and sanitary district's debts. The city's **net total debt**, also called **net overall debt**, is the sum of the overlapping debt and the net direct debt.

3. 3. 1. 6. 3   Calculating a Municipality's Net Total Debt

A municipality's net total debt can be calculated as follows:

	Total Debt
−	Self-supporting debt
−	Sinking fund accumulations
=	Net direct debt
+	Overlapping debt
=	Net total debt

TEST TOPIC ALERT   A question might ask about what is or is not included in the various categories on the debt statement. A good rule: for any category that uses the word *net*, self-supporting debt and sinking fund accumulations are not included. For instance, net total debt includes all GOs and overlapping debt but does not include the self-supporting and sinking fund accumulations.

Do not expect a calculation question on this topic. The exam will test your understanding of the concept.

3. 3. 2   REVENUE BONDS

Revenue bonds are rated according to a facility's potential to generate sufficient money to cover operating expenses and principal and interest payments. Revenue bonds are not repaid from taxes, so they are not subject to statutory debt limits. Revenue bonds are meant to be self-supporting, and if the facility they finance does not make enough money to repay the debts, the bondholders, not the taxpayers, bear the risk. When assessing the quality of revenue bonds, an investor should consider the following factors.

- **Economic justification:** the facility being built should be able to generate revenues.
- **Competing facilities:** a facility should not be placed where better alternatives are easily available.
- **Sources of revenue:** the sources should be dependable.
- **Call provisions:** with callable bonds, the higher the call premium, the more attractive a bond is to an investor.
- **Flow of funds:** revenues generated must be sufficient to pay all of the facility's operating expenses and to meet debt service obligation.

3. 3. 2. 1   Applications of Revenues

Principal and interest on revenue bonds are paid exclusively from money generated by the facility the issue finances. The issuer pledges to pay expenses in a specific order, called the **flow of funds**.

In most cases, a **net revenue pledge** is used, meaning that operating and maintenance expenses are paid first. The remaining funds (or net revenues) are used to pay debt service and meet other obligations.

3. 3. 2. 1. 1   Flow of Funds in a Net Revenue Pledge

In a net revenue pledge, total receipts from operating the facility are usually deposited in the **revenue fund**, and funds are disbursed as follows:

■ **Operations and maintenance**—used to pay current operating and maintenance expenses; remaining funds are called **net revenues**

■ **Debt service account**—used to pay the interest and principal maturing in the current year and serves as a sinking fund for term issues

■ **Debt service reserve fund**—used to hold enough money to pay one year's debt service

■ **Reserve maintenance fund**—used to supplement the general maintenance fund

■ **Renewal and replacement fund**—used to create reserve funds for major renewal projects and equipment replacements

■ **Surplus (sinking) fund**—used for a variety of purposes, such as redeeming bonds or paying for improvements

If the issuer has not pledged to pay operating and maintenance expenses first, debt service is the priority expense. When debt service is paid first, the flow of funds is called a **gross revenue pledge**.

The debt service includes current principal and interest due, plus any sinking fund obligations. If revenues exceed operating and other obligations, the money is usually placed in a surplus fund.

Gross and Net Revenue Pledges

Gross Revenue Pledge	Net Revenue Pledge
Issuer pays debt service first from gross revenues.	Issuer pays expenses first from gross revenues.
User pays operations and maintenance.	Issuer pays debt service second from net revenues.

TEST TOPIC ALERT   If you see questions that require differentiating gross revenue and net revenue pledges, maybe this will help: the name of the pledge tells you how debt service is paid. In a gross revenue pledge, debt service is paid first, from gross revenues. Operations and maintenance expenses are paid after debt service. In a net revenue pledge, debt service is paid from the net revenues, meaning operations and maintenance costs are paid first. This is the more common of the two pledges.

3. 3. 3   MUNICIPAL DEBT RATIOS

A community's ability to meet its debt service is reflected in the following mathematical ratios based on information in the debt statement and other documents.

- **Net debt to assessed valuation:** a ratio of 5% ($5,000 of debt per $100,000 of assessed property value) is considered reasonable for a municipality.

- **Net debt to estimated valuation:** assessed valuation varies among municipalities, so most analysts prefer to use **estimated valuation** of property.

- **Taxes per person or per capita:** this ratio equals the city's tax income divided by the city population; it is used to evaluate the population's tax burden.

- **Debt per capita:** larger cities can assume more debt per capita because their tax bases are more diversified.

- **Debt trend:** this number indicates whether the ratios are rising or falling. Bonds can be long-term investments, so it is important to anticipate the community's future financial position.

- **Collection ratio:** this ratio equals the taxes collected divided by the taxes assessed; it can help detect deteriorating credit conditions.

- **Coverage ratio:** this ratio shows how many times annual revenues will cover debt service. A coverage of 2:1 is considered adequate for a typical municipal revenue bond. For utility revenue bonds (i.e., sewer, water, and electricity), a coverage of 5:4 (125%) of fixed charges is considered adequate.

Basic demographic information (e.g., average age, average income, or number of children in or expected to be in public schools) for a population living in a particular area is also used to evaluate GO bonds.

TEST TOPIC ALERT   Memorizing the ratios is less important than understanding them. A question might ask if a ratio is used to analyze GOs or revenues. Associate all ratios with GOs, except for debt service coverage ratio, which analyzes revenues.

A municipal revenue bond indenture contains a net revenue pledge. The following are reported for the year: $30 million of gross revenues, $18 million of operating expenses, $4 million of interest expense, and $2 million of principal repayment. What is the debt service coverage ratio?

A. 2:1
B. 3:1
C. 5:1
D. 9:1

Answer: A. Under a net revenue pledge, bondholders are paid from net revenue, which equals gross revenue minus operating expenses. Net revenue is $12 million ($30 million – $18 million). Debt service is the combination of interest and principal repayment. The debt service is $6 million ($4 million + $2 million). To compute the debt service ratio, divide net revenue by debt service: $12 million ÷ $6 million = a ratio of 2:1.

3. 3. 4 OTHER SOURCES OF INFORMATION FOR MUNICIPAL BOND ANALYSIS

3. 3. 4. 1 Interest Rate Comparisons

In addition to issuer-specific information, the value of any bond is affected by trends in the overall bond market. Municipal bond prices tend to fluctuate more than government and corporate bond prices because each issue is unique and may have few regular market makers. Because fewer market makers exist in the municipal bond market than exist in the OTC equity market, the market for any specific municipal bond is typically thinner than the market for comparable corporate or government bonds.

3. 3. 4. 2 Municipal Bond Insurance

Municipal bond issuers can insure their securities' principal and interest payments by buying insurance from a number of insurers. Amongst those specializing in insuring municipal issues are National Public Finance Guarantee Corp. (formerly the Municipal Bond Investors Assurance Corporation—MBIA), Financial Guaranty Insurance Company (FGIC), Assured Guaranty Corporation (AGC), and AMBAC Indemnity Corporation (AMBAC). While AMBAC is not currently insuring new municipal issues, there are many AMBAC insured municipal bonds still outstanding.

Insured bonds are generally issued with lower coupon rates because investors will accept lower rates of return for the added safety insurance affords. In addition, the cost of insurance may also lessen the yield a municipal issuer is willing to pay. If not rated, insured bonds are typically implied to be rated AAA.

TEST TOPIC ALERT   Insured bonds should be delivered with evidence of insurance either on the certificate or in a separate document.

3. 3. 4. 3 Bond Ratings

Rating services, such as Standard & Poor's, Moody's, and Fitch, evaluate the credit quality of municipal bonds and publish their ratings. They also provide ratings for short-term municipal notes.

Moody's short-term MIG ratings are from MIG 1 (best quality) through MIG 4 (adequate quality). If a note is speculative, it is listed as SG. S&P's rates notes as SP-1, SP-2, and SP-3, and Fitch rates notes as F-1, F-2, and F-3.

EXAMPLE   All municipalities have **pension liabilities**, which are their legal obligation to pay retirement benefits to future retirees. An **unfunded pension liability** is one where adequate reserves have not been set aside to meet this future obligation. Poor investment performance of the monies set aside today can lead to an unfunded liability later. This type of liability will be noted by municipal bond credit rating agencies and ultimately have an adverse affect on the municipalities credit rating.

QUICK QUIZ 3.C

1. If an insured municipal bond defaults, the insurance company must pay

   A. interest only
   B. principal only
   C. both A and B
   D. neither A nor B

2. Which of the following are considered sources of debt service for GO bonds?

   I.   Personal property taxes
   II. Real estate taxes
   III. Fees from delinquent property taxes
   IV. Liquor license fees

   A. I and IV
   B. II and III
   C. II, III and IV
   D. I, II, III and IV

3. In rating a general obligation bond, an analyst must consider

   I.   debt per capita
   II. total outstanding debt
   III. tax collection ratio
   IV. political attitude

   A. I and II
   B. I and III
   C. II, III and IV
   D. I, II, III and IV

4. Which of the following is NOT considered when evaluating municipal revenue bond credit risk?

   A. Competing facilities
   B. Quality of management
   C. Coverage ratios
   D. Interest rate movements

5. A municipal bond issue would be nonrated when

   A. the municipality's credit is not good
   B. the municipality's debt is too small to be rated
   C. the issue is a term bond
   D. the municipality has an outstanding bond in default

6. A qualitative analysis of a general obligation bond that is to be issued would take into consideration all of the following factors EXCEPT

   A. the tax base of the community
   B. the economic character of the community
   C. the dollar denominations of the bonds to be issued
   D. the makeup of the community's population

7. Which of the following would a customer examine to evaluate the credit quality of a new municipal security?

    A. Official statement
    B. Legal opinion
    C. Prospectus
    D. Trust indenture

8. An increase in any of the following would indicate deteriorating credit conditions EXCEPT

    A. bankruptcies
    B. consumer debt
    C. bond defaults
    D. assessed valuations

9. Which of the following could insure payment of principal and interest on a municipality's outstanding debt?

    I.   FGIC
    II.   AGC
    III. SIPC
    IV.   FDIC

    A. I and II
    B. I, II and III
    C. III and IV
    D. I, II, III and IV

3. 4   MUNICIPAL TRADING AND TAXATION

The following sections will cover some of the trading terminology and concepts associated with municipals as well as their unique tax consequences.

3. 4. 1   QUOTATIONS

Municipal bonds are bought and sold in the over-the-counter (OTC) market. Most large brokerages maintain trading departments that deal exclusively in municipal bonds. Many of the rules governing the trading of other OTC securities also apply to municipal bond transactions.

Municipal dealers are called upon regularly to provide current quotations for municipal securities. The term **quotation** means any bid for or offer of municipal securities. Any indication of interest or solicitation by a municipal dealer (such as **bid wanted** or **offer wanted**) would be considered a quotation request.

Municipal bonds are usually priced and offered for sale on a **yield-to-maturity (YTM)** basis rather than a dollar price. This is called a **basis quote**. Municipal bonds with serial maturities are quoted in basis (YTM).

If a question mentions a 6% bond quoted on a 6.5 basis, you should be able to determine that the coupon of the bond is 6% and its YTM is 6.5%. Because the YTM is higher than the coupon, the bond is trading at a discount.

YTM/YTC and Premium and Discount

Are the following bonds trading at premium or a discount?

1. 7% bond, 6.25% basis
2. 7% bond, 7.64% basis
3. 5% bond, 4.85% basis
4. 6% bond, 6.45% basis

Answers: 1. Premium; 2. Discount; 3. Premium; 4. Discount

3. 4. 1. 1   Dollar Bonds

Some municipal revenue bonds are quoted on a percentage of par dollar basis rather than a yield basis. Such bonds are commonly called dollar bonds. Dollar bonds are usually term bonds callable before maturity.

Be sure to recognize that a bond quoted at 104 for example is a dollar bond, and that the "104" actually represents its price expressed as a percentage of PAR value. Therefore, a quote of 104 = 104% of PAR or 104%($1,000) = $1,040.

3. 4. 1. 2   Bona Fide Quotes

If a municipal dealer gives, distributes, or publishes a quotation for a security, that quote must be **bona fide**. For a quote to be considered bona fide, or **firm**, the dealer must be prepared to trade the security at the price specified in the quote and under the conditions and restrictions (if any) accompanying the quote. A bona fide quote:

■ must reflect the dealer's best judgment and have a reasonable relationship to the fair market value for that security; and

■ may reflect the firm's inventory and expectations of market direction.

In other words, a quotation need not represent the best price, but it must have a reasonable relationship to fair market value. A quotation may take into consideration such other factors as the dealer's inventory position and any anticipated market movement.

If the dealer distributes or publishes the quotation on behalf of another dealer, it must have reason to believe that the quote is bona fide and based on the other dealer's best judgment of fair market value. Dealers cannot knowingly misrepresent a quote made by another municipal securities dealer.

Quotations are always subject to prior sale or change in price. Any means of communication, including print, voice, and electronic media, can be used to disseminate, distribute, or publish quotations.

TAKE NOTE   Municipal dealers can make offers to sell securities by providing quotes without owning the bonds. The dealer, however, must know where to obtain the bonds if such offers are accepted.

3. 4. 2   REPORTS OF SALES

MSRB rules prohibit dealers from distributing or publishing any report of a municipal security's purchase or sale unless they know or have reason to believe that the transaction took place. Broker-dealers reporting the sale must believe that the reported trade is real and not fictitious, fraudulent, or deceitful.

Municipal securities dealers must report trades with other dealers to the **National Securities Clearing Corporation (NSCC)**. The report must include the two executing firms' names and the amount of accrued interest, if known.

TAKE NOTE   A round lot for municipal bonds is usually $100,000 face amount.

3. 4. 2. 1   Broker's Broker

Some municipal brokers specialize in trading only with institutional customers, such as banks and other municipal brokers, not with the retail public. These firms are called **broker's brokers** because their business focuses on helping other municipal dealers place unsold portions of new bond issues. They do not disclose the identity of the customers they represent. Furthermore, they act solely as agents and do not maintain an inventory of bonds.

TEST TOPIC ALERT   Broker's brokers protect the identity of their customers.

3. 4. 3   BROKER-DEALER REGULATION

3. 4. 3. 1   Reciprocal Dealings (Antireciprocal Rule)

A dealer cannot solicit trades in municipal securities from an investment company in return for sales by the dealer of shares or units in the investment company (**antireciprocal rule**).

If a municipal bond fund makes a large number of trades every month in its portfolio, a municipal dealer cannot be selected to execute the fund's portfolio trades only on the basis of the firm's promise that its account executives will increase sales of the bond fund's shares. The firm can be selected to execute those trades on the basis of the services the dealer offers to the fund, such as prompt execution and research.

3. 4. 3. 2   Customer Recommendations and Suitability

MSRB rules require municipal securities broker-dealers to make suitable recommendations to customers. Before making a recommendation, a municipal securities firm must make a reasonable effort to learn the customer's financial status, tax status, investment objectives, and other holdings. The **suitability test** applies to discretionary accounts as well as to all other accounts.

Regarding suitability, one should always remember that the tax-free interest paid by municipal bonds makes them better suited to those in higher tax brackets. In addition, the ability to receive tax-free interest payments means that these bonds have no place in an investor's tax-advantaged accounts like IRAs or 401(k) plans. Of course, because they are bonds, and bonds pay interest income, they are best suited to those who list income as an investment objective.

Any recommendations beyond these parameters would be unusual and the practice of increasing commissions through excessive trading, known as **churning**, is specifically prohibited. Before an account is opened, it must be approved in writing by a principal and if investment objectives noted when the account was approved do not align with transactions in the account later, this would present a red flag to be addressed.

TAKE NOTE   If a customer refuses to disclose net worth, income, or both, the account can still be opened. However, in this situation, recommendations cannot be made.

3. 4. 3. 2. 1   Protecting Customer Accounts

Municipal securities dealers cannot misuse securities or funds held for another person. Dealers also may not guarantee customers against loss (put options and repurchase agreements are not considered guarantees against loss) or share in the profits or losses of a customer's account. An exception to this rule applies in the case of an associated person who establishes a personal joint account with a customer and obtains written permission from the firm. In this situation, the associated person may share in the account's profits and losses only in proportion to the amount of capital contributed to the account.

3. 4. 3. 2. 2   Disclosure of Control

A municipal securities firm that has a control relationship with respect to a municipal security is subject to additional disclosure requirements. A **control relationship** exists if the dealer controls, is controlled by, or is under common control with that security's issuer.

An officer of a municipal dealer sits on the board of directors of an issuer.

The dealer must disclose the control relationship to the customer before it can effect any transaction in that security for that customer. Although, initially, this disclosure can be verbal, the dealer must make a written disclosure at or before the transaction's completion. The disclosure is normally made on the confirmation. If the transaction is for a discretionary account, the customer must give express permission before the transaction can be executed.

3. 4. 4 MARKUPS AND COMMISSIONS

A dealer acts as an agent when it arranges trades for customers and charges **commissions**. A dealer acts as a principal when it buys for or sells securities from its own inventory. The dealer charges a **markup** for principal transactions when it sells securities to customers and a **markdown** when it buys securities from customers.

3. 4. 4. 1 Principal Transactions

Each **principal transaction** is executed at a net price, which includes the markup or markdown. Some of the factors taken into consideration include the:

- dealer's best judgment of fair market value;
- expense of effecting the transaction;
- fact that the dealer is entitled to a markup or markdown (profit);
- total dollar amount of the transaction; and
- value of any security exchanged or traded.

TAKE NOTE   Markups or markdowns are not disclosed separately on a customer's confirmation.

3. 4. 4. 2 Agency Transactions

Each agency transaction is executed for a commission that is not in excess of a fair and reasonable amount, considering all relevant factors. For an agency commission calculation, a dealer takes into consideration the:

- security's availability;
- expense of executing the order;
- value of services the dealer renders; and
- amount of any other compensation received or to be received in connection with the transaction.

3. 4. 4. 2. 1 Best Execution

When executing an order as an agent, a dealer must make a reasonable effort to obtain a fair and reasonable price.

TAKE NOTE   Commissions are disclosed on customer confirmations.

3. 4. 5 CONFIRMATIONS

Customers must receive a written **confirmation** of each municipal securities transaction they have entered. The confirmation must describe the security; list the trade date, settlement date, and amount of accrued interest; state the firm's name, address, and phone number; and indicate whether the firm acted as agent or principal in the trade. A confirmation that does not include the time of execution must indicate that this information will be provided if the customer requests it.

3. 4. 5. 1 Disclosing Yield

In disclosing yield on a customer confirmation, the following rules apply. If the bond is noncallable, the actual life of the bond is known with certainty. Therefore, the yield shown is the yield to maturity.

If the bond is callable, the problem is the uncertainty surrounding a possible call. Will the bond be called? We do not know the answer. If interest rates have risen since the bond's issuance, causing the price to fall and trade at a discount, the issuer is not likely to call the bonds because any refunding bonds would have to be sold at higher yields. If rates have fallen since the bond's issuance, causing the price to rise and trade at a premium, the issuer is more likely to call the bonds because any refunding bonds can be sold at lower yields.

Therefore, discount bonds are not likely to be called, whereas premium bonds are likely to be called.

To deal with all of this, the MSRB requires that the yield shown on a customer confirmation be the lower of YTM or YTC. For discount bonds, the lower is YTM. For premium bonds, the lower is YTC. If a premium bond has a number of call dates and prices, rather than computing yield to all of the possible call dates and prices to determine which is the lowest, the MSRB permits firms to show yield to the near-term (closest in) in-whole call.

Furthermore, if the issuer has announced an in-whole call, there is no longer any uncertainty. Therefore, the confirmation should show yield computed to the announced call date and price, which is the new maturity of the bond. If an issue is subject to a partial call, there is uncertainty as to whether the bond being sold to the customer will be one of the bonds selected for the call. In this situation, the basic rule applies: show the lower of YTM or YTC.

There are three cases where no separate yield disclosure is required.

- **Variable rate bonds (reset bonds):** As the coupon is adjusted periodically, a yield computation is impossible.
- **Bonds in default:** If a bond is no longer paying interest, a yield computation is impossible.
- **Bonds sold at par:** For bonds sold at par, no separate yield disclosure is required because the yield cannot be anything other than the coupon rate. Remember: at par, all yields are the same.

3. 4. 5. 1. 1 Zero-Coupon Municipal Securities

A zero-coupon bond is issued at a deep discount from par and pays no current interest. The confirmation must indicate an interest rate of 0% and state that accrued interest is not calculated.

3. 4. 5. 1. 2 Required Information on Confirmations

Each confirmation must also include the following information:

- In an agency transaction, the name of the party on the other side of the transaction and the source and amount of any commission (the name of the other party must be disclosed on request if it is not listed on the confirmation)
- The dated date if it affects the interest calculation
- Whether the securities are fully registered, registered as to principal only, in book-entry form, or in bearer form
- Whether the securities are called or pre-refunded, as well as the date of maturity fixed by the call notice and the amount of the call price
- Any special qualification or factor that might affect payment of principal or interest
- Whether the bond interest is taxable or subject to the alternative minimum tax (AMT)

3. 4. 6 ADVERTISING

Any material designed for use in the public media is considered **advertising**. This includes abstracts and summaries of the official statement; offering circulars; reports; market letters; and form letters, including professional, product, and new issue advertisements.

A municipal securities principal or general securities principal of the dealer must approve all advertising before use, and a copy of each advertisement must be kept on file for three years.

TAKE NOTE Preliminary and final official statements are not considered advertising because they are prepared by or on behalf of an issuer. Also note that copies of advertising are never filed with the MSRB.

3. 4. 7 THE BROKER-DEALER AS FINANCIAL ADVISER

3. 4. 7. 1 Financial Advisers

The MSRB has established ethical standards and disclosure requirements for municipal securities dealers that act as **financial advisers** to municipal securities' issuers. A financial advisory relationship exists when a municipal dealer provides financial advisory or consulting services to an issuer with respect to a new issue for a fee or other compensation. This includes advice regarding the structure, timing, and terms of, as well as other matters concerning, the issue or issuer.

3. 4. 7. 1. 1 Basis of Compensation

Each financial advisory relationship must be documented in writing before, upon, or promptly after its inception. This document establishes the basis of compensation for the advisory services to be rendered.

3. 4. 7. 2   Conflicts of Interest

Potential **conflicts of interest** arise if a firm acts as both underwriter and financial adviser for the same issue. The MSRB has the following requirements.

The MSRB simply prohibits a broker-dealer that serves as a financial advisor to a municipal issuer for any issue sold on either a negotiated or competitive bid basis from switching roles and underwriting the same issue. In other words, if a broker-dealer is acting as a financial advisor to the issuer, generally they may not participate in underwriting the bonds of the issuing municipality.

However, there are some allowable exceptions. For example, a broker-dealer that has a financial advisory relationship with an issuer with respect to the issuance of municipal securities will still be permitted to assist with preparing the official statement and other similar duties normally associated with underwriting. They can also purchase the bonds from an underwriter either for their own trading account or for the accounts of their customers. But in all cases, if performing such functions or acting in such a capacity as described above, the broker-dealer may not receive any compensation other than for financial advisory services to the issuer. In other words, no underwriting compensation can be received by the broker-dealer who is acting in an advisory capacity.

Customers who might be purchasing new securities from a broker-dealer that is acting in an advisory capacity to a municipality must be informed that the advisory relationship exists at or before confirmation of the sale.

3. 4. 7. 2. 1   Assistance with Official Statement

As part of its financial advisory services to an issuer, a municipal securities dealer may help prepare the final official statement for a new issue. If it prepares the official statement, the adviser must make a copy of that statement available to the managing underwriter promptly after the award is made and at least two days before the syndicate manager delivers the securities to the syndicate members.

3. 4. 7. 2. 2   Use of Ownership Information

While acting in a fiduciary capacity for an issuer, a municipal securities dealer often obtains confidential information about its bondholders. The dealer cannot use this information to solicit purchases or sales of municipal securities or to pursue other financial gain without the issuer's consent.

Examples of fiduciary capacities include but are not limited to acting as paying agent, transfer agent, registrar, or indenture trustee for an issuer.

3. 4. 8   TAXATION OF MUNICIPAL ISSUES

3. 4. 8. 1   Tax-Exempt Interest Payments

The **Tax Reform Act of 1986** restricted the federal income tax exemption of interest for municipal bonds to public purpose bonds, which are bonds issued to finance projects that benefit citizens in general rather than particular private interests. If a bond channels more than 10% of its proceeds to private parties, it is considered a private activity bond and is not automatically granted tax exemption.

3. 4. 8. 1. 1   Calculating Tax Benefits

An investor considering the purchase of a tax-exempt bond should compare its yield carefully with that of taxable securities. The tax savings of the tax-free bond may be more attractive than a taxable bond with a higher interest rate. This depends, in part, on the investor's tax bracket: the higher the tax bracket, the greater the tax exemption's value.

To determine a municipal bond investment's tax benefit, an investor must calculate the tax-equivalent yield. To do so, divide the tax-free yield by 100% less the investor's tax rate.

TEST TOPIC ALERT   When answering a tax equivalent yield question, keep in mind that the municipal yield will always be less than the corporate yield.

An investor is in the 30% tax bracket. A municipal bond currently yields 7%. To offer an equivalent yield, what must a corporate bond yield?

Divide the municipal yield by 100% minus the investor's tax bracket. This is known as the tax-equivalent yield formula.

$$7\% \div (100\% - 30\%) = 10\%$$

Assume the same investor is in the 30% tax bracket. If a corporate bond currently yields 11%, what would be the equivalent municipal yield?

To find the answer, multiply the corporate yield by 100% minus the investor's tax bracket. This is known as the tax-free equivalent yield formula.

$$11\% \times (100\% - 30\%) = 7.7\%$$

3. 4. 8. 2   No Interest Deductions

The expenses associated with purchasing or holding municipal bonds are not deductible. This includes interest on loans to acquire bonds, such as margin loans, and safe deposit box rental. These rules apply because of the tax-free nature of the interest income at the federal government level.

3. 4. 8. 2. 1   Exception for Banks

When banks purchase certain issues of GO bonds (limited to a maximum face amount of $10 million), they are allowed to deduct 80% of the interest carrying cost of the deposits funding the purchase of the bonds.

EXAMPLE   A bank buys municipal bonds with $1 million of deposits paying 3% interest. Because these bonds are bank qualified, the bank can deduct 80% of the interest paid (1 million × .03 × .8 = $24,000). The bank also receives interest on the newly purchased municipal bonds free of federal income tax.

3. 5 MUNICIPAL SECURITIES RULES AND REGULATIONS

Rules and regulations applicable to all firms and individuals having to do with municipal securities are written by the Muncipal Securities Rulemaking Board (MSRB).

3. 5. 1 MUNICIPAL SECURITIES RULEMAKING BOARD (MSRB)

The Securities Acts Amendments of 1975 established the **Municipal Securities Rulemaking Board** as an independent SRO. The MSRB governs the issue and trade of municipal securities. The rules require municipal securities underwriters and dealers to protect investors' interests, be ethical in offering advice, and be responsive to complaints and disputes. The MSRB rules apply to all firms and individuals engaged in the conduct of municipal securities business. The MSRB does not regulate issuers.

3. 5. 1. 0. 1 Rule Enforcement

The MSRB has no authority to enforce the rules it makes. While the SEC oversees all securities-related rule enforcement, the MSRB rules concerning municipal securities dealers (e.g., NYSE member firms) are specifically enforced by FINRA; the Office of the Comptroller of the Currency enforces those rules that apply to national banks.

The **Federal Reserve Board (FRB)** enforces MSRB rules governing any nonnational banks that are members of the Federal Reserve System. The **Federal Deposit Insurance Corporation (FDIC)** enforces MSRB rules for non-national banks that are not members of the Federal Reserve System.

3. 5. 1. 0. 2 Municipal Finance Professional

As defined by the Municipal Securities Rulemaking Board (MSRB), a Municipal Finance Professional is an associated person of a broker dealer who is primarily engaged in municipal securities activities other than retail sales to individuals, or who solicits municipal securities business for the broker dealer or who is in the supervisory chain above MFPs as described. This can include senior officials of the broker dealer, or executives or management committee members of the broker dealer having the previously noted responsibilities.

Of note, the MSRB is clear that anyone designated as an MFP is subject to the rules regarding political contributions (as stated in Rule G-37 later in this unit) and are required to report those contributions to the MSRB as well as any payments made to a state or local political party. There are exceptions for "de minimis" contributions.

TAKE NOTE This final section of the Municipal Securities unit addresses the rules of the MSRB. Each rule is identified with a G-number, such as G-12. It is unnecessary to memorize these rules by their numbers; instead, be comfortable with the concepts they convey.

3. 5. 1. 1 General Regulations

The three categories of MSRB rules include (1) rules that provide consistent legal definitions of terms used in the business of trading municipal securities, (2) administrative rules that cover the organization and functions of the MSRB, and (3) general rules and regulations that describe MSRB policies. The following sections highlight the important MSRB rules.

Rule G-1. A bank that has a separately identifiable department or division engaged in any activity related to the municipal securities business is classified as a municipal securities dealer and must comply with MSRB regulations. A separately identifiable division is one under the direct supervision of an officer of the bank responsible for the day-to-day conduct of municipal securities business.

Municipal securities-related activity includes underwriting, trading or selling municipal securities, or serving as an issuer's financial adviser. In addition, a firm that provides research or advisory services for municipal securities investors or that communicates with the public in any way about investing in municipal securities is considered a municipal securities dealer and must register with the MSRB.

Rules G-2 and G-3. Those who must qualify by examination under MSRB rules include municipal securities principals, financial and operations principals, and municipal securities representatives. A municipal securities representative is any person who gives financial advice to municipal securities issuers or investment advice to investors. Anyone who communicates with the public about municipal securities acts as a representative.

A person must pass the Municipal Securities Representative Qualification Exam (Series 52) or the General Securities Representative Exam (Series 7) to be qualified as a municipal securities representative. To qualify as a municipal securities principal, a person must pass the Municipal Securities Principal Qualification Exam (Series 53).

TAKE NOTE

Excluded from the licensing requirements are persons acting in a clerical or ministerial capacity who:

- read approved quotes;
- provide trade reports; or
- record or enter orders.

Persons who take a qualification exam and fail cannot retake the exam for 30 days. After failing the exam three or more times, a six-month wait is imposed before another attempt is allowed. FINRA has adopted this rule.

Rule G-6. The MSRB requires municipal broker-dealers to maintain blanket fidelity bonds as mandated by the SRO to which a broker-dealer belongs. The dollar amount of coverage required varies according to the firm's size. Banks are not affected by this rule.

Rule G-7. A municipal securities dealer must obtain and keep on file specific information about its associated persons. Most of the required information (e.g., employment history, disciplinary actions, residence, and personal data) is contained on the U-4 and U-5 forms.

Rule G-10. Any time a municipal securities firm receives a written complaint from a customer, the firm must enter the complaint in a complaint file, indicating what action, if any, the firm has taken. It must also deliver a copy of the MSRB's *Investor Brochure* to that customer.

Rule G-11. During the underwriting period, a syndicate must establish a priority for allocating orders and identify conditions that might alter the priority.

Rule G-12. This rule outlines the procedures, or **uniform practices**, for settling transactions between municipal securities firms. The MSRB uniform practices include regulations regarding settlement dates, which are the same for municipal securities firms as they are for the rest of the securities industry.

■ **Cash trades** settle on the trade date.

■ **Regular way trades** settle on the second business day after the trade date.

Rule G-12 also discusses **good delivery requirements**. Securities that are not in good delivery form are rejected (buyer does not accept delivery) or reclaimed (buyer accepts delivery only to find the bonds are not good delivery). This does not invalidate the trade; the seller is still obligated to sell the securities.

Delivery is made in denominations of $1,000 or $5,000 for bearer bonds. Registered bonds are delivered in multiples of $1,000 par value, with a maximum par value on any one certificate of $100,000.

Mutilated certificates are not good delivery unless the transfer agent or some other acceptable official of the issuer validates the security. The issuer or a commercial bank must endorse mutilated coupons for them to be considered good delivery. Coupon bonds must have all unpaid coupons attached in proper order.

In the case of an issue's **partial call**, the called securities are not good delivery unless they are identified as called when traded. Municipal securities without legal opinions attached are not good delivery unless it is specified on the trade date that the transaction is ex-legal.

Rule G-13. Dealers can publish quotations only for bona fide bids or offers. Nominal quotes (informational only) are permissible if identified as such. No dealer participating in a joint account may distribute a quotation indicating more than one market for that security.

Rule G-15. Confirmations of trades must be sent or given to customers at or before a transaction's completion. Each confirm must include:

■ broker-dealer's name, address, and telephone number;

■ customer's name;

■ detailed description of the security, including issuer, interest rate and maturity, whether it is callable, and so forth;

■ trade date and time of execution;

■ settlement date;

■ CUSIP number, if any;

■ yield and dollar price;

■ amount of accrued interest;

■ extended principal amount (the total principal of all securities the information covers);

■ total dollar amount (the extended principal plus any accrued interest);

■ whether the firm acted as broker or dealer (if it acted as broker, the name of the person on the other side of the trade must be given, if requested, and the dollar amount of commission earned from both parties must be disclosed);

■ dated date, if it affects the interest calculation and the first interest payment date;

- level of registration of the security (fully registered, registered as to principal only, or book-entry);
- whether the bonds are called or pre-refunded; and
- any other special fact about the security traded (e.g., escrowed to maturity, ex-legal trade, federally taxable, or odd denominations).

Rule G-16. Each municipal broker-dealer must be examined at least once every two calendar years to ensure that the firm is in compliance with MSRB regulations, SEC rules, and the Securities Exchange Act of 1934. Because the MSRB does not enforce its own rules, it does not examine municipal securities firms. The appropriate enforcement agency (e.g., FINRA, FDIC, Comptroller of the Currency, or FRB) administers the examinations.

Rule G-17. Municipal securities dealers must deal fairly with everyone in transacting municipal securities business and must not engage in deceptive, dishonest, unfair, or manipulative practices.

Rule G-18. Dealers must try to obtain prices for customers that are reasonable and fairly related to the market. This rule also applies to broker's brokers, which regularly effect trades for the accounts of other municipal brokers and dealers.

Rule G-19. A municipal securities firm, through its representatives, must obtain extensive financial, personal, and investment information about a client to ensure suitable recommendations and transactions. A representative must obtain and use as much information as possible when making recommendations and must have reasonable grounds for recommending any particular security or transaction.

The MSRB prohibits broker-dealers from recommending municipal securities to a customer if a broker-dealer has not obtained the customer's financial information, tax status, and investment objectives, even if the broker-dealer has reasonable grounds to believe that the recommendation is suitable for the customer.

Rule G-20. Municipal securities dealers cannot give gifts valued at more than $100 to any person in one year other than their employees. Payments for services rendered are allowed. Gifts of occasional meals or tickets to sporting events or concerts (not season passes) are permitted. Sponsorship of legitimate business functions is also permissible.

Rule G-21. Municipal securities firms must be truthful in their advertising. They must not publish advertisements that are false or misleading in regard to their services, skills, or products. An advertisement for a new issue can show the original reoffering price, even though it may have changed, if the advertisement contains the sale date. A firm's municipal or general securities principal must approve each advertisement in writing before first use.

Rule G-22. Clients must be informed if a control relationship exists between a municipal firm and an issuer. A **control relationship** means the dealer or one of its officers is in a position to influence the issuer or is in a position to be influenced by the issuer. The phrase "controls, is controlled by, or is under common control with" allows the broadest interpretation of control. Verbal disclosure is required before the trade is effected, with written disclosure following no later than at the time of the confirmation.

TAKE NOTE   Particular care must be taken in a discretionary account. If a control relationship exists, no transaction is permitted without prior authorization from the customer.

Rule G-23. Prohibits a broker-dealer or municipal securities dealer that serves as financial advisor to a municipal issuer from underwriting the issuer's bonds in either a negotiated or competitive bid underwriting except in the instance of certain defined allowable functions (i.e., assisting with the preparation of the official statement).

Rule G-24. In the normal course of business, dealers gain access to confidential, nonpublic information about their customers. Municipal securities firms may not use this confidential information to solicit trades of municipal securities except with an issuer's express consent.

Rule G-25. Like other types of broker-dealers, municipal securities firms and their representatives may not misuse securities or money held for other people. They must not guarantee a customer against loss or share in the profits or losses of a customer's account, although joint accounts in a private capacity are allowed. Bona fide put options and repurchase agreements are not considered guarantees against loss.

Rule G-27. Each municipal securities firm must designate a principal to supervise the firm's representatives and must create and maintain a written supervisory procedures manual. The designated principal for the firm must approve in writing:

- the opening of new customer accounts;
- every municipal securities transaction;
- actions taken on customer complaints; and
- correspondence regarding municipal securities trades.

Every broker-dealer, but not bank dealers, must have a **financial and operations principal (FinOp)** who maintains the financial books and records.

Rule G-28. If a municipal securities dealer employee opens an account with another municipal securities firm, MSRB rules require the firm opening the account to notify the employer in writing and to send duplicate confirmations to the employer. The firm opening the account must comply with any other requests the employer makes.

Rule G-29. Every municipal securities dealer's office must keep a copy of MSRB regulations so that it may provide a copy of these rules for review to any customer upon request.

Rule G-30. The markups or markdowns that municipal securities dealers charge must be fair and reasonable, taking into account all characteristics of a trade, such as:

- fair market value of the securities at trade time;
- total dollar amount of the transaction;
- any special difficulty in doing the trade; and
- the fact that the dealer is entitled to a profit.

Rule G-31. A municipal securities broker-dealer may not solicit business from an investment company on the basis of the broker-dealer's record of sales of the investment company's shares.

Rule G-32. When a new issue of municipal securities is delivered to a customer, a copy of the official statement must accompany or precede the delivery.

If the issue is a negotiated underwriting, the municipal firm must disclose in writing to the customer the amount of the spread, the amount of any fee received if the firm acted as an agent in the sale, and the initial offering price for each maturity in the issue. There is no requirement to disclose the spread in competitive underwritings.

Rule G-33. Municipal dealers must calculate accrued interest when a municipal security trades and interest. Municipal bonds, like corporates, use a 360-day year with 30-day months.

Rule G-37. Rule G-37 prohibits municipal firms from engaging in municipal securities business with an issuer for two years after any political contribution is made to an official of that issuer. In this context, municipal securities business refers to negotiated underwritings, not to competitive underwritings. The idea is to prevent firms from making large political contributions in return for being selected as underwriter for that issuer.

The rule applies to contributions by the firm, its municipal finance professionals (MFPs), and by political action committees controlled by the firm or its representatives. Contributions of up to $250 per election are permitted by municipal finance professionals as long as these individuals are eligible to vote for the issuer official. This exemption does not apply to firms.

Rule G-39. Telemarketers calling on behalf of a firm may not call a person before 8:00 am or after 9:00 pm in the called person's time zone. The caller must disclose his name and the firm's name, the firm's telephone number or address, and the fact that he is calling to solicit the purchase of municipal bonds or investment services.

The requirements do not apply if the person called is an established customer. Calls made to other brokers or dealers are also exempt.

Rule G-41. Every broker, dealer, or municipal securities dealer must establish and implement an anti-money laundering compliance program reasonably designed to achieve and monitor ongoing compliance with the requirements of the Bank Secrecy Act.

Rule G-42. Limits political contributions by advisors.

UNIT TEST

1. The call premium on a municipal bond trading above par is best described as the difference between

   A. the market price and par
   B. the market price and the call price
   C. par and the call price
   D. the amortized premium and the annual interest

2. The interest from which of the following bonds is exempt from federal income tax?

   I. State of California
   II. City of Anchorage
   III. Treasury bonds
   IV. GNMA

   A. I and II
   B. I and III
   C. II and III
   D. III and IV

3. A couple's home has an assessed valuation of $40,000 and a market value of $100,000. What will the tax be if a rate of 5 mills is used?

   A. $200
   B. $500
   C. $2,000
   D. $5,000

4. The document that establishes the municipal syndicate as either Eastern or Western and establishes the terms for operation of the syndicate is known as

   A. the underwriting agreement
   B. the trust indenture
   C. the agreement among underwriters
   D. the bond resolution

5. All of the following deal with the secondary market EXCEPT

   A. dealer quotes
   B. broker's broker
   C. notice of sale
   D. Thomson Municipal Market Monitor

6. The MSRB is authorized to adopt rules concerning all of the following EXCEPT

   A. form and content of price quotations
   B. sale of new issues to related portfolios
   C. information to be provided by municipal issuers
   D. records to be maintained by municipal dealers

7. All of the following have the authority to enforce MSRB rules EXCEPT

   A. FINRA
   B. FDIC
   C. Federal Reserve Board
   D. MSRB

8. Municipal broker's brokers deal with all of the following EXCEPT

   A. bank dealers
   B. municipal dealers
   C. individuals
   D. institutions

9. Which of the following projects is most likely to be financed by a general obligation rather than a revenue bond?

   A. Municipal hospital
   B. Expansion of an airport
   C. New high school
   D. Public golf course

10. All of the following characteristics regarding industrial development bonds are true EXCEPT

    A. the bonds are issued by municipalities or other governmental units
    B. the funds are used to construct a facility for a private corporation
    C. these bonds are normally backed by the full faith and credit of the municipality
    D. funds from the lease are used to pay the principal and interest on the bonds

11. Which of the following statements regarding the good faith deposit submitted by interested bidders are TRUE?

    I.   It is usually 1–2% of the total par value of the bonds offered.
    II. It is usually 10% of the total par value of the bonds offered.
    III. If the bid is unsuccessful, it is returned to the underwriting syndicate.
    IV. If the bid is unsuccessful, it is retained by the issuer.

    A. I and III
    B. I and IV
    C. II and III
    D. II and IV

12. If IDB bonds are called because of condemnation, this would be covered under which of the following clauses in the bond indenture?

    A. Defeasance
    B. Refunding
    C. Catastrophe
    D. Refinancing

13. Which of the following would be found in the agreement among underwriters for a municipal bond offering?

    I.   Legal opinion
    II. Amount of the concession
    III. Appointment of the bond counsel
    IV. Establishment of the takedown

    A. I and III
    B. I and IV
    C. II and III
    D. II and IV

14. New Housing Authority (NHA) bonds are a relatively safe investment because

    A. rental income provides a hedge against inflation
    B. the U.S. government guarantees a contribution to secure the bonds
    C. they are backed by the full faith and credit of the issuing municipalities
    D. banks buy these bonds

15. Which of the following types of municipal bond issues are associated with a flow of funds?

    A. TANs
    B. General obligation bonds
    C. Revenue bonds
    D. All of the above

16. New issues of municipal securities are available in

    I.   bearer form
    II. book-entry form
    III. registered form
    IV. registered as to principal only form

    A. I and II
    B. II and III
    C. II and IV
    D. III and IV

17. All of the following statements regarding a municipality's debt limit are true EXCEPT

    A. the purpose of debt restrictions is to protect taxpayers from excessive taxes
    B. revenue bonds are not affected by statutory limitations
    C. the debt limit is the maximum amount a municipality can borrow in any one year
    D. unlimited GO bonds may be issued when a community's taxing power is not restricted by statutory provisions

18. An issuer's proportionate share of the debt of other local governmental units in the area in which the issuer is located is defined as

    A. net direct debt
    B. overlapping debt
    C. bonded debt
    D. reversionary working interest

19. Nonmembers of a syndicate buy the bonds at a discount called

    A. a takedown
    B. a net designated price
    C. a concession
    D. the basis price

20. The Bond Buyer Revenue Bond Index

    I. includes 30-year bonds
    II. includes 20 bonds
    III. is compiled weekly
    IV. is compiled monthly

    A. I and II
    B. I and III
    C. II and III
    D. II and IV

21. Special tax bonds are

    A. general obligation bonds
    B. self-supporting bonds
    C. backed by property taxes
    D. backed by sales and/or excise taxes

22. In a municipal underwriting, total takedown can be described as

    A. additional takedown + concession
    B. underwriting fee + additional takedown
    C. underwriting fee + manager's fee
    D. concession + manager's fee

23. Which of the following is a double-barreled bond?

    A. New Housing Authority bond
    B. Project note
    C. Hospital bond backed by revenues and taxes
    D. GO bond to construct a new grade school

24. Which of the following statements regarding callable municipal bonds is TRUE?

    A. Noncallable bonds usually yield more than callable bonds.
    B. Bonds are typically called when interest rates are rising.
    C. Bond call premiums generally compensate the bondholder for interest payments lost if the bond is called.
    D. As interest rates rise, callable bonds trading at a premium will generally rise in value.

25. Seventy-five basis points is equal to

    I. 7.5%
    II. .75%
    III. $7.50
    IV. $75.00

    A. I and III
    B. I and IV
    C. II and III
    D. II and IV

26. An unqualified legal opinion means that

    A. the issue is legal, but certain contingencies may limit the flow of funds in the future
    B. the interest is not exempt from state or local taxes
    C. the bond counsel has rendered an opinion without any qualifying limitations
    D. the underwriter has failed to disclose sufficient information to qualify the issue

27. Which of the following should a registered representative consider before recommending a municipal security?

    A. Customer's state of residence
    B. Customer's tax status
    C. Municipal security's rating
    D. All of the above

28. All of the following statements regarding municipal bond official statements are true EXCEPT

    A. all purchasers of a new municipal bond issue must receive a final official statement
    B. a customer must receive an official statement no later than the settlement date
    C. an official statement must be delivered only upon customer request
    D. the MSRB does not require the preparation of a final official statement for new municipal bond issues

29. In the context of municipal bond underwritings, what distinguishes the true interest cost from the net interest cost?

    A. TIC reflects the time value of money.
    B. TIC reflects the credit risk.
    C. TIC is the method required by the IRS.
    D. TIC produces a lower cost of borrowing for the issuer.

30. Which of the following governmental bodies receive the least amount of their revenues from property taxes?

    A. State governments
    B. County governments
    C. Municipalities
    D. School districts

31. TANs, RANs, and BANs are issued by municipalities seeking

    A. short-term financing
    B. special tax assessments for GO bonds
    C. bond insurance
    D. financing for low-cost housing

32. A municipal securities representative intends to give $50 crystal vases to 10 of his favorite clients. According to MSRB rules, this is

    A. not permitted because the representative is not allowed to give gifts to customers
    B. not permitted because the aggregate amount exceeds the permissible annual limit
    C. permitted
    D. only permitted with written permission from the MSRB

33. A bank doing all of the following would be required to register as a municipal broker-dealer with FINRA EXCEPT

    A. underwriting municipal securities for municipal issuers
    B. purchasing or selling municipal securities for public customers
    C. providing investment research regarding municipal securities to public investors
    D. holding municipal securities as custodian for public customers

34. Which of the following describes the responsibilities of a municipal finance professional (MFP)?

    I. An associated person of a broker-dealer engaged in municipal securities representative activities other than retail sales
    II. A registered representative engaged in the retail sale of municipal securities to individual investors
    III. Is subject to the political contribution rules as outlined in MSRB Rule G-37
    IV. Is not subject to the political contribution rules as outlined in MSRB Rule G-37
    A. I and III
    B. I and IV
    C. II and III
    D. II and IV

35. A legal opinion evaluates which of the following features of a municipal issue?

    I. Marketability
    II. Legality
    III. Tax-exempt status
    IV. Economic feasibility

    A. I and II
    B. II and III
    C. II and IV
    D. III and IV

36. The interest from which of the following bonds would be included in the alternative minimum tax calculation?

    A. General obligation bonds
    B. Industrial development revenue bonds
    C. TANs
    D. Special assessment bonds

37. Which of the following investors could be allowed to deduct margin interest charged on funds borrowed to purchase municipal bonds on an income tax return?

    A. Mutual funds on all municipal issues
    B. Those who are in a very low income tax bracket for all municipal issues
    C. Those who are in a very high income tax bracket for some municipal issues
    D. Banks for certain municipal issues only

38. Auction Rate Securities (ARS) are associated with

    I. U.S. government securities
    II. Dutch auctions
    III. reset rates
    IV. being noncallable

    A. I and III
    B. I and IV
    C. II and III
    D. III and IV

39. Arrange the following bonds in order of safety, from safest to most speculative.

    I.   AA rated unlimited tax general obligation
    II. PHA
    III. IDR
    IV. AAA rated revenue bond

    A. I, IV, II, III
    B. II, I, IV, III
    C. II, IV, I, III
    D. IV, I, II, III

40. A bond that is a general obligation, is secured by ad valorem taxes, and has specific pledged revenues underlying payment of principal interest is known as

    A. a moral obligation bond
    B. a double-barreled bond
    C. a dual-backing bond
    D. a special assessment bond

ANSWERS AND RATIONALES

1. **C.** The call premium represents the difference between the call price and par.

2. **A.** Municipal bonds are exempt from federal income tax. Direct federal debt, such as Treasury bonds, is subject to federal income tax but is exempt from state tax. GNMA bonds are subject to federal, state, and local taxes.

3. **A.** Real property tax is based on the assessed value assigned to the property by the municipality's tax assessor (in this case, $40,000). Property tax rates use the mill (or mil) as a base unit. One mill = $1 of tax per year for each $1,000 of assessed value. Five mills would equal $5 for each $1,000 of assessed value. Because there are 40 thousands, 40 × $5 = $200 in annual tax. A short-cut method: take the assessed value, remove the last three 0s, and multiply by the number of mills of tax ($40 × 5 mills = $200).

4. **C.** The agreement among underwriters (the syndicate agreement) spells out the rights and obligations of each syndicate member. It also details how the responsibility for unsold bonds will be handled. In a Western account, liability is divided, which means each syndicate member is responsible for only its participation. In an Eastern account, each syndicate member assumes pro rata responsibility for unsold bonds.

5. **C.** A notice of sale is published to provide syndicates with information on proposed new, or primary market, issues.

6. **C.** The MSRB does not regulate issuers. Rather, it regulates the underwriting of municipal securities and the subsequent secondary market trading. Disclosure requirements for issuers are mandated by the SEC.

7. **D.** The MSRB has no enforcement authority. The Comptroller of the Currency, the FRB, and the FDIC regulate banks that trade municipals. FINRA enforces MSRB rules for broker-dealers that trade municipals.

8. **C.** As the term suggests, a municipal broker's broker deals with other dealers and institutions, not with the general public.

9. **C.** Hospitals, airports, and golf courses all generate revenue and can be financed with revenue bond issues. Schools are financed through GO bond sales.

10. **C.** IDBs are issued by a municipality, and the proceeds are used to construct facilities or purchase equipment for a private corporation. The corporation leases the facilities and equipment; funds from the lease are used to repay investors. In addition to a first mortgage on the property, IDBs are backed by the full faith and credit of the corporation, not the municipality.

11. **A.** A good faith deposit is required when the syndicate places a bid on a competitive offering. It is generally 1–2% of the par value of the bonds offered for sale. If the bid is unsuccessful, the deposit is returned by the issuer to the syndicate manager.

12. **C.** Condemnation is considered a catastrophe and applies only to revenue bonds.

13. **D.** The agreement among underwriters describes the rights, duties, and commitments of the syndicate members with respect to the securities being underwritten. It appoints the syndicate manager to act on behalf of the syndicate and includes provisions dealing with underwriting compensation (takedown and concession). The legal opinion is a document prepared by the bond counsel, and the appointment of the bond counsel is the responsibility of the issuer.

14. **B.** NHAs are considered to have a high degree of safety because, in addition to the backing of rental income, they are secured by an annual contribution from the U.S. government. Thus, they are rated AAA.

15. **C.** The flow of funds relates only to municipal revenue bonds. It describes the priority of disbursing revenues from the project. Tax anticipation notes (TANs) are backed by taxes to be collected, whereas GO bonds are backed by the taxing authority of the issuer.

16. **B.** Although municipal bonds were previously issued in bearer form, this is no longer permitted. The same is true of bonds registered as to principal only. Newly issued bonds can be either fully registered or book entry, which is a certificateless form of ownership.

17. **C.** The debt limit is the maximum amount of debt a municipality can have outstanding.

18. **B.** Overlapping, or coterminous, debt is an issuer's proportionate share of debt. This debt is used in calculating a municipality's net overall debt.

19. **C.** Members of the syndicate buy the bonds at the offering price less the takedown, non-members less a concession. The basis price is the yield to maturity.

20. **B.** The Bond Buyer Revenue Bond Index (Revdex) is computed weekly just like *The Bond Buyer's* GO index. It consists of 25 revenue bonds with 30-year maturities. The Bond Buyer GO index includes 20 bonds each with approximately 20 years to maturity. The Revdex measures yields of revenue bonds in the secondary market, whereas the GO index measures yields of GO bonds in the secondary market.

21. **D.** A special tax bond is backed by one or more designated taxes (e.g., sales, cigarette, fuel, or alcohol) other than ad valorem taxes. The designated tax does not need to be directly related to the project purpose. These bonds are not considered self-supporting debt.

22. **A.** The total takedown has two components: concession plus additional takedown.

23. **C.** A double-barreled bond is backed by a defined source of revenue other than property taxes, plus the full faith and credit of an issuer with taxing authority. NHA bonds are not double barrelled. If rental income from the housing is insufficient to meet servicing costs, the shortfall is covered by the U.S. Department of Housing and Urban Development (HUD). To be double barreled, the issue must be backed by more than one municipal source.

24. **C.** Because callable bonds represent more risk to the investor, they generally trade at higher yields than comparable noncallable bonds. Bonds are called when rates are falling or have fallen, allowing the issuer to replace the called issue with one with a lower coupon. As rates rise, bond prices fall. The call premium on a callable bond, which represents the difference between the call price and par, compensates bondholders for lost interest if the bond is called.

25. **C.** There are 100 basis points in each point. One point represents 1% of the value of a bond, so 75 basis points represents .75%. Also, each point is worth $10. Therefore, 75 basis points represents $7.50.

26. **C.** An unqualified legal opinion means that the bond counsel found no problems with the issue. A qualified opinion means that the issue is legal, but certain contingencies exist. For example, the bond counsel might render a qualified opinion because competing facilities may restrict the flow of funds in the future. If the issuer does not have clear title to the property, the legal opinion may be qualified.

27. **D.** The customer's state of residence and tax status are essential when determining the suitability of a municipal security. The security's rating is also important because it measures the safety and quality of the bond.

28. **C.** A final official statement must be delivered to buyers of a new issue on or before settlement date. The MSRB does not regulate issuers.

29. **A.** The true interest cost method uses present value calculations, which take into consideration the time value of money (as opposed to net interest cost, which does not consider the timing of interest payments). It is a more complicated calculation than net interest cost. The IRS does not stipulate which should be used.

30. **A.** State governments generally do not assess property (ad valorem) taxes. These are assessed by local governments. Generally, state governments receive most of their income from sales and income taxes.

31. **A.** Municipal short-term notes (tax anticipation notes, revenue anticipation notes, and bond anticipation notes) are used as interim financing until a permanent long-term issue is floated.

32. **C.** Provided each gift does not exceed the $100 annual gift limitation, the gifts are permitted.

33. **D.** A bank doing any of these activities must register as a municipal securities broker-dealer with FINRA except a bank simply holding municipal securities as custodian for public customers.

34. **A.** As defined by the Municipal Securities Rulemaking Board (MSRB), a municipal finance professional (MFP) is an associated person of a broker-dealer who is primarily engaged in municipal securities representative activities, other than retail sales to individuals, who solicits municipal securities business for the broker-dealer, or who is in the supervisory chain above MFPs. MFPs are subject to the political contribution reporting rules as outlined in MSRB Rule G-37. Though there are exceptions for de minimis contributions, exceeding the allowable contribution limits may trigger restrictions on engaging in municipal securities business by the broker-dealer for 2 years.

35. **B.** A legal opinion, rendered by bond counsel, deals with the tax-exempt status of the proposed issue and the legality of the issue. The marketability of the new issue of bonds is dealt with by the syndicate. Economic feasibility relates to revenue bond issues and is performed by independent consultants.

36. **B.** Industrial revenue bonds (IRBs), sometimes called industrial development bonds (IDBs), are nonpublic purpose bonds, and the proceeds are used to benefit private corporations. As such, the interest income from these bonds is a tax-preference item in the AMT calculation.

37. **D.** Margin interest charged for loans to purchase municipal bonds is generally not deductible. However, for certain GO municipal issues (known as bank qualified municipal issues), a bank may deduct up to 80% of the margin interest for funds the bank borrowed to purchase the bonds.

38. **C.** Auction rate securities, typically issued by municipalities, utilize a Dutch auction method at predetermined short term intervals to establish a reset rate known as the clearing rate.

39. **C.** Public Housing Authority (PHA) bonds are the safest because they are the only municipal bond with a federal government guarantee. Any AAA bond is deemed safer than an AA bond, and IDRs are generally less safe, especially one unrated, as this one is.

40. **B.** This is the pure definition of a double-barreled bond.

QUICK QUIZ ANSWERS

Quick Quiz 3.A

1. **B.** A variable-rate bond has no fixed coupon rate. The interest rate is tied to a market rate (for example, T-bill yields) and is subject to change at regular intervals. Because the interest paid reflects changes in overall interest rates, the price of the bond remains relatively close to its par value.

2. **A.** Property taxes are a primary source of cash flow for most municipalities, but property taxes are collected at established intervals. Issuing tax anticipation notes (TANs) backed by future tax revenues can help a municipality maintain an even cash flow throughout its fiscal year.

3. **C.** The debt limit is the maximum amount of debt a municipality can incur. Such restrictions have made revenue bonds increasingly popular because they are normally not subject to statutory debt limitations.

4. **C.** A double-barreled bond is backed by a defined source of revenue, other than property taxes, plus the full faith and credit of an issuer with taxing authority.

5. **C.** The interest income from most U.S. government and agency securities is exempt from state and local taxes, but not federal taxes. The interest on municipal issues (like the Minneapolis Housing Authority bonds) is exempt from both federal taxes and, because this investor is a Minnesota resident, state taxes. Ginnie Maes are subject to taxation on all levels.

Quick Quiz 3.B

1. **D.** The priority of filling municipal orders is established by the managing underwriter in the release terms letter sent to the syndicate once the bid is won. This letter is an amendment to the syndicate agreement.

2. **D.** The syndicate agreement is signed by all members of the syndicate, including the managing underwriter. It is not signed by the issuer, the bond counsel, or the trustee.

3. **C.** The scale, or reoffering scale, is the yield(s) to maturity at which the syndicate will reoffer the bonds to the public. Syndicate participants consider the market for bonds of similar quality in deciding at what yield to market the issue on which they are bidding.

4. **A.** Net interest cost (NIC) measures an issuer's overall cost of borrowing for a particular bond issue. It is therefore the most important item considered by an issuer when evaluating competing bids. Coupon rate, par value, and maturity length are elements of the net interest cost calculation. The reoffering scale is the arrangement of yields at which the bonds will be sold to the public and is unrelated to the issuer's cost of borrowing. Takedown and concession refer to the arrangements for allocating bonds and assigning underwriting profit to the various underwriters once the winning bid has been awarded. These do not affect the net interest cost.

5. **A.** A municipal group net order is credited to syndicate members according to their percentage participation in the account. This order type is given priority over designated or member takedown orders, but not over presale orders. By placing this type of order, syndicate members are stipulating that they want those bond orders to have the highest priority still available. Note that presale orders are also confirmed for the benefit of the entire syndicate, but these are placed before the time the winning bid is awarded.

6. **D.** The spread is the difference between the reoffering price and the amount bid on an issue in competitive bidding. MSRB rules state that a dealer is entitled to make a profit in an underwriting. Therefore, the dealer can take into account such factors as market conditions, the type and size of the issue, the dollar volume of the transaction, and any extraordinary costs incurred by the syndicate. The amount of the good faith check deposited before bidding on the issue has no relevance to the bid or to the reoffering price.

7. **C.** An unqualified legal opinion means that the bond counsel found no problems with the issue. A qualified opinion means that the issue is legal, but some qualification is necessary because certain contingencies exist. For example, the bond counsel might render a qualified opinion because competing facilities may restrict the flow of funds in the future. If the issuer does not have clear title to the property, the legal opinion may be qualified. The legal opinion has nothing to do with broker-dealer disclosure.

8. **D.** In a competitive bidding situation, each syndicate submits a sealed written bid. The price at which the bonds are sold is called the reoffering yield.

Quick Quiz 3.C

1. **C.** Municipal bond insurance is purchased to insure the payments of principal and interest in the event the issuer defaults.

2. **D.** All of the fees and taxes listed are payments received by the municipality that are not the result of a revenue-producing facility. General revenues of the municipality may be used to pay the debt service on a general obligation bond.

3. **D.** General obligation bonds are backed by the full faith and credit of an issuer, which is based on its ability to levy and collect taxes. Although these quantitative factors, are important to an analyst, qualitative factors such as a community's attitude toward borrowing and repaying debt, are also important considerations.

4. **D.** Interest rate movements have no bearing on determining the quality of revenue bond issues.

5. **B.** The size of the municipality does not count, but the size of the debt outstanding for a municipality does. A municipality with a small amount of debt will not have enough activity in those debt instruments to warrant a rating by a rating agency.

6. **C.** The dollar denomination of bonds to be issued has no bearing on a GO bond analysis. The tax base, economic character, and population makeup would all be considered.

7. **A.** The official statement is an offering document that discloses material information on a new issue of municipal securities. Because it commonly includes information concerning the purpose of the issue, how the securities will be repaid, and the financial, economic, and social characteristics of the issuer, it is an appropriate place to review the creditworthiness of an issue. The legal opinion reviews the legality of the issue, including certain legal exemptions. A prospectus is the document that provides material information about a nonexempt security being publicly distributed. The trust indenture is the basic bond contract between the issuer and the trustee.

8. **D.** When credit conditions deteriorate, bankruptcies rise, bond defaults increase, and consumer debt increases. An increase in assessed valuation, or property value, would indicate a strengthening economy.

9. **A.** FGIC and AGC insure municipal bonds.

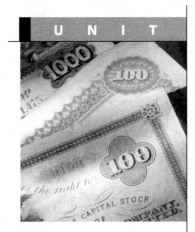

4

Options

For many Series 7 candidates, this is one of the more challenging sections. Be sure to review each section of the Unit thoroughly.

Options account for approximately 25–30 questions on the Series 7 exam. The majority of questions will be on equity options (options on stock), but expect some to involve nonequity options such as index, interest rate, and foreign currency option contracts. As you review the Unit, concentrate on the basic concepts. If you are well grounded in the basics, proficiency with the more complex concepts and strategies will follow. ■

When you have completed this Unit, you should be able to:

- **list** the basic features of option contracts;

- **name** the components of an options premium and calculate intrinsic value;

- **calculate** breakeven, maximum gain, and maximum loss for single options, hedging strategies, spreads, and straddles;

- **calculate** profit and loss on options transactions involving exercise, expiration, or closing a position;

- **identify** investor strategies for single options, hedges, and multiple option positions;

- **describe** the functions of the Options Clearing Corporation (OCC);

- **describe** the process of opening an options account;

- **describe** the unique features and usage of nonequity options; and

- **identify** tax consequences of exercise, expiration, or closing of a position.

4. 1 THE OPTIONS CONTRACT

An **option** is a two-party contract that conveys a right to the buyer and an obligation to the seller. The **terms** of option contracts are standardized by the Options Clearing Corporation (OCC), which allows options to be traded easily on an exchange such as the Chicago Board Options Exchange (CBOE). The underlying security for which an option contract is created may be a stock, stock market index, foreign currency, interest rate, or government bond.

4. 1. 0. 1 Type

The two types of options are calls and puts.

4. 1. 0. 2 Class

All calls of one issuer, or all puts of one issuer, are **classes** of options.

4. 1. 0. 3 Series

All options of one issuer with the same class, exercise price, and expiration month are in the same **series** (e.g., all XYZ Jan 40 calls).

4. 1. 0. 4 Style

Call or put buyers can exercise a contract any time before expiration if the contract is an **American-style** option. **European-style** options can be exercised on expiration day only. Nearly all equity options are American style. Foreign currency options may be either American style or European style.

4. 1. 0. 5 The Options Contract

The most common type of options contracts are **equity options**. Each contract includes **100 shares** when issued.

Two Parties Are Involved in an Options Contract

Buyer = Long = Holder = Owner	Seller = Short = Writer
Pays premium (the cost of the contract) to seller. There is a debit (DR) to the account of the buyer when the premium is paid. The buyer *opens his position* with a debit to his account.	*Receives premium* from buyer. There is a credit (CR) to the account of the seller when the premium is received. The seller *opens his position* with a credit to his account.
Has *rights* to exercise (buy or sell stock)	Has *obligations* at exercise (must buy or sell as required by contract)

TAKE NOTE

The Chicago Board Options Exchange (CBOE) also offers option contracts known as mini-options. These contracts overlay only 10 shares of the underlying security instead of 100 shares as is the case for standard options contracts.

With standard contracts the multiplier is 100 (Ex: 2 premium = $200). With mini-option contracts the multiplier is only 10. Therefore mini-option contract premium of 2 represents only $20.

4. 1. 0. 5. 1 Every Options Contract Has Three Specifications

- **Underlying instrument:** anything with fluctuating value can be the underlying instrument of an option contract.
- **Price:** the contract specifies a strike or exercise price at which purchase or sale of the underlying security will occur.
- **Expiration:** all contracts have a specified life cycle and expire on a specified date. Once a contract is issued, it can be bought or sold any time during its life cycle.

  — Standard contracts are issued with nine-month expirations and expire on the third Friday of the expiration month at 11:59 pm ET.

  — Long-term equity anticipation securities (LEAPS) have maximum expirations up to 39 months. Though the maximum is 39 months, most trade with a 30 month life-cycle. The length of time until the contract expires is the one contract specification that can be customized between buyer and seller when the contract first trades.

  — Weekly contracts are issued on a Thursday and expire on the Friday of the following week. They have much lower premiums as a result of the shorter time span between the day of issue and the day they expire. New weeklies are listed each week, except the week that standardized contracts expire.

Options are called **derivative securities** because their value is derived from the value of the underlying instrument, such as stock, an index, or a foreign currency.

4. 1. 1 CALLS AND PUTS

There are two types of options contracts: the **call** and the **put**.

4. 1. 1. 1 Calls

An investor may buy calls (go long) or sell calls (go short). The features of each side of a call contract are noted below.

- **Long call:** a call buyer owns the **right to buy** 100 shares of a specific stock at the strike price before the expiration if he chooses to exercise.
- **Short call:** a call writer (seller) has the **obligation to sell** 100 shares of a specific stock at the strike price if the buyer exercises the contract.

4. 1. 1. 2   Puts

An investor may buy puts (go long) or sell puts (go short). The features of each side of a put contract are noted below.

- **Long put:** a put buyer owns the **right to sell** 100 shares of a specific stock at the strike price before the expiration if he chooses to exercise.
- **Short put:** a put writer (seller) has the **obligation to buy** 100 shares of a specific stock at the strike price if the buyer exercises the contract.

TAKE NOTE

Buyers of options call the shots; they choose to exercise or not to exercise. That is why buyers pay premiums. The writer is at the mercy of the buyer's decision. Writers are only exercised against; they do not have the opportunity to choose to exercise.

- The buyer wants the contract to be **exercised**. He wins, and the seller loses at exercise.
- The seller wants the contract to **expire**. The seller wins at expiration because he gets to keep the premium. No purchase or sale of stock is required.

A significant number of test questions can be answered by knowing that buyers have **rights** and sellers have **obligations**.

4. 1. 2   SINGLE OPTION STRATEGIES

There are four basic strategies available to options investors:

- buying calls;
- writing calls;
- buying puts; and
- writing puts.

The Four Basic Options Transactions

Calls	
Buy a Call	Write a Call
Buy	**Sell**
Buy a Put	Write a Put
Puts	

4. 1. 2. 1   Calls

Identified below are the key features of call contracts.

Long XYZ Jan 60 call at 3

Long   The investor has bought the call and has the right to exercise the contract.

XYZ   The contract includes 100 shares of XYZ stock.

Jan   The contract expires on the third Friday of January at 11:59 pm ET.

60   The strike price of the contract is 60.

Call   The type of option is a call, and the investor has the right to buy the stock at 60 since he is long the call.

3   The premium of the contract is $3 per share. Contracts are issued with 100 shares, so the total premium is $300. The investor paid the premium to buy the call.

Buyers of calls want the market price of the underlying stock to rise. The investor who owns this call hopes that the market price will rise above 60. He then has the right to buy the stock at the strike price of 60, even if the market price is higher (e.g., 80).

Short XYZ Jan 60 call at 3

Short   The investor has sold the call and has obligations to perform if the contract is exercised.

XYZ   The contract includes 100 shares of XYZ stock.

Jan   The contract expires on the third Friday of January at 11:59 pm ET. If expiration occurs, the writer keeps the premium without any obligation.

60   The strike price of the contract is 60.

Call   The type of option is a call, and the investor is obligated to sell the stock at 60, if exercised, because he is short the call.

3   The premium of the contract is $3 per share. Options contracts are issued with 100 shares, so the total premium is $300.

Writers of calls want the market price of the underlying stock to fall or stay the same. The investor who owns this call hopes that the market price will rise or go above 60. The contract will not be exercised if the market price is at or below 60 at expiration, and the writer keeps the premium of $300 with no obligation.

4. 1. 2. 1. 1   Market Attitude

A call **buyer** is a bullish investor because he wants the market to rise. The call is exercised only if the market price rises.

A call **writer** is a bearish investor because he wants the market to fall. The contract is not exercised if the market price falls below the strike price.

QUICK QUIZ 4.A

Consider the following contract:

Long XYZ Jan 60 call at 3

At expiration, the market price of XYZ is 70.

1. Which of the following will occur?
    A. Exercised by the buyer
    B. Expires worthless

2. Which of the following will the seller do if exercised?
    A. Buy 100 shares of XYZ at 60
    B. Sell 100 shares of XYZ at 60
    C. Buy 100 shares of XYZ at 70
    D. Sell 100 shares of XYZ at 70

3. Which of the following will the buyer do if he elects to exercise?
    A. Buy 100 shares of XYZ at 60
    B. Sell 100 shares of XYZ at 60
    C. Buy 100 shares of XYZ at 70
    D. Sell 100 shares of XYZ at 70

Quick Quiz answers can be found at the end of the Unit.

QUICK QUIZ 4.B

Consider the following contract:

Short XYZ Oct 25 call at 4.50

At expiration the market price of XYZ is 20.

1. Which of the following will occur?
    A. Exercised by the buyer
    B. Expires worthless

2. Which of the following will the seller do at expiration?
    A. Buy 100 shares of XYZ at 25
    B. Sell 100 shares of XYZ at 25
    C. Pay $450 to the buyer
    D. Keep the $450 premium, no further obligation

3. Which of the following will the buyer do at expiration?
    A. Buy 100 shares of XYZ at 25
    B. Sell 100 shares of XYZ at 25
    C. Neither buy nor sell, but lose the $450 premium paid for the option
    D. Receive $450 premium from the seller

4.1.2.2   Puts

Identified below are the key features of put contracts.

Long XYZ Jan 60 put at 3

Long The investor has bought the put and has the right to exercise the contract.

XYZ The contract includes 100 shares of XYZ stock.

Jan The contract expires on the third Friday of January at 11:59 pm ET.

60 The strike price of the contract is 60.

Put The type of option is a put, and the investor has the right to sell the stock at 60 since he is long the put.

3 The premium of the contract is $3 per share. Contracts are issued with 100 shares, so the total premium is $300. The investor paid the premium to buy the put.

Buyers of puts want the market price of the underlying stock to fall. The investor who owns this put hopes that the market price will fall below 60. He then has the right to sell the stock at the strike price of 60, even if the market price is lower (e.g., 40).

Short XYZ Jan 60 put at 3

Short The investor has sold the put and has obligations to perform if the contract is exercised.

XYZ The contract includes 100 shares of XYZ stock.

Jan The contract expires on the third Friday of January at 11:59 pm ET. If expiration occurs, the writer keeps the premium without any obligation.

60 The strike price of the contract is 60.

Put The type of option is a put, and the investor is obligated to buy the stock at 60, if exercised, because he is short the put.

3 The premium of the contract is $3 per share. Options contracts are issued with 100 shares, so the total premium is $300.

Writers of puts want the market price of the underlying stock to rise or stay the same. If the market price is at or above 60, the investor keeps the premium of $300 with no obligation because the contract will not be exercised.

4.1.2.2.1   Market Attitude

A put **buyer** is a bearish investor because he wants the market to fall. The put is exercised only if the market price falls below the strike price.

A put **writer** is a bullish investor because he wants the market to rise or remain unchanged. The contract is not exercised if the market price rises above the strike price.

QUICK QUIZ 4.C

Consider the following contract:

Long XYZ Jan 60 put at 3

At expiration, the market price of XYZ is 70.

1. Which of the following will occur?

   A. Exercised by the buyer
   B. Expires worthless

2. Which of the following will the seller do at expiration?

   A. Buy 100 shares of XYZ at 60
   B. Sell 100 shares of XYZ at 60
   C. Do nothing; keep the premium of $300 already received
   D. Pay the premium of $300 to the buyer

3. Which of the following will the buyer do at expiration?

   A. Buy 100 shares of XYZ at 60
   B. Sell 100 shares of XYZ at 60
   C. Do nothing; the put expires and the buyer loses the $300 premium
   D. Pay the premium of $300 to the buyer

QUICK QUIZ 4.D

Consider the following contract:

Short XYZ Oct 25 put at 4.50

At expiration the market price of XYZ is 20.

1. Which of the following will occur?

   A. Exercised by the buyer
   B. Expires worthless

2. Which of the following will the seller do at expiration of the option?

   A. Buy 100 shares of XYZ at 25
   B. Sell 100 shares of XYZ at 25
   C. Pay $450 to the buyer
   D. Keep the $450 premium with no further obligation

3. Which of the following will the buyer do at expiration?

   A. Buy 100 shares of XYZ at 25
   B. Sell 100 shares of XYZ at 25
   C. Neither buy nor sell, but lose the $450 premium paid for the option
   D. Receive $450 premium from the seller

4. 1. 3   BASIC OPTIONS DEFINITIONS

Options contracts are described with various terms unique to the options marketplace. Basic terms in the discussion of options contracts are:

■ in the money;

■ at the money;

- out of the money;
- intrinsic value; and
- breakeven.

These terms are defined differently for calls and puts.

4. 1. 4   CALLS

For both long and short calls, the definitions are as follows.

4. 1. 4. 1   In the Money Call

A call is **in the money** when the market price exceeds the strike price. A buyer will exercise calls that are in the money at expiration. Buyers want options to be in the money; sellers do not.

4. 1. 4. 2   At the Money Call

A call is **at the money** when the market price equals the strike price. A buyer will not exercise contracts that are at the money at expiration. Sellers want at the money contracts at expiration; buyers do not. Sellers then keep the premium without obligations to perform.

4. 1. 4. 3   Out of the Money Call

A call is **out of the money** when the market price is lower than the strike price. A buyer will not exercise calls that are out of the money at expiration. Sellers want contracts to be out of the money; buyers do not. Sellers then keep the premium without obligations to perform.

4. 1. 4. 4   Intrinsic Value: Calls

Intrinsic value is the in the money amount. A call has intrinsic value when the market price is above the strike price. The amount of intrinsic value is found by subtracting the strike price from the market price. Options never have negative intrinsic value; intrinsic value is always a positive amount or zero. Options that are at the money or out of the money have an intrinsic value of zero. Buyers like calls to have intrinsic value; sellers do not. A call that has intrinsic value at expiration will be exercised.

During the lifetime of an option contract, buyers want the contract to move in the money; sellers want the contract to move out of the money.

EXAMPLE   XYZ 30 call with XYZ stock trading at 35.
Intrinsic value (IV) of call = 5 (stock price 35 – strike price 30 = 5 IV).

4.1.4.5   Parity: Calls

An option is at **parity** when the premium equals intrinsic value.

EXAMPLE   An ABC June 60 call trading at 2 when ABC is at 62 is at parity.

4.1.4.6   Breakeven: Calls

The **breakeven point** is the point at which the investor neither makes nor loses money. For calls, the breakeven is found by adding the strike price and the premium. For the call buyer, the contract is profitable above the breakeven; for the call seller, the contract is profitable below the breakeven.

TAKE NOTE   Note that the definitions are the same whether the contract is long or short. An easy way to remember the call definitions is CALL UP. A call has intrinsic value, or is in the money, when the market price is up above the strike price, whether it is long or short. Also, the call breakeven is above the strike price (strike price plus premium).

QUICK QUIZ 4.E   Consider the following contracts (CMV = current market value):

Long XYZ Jan 65 call at 7, CMV of XYZ is 70

_in_   1.   Is this contract in-, at-, or out of the money?

_72_   2.   What is the breakeven point?

_5_   3.   How much intrinsic value does the contract have?

Short XYZ Jan 65 call at 7, CMV of XYZ is 70

_in_   4.   Is this contract in-, at-, or out of the money?

_72_   5.   What is the breakeven point?

_____   6.   How much intrinsic value does the contract have?

Short XYZ Sep 45 call at 4, CMV of XYZ is 39

out   7.   Is this contract in-, at-, or out of the money?

_49_   8.   What is the breakeven point?

_0_   9.   How much intrinsic value does the contract have?

An option that is in the money is not necessarily at breakeven. Options that are in the money are not always profitable. Review these terms carefully, as it is very easy to confuse them.

4. 1. 5   PUTS

The basic definitions for **puts** are listed below. For puts, the definitions are the opposite of what they are for calls.

4. 1. 5. 1   In the Money Put

A put is **in the money** when the market price is lower than the strike price. A buyer will exercise puts that are in the money at expiration. Buyers want in-the-money contracts; sellers do not.

4. 1. 5. 2   At the Money Put

A put is **at the money** when the market price equals the strike price. A buyer will not exercise contracts that are at the money at expiration. Sellers want at the money contracts; buyers do not.

4. 1. 5. 3   Out of the Money Put

A put is **out of the money** when the market price is higher than the strike price. A buyer will not exercise puts that are out of the money at expiration. Sellers want out of the money contracts; buyers do not.

4. 1. 5. 4   Intrinsic Value: Puts

Intrinsic value is the in the money amount. A put has intrinsic value when the market price is below the strike price. The amount of intrinsic value is found by subtracting the market price from the strike price. Options never have negative intrinsic value; it is always a positive number or zero. Buyers like options to have intrinsic value; sellers do not. An option (call or put) that has intrinsic value at expiration will be exercised.

EXAMPLE
XYZ 40 put with XYZ stock trading at 35.
Intrinsic value (IV) of put = 5 (strike price 40 – stock price 35 = 5 IV).

As with calls, a put is at parity when the premium equals intrinsic value.

4. 1. 5. 5   Breakeven: Puts

The **breakeven point** is the point at which the investor neither makes nor loses money. For puts, the breakeven is found by subtracting the premium from the strike price. For the put buyer, the contract is profitable below the breakeven at expiration; for the put seller, the contract is profitable above the breakeven at expiration.

Comparison of In, At, and Out of the Money Options

When the price of a security is above an option's strike price, a call option is in the money; a put option is out of the money.

When the market price of a security equals the strike price, an option is at the money.

When the market price of a security is below the strike price, a call is out of the money; a put is in the money.

TAKE NOTE

An easy way to remember the put definitions is PUT DOWN. A put has intrinsic value, or is in the money, when the market price is below the strike price, whether it is long or short. Also, the put breakeven is below the strike price (strike price minus premium). These put definitions are the opposite of the call definitions; options are a game of opposites. Calls are opposites of puts, and buyers are opposites of sellers.

QUICK QUIZ 4.F

Consider the following contracts:

Long XYZ Sep 65 put at 2, CMV of XYZ is 70

Out~~At~~ 1.   Is this contract in-, at-, or out of the money?

_63_ 2.   What is the breakeven point?

_0_ 3.   How much intrinsic value does the contract have?

Short XYZ Jan 65 put at 2, CMV of XYZ is 70

out 4.   Is this contract in-, at-, or out of the money?

_63_ 5.   What is the breakeven point?

_0_ 6.   How much intrinsic value does the contract have?

Short XYZ Sep 45 put at 8, CMV of XYZ is 39

_____ 7. Is this contract in-, at-, or out of the money?

31 8. What is the breakeven point?

_____ 9. How much intrinsic value does the contract have?

4. 1. 5. 6   Quick Summary of Basic Definitions

The following table summarizes the basic definitions for calls and puts (CMV = current market value, SP = strike price).

Basic Definitions for Calls and Puts

Calls		Puts
CMV > SP	In the Money	CMV < SP
CMV = SP	At the Money	CMV = SP
CMV < SP	Out of the Money	CMV > SP
CALL UP	Intrinsic Value	PUT DOWN
SP + Premium	Breakeven	SP − Premium

TAKE NOTE

The following chart will help you remember the basics of options. When you take the exam, consider drawing and referring to it when you encounter options questions. Each quadrant represents one of the four basic options positions.

- Buyers are on the left side; sellers are on the right.

- The arrow identifies the investor's market attitude. Up arrows represent bullish investors; down arrows represent bearish investors.

- The information in the parentheses identifies what occurs at the exercise of the option.

- The solid horizontal line represents the strike price (SP). The dashed horizontal lines represent the breakevens. For calls, the breakeven is strike price plus premium, long or short, and for puts, the breakeven is strike price minus premium, long or short.

- Calls are above the horizontal line because they are in the money when the market price is above the strike price, long or short (CALL UP).

- Puts are below the horizontal line because they are in the money when the market price is below the strike price, long or short (PUT DOWN).

Basic Options Chart

- ■ Buy = Long = Hold = Open the position with a debit (DR) to the account
- ■ Sell = Short = Write = Open the position with a credit (CR) to the account

4. 1. 6   OPTIONS PREMIUMS

As stated earlier, the price of an option contract is known as the **premium**. Both bid and ask prices are quoted in cents, with a minimum price interval of $.05. An option buyer will pay the **ask**, or **offer** price, and the option seller will receive the **bid** price. An option's premium reflects two types of values: **intrinsic value**, or the amount by which the option is in the money, and **time value,** which is the market's perceived worth of the time remaining to expiration.

4. 1. 6. 1   Options Quotes

Options premiums are quoted on a **per share** basis. Options contracts are issued to include 100 shares of stock, so the total premium is calculated by multiplying by 100. However, some contracts may be subject to stock splits and stock dividends and may include more than 100 shares. This is discussed later in this Unit.

4. 1. 6. 2   Factors Affecting Premium

The premium of an option is affected by many factors, including:
- ■ volatility;
- ■ amount of intrinsic value;
- ■ time remaining until expiration; and
- ■ interest rates.

The factor with the greatest influence is the **volatility** of the underlying stock. A stock that is highly volatile has the potential to experience greater price movement; it has the possibility of greater profit because of high volatility.

Premiums for options fluctuate constantly, like stock prices. If the underlying stock price fell from one day to the next, a call premium would fall and a put premium would rise. The amount of intrinsic value is affected by any change in the stock's price.

For AOL, note that the closing price on the previous day was $49.00. The strike prices range from $42.50 to $60.00. The next column shows the expiration month followed by volume and premium on the AOL calls and by volume and premium on the AOL puts.

From the chart below, find the premium for the AOL July 45 call. The premium of $7.40 is made up of two components: intrinsic value and time value. Once you know intrinsic value, it is easy to back into time value.

Intrinsic value + time value = premium

STOCK/ PRICE	OPTION/ STRIKE	EXP	-CALL- VOL	LAST	-PUT- VOL	LAST
AmOnline	4250	Apr	2431	650	49	010
49	4250	May	902	760	409	090
49	45	Apr	5790	420	3298	020
49	45	May	1376	530	1573	150
49	45	Jul	1371	740	94	150
49	4750	Apr	3169	205	1229	055
49	4750	May	3333	340	530	230
49	4750	Oct	294	820	2696	570
49	50	Apr	7618	050	1031	165
49	50	May	5307	220	1017	320
49	50	Jul	2436	450	197	520
49	55	May	3548	050	57	660
49	55	Jul	2574	230	18	8
49	55	Oct	86010	420	251	970
49	60	Jul	2869	110	22	12
ASM Litho	25	Apr	1060	165	...	...
ATT Wris	20	May	1752	130	3360	180
AT&T	20	Apr	1885	2	11	005
22	2250	Apr	1396	020	445	065

* This sample comprises formats, styles, and abbreviations from a variety of currently available sources and has been created for educational purposes.

A call option has intrinsic value if the market price of the underlying stock is higher than the strike price. In the case of the July 45 call, the intrinsic value (in the money amount) is $4.00 ($49.00 – $45.00). The intrinsic value of $4.00 when added to the time value must equal $7.40. The time value of the July 45 call is $3.40 ($7.40 – $4.00).

TAKE NOTE

If an option is at the money or out of the money, the intrinsic value is zero. There is no such thing as negative intrinsic value. Therefore, the premium on any out of the money option is composed entirely of time value.

From the chart, compare the premium of the May 45 call ($5.30) to the premium of the July 45 call ($7.40). Both contracts are in the money by the same amount ($4.00), but the July contract has a higher premium because it has a greater time value. The further to expiration, the greater the time value.

The May 50 call is at 2.20, whereas the premium on the July 50 call is 4.50. Both of these contracts are out of the money by $1. Again, the further to expiration, the greater the time value.

The May 50 put is trading at 3.20, whereas the July 50 put is at 5.20. Both of these contracts are in the money by $1. The time value of these options is $2.20 and $4.20, respectively. Again, the further to expiration, the greater the time value.

TEST TOPIC ALERT   You are likely to see a question or two on option premiums. Be prepared to calculate the time value of an option premium and recognize the features that affect premiums. In calculating the premium, remember to determine intrinsic value by thinking CALL UP or PUT DOWN. What's left of the premium is the time value.

A likely test question might be: An XYZ Jan 50 put is trading for a premium of 5. The current market value of XYZ stock is 55. What is the time value and intrinsic value of the premium?

Think PUT DOWN. A put has intrinsic value when the market price of the stock is below the strike price. In this example, that market price is up, so this option has no intrinsic value. The premium of 5 is all time value.

The solution is: intrinsic value = 0, time value = 5.

QUICK QUIZ 4.G   RST is trading for $54.

What are the intrinsic values and time values of the following options?

1.   RST September 50 call for 6

2.   RST October 55 call for 2.25

3.   RST September 60 put for 7.25

4.   RST October 50 put for 1.15

(handwritten notes: IV / TV columns — 1. 4 / 2; 2. 0 / 2.25; 3. 6 / 1.25; 4. 0 / 1.15)

TEST TOPIC ALERT   Your customer buys 1 MCS Jul 70 call at 2.50 when the market is at 71. As time passes, the market price of MCS remains stable at 71. The premium, therefore, will probably

A.   stay the same
B.   go up
C.   go down
D.   exhibit extreme volatility

Answer: C. Remember that options are wasting assets. As the expiration date approaches, the option's time value diminishes. Time, therefore, is against the option owner. In this case, the intrinsic value stays the same because the stock price remains stable at 71. Intrinsic value for a call is the difference between the strike price and the market price, if the market price is higher.

4. 2   BASIC OPTIONS TRANSACTIONS

Four basic options positions are available to the options investor. Investors use these strategies to accomplish a variety of objectives. An overview of these strategies and their potential risks and rewards follows.

4. 2. 1   BUYING CALLS

Call buyers are **bullish** on the underlying stock. By purchasing calls, an investor can profit from an increase in a stock's price while investing a relatively small amount of money. There are many reasons why investors purchase calls.

4. 2. 1. 1   Speculation

Speculation is the most common reason for buying calls. Investors can speculate on the upward price movement of the stock by paying only the premium. Buying the actual stock would require a far greater investment.

4. 2. 1. 2   Deferring a Decision

An investor can buy a call on a stock and lock in a purchase price until the option expires. This allows him to postpone making a financial commitment other than the premium until the expiration date of the option.

4. 2. 1. 3   Diversifying Holdings

With limited funds, an investor can buy calls on a variety of stocks and possibly profit from any rise in the options premium.

4. 2. 1. 4   Protection of a Short Stock Position

Investors can use calls to protect a short stock position. The option acts as an insurance policy against the stock rising in price.

4. 2. 1. 5   Maximum Gain

Theoretically, the potential gains available to call owners are unlimited because there is no limit on the rise in a stock's price.

4. 2. 1. 6   Maximum Loss

The most the call buyer can lose is the premium paid; this happens if the market price is at or below the strike price at the option's expiration.

4. 2. 2   WRITING CALLS

Call writers are **bearish** or neutral on the price of the underlying stock. An investor who believes a stock's price will decline or stay the same can write calls for any of the following reasons.

4.2.2.1 Speculation

By writing calls, an investor can profit if the stock's price falls below or stays at the strike price. The investor can earn the amount of the premium.

4.2.2.2 Increasing Returns

Additional income can be earned for a portfolio by writing calls. Investors hope for expiration of the calls so they can keep the premiums.

4.2.2.3 Locking in a Sale Price

If an investor has an unrealized profit in a stock and is interested in selling it, a call can be written at a strike price that will attempt to lock in that profit.

4.2.2.4 Protection of a Long Stock Position

The premium collected from writing a call provides limited downside protection to the extent of the premium received.

4.2.2.5 Maximum Gain

An uncovered call (or naked call) writer's maximum gain is the premium received. If a call is uncovered, the investor does not own the underlying stock. The maximum gain is earned when the stock price is at or below the exercise price at expiration.

4.2.2.6 Maximum Loss

An uncovered call (or naked call) writer's maximum loss is unlimited because the writer could be forced to buy the stock at a potentially unlimited price, if the option is exercised against him, for delivery at the strike price.

Long Call/Short Call

Position	Maximum Gain	Maximum Loss
Long call	Unlimited	Premium
Short call	Premium	Unlimited

QUICK QUIZ 4.H

1. An investor buys 1 DWQ May 60 call at 3.50. What is the investor's maximum potential gain?

   A. $350
   B. $5,650
   C. $6,350
   D. Unlimited

2. An investor buys 1 DWQ May 60 call at 3.50. What is the investor's maximum potential loss?

    A. $350
    B. $5,650
    C. $6,350
    D. Unlimited

3. An investor sells 1 KLP Dec 45 call at 3. What is the investor's maximum potential gain?

    A. $300
    B. $4,200
    C. $4,800
    D. Unlimited

4. An investor sells 1 KLP Dec 45 call at 3. What is the investor's maximum potential loss?

    A. $300
    B. $4,200
    C. $4,800
    D. Unlimited

5. All of the following will usually result in a profit to a naked call writer EXCEPT

    A. when the option contract expires without being exercised
    B. when the price of the underlying security falls below and remains below the exercise price of the option
    C. when the call is exercised and the price of the underlying security is greater than the exercise price plus the premium received
    D. when the price of the option contract declines

6. In buying listed call options, compared with buying the underlying stock, which of the following is NOT an advantage?

    A. Buying a call would require a smaller capital commitment.
    B. Buying a call has a lower dollar loss potential than buying the stock.
    C. The call has a time value beyond an intrinsic value that gradually dissipates.
    D. Buying a call allows greater leverage than buying the underlying stock.

7. All of the following are objectives of call buyers EXCEPT

    A. speculating for profit on the rise in price of stock
    B. delaying a decision to buy stock
    C. hedging a long stock position against falling prices
    D. diversifying holdings

4. 2. 3   BUYING PUTS

Put buyers are **bearish** on the underlying stock. By purchasing puts, an investor can profit from a decrease in a stock's price while investing a relatively small amount of money. Reasons that investors purchase puts are listed below.

4. 2. 3. 1   Speculation

Investors can speculate on the downward price movement of the stock that is not owned by paying only the premium.

4. 2. 3. 2   Deferring a Decision

An investor can buy a put on a stock and lock in a sale price until the option expires. This allows him to postpone a selling decision until the expiration date of the option. With this strategy, an investor can not only lock in an acceptable sales price for stock that is owned but also protect its appreciation potential until the expiration date.

4. 2. 3. 3   Protection of a Long Stock Position

Investors can use puts to protect a long stock position. The option acts as an insurance policy against the stock declining in price.

4. 2. 3. 4   Maximum Gain

The maximum potential gain available to put owners is the option's strike price less the amount of the premium paid (same as the breakeven). A stock's price can fall no lower than zero.

4. 2. 3. 5   Maximum Loss

The most the put buyer can lose is the premium paid. This happens if the market price is at or above the strike price at the option's expiration.

4. 2. 4   WRITING PUTS

Put writers are **bullish** or neutral on the price of the underlying stock. An investor who believes a stock's price will increase or stay the same can write puts for the following reasons.

4. 2. 4. 1   Speculation

By writing puts, an investor can profit if the stock's price rises above or stays at the strike price. The investor can earn the amount of the premium.

4. 2. 4. 2   Increasing Returns

Additional income can be earned for a portfolio by writing puts. Investors hope for expiration of the puts so that they can keep the premium.

4. 2. 4. 3   Buying Stock Below Its Current Price

The premium received from writing puts can be used to offset the cost of stock when the put is exercised against the writer. The writer buys his stock at a price that is reduced by the premium received.

4. 2. 4. 4   Maximum Gain

An uncovered put (naked put) writer's maximum gain is the premium received. The maximum gain is earned when the stock price is at or above the exercise price at expiration.

4. 2. 4. 5   Maximum Loss

An uncovered put (naked put) writer's maximum loss is the put's strike price less the premium received (the same as the breakeven); it occurs when the stock price drops to zero. The investor is forced to buy the worthless stock at the option's strike price. The investor's loss is reduced by the premium received.

Position	Maximum Gain	Maximum Loss
Long put	Strike price – premium	Premium
Short put	Premium	Strike price – premium

QUICK QUIZ 4.1

1. An investor buys 1 ABC Jan 50 put at 2. What is the investor's maximum potential gain?

    A. $200
    B. $4,800
    C. $5,200
    D. Unlimited

2. An investor buys 1 ABC Jan 50 put at 2. What is the investor's maximum potential loss?

    A. $100
    B. $200
    C. $4,800
    D. $5,200

3. An investor sells 1 DWQ Feb 30 put at 4.50. What is the investor's maximum potential gain?

    A. $450
    B. $2,550
    C. $3,450
    D. Unlimited

4. An investor sells 1 DWQ Feb 30 put at 4.50. What is the investor's maximum potential loss?

    A. $450
    B. $2,550
    C. $3,450
    D. Unlimited

TEST TOPIC ALERT   Options offer investors a great deal of flexibility. You will typically see several test questions that require you to know the strategies just reviewed. Maximum gain and loss are concepts that are normally heavily tested. When learning them, focus on the long positions. If you know the long position definitions, you can always remember the short position definitions because they are the opposite. The following chart summarizes this relationship.

Position	Maximum Gain	Maximum Loss
Long call	Unlimited	Premium
Short call	Premium	Unlimited
Long put	Strike price – premium	Premium
Short put	Premium	Strike price – premium

4. 2. 5   CHOICES AT EXPIRATION

The owner of a put or call option contract has three choices before the expiration of the contract. The investor can exercise the option, let the option expire, or sell the option contract before the expiration date.

4. 2. 5. 1   Exercise the Option

The holder of a call will buy the stock at the strike price.
The holder of a put will sell the stock at the strike price.

4. 2. 5. 2   Let the Option Expire

The holder of a call will allow the option to expire if the market price of the stock is equal to or less than the strike price.

The holder of a put will allow the option to expire if the market price of the stock is equal to or greater than the strike price.

4. 2. 5. 3   Sell the Option Contract Before the Expiration Date

The holder can sell the option for its current premium; there is no purchase or sale of underlying stock in this situation. The investor has profit or loss based on the increase or decrease of the option's premium from the time the option was purchased (**closing the position**).

TEST TOPIC ALERT
A significant number of your options questions will require determining the amount of profit or loss in an options transaction. Consider using the following T-chart to compare money paid out to money received in a transaction. Money paid out is identified as a **debit (DR)** to the investor's account. Money received is a **credit (CR)** to the investor's account.

DR	CR

If an investor pays a premium to buy an option, he opens his position with a debit to the account in the amount of the premium.

EXAMPLE

An investor buys one XYZ January 50 call for 3. The T-chart is filled out like this:

DR	CR
3	

If the investor had instead sold the XYZ January 50 call for 3, the T-chart would reflect that:

DR	CR
	3

Try using the T-chart on any option question that requires a calculation. It will keep your accounting organized, making it easy to determine profit and loss.

4. 2. 6   OPTION EXERCISE

Option contracts are **exercised** if they are in the money. Writers are required to fulfill their obligations as required. Exercises of listed equity options settle regular way: two business days from the exercise date.

4. 2. 7   OPTION EXPIRATION

Option contracts **expire** worthless if they are at the money or out of the money at expiration. At expiration, the buyer of the option loses the premium paid; the seller of the option profits by the amount of the premium received.

TEST TOPIC ALERT

Answer this question using the T-chart:

An investor with no other positions buys 1 DWQ May 75 call at 6.50. The investor exercises the call when the stock is trading at 77 and immediately sells the stock in the market. What is the investor's profit or loss?

The solution is a calculation, so draw a T-chart.

-6.50
2

DR	CR
6.50	
75	77
81.50	77
4.50	

The position is opened by buying; a debit of the premium is made. The call is exercised. Exercise of a long call requires the investor to buy the stock at the strike price. A debit of 75 must be made to the account.

When the stock is trading at 77, the investor sells. A credit of 77 must be made to the account. The resulting loss is $450 (4.50 x 100) because the investor paid out 81.50 and received only 77.

QUICK QUIZ 4.J

1. An investor with no other positions sells 1 KLP Jul 40 call at 3.50. The call is exercised when the stock is trading at 47. What is the investor's profit or loss?

    A. $350 profit 3.50
    B. $350 loss -700
    C. $450 profit
    D. $450 loss

2. An investor with no other positions buys 1 COD May 65 put at 3.50. The investor buys the stock in the market and exercises the put when the stock is trading at 63.50. What is the investor's profit or loss?

    A. $200 profit -3.50
    B. $200 loss 1.50
    C. $350 profit
    D. $350 loss

3. An investor with no other positions sells 1 ALF 95 Jan put at 5.50. The put is exercised when the stock is trading at 79, and the investor immediately sells the stock in the market. What is the investor's profit or loss?

    A. $550 profit $+5.50$
    B. $550 loss -16.00
    C. $1,050 profit
    D. $1,050 loss

4. 2. 8 CLOSING TRANSACTIONS

If an investor has purchased an option before expiration, the investor can sell the option. A profit is made if the premium is greater than originally paid. In this situation, the sale of the option is known as the **closing transaction**.

If an investor initially sold an option, the investor can close the position by buying the option. This closing transaction is profitable if the investor is able to buy the option for a premium less than was received for its sale. Trading options accounts for a very large portion of activity in the options market.

TEST TOPIC ALERT

If an investor opens an option position by buying, he must close it by selling; if the position is opened by selling, he must close it by buying. Opening and closing transactions are always opposites of each other.

Opening and Closing Transactions

	Open	Close
Long	Buy contract	Sell contract
Short	Sell contract	Buy contract

The test may ask you to close transactions for their intrinsic value.

Normally, a transaction is closed for its premium amount, but if an option is about to expire, it has no time value—intrinsic value is all that is left. Use a T-chart on questions that require you to close out options positions.

4. 2. 8. 1 Cabinet or Accommodation Transactions

Options exchanges allow an accommodation procedure for closing out worthless options before expiration. Orders to liquidate worthless options are kept, so to speak, in a cabinet to be executed by the market maker or the electronic book. The rules are as follows.

- The closing transaction can be placed only at a price of $1 per contract ($.01 per share); these transactions are considered limit orders.
- All closing transactions must be handled in priority, based on time of receipt.
- Bids and offers at $1 per contract ($.01 per share) must be submitted in writing, to be matched by the market maker or electronic book.
- Cabinet trades are not reported to the consolidated tape system (CTS) but must be reported to the exchange at the close of business.
- Cabinet trades can be used by both firm (proprietary) and public customer accounts to close worthless positions before expiration.

Cabinet trades produce a confirmation to the customer showing a closeout for the sum of $1, which can be useful for transaction and tax records.

TAKE NOTE

Cabinet trades are also referred to as **accommodation liquidations** because, for tax purposes, they provide customers, including proprietary accounts, with a record of worthless options.

QUICK QUIZ 4.K

1. A customer with no other positions sells 1 MTN Jul 80 call for 10 and buys 100 shares of MTN stock for $85 per share. If the customer enters into a closing purchase for $10 for the MTN Jul call and sells 100 shares of MTN stock for $88 per share, he would realize

    300

    A. a $300 loss
    B. a $300 profit
    C. a $800 loss
    D. a $800 profit

2. In April, a customer buys 1 MTN Oct 50 call for 9 and sells 1 MTN Jul 50 call for 4. What will the customer's pretax profit or loss be if he buys back the July call for $1 and sells the October call for $12?

    A. $100 loss
    B. $100 profit
    C. $600 loss
    D. $600 profit

3. In April, a customer purchases 1 TCB Jul 85 call for 5 and purchases 1 TCB Jul 90 put for 8. TCB stock is trading at 87. If TCB stays at 87 and both options are sold for their intrinsic value, the customer will realize

    −5   +2
    −8   +3

    A. a $500 profit
    B. an $800 loss
    C. a $1,000 profit
    D. an $1,100 profit

TEST TOPIC ALERT

Use a T-chart to simplify all questions that ask the investor's profit or loss.

If you feel comfortable with what you have done so far, advance to a different use of options—hedging. If not, go back and review before proceeding.

With hedging, options can be used to protect a stock position. Expect up to 10 questions on this concept. Even though hedging appears to be a short part of this Unit, learn it well—it is a heavily tested portion of the options Unit.

4. 3   USING OPTIONS TO PROTECT A POSITION—HEDGING

An investor with an established stock position can use options to help protect against the risk of the position. The option helps insure the investor against some of the possible loss from the stock position.

The investor who has a long stock position hopes for the market price of the stock to increase. The risk of the position, a market price decline, can be offset by the purchase of a put or, to a limited degree, the sale of a call.

The investor who has a short stock position hopes for the market price of the stock to decline. The risk of the position, a market price increase, can be offset by the purchase of a call or, to a limited degree, the sale of a put.

TAKE NOTE

Here's an easy way to think about hedging strategy using the master options chart.

An investor has a long stock position that he wishes to protect. What is the risk of the long stock position?

The risk is that the market price will fall (a downward arrow). To hedge the position, select an option position with a downward (bearish) arrow. The investor can protect a long stock position with a long put or short call.

Try this with a short stock position. If an investor has a short stock position, it is profitable when the market price declines. Remember, in a short stock position, the investor has borrowed stock from the broker-dealer. He needs to buy back the shares to return to the broker-dealer. If he can buy them back at a price lower than the price at which he sold them, he makes a profit. What is the risk of the short stock position?

The risk is that the market price will rise (an upward arrow). To hedge the position, select an option position with an upward (bullish) arrow. The investor can protect a short stock position with a long call or short put.

Sometimes the hedging strategy questions on the exam will ask you to determine which option will best or fully protect a stock position. The best protection is to buy an option (remember "Best Buy").

If the question asks for partial protection, or how the investor could improve his rate of return, select a short option position. The sale of the option generates premium income to improve the investor's rate of return. The risk of the stock position is reduced by the amount of the premium received, which is partial protection only.

The Use of Option Positions to Protect Stock Positions

Stock Position	Full Protection	Partial Protection
Long stock position	Long put	Short call
Short stock position	Long call	Short put

If an investor holds a long stock position, buying puts provides nearly total downside protection. The upside potential of the stock is reduced only by the amount of premiums paid.

Selling calls when holding a long stock position, also known as **covered call writing**, is partial protection that generates income and reduces the stock's upside potential.

The following examples explain the use of options to protect a long stock position.

4. 3. 1 LONG STOCK, LONG PUT

An investor buys 100 shares of RST at 53 and buys an RST 50 put for 2. The maximum gain is unlimited. Should the stock price fall below the strike price of 50, the investor will exercise the put to sell the stock for 50. The investor loses $3 per share on the stock and has spent $2 per share for the put. The total loss equals $500. The breakeven point is reached when the stock rises by the amount paid for the put; in this case, 53 + 2 = 55.

TAKE NOTE

In the above example, no matter how far the stock falls, the investor can get out at 50 by exercising the put. Therefore, the most the investor can lose on the stock position is $3 per share. The cost of this protection is $2 per share. Therefore, maximum potential loss is $5 per share or $500. On the other hand, maximum gain is unlimited because the stock price could rise infinitely. To break even, the stock must rise by the cost of the put option purchased. The breakeven point for long stock-long put is cost of stock purchased plus premium.

4. 3. 2 LONG STOCK, SHORT CALL

An investor buys 100 shares of RST at 53 and writes 1 RST 55 call for 2. The maximum gain equals $400: if the stock price rises above 55, the call will be exercised; thus, the investor will sell the stock for a gain of $200, in addition to the $200 premium received. The maximum loss is $5,100. Should the stock become worthless, the $200 premium reduces the loss on the stock. The breakeven point is reached when the stock falls by the amount of the premium received. Therefore, 53 − 2 = 51.

TAKE NOTE

In the above example, the customer is protected only on the downside by the amount of the premium received for writing the call. Thus, the stock could fall to $51, at which point the customer breaks even; the $2 loss on the stock is offset exactly by the premium received. Below $51, losses begin. If the stock becomes worthless, the customer could lose $5,100 (which is maximum loss). If the stock rises above $55, the customer will be exercised, forced to sell stock at $55 for a $2 per share gain. Combined with the $2 per share premium received, the maximum potential gain is $400. One of the drawbacks of writing calls against a long stock position is that it limits upside potential. Therefore, covered call writing is normally done in a stable market. The breakeven point for long stock-short call is cost of stock purchased minus premium.

4. 3. 3 SHORT STOCK, LONG CALL

An investor sells short 100 shares of RST at 58 and buys an RST 60 call for 3. The inves-tor's maximum gain is $5,500; if the stock becomes worthless, the investor gains $5,800 from the short sale minus the $300 paid for the call. The maximum loss is $500; if the stock price rises above $60, the investor will exercise the call to buy the stock for 60, incurring a $200 loss on the short sale, in addition to the $300 paid for the call. The breakeven point is the stock's sale price minus the premium paid in this case, 58 – 3, or 55.

TAKE NOTE   In the previous example, no matter how high the stock rises, the investor can buy back his short position at 60 by exercising the call. Therefore, the most the investor can lose on the short stock position is $2 per share. The cost of this protection is $3 per share. Therefore, maximum potential loss is $5 per share or $500. On the other hand, maximum gain will occur if the stock becomes worthless. If the stock falls to zero, the customer will make $5,800 on the short stock position less the $300 paid to buy the call. Overall, maximum potential gain is $5,500. The breakeven point for short stock-long call is short sale price minus premium.

4. 3. 4 SHORT STOCK, SHORT PUT

A customer sells short 100 RST at 55 and writes an RST 55 put for 2.50 for partial protec-tion. The maximum gain is $250. If the stock declines to zero and the put is exercised against him, the customer is obligated to pay $5,500 to buy the stock, losing $5,500. However, he receives a $5,500 gain from the short sale. Because he received the $250 premium, the stock can increase to 57.50, the breakeven point, before the short stock position generates a loss, which is potentially unlimited.

TAKE NOTE   In the above example, the customer is protected only on the upside by the amount of the premium received for writing the put. Thus, the stock could rise to $57.50, at which point the customer breaks even; the $2.50 per share loss on the short position is offset exactly by the premium received. Potentially unlimited losses could result if the stock rises above the breakeven point. If the stock falls below $55, the put will be in the money, at which point the customer will be exercised and forced to buy stock at $55 to close out his short position. Therefore, there is no gain or loss on the short stock position. The customer's gain is limited to $250, the premium received. The breakeven point for short stock-short put is the short sale price plus premium.

4. 3. 4. 1 Ratio Call Writing

Ratio call writing involves selling more calls than the long stock position covers. This strategy generates additional premium income for the investor, but also entails unlimited risk because of the short uncovered calls.

TEST TOPIC ALERT   The following Quick Quiz questions require you to compute the breakeven, maximum gain, and maximum loss of hedged positions. To find breakeven, draw a T-chart and identify the debit/credit for both the stock position and the option position. The result is the breakeven point. To find maximum gain and maximum loss, focus on the stock position. What happens if the market goes up or down? Will the option be exercised?

QUICK QUIZ 4.L

1. A customer holds the following positions:
    Long 100 XYZ shares at 62
    Long 1 XYZ 60 put at 3
    The customer breaks even if XYZ trades at

    A. 57
    B. 59
    C. 63
    D. 65

2. **Long 100 XYZ shares at 62**
    Long 1 XYZ 60 put at 3
    What is the maximum gain the customer can realize on these positions?

    A. $5,700
    B. $6,500
    C. $11,900
    D. Unlimited

3. **Long 100 XYZ shares at 62**
    Long 1 XYZ 60 put at 3
    What is the most the customer can lose on these positions?

    A. $300
    B. $500
    C. $1,000
    D. Unlimited

4. **Short 100 shares of XYZ at 26**
    Long XYZ 30 call at 1
    The customer breaks even if XYZ trades at

    A. 25
    B. 27
    C. 29
    D. 31

5. **Short 100 shares of XYZ at 26**
    Long XYZ 30 call at 1
    What is the maximum potential gain for the customer?

    A. $2,500
    B. $2,700
    C. $2,900
    D. $3,100

6. **Short 100 shares of XYZ at 26**
   Long XYZ 30 call at 1
   What is the maximum potential loss on the positions?

   A. $400
   B. $500
   C. $2,500
   D. Unlimited

7. **Long 100 XYZ shares at 62**
   Short 1 XYZ 65 call at 3
   The customer breaks even if XYZ trades at

   A. 57
   B. 59
   C. 63
   D. 65

8. **Long 100 XYZ shares at 62**
   Short 1 XYZ 65 call at 3
   What is the maximum gain the customer can realize on these positions?

   A. $300
   B. $600
   C. $5,900
   D. Unlimited

9. **Long 100 XYZ shares at 62**
   Short 1 XYZ 65 call at 3
   What is the most the customer can lose on these positions?

   A. $300
   B. $600
   C. $5,900
   D. Unlimited

10. **Short 100 shares of XYZ at 54**
    Short XYZ 50 put at 2
    What is the maximum potential loss to the customer?

    A. $60
    B. $200
    C. $5,200
    D. Unlimited

11. A customer is long 200 shares of XYZ at 90 and simultaneously writes 3 XYZ July 90 calls at 3. What is the maximum loss?

    A. $900
    B. $1,800
    C. $18,000
    D. Unlimited

4. 4 MULTIPLE OPTIONS TRANSACTIONS

Investors can simultaneously buy or sell more than one option contract on opposite sides of the market. These positions, known as **spreads**, **straddles**, and **combinations**, can be used to speculate on a security's price movement and limit position costs and risks.

4. 4. 1   SPREADS

A **spread** is the simultaneous purchase of one option and sale of another option of the same class.

■ A call spread is a long call and a short call.

■ A put spread is a long put and a short put.

You may see questions on the exam that ask you to identify what position the investor has established. Again, the master options chart will give you the answer. The horizontal ovals shown in the following chart identify the two types of spreads: call spreads and put spreads.

As you solve questions, point at the investor's options positions on your chart. You will easily identify what type of position has been created.

Price Spread

Master Options Chart

4. 4. 1. 1   Types of Spreads

Investors can buy or sell three types of spreads: a price or vertical spread, a time or calendar spread, or a diagonal spread.

A **price spread** or **vertical spread** is one that has different strike prices but the same expiration date. It is called a vertical spread because strike prices on options reports are reported vertically.

EXAMPLE Example of a price spread/vertical spread:

Long RST Nov **50** call for 7

Short RST Nov **60** call for 3

TAKE NOTE The most common spread, and the one most likely to occur on the Series 7 exam, is the price spread (vertical spread), in which the two options have the same expiration date but different exercise prices.

A **time spread** or **calendar spread,** also known as a **horizontal spread,** includes option contracts with different expiration dates but the same strike prices. Investors who establish these do not expect great stock price volatility; instead they hope to profit from the different rates at which the time values of the two option premiums erode. Time spreads are called horizontal spreads because expiration months are arranged horizontally on options reports.

EXAMPLE Example of a time spread/calendar spread:

Long RST **Nov** 60 call for 3

Short RST **Jan** 60 call for 5

A **diagonal** spread is one in which the options differ in both time and price. On an options report, a line connecting these two positions would appear as a diagonal.

EXAMPLE Example of a diagonal spread:

Long RST **Jan 55** call for 6

Short RST **Nov 60** call for 3

Spreads are categorized as either **debit spreads** or **credit spreads**. A spread is a debit spread if the long option has a higher premium than the short option; a spread is a credit spread if the short option has a higher premium than the long option.

EXAMPLE Long RST Jan 55 call for 6

Short RST Jan 65 call for 2

DR	CR
6	
	2
4	

This spread is a debit spread because more premium was paid than received.

EXAMPLE

Long RST Jan 55 call for 2

Short RST Jan 45 call for 6

DR	CR
2	
	6
	4

Price vertical
time horizontal calendar

This spread is a credit spread because more premium was received than paid.

4. 4. 1. 2   Debit Call Spread

Debit call spreads are used by investors to reduce the cost of a long option position. There is, however, a trade-off, because the potential reward of the investor is also reduced. The investor who establishes a debit call spread is bullish.

EXAMPLE

Buy 1 RST Nov 55 call for 6

Sell 1 RST Nov 60 call for 3

DR	CR
6	
	3
3	

Instead of paying $600 to buy the call, the investor reduced its cost to $300 by also selling a call. If the market price of the stock rises above 60, both calls will be exercised. The investor has the right to buy the stock for 55 but must then sell the stock for 60. The $500 profit on the stock is reduced by the $300 net premium paid, for a net profit of $200. This is the investor's maximum gain on the position.

If the stock price remains below 55, both options will expire, and the investor will lose the net premium paid. The investor's maximum loss is the $300 net premium.

The investor's breakeven point is always between the two strike prices in a spread. For call spreads, breakeven is found by adding the net premium to the lower strike price. Adding the net premium of 3 to the lower strike price of 55 results in a breakeven point of 58.

Because this is a debit spread, the investor profits if exercise occurs. The difference in premiums on the two options widens as exercise becomes likely. Investors always want net debit spreads to widen.

CAL
PSH

TEST TOPIC ALERT

The following tips may be helpful with spread questions:

Debit = widen = exercise (When you begin to widen, you need to exercise.)

This reminds you that debit spreads are profitable if widening of premiums or exercise occurs. The test may ask you in which type of spread the investor wants the premiums to widen. Look for the debit spread.

Credit = narrow = expire (When you become too narrow, you may expire.)

This reminds you that credit spreads are profitable if premiums narrow and expiration occurs. This is logical because sellers want expiration, and option premiums decline as expiration approaches. In which type of spread does the investor want premiums to narrow? Look for the credit spread.

In finding breakeven points on spreads, remember CAL and PSH:

For **C**all spreads: **A**dd the net premium to the **L**ower strike price.

For **P**ut spreads: **S**ubtract the net premium from the **H**igher strike price.

A final tip on finding maximum gain and maximum loss: Start by completing a T-chart. If the result is a net debit, the net debit equals maximum loss. Find the maximum gain by subtracting the net debit from the difference in the two strike prices of the spread.

EXAMPLE

Long XYZ 50 call at 9
Short XYZ 60 call at 5

DR	CR
9	
	5
4	

The maximum loss is 4 because buyers of options lose premiums paid. The difference in strike prices is 10 (60 − 50); 10 − 4 leaves 6 for the maximum gain.

Remember, the maximum loss plus the maximum gain must always total the difference in the strike prices.

Breakeven for the investor is found by CAL: 50 + 4 = 54.

If this had been a credit spread, the net premium would represent the maximum gain. The maximum loss would be found by subtracting the maximum gain from the difference in strike prices.

4. 4. 1. 3   Credit Call Spread

Credit call spreads are created by investors to reduce the risk of a short option position. Again, there is a trade-off; the potential reward of the investor is reduced. The investor who establishes a credit call spread is bearish.

EXAMPLE

Buy 1 RST Nov 55 call for 2
Sell 1 RST Nov 45 call for 9

DR	CR
2	
	9
	7

The investor reduced the unlimited risk of the short naked call by also purchasing a call. The long call gives the investor the right to purchase the stock at 55 if forced to sell at 45. The investor in this situation is bearish; if the stock price declines below the lower strike price of 45, both options will expire worthless and the investor keeps the net premium. The net premium (in this case, $700) is the maximum gain for a credit spread.

If the market price of the stock rises above 45, the investor's loss is limited. The investor's long call can be exercised to buy the stock at 55. The loss on the stock is limited to 10, less the net premium of 7 collected. The maximum loss to the investor in a credit spread is the difference in the strike prices minus the net premium (in this case $300).

The investor's breakeven point is always between the two strike prices in a spread. For call spreads, breakeven is found by adding the net premium to the lower strike price. Adding the net premium of 7 to the lower strike price of 45 results in a breakeven point of 52.

Because this is a credit spread, the investor profits when the options expire. The difference in premiums on the two options narrows as the options are about to expire. Investors always want net credit spreads to narrow.

QUICK QUIZ 4.M

1. Buy 1 QRS Jan 40 call at 2.35; write 1 QRS Jan 45 call at .85. What is the breakeven point?

    A. 3.25
    B. 39.50
    C. 41.50
    D. 95.00

2. Write 1 MCS Dec 50 call at 5.25; buy 1 MCS Dec 55 call at 2. What is the breakeven point?

    A. 7.25
    B. 50.00
    C. 53.25
    D. 57.00

3. Write 1 ABC Oct 30 call at 3.25; buy 1 ABC Oct 40 call at .25. What is the maximum gain and the maximum loss?

    I.   Maximum gain $300
    II. Maximum gain $325
    III. Maximum loss $700
    IV. Maximum loss $7,025

    A. I and III
    B. I and IV
    C. II and III
    D. II and IV

4. Buy 1 LMN Oct 80 call at 8; write 1 LMN Oct 90 call at 2.75. What is the maximum gain and the maximum loss?

 I. Maximum gain $475
 II. Maximum gain $525
 III. Maximum loss $475
 IV. Maximum loss $525

 A. I and III
 B. I and IV
 C. II and III
 D. II and IV

5. Write 1 XYZ Jan 130 call at 26.75; buy 1 XYZ Jan 140 call at 19.50. What is the maximum gain and the maximum loss?

 I. Maximum gain $275
 II. Maximum gain $725
 III. Maximum loss $725
 IV. Maximum loss $275

 A. I and III
 B. I and IV
 C. II and III
 D. II and IV

4. 4. 1. 4 Debit Put Spread

Debit put spreads are used by investors to reduce the cost of a long put position. The investor who establishes a debit put spread is bearish.

EXAMPLE

Buy 1 RST Nov 55 put for 6
Sell 1 RST Nov 50 put for 3

DR	CR
6	
	3
3	

Instead of paying $600 to buy the put, the investor reduced its cost to $300 by also selling a put. If the market price of the stock falls below 50, both puts will be exercised. The investor will sell the stock for 55 but will buy the stock for 50. The $500 profit on the stock is reduced by the $300 net premium paid for a net profit of $200. This is the investor's maximum gain on the position.

If the stock price remains above 55, both options will expire and the investor will lose the net premium paid. The investor's maximum loss is the $300 net premium.

The investor's breakeven point is always between the two strike prices in a spread. For put spreads, breakeven is found by subtracting the net premium from the higher strike price. Subtracting the net premium of 3 from 55 results in a breakeven point of 52.

This is a debit spread, so the investor profits if exercise occurs. The difference in premiums on the two options widens as exercise becomes likely. Investors always want net debit spreads to widen.

4. 4. 1. 5 Credit Put Spread

Credit put spreads are created by investors to reduce the risk of a short put position. Again, there is a trade-off: the potential reward of the investor is reduced. The investor who establishes a credit put spread is bullish.

EXAMPLE

Buy 1 RST Nov 55 put for 2

Sell 1 RST Nov 65 put for 9

DR	CR
2	
	9
	7

The investor reduced the substantial risk of the short naked put by also purchasing a put. The long put gives the investor the right to sell stock if necessary to provide cash the investor needs to buy stock when the short put is exercised. The investor in this situation is bullish; if the stock price rises above the upper strike price of 65, both options will expire worthless and the investor keeps the net premium. The net premium is the maximum gain for a credit spread.

If the market price of the stock falls below 55, the investor's loss is limited. The exercise of the investor's short put will require purchase of the stock at 65. The loss is limited to 10, less the net premium of 7 collected. The maximum loss to the investor in a credit spread is the difference in the strike prices minus the net premium.

The investor's breakeven point is always between the two strike prices in a spread. For put spreads, breakeven is found by subtracting the net premium from the higher strike price. Subtracting the net premium of 7 from 65 results in a breakeven point of 58.

This is a credit spread, so the investor profits when the options expire. The difference in premiums on the two options narrows as the options are about to expire. Investors always want net credit spreads to narrow.

Maximum Gain and Maximum Loss for Debit and Credit Spreads

Calculation	Credit Spread	Debit Spread
Maximum gain	The net credit	The difference between the strike prices – the net debit
Maximum loss	The difference between the strike prices – the net credit	The net debit

---

TEST TOPIC ALERT   Note that all spreads (debit and credit, put and call) have a limited (defined) maximum loss and maximum gain potential. From a suitability perspective, no spread would expose an investor to an unlimited maximum loss potential.

QUICK QUIZ 4.N

1. Which of the following are spreads?

    I. Long 1 ABC May 40 call; short 1 ABC May 50 call
    II. Long 1 ABC May 40 call; long 1 ABC May 50 call
    III. Long 1 ABC Aug 40 call; short 1 ABC May 40 call
    IV. Long 1 ABC Aug 40 call; short 1 ABC Aug 50 put

    A. I and II
    B. I and III
    C. II and III
    D. II and IV

2. Buy 1 XYZ Apr 30 put at 3.30; write 1 XYZ Apr 35 put at 5.80. What is the breakeven point?

    A. 21.00
    B. 26.00
    C. 27.50
    D. 32.50

3. Buy 1 LMN Jan 40 put at 6.50; write 1 LMN Jan 30 put at 2.25. What is the maximum gain and the maximum loss?

    I. Maximum gain $425
    II. Maximum gain $575
    III. Maximum loss $425
    IV. Maximum loss $575

    A. I and III
    B. I and IV
    C. II and III
    D. II and IV

4. An investor who has entered into a debit spread will profit if

    A. the spread widens
    B. the spread narrows
    C. the spread remains unchanged
    D. both contracts expire unexercised

5. In March, a customer sells 1 CW Oct 50 put for 3 and buys 1 CW Oct 60 put for 11. The customer will experience a pretax profit from these positions if

    I. the difference between the premiums narrows to less than $8 per share
    II. the difference between the premiums widens to more than $8 per share
    III. both puts are exercised at the same time
    IV. both puts expire unexercised

    A. I and III
    B. I and IV
    C. II and III
    D. II and IV

4. 4. 1. 6   Determining a Spread Investor's Market Attitude

The **market attitude** of a spread investor is determined by the option that is the more costly of the two.

With **call** spreads, the option with the *lower strike price* has the *higher premium*. It depends on if you purchased the option with the lower strike price or sold it. That is how you know if it is a *debit* (purchased the one with the lower strike price) or a *credit* (sold the one with the lower strike price).

Examples:
Long 1 July 40 call
Short 1 July 45 call
Purchased the one with the lower strike price (higher premium), so this is a *debit*, and debit call spreads are *bullish*.

Long 1 Aug. 40 call
Short 1 Aug. 30 call
Sold the one with the lower strike price (higher premium), so this is a *credit*, and credit call spreads are *bearish*.

With **put** spreads, it is just the opposite. The option with the *higher strike price* has the *higher premium*. So again, it depends on if you purchased the option with the higher strike price or sold it. That is how you know if it is a *debit* (purchased the one with the higher strike price) or a *credit* (sold the one with the higher strike price).

Examples:
Long 1 Sept. 40 put
Short 1 Sept. 30 put
Purchased the one with the higher strike price (higher premium), so this is a *debit*, and debit put spreads are *bearish*.

Long 1 Dec. 20 put
Short 1 Dec. 25 put
Sold the one with the higher strike price (higher premium) so this is a *credit*, and credit put spreads are *bullish*.

TEST TOPIC ALERT   You may be asked to determine whether a spread is bullish or bearish. With premiums shown, use a T-chart to determine debit or credit. If no premiums are shown, it is up to you to determine which of the options is more valuable. Expect to see one or two questions on this concept.

A quick way to determine whether a spread is bullish or bearish is the following: in any spread, put or call, if you are buying the lower strike price, you are a bull.

Buy XYZ Jan 20 call at 7; sell XYZ Jan 30 call at 3: bull call spread – debit spread

Buy ABC Aug 35 call at 1; sell ABC Aug 25 call at 8; bear call spread – credit spread

Buy DEF Mar 70 put at 6; sell DEF Mar 90 put at 17; bull put spread – credit spread

Buy LRK Sep 30 put at 9; sell LRK Sep 20 put at 3; bear put spread – debit spread

QUICK QUIZ 4.0

1. A customer buys 1 DOH Nov 70 put and sells 1 DOH Nov 60 put when DOH is selling for 65. This position is
   A. a bull spread
   B. a bear spread
   C. a combination
   D. a straddle

2. All of the following are credit spreads EXCEPT
   A. write 1 Nov 35 put and buy 1 Nov 30 put
   B. buy 1 Apr 40 call and write 1 Apr 30 call
   C. buy 1 Jul 50 call and write 1 Jul 60 call
   D. buy 1 Jan 50 put and write 1 Jan 60 put

In Questions 3–10, answer A to identify a bear spread and B for a bull spread.

____ 3. Write 1 Nov 35 put; buy 1 Nov 30 put

____ 4. Buy 1 Jan 70 call; write 1 Jan 75 call

____ 5. Write 1 Apr 30 call; buy 1 Apr 40 call

____ 6. Write 1 Dec 45 put; buy 1 Dec 60 put

____ 7. Buy 1 Jul 50 call; write 1 Jul 60 call

____ 8. Buy 1 Dec 45 put; write 1 Dec 40 put

____ 9. Write 1 Jan 60 put; buy 1 Jan 50 put

____ 10. Buy 1 May 25 put; write 1 May 20 put

11. In which of the following cases would the investor want the spread to widen?
    I. Write 1 May 25 put; buy 1 May 30 put
    II. Write 1 Apr 45 put; buy 1 Apr 55 put
    III. Buy 1 Nov 65 put; write 1 Nov 75 put
    IV. Write 1 Jan 30 call; buy 1 Jan 40 call

    A. I and II
    B. I and IV
    C. II and III
    D. II and IV

4. 4. 2   STRADDLES

A **straddle** is composed of a call and a put with the same strike price and expiration month. Straddles can be long or short and are used by investors to speculate on the price movement of stock.

Like spreads, straddles can also be identified easily with the master options chart. Straddles are identified by vertical ovals rather than horizontal ovals on the chart.

Straddles Chart

The chart also provides a tip about the strategy behind straddles. Notice the market attitude arrows pushing away from each other on the long straddle. This reminds you that the investor who buys a straddle expects a large amount of movement in the price of the stock.

The arrows on the short side are pointing toward each other and signify little or no market price movement: the objective of the seller of the straddle.

4. 4. 2. 1   Long Straddles

An investor who uses a **long straddle** expects substantial volatility in the stock's price but is uncertain of the direction the price will move. To be ready for either occurrence, the investor purchases both a call and a put.

EXAMPLE

Buy 1 ABC Jan 50 call at 3

Buy 1 ABC Jan 50 put at 4

Maximum gain = unlimited

Maximum loss = $700

Breakevens = 57, 43

The investor has created a long straddle by purchasing a call and a put with the same strike and expiration. If the market price of the stock rises sufficiently, the call will be profitable and the put will expire. The investor's gain on the call will be reduced by the premiums paid on both the call and the put.

If the market price of the stock falls substantially instead, the put will be profitable and the call will expire. The investor's gain on the put will be reduced by the premiums paid on both the call and the put.

The maximum gain of the long straddle is unlimited because the potential gain on a long call is unlimited. The maximum loss of the long straddle is both premiums paid. There are two breakeven points because there are two options. The breakeven for the call is the strike price plus both premiums paid; the breakeven for the put is the strike price minus both premiums paid. The investor does not experience profit unless the market price is above the breakeven of the call or below the breakeven of the put.

4. 4. 2. 2   Short Straddles

An investor who writes a short straddle expects that the stock's price will not change or will change very little. The investor collects two premiums for selling a straddle.

E X A M P L E

Sell 1 ABC Jan 45 call at 4

Sell 1 ABC Jan 45 put at 5

Maximum gain = $900

Maximum loss = unlimited

Breakevens = 54, 36

The investor has created a short straddle by selling a call and a put with the same strike and expiration. If the market price of the stock changes little or not at all, the call and put will expire. The investor's maximum profit is the two premiums collected.

If the market price of the stock rises or falls substantially, either the put or call will be exercised against the investor. The investor's maximum loss in this position is unlimited because of the short naked call.

The breakeven points for the short straddle are found the same way as for the long straddle. The call breakeven is the strike price plus both premiums paid; the breakeven for the put is the strike price minus both premiums paid. The investor does not experience profit unless the market price stays within the breakeven points at expiration.

Straddle Calculations

Calculation	Long Straddle	Short Straddle
Maximum gain	Unlimited	Total premiums received
Maximum loss	Total premiums paid	Unlimited
Breakevens	Call: strike + both premiums Put: strike – both premiums	Call: strike + both premiums Put: strike – both premiums

4. 4. 2. 3   Combinations

A **combination** is composed of a call and a put with different strike prices, expiration months, or both. Combinations are similar to straddles in strategy. Investors typically use combinations because they are cheaper to establish than long straddles if both options are out of the money.

EXAMPLE

An investor could establish a long combination by buying an XYZ Jan 40 call and buying an XYZ Jan 45 put. If the investor were to write both options, a short combination would result. Breakeven points are computed in the same manner as straddles. Add the combined premiums to the strike price of the call and subtract combined premiums from the strike price of the put. As with straddles, the holder of a long combination makes money if the underlying stock trades outside the breakeven points. The writer of a short combination makes money if the stock stays inside the breakeven points.

EXAMPLE

With XYZ trading at 25, a customer writes 1 XYZ Jan 20 call at 6 and writes 1 XYZ Jan 30 put at 7. This is an example of a short combination where both contracts are in the money. Both the call and the put are in the money by 5 points. The Series 7 exam could ask you the following question: Just before expiration, with XYZ now trading at 27, the customer closes his positions at intrinsic value. How much did the customer make or lose?

In this example, closing means buying back the two options that were originally sold. What will be the cost of buying back both options? The answer is their intrinsic value. With XYZ now at 27, the call is in the money by 7 points and the put is in the money by 3 points. Now it is just a simple computation. The call was sold for 6 and bought back for 7, a loss of $100. The put was sold for 7 and bought back for 3, a gain of $400. Overall, the gain is $300.

QUICK QUIZ 4.P

1. Your customer sells a DOH Mar 35 call. To establish a straddle, he would

   A. sell a DOH Mar 40 call
   B. buy a DOH Mar 35 put
   C. sell a DOH Mar 35 put
   D. buy a DOH Mar 40 call

2. ACM issues a news release that your customer believes will strongly affect the market price of ACM stock. However, your customer is not sure whether the effect will be positive or negative. In this situation, which of the following strategies would be best?

   A. Buy a call
   B. Write a call
   C. Write a straddle
   D. Buy a straddle

3. Your customer buys 2 QRS Jul 30 calls at 2 and 2 QRS Jul 30 puts at 2.50. The customer will break even when the price of the underlying stock is

   I. 25.50
   II. 27.50
   III. 32
   IV. 34.50
   A. I and IV
   B. II and III
   C. III only
   D. IV only

Identify the positions described by indicating one of the following terms.

A. Price spread
B. Long straddle
C. Time spread
D. Short straddle
E. Diagonal spread
F. Combination

___ 4. Buy 1 QRS May 40 call; sell 1 QRS May 50 call

___ 5. Buy 1 QRS May 40 call; buy 1 QRS May 40 put

___ 6. Buy 1 QRS Aug 40 call; sell 1 QRS Dec 40 call

___ 7. Buy 1 DOH May 30 call; buy 1 DOH Jul 40 put

___ 8. Write 1 DOH Jan 30 call; write 1 DOH Jan 40 put

___ 9. Buy 1 DOH Mar 35 call; write 1 DOH Jun 45 call

4. 5 NONEQUITY OPTIONS

Nonequity options function nearly the same as equity options. However, because the underlying instruments are not shares of stock, nonequity options have different contract sizes and delivery and exercise standards.

4. 5. 1 INDEX OPTIONS

Options on indexes allow investors to profit from the movements of markets or market segments and hedge against these market swings. They may be based on broad-based, narrow-based, or other indexes with a particular focus.

Broad-based indexes reflect movement of the entire market and include the S&P 100 (OEX), S&P 500, and the Major Market Index (XMI).

Narrow-based indexes track the movement of market segments in a specific industry, such as technology or pharmaceuticals.

Some indexes have a very particular focus, such as the VIX (volatility market index). This index is a measure of the implied volatility of the S&P 500 Index options traded on the CBOE. VIX index options, also traded on the CBOE, are designed to reflect investor expectations of market volatility over the next 30 days. It is often referred to as the "fear" gauge or index. High readings are not bullish, nor are they bearish, but instead are a measure of the expectation (fear) that the market will be volatile. The expectation of greater volatility generally translates into higher premiums for options contracts.

4. 5. 1. 1   Index Option Features

4. 5. 1. 1. 1   *Multiplier*

Index options typically use a multiplier of $100. The premium amount is multiplied by $100 to calculate the option's cost, and the strike price is multiplied by $100 to determine the total dollar value of the index.

4. 5. 1. 1. 2   *Trading*

Purchases and sales of index options, like equity options, settle on the next business day. Index options stop trading at 4:15 pm ET if they are broad-based. Narrow-based index options stop trading at 4:00 pm ET.

4. 5. 1. 1. 3   *Exercise*

The exercise of an index option settles in cash rather than in delivery of a security, and the cash must be delivered on the next business day. If the option is exercised, the writer of the option delivers cash equal to the intrinsic value of the option to the buyer.

4. 5. 1. 1. 4   *Settlement Price*

When index options are exercised, their settlement price is based on the closing value of the index on the day of exercise, not the value at the time of exercise.

4. 5. 1. 1. 5   *Expiration Dates*

Index options expire on the third Friday of the expiration month, just as equity options do.

TAKE NOTE   With regard to settlement, there is one major difference between index options and equity options. The exercise of an index option settles next business day, whereas the exercise of an equity option settles regular way (two business days). With regard to trading (i.e., buying or selling), settlement is the next business day for both.

4. 5. 1. 1. 6   *Index Option Exercise*

Following is an example to take you through the process from purchase through exercise, or through expiry, for an index option.

EXAMPLE   A customer buys 1 OEX Jan 460 call at 3.20 when the OEX index is trading at 461.

What is the premium?	$320 (3.20 x $100)
What is the breakeven point?	463.20 (strike price + premium)
What is the intrinsic value?	$100 (461 − 460)
What is the time value?	$220 ($320 − $100)

One month later, with the index at 472 and the Jan 460 call trading at 13.70, the customer elects to exercise.

How much cash will the customer receive from the writer?	$1,200, the intrinsic value of the option (472 – 460)
How much profit did the customer make?	$880, which is the cash received from the writer less the premium paid ($1,200 – $320)

Now, instead of exercising, assume the customer closes the position.

How much profit would the customer make?	$1,050, which is the difference between the premium received on selling ($1,370) and the premium paid to open the position ($320)

Note that instead of making $880 by exercising, the customer would have made $1,050 by closing the position. Why the $170 difference? As long as there is time value in the option, the customer will always make more by closing an index option rather than by exercising. The time value of the 460 call trading at 13.70 is $170 when the index is at 472.

4. 5. 1. 2   Index Options Strategy

Index options may be used to speculate on movement of the market overall. If an investor believes the market will rise, he can purchase index calls or write index puts. If an investor believes the market will fall, he can purchase index puts or write index calls.

Hedging a portfolio is an important use of index options. If a portfolio manager holds a diverse portfolio of equity, he can buy a put on the index to offset loss if the market value of the stocks fall. This use of index puts is known as **portfolio insurance**. Index options protect against the risk of a decline in the overall market, which is **systematic** or **systemic risk**.

TEST TOPIC ALERT   Using index options can be more cost efficient than hedging positions individually due to commission costs. When a portfolio contains several positions in need of hedge protection, an investor may be able to use index options and adequately hedge the entire portfolio with fewer transactions.

EXAMPLE   A customer has a broad-based stock portfolio worth $920,000 and is concerned about a possible market downturn. In order to hedge, the customer could buy broad-based index puts (e.g., the OEX). If the market does turn downward, the loss on the portfolio would be offset by a gain on the puts. Remember, a put increases in value as the underlying security or portfolio goes down in value. If the OEX is trading at 460, each contract has a value of $46,000 (460 x $100). Therefore, to hedge a $920,000 stock portfolio, the customer would buy 20 OEX 460 puts (20 x $46,000).

4. 5. 1. 3   Beta

Beta is a measure of the volatility of a stock or a portfolio related to the volatility of the market in general. If a portfolio has a beta of 1.0, it has the same volatility characteristics as the market in general. In other words, if the market were to rise by 5%, the portfolio should rise by the same amount. If a portfolio has a beta of 1.2, it is 20% more volatile than the market in general. For example, if the market were to rise by 10%, a portfolio with a beta of 1.2 should rise by 20% more, or 12%. Conversely, should the market decline, a portfolio with a beta of more than 1.0 will fall more than the overall market.

EXAMPLE   Back to our original example: if the $920,000 portfolio has a beta of 1.2, instead of purchasing 20 OEX 460 puts to hedge, the customer must purchase 24 OEX 460 puts. Because the portfolio is 20% more volatile, the customer needs 20% more protection (1.2 × 20 puts = 24).

Portfolio managers may also choose to write index options to generate income.

QUICK QUIZ 4.Q

1. Your customer is bullish on the market. If he buys 1 Jul 490 call on the XMI, which of the following options might he write to create a debit spread?

    I.   Jul 485 call
    II. Jul 480 call
    III. Jul 500 call
    IV. Jul 505 call

    A. I only
    B. I and II
    C. II, III and IV
    D. III and IV

2. Your client owns a portfolio of blue-chip stocks. He tells you that he believes the securities will provide good, long-term appreciation but also believes that the market will decline over the short term. Which index options strategy should you recommend that will protect against the expected decline and still allow for long-term capital appreciation?

    A. Buy puts
    B. Buy calls
    C. Sell covered puts
    D. Sell covered calls

3. When an investor exercises an OEX option, he receives

    A. common stock
    B. cash equal to the strike price
    C. cash equal to the intrinsic value
    D. It cannot be exercised.

4. Which of the following statements regarding stock index options are TRUE?

   I. Trades are settled the next business day.

   II. Trades are settled on the third business day.

   III. Exercise settlement involves the delivery of stock.

   IV. Exercise settlement involves the delivery of cash.

   A. I and III

   B. I and IV

   C. II and III

   D. II and IV

4. 5. 2 INTEREST RATE OPTIONS

Interest rate options are yield based (i.e., they have a direct relationship to movements in interest rates). These options are based on yields of T-bills, T-notes, and T-bonds. A yield-based option with a strike price of 35 reflects a yield of 3.5%. Assume an investor believes that rates on T-notes, currently at 3.5%, will rise in the near term. The investor could purchase a call option with a 35 strike price (at the money). If rates rise to 4.5%, the investor could exercise and receive cash equal to the intrinsic value of the option.

Rates have gone up by 10 points—35 to 45—so the investor would receive $1,000 because each point is worth $100. Profit would be the $1,000 received on exercise less the premium paid. On the other hand, the investor could have closed his position, profiting from the difference between the premium paid and the premium received on closing.

The strategy is straightforward. If a portfolio manager believes rates will fall, the manager will buy puts or write calls. If the manager believes rates will rise, buying calls and writing puts would be appropriate.

TAKE NOTE
     All yield-based options are European-style exercise. That is, they may be exercised only on expiration day.

4. 5. 3 FOREIGN CURRENCY OPTIONS

Currency options allow investors to speculate on the performance of currencies other than the U.S. dollar or to protect against fluctuating currency exchange rates against the U.S. dollar. Currency options are available for trading on U.S. listed exchanges on the Australian dollar, the British pound, the Canadian dollar, Swiss francs, Japanese yen, and the Euro. Importers and exporters frequently use currency options to hedge currency risk.

4. 5. 3. 1 Features of Foreign Currency Options

TAKE NOTE
     Foreign Currency Options contracts are cash settled in U.S. dollars with no physical delivery of foreign currency.

4. 5. 3. 1. 1 Contract Sizes

Currency options contracts sizes are now smaller to accommodate retail investors. A British pound contract, for instance, covers 10,000 pounds. Each currency has its own contract size as follows:

New World Currency

Currency		Options Contract Size
Australian $	(XDA)	10,000
British £	(XDB)	10,000
Canadian $	(XDC)	10,000
Euro €	(XDE)	10,000
New Zealand $	(XDZ)	10,000
Swiss Fr	(XDS)	10,000
Japanese ¥	(XDN)	1,000,000

4. 5. 3. 1. 2 Strike Prices

Strike prices of most foreign currency options are quoted in U.S. cents. The Japanese yen is an exception and is quoted in 1/100th of a cent.

EXAMPLE   Strike price of .85 = 85 U.S. cents except for Japanese yen where a strike price denoted as 121 = 1.21 U.S. cents (121 × 1/100).

4. 5. 3. 1. 3 Premiums

Currency options are quoted in cents per unit. Just as with equity options, one point of premium = $100. The total premium of the contract is found by multiplying the premium by the number of units. If a Swiss franc contract (10,000 units) is quoted with a premium of 1.5, the cost of the contract is 10,000 × .015, or $150.

4. 5. 3. 1. 4 Trading

Listed currency options are primarily traded on the NASDAQ OMX PHLX (formerly the Philadelphia Stock Exchange). Trading hours are 9:30am–4:00pm ET.

4. 5. 3. 1. 5 Expiration Date

Currency options expire on the third Friday of the expiration month, just as equity options do.

4. 5. 3. 1. 6 Settlement

Currency options settle, like equity options, on the next business day. When a foreign currency option is exercised, settlement occurs on the next business day as well.

4. 5. 3. 1. 7 Styles

Exchange listed foreign currency options are European style exercise only.

4. 5. 3. 1. 8 Strategies

If an investor believes the value of a currency is going to rise, he will buy calls or sell puts on the currency. If an investor expects the value of a currency to fall, he will buy puts or sell calls on the currency. Currency options are measured relative to the U.S. dollar, and an inverse relationship exists between their exchange rates. Therefore, if the U.S. dollar is rising, relative to other currencies, then those currencies are falling. Conversely, if the U.S. dollar is falling against other currencies, then those currencies are rising.

EXAMPLE

A U.S. importer must pay for Swiss chocolates in Swiss francs within three months. The importer is fearful that the value of the dollar will fall. Using foreign currency options, what should this investor do?

If the importer believes the U.S. dollar will fall, then foreign currency values will rise. The investor should buy calls on the Swiss franc to lock in the purchase price for the francs needed in three months.

TAKE NOTE

As a general rule, importers buy calls on the foreign currency to hedge; exporters buy puts to hedge. However, keep in mind that there are no options available on the U.S. dollar. As an example, consider a Japanese company that exports stereos to the United States. The company will be paid in dollars upon delivery. The risk to the Japanese company is that the dollar will decline between now and the delivery, which means $1 will be worth fewer yen. How should this company hedge this risk?

The rule of thumb is that exporters should buy puts on the foreign currency. However, because there are no options on the U.S. dollar, the Japanese company should buy calls on its own currency, the yen.

EXAMPLE

A British company is exporting sweaters to the United States. How should the company hedge its foreign exchange risk?

A. Buy BP calls
B. Sell BP calls
C. Buy BP puts
D. Sell BP puts

Answer: A: As options on the U.S. dollar are not available, exporters to the United States should buy calls on their own currency.

1. Which of the following currency options is NOT listed for trading on U.S. exchanges?

    A. British pound
    B. Japanese yen
    C. Canadian dollar
    D. U.S. dollar

2. An investor is long 5 PHLX Dec puts on the Canadian dollar. These options will expire in December on

    A. the 3rd Friday of the month
    B. the Saturday after the 3rd Friday
    C. the Wednesday after the 3rd Saturday
    D. the Friday preceding the 3rd Wednesday

3. A U.S. company expects to receive British pounds upon delivery of manufactured goods to a British distributor. How can the company best hedge against the risk of a strengthened U.S. dollar?

    A. Buy puts on the pound
    B. Buy calls on the pound
    C. Sell puts on the pound
    D. Sell calls on the pound

4. An investor who believes the U.S. dollar will soon strengthen in relation to the Canadian dollar might profit from which of the following strategies?

    I.   Buying puts on the Canadian dollar
    II. Writing puts on the Canadian dollar
    III. Writing a straddle on the Canadian dollar
    IV. Establishing a call credit spread on the Canadian dollar

    A. I and III
    B. I and IV
    C. II and IV
    D. I, II, III and IV

5. An investor purchases 2 Dec .56 Swiss franc calls at 2.5. One SF contract includes 10,000 units. How much does the investor pay for this position?

    A. $56
    B. $250
    C. $500
    D. $560

6. A customer opens a spread on Canadian dollars (10,000 units) by purchasing 1 Dec .74 call for 1.30 and selling 1 Dec .77 call for .50. What is the total cost of this debit spread?

    A. $80
    B. $125
    C. $135
    D. $400

4. 6 HOW THE OPTIONS MARKET FUNCTIONS

Options trade on the major U.S. exchanges and OTC.

Exchange-traded options are known as **listed options** and have standardized strike prices and expiration dates. OTC options are not standardized; as a result, little secondary market activity exists. Contract terms are individually negotiated between buyer and seller.

TAKE NOTE   If a security is subject to a trading halt, options on that security stop trading as well.

4. 6. 1 STANDARD FEATURES OF OPTIONS TRADING AND SETTLEMENT

4. 6. 1. 1 Trading Times

Listed stock options trade from 9:30 am–4:00 pm ET (3:00 pm CT). Note that broad based index options trade until 4:15 pm ET (3:15 pm CT).

4. 6. 1. 2 Expiration

Listed options (equity, index, interest rate, and currency) expire on the third Friday of the expiration month at 11:59 pm ET. Final trades may be made until 4:00 pm ET on the final day of trading (expiration).

4. 6. 1. 3 Settlement

Listed options transactions settle on the next business day. Stock delivered as a result of exercise is settled on a **regular way basis** (two business days).

4. 6. 1. 4 Automatic Exercise

Contracts that are in the money by at least .01 at expiration are automatically exercised as a service to the customer unless other instructions have been given. Automatic exercise applies to both customer and institutional accounts. Customers may give "do not exercise" instructions for any contract in the money if they do not want to have their contract exercised. All instructions must be received by OCC no later than 5:30 pm ET on the third Friday of the expiration month (last day of trading).

Exercise, Trading, or Expiration of Options

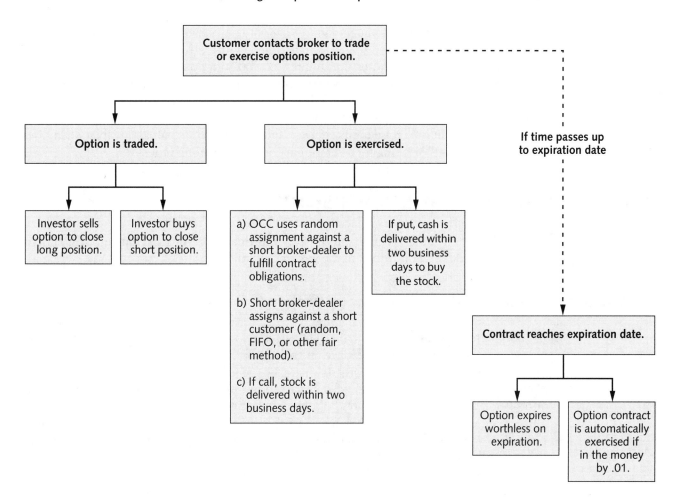

4. 6. 1. 5   Position Limits

For the most heavily traded equity options contracts, position limits are 250,000 contracts on the same side of the market. This limit is subject to frequent adjustment. No more than 250,000 contracts on the same side of the market may be exercised within a five-business-day period.

Position limits apply to individuals, registered representatives acting for discretionary accounts, and individuals acting in concert (acting together as one person). LEAPS are added to traditional options to determine whether a violation of the position limit rules has occurred.

Position limits are measured by the number of contracts on the same side of the market. There are two sides: the bull side and the bear side. Long calls and short puts represent the former; long puts and short calls, the latter.

Take a company subject to a 250,000 contract limit. If a customer were long 140,000 calls and 140,000 puts, there would be no violation. However, if the same customer were long 140,000 calls and short 140,000 puts, the customer would have 280,000 contracts on the bull side of the market, a violation. In determining whether a violation has occurred, long calls are aggregated with short puts and long puts are aggregated with short calls.

4. 6. 1. 6   Exercise Limits

OCC exercise limits are the maximum number of contracts that can be exercised on the same side of the market within a specified time frame. Currently, the time frame is five consecutive business days. As with position limits, the maximum number applicable to exercise limits can vary from one underlying security to another, and to determine if a violation has occurred, long calls and short puts (bullish contracts) are aggregated, and short calls and long puts (bearish contract) are aggregated.

Like position limits, exercise limits apply to individuals, individuals acting in concert, and registered representatives acting for discretionary accounts, among others.

4. 6. 2   OPTIONS TRADING PERSONNEL

Options are traded most heavily on the **Chicago Board Options Exchange (CBOE)** in a double-auction market. Following are the key trading roles.

4. 6. 2. 1   Designated Primary Market Maker

A **designated primary market maker (DPM)** is a floor trader responsible for maintaining a two-sided market for a specific product on the CBOE and is the trading firm designated by the exchange to ensure a fair and orderly market—the CBOE's equivalent to a specialist on the NYSE-Amex options exchange. A DPM can perform the roles of a market maker and/or a floor broker, if the conditions warrant. All equity options on the CBOE have a DPM.

Also note that an electronic designated market maker (eDPM) functions with the same responsibilities as a DPM, except that they are permitted to conduct business electronically from off-floor locations.

4. 6. 2. 2   Market Makers

Options market makers are registered with the exchange to trade for their own accounts. They must stand ready to buy or sell options in which they make markets to maintain an orderly market.

4. 6. 2. 3   Floor Brokers

Floor brokers are a firm's representatives on the floor of the exchange. They execute orders on behalf of the firm and its customers.

4. 6. 2. 4   Order Routing Systems

Computerized order routing systems are often used to route customer orders directly to the trading post and back to the firm. Notice of execution is sent directly to the broker-dealer.

4. 6. 3   OPTIONS CLEARING CORPORATION (OCC)

The **Options Clearing Corporation (OCC)** is the clearing agent for listed options contracts and is owned by the exchanges that trade options. Its primary functions are to standardize, guarantee the performance of, and issue option contracts. The OCC determines when new option contracts should be offered to the market. It designates the strike prices and expiration months for new contracts within market standards to maintain uniformity and liquidity. The market determines the premium for the contracts.

The exercise of options contracts is guaranteed by the OCC. If a holder of an option wishes to exercise, his broker-dealer notifies the OCC. The OCC then assigns exercise notice against a short broker-dealer, who assigns to a short customer.

The OCC assigns exercise notices on a **random** basis. Broker-dealers may then assign exercise notices to customers on a random basis, on a first in, first out (FIFO) method, or any other method that is fair and reasonable.

Options contracts are traded without a certificate. An investor's proof of ownership is the trade confirmation.

4. 6. 3. 1   Documentation of Customer Accounts

The OCC requires that certain documents be provided to customers that open options accounts. The **OCC Options Disclosure Document** must be provided at or before the account approval. This document explains options strategies, risks, and rewards and is designed to provide full and fair disclosure to customers before they begin options trading.

Before any trading can take place, an options account must be approved by the branch manager. Then, not later than 15 days after the account approval, the customer must return the signed **options agreement**. This document states that the customer has read the disclosure document, understands the risks of options trading, and will honor position limit rules. By signing, the customer also agrees to advise the firm if any changes occur in his financial situation, investment objectives, and so forth.

If the signed options agreement is not returned within 15 days of account approval, the investor cannot open new options positions. Only closing transactions are allowed if the options agreement is not returned as required.

4. 6. 3. 2   Supervision and Compliance

Member firms are required to integrate the responsibility for supervision and compliance of their public customer options business into their overall supervisory and compliance programs. A registered option principal (ROP) must be designated by a firm to handle compliance and supervisory issues regarding customer options business. An ROP is Series 4 licensed.

Any options literature (advertising or sales) intended to communicate with the public must be approved by the ROP before distribution. Options worksheets, which identify the risks, rewards, and costs of various option strategies, or any material considered educational in nature regarding options, is considered communications. While OCC distinguishes between advertising and sales literature, how any communications piece will be regulated depends on if it is considered retail, institutional, or correspondence. These categories will be discussed later in Unit 17.

EXAMPLE   In accordance with the distinction that OCC makes between options advertising and sales literature recommendations, past performance and projected performance are not permitted in options advertising, but they are permitted in sales literature. In general, sales literature must be preceded or accompanied by a copy of the Options Disclosure Document (ODD) if it includes past or projected performance figures or it constitutes a recommendation pertaining to options. Communications that are educational in nature but do not contain projected performance figures or make recommendations pertaining to options need not be preceded by the ODD but instead must be accompanied by a notice providing the name and address where an ODD can be obtained.

Options Account Diagram

Customer wishes to trade options.

Registered representive determines suitability of options trading.

OCC Options Disclosure Document is provided at or before account approval.

Option account is approved by ROP.

First trade may take place immediately following account approval.

Option contracts are bought or sold T + 1 (payments of premiums).

Signed option agreement returned within 15 days of account approval.

Closing transactions only if option agreement is not returned or is late.

4. 6. 3. 3 Options Contract Adjustments

Options contracts are adjusted for stock splits, reverse stock splits, stock dividends, and rights offerings. They are not adjusted for ordinary cash dividends or for cash distributions of less than $12.50 per option contract. Adjustments to the number of shares are rounded down to the next whole share.

When **even** stock splits occur, additional options contracts are created. An even split ends in 1—such as a 2:1, 3:1, or 4:1 split.

EXAMPLE

After a 2:1 split, 1 ALF 60 call becomes 2 ALF 30 calls. A 2:1 creates 200 shares instead of 100, so the owner has twice as many contracts as before, at half the exercise price.

The total exercise value remains the same:

Original contract: 100 x 60 = $6,000
New contracts: 200 x 30 = $6,000

An **uneven split,** also known as a **fractional split,** such as a 3:2 or 5:4, does not create additional options contracts. Contracts adjusted for uneven splits include a larger number of shares and will receive a new option contract symbol.

EXAMPLE

After a 3:2 split, 1 ALF 60 call will effectively be represented by 1 ALF 40 call with 150 shares in the contract.

The total exercise value effectively remains the same as before:

Original contract: 100 x 60 = $6,000
New contract when closed or exercised: 150 x 40 = $6,000

TEST TOPIC ALERT

Expect to see five to seven questions on the information presented in the previous section. Be familiar with documentation of options accounts, the contract adjustments, and the times and dates discussed. Note that stock dividends are treated as uneven splits; the number of contracts remains the same, the strike price is adjusted, and the contract now covers more shares.

4. 6. 3. 4 Opening vs. Closing

When filling out an order ticket for an option transaction, the representative must indicate whether the trade is an opening or closing transaction. An opening transaction establishes a position, whereas a closing transaction eliminates a position. Furthermore, if an opening transaction involves the sale of an option, the representative must indicate whether it is covered or uncovered.

EXAMPLE   If you enter an order to sell 1 XYZ Jan 30 call at the market, are you establishing a short position or closing out an existing long position in that contract? If you are establishing a short position, the order ticket must be marked as an opening sale. If you are closing out an existing long position, the ticket must be marked as a closing sale.

EXAMPLE   If you are writing a call against an existing long position in the stock, the ticket must be marked as an opening sale covered.

4. 6. 3. 5   Open Interest

The open interest in an option is the number of contracts outstanding. The higher the open interest, the more liquid the option. As an option approaches expiration, open interest begins to decline as investors close out or exercise existing positions.

4. 6. 3. 5. 1   Put-Call Ratio

The put-call ratio reflects the current open interest in the trading of put options to call options. The ratio can be used as a gauge of investor sentiment (bullish or bearish) and can be calculated to measure broad sectors of the market across many underlying securities or indexes, or it can be used to gauge investor sentiment for just one underlying security.

The ratio is calculated by dividing the number of traded put options by the number of traded call options. The higher the ratio, the more bearish investors have been up to that point in time. For instance, as the ratio increases, it can be interpreted as an indication that investors have felt the market sector or underlying security would move lower and were buying more puts, or that investors were purchasing puts to hedge existing long portfolios in anticipation of a downward move.

However it should also be noted that the ratio can be used as a contrarian indicator by traders. For example, the higher the ratio becomes it is likely that traders may feel it is time to close or cover short positions in favor of long positions. In other words, the ratio may have become so high that the continued bearish sentiment begins to diminish indicating that a reversal may be near.

4. 6. 3. 6   Market Manipulation

Any attempt to manipulate options' markets is considered unlawful. There is no regard for market impact or the economic result, profit, or loss caused by the activity once evidence presented support that the offense has occurred.

Although manipulation can be attempted by any investor, these violations most often occur where large positions are at stake more likely among traders and institutional trading entities. Following are the most common types of market manipulation involving options.

■ **Capping:** This is the act of entering sell orders in a stock for the purpose of keeping the stock from rising above the strike price of calls one is short. If successful, the stock will stay below the strike price and the short call options will be out of the money and not be exercised.

■ **Supporting:** This is the act of entering purchase orders in a stock for the purpose of keeping the price from falling below the strike price of puts one is short. The intent is to keep the puts out of the money and unexercised.

■ **Pegging:** This is a generic term that applies to any activity intended to keep the price of a stock from moving. This can involve entering either buy or sell orders or both. For example, a short straddle writer will profit most if the stock price and strike prices of the position are the same at expiration—that is, the short options are right at the money.

■ **Front running:** This is the act of taking an option position when a firm has received a block order but before the block has been entered for execution. The intent is to establish an option position likely to profit or protect against loss once the block is executed.

QUICK QUIZ 4.S

1. An investor buys 1 DWQ Apr 70 call at 5, giving him the right to buy 100 shares of DWQ at $70 per share. Which aspect of the transaction is NOT set or standardized by the OCC?

   A. Contract size of 100 shares
   B. Premium of 5
   C. Exercise price of 70
   D. Expiration date in April

2. A customer first discusses options trading with a registered representative on July 3. On July 7, the customer is approved for trading listed options, and on July 12, he enters the first trade. The investor must receive an options disclosure document no later than

   A. July 3
   B. July 7
   C. July 12
   D. July 13

3. When applying the exercise limit rules, which of the following could be considered as acting in concert?

   A. Registered representative who has discretionary control over 10 customer accounts
   B. Many options customers of the same brokerage firm acting independently on a recent recommendation published by the firm
   C. Registered representatives making recommendations to nondiscretionary customers
   D. All of the above

4. SSS is a stock subject to a 25,000 options position limit. Which of the following positions violate the rules governing position limits?

   I.   Long 14,000 SSS Aug 40 calls; short 12,000 SSS Aug 40 puts
   II. Long 14,000 SSS Aug 40 calls; short 12,000 SSS Jan 40 puts
   III. Long 14,000 SSS Aug 40 calls; short 12,000 SSS Aug 40 calls

   A. I and II
   B. I and III
   C. II and III
   D. I, II and III

5. If a 50% stock dividend is declared, the owner of 1 XYZ Jul 30 call now owns

    A.   1 contract for 100 shares with an exercise price of 20
    B.   1 contract for 150 shares with an exercise price of 20
    C.   2 contracts for 100 shares with an exercise price of 20
    D.   2 contracts for 150 shares with an exercise price of 30

6. When must a new options customer who has not yet traded options receive the Options Clearing Corporation's current disclosure document?

    A.   At or before the time the registered representative signs the customer approval form
    B.   Within 15 days after the registered representative has approved the customer's account for options trading
    C.   At or before the time the account receives the registered options principal's final approval for options trading
    D.   No later than 15 days after the registered options principal's signs the options customer approval form

7. Equity options can be traded up until

    A.   4:00 pm ET the day prior to expiration
    B.   4:00 pm ET on the expiration date
    C.   11:00 pm ET on the expiration date
    D.   11:59 pm ET on the day prior to expiration

8. The Options Clearing Corporation uses which of the following methods in assigning exercise notices?

    I.   Random selection
    II.   First in, first out
    III. To the member firm holding a long position that first requests an exercise
    IV.   On the basis of the largest position

    A.   I only
    B.   I, II and III
    C.   I and III
    D.   II and IV

4. 7   TAX RULES FOR OPTIONS

Because options are capital assets, capital gains tax rules apply. The tax consequences will vary depending on how an existing position is handled.

There are three ways to handle an existing (open) option position. An open position can expire, be closed in the open market, or be exercised by the party who is long.

4. 7. 0. 1   Expiration

At the expiration of an options contract, the buyer loses the premium; the seller profits from the premium. The buyer reports a capital loss equal to the premium amount; the seller reports a capital gain equal to the premium amount.

The tax treatment for LEAPS writers at expiration is unique. Although investors may have held the contract for more than 12 months, LEAPS writers must report **short-term capital gains** at expiration. LEAPS buyers will report long-term losses and gains if the contract is held for more than 12 months. Essentially, LEAP contracts for buyers are handled like most other securities regarding long- and short-term gains and losses.

4. 7. 0. 2   Closing Out

Closing sales or purchases generate a capital gain or loss equal to any price difference. This gain or loss must be reported on the basis of the date of the closing transaction.

4. 7. 0. 3   Exercise

The exercise of options does not generate a capital gain or loss until a subsequent purchase or sale of the stock occurs. If a long call is exercised, the option holder buys the stock. Because the investor paid a premium for the stock, the total cost basis for the stock includes the premium and strike price. The chart identifies the tax consequences of these options strategies.

Possible Tax Consequences of Options Strategies

Strategy	Option Expires	Option Exercised	Position Closed
Buy a call	Capital loss	Strike price + premium = cost basis	Capital gain or loss
Sell a call	Capital gain	Strike price + premium = sale proceeds	Capital gain or loss
Buy a put	Capital loss	Strike price − premium = sale proceeds	Capital gain or loss
Sell a put	Capital gain	Strike price − premium = cost basis	Capital gain or loss

4. 7. 1   STOCK HOLDING PERIODS

The IRS does not allow the use of options to postpone the sale of stock for the purpose of generating long-term capital gains treatment. Options that allow an investor to lock in a sale price are long puts. If stock has been held 12 months or less before the purchase of a put, the gain will be classified as short term.

EXAMPLE   An investor bought XYZ 11 months ago at 50. It now trades for 70. If the investor were to sell it now, the gain would be classified as short term.

Assume the investor buys a 70 put that will expire in nine months. Even though the sale of the stock is postponed until up to 20 months have elapsed, the IRS still requires the holding period to be classified as short term for tax purposes. If the stock had already been held for more than 12 months, its holding period would not be affected by the purchase of a put.

TEST TOPIC ALERT   Expect to see about five to seven questions on options taxation. Many of these questions are a matter of finding the profit or loss, so use a T-chart. Remember that option exercise alone does not create a taxable event.

QUICK QUIZ 4.T

1. In September, an investor sells 2 AMF Jan 60 puts at 3. If the investor buys the 2 puts back at 4.50, the result for tax purposes is

A. a $150 capital gain
B. a $150 capital loss
C. a $300 capital gain
D. a $300 capital loss

2. In September, an investor sells 2 AMF Jan 60 puts at 3. If the 2 AMF Jan 60 puts expire in January, what are the tax consequences for the seller?

A. $600 gain realized in September
B. $600 loss realized in September
C. $600 gain realized in January
D. $600 loss realized in January

3. Your customer buys 1 FLB Oct 50 call at 3. He exercises the option to buy 100 shares when the market is at 60. What is the cost basis of the 100 shares?

A. $5,000
B. $5,300
C. $6,000
D. $6,300

4. A customer writes 1 Jul 50 put at 7. The put is exercised when the market price is 40. For tax purposes, what is the effective cost basis of the stock put to the seller?

A. $40
B. $43
C. $50
D. $57

5. Your customer buys 100 shares of TIP stock at 59 and sells a TIP 60 call at 4. The stock's price rises to 70 and the option is exercised. For tax purposes, the customer must report sales proceeds of

A. $6,400 and cost basis of $5,900
B. $6,000 and cost basis of $5,500
C. $7,000 and cost basis of $5,900
D. $7,000 and cost basis of $6,500

6. An investor buys a LEAPS contract at issuance and allows it to expire unexercised. What is the investor's tax consequence at expiration?

A. Short-term capital gain
B. Short-term capital loss
C. Long-term capital gain
D. Long-term capital loss

7. A customer buys 100 shares of stock at 67 and sells a 70 call for 4. The stock rises to 75, and the option is exercised. For tax purposes, this investor reports sales proceeds of

A. $7,000 and cost basis of $6,300
B. $7,400 and cost basis of $6,700
C. $7,500 and cost basis of $6,700
D. $7,500 and cost basis of $7,400

UNIT TEST

1. A customer sells an FLB Mar 35 call. To establish a straddle, he would

   A. sell an FLB Mar 40 call
   B. buy an FLB Mar 35 put
   C. sell an FLB Mar 35 put
   D. buy an FLB Mar 40 call

2. All of the following procedures are required when opening an options account EXCEPT

   A. the registered representative must document that the client has received a current OCC disclosure document
   B. the background and financial information provided by the client must be verified by the client and returned within 15 days of the time the account was approved
   C. the client must agree that any material change in financial status requires the broker-dealer be notified, and the options agreement will be amended
   D. trades may not occur until OCC verifies the financial information supplied by the client and ultimately approves the account

3. An investor with no other positions sells 1 ABC Jan 45 call at 2.50. If the option expires when the stock is trading at 44.50, what is the investor's profit or loss?

   A. $50 profit
   B. $50 loss
   C. $250 profit
   D. $250 loss

4. An investor buys 1 ABC Jun 55 call at 4. What is the investor's breakeven point?

   A. 51
   B. 55
   C. 59
   D. 60

5. If an investor maintaining a short equity option is assigned an exercise notice, which of the following statements is TRUE?

   A. He may refuse exercise under certain circumstances.
   B. He must accept the exercise notice.
   C. He may offset his obligation with a closing transaction up to the end of trading on the same day.
   D. He may offset his obligation with a closing transaction within 3 days.

6. A customer buys 1 ABC Jan 60 put at 6 and writes 1 ABC Jan 75 put at 13. The maximum loss is

   A. $700
   B. $800
   C. $900
   D. $1,500

7. A customer is short 100 XYZ shares at 26 and long 1 XYZ 30 call at 1. The customer breaks even if XYZ trades at

   A. 25
   B. 27
   C. 29
   D. 31

8. In which of the following strategies would the investor want the spread to widen?

   I. Buy 1 RST May 30 put; write 1 RST May 25 put
   II. Write 1 RST Apr 45 put; buy 1 RST Apr 55 put
   III. Buy 1 RST Nov 65 put; write 1 RST Nov 75 put
   IV. Buy 1 RST Jan 40 call; write 1 RST Jan 30 call

   A. I and II
   B. I and IV
   C. II and III
   D. III and IV

9. The market attitude of a customer who sells a call spread is

   A. bullish
   B. bearish
   C. speculative
   D. neutral

10. After selling short ABC at 70, a customer holds the position as ABC gradually falls to $53 per share. Which of the following strategies would best protect his gain?

    A. Write 55 calls
    B. Buy 55 calls
    C. Write 55 puts
    D. Buy 55 puts

11. An investor buys 1 LMN Jan 50 put at 2. What is the investor's maximum potential loss?

    A. $100
    B. $200
    C. $4,800
    D. $5,200

12. An investor wants to purchase TCB stock (currently trading at 38), and he expects the price of TCB stock to decline in the short term before rising. If he wants to purchase the stock below its current market value and generate additional income, he should

    A. write a call at 35
    B. buy a put and exercise the option
    C. write a put at 35
    D. buy a 40 call and exercise the option

13. A customer sells 3 ABC Feb 25 puts at 4 when ABC is at 24. If the contracts are closed out at intrinsic value when ABC is at 19, the customer has a

    A. $600 loss
    B. $600 gain
    C. $200 loss
    D. $200 gain

14. Options listed on U.S. exchanges are available on all of the following currencies EXCEPT

    A. euro
    B. Japanese yen
    C. Canadian dollar
    D. U.S. dollar

15. All of the following would affect option premiums EXCEPT

    A. volatility of the stock
    B. stock price
    C. time to expiration
    D. account position

16. If a customer writes 1 ABC April 60 put at 5 when ABC is trading at 58, which of the following statements are TRUE?

    I. The time value of the option is 2 points.
    II. The time value of the option is 3 points.
    III. Breakeven is 65.
    IV. Breakeven is 55.

    A. I and III
    B. I and IV
    C. II and III
    D. II and IV

17. A customer buys 100 XYZ at 49 and writes 1 XYZ Nov 50 call, receiving $350 in premiums. The breakeven point is

    A. 45.50
    B. 46.50
    C. 52.50
    D. 53.50

18. In a volatile market, which of the following option strategies carries the most risk?

    A. Long straddle
    B. Short straddle
    C. Debit spread
    D. Credit spread

19. Which of the following strategies is considered most risky in a strong bull market?

    A. Buying calls
    B. Writing naked calls
    C. Writing naked puts
    D. Writing either naked calls or puts

20. A customer purchases OEX puts to protect his stock portfolio from an expected downturn. This use of index options to hedge reduces

    A. systematic risk
    B. nonsystematic risk
    C. rate risk
    D. credit risk

21. A customer should receive a current option disclosure document before or at the date of

    A. the first trade
    B. settlement
    C. final account approval
    D. the first monthly statement

22. When an index option is exercised, cash settlement must take place how many business days after exercise?

    A. 1
    B. 2
    C. 3
    D. 5

23. When comparing a short call to a short call spread, all of the following are true EXCEPT

    A. maximum gain is limited
    B. maximum loss is limited
    C. both positions are bearish
    D. both positions generate premium income

24. A Japanese exporter wants to hedge a recent sale of stereo equipment to a U.S. buyer. The exporter will be paid in U.S. dollars upon delivery of the goods. The best hedge would be to

    A. sell Japanese yen calls
    B. sell Japanese yen puts
    C. buy Japanese yen calls
    D. buy Japanese yen puts

25. An investor sells 1 DWQ Feb 30 put at 4.50. What is the investor's breakeven point?

    A. 25.50
    B. 27.50
    C. 30.50
    D. 34.50

26. Which of the following has unlimited risk if it is the only position in an account?

    A. Long put
    B. Long call
    C. Short put
    D. Short call

27. Which of the following statements regarding a March .80 Canadian dollar call option trading at 6 if the Canadian dollar is at $.85 is TRUE?

    A. The contract is out of the money.
    B. The contract has intrinsic value.
    C. The contract is at parity.
    D. The contract has no time value.

28. What is the following position?

    Buy 1 QRS May 40 call
    Sell 1 QRS May 50 call
    A. Price spread
    B. Time spread
    C. Diagonal spread
    D. Combination

29. If a customer wishes to take an option position on a company and does not anticipate that the price of the stock will change, he would most likely

    A. buy a call
    B. buy a put
    C. buy a straddle
    D. sell a straddle

30. A customer buys 1 XYZ Nov 70 put and sells 1 XYZ Nov 60 put when XYZ is selling for 65. This position is

    A. a bull spread
    B. a bear spread
    C. a combination
    D. a straddle

31. If a customer writes 10 DEF Aug 50 calls at 1 when DEF is trading at 44, what is the maximum gain?

    A. $100
    B. $500
    C. $1,000
    D. Unlimited

32. Which of the following investors are bearish?

    I. Buyer of a call
    II. Writer of a call
    III. Buyer of a put
    IV. Writer of a put

    A. I and II
    B. I and IV
    C. II and III
    D. III and IV

33. Which of the following statements regarding stock index options are TRUE?

    I. Trades are settled the next business day.
    II. Trades are settled on the third business day.
    III. Exercise settlement involves the delivery of stock.
    IV. Exercise settlement involves the delivery of cash.

    A. I and III
    B. I and IV
    C. II and III
    D. II and IV

34. The holder of a yield-based call option will profit if

    I. rates rise
    II. rates fall
    III. debt prices rise
    IV. debt prices fall

    A. I and III
    B. I and IV
    C. II and III
    D. II and IV

35. A customer who was recently approved to trade options writes an OEX put, which is the initial transaction in the account. The customer fails to return the signed option agreement within 15 days of account approval. Which of the following transactions would the customer be permitted to make?

    A. Opening sale
    B. Closing sale
    C. Opening purchase
    D. Closing purchase

ANSWERS AND RATIONALES

1. **C.** Straddles involve options of different types, but both options must be long or both must be short. They must have the same expiration date and strike price.

2. **D.** The client must have a current OCC disclosure document. The option agreement form must be signed and returned within 15 days of account approval. Any changes in the client's financial status must be updated as soon as possible and the options agreement amended if necessary. OCC approval for an options account is not required nor do they verify any information given by the client.

3. **C.** The option expired because it was out of the money. When the option expires, the writer profits by the amount of the premium received, which is 2.50 (2.50 × 100 = $250).

4. **C.** The breakeven point on a call is calculated by adding the premium to the strike price. Add the premium of 4 to the strike price of 55 to determine the breakeven point of 59. The breakeven point of 59 applies to both buyers and writers of calls.

5. **B.** Once exercised, a contract can no longer be traded to another individual. The exercised party must either deliver the stock in 2 business days (when assigned on a call) or buy the stock in 2 business days (when assigned on a put).

6. **B.** This is a credit spread (more premium was received than was paid). The maximum gain to a seller is the premium received, which is the net credit of 7. In a spread, the maximum gain plus the maximum loss equals the difference in strike prices (75 – 60 = 15): 15 – maximum gain of 7 = maximum loss of 8 × $100, or $800. In a credit spread, the net credit always represents maximum gain. In a debit spread, the net debit always represents maximum loss.

7. **A.** The customer must recover the cost of the premium paid to be at the breakeven. Since this is a short position, the price of the stock must decline 1 point for this to occur. Therefore, the breakeven on this hedged position is found by subtracting the premium of the option from the short sale price of the stock (26 – 1 = 25).

8. **A.** Strategies I and II are debit spreads. An investor wants a debit spread to widen. As the distance between premiums increases, the investor's potential profit also increases. This is because the investor intends to sell the option with the higher premium and buy back the option with the lower premium. With credit spreads, investors profit if the spread between the premiums narrows.

9. **B.** In a call spread, a customer is buying a call and selling a call with different strike prices, expirations, or both. In any spread, one of the options is dominant. In a short call spread, it is the short call position that is dominant because it has the higher premium; writing calls is bearish.

10. **B.** If the investor buys the 55 calls, he has the right to purchase the stock at $55 per share. If exercised, the investor has a 15-point gain less the premium paid.

11. **B.** The maximum loss on a long put is equal to the premium paid for the option. One contract represents 100 shares and the buyer paid a $2 per share premium, which equals $200.

12. **C.** If the investor writes a put, he collects a premium. If the stock price rises, the put expires worthless and the investor keeps the premium. However, if the stock price declines, as the customer anticipates, the put will be exercised, forcing the customer to buy stock at 35. His effective cost of the stock is the breakeven point, which is strike price minus premium.

13. **A.** Because the investor sold the puts for a total of $1,200 to open his position, he must buy the options to close out his position. If he buys when ABC is at 19, the intrinsic value at that time is 6 because puts are in the money when the market price is below the strike price (25 – 19 = 6). He pays a total of $1,800 to close out his three contracts. Because he paid more than he received, he has a loss of $600 on the transaction.

14. **D.** Option contracts exist on foreign currencies, not on the U.S. dollar.

15. **D.** The number of contracts a client is long or short would not affect option premiums. The volatility of the stock, the price of the stock, and the time to expiration are all factors that would affect option premiums.

16. **D.** Puts (long or short) are in the money if the market price is below the strike price. In this case, the put is in the money by 2 points. Because the total premium is 5 points, the time value is 3 points. Remember, option premiums consist of two components: intrinsic value and time value. Once the in the money amount is determined, it is easy to back into time value. Breakeven for puts (long or short) is strike price minus premium.

17. **A.** This is a covered call. The investor has protection in the event the stock drops to the extent of the premium received, and the breakeven is 45.50 (49 – 3.50).

18. **B.** To establish a short straddle, the investor sells a call and sells a put. The short call exposes the investor to unlimited loss potential.

19. **B.** Writing naked calls gives unlimited risk, and writing naked puts results in the puts expiring if the market rises. In the latter case, the writer profits by the premiums received.

20. **A.** Systematic risk is market risk, and the S&P 100 Index (OEX) is a widely used measure of stock market performance.

21. **C.** The customer must receive a current disclosure document either before or at the time that the account receives final approval for option trading.

22. **A.** Exercised stock index options settle on the next business day.

23. **B.** In any spread, both maximum gain and maximum loss are limited. In a short call, gain is limited to the premium received, but loss is unlimited. Short calls and short call spreads are bearish, and both generate premium income. The investor who writes a call spread receives premium income (a short call spread is a credit spread).

24. **C.** The Japanese exporter will be paid in U.S. dollars upon delivery of the equipment. He would be adversely affected if the dollar dropped in value in relation to the yen. Therefore, to protect his position in the dollar from falling against the yen, he should buy calls on his own currency, the yen. Then, if the yen appreciates, his loss on the dollar will be offset by his gain on the calls. Remember, exporters buy puts on the foreign currency to hedge, but there are no options on the U.S. dollar, so the next best strategy is to buy calls on the home currency.

25. **A.** The breakeven point on a put (long or short) is calculated by subtracting the premium from the strike price. Subtract the premium of 4.50 from the strike price of 30 to determine the breakeven point of 25.50.

26. **D.** Uncovered short calls entail unlimited risk.

27. **B.**   A call is in the money whenever the market value of the underlying instrument is above the strike price. The Canadian dollar is currently at $.85, which is above the strike price of $.80, so this call is in the money. The contract does have time value ($.01). Also, the contract is not at parity. Parity means the premium equals the in the money amount.

28. **A.**   A price spread is composed of a long and short option of the same type with the same expiration, but different strike prices. A price spread is also termed a vertical spread.

29. **D.**   When selling a straddle (sale of a call and put with same terms), the customer earns combined premiums. He hopes that the market price will not move and both positions will expire unexercised, so he keeps the premiums.

30. **B.**   This put spread is established at a debit because the customer pays more for the 70 put than he receives for the 60 put; bears buy puts. A debit spread is a net buy, whereas a credit spread is a net sale. Therefore, a debit put spread is like buying a put, which is bearish.

31. **C.**   When writing options, the maximum gain is equal to the premium received. Because there are 10 calls with a premium of $100 each, the maximum gain is 10 × $100, or $1,000.

32. **C.**   Buyers of puts and writers of calls are bearish investors. Buyers of calls and writers of puts are bulls.

33. **B.**   Index option trades settle on the next business day, and cash is delivered upon exercise of the option. Note that exercises of index options also settle on the next business day.

34. **B.**   Holders of yield-based call options profit if rates rise. If rates rise, prices of debt securities fall.

35. **D.**   If a customer fails to return the signed option agreement within 15 days of the account approval, the customer is permitted to make closing transactions only. No opening transactions are allowed. Because the customer opened a position by selling, the only transaction permitted would be a closing purchase.

QUICK QUIZ ANSWERS

Quick Quiz 4.A

1. **A.** A call is exercised when the market price is higher than the strike price.

2. **B.** The seller of a call is required to sell 100 shares of stock at the strike price when the call is exercised. Exercise occurs in this situation because the market price of the stock is greater than the strike price.

3. **A.** The buyer of the call has the right to buy 100 shares of stock at the strike price if he elects to exercise.

Quick Quiz 4.B

1. **B.** Expiration occurs in this situation because the market price of the stock is lower than the strike price. There is no value for the holder in exercising a call with a strike price that is more than the market price.

2. **D.** The seller has no obligation to perform at expiration because the market price of the stock is lower than the strike price. The option will expire, and the seller will keep the premium received without obligation.

3. **C.** Because the market price of the stock is lower than the strike price, the buyer will not exercise the call. The buyer will lose the premium of $450 paid.

Quick Quiz 4.C

1. **B.** A put is exercised when the market price is lower than the strike price. In this situation, the put is not exercised. The buyer will lose the premium; the seller will keep the premium with no obligation.

2. **C.** The put will expire because the market price is greater than the strike price. The seller has no obligation to perform and keeps the premium received.

3. **C.** The buyer of the put will not exercise this put because the market price is higher than the strike price. The buyer will lose the premium of $300.

Quick Quiz 4.D

1. **A.** A put is exercised by the owner of the put when the market price is lower than the strike price. The writer of the put (the premise in this question "short") is obligated to buy 100 shares of XYZ at the strike price of $25 per share when the owner of the put exercises the right to sell the stock at $25 per share.

2. **A.** The put will be exercised because the market price is lower than the strike price. The seller of the put is obligated to buy 100 shares of XYZ at a price of $25.

3. **B.** Because the market price of the stock is lower than the strike price of the put, the buyer will exercise the put. The buyer of the put has the right to sell 100 shares of XYZ at the strike price of $25. The buyer of the put can buy the stock in the marketplace at 20 and exercise his right to sell the stock at 25.

Quick Quiz 4.E

1. **In**   Market price is higher than the strike price.

2. **72**   Strike price + premium

3. **500** Market price is higher than strike price by $5; $5 × 100=$500.

4. **In**   Market price is higher than the strike price.

5. **72**   Strike price + premium

6. **500** With the stock price at 70, a Jan 65 call with a market value of 70 has 5 points of intrinsic value.

7. **Out** Market price is lower than the strike price.

8. **49**   Strike price + premium

9. **0**   Intrinsic value is never negative.

Quick Quiz 4.F

1. **Out**   Market price is higher than the strike price.

2. **63**   Strike price – premium

3. **0**   Intrinsic value is never negative.

4. **Out**   Market price is higher than the strike price.

5. **63**   Strike price – premium

6. **0**   Intrinsic value is never negative.

7. **In**   Market price is lower than the strike price.

8. **37**   Strike price – premium

9. **600**   Market price is lower than the strike price by $6; $6 × 100 shares = $600.

Quick Quiz 4.G

1. $4 intrinsic; $2 time

2. No intrinsic; $2.25 time

3. $6 intrinsic; $1.25 time

4. No intrinsic; $1.15 time

Quick Quiz 4.H

1. **D.**   The maximum gain on a long call is unlimited because, theoretically, there is no limit on a rise in stock price.

2. **A.**   The maximum loss on a long call is equal to the premium paid for the option. One contract represents 100 shares, and the buyer paid a $3.50 per share premium, which equals $350.

3. **A.**   The maximum gain on a short call is equal to the premium received by the seller. One contract represents 100 shares, and the seller received a $3 per share premium, which equals $300.

4. **D.**   The maximum loss on a short call is unlimited because, theoretically, there is no limit on a rise in stock price.

5. **C.**   If the option expires out of the money, the naked call writer keeps the premium. This occurs when the market price stays below the strike price. Breakeven is the strike price plus the premium. If the price rises above this, the naked call writer, when exercised, will lose.

6. **C.**   Call options allow greater leverage than buying the underlying stock, and the capital requirements are smaller, allowing for a smaller loss potential. The fact that options expire (i.e., have a time value that erodes as the option nears expiration) is a disadvantage of options. Stock purchases have no time value component—there is no expiration and therefore no value erosion due to this factor.

7. **C.**   The right to purchase more shares of stock does not provide a hedge against falling prices.

Quick Quiz 4.I

1. **B.**   The maximum gain on a long put is calculated by subtracting the premium from the strike price. Subtract the premium paid of 2 from the strike price of 50 and multiply by the number of shares to determine the maximum potential gain. One contract represents 100 shares, so the buyer's maximum gain is $4,800.

2. **B.**   The maximum loss on a long put is equal to the premium paid for the option. One contract represents 100 shares, and the buyer paid a $2 per share premium, which equals $200.

3. **A.**   The maximum gain on a short put is equal to the premium received by the seller. One contract represents 100 shares, and the seller received a $4.50 per share premium, which equals $450.

4. **B.** The maximum loss on a short put occurs when the stock drops to $0 and is calculated by subtracting the premium from the strike price. Subtract the premium received by the seller of 4.50 from the strike price of 30 to determine the maximum loss of 25.50 per share. One contract represents 100 shares, so the seller's maximum loss is $2,550.

Quick Quiz 4.J

1. **B.** The solution is a calculation, so draw a T-chart.

DR	CR
	3.50
	40
47	
47	43.50
3.50	

1. The position is opened by selling; a credit of the premium is made.

2. The call is exercised. Exercise of a short call requires the investor to sell the stock at the strike price. A credit of 40 must be made to the account.

3. The investor must buy the stock at the current price to have it to sell. A debit of 47 must be made.

2. **B.** The solution is a calculation, so draw a T-chart.

DR	CR
3.50	
63.50	
	65
67	65
2	

1. The position is opened by buying; a debit of the premium of 3.50 is made.

2. The investor buys the stock at the current price; a debit of 63.50 must be made.

3. The put is exercised. Exercise of a long put enables the investor to sell the stock at the strike price. A credit of 65 must be made to the account.

3. **D.** The position is a calculation, so draw a T-chart.

DR	CR
	5.50
95	79
95	84.50
10.50	

1. The position is opened by selling; a credit of the premium is made.

2. The put is exercised. Exercise of a short put requires the investor to buy the stock at the strike price. A debit of 95 must be made to the account.

3. The investor sells the stock at the current price. A credit of 79 must be made.

Quick Quiz 4.K

1. **B.** The customer bought and sold the call for 10, experiencing no gain or loss. Because the stock purchased for $85 was sold for $88, the gain is $300.

DR	CR
	10
85	88
10	
95	98
	3

2. **D.** $600 profit.

DR	CR
9	4
1	
	12
10	16
	6

3. **B.** The opening purchase of the Jul 85 call was made at 5, and the closing sale of that call was made at 2; the difference of 3 represents a $300 loss. The opening purchase of the Jul 90 put was made at 8, and the closing sale of that put was made at 3; the difference of 5 represents a $500 loss. The total loss for the account was $800.

DR	CR
5	
8	
	2 (87 – 85)
	3 (90 – 87)
13	5
8	

With the stock at 87, the intrinsic value of the 85 call is 2 and the intrinsic value of the 90 put is 3.

Quick Quiz 4.L

1. **D.** The customer must recover the cost of the premium paid to be at the breakeven. Since this is a long stock position, the market must advance 3 points for this to occur. Therefore, the breakeven of this hedged position is found by adding the premium of the option to the price of the stock (62 + 3 = 65).

DR	CR
62	
3	
65	

2. **D.** The customer has protected his stock position from downside loss by purchasing the put. If the market rises, the put is not exercised and the unlimited upside potential of the stock is not affected. If the market falls, the put will be exercised, allowing the customer to sell his stock at the option strike price.

3. **B.** The customer has protected his stock position from downside loss by purchasing the put. If the market falls, the put will be exercised, allowing the customer to sell his stock at the option strike price of 60. Therefore, the most the customer can lose is $200 on the stock position (62 – 60), plus the premium paid for the option ($200 + $300 = $500).

DR	CR
62	60
3	
65	60
5	

4. **A.** The customer must recover the cost of the premium paid to be at the breakeven. Because this is a short stock position, the price of the stock must decline 1 point for this to occur. Therefore, the breakeven of this hedged position is found by subtracting the premium of the option from the price of the stock (26 – 1 = 25).

DR	CR
	26
1	
	25

5. **A.** The customer has protected his short stock position from a market advance by buying the call. If the market rises, the call will be exercised, allowing the customer to buy the stock and cover his short position at the option strike price. But because a premium was paid to buy the option, the premium reduces the gain. The maximum gain is the stock price minus the option premium (26 – 1 = 25). On 100 shares, this translates into a $2,500 maximum potential gain, which occurs if the stock becomes worthless.

6. **B.** The customer has protected his short stock position from loss by purchasing a call. If the market rises, the call would be exercised, allowing the customer to buy the stock at the option strike price of 30 to cover the short position. Therefore, the most the customer can lose is $400 on the stock position (the difference between the option strike price and the short sale price), plus the premium paid for the option ($400 + $100 = $500).

DR	CR
	26
30	
1	
31	26
5	

7. **B.** Even if the market falls by 3, the investor has not lost money on his overall position. Therefore, the breakeven of this hedged position is found by subtracting the premium of the option from the price of the stock (62 − 3 = 59).

DR	CR
62	
	3
59	

8. **B.** The customer makes money on the long stock position if the market price of the stock increases. If the stock rises above the strike price of the call, the call will be exercised, requiring the customer to sell his stock at the option strike price and capping the upside potential of the stock position. The premium received adds to the amount of investor profit.

DR	CR
62	
	3
	65
62	68
	6

9. **C.** The customer has protected his stock position from downside loss only by the amount of the premium received from the short call. The investor can lose $5,900 (62 − 3 = 59).

10. **D.** The customer has protected his short stock position from loss by the amount of the premium received from writing the put. The premium does little to offset the unlimited risk of the short stock position. The maximum loss is unlimited in this situation.

11. **D.** This is a ratio write. There are three short calls to only 200 shares. Two of the calls are covered; one is uncovered (naked). This is an inappropriate recommendation for a risk-averse customer.

Quick Quiz 4.M

1. **C.** This is a call spread, so the breakeven point is found by adding the net debit of 1.50 to the lower strike price: 40 + 1.50 = 41.50.

2. **C.** To find the breakeven point on this call credit spread, add the net credit of 3.25 to the lower strike price of 50.

3. **A.** The maximum gain is $300. The maximum potential gain on a credit spread is the net credit. The maximum loss is $700. The maximum potential loss on a credit spread is the difference between the strike prices minus the net credit: 10 − 3 = 7; 7 × 100 shares = $700.

4. **B.** The maximum loss is $525. In a debit spread, the net debit represents maximum loss. To find maximum gain, subtract the maximum loss from the difference between the strike prices.

5. **D.** The maximum gain is $725. The maximum gain on a credit spread is the net credit received. The maximum loss is $275. The maximum loss on a credit spread is the difference between the strike prices minus the net credit: 10 − 7.25 = 2.75; 2.75 × 100 shares = $275.

Quick Quiz 4.N

1. **B.** Choices I and III fit the definition of a call spread because each includes one long and one short option of the same type with either different strike prices or different expiration dates. Choice II involves options of the same type, but both are long. Choice IV involves options of different types.

2. **D.** This is a put spread established at a credit of 2.50. To find the breakeven point on a put spread, subtract the net credit or debit from the higher strike price. (PSH: Puts Subtract from Higher). In this case, subtract the credit of 2.50 from the higher strike price of 35.

3. **C.** The maximum loss on a debit spread is the net debit. The maximum gain on a debit spread is the difference between the strike prices minus the net debit: 10 – 4.25= 5.75; 5.75 × 100 shares = $575. The maximum loss is $425.

4. **A.** Debit spreads are profitable if the spread between the premiums widens.

5. **C.** This is a debit spread that will be profitable if the spread between the premiums widens. If both puts are exercised, the spread is profitable. If the short 50 put is exercised, the customer buys the stock that is then sold for 60 by exercising the long 60 put. The $1,000 profit less $800 paid in premiums equals a net $200 profit.

Quick Quiz 4.O

1. **B.** This put spread is established at a debit because the investor pays more for the 70 put than he receives for the 60 put. Bears buy puts and put spreads. Another easy way to think of this: long the lower strike price is bullish so the investor is short the lower strike price; the position is bearish.

2. **C.** The lower the strike price, the more expensive the call option. The higher the strike price, the more expensive the put option. In answer choice C., the investor has bought the call option with the lower strike price which is the more expensive, so this is a debit spread.

3. **B.** This is a credit put spread. The investor receives more for the Nov 35 put than he paid for the Nov 30 put. Bulls sell put spreads. The put with the higher strike price is more likely to be in the money as the market falls.

4. **B.** This is a debit call spread. Bulls buy calls. A lower strike price call is more likely to be in the money as the market rises.

5. **A.** This is a credit call spread. Bears sell calls.

6. **A.** This is a debit put spread. Bears buy puts. The 60 put is worth more because it has a higher strike price.

7. **B.** This is a debit call spread. Bulls buy calls.

8. **A.** This a debit put spread. Bears buy puts.

9. **B.** This is a credit put spread. Bulls sell puts.

10. **A.** This is a debit put spread. Bears buy puts.

11. **A.** Choices I and II are debit spreads: an investor wants a debit spread to widen. As the distance between the premiums increases, the investor's potential profit also increases.

Quick Quiz 4.P

1. **C.** Straddles involve options of different types, but both options must be long or both must be short. They must have the same expiration date and strike price.

2. **D.** Investors who are unsure of market attitude but expect substantial volatility may profit from buying straddles.

3. **A.** The customer buys calls and puts with the same strike price and expiration date, so the position is a straddle. Straddles have two breakeven points: the strike price plus and minus the sum of the two premiums.

4. **A.** The most common spread, and the one most likely to occur on the Series 7 exam, is the price spread (vertical spread), in which the two options have the same expiration date but different exercise prices.

5. **B.** The investor is long a call and long a put with the same strike price and expiration date; this is a long straddle.

6. **C.** Also called a horizontal or calendar spread, a time spread involves two options with different expiration dates.

7. **F.** A combination is similar to a straddle in that the investor buys or sells a call and a put. With a combination, however, the strike prices, expiration dates, or both are different. This is a long combination.

8. **F.** The investor is selling a call and a put with different strike prices. This is a short combination.

9. **E.** A diagonal spread involves the purchase and sale of two options of the same type with different expiration dates and strike prices.

Quick Quiz 4.Q

1. **D.** If the customer sold either a 500 call or a 505 call, he would have a debit spread because he has purchased the more expensive call—the one with a lower strike price. The customer would create a credit spread by selling the 480 call or the 485 call. Because they have lower strike prices, they would be more expensive than the 490 call.

2. **A.** Because your client is long stock, his position would be hurt by a drop in the market. To hedge against that risk, he must take an option position that appreciates in value as the market declines: long puts or short calls. Because your client also wishes to benefit from any appreciation, the long put is the better hedging vehicle. If the market averages increase, the put position will lose only the premium, and your client could still gain on the portfolio.

3. **C.** Exercise settlement on index options is in cash, not stock. When the owner of an option exercises, the person who has a short position must deliver cash equal to the intrinsic value (the in the money amount). This is computed on the basis of the closing value of the index on the day the option is exercised.

4. **B.** Index option trades settle on the next business day, and cash is delivered upon exercise of the option. Exercise of index options is also on the next business day.

Quick Quiz 4.R

1. **D.** Option contracts exist on foreign currencies, not on the U.S. dollar.

2. **A.** Foreign currency options expire on the third Friday of the expiration month.

3. **A.** The long puts guarantee that the British pounds, when received, can be exercised for a number of U.S. dollars at the strike price.

4. **B.** The investor is bearish on the Canadian dollar. Bears buy puts and write calls and call spreads. Short straddles pay off when the market does not move either way.

5. **C.** Swiss franc options are quoted in cents per unit. One call at 2.5 cents × 10,000 units (.025 × 10,000) = $250. The investor has purchased two contracts, so the total premium is $500.

6. **A.** The customer pays a premium of 1.30 and receives a premium of .50, for a net payment of .80. Multiply the net premium by the number of units in the contract for the answer: 10,000 × .008 (.8 cents) = $80.

Quick Quiz 4.S

1. **B.** The OCC sets standard exercise prices and expiration dates for all listed options, but the premiums that buyers pay for options are determined by the market.

2. **B.** The OCC disclosure document must be given to the customer no later than at the time the account is approved for options trading.

3. **A.** Acting in concert rules apply to position limits and exercise limits. Acting in concert means acting together with knowledge of each other's activities or having one person control a number of accounts.

4. **A.** The expiration dates and strike prices may be different or the same. However, the total number of contracts on the same side of the market on this stock is limited to 25,000. The OCC considers long calls and short puts to be on the same side of the market.

5. **B.** When a company pays a stock dividend or effects a fractional stock split, the number of contracts will remain the same but the number of shares the contract represents increases. The effective strike price will be adjusted accordingly, in this case downward.

6. **C.** Customers must be furnished with options disclosure documents before or at the time their accounts receive a registered options principal's approval.

7. **B.** Equity options cease trading at 4:00 pm ET on the expiration date.

8. **A.** The OCC assigns exercise notices to member firms on a random basis. The members may choose the customers to be exercised on either a random or FIFO basis.

Quick Quiz 4.T

1. **D.** The closing cost of $900 minus $600 opening sale proceeds equals a $300 loss.

2. **C.** Expiration of a short option generates a gain at the time the option expires.

3. **B.** The cost basis of the 100 shares is the total amount the investor spent to acquire them. He paid $300 to buy the call option. When he exercised the call, he purchased 100 shares of FLB at $50 per share, for a total price of $5,000. The cost basis, therefore, is $5,300.

4. **B.** The cost basis is 50 (the price at which the writer must buy) minus 7 (the premium the writer was paid), or $43 per share.

5. **A.** When a call option is exercised, the writer's sale proceeds are equal to the sum of the strike price plus the call premium ($6,000 + $400 = $6,400). The cost basis of the stock is the original purchase price, which equals $5,900. The investor's total gain is $500.

6. **D.** A LEAPS contract has an expiration of more than one year. Upon expiration, the buyer incurs a long-term capital loss equal to the amount of the premium paid.

7. **B.** When the call is exercised, the investor must sell the stock at $70 per share. The investor reports sales proceeds of $7,400 ($7,000 from the sale of stock + $400 premium) and cost basis of $6,700 (the original cost to purchase the stock).

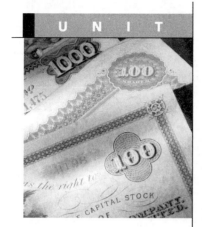

5

Customer Accounts

C ustomer accounts are the foundation of a brokerage business. The customer account is the record of all customer investment activity, and strict recordkeeping requirements apply to all accounts that have been opened.

The customer account serves as the repository for the customer's cash and securities and as a record of the customer's investment objectives and activity. There are many types of accounts, each requiring its own documentation and, in some instances, authorization. All new accounts must be accepted on behalf of the firm by a principal.

Account information is also to be kept in strict confidence. In addition, no one except specifically authorized individuals may make investment decisions for an account.

You can expect to see approximately 15–25 questions on customer accounts on the Series 7 exam. ■

When you have completed this Unit, you should be able to:

■ **describe** the process when opening new accounts;

■ **describe** required brokerage account documentation;

■ **identify** specific account recordkeeping requirements;

■ **define** special procedures for opening accounts for employees of other broker-dealers;

■ **list** discretionary account requirements;

■ **describe** procedures at the death or incompetence of an account holder; and

■ **identify** unique features of custodial accounts.

5. 1   NEW ACCOUNTS

The following procedures must be followed and taken into consideration by a broker-dealer when opening a new account.

5. 1. 1   NEW ACCOUNT FORM

An account opened by a broker-dealer requires a completed **new account form** or new account card.

A registered representative must fill out the following information on all new account forms:

- Full name of each customer who will have access to the account
- Date of birth
- Address and telephone number (business and residence)
- Social Security number if the customer is an individual, or tax identification number if the customer is another legal entity
- Occupation, employer, and type of business
- Citizenship
- Whether the customer is of legal age
- Annual income and net worth (excluding value of primary residence)
- Investment objectives
- Bank and brokerage references
- Whether the customer is an employee of another broker-dealer
- How the account was acquired
- Name and occupation of the person(s) with authority to make transactions in the account
- Signature of the principal or branch manager accepting the account

---

TAKE NOTE   FINRA rules do not require the signatures of the registered representative or the customer on the new account form.

All of the items listed are required by FINRA rules. The Municipal Securities Rulemaking Board (MSRB) also requires the customer's tax status.

5. 1. 1. 1   Customer Information and Suitability

Accounts may be opened by any legally competent person above the age of majority. Legally incompetent individuals may not open accounts.

TAKE NOTE   Rules also require the new account form to identify whether the customer is a director, officer, or shareholder of 10% or more of a publicly traded company. This helps monitor potentially unusual trading activity associated with insiders.

When opening an account, rules generally referred to as the "Know Your Customer" rules require representatives to know all essential facts about a customer's current financial situation, present holdings, risk tolerance, needs, and objectives. Such information should be updated periodically as situations change.

If a customer refuses to provide all information requested, the account may still be opened if the firm believes the customer has the financial resources necessary to support the account. The registered representative can make recommendations only if sufficient information has been given to determine **suitability**. Customers may place transactions that the registered representative considers unsuitable or has not recommended. In this case, the registered representative should mark the order ticket *Unsolicited*. Unmarked order tickets are assumed to be solicited transactions.

5. 1. 1. 2   USA PATRIOT Act of 2001

Under provisions of the USA PATRIOT Act, broker-dealers are required to:

- verify the identity of any new customer;
- maintain records of the information used to verify identity; and
- determine whether the person appears on any list of known or suspected terrorists or terrorist organizations.

These rules are designed to prevent, detect, and prosecute money laundering and the financing of terrorism. Under the Act, financial institutions are encouraged to share information regarding terrorism and money laundering activity.

As part of its customer identification program, a broker-dealer must, before opening an account, obtain at least:

- customer name;
- date of birth;
- physical address (no PO box); and
- Social Security number.

An exception is granted to persons who do not currently have but who have applied for a Social Security number. The firm, in this instance, must obtain the number within a reasonable period of time.

5. 1. 1. 2. 1   Customer Identification Programs (CIPs)

The USA PATRIOT Act requires financial institutions to maintain **Customer Identification Programs (CIPs)** to prevent financing of terrorist operations and money laundering. Financial institutions, such as banks and broker dealers, must keep records of identification information and check customer names against the Specially Designated Nationals (SDN) list maintained by the Office of Foreign Asset Control (OFAC).

5. 1. 1. 2. 2 *Specially Designated Nationals (SDN) List*

The **Office of Foreign Assets Control (OFAC)** publishes and maintains a list of individuals and companies owned or controlled by, or who are acting for, or on behalf of, targeted countries and individuals, groups, or entities that are designated under programs that are not country specific, such as terrorists and those trafficking in narcotics. When individuals or groups appear on the SDN list, their assets are blocked, and U.S. persons and businesses, which include registered representatives and broker dealers, are generally prohibited from dealing with or conducting business with them.

Finally, new customers must be advised, before the account is opened, that the firm is requesting information to verify their identities. This notification may be placed on the firm's website, delivered verbally, or placed on the new account form.

5. 1. 1. 3 Updating Customer Information

To ensure that the information obtained from each new customer is accurate, firms must furnish to each customer, within 30 days of opening the account, a copy of the account record. The firm must include a statement that the customer should mark any corrections on the record and return it along with a statement that the customer should notify the firm of any future changes to information in the account record. Two examples, for instance, of changes that one would expect be noted are changes in employment and financial status. If the customer indicates any changes, the firm must furnish the customer with an updated account record within 30 days of receipt of the notice of change. Furthermore, this account updating must occur at least every 36 months thereafter.

5. 1. 1. 4 Regulation S-P (Privacy Notices)

This regulation was enacted by the SEC to protect the privacy of customer information. In particular, the regulation deals with nonpublic personal information. Examples of nonpublic personal information include a customer's Social Security number, account balances, transaction history, and any information collected through an internet cookie. Your firm must provide a privacy notice describing its privacy policies to customers whenever a new account is opened and annually thereafter.

If your firm reserves the right to disclose to unaffiliated third parties nonpublic personal information, the notice must provide customers a reasonable means to opt out of this disclosure. Reasonable opt-out means include providing customers with a form with check-off boxes along with a prepaid return envelope, providing an electronic means to opt out for customers who have agreed to the electronic delivery of information, and providing a toll-free telephone number. Asking customers to write a letter to express their disclosure preferences or to opt-out would not be considered reasonable under Regulation S-P.

In addition, the regulation embodies the obligation of financial institutions to safeguard customer information as related to all forms of existing and developing technology. For example, this would include, but not be limited to, securing desktop and laptop computers and encrypting email.

5. 1. 1. 5 Account Ownership and Authority

Accounts may be opened with various types of ownership. The principal types of ownership are **individual**, **joint**, **corporate**, and **partnership**.

Accounts may be opened with someone other than the owner having the authority to buy and sell securities on behalf of the owner. This is known as **trading authorization** or **power of attorney**. The primary types of trading authorization are as follows:

- **Discretionary**—a registered representative or other person who has been given written authorization from a customer to make trading decisions for the customer
- **Custodial**—an adult who has been designated to act on behalf of a child, who is the beneficial owner of the account
- **Fiduciary**—a third party who has been legally appointed to prudently manage the account on behalf of another person or entity

5. 1. 2   OPENING NEW ACCOUNTS

Generally, any competent person of age may open an account. Any person declared legally incompetent may not. Fiduciary or custodial accounts may be opened for minors or legally incompetent individuals.

5. 1. 2. 1   Payment and Delivery Instructions

After opening an account, the customer and the registered representative establish payment and delivery instructions. Although these instructions may be changed for individual transactions or at any time to be applied going forward, the customer selects any of the following when initially opening the account.

- **Transfer and ship:** Securities are registered in the customer's name and shipped to them.
- **Transfer and hold in safekeeping:** Securities are registered in the customer's name, and the broker-dealer holds them in safekeeping.
- **Hold in street name:** Securities are registered in the broker-dealer's name and held by the broker-dealer. Although the broker-dealer is the securities' nominal owner, the customer is the beneficial owner.
- **Delivery versus payment (DVP):** DVP securities are delivered to a bank or depository against payment. Normally used for institutional accounts, this is a **cash-on-delivery (COD) settlement**. The broker-dealer must verify the arrangement between the customer and the bank or depository, and the customer must notify the bank or depository of each purchase or sale. In addition, the customer designates whether the broker-dealer should hold or forward any cash balance.

5. 1. 2. 1. 1   Direct Registration System (DRS)

The Direct Registration System (DRS) is an offering of the Depository Trust Company (DTC) that provides registered owners the option of holding their assets on the books and records of the issuer or their transfer agent in book-entry form. An investor electing to hold a security in a DRS book-entry position will receive a statement from the issuer or its transfer agent evidencing ownership of the security. In this light, DRS can offer investors an alternative to having assets registered and held in "street name" or their own name.

Its primary function is to facilitate the direct transfer of assets electronically between transfer agents and broker dealers. Among its benefits are accurate, fast, and cost efficient transfers between issuers and their transfer agents and broker dealers, and the security that comes with electronic transfer as opposed to physical transfer, where paper processing delays, lost certificates, or stolen, forged, or counterfeit certificates can be considered issues of risk.

Instructions to transfer shares are sent via the DRS Profile system, which provides an indemnification against false instructions.

The service is available to issuers who act as their own transfer agent, transfer agents, and Depository Trust Company participants in general. Issuers and transfer agents would apply for DRS eligibility.

5. 1. 2. 2   Mailing Instructions

A customer gives specific mailing instructions when opening a new account. Statements and confirmations may be sent to someone who holds power of attorney for the customer if the customer requests it in writing and if duplicate confirmations are also sent to the customer.

5. 1. 2. 3   Holding Customer Mail

Your firm is permitted to hold mail for a customer (e.g., statements and confirmations) who will not be receiving mail provided that:

- the member firm receives written instructions that include the time period the request is being made for up to three months (requests may be granted for periods longer than three months for an acceptable reason such as safety or security concerns but not merely for the sake of of convenience);
- the member firm informs the customer of any alternate methods that the customer may use to receive or monitor account activity such as email or through the member firm's website (the member must obtain customer confirmation that this information regarding alternate methods was received); and
- the member verifies at reasonable intervals that the customer's instructions still apply.

Additionally, during that time that a member firm is holding mail for a customer, the firm must be able to communicate with the customer in a timely manner to provide important account information. The firm must take actions reasonably designed to ensure that a customer's mail is not tampered with or used in a manner that would violate FINRA rules or federal securities laws.

While holding mail is a courtesy that firms are permitted to extend to customers, the rule does not require them to. If extending the courtesy is consistent with the broker-dealer's in-house rules, the written request by the customer to do so implies that the customer is also giving the broker-dealer permission to do so.

5. 1. 2. 4   Instructions From Customers by Email

All firms are required to establish, maintain, and enforce written supervisory control policies and procedures for reviewing and monitoring the transmittal of funds or securities. Specifically regarding instructions from customers sent to a firm by email, FINRA recommends that such policies and procedures should:

- include a method for verifying that the email was in fact sent by the customer; and
- be designed to identify and respond to "red flags," including transfer requests that are out of the ordinary, requests that funds be transferred to an unfamiliar third party account, or requests that indicate urgency or otherwise appear designed to deter verification of the transfer instructions.

Additionally, firms must train their employees to follow all applicable policies and procedures rigorously.

5. 1. 3   TYPES OF ACCOUNTS

5. 1. 3. 1   Cash Accounts

A **cash account** is the basic investment account. Anyone eligible to open an investment account can open a cash account. In a cash account, a customer pays in full for any securities purchased.

Certain accounts must be opened as cash accounts, such as personal retirement accounts (individual retirement accounts, Keoghs, and tax-sheltered annuities), corporate retirement accounts, and custodial accounts (Uniform Gift to Minors Act and Uniform Transfers to Minors Act accounts).

TEST TOPIC ALERT   When opening a cash account, the only signature required is that of the principal accepting the account. Neither the registered representative nor the customer are required to sign the new account agreement. By contrast, if the account to be opened is a margin account, the customer's signature is required on the margin agreement.

5. 1. 3. 2   Margin Accounts

A **margin account** allows a customer to borrow money for investing. The term **margin** refers to the minimum amount of cash or marginable securities a customer must deposit to buy securities. Margin accounts will be discussed in detail in the following Unit.

5. 1. 3. 3   Corporate Accounts

A registered representative who opens a corporate account must establish:

- the business's legal right to open an investment account;
- an indication of any limitations that the owners, the stockholders, a court, or any other entity has placed on the securities in which the business can invest; and
- who will represent the business in transactions involving the account.

When opening an account for a corporation, a firm must obtain a copy of the corporate charter as well as a corporate resolution. The charter is proof that the corporation does exist and the resolution authorizes both the opening of the account and the officers designated to enter orders.

5. 1. 3. 4   Fee-Based Accounts

Many firms offer investors fee-based accounts that charge a single fee (either fixed or a percentage of assets in the account) instead of commission-based charges for brokerage services. Fee-based accounts are not wrap accounts. Wrap accounts are accounts for which firms provide a group of services, such as asset allocation, portfolio management, executions, and administration, for a single fee. Wrap accounts are generally investment advisory accounts.

Fee-based accounts are appropriate only for investors who engage in at least a moderate level of trading activity. Accounts with a low level of trading activity may be better off with commission-based charges. Rules require that, before opening a fee-based account, investors be given a disclosure document describing the services to be provided and the cost.

5. 1. 3. 5   Prime Brokerage Accounts

A prime brokerage account is one in which a customer, generally an institution, selects one member firm (the prime broker) to provide custody and other services, while other firms, called executing brokers, handle all trades placed by the customer.

To open a prime brokerage account for a customer, a member (the prime broker) must sign an agreement with the customer spelling out the terms of the agreement as well as names of all executing brokers the customer has contracted with. The prime broker will then enter into written agreements with each executing broker named by the customer. The customer receives trade confirmations and account statements from the prime broker, who facilitates the clearance and settlement of the securities transactions. Responsibility for compliance of certain trading rules rests with the executing brokers.

The key advantage of a prime brokerage account is that it usually provides a client with the ability to trade with multiple brokerage houses while maintaining a centralized master account with all of the client's cash and securities. A prime brokerage account often includes a list of specialized services, such as securities lending, margin financing, trade processing, cash management, and operational support. Prime brokerage accounts are likely to be offered to a broker-dealer's more active trading clients, like hedge funds for example, who may require a number of executing broker outlets to conduct their transactions and who can benefit by having margin requirements that are netted across all of the prime broker's positions.

5. 1. 4   SPECIAL ACCOUNT SITUATIONS

Sometimes, account owners request that their accounts be handled in a special manner. The most commonly requested situations are numbered accounts, multiple accounts, and account transfers.

5. 1. 4. 1   Numbered Accounts

At a customer's request, his account may be identified by only a number or symbol. The customer must sign a form certifying that he owns the account(s) identified by the number or symbol and must supply other information identifying himself as the owner.

EXAMPLE   Celebrities sometimes use numbered accounts to preserve anonymity.

5. 1. 4. 2 Multiple Accounts

A customer who has both a cash and a margin account is considered to have only one account. If a customer wishes to open more than one individual account with a broker-dealer, the representative must get a statement from the customer attesting that no one else has any interest in the second and subsequent accounts and that each account unreservedly guarantees the others. These are sometimes called **guaranteed accounts**.

5. 1. 4. 3 Account Transfers

To transfer a customer's account from one broker-dealer to another, a customer submits transfer instructions to the new broker-dealer. The transfer instructions are then sent to the firm currently carrying the account. The firm has one business day to **validate** or to **take exception** to the transfer instructions. The firm may take exception to the transfer instructions if the account number is invalid, the Social Security number on the instruction does not match, the account title does not match, or the customer's signature is improper. The firm may not take exception solely because of a dispute about the value of the cash or securities in the account.

Transfer instructions are validated when the current firm returns them to the new firm with an attachment detailing the customer's securities positions. The account is then **frozen**, except for options expiring within seven business days. Account transfers must be completed within three business days of validation. Once the transfer instructions are validated by the current firm, any orders to buy or sell must be placed with the new firm, even though the positions, securities, and cash may still be in the possession of the current firm.

TAKE NOTE   Broker-to-broker transfers can be accomplished via the Automated Customer Account Transfer Service (ACATS). When using this service to communicate instructions on form ACAT, both validation and transfer can occur. Once the receiving broker has received written instructions from the customer regarding the positions to be transferred, the receiving broker must immediately submit the instructions to the carrying firm member through the ACATS service using form ACAT.

5. 1. 5   OPENING ACCOUNTS FOR OTHER BROKERS' EMPLOYEES

Regulatory bodies have rules and special procedures regarding the establishment of accounts for certain individuals, including:

■ employees of broker-dealers; and

■ spouses or minor children of broker-dealer employees.

5. 1. 5. 1   FINRA Requirements

The FINRA rule requires that a person associated with a member, before opening an account or placing an initial securities order with another member, notify the employer and the executing member (where the new account is to be maintained), in writing, of her association with the other member.

Before the account can be opened, the employing FINRA member firm must grant written permission. Prior written consent from the employer is specified within the rule.

Upon written request from the employing member firm, the executing member must supply to the employing member duplicate copies of confirmations, account statements, or any other account information requested.

5. 1. 5. 2   MSRB Requirements

The MSRB does not require an employee of a member firm to obtain prior permission from the employer to open an account with another firm. However, the broker-dealer must notify the employer in writing that the account is being opened and must supply the employer with duplicate confirmations and any other account documentation if requested such as account statements.

SRO Notification and Confirmation Requirements

Rule	Margin Account	Cash Account	Duplicate Confirm
FINRA	Written notification and permission	Written notification and permission	Upon written request
MSRB	Notification (not permission)	Notification (not permission)	■ Must supply confirms ■ Other account information if requested

TEST TOPIC ALERT

Testable points include the following.

■ A principal must approve every new account opened for the firm.

■ Account approval does not have to take place before the first trade; it can be done promptly after the completion of the first transaction.

■ In account transfers, the firm has one day to validate positions and three more days to complete the transfer. (Assume business days any time the number is less than 30.)

■ Cash accounts are sometimes called special cash accounts. Before the crash of 1929, margin accounts were the normal type of account opened. Because cash accounts were unusual, they were referred to as "special."

QUICK QUIZ 5.A

1. An employee of another FINRA member broker-dealer would like to open an account with your firm. All of the following statements regarding the employee and the account are true EXCEPT

   A. the employer must receive duplicate copies of all trade confirmations if requested
   B. notification to and prior written consent from the employing member is needed for a cash account
   C. notification to and prior written consent from the employing member is needed for a margin account
   D. the broker-dealer holding the account must approve each transaction made by the person before entry of the order

2. A registered representative is permitted to open all of the following customer accounts EXCEPT

   A. an individual account opened by the individual's spouse
   B. a minor's account opened by a custodian
   C. a corporate account opened by the designated officer
   D. a partnership account opened by the designated partner

3. A registered representative who receives instructions from a customer to transfer and ship will instruct the margin department to transfer ownership into

   A. the customer's name and deliver the securities to the customer
   B. the brokerage firm's name and deliver the securities to the customer
   C. the brokerage firm's name and deliver the securities to the brokerage firm's commercial bank for safekeeping
   D. the customer's name and deliver the securities to the customer's bank for safekeeping

4. Which of the following must sign a new account form?

   I. Principal
   II. Registered representative
   III. Customer
   IV. Spouse of the customer

   A. I only
   B. I, II and III
   C. II and III
   D. I, II, III and IV

Quick Quiz answers can be found at the end of the Unit.

5. 2 ACCOUNT DESIGNATIONS

There are different designations for accounts held at broker-dealers, including how the account is registered in name or whether it is a cash or margin account.

5. 2. 1   ACCOUNT REGISTRATION

When an account is opened, it is **registered** in the name(s) of one or more persons. These persons are the account owners and the only individuals allowed access to and control of the investments in the account.

5. 2. 1. 1   Single Accounts

A **single account** has one beneficial owner. The account holder is the only person who can control the investments within the account and request distributions of cash or securities from the account.

5. 2. 1. 1. 1   Transfer on Death (TOD)

This is an account that allows the registered owner of the account to pass all or a portion of it, upon death, to a named beneficiary. This account avoids probate (having the decedent's will declared genuine by a court of law) because the estate is bypassed. However, the assets in the account do not avoid estate tax, if applicable.

TAKE NOTE
Naming beneficiaries requires the account holder to complete a beneficiary form supplied by the financial institution holding the account.

5. 2. 1. 2   Joint Accounts

In a **joint account**, two or more adults are named on the account as co-owners, with each allowed some form of control over the account.

In addition to the appropriate new account form, a **joint account agreement** must be signed, and the account must be designated as either **tenants in common (TIC)** or **joint tenants with right of survivorship (JTWROS)**.

The account forms for joint accounts require the signatures of all owners. Both types of joint account agreements provide that any or all tenants may transact business in the account. Checks must be made payable to the names in which the account is registered and endorsed for deposit by all tenants, although mail need be sent to only a single address. To be in **good delivery form**, securities sold from a joint account must be signed by all tenants.

5. 2. 1. 2. 1   Tenants in Common

TIC ownership provides that a deceased tenant's fractional interest in the account is retained by that tenant's estate and is not passed to the surviving tenant(s).

5. 2. 1. 2. 2 *Joint Tenants with Right of Survivorship*

JTWROS ownership stipulates that a deceased tenant's interest in the account passes to the surviving tenant(s).

TEST TOPIC ALERT

- JTWROS—all parties have an undivided interest in the account

- TIC—each party must specify a percentage interest in the account

Checks or distributions must be made payable to all parties and endorsed by all parties.

5. 2. 1. 2. 3 *Community Property*

Community property is a marital property classification recognized by some, but not all, states. In these jurisdictions, most property acquired during the marriage is considered to be owned jointly by both spouses and would be divided at the time of divorce, annulment, or death. Joint ownership is therefore automatically presumed by law in these jurisdictions, absent of any specific evidence that would point to a contrary conclusion for any item of ownership. Exceptions are made for inheritances, gifts, or any property that is owned by one spouse prior to marriage, which is considered the separate property of that spouse, unless it was designated to be owned jointly by both spouses during the marriage.

It is important to know that laws in jurisdictions where community property is presumed differ from state to state. Additionally, community property can have certain federal tax implications. Generally, community property may result in lower federal capital gains taxes after the death of one spouse when the property is dissolved by the surviving spouse. Some states have created separate classifications called "community property with rights of survivorship" that are similar to joint tenancy with rights of survivorship property designations.

5. 2. 1. 3 Partnership Accounts

A **partnership** is an unincorporated association of two or more individuals. Partnerships frequently open cash, margin, retirement, and other types of accounts necessary for business purposes.

The partnership must complete a **partnership agreement** stating which of the partners can make transactions for the account. If the partnership opens a margin account, the partnership must disclose any investment limitations.

An amended partnership agreement must be obtained each year if changes have been made. A partnership agreement is similar to a corporate resolution.

5. 2. 1. 4 Fiduciary and Custodial Accounts

When securities are placed in a **fiduciary**, or **custodial**, **account**, a person other than the owner initiates trades. The most familiar example of a fiduciary account is a **trust account**. Money or securities are placed in trust for one person, often a minor, but someone else manages the account. The manager or trustee is a fiduciary.

In a fiduciary account, the investments exist for the owner's beneficial interest, yet the owner has little or no legal control over them. The fiduciary makes all of the investment, management, and distribution decisions and must manage the account in the owner's best interests. The fiduciary may not use the account for his own benefit, although he may be reimbursed for reasonable expenses incurred in managing the account.

Securities bought in a custodial account must be registered in such a way that the custodial relationship is evident.

EXAMPLE

Marilyn Johnson, the donor, has appointed her daughter's aunt, Barbara Wood, as custodian for the account of her minor daughter, Alexis. The account and the certificates would read "Barbara Wood as custodian for Alexis Johnson."

The beneficial owner's Social Security number is used on the account.

A **fiduciary** is any person legally appointed and authorized to represent another person, act on his behalf, and make whatever decisions are necessary to the prudent management of his account. Fiduciaries include a(n):

- trustee designated to administer a trust;

- executor designated in a decedent's will to manage the affairs of the estate;

- administrator appointed by the courts to liquidate the estate of a person who died intestate (without a will);

- guardian designated by the courts to handle a minor's affairs until the minor reaches the age of majority or to handle an incompetent person's affairs;

- custodian of an UGMA or UTMA account;

- receiver in a bankruptcy; and

- conservator for an incompetent person.

Any trades the fiduciary enters must be compatible with the investment objectives of the underlying entity.

5. 2. 1. 4. 1   Opening a Fiduciary Account

Opening a fiduciary account may require a court certification of the individual's appointment and authority. An account for a trustee must include a **trust agreement** detailing the limitations placed on the fiduciary. No documentation of custodial rights or court certification is required for an individual acting as the custodian for an UGMA or UTMA account.

The registered representative for a fiduciary account must be aware of the following rules.

- Proper authorization must be given—the necessary court documents must be filed with and verified by the broker-dealer.

- Speculative transactions are generally not permitted.

- Margin accounts are only permitted if authorized by the legal documents establishing the fiduciary accounts.

- The **prudent investor** rule requires fiduciaries to make wise and safe investments.

- Many states publish a **legal list** of securities approved for fiduciary accounts.

- A fiduciary may not share in an account's profits but may charge a reasonable fee for services.

5. 2. 1. 5   Power of Attorney

If a person not named on an account will have trading authority, the customer must file written authorization with the broker-dealer giving that person access to the account. This trading authorization usually takes the form of a power of attorney. Two basic types of trading authorizations are full and limited powers of attorney. Both would be cancelled upon the death of either party.

5. 2. 1. 5. 1   Full Power of Attorney

A **full power of attorney** allows someone who is not the owner of an account to:

■ deposit or withdraw cash or securities; and

■ make investment decisions for the account owner.

Custodians, trustees, guardians, and other people filling similar legal duties are often given full powers of attorney.

5. 2. 1. 5. 2   Limited Power of Attorney

A **limited power of attorney** allows an individual to have some, but not total, control over an account. The document specifies the level of access the person may exercise. Limited power of attorney, also called **limited trading authorization**, allows the entering of buy and sell orders but no withdrawal of assets. Entry of orders and withdrawal of assets is allowed if full power of attorney is granted.

TEST TOPIC ALERT   A **durable** power of attorney (POA) will survive a declaration of mental incompetence.

5. 2. 2   DISCRETIONARY ACCOUNTS

An account set up with preapproved authority for a registered representative to make transactions without having to ask for specific approval is a **discretionary account**. **Discretion** is defined as the authority to decide:

■ what security;

■ the number of shares or units; or

■ whether to buy or sell.

Discretion does not apply to decisions regarding the timing of an investment or the price at which it is acquired.

EXAMPLE   An order from a customer worded "Buy 100 shares of ABC for my account whenever you think the price is right" is not a discretionary order.

5. 2. 2. 1   Discretionary Authority

A customer can give discretionary power over his account(s) only by filing a **trading authorization** or a limited power of attorney with the broker-dealer. No transactions of a discretionary nature can take place without this document on file. Once authorization has been given, the customer is legally bound to accept the decision made by the person holding discretionary authority, although the customer may continue to enter orders on his own.

5. 2. 2. 2   Regulation of Discretionary Accounts

In addition to requiring the proper documentation, discretionary accounts are subject to the following rules.

- Each discretionary order must be identified as such at the time it is entered for execution.
- An officer or a partner of the brokerage house must approve each order promptly and in writing, but not necessarily before order entry.
- A record must be kept of all transactions.
- No excessive trading, or **churning**, may occur in the account relative to the size of the account and the customer's investment objectives.
- To safeguard against the possibility of churning, a designated supervisor or manager must review all trading activity frequently and systematically.

5. 2. 2. 3   Discretionary Accounts and Non Conventional Investments

Non Conventional Investments (NCIs) are alternative investments that do not fit a common category. Examples would include the following.

- **Hedge funds:** Aggressively managed and unregulated portfolio of investments that uses advanced investment strategies.
- **Distressed debt:** Debt instruments of companies that have declared bankruptcy or are considering declaring bankruptcy.
- **Equity-linked notes (ELNs):** A debt instrument where the final payment at maturity is based on the return of a single stock, a basket of stocks or an equity index.

FINRA is concerned that retail investors do not fully understand the risks associated with these NCIs. Accordingly, FINRA requires members that sell these products to conduct the appropriate due diligence. Regarding discretionary accounts and these products, appropriate due diligence may require members to receive prior written consent before purchasing them.

TEST TOPIC ALERT   If you are having difficulty identifying a discretionary order, try this method: An order is discretionary if any one of the **three As** is missing. The three As are:

- activity (buy or sell);
- amount (number of shares); and
- asset (the security).

EXAMPLE   If a customer asks a representative to sell 1,000 shares of XYZ stock, the order is not discretionary even though the customer did not specifically say when or at what price.

Activity = sell

Amount = 1,000 shares

Asset = XYZ stock

All three As were defined.

However, if a customer asks a representative to buy 1,000 shares of the best computer company stock available, the order is discretionary. The asset is missing because the company was not defined.

EXAMPLE   A customer wishes to buy 1,000 shares of XYZ whenever you think he can get the best price. The order is nondiscretionary. The three As were all defined. Omitting the time or price does not make an order discretionary.

Any order for which the customer gives you authority over price or time, as above, is not discretionary. Rather, it is termed a **market not held** order. In other words, you are not held to secure a specific price for the order. Market not held orders must be executed on the day received (day orders) unless the customer has given written instructions to the contrary.

5. 2. 3   DEATH OF AN ACCOUNT HOLDER

With regard to individual accounts, once a firm becomes aware of the death of the account owner, the firm must cancel all open orders, mark the account *Deceased,* and freeze the assets in the account until receiving instructions and the necessary documentation from the executor of the decedent's estate. If the account has a third-party power of attorney, the authorization is revoked.

TAKE NOTE   Discretionary authority ends at the death of the account owner.

Depending on the type of account, the documents necessary to release the assets of a decedent are:

■ a certified copy of the death certificate;

■ inheritance tax waivers; and

■ letters testamentary.

If one party in a JTWROS account dies, the account cannot be transferred to the name of the new owner (the other party) until a certified copy of the death certificate is presented to the member firm. The other documents noted above are not needed to transfer ownership at death in a JTWROS account.

If one party in a TIC account dies, the decedent's interest in the account goes to his estate. The executor for the decedent must present the proper documents before the assets belonging to the decedent can be released. In some states, the death of a tenant in a TIC account requires that the executor present an affidavit of domicile to the member that shows the decedent's estate will be handled under the laws of that state.

Also note that in TIC accounts, the death of a tenant requires that the member firm freeze the account and acceptance of orders until the required documents are presented. Compare this with a JTWROS account, for which the death of one tenant does not preclude the remaining tenant from entering orders.

With regard to partnership accounts, if one partner dies, the member needs written authority from the remaining partners before executing any further orders. This written authorization generally takes the form of an amended partnership agreement.

TEST TOPIC ALERT

Three basic steps apply at the death of a customer:

- Cancel open orders

- Freeze the account (mark it *deceased*)

- Await instructions from the executor of the estate

5. 3 UNIFORM GIFT AND UNIFORM TRANSFERS TO MINORS ACT

Uniform Gift to Minors Act (UGMA) and **Uniform Transfers to Minors Act (UTMA)** accounts require an adult to act as custodian for a minor (the beneficial owner). Any kind of security or cash may be given to the account without limitation.

Under UGMA, when the minor reaches the age of majority, the property in the account is transferred into the name of the new adult. Under UTMA, the custodian can withhold transfer of property in the account until the new adult reaches age 25 (21 in some states).

5. 3. 1 CHARACTERISTICS OF CUSTODIAL ACCOUNTS

5. 3. 1. 1 Donating Securities

When a person makes a gift of securities to a minor under the UGMA or UTMA laws, that person is the **donor** of the securities. A gift under these acts conveys an **indefeasible title**; that is, the donor may not take back the gift, nor may the minor return the gift. Once the gift is donated, the donor gives up all rights to the property.

5. 3. 1. 2 Custodian

Any securities given to a minor through an UGMA or UTMA account are managed by a **custodian** until the minor reaches the age of majority. The custodian has full control over the minor's account and can:

- buy or sell securities;

- exercise rights or warrants; or
- liquidate, trade, or hold securities.

The custodian may also use the property in the account in any way deemed proper for the minor's support, education, maintenance, general use, or benefit. However, the account is not normally used to pay expenses associated with raising a child because the parents can incur negative tax consequences.

Registered representatives must know the following rules of custodial accounts.

- An account may have only one custodian and one minor or beneficial owner.
- Only an individual can be a custodian for a minor's account.
- A minor can be the beneficiary of more than one account, and a person may serve as custodian for more than one account as long as each account benefits only one minor.
- The donor of securities can act as custodian or can appoint someone else to do so.
- Unless they are acting as custodians, parents have no legal control over a custodial account or the securities in it.

5. 3. 1. 3   Opening a Custodial Account

When opening a custodial account, a representative must ensure that the account application contains the custodian's name, the minor's name and Social Security number, and the state in which the account is registered.

5. 3. 1. 4   Registration of Custodial Securities

Any securities in a custodial account are registered in the custodian's name for the benefit of the minor; they cannot be registered in street name. Typically, the securities are registered to "Joan Smith as custodian for Brenda Smith," for example, or a variation of this form.

5. 3. 1. 5   Fiduciary Responsibility

A custodian is charged with **fiduciary responsibilities** in managing the minor's account. Certain restrictions have been placed on what is deemed to be proper handling of the investments in these accounts. The most important limitations follow.

- Custodial accounts may be opened and managed as cash accounts only.
- A custodian may not purchase securities in an account on margin or pledge them as collateral for a loan.
- A custodian must reinvest all cash proceeds, dividends, and interest within a reasonable time. Cash proceeds from sales or dividends may be held in a non-interest bearing custodial account for a reasonable period but should not remain idle for long.
- Investment decisions must take into account a minor's age and the custodial relationship. Commodities futures, naked options, and other high-risk securities are examples of inappropriate investments. Options may not be bought in a custodial account because no evidence of ownership is issued to an options buyer. Covered call writing is normally allowed.
- Stock subscription rights or warrants must be either exercised or sold if they have any value.

- A custodian cannot delegate away fiduciary responsibility but can grant trading authority and investment decisions to a qualified third party.
- A custodian may loan money to an account but cannot borrow from it.

A custodian may be reimbursed for any reasonable expenses incurred in managing the account unless the custodian is also the donor.

5. 3. 1. 6   Taxation

The minor's Social Security number appears on a custodial account, and the minor must file an annual income tax return and pay taxes on any investment income produced by the account at the parent's tax rate until the minor reaches the age of 18, and in the case of full time students, until the age of 24. Exclusions are available, and they are indexed for inflation.

TAKE NOTE   When the minor reaches age 18, the account will be taxed at the minor's tax rate.

Although the minor is the account's beneficiary and is responsible for any and all taxes on the account, in most states, it is the parent's or legal guardian's responsibility to see that the taxes are paid.

5. 3. 1. 7   Death of the Minor

If the beneficiary of a custodial account dies, the securities in the account pass to the minor's estate, not to the parents' or custodian's estate.

5. 3. 1. 8   Death of the Custodian

In the event of the custodian's death or resignation, either a court of law or the donor must appoint a new custodian.

QUICK QUIZ 5.B

1. Which of the following persons are considered fiduciaries?

    I.   Executor of an estate
    II. Administrator of a trust
    III. Custodian of an UGMA/UTMA account
    IV. Conservator for a legally incompetent person

    A. I and II
    B. I, II and III
    C. III and IV
    D. I, II, III and IV

2. If a customer would like to open a custodial UGMA or UTMA account for his nephew, a minor, the uncle

   A. can open the account provided the proper trust arrangements are filed first
   B. can open the account and name himself custodian
   C. needs a legal document evidencing the nephew's parents' approval of the account
   D. can be custodian for the account only if he is also the minor's legal guardian

3. All of the following statements regarding customer accounts are true EXCEPT

   A. stock held in a custodial account may not be held in street name
   B. the customer who opens a numbered account must sign a statement attesting to ownership
   C. stock held under JTWROS goes to the survivor(s) in the event of the death of one of the tenants
   D. margin trading in a fiduciary account does not require any special consideration

4. Which of the following individuals may NOT open a joint account?

   A. Two spouses
   B. Three sisters
   C. Two strangers
   D. Parent and a minor

5. Securities owned by a donor and given to a minor under the Uniform Gift to Minors Act become the property of the minor

   A. when the securities are paid for by the minor
   B. on the settlement date
   C. when the securities are registered in the custodian's name for the benefit of the minor
   D. when the donor decides to give the securities to the minor

UNIT TEST

1. If a customer wishes to open a numbered account, you should inform him that
   A. it may be opened only with prior permission from the SEC
   B. numbered accounts are restricted to cash accounts
   C. he will have to supply a written statement attesting to his ownership of the account
   D. he will have to supply proof of U.S. citizenship and reside permanently in the United States

2. Which of the following occurs in a partnership account if one partner dies?
   A. The surviving partners receive the deceased partner's share.
   B. The account is frozen until an amended partnership agreement is received.
   C. The surviving partners are considered joint tenants.
   D. The surviving partners are considered joint tenants and receive the deceased partner's share.

3. Three individuals have a tenants in common account with your firm. If one individual dies, which of the following statements is TRUE?
   A. The account must be liquidated and the proceeds split evenly among the two survivors and the decedent's estate.
   B. Two survivors continue as cotenants with the decedent's estate.
   C. Trading is discontinued until the executor names a replacement for the deceased.
   D. The account is converted to joint tenants with rights of survivorship (JTWROS).

4. Who must sign a new account form for a cash account?
   A. Principal only
   B. Registered representative and principal
   C. Registered representative and customer
   D. Customer only

5. A dealer must use special procedures whenever it opens a municipal securities account for
   A. a clerical employee of another dealer
   B. the spouse of a trader employed by another dealer
   C. the minor child of an operations supervisor employed by another dealer
   D. all of the above

6. Which of the following would be considered discretionary?
   A. Order that specifies the size of the trade and name of the security but leaves the choice of price and time up to the registered representative
   B. Account in which the broker has the power to decide when and what to trade, without specific customer authorization for those trades
   C. Joint account with right of survivorship
   D. Joint tenants in common account

7. One of your clients dies. Upon notification of the death, you should immediately do all of the following EXCEPT
   A. mark the account *Deceased* until proper documents are received
   B. obtain the names of beneficiaries of the estate for the purpose of notification
   C. cancel all GTC orders for the account
   D. cancel all day orders for the account

8. Under which of the following circumstances may a gift given to a minor under UGMA or UTMA be revoked?
   A. At any time before the minor reaches the age of majority
   B. If the minor dies before reaching the age of majority
   C. If the custodian dies before the minor reaches the age of majority
   D. Under no circumstances

9. The documents required to open a cash account for a customer and give a sibling trading authorization include

    I. a new account form
    II. a loan consent agreement
    III. a customer margin agreement
    IV. a limited power of attorney

    A. I and III
    B. I and IV
    C. II and III
    D. II and IV

10. Which of the following are fiduciaries?

    I. Executor of an estate
    II. Administrator of a trust
    III. Custodian of an UGMA account
    IV. Registered representative granted the authority to choose the security, quantity, and action in a customer's account

    A. I and II
    B. I, II and III
    C. II, III and IV
    D. I, II, III and IV

11. For custodial accounts, all of the following statements are true EXCEPT

    A. an UGMA account may have only one custodian for only one minor
    B. only an adult can make a gift to a minor
    C. the maximum amount of money an adult can give to a minor in any one year is limited
    D. once a gift is given to a minor, it cannot be reclaimed

12. An employee of another broker-dealer would like to open an account with your firm. Under FINRA rules, all of the following statements regarding the employee and the account are true EXCEPT

    A. the employer must receive duplicate copies of all transactions made in the account if requested
    B. prior notice to the employer is needed for a cash account
    C. prior notice to the employer is needed for a margin account
    D. the broker-dealer holding the account must approve each transaction made by the person before entry of the order

13. A new account is opened joint tenants with rights of survivorship. All of the following statements are true EXCEPT

    A. orders may be given by either party
    B. mail can be sent to either party with the permission of the other party
    C. checks can be drawn in the name of either party
    D. in the event of death, the decedent's interest in the account goes to the other party

14. All of the following information must be obtained from new customers EXCEPT

    A. employer name and address
    B. date of birth
    C. educational background
    D. citizenship

15. All of the following are true of custodial accounts EXCEPT

    A. the account should contain the Social Security number of the minor
    B. securities in a custodial account may be kept in street name
    C. custodial property may be used for support of the minor
    D. only an adult may make a gift under the act

ANSWERS AND RATIONALES

1. **C.** Numbered or symbol accounts require a signed, written statement from the client to be kept on file. This type of account is opened for anonymity, not tax evasion.

2. **B.** Upon a partner's death, a partnership account is automatically frozen until an amended partnership agreement is received. The deceased partner's share usually goes to an estate; the other partners do not receive it.

3. **B.** The decedent's estate becomes a tenant in common with the survivors.

4. **A.** To open a cash account, only the signature of the principal accepting the account is required. For margin accounts, the signature of the customer is required on the margin agreement.

5. **D.** The firm must follow special procedures whenever it opens an account for the employee of another broker-dealer. The firm must give the employing broker-dealer written notice that it is opening the account. Also, the firm must send copies of all confirmations to the employer.

6. **B.** An order is discretionary when it is placed by the member firm or its representative for a customer's account without the customer's express authorization for that order. Also, for the order to be considered discretionary, the firm must choose more than just the price or time of execution; that is, the size of the trade, whether to buy or sell, or the security must be chosen by the firm.

7. **B.** The account registered representative should cancel all open orders and mark the account *Deceased*. The firm should not permit any trades until proper documents are received from the estate representative. It is not the responsibility of the firm to contact the decedent's attorney or the beneficiaries.

8. **D.** The Uniform Gift and Uniform Transfer to Minors Acts state that all gifts to minors are irrevocable.

9. **B.** If one party wants to give discretionary privileges to a third party in a cash account, a member firm requires a new account form and a limited power of attorney. A limited power of attorney gives the third party trading authority but prohibits that party from withdrawing cash or securities from the account.

10. **D.** Each of these has a fiduciary relationship to the customer and is required to act prudently in the customer's best interest.

11. **C.** Any adult can give a gift to a minor in a custodial account, and there is no limitation on the size of the gift. There is, however, a limitation regarding the gift tax exclusion, which is subject to change in accordance with current tax law.

12. **D.** The FINRA rule does not require prior approval of individual transactions by the broker-dealer at which the account has been opened.

13. **C.** Although either party may enter an order, any money or securities delivered out of the account must be in the names of both owners.

14. **C.** A customer's educational background need not be ascertained when opening an account.

15. **B.** All custodial account securities must be registered in the formal designation *custodian for a minor*. They can never be kept in street name.

QUICK QUIZ ANSWERS

Quick Quiz 5.A

1. **D.** The broker-dealer has no obligation to approve every transaction before entry.

2. **A.** A representative is not permitted to open an individual account in the name of another individual, even in the name of a spouse.

3. **A.** Transfer and ship means to transfer the securities into the name of the customer and ship (deliver) the securities to the customer. Hold in street name would require the securities to be transferred into the name of the broker-dealer and held for safekeeping.

4. **A.** To open a cash account, only the signature of the principal accepting (approving) the account is required. For margin accounts, the signature of the customer is required on the margin agreement. The signature of the spouse is required only for a joint account.

Quick Quiz 5.B

1. **D.** All of the persons listed have fiduciary responsibilities because of the authority with which they are entrusted.

2. **B.** The donor may name himself the custodian of an UGMA or UTMA account. No documentation of custodial status is required to open a custodial account, and the custodian is not required to be the minor's legal guardian.

3. **D.** Trading on margin is prohibited in fiduciary accounts except with the appropriate documentation.

4. **D.** A minor may not be a party in a joint account because a minor cannot legally exercise control over the account. A custodial account should be set up for the minor.

5. **C.** Transfer of securities into the custodial account completes the gift. At that time, the minor becomes the owner of the securities.

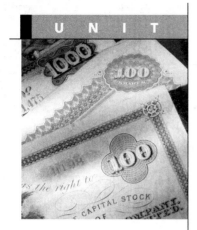

U N I T

6

Margin Accounts

Margin accounts allow investors to leverage their investment dollars. Through margin accounts, investors can borrow money from brokerage firms by pledging collateral. The Federal Reserve Board regulates margin transactions.

Broker-dealers are required to impose initial and maintenance requirements on all margin accounts. They must mark to market all positions daily to ensure that account equity meets the minimum requirements.

Although this margin accounts Unit involves substantial calculation and accounting scenarios, only about one-third to one-half of your margin test questions will involve computations. The others will test your mastery of definitions and regulations associated with margin accounts. Series 7 margin questions are likely to ask about the initial and maintenance requirements for long and short margin transactions. The margin accounting charts presented in this Unit will assist you in any calculation questions you encounter.

The information on margin accounts in this Unit will account for approximately 3–7 questions on the Series 7 exam. ■

When you have completed this Unit, you should be able to:

- **identify** documentation required when extending credit to customers

- **calculate** initial and maintenance requirements for long and short margin accounts;

- **identify** regulations and regulatory bodies that affect margin account transactions;

- **define** Regulation T and its importance to margin accounts;

- **compute** SMA; and

- **calculate** equity in long, short, and combined margin accounts.

6. 1 EXTENSION OF CREDIT IN THE SECURITIES INDUSTRY

Buying **on margin** is a common practice in the securities industry. It allows customers to increase their trading capital by borrowing from broker-dealers.

6. 1. 1 TYPES OF MARGIN ACCOUNTS

There are two types of margin accounts: long and short. In a **long margin account**, customers purchase securities and pay interest on the money borrowed until the loan is repaid. In a **short margin account**, stock is borrowed and then sold short, enabling the customer to profit if its value declines. All short sales must be executed through and accounted for in a margin account.

TAKE NOTE   In long margin accounts, customers borrow money; in short margin accounts, customers borrow securities.

Advantages of margin accounts for customers are that the customer can:

- purchase more securities with a lower initial cash outlay; and
- **leverage** the investment by borrowing a portion of the purchase price.

Leveraging magnifies the customer's rate of return, or rate of loss in adverse market conditions.

Cash/Margin Purchase

	Cash Purchase	Margin Purchase
Purchase of 1,000 shares of ABC for $20	Customer pays $20,000 for purchase	Customer borrows 50% ($10,000) from broker-dealer, deposits equity of $10,000
Return after increase from $20 to $30 per share	Customer experiences 50% return (gain/initial investment: $10,000 ÷ $20,000 = 50%)	Customer experiences 100% return (gain/initial investment: $10,000 ÷ $10,000 = 100%)
Return after decrease from $20 to $15 per share	Customer experiences 25% loss (loss/initial investment: – $5,000 ÷ $20,000 = – 25%)	Customer experiences 50% loss (loss/initial investment: – $5,000 ÷ $10,000 = – 50%)

The advantages of margin accounts for broker-dealers are:

- margin account loans generate interest income for the firm; and
- margin customers typically trade larger positions because of increased trading capital, generating higher commissions for the firm.

6. 1. 2   MARGIN AGREEMENT

Customers who open margin accounts must sign a **margin agreement** before trading can begin. The agreement consists of three parts: the credit agreement, the hypothecation agreement, and the loan consent form.

6. 1. 2. 1   Credit Agreement

The **credit agreement** discloses the terms of the credit extended by the broker-dealer, including the method of interest computation and situations under which interest rates may change.

6. 1. 2. 2   Hypothecation Agreement

The **hypothecation agreement** gives permission to the broker-dealer to pledge customer margin securities as collateral. The firm hypothecates customer securities to the bank, and the bank loans money to the broker-dealer on the basis of the loan value of these securities. All customer securities must be held in **street name** (registered in the name of the firm) to facilitate this process. When customer securities are held in street name, the broker-dealer is known as the **nominal, or named, owner**. The customer is the **beneficial owner**, because he retains all rights of ownership.

6. 1. 2. 3   Loan Consent Form

If signed, the loan consent form gives permission to the firm to loan customer margin securities to other customers or broker-dealers, usually for short sales.

TAKE NOTE   It is mandatory that the customer signs the credit agreement and hypothecation agreement. The loan consent form is optional.

TEST TOPIC ALERT   The interest paid by margin customers on money borrowed is a variable rate based on the **broker call rate**.

6. 1. 2. 4   Risk Disclosure

Before opening a margin account, you must provide customers with a risk disclosure document. This information must also be provided to margin customers on an annual basis. The document discusses the risks associated with margin trading, some of which are shown in the following.

- Customers are not entitled to choose which securities can be sold if a maintenance call is not met.
- Customers can lose more money than initially deposited.
- Customers are not entitled to an extension of time to meet a margin call.
- Firms can increase their in-house margin requirements without advance notice.

6. 1. 3   REGULATION T

The Securities Act of 1934 gives the Federal Reserve Board the authority to regulate the extension of credit in the securities industry. For margin accounts, Regulation T states that customers must deposit a minimum of 50% of the market value of the transaction within two days of settlement. Because most transactions settle regular way (T+2), this would be within four business days. The minimum required is 50%; a customer can choose to pay a larger percentage of the purchase price.

TAKE NOTE

Regulation T applies to both cash and margin accounts; customers have four business days (two additional days past regular way T+2 settlement) to pay for the purchase regardless of the account type. Firms, however, expect payment to be made regular way: within two business days of trade date.

6. 1. 3. 1   Marginable Securities

Regulation T also identifies which securities are eligible for purchase on margin and which may be used as collateral for loans for other purchases.

TAKE NOTE

Differentiate between use of the terms *margin* and *marginable*.

■ **Margin** is the amount of equity that must be deposited to buy securities in a margin account.

■ **Marginable** refers to securities that can be used as collateral in a margin account.

May be purchased on margin and used as collateral:
• Exchange-listed stocks, bonds
• Nasdaq stocks
• Non-Nasdaq OTC issues approved by the FRB
• Warrants

Cannot be purchased on margin and cannot be used as collateral:
• Put and call options
• Rights
• Non-Nasdaq OTC issues not approved by the FRB
• Insurance contracts

Cannot be bought on margin but can be used as collateral after 30 days:
• Mutual funds
• New issues

TEST TOPIC ALERT

With the exception of LEAPS options, options cannot be purchased on margin. When buying options, customers must deposit 100% of the premium. When writing a covered call, there is no Regulation T requirement for writing the call. All the customer must do is have 50% of the purchase price of the stock in the account. If you see a margin question on covered call writing, be sure to focus on what is being asked: Is it the Regulation T requirement, or is it the margin deposit? Consider the following examples.

If a customer buys stock and receives a premium by writing a call against that stock, the premium received for the call reduces the margin deposit that would be required for the stock.

Question: A customer purchases 100 ABC at 62 and also writes an ABC 65 call at 3. What is the margin deposit?

Answer: The Regulation T requirement for establishing both positions is $3,100 (50% × $6,200). The margin deposit is $2,800, which is the Regulation T requirement reduced by the premium received.

Question: A customer in a cash account purchases 100 ABC at 62 and also writes an ABC 65 call at 3. What is the required deposit?

Answer: In a cash account, the Regulation T requirement is 100% of the purchase price of the stock—that is, $6,200. The required deposit, however, is $5,900.

If, in a margin account, a customer buys stock and simultaneously buys an option, the customer must deposit 50% of the purchase price of the stock and 100% of the premium.

Question: A customer purchases 100 ABC at 62 and at the same time buys an ABC 60 put at 3. What is the margin deposit?

Answer: The margin deposit is $3,400. The 50% requirement on the stock is $3,100. Because options cannot generally be purchased on margin, the customer must pay the entire premium of $300.

TAKE NOTE

LEAPS options with more than nine months to expiration can be purchased on margin. The initial (and maintenance) requirement is 75%.

EXAMPLE

A customer buys 10 XYZ LEAPS at $4.50 each. The LEAPS expire in 24 months. What must the customer deposit?

The customer must deposit $3,375, which is 75% of the total cost of $4,500. When the time remaining to expiration reaches nine months, the maintenance requirement is 100% of the current market value.

With regard to option spreads, Regulation T requires customers to deposit the maximum loss. In debit spreads, the net debit represents maximum loss. In credit spreads, subtract the net credit from the difference between the strike prices to determine maximum loss.

Question: A customer buys 1 XYZ Jan 60 put at 8.50 and writes 1 XYZ Jan 50 put at 2.25. What must the customer deposit?

Answer: This a bear put spread established at a net debit of 6.25. Because the net debit represents maximum loss, the customer must deposit $625.

6. 1. 3. 2   Exempt Securities

Certain securities are exempt from Regulation T margin requirements. If they are bought or sold in a margin account, they are subject to the firm's determination of an initial requirement, and firms must follow maintenance requirements established by FINRA or their SRO rules.

Securities exempt from Regulation T include:

- U.S. Treasury bills, notes, and bonds;
- government agency issues; and
- municipal securities.

[handwritten: $X < 2000$ X]
[handwritten: $2000 < X < 4,000$ $2,000$]
[handwritten: $X > 4,000$ 50%]

TAKE NOTE   The FRB can change Regulation T, but the current requirement has been in place for more than 20 years. Assume Regulation T equals 50% in test questions.

6. 1. 4   INITIAL REQUIREMENTS

Customers are required to deposit a minimum amount of equity for their **first purchase** in a margin account. Although Regulation T states that a deposit of 50% of the market value of the purchase is required, FINRA rules require that this initial deposit cannot be less than $2,000.

Initial Requirements Example

Customer Purchase	Regulation T Requirement	FINRA Minimum Rule	Customer Deposit Required
100 shares at $50/share	$2,500	$2,000	$2,500
100 shares at $30/share	$1,500	$2,000	$2,000
100 shares at $15/share	$750	$1,500	$1,500

The customer is required to deposit the greater of the Regulation T requirement or the FINRA minimum. The exception occurs when the customer's initial purchase is less than $2,000; the customer is not required to deposit $2,000, only the full purchase price.

There is another way to look at this: if the customer's first purchase in a margin account is less than $2,000, deposit 100% of the purchase price. If the first purchase is between $2,000 and $4,000, deposit $2,000. If the first purchase is greater than $4,000, deposit 50%.

TAKE NOTE   The FINRA minimum rule also applies to short margin accounts. However, because short transactions are more speculative, the minimum of $2,000 is never waived. If a short sale margin requirement is less than $2,000, the required deposit is still $2,000.

6. 1. 5   DEADLINES FOR MEETING MARGIN CALLS

As previously discussed, Regulation T requires margin account customers to meet initial margin deposit requirements no more than four business days after the trade date. The deposit may be made in cash or in fully paid marginable securities valued at twice (200%) the amount of the Regulation T cash call.

If payment is late, the broker-dealer may apply to the designated examining authority (DEA) for an extension, as it may do on behalf of cash account customers. The DEA for a broker-dealer can be FINRA, an exchange, or the Federal Reserve Bank in some cases. For introducing broker-dealers, who do not clear their own trades, the request is made by the clearing firm. For an amount less than $1,000, the broker-dealer can choose to take no action.

If no extension is requested on the morning of the fifth business day, the firm must sell out the securities purchased and freeze the account for 90 days. If the customer wants to purchase securities in a frozen account, the customer must have good funds in the account before order entry.

TAKE NOTE   "Freeriding" is a term used when securities are purchased and then sold before making payment for the purchase. Freeriding is generally prohibited in both cash and margin accounts. As a penalty, the account will be frozen for 90 days and no new transactions can occur unless there is cash or marginable securities in the account before the purchase is made.

6. 2   MARGIN ACCOUNTING

After margin accounts have been opened, broker-dealers must verify that equity in the account still meets minimum requirements following fluctuations in market value.

The practice of recalculation to check the status of the equity in the account is called **marking to the market**. It is typically done every business day on the basis of the closing price of the stock. This concept applies to both long and short margin accounts, which will be discussed separately.

6. 2. 1   LONG MARGIN ACCOUNTING

The Series 7 examination uses the following terms to describe activity in long margin accounts:

■ **Long market value (LMV)**—the current market value of the stock position the investor purchased

■ **Debit register (DR)**—the amount of money borrowed by the customer

■ **Equity (EQ)**—the customer's net worth in the margin account; it represents the portion of the securities the customer fully owns

The amount of equity in the account is determined by this equation:

$$LMV - DR = EQ$$

LMV − DR = EQ (handwritten)

To simplify long margin accounts, think of them as a house with a mortgage. If the market value of a house goes up or down, the mortgage amount does not change, but the equity goes up or down. The same is true in a margin account; when market value of securities goes up, the debit balance (what the customer owes the broker-dealer) stays the same, while the equity increases. When market value of securities goes down, the debit balance stays the same and the equity decreases.

Continuing the analogy, consider a house payment. The payment does not affect the market value of the house but reduces the debit balance and consequently increases the equity. When money is paid into a margin account, the debit balance is decreased, and the equity is increased.

6. 2. 1. 1   Analyzing Long Margin Accounts

To analyze long margin account activity, a simplified balance sheet will be used, as shown below.

LMV	DR
	EQ

(handwritten margin chart: LMV | DR / EQ)

TAKE NOTE

Draw a chart whenever you are asked to compute equity in a margin account. Remember the master margin account equation: **LMV – DR = EQ**. Be sure that your account is balanced before going to the next step.

EXAMPLE

A customer purchases 1,000 shares of XYZ at 60 on margin and borrows the maximum 50% from the broker-dealer.

The margin chart is set up as follows:

LMV	DR
60,000	30,000
	EQ
	30,000

(handwritten margin chart: LMV DR / 60,000 | 30,000 / EQ 30,000)

In this instance, the customer must deposit $30,000. The customer may deposit cash or fully paid securities. Meeting the margin requirement in securities requires double the necessary cash margin when Regulation T is 50%. For a margin requirement of $30,000, the customer may pay $30,000 in cash or deposit $60,000 of fully paid securities to meet the Regulation T requirement.

When the market value of securities changes, the broker-dealer must mark to market the positions to ensure that enough equity remains in the account. The customer's account must always meet the **maintenance requirement** of FINRA. In a long margin account, minimum maintenance is 25% of the long market value.

Marking to the market identifies the status of the customer's account. The determination of the status requires the computation of two benchmarks:

- **Regulation T** (50% of LMV)
- **Minimum maintenance** (25% of LMV)

If XYZ declines to 50, both of these benchmarks are computed on the basis of the new market value of the account, as shown below:

	LMV	DR
		30,000
	~~60,000~~	
	50,000	
Regulation T = 25,000		**EQ**
Minimum Maintenance = 12,500		~~30,000~~
		20,000

TAKE NOTE

Here are some helpful tips in long margin accounting.

- When the market value of securities goes up or down, the DR does not change.

- When marking to the market, the calculation of Regulation T and minimum maintenance is based on the new long market value.

6.2.1.2 Restricted Accounts

If the equity in the account is less than the Regulation T amount but greater than or equal to the minimum maintenance requirement, the account is **restricted**.

TAKE NOTE

If an account becomes restricted, there is no requirement for the customer to take any action to unrestrict the account. A maintenance call will be sent only if the account falls below the minimum maintenance requirement.

6.2.1.3 Maintenance Requirements

When the equity in the account falls below the minimum maintenance requirement, the customer receives a maintenance margin call. **Maintenance calls** are a demand that the customer make a payment to bring the account back to minimum. If payment is not made, the broker-dealer will liquidate enough of the securities in the account to bring the account back to minimum. The customer can meet a maintenance call by depositing cash or fully paid marginable securities.

TAKE NOTE

A firm can impose a maintenance level higher than the FINRA minimum maintenance rule levels. This is a **house minimum**. Many firms today impose 30–35% minimum maintenance requirements.

Consider the previous example. By evaluating the amount of equity in the account relative to the Regulation T and minimum maintenance benchmarks, it can be determined that the account is in **restricted status**.

The new equity of $20,000 is less than the Regulation T requirement of $25,000, but more than the minimum maintenance of $12,500.

LMV	DR
	30,000
~~60,000~~ 50,000	
Regulation T = 25,000 **EQ**	
Minimum Maintenance = 12,500	~~30,000~~ 20,000

TAKE NOTE

When calculating equity in the margin account using a T-chart, be sure to follow the steps below:

- Calculate the equity after a market value change: LMV – DR = EQ.

- Calculate the new Regulation T: 50% of the new LMV.

- Calculate the new minimum maintenance: 25% of the new LMV.

6. 2. 1. 4   Maintenance Call

Assume that the market value of the securities falls from $50,000 to $36,000. To find the status of the account, the chart would be adjusted as follows:

LMV	DR
~~50,000~~ 36,000	30,000
Regulation T = 18,000 **EQ**	
Minimum Maintenance = 9,000	~~20,000~~ 6,000

Note the adjustment to the LMV. The LMV has fallen to $36,000, so the EQ must be changed to $6,000 ($36,000 – $30,000 = $6,000). After adjusting EQ in the account, the new Regulation T and minimum maintenance levels are calculated. (Regulation T = 50% of $36,000, or $18,000; Minimum Maintenance = 25% of $36,000, or $9,000).

This account is subject to a maintenance call because the equity is below the minimum requirement by $3,000. If the call is not met promptly, the broker-dealer will liquidate the customer's securities as needed.

A formula can be applied to calculate the market value to which securities can fall before there is a maintenance call. This formula is known as the **market value at maintenance formula** and is calculated as follows:

$$DR \div .75$$

EXAMPLE

A customer buys $90,000 worth of stock on margin and meets the initial Regulation T requirement by depositing $45,000. The debit balance is $45,000. To what level would the market value have to fall in order for the account to be at minimum maintenance?

Divide the debit balance of $45,000 by .75, which results in a maintenance market value of $60,000. If the market value does fall to $60,000, the account will look like this: LMV $60,000; DR $45,000; EQ $15,000. At this point, the account is exactly at 25% equity.

TAKE NOTE

If an account falls below minimum, a maintenance call will be sent in an amount sufficient to bring the account back up to minimum.

EXAMPLE

A customer has a long margin account with a market value of $12,000 and a debit balance of $10,000. The equity in the account is $2,000, which is approximately 16% of the market value. To bring the account back to minimum, which is $3,000 (25% × $12,000), the customer will receive a maintenance call for $1,000. Once the call is met, the account will look like this: LMV $12,000; DR $9,000; EQ $3,000.

6. 2. 1. 5   Excess Equity and Special Memorandum Account (SMA)

Excess equity in a margin account is the amount of equity exceeding the Regulation T requirement.

To illustrate, return to the example account:

LMV	DR
60,000	30,000
	EQ
	30,000

Handwritten notes (top left):
$LMV - DR = EQ$
$X - DR = .25X$
$.75X = DR$
$X = \frac{DR}{.75}$

$\frac{4}{3}$

$Y = 60,000$

90,000   45,000

45,000

12,000   9,000
3,000

Assume that the market value of the securities increases to $80,000. After marking to the market, the account appears as shown below:

LMV	DR	
	30,000	(2) SMA = 10,000
~~60,000~~		Special
80,000		memorandum
		account
Regulation T = 40,000	**EQ**	
Minimum Maintenance = 20,000	~~30,000~~	(1) EE = 10,000
	50,000	Excess Equity

The increase in market value creates equity of $50,000 because the DR does not change. The new Regulation T requirement is $40,000 (50% of $80,000), and the new minimum maintenance is $20,000 (25% of $80,000). Because the equity exceeds Regulation T, this account has excess equity of $10,000 ($50,000 – $40,000 = $10,000).

Item 1 in the example shows the excess equity. Item 2 shows the SMA, discussed below.

TAKE NOTE   A rule to determine SMA is as follows: for every $1 increase in market value, $.50 of SMA is created. In the previous example, market value increased by $20,000, which created SMA of $10,000.

Excess equity creates **SMA**, or **buying power**, in the account.

Item 1 above shows the excess equity. Item 2 above shows the SMA.

SMA stands for **special memorandum account**, a line of credit that a customer can borrow from or use to purchase securities.

SMA is perhaps the most complicated margin concept. The house analogy can also help simplify SMA. Assume that a house has increased substantially in value. Homeowners with large amounts of equity sometimes borrow against their equity through home equity loans. When they take a loan, the amount they owe on their house is more than before and the equity falls. SMA is like a home equity loan. It is created because of increased equity in the account and is an additional line of credit. When the SMA line of credit is used, the debit balance in the customer's account is increased and the equity falls.

TAKE NOTE   The amount of SMA in the account is equal to the greater of the excess equity or the amount already in SMA.

Until this transaction, our example account had no excess equity. The excess equity of $10,000 generated SMA of $10,000.

What happens to SMA if the market value of the securities falls? The example below depicts the market value falling to $70,000:

LMV	DR	
~~80,000~~	30,000	(2) SMA = 10,000
70,000		
	EQ	
Regulation T = 35,000		
Minimum Maintenance = 17,500	~~50,000~~	(1) EE = 5,000
	40,000	~~10,000~~

The decrease in market value creates equity of $40,000. The new Regulation T requirement is $35,000 (50% of $70,000), and the new minimum maintenance is $17,500 (25% of $70,000). Because the equity exceeds Regulation T, this account has **excess equity** of $5,000 ($40,000 – $35,000 = $5,000).

What is the new SMA amount? Regulation T states that the SMA amount is equal to the greater of the excess equity or the SMA already in the account. Because the SMA of $10,000 is greater than the excess equity of $5,000, the SMA remains at $10,000. In summary, remember that although SMA increases when market value in the account increases, it does not decrease as a result of a market value decline.

TAKE NOTE   SMA may be more than excess equity and may exist even if there is no excess equity in the account.

TAKE NOTE   Although the SMA is not reduced by a decline in market value, its use may be restricted under certain conditions.

SMA can always be used, even in a restricted account, as long as its use does not bring the account below minimum.

The following is one last example in calculating the SMA balance. Assuming the market value of securities rises to $100,000, what is the new SMA balance?

LMV	DR	
~~70,000~~	30,000	(2) SMA = ~~10,000~~
100,000		20,000
	EQ	
Regulation T = 50,000		
Minimum Maintenance = 25,000	~~40,000~~	(1) EE = ~~5,000~~
	70,000	20,000

The increase in market value creates equity of $70,000. The new Regulation T requirement is $50,000 (50% of $100,000), and the new minimum maintenance is $25,000 (25% of $100,000). Because the equity exceeds Regulation T, this account has excess equity of $20,000

($70,000 − $50,000 = $20,000). What is the new SMA amount? The SMA rule explains that the SMA amount is equal to the greater of the excess equity or the SMA already in the account. Because the excess equity of $20,000 is greater than the existing SMA of $10,000, the SMA balance becomes $20,000.

We have illustrated that SMA is increased by excess equity from market value increases. Any of the following also generate SMA.

- **Nonrequired cash deposits:** If a customer deposits cash that is not required to meet a margin call, the full amount reduces the debit and is also credited to SMA.
- **Dividends:** Dividends received on securities in the margin account are added to SMA. The customer can withdraw these income distributions, even if the account is restricted.

TAKE NOTE

If a customer wants to remove cash dividends coming into his margin account, he must do so within 30 days of receipt. Otherwise, the cash dividend will be applied against the debit balance, thereby increasing the equity in the account.

- **Loan value:** If a customer makes a nonrequired deposit of marginable stock, the stock's loan value is credited to SMA. The credit is equal to half the value of a cash deposit.
- **Sale of stock:** When stock is sold, 50% of the sales proceeds is credited to SMA.

6. 2. 1. 6   Using SMA

SMA is a line of credit; therefore, the investor can use it to withdraw cash or meet the margin requirement on stock purchases.

EXAMPLE

Assume a margin account as follows:

LMV	DR	
70,000	30,000	SMA = 20,000
	EQ	
Regulation T = 35,000	40,000	
Minimum Maintenance = 17,500		

The customer can withdraw cash by borrowing against the credit line of $20,000, which will increase the debit balance by $20,000. If the full $20,000 is withdrawn, the account will appear as follows:

LMV	DR	
70,000	~~30,000~~	SMA = ~~20,000~~
	50,000	0
	EQ	
Regulation T = 35,000	~~40,000~~	
Minimum Maintenance = 17,500	20,000	

The use of $20,000 of SMA reduces the SMA balance to zero. The debit balance is increased to $50,000, because SMA is a loan. The equity balance falls to $20,000, and the account is in restricted status. The customer can use SMA as long as it does not cause a maintenance call.

SMA can be used when the account has excess equity or is in restricted status. SMA can also be used to meet the initial margin requirements on stock purchases. SMA gives the investor buying power. Assume a margin account as follows:

LMV	DR	
70,000	30,000	SMA = 20,000
	EQ	
Regulation T = 35,000		
Minimum Maintenance = 17,500	40,000	

The SMA of $20,000, when used as the margin requirement, allows the customer to purchase $40,000 of stock. In other words, for every $1 of SMA, the customer can purchase $2 of stock. SMA has a buying power of 2 to 1. After the purchase of $40,000, the account appears as follows:

LMV	DR	
~~70,000~~	~~30,000~~	SMA = ~~20,000~~
110,000	70,000	0
	EQ	
Regulation T = 55,000		
Minimum Maintenance = 27,500	40,000	

The $40,000 purchase was paid for by a debit balance increase of $40,000. Any time SMA is used to buy stock, the debit balance increases by the full amount of the purchase.

The use of SMA to meet the purchase price is like borrowing on a credit card. The customer owes more money. This account is in restricted status after the purchase of $40,000 of stock.

TEST TOPIC ALERT

Here is a quick review of critical long margin account concepts.

- The first transaction in a margin account requires a deposit of the greater of 50% of the LMV or $2,000. The $2,000 minimum is waived if 100% of the transaction is less than $2,000.

- The basic margin equation is: LMV − DR = EQ.

- Regulation T = 50% of the LMV.

- Minimum maintenance = 25% of the LMV (50% of Regulation T requirement).

- SMA can be borrowed from the account, dollar for dollar.

- Utilizing SMA increases the debit balance.

- The buying power of SMA is 2 to 1.

- Excess equity and SMA are not necessarily equal.

- SMA cannot be used to meet a maintenance margin call.

- The market value at maintenance equation for long margin accounts is DR ÷ .75. This calculates what the market value can fall to before a maintenance call is sent.

- Exempt securities are not subject to Regulation T but are subject to the maintenance requirements of FINRA.

6. 2. 1. 7   Restricted Accounts Revisited

If an account is restricted, the following rules apply.

- To purchase additional securities, put up 50%.
- To withdraw securities from the account, the customer must deposit cash equal to 50% of the value of the securities to be withdrawn.
- If securities are sold in a restricted account, at least half the proceeds must be retained in the account to reduce the debit balance. This is called the **retention requirement**. Also, 50% of the proceeds are credited to SMA.

The sale of securities in a restricted account can be complicated.

EXAMPLE

LMV $50,000; DR $30,000; EQ $20,000

This account is restricted by $5,000; if the equity were $5,000 higher, the account would be at 50% and therefore not restricted. The customer wants to sell $10,000 worth of stock.

Initially, all of the proceeds are applied against the debit balance, and a credit of $5,000 is made to SMA. The account now looks as follows:

LMV $40,000; DR $20,000; EQ $20,000; SMA $5,000

If the customer wants to withdraw half the proceeds (remember, at least 50% must be retained in the account to reduce the debit balance, and the customer can remove the other half), he does so by using SMA and borrowing from the account. After the customer withdraws $5,000, the account looks like this:

LMV $40,000; DR $25,000; EQ $15,000; SMA 0

The reason all of the proceeds of the sale are initially applied against the debit balance is this: what if the customer does not want any of the proceeds to be sent to him? In this case, the firm has the obligation to reduce the debit and thus his interest charges. If, however, the customer changes his mind and wants half the proceeds, he can always take out the $5,000 by using SMA.

TEST TOPIC ALERT

For the Series 7 exam, watch for the following: if securities are sold in a restricted account, which of the following are affected? LMV, DR, EQ, SMA?

All but equity are affected: LMV, DR, and SMA. Equity is affected only if the customer elects to remove half the proceeds.

1. An investor opens a new margin account and buys 200 shares of DWQ at 50, with Regulation T at 50%. What is the investor's initial margin requirement?

    A. $2,500
    B. $3,000
    C. $5,000
    D. $10,000

2. An investor has an established margin account with a current market value of $4,000 and a debit balance of $2,250, with Regulation T at 50%. How much equity does the investor have in the account?

    A. $1,750
    B. $2,000
    C. $2,250
    D. $4,000

3. An investor has an established margin account with a current market value of $6,000 and a debit balance of $2,500. With Regulation T at 50%, how much excess equity does the investor have in the account?

    A. $500
    B. $2,500
    C. $3,500
    D. $6,000

4. In a new margin account, a customer buys 100 shares of GGG, Inc., at $30 per share and meets the initial margin requirement. If the stock falls to $25 per share, the equity in the account is equal to

    A. $1,000
    B. $1,500
    C. $2,000
    D. $2,500

5. A margin account has long market value of $6,000 and a debit of $5,000. How much money must the investor deposit to satisfy the maintenance requirement?

    A. $500
    B. $1,000
    C. $2,000
    D. $5,000

6. A margin account is restricted by $2,000. Which of the following actions may the customer take to bring the account to the Regulation T requirement?

    I.   Cancel $2,000 of SMA
    II. Deposit $2,000 cash
    III. Deposit $4,000 of fully paid marginable stock

    A. I only
    B. I and II
    C. II and III
    D. I, II and III

7. When stock held in a long margin account appreciates, which of the following increase(s)?

   I.   Current market value
   II. Debit balance
   III. Equity

   A. I only
   B. I and III
   C. II only
   D. I, II and III

8. A client has a margin account with $23,000 in securities and a debit of $12,000. If Regulation T is 50%

   I.   the account is restricted
   II. the client will receive a margin call for $500
   III. the client may withdraw securities if he deposits 50% of the securities' value
   IV. the account has excess equity of $5,250

   A. I and II
   B. I and III
   C. II, III and IV
   D. I, II, III and IV

9. A client has a margin account with $23,000 in securities and a debit of $12,000. The stock increases in value to $26,000. How much money may the client withdraw from the account?

   A. $1,000
   B. $2,000
   C. $3,000
   D. $4,000

10. Which of the following can change the SMA balance in a long account?

   I.   Sale of securities in the account
   II. Market appreciation of securities in the account
   III. Interest and cash dividends deposited in the account
   IV. Decrease in value of securities in the account

   A. I only
   B. I and II
   C. I, II and III
   D. I, II, III and IV

Quick Quiz answers can be found at the end of the Unit.

6. 2. 2   PATTERN DAY TRADERS

A **day trader** is one who buys and sells the same security on the same day to try to take advantage of intraday price movements. A **pattern day trader** is one who executes four or more day trades in a five-business-day period.

The minimum equity requirement for pattern day traders is $25,000; pattern day traders must have on deposit in the account equity of at least $25,000 on any day on which day trading occurs. The minimum maintenance margin requirement for pattern day traders is 25%, the same as for regular customers.

Pattern day traders are also treated differently when it comes to **buying power**. Buying power for day traders is four times the maintenance margin excess. *Maintenance margin* **excess** is defined as the equity in the account above the 25% minimum requirement. For regular customers, buying power is two times SMA.

Margin rules also prohibit day trading accounts from using **account guarantees,** which are otherwise permitted. A **cross guarantee** is one for which another customer, in writing, agrees to the use of money or securities in his account to carry the guaranteed accounts (i.e., to meet any margin calls).

6. 2. 2. 1   Approval for Day Trading Accounts

Member firms who promote day trading strategies must now implement procedures to approve day trading accounts.

Before opening an account, the member must:

- provide the customer with a risk disclosure statement that outlines all of the risks associated with day trading (the statement can be furnished in writing or electronically); and

- approve the account for a day trading strategy or receive from the customer a written statement that the customer does not intend to engage in day trading.

6. 2. 3   SHORT SALES AND MARGIN REQUIREMENTS

Selling short is a strategy an investor uses to profit from a decline in a stock's price. Selling short must always be done through a margin account. The investor then sells the borrowed stock at the market price with the hope of buying back the shares at a lower price. The short seller profits when the loan of stock can be repaid with shares purchased at a lower price.

In a short sale, there is a **short seller**, a **stock lender** (from whom the shares are borrowed), and a **buyer** who purchases the shares being sold short. One of the basic requirements of short selling is that the short seller, on the dividend payment date, must make good to the stock lender for the dividends the lender is no longer receiving from the issuer. The buyer of the shares is receiving the dividends directly from the issuer. Therefore, on the dividend payment date, the short seller's account is debited the amount of the cash dividend for remittance to the stock lender.

6. 2. 3. 1   Margin Deposits

To borrow shares for short sales, an investor must make **margin deposits**. Regulation T specifies that the initial margin for short sales can be met with either cash or marginable securities, just as in long margin transactions.

6. 2. 3. 2   Terminology

The Series 7 examination uses the following terms to describe activity in short margin accounts:

- **Short market value (SMV)**—the current market value of the stock position the investor sells short

- **Credit register (CR)**—the amount of money in the customer's account; equal to the sales proceeds plus the margin deposit requirement
- **Equity (EQ)**—the customer's net worth in the margin account; the amount by which the credit balance exceeds the current short market value of the securities in the account

The amount of equity in the account is determined by this equation:

$$CR - SMV = EQ$$

6. 2. 3. 3   Analyzing Short Margin Account Activity

To analyze short margin account activity, a simplified balance sheet will be used, as shown here:

CR	SMV
	EQ

When establishing a short margin account, there is a minimum deposit of $2,000. This minimum must be met even if the customer sells short less than $2,000 worth of securities. The Regulation T requirement for short sales is the same as it is for long purchases: 50%.

Customer Sells Short

Customer Sells Short	Regulation T Requirement	FINRA Minimum Rule	Customer Deposit Required
100 shares at $50/shares	$2,500	$2,000	$2,500
100 shares at $30/shares	$1,500	$2,000	$2,000
100 shares at $15/shares	$750	$2,000	$2,000

TAKE NOTE

Shorting stock that is below $5 per share requires an initial deposit of $2,000 or $2.50 per share, whichever is greater.

6. 2. 3. 4   Minimum Maintenance

FINRA **minimum maintenance requirement** rules on short positions is 30%, compared with 25% on long positions. As with long margin accounts, the firm may impose a higher house minimum.

6. 2. 3. 5   Short Margin Account

To illustrate how a short margin account works, assume the following:

A client sells short 1,000 shares of ABC at $70,000 and meets the Regulation T requirement. The market value of securities falls to $60,000. What is the new equity in the account? The accounting in the short margin chart should appear as follows:

CR	SMV
105,000 (3)	70,000 (1)
	EQ
	35,000 (2)

■   The market value of the securities sold short is entered as the SMV.

■   The Regulation T requirement of 50% of the short market value is entered as equity.

■   The credit balance (CR) is the stock sales proceeds plus the equity deposited (SMV + EQ).

The **credit balance (CR)** provides security to the broker-dealer that there will be cash available for the customer to purchase the securities if the market value of the securities rises. The risk of a short account is a stock price increase; a short seller profits only if the market value of the securities declines.

The following illustrates the accounting for the market value decline and the resulting new equity:

CR	SMV
105,000	~~70,000~~
	60,000 (1)
	EQ
	~~35,000~~
	45,000 (2)

- The market value of the securities sold short declines to $60,000.
- The equity increases to $45,000 as a result of the decline. This is determined as follows: CR – SMV = EQ ($105,000 – $60,000 = $45,000).

TAKE NOTE
Short positions, like long positions, are marked to market daily to reflect any change in position value.

What is the status of this investor's account? Just as in long margin accounts, the short margin account statuses are as follows:

- **Excess equity**—equity in excess of Regulation T (50% of the current SMV)
- **Restricted**—equity less than Regulation T, and greater than or equal to minimum maintenance
- **Maintenance call**—equity less than minimum maintenance (30% of the SMV)

By calculating the Regulation T benchmark, we can see that this account has excess equity and has created SMA of $15,000, as shown:

CR	SMV	
105,000	~~70,000~~	SMA = 15,000
	60,000	
	(1)	

Regulation T = 30,000	**Eq**	
Minimum Maintenance = 18,000	~~35,000~~	EE = 15,000
	45,000	
	(2)	

TAKE NOTE
Multiply the decrease in short market value (SMV) by 1.5 to arrive at the excess equity (EE) and the amount that would be credited to the special memorandum account (SMA).

The excess equity and SMA of $15,000 are available because the equity in the account ($45,000) exceeds the Regulation T requirement ($30,000) by $15,000. Now assume that the market value of the securities in this account rises to $80,000. How much cash must the customer deposit?

CR	SMV	
	~~60,000~~	The increase of short market
	80,000	value to $80,000 causes the
		equity to fall to $25,000
		(CR – SMV = EQ).

Regulation T = 40,000   105,000   EQ
Minimum Maintenance = 24,000

~~45,000~~	
25,000	

The new Regulation T requirement is $40,000 (50% of $80,000); the new minimum maintenance is $24,000 (30% of $80,000).

Because the equity of $25,000 exceeds the minimum mainte-nance of $24,000, there is no cash deposit required.

To find the maximum market value to which a short sale position can increase before a maintenance call is issued, apply the following formula:

$$\text{Total credit balance} \div 130\% \ (1.3)$$

This is known as the **short market value at maintenance**.

6. 2. 3. 6   Minimum Maintenance in a Short Account

The minimum maintenance margin requirement for short accounts is 30%. However, there are exceptions based on price per share.

- For stock trading under $5 per share, a customer must maintain 100% of SMV or $2.50 per share, whichever is greater.

- For stock trading at $5 per share and above, the minimum requirement is $5 per share or 30%, whichever is greater.

EXAMPLE

A customer sells short 1,000 shares of stock at $4 per share. The margin deposit would be $4,000, not $2,000.

A customer sells short 1,000 shares at $2 per share. The margin deposit would be $2,500.

In both cases, the minimum maintenance margin requirement exceeds the initial requirement. Therefore, each customer must deposit the higher amount.

EXAMPLE

A customer has a short margin account. In it, there is one stock currently trading at $10 per share. The minimum maintenance requirement for this account is

A.   100%

B.   30%

C. $5/share

D. $2.50/share

Answer: C. With the stock at $10, $5 per share is greater than 30%.

QUICK QUIZ 6.B

1.   An investor opens a new margin account, sells short 100 shares of KLP at $45 per share, and meets the Regulation T requirement of 50%. How much equity does the investor have in the account?

A. $2,000

B. $2,250

C. $4,500

D. $6,750

2.   An investor has an established margin account with a short market value of $4,000 and a credit balance of $6,750, with Regulation T at 50%. How much excess equity does the investor have in the account?

A. $750

B. $1,500

C. $2,000

D. $2,750

3.   An investor opens a new margin account and sells short 100 shares of COD at 32.50, with Regulation T at 50%. What is the investor's required deposit?

A. $812.50

B. $1,625

C. $2,000

D. $3,250

4.   A customer sells short 100 shares of ABC at $80 per share and meets the minimum Regulation T requirement. Two months later, he covers the short position by buying ABC at $70 per share. This was the only transaction in the account. What is the maximum amount he can withdraw from the account after closing the short position (Regulation T is 50%)?

A. $1,000

B. $4,000

C. $5,000

D. $12,000

6. 2. 4   COMBINED ACCOUNTS

A client who has a margin account with both long and short positions in different securities has a **combined account**. In combined accounts, equity and margin requirements are determined by calculating the long and short positions separately and combining the results.

The following example shows the use of the long and short margin charts in calculating combined equity.

An investor has the following margin account positions:

LMV = $50,000; SMV = $40,000; CR = $60,000; DR = $20,000
SMA = $5,000 (The combined equity in this example is $50,000.)

	LMV	DR			CR	SMV
		20,000				40,000
Regulation T = 25,000	50,000	EQ		Regulation T = 20,000	60,000	EQ
Minimum Maintenance = 12,500		30,000		Minimum Maintenance = 12,000		20,000

The basic equation for the calculation of combined equity is:

$$LMV + CR - DR - SMV = EQ$$

TEST TOPIC ALERT   Besides asking about the calculation of combined equity, questions may ask for combined Regulation T requirement or combined minimum maintenance requirements. As with combined equity questions, first calculate the long, then the short, and add the two together.

6. 3 SPECIAL MEMORANDUM ACCOUNT

As discussed in both the long and short margin accounting sections, SMA is generated from excess equity in margin accounts. The following table reviews the effects on SMA of various account activities in a long margin account.

Activity	Effect on SMA	Remarks
Rise in market value	Increase	SMA increases only if the new excess equity is higher than the old SMA.
Sale of securities	Increase	The client is entitled to excess equity in the account after the sale, or to 50% of the sale proceeds, whichever is greater.
Deposit of cash	Increase	The full amount of the deposit is credited to SMA.
Deposit of marginable securities	Increase	SMA is increased by the loan value of the securities deposited, as prescribed by Regulation T at the time of the deposit (50%).
Dividends or interest	Increase	100% of a cash dividend or interest (a nonrequired deposit) is credited to SMA.
Purchase of securities	Decrease	The margin requirement on new purchases is deducted from SMA. If SMA is insufficient to meet the charge, a Regulation T call is issued for the balance.
Withdrawal of cash	Decrease	The full amount of the cash withdrawal is deducted from SMA. Remaining equity may not fall below FINRA rules or house equity requirement.
Fall in long account market value	No effect	After the SMA balance is established, it is not affected by a fall in market value in a long account.
Interest charges to account	No effect	SMA remains the same.
Stock dividend or split	No effect	SMA remains the same.

6. 4 PLEDGING CUSTOMER SECURITIES FOR LOANS

Hypothecation is the pledging of customer securities as collateral for margin loans.

When customers sign margin agreements, permission is given for this process to occur. After customers pledge their securities to the broker-dealer, the broker-dealer **rehypothecates** (repledges) them as collateral for a loan from the bank. Regulation U oversees the process of banks lending money to broker-dealers based on customer securities as collateral.

Broker-dealers are limited to pledging 140% of a customer's debit balance as collateral. Any customer securities in excess of this amount must be physically segregated. The firm cannot commingle customer securities with securities owned by the firm.

Firms can only commingle one customer's securities with another customer's securities for hypothecation if customers have given specific permission by signing the hypothecation agreement.

Rehypothecation of Customer Securities

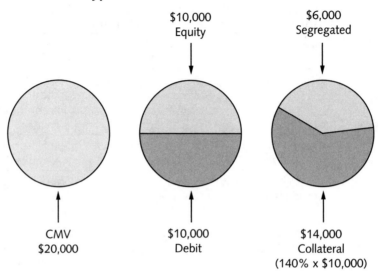

$10,000
Equity

$6,000
Segregated

CMV
$20,000

$10,000
Debit

$14,000
Collateral
(140% x $10,000)

UNIT TEST

1. An investor opens a new margin account and sells short 200 shares of ALF at $56 per share, with Regulation T at 50%. The investor deposits the initial margin requirement. What is the investor's credit balance?

    A. $2,000
    B. $5,600
    C. $11,200
    D. $16,800

2. According to Regulation T and FINRA rules, initial and maintenance margin requirements for a short account are

    A. 50% initial; 25% maintenance
    B. 50% initial; 30% maintenance
    C. 50% initial; 50% maintenance
    D. 70% initial; 50% maintenance

3. A customer purchases 200 shares of ABC Health Care at $60 per share and meets the initial margin requirement. If ABC announces an acquisition and its stock appreciates on the news to $75 per share, how much cash can the customer withdraw after this market move?

    A. $0
    B. $1,000
    C. $1,500
    D. $3,000

4. SMA in a long account will be affected by

    I.   the sale of securities in the account
    II. the decline in market value of securities
    III. the cash deposited by the customers
    IV. the interest charged on debit balances

    A. I, II and III
    B. I and III
    C. I and IV
    D. II, III and IV

5. A member firm may commingle the securities of 2 or more customers

    A. with the customers' written permission
    B. with the SEC's written permission
    C. with FINRA's written permission
    D. under no circumstances

6. An investor sells stock short to

    A. profit if prices decline
    B. establish a permanent tax loss
    C. defer taxes
    D. liquidate a long stock position

7. The formula for computing equity in a combined margin account is

    A. long market value – short market value + credit balance + debit balance
    B. long market value – short market value + debit balance – credit balance
    C. long market value + credit balance – short market value – debit balance
    D. long market value + short market value – debit balance + credit balance

8. A customer's margin account contains the following securities:

    100 shares of DEF, CMV $40 per share
    100 shares of AMF, CMV $50 per share
    100 shares of KLP, CMV $80 per share

    The account has a debit balance of $10,800. How much equity is in the account?

    A. $4,030
    B. $6,200
    C. $11,050
    D. $17,000

9. A customer is long 200 shares of MTN at $30 per share and 400 shares of DWQ at 20 in a margin account. The debit balance in the account is $8,000. The customer sells 200 of the DWQ shares for $4,000. The credit to SMA is

    A. $0
    B. $1,000
    C. $2,000
    D. $4,000

10. An investor opens a new margin account and sells short 200 shares of DWQ at $65 per share, with Regulation T at 50%. What is the investor's required deposit?

   A. $2,775
   B. $3,250
   C. $6,500
   D. $13,000

11. In a new margin account, a customer buys 300 XYZ at 48 and simultaneously writes 3 XYZ Jan 50 calls at 1. The Regulation T margin requirement is

   A. $6,900
   B. $7,200
   C. $7,350
   D. $7,500

12. A customer has a restricted margin account with SMA of $2,500. If the customer wishes to purchase $10,000 worth of stock, the customer must deposit

   A. $0
   B. $2,500
   C. $5,000
   D. $10,000

13. A customer has a margin account with market value of $50,000 and a debit balance of $20,000. Your firm is permitted to rehypothecate stock with a total market value of

   A. $20,000
   B. $25,000
   C. $28,000
   D. $50,000

14. Extensions of time in which to make payments of balances due on purchases made in cash accounts can be granted by

   A. application to the SEC, in which the circumstances requiring the extension are set forth clearly
   B. application to the State Securities Commission in the state in which the transaction took place using Form EXT-FRB-T
   C. FINRA, registered stock exchanges, and the Federal Reserve banks when exceptional circumstances have prevented payment within the periods specified by Regulation T
   D. the broker-dealer concerned, when, in his opinion, exceptional circumstances warrant such action

15. The term *hypothecation* usually refers to

   A. pledging customers' securities as collateral for a loan in a margin account
   B. forecasting the future of the market
   C. determining a reasonable offering price of a new security issue
   D. a security trading on more than one stock exchange

ANSWERS AND RATIONALES

1. **D.** The investor's credit balance is calculated by adding the short sale price of $11,200 to the initial margin deposit of $5,600 ($16,800).

2. **B.** Initial Regulation T margin is 50% and the maintenance margin is 30% for short accounts.

3. **C.** The customer could withdraw cash equal to the SMA. A purchase of 200 shares at $60 per share would require an initial deposit of $6,000 on a market value of $12,000. The customer would have $6,000 in equity and a $6,000 debit. After a rise to $75 a share, the stock's market value would be $15,000. The customer's debit balance would remain unchanged at $6,000, but the equity would increase to $9,000 ($15,000 CMV − $6,000 DR). For every $1 increase in market value, $.50 of SMA is created.

4. **B.** Whenever stock is sold, half of the sales proceeds are credited to SMA. Nonrequired cash deposits are credited to SMA in full. SMA goes down only when a customer uses it to borrow from the account or purchase securities; it is not affected by declines in market value or by interest charges.

5. **A.** A member may commingle a customer's securities with those of other customers only if all of the customers involved have given their written consent. This occurs in margin accounts where the margin securities of multiple customers are commingled at a bank for debit balance financing purposes.

6. **A.** Short sales are used to profit if prices fall.

7. **C.** The formula for equity in a long account is the long market value minus the debit balance. The formula for equity in a short account is the credit balance minus the short market value.

8. **B.** The total market value in the account is $17,000: CMV − DR = EQ; $17,000 CMV − $10,800 DR = $6,200.

9. **C.** Because this account is below 50% margin, the account is restricted ($6,000 equity divided by $14,000 market value = 42.8% equity). When securities are sold in a restricted account, 50% of the proceeds are released to SMA. Because $4,000 worth of securities were sold, $2,000 (50%) is credited to SMA.

10. **C.** The required deposit is calculated by multiplying the short market value of $13,000 by the Regulation T requirement of 50%, which equals $6,500.

11. **B.** The Regulation T requirement for purchasing $14,400 of stock (300 × 48) is $7,200. The Regulation T requirement for writing covered calls is zero. Therefore, the Regulation T requirement for establishing both these positions is $7,200. The margin call (deposit) would be $6,900. The requirement can be reduced by the $300 premiums received. By depositing the $6,900, the customer will have $7,200 in the account.

12. **B.** With SMA of $2,500, the customer can purchase $5,000 of stock without having to make a deposit. Buying power is twice SMA. This leaves $5,000 to purchase, which requires a deposit of $2,500. Or, alternatively, the purchase of $10,000 requires a $5,000 deposit, which can be reduced dollar for dollar by the existing SMA.

13. **C.** 140% × $20,000 debit balance = $28,000 worth of customer stock that may be rehypothecated.

14. **C.** These are the sources for a broker-dealer obtaining an extension under Regulation T if exceptional circumstances warrant it.

15. **A.** This is the definition of hypothecation. Remember that a broker-dealer may not rehypothecate securities in excess of 140% of the customer's debit balance.

QUICK QUIZ ANSWERS

Quick Quiz 6.A

1. **C.** The initial margin requirement is calculated by multiplying the market value of $10,000 by the Regulation T requirement of 50%, which equals $5,000.

2. **A.** Equity is calculated by subtracting the debit balance of $2,250 from the current market value of $4,000, which equals $1,750.

3. **A.** The Regulation T requirement is 50% of the current market value of $6,000, which equals $3,000. Equity is equal to the current market value of $6,000 minus the debit balance of $2,500, which equals $3,500. Excess equity is then calculated by subtracting the Regulation T requirement of $3,000 from the equity of $3,500, which equals $500.

4. **B.** FINRA rules require a minimum equity deposit of $2,000 on the first transaction in a new margin account. After the customer sends in the required deposit, the equity is $2,000 (LMV of $3,000 – DR of $1,000 = EQ of $2,000). When the market value falls to $2,500 (a decrease of $500), the equity also declines by $500, leaving $1,500 of equity in the account.

5. **A.** The maintenance requirement in a long margin account is 25% of the market value of the stock. The equity in the account is $1,000, and the required maintenance margin is $1,500 (25% of the $6,000 long market value). Therefore, the account will receive a margin call for $500.

6. **C.** Equity may be increased by depositing cash or fully paid securities. SMA represents a line of credit, but there is no such thing as cancellation of an SMA balance.

7. **B.** The debit balance changes only when money is borrowed or deposited. A withdrawal of cash is borrowed against the loan value of the securities in the account, increasing the debit balance. A deposit of cash into the account reduces the debit balance.

8. **B.** The account is restricted by $500. The client will not, however, receive a margin call for the $500 because Regulation T applies only to the initial purchase. Because the account is restricted, withdrawal of securities requires a cash deposit of 50% or a deposit of securities with a loan value of 50% of the value of the securities withdrawn. The account is $5,250 above the required minimum, but this amount is not considered excess equity.

9. **A.** The account now has equity of $14,000. The Regulation T requirement is $13,000. This leaves $1,000 in excess equity that may be withdrawn.

$26,000	CMV
– 12,000	DR
$14,000	EQ
– 13,000	Regulation T
$1,000	EE

10. **C.** The sale of securities in the account results in an automatic release of funds to SMA. Nonrequired cash deposits, such as interest and dividends, are also automatically credited to SMA. An increase in the value of the securities will increase SMA if the excess equity becomes greater than existing SMA. A decrease in the market value of the securities will not increase or decrease SMA.

Quick Quiz 6.B

1. **B.** Equity in a short margin account is calculated by subtracting the short market value of $4,500 from the credit balance of $6,750 ($4,500 stock sales proceeds + $2,250 initial margin deposit of 50% = $6,750 credit balance). The initial deposit of $2,250 is the equity.

2. **A.** The Regulation T requirement and equity must be calculated before excess equity can be determined. The Regulation T requirement is 50% of the short market value of $4,000, which equals $2,000. Equity is calculated by subtracting the short market value of $4,000 from the credit balance of $6,750, which equals $2,750. Excess equity is then calculated by subtracting the Regulation T requirement of $2,000 from the equity of $2,750, which equals $750.

3. **C.** When selling stock short in a new account, an investor must meet the FINRA initial minimum requirement rules of $2,000. This is required although the Regulation T requirement is $1,625 ($3,250 × 50%).

4. **C.** The customer originally sold the stock at $80 per share and deposited $4,000 per the Regulation T requirement ($8,000 × 50%). He now has an SMV of $8,000 and a credit balance of $12,000 ($8,000 sale proceeds + $4,000 deposit). The market value of the stock is now down to $7,000. The customer may withdraw the equity of $5,000 when the position is closed.

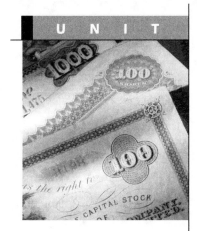

7

Issuing Securities

This Unit describes the process of bringing new issues to the marketplace. It focuses on registering securities, regulations that affect investment bankers, and special exemptions from the normal registration process.

New securities are sold in the primary market. The new issue market is regulated primarily by the Securities Act of 1933, which requires issuers of securities to provide sufficient information to the investing public in a prospectus so that investors may make informed investment decisions. The information must be filed with the SEC before an issue can be offered to the public. The Act of 1933 strictly prohibits fraudulent information or activity in connection with the underwriting and distribution of new issues.

This Unit accounts for about 10–15 questions on the Series 7 exam. ■

When you have completed this Unit, you should be able to:

■ **describe** the scope of the Securities Act of 1933 and the role of the SEC;

■ **identify** the steps in the registration process of nonexempt securities;

■ **describe** the role of investment bankers and syndicates in primary offerings;

■ **compare** and contrast firm commitment and best efforts underwriting agreements;

■ **list** and describe transactions that are exempt from the registration and prospectus requirements of the Securities Act of 1933; and

■ **define** rules that apply to the sale of a new issue of common stock.

Securities Act 1933
Securities Exchange act 1934 SEC
1938 Maloney act

7. 1 THE REGULATION OF NEW ISSUES

After the stock market crash of 1929, Congress examined the causes of the debacle and passed several laws designed to prevent its recurrence. This legislation included the Securities Act of 1933 and the Securities Exchange Act of 1934, among others.

7. 1. 1   THE LEGISLATIVE FRAMEWORK

7. 1. 1. 1   The Securities Act of 1933

The **Securities Act of 1933** regulates new issues of corporate securities sold to the public and requires securities issuers to provide enough information for investors to make fully informed buying decisions. This information must be filed with the SEC and published in a prospectus. The act prohibits any fraudulent activity in connection with the underwriting and issuing of all securities.

7. 1. 1. 2   The Securities Exchange Act of 1934

The **Securities Exchange Act of 1934** addresses secondary trading of securities, personnel involved in secondary trading, and fraudulent trading practices. It also created the **Securities and Exchange Commission (SEC)** to oversee the industry.

In 1938, the act was amended by the **Maloney Act**, which provides for the establishment of self-regulatory bodies to help police the industry. Each SRO, such as FINRA, MSRB, and CBOE, regulates its own members.

7. 2 THE THREE PHASES OF AN UNDERWRITING

When a security is first sold to the investing public, it goes through an underwriting process. Essentially, this process brings the new securities from the issuer to the marketplace.

7. 2. 1   REGISTRATION OF SECURITIES

The Securities Act of 1933 is also referred to as the **Paper Act**, **Full Disclosure Act**, **New Issues Act**, **Truth in Securities Act**, and **Prospectus Act**. The act's main purpose is to ensure that the investing public is fully informed about a security and its issuing company when the security is first sold in the primary market. The 1933 Act protects investors who buy new issues by:

- requiring registration of new issues that are to be distributed interstate;
- requiring an issuer to provide full and fair disclosure about itself and the offering;
- requiring an issuer to make available all material information necessary for an investor to judge the issue's merit;
- regulating the underwriting and distribution of primary and secondary issues; and
- providing criminal penalties for fraud in the issuance of new securities.

7. 2. 1. 1   The Registration Statement

An issuer must file with the SEC a **registration statement** disclosing material information about the issue. Part of the registration statement is a **prospectus**, which must be provided to all purchasers of the new issue.

The registration statement must contain:

- a description of the issuer's business;
- the names and addresses of company officers and directors, their salaries, and a five-year business history of each;
- the amount of corporate securities company officers and directors own and identification of investors who own 10% or more of the company;
- the company's capitalization, including its equity and debt;
- a description of how the proceeds will be used; and
- whether the company is involved in any legal proceedings.

The underwriter may assist the issuer in preparing and filing the registration statement and prospectus. However, the accuracy and adequacy of these documents is the responsibility of the issuer.

The registration statement must be signed by the issuer's chief executive officer, chief financial officer, and chief accounting officer, as well as a majority of the issuer's board of directors.

7. 2. 2   THE COOLING-OFF PERIOD

After the issuer files a registration statement with the SEC, a 20-day **cooling-off period** begins. After the issuer (with the underwriter's assistance) files with the SEC for registration of the securities, the cooling-off period ensues before the registration becomes effective.

The registration can become effective as early as 20 calendar days after the date the SEC has received it. In practice, however, the cooling-off period is seldom the minimum 20 days; the SEC usually takes longer to clear registration statements.

The Three Phases of an Underwriting

| Issuer files registration statement with the SEC | Cooling-off period | Effective date—offering period may begin |

| Prior to the filing of the registration statement, no sales can be solicited and no prospectus can circulate. | No one can solicit sales during the cooling-off period, but indications of interest can be solicited with a red herring. | Sales can now be solicited, but the firm must use a final prospectus. |

If it finds that the registration statement needs revision or expansion, the SEC may suspend the review and issue a deficiency letter. The 20-day cooling-off period resumes when the issuer submits a corrected registration statement.

The cooling-off period can last several months because of the time it takes to make additions and corrections. The SEC sometimes issues a **stop order**, which demands that all underwriting activities cease. This may be done if requirements of the 1933 Act have not been met or if fraud is suspected.

7. 2. 2. 1   Preliminary Prospectus

The **preliminary prospectus, or red herring**, can be used as a prospecting tool, allowing underwriters and selling group members to gauge investor interest and gather indications of interest. There is no final price included in the preliminary prospectus. The preliminary prospectus must be made available to any customer who expresses interest in the securities between the SEC registration filing date and when the SEC clears the issue for sale, the effective date.

An indication of interest is an investor's declaration that he might be interested in purchasing some of the issue from the underwriter after the security comes out of registration. An investor's indication of interest is not a commitment to buy because sales are prohibited until after the registration becomes effective (the **effective date**).

TAKE NOTE
Two items missing from the preliminary prospectus (red herring) are the public offering price and the effective date.

TEST TOPIC ALERT
During the cooling-off period, underwriters may not:

■ make offers to sell the securities;

■ take orders; or

■ distribute sales literature or advertising material.

However, they may:

■ take indications of interest;

■ distribute preliminary prospectuses; or

■ publish tombstone advertisements to provide information about the potential availability of the securities.

TAKE NOTE
A tombstone advertisement will show the anticipated gross proceeds of the issue. A final prospectus will show both the gross and net proceeds to the issuer.

7. 2. 2. 2   Advertising a New Issue

Advertising and **sales literature** include any notice, circular, advertisement, letter, or other communication published or transmitted to any person. The only advertising allowed during the cooling-off period is a **tombstone advertisement**, a simple statement of facts regarding the issue. The tombstone advertisement announces a new issue, but does not offer the securities for sale. The tombstone may appear before or after the effective date. Issuers or underwriters are not required to publish tombstone advertisements.

7. 2. 2. 3   Due Diligence

Near the end of the cooling-off period, the underwriter holds a **due diligence** meeting. The preliminary studies, investigations, research, meetings, and compilation of information about a corporation and a proposed new issue that go on during an underwriting are known collectively as due diligence.

The underwriter must conduct a formal due diligence meeting to provide information about the issue, the issuer's financial background, and the intended use of the proceeds. Representatives of the issuer and the underwriter attend these meetings and answer questions from brokers, securities analysts, and institutions.

As part of the due diligence process, investment bankers must:

■ examine the use of the proceeds;

■ perform financial analysis and feasibility studies;

■ determine the company's stability; and

■ determine whether the risk is reasonable.

7. 2. 2. 4   The Final Prospectus

When the registration statement becomes effective, the issuer amends the preliminary prospectus and adds information, including the final offering price and the underwriting spread for the **final prospectus**. Registered representatives may then take orders from those customers who indicated interest in buying during the cooling-off period.

A copy of the final prospectus must precede or accompany all sales confirmations. The prospectus must include the:

■ description of the offering;

■ offering price;

■ selling discounts;

■ offering date;

■ use of the proceeds;

■ description of the underwriting, but not the actual contract;

■ statement of the possibility that the issue's price may be stabilized;

■ history of the business;

■ risks to the purchasers;

■ description of management;

■ material financial information;

■ legal opinion concerning the formation of the corporation; and

■ SEC disclaimer.

7. 2. 2. 5   SEC Review

The SEC examines the prospectus for completeness. It does not guarantee the disclosure's accuracy nor does it approve the security; rather it clears it for distribution. Implying that the SEC has approved the issue violates federal law. The front of every prospectus must contain a clearly printed SEC disclaimer specifying the limits of the SEC's review procedures. A typical SEC disclaimer clause reads as follows:

> These securities have not been approved or disapproved by the Securities and Exchange Commission or by any State Securities Commission, nor has the Securities and Exchange Commission or any State Securities Commission passed upon the accuracy or adequacy of this prospectus. Any representation to the contrary is a criminal offense.

The information supplied to the SEC becomes public once a registration statement is filed.

7. 2. 2. 5. 1   Aftermarket Sales by Prospectus

In certain offerings, a final prospectus must be delivered by all members to buyers in the secondary market for a specified time following the effective date. This is termed the **prospectus delivery requirement period**.

For initial public offerings (IPOs), this period is:

- 90 days if the security is to be quoted on the OTC *Pink* or over the OTCBB (non-Nasdaq); or

- 25 days if the security is to be listed on an exchange or quoted over Nasdaq.

For additional issue offerings, the following apply.

- If the security is listed or quoted over Nasdaq, a prospectus must be delivered only in connection with purchases at the public offering price. Once the distribution is complete, there is no obligation to deliver a prospectus in secondary market transactions.

- If the security is non-Nasdaq, the prospectus delivery requirement period is 40 days.

7. 2. 2. 6   Access Equals Delivery

New rules acknowledge the widespread use of the internet and the use of electronic communications by adopting an access equals delivery model for meeting prospectus delivery obligations. A prospectus will be deemed to precede or accompany a security for sale if the final prospectus has been filed with the SEC. In other words, an investor can see a copy of the final prospectus by logging on to the SEC's website. The access equals delivery rule applies to the final prospectus and aftermarket prospectus delivery obligations.

TAKE NOTE   If a prospectus delivery requirement period exists in the secondary market, a prospectus must be delivered by all dealers, including those that did not participate in the distribution.

TAKE NOTE

An associated person may never mark (or use a highlighter on) a prospectus, whether preliminary or final. Doing so violates federal securities law.

QUICK QUIZ 7.A

1. Which of the following is NOT required in a preliminary prospectus?

    A. Written statement in red that the prospectus may be subject to change and amendment and that a final prospectus will be issued
    B. Purpose for which the funds being raised will be used
    C. Final offering price
    D. Financial status and history of the company

2. Which of the following statements about a red herring is NOT true?

    A. A red herring is used to obtain indications of interest from investors.
    B. The final offering price does not appear in a red herring.
    C. Additional information may be added to a red herring at a later date.
    D. A registered representative may send a copy of a company's research report with it.

3. As a registered representative, you can use a preliminary prospectus to

    A. obtain indications of interest from investors
    B. solicit orders from investors for the purchase of a new issue
    C. solicit an approval of the offering from the SEC
    D. obtain FINRA's authorization to sell the issue

4. If the SEC has cleared an issue, which of the following statements is TRUE?

    A. The SEC has guaranteed the issue.
    B. The underwriter has filed a standard registration statement.
    C. The SEC has endorsed the issue.
    D. The SEC has guaranteed the accuracy of the information in the prospectus.

Quick Quiz answers can be found at the end of the Unit.

7. 3 THE UNDERWRITING PROCESS

The issuer will enlist the help of an **underwriter**, a broker-dealer that specializes in investment banking and the distribution of new issues. The underwriter will often advise the issuer regarding the best financing mechanism (equity or debt) in light of current market conditions and tax considerations.

The underwriter will also normally form an **underwriting syndicate**, a group of other broker-dealers, to assist in the distribution of the new issue. An underwriter may commit to distribute a new issue in several different ways, each involving a different degree of risk to the underwriter. The degree of risk the underwriter assumes in the distribution of a new issue also affects the level of compensation it receives for the underwriting.

7. 3. 1   INVESTMENT BANKING

A business or municipal government that plans to issue securities usually works with an **investment bank**, a securities broker-dealer that underwrites new issues. An investment bank's functions may include the following:

- Advising corporations on the best ways to raise long-term capital
- Raising capital for issuers by distributing new securities
- Buying securities from issuers and reselling them to the public
- Distributing large blocks of stock to the public and to institutions
- Helping issuers comply with securities laws

7. 3. 2   PARTICIPANTS IN A CORPORATE NEW ISSUE

The main participants in a new issue are the company selling the securities and the broker-dealer acting as the underwriter.

7. 3. 2. 1   The Issuer

The **issuer** (the party selling the securities to raise money) is responsible for:

- filing the registration statement with the SEC;
- filing a registration statement with the states in which it intends to sell securities (also known as **blue skying** the issue); and
- negotiating the securities' price and the amount of the spread with the underwriter.

7. 3. 2. 2   The Underwriter

The **underwriter** assists with registration and distribution of the new security and may advise the corporate issuer on the best way to raise capital. The underwriter's considerations include the following.

- **Stocks or bonds:** Although debt financing comprises the bulk of corporate financing, if bonds are currently selling with high coupon rates, the company may choose to issue stock. Determining the cheapest cost of capital is a very important role of the investment bank.
- **Tax consequences of the offering:** The interest a corporation pays on its bonds is tax deductible; cash dividends to stockholders are paid out of after-tax profits.
- **Money market financing:** Money market instruments are a short-term financing mechanism, typically one year or less.
- **Capital market financing:** The capital markets represent long-term financing for secured bonds, debentures, and preferred or common stock. These securities require registration and sale by prospectus.

TEST TOPIC ALERT   Underwriters of nonexempt corporate securities are required to be FINRA member firms. U.S. nonmember firms, like banks, cannot participate as investment bankers in corporate issues. Banks may participate in municipal underwritings.

---

7. 3. 3   TYPES OF OFFERINGS

An **offering** is identified by who is selling the securities and whether the company is already publicly traded.

7. 3. 3. 1   New Issues

The **new issue market** is composed of companies going public by selling common stock to the public for the first time in an **initial public offering (IPO)**. Generally, their business purpose and products or services offered are clearly defined.

TAKE NOTE   Both the NYSE and Nasdaq allow the listing of Special Purpose Acquisition Companies (SPACs). These companies, also known as blank-check companies, are companies without business operations that raise money through IPOs in order to have their shares publicly traded for the sole purpose of seeking out a business or combination of businesses. When a business is located, they will present proposals to holders of their shares for approval.

---

7. 3. 3. 2   Additional Issues

The **additional issue market** is made up of new securities issued by companies that are already publicly owned. For instance, these companies may increase their equity capitalization by issuing more stock and having an underwriter either distribute the stock in a public offering or arrange for the shares to be sold in a private placement. In addition to being classified as new or additional issues of stock, offerings can be classified by the final distribution of their proceeds.

7. 3. 3. 3   Primary Offering

A **primary offering** is one in which the proceeds of the underwriting go to the issuing corporation. It may do this at any time and in any amount, provided the total stock outstanding does not exceed the amount authorized in the corporation's bylaws.

7. 3. 3. 4   Secondary Offering

A **secondary offering** is one in which one or more major stockholders in the corporation are selling all or a major portion of their holdings. The underwriting proceeds are paid to the stockholders rather than to the corporation.

7. 3. 3. 5 Split Offering (Combined Distribution)

A **split offering** is a combination of a primary and a secondary offering. The corporation issues a portion of the stock offered, and existing shareholders offer the balance.

7. 3. 3. 6 Shelf Offering

Through a **shelf offering**, an issuer who is already a publicly traded company can register new securities without selling the entire issue at once. Once filed, the registration is good for two years and allows the issuer to sell portions of a registered shelf offering over a three-year period without having to reregister the security. However, a supplemental prospectus must be filed before each sale. Shelf registrations can be used for both equity and debt offerings.

Offerings and Markets

	New Issue (IPO) Market	Additional Issue Market
Primary Offering	Company is going public; underwriting proceeds go to the company	Company is already public; underwriting proceeds go to the company
Secondary Offering	Company is going public; underwriting proceeds go to the selling stockholders	Company is already public; underwriting proceeds go to the selling stockholders

7. 3. 4 PUBLIC OFFERINGS AND PRIVATE PLACEMENTS

Corporate securities are sold to investors through either public offerings or private placements.

7. 3. 4. 1 Public Offering

In a **public offering**, securities are sold to the investing public through one or more broker-dealers.

7. 3. 4. 2 Private Placement

A **private placement** occurs when the issuing company, usually with the assistance of its investment bank, sells securities to private investors as opposed to the general investing public. Although private placement buyers tend to be institutional investors, securities may be sold to small groups of wealthy individuals. When an issuer privately places securities with investors, there can be no solicitation of the general public. Private placements are generally exempt from the registration requirements of the Securities Act of 1933.

Private Placements are exempt for Securities Act of 1933

7. 3. 5 UNDERWRITING SEQUENCE

7. 3. 5. 1 Forming the Syndicate

The syndicate and selling group may be assembled either before or after the issue is awarded to the underwriter. In **competitive bidding**, the syndicate is assembled first, and syndicate members work together to arrive at the bid. In **negotiated underwriting**, the syndicate may be formed after the issuer and the underwriting manager have negotiated the terms of the offering.

7. 3. 5. 2 Pricing the New Issue of Publicly Traded Securities

The underwriter advises the issuing corporation on the best price at which to offer securities to the public. The following variables may be considered when pricing new issues:

- Indications of interest from the underwriter's book
- Prevailing market conditions, including recent offerings and the prices of similar new issues
- Price that the syndicate members will accept
- **Price-to-earnings (PE) ratios** of similar companies and the company's most recent earnings report (at what price the shares must be offered so that the PE ratio is in line with the PE ratios of other similar publicly traded stocks)
- The company's dividend payment record (if any) and financial health
- The company's debt ratio

An issue's price or yield must be determined by the effective date of the registration. The **effective date** is when the security begins to trade.

7. 3. 5. 3 Stabilizing Price

In the case of a stock offering, when demand is considerably lower than supply for a new issue, the price in the aftermarket is likely to fall. Under these circumstances, the underwriter can stabilize the security by bidding for shares in the open market. These bids may be placed at or just below the public offering price. The managing underwriter can enter or appoint a syndicate member to enter stabilizing bids for the security until the end of the offering period.

7. 3. 5. 3. 1 Syndicate Penalty Bid

Stabilizing after an issue is sold out is not permitted. If syndicate members' clients turn in shares on a stabilizing bid after the issue is sold out, the syndicate manager will levy a **syndicate penalty bid** against those members.

TEST TOPIC ALERT Stabilizing bids must not be made at a price higher than the public offering price (POP). Stabilization is not illegal; however, if the stabilization bid is made at a price higher than the public offering price, it is called **pegging**, or **fixing**, and is strictly prohibited. If public buying interest does not increase, the managing underwriter may have no choice but to abandon the POP, pull the stabilizing bid, and let the stock find its own price level.

7. 4   THE UNDERWRITING SYNDICATE

Corporate underwriting normally takes the form of a **negotiated agreement** between the issuer and investment banker. This negotiated agreement, known as the **underwriting agreement**, is signed before the effective date.

7. 4. 0. 1   Underwriting Agreement

The **underwriting agreement (UA)** is the contract that establishes the relationship between the issuer and the underwriters, setting forth their respective rights and obligations and the terms and conditions upon which the issuer is required to sell and the underwriters are required to purchase the securities. The UA is executed and signed by all underwriters.

7. 4. 1   SYNDICATE FORMATION

Depending on the offering size, the underwriter may want to form a **syndicate**, or a **joint account**, for the purposes of the underwriting. The underwriting syndicate includes a syndicate manager and an association of underwriters.

7. 4. 1. 1   Underwriting Manager

The investment banker who negotiates with the issuer is known as the **underwriting manager** or **syndicate manager**. The underwriting manager directs the entire underwriting process, including signing the underwriting agreement with the issuer and directing the due diligence meeting and distribution process. A syndicate may have more than one manager.

7. 4. 1. 2   Syndicate Members

Underwriting syndicate members make a financial commitment to help bring the securities public. In a firm commitment offering, all syndicate members commit to purchase from the issuer and then distribute an agreed-on amount of the issue (their **participation** or **bracket**). Syndicate members sign a **syndicate agreement**, or **syndicate letter**, that describes the participants' responsibilities and allocation of syndicate profits, if any.

7. 4. 1. 2. 1   Agreement Among Underwriters

The agreement among underwriters details each underwriter's commitment and liability, particularly for any shares that remain unsold at the underwriting syndicate's termination (Western/divided, Eastern/undivided).

The agreement designates the syndicate manager to act on behalf of the syndicate members. The manager's authority to manage the underwriting, which includes establishing the offering price with the issuer, deciding the timing of the offering, controlling advertising, and making all required filings, comes via this agreement.

7. 4. 1. 3   Selling Group Formation

Although the members of an underwriting syndicate agree to underwrite an entire offering, they frequently enlist other firms to help distribute the securities as members of the selling group. **Selling group** members act as agents with no commitment to buy securities.

The managing underwriter is normally responsible for determining whether to use a selling group and, if so, which firms to include. If the securities to be issued are attractive, broker-dealers will want to participate. If the securities are not attractive, the manager may have to persuade broker-dealers to join.

Selling group members sign a **selling group agreement** with the underwriters, which typically contains:

- a statement that the manager acts for all of the underwriters;
- the amount of securities each selling group member will be allotted and the tentative public offering price at which the securities will be sold (this price is firmed up just before the offering date);
- provisions as to how and when payment for shares is to be made to the managing underwriter; and
- legal provisions limiting each selling group member's liability in conjunction with the underwriting.

TEST TOPIC ALERT   Syndicate members take on financial liability and act in a principal capacity. Selling group members have no financial liability and act as agents because they have no commitment to buy securities from the issuer.

7. 4. 1. 4   Negotiated Underwriting

In a **negotiated underwriting**, the issuer and the investment banker negotiate the offering terms, including the amount of securities to be offered, offering price or yield, and underwriting fees.

Negotiated underwritings are standard in underwriting corporate securities because of close business relationships between issuing corporations and investment banking firms.

7. 4. 1. 5   Competitive Bid

Competitive bid arrangements are the standard for underwriting most municipal securities and are often required by state law. In a competitive bid, a state or municipal government invites investment bankers to bid for a new issue of bonds. The issuer awards the securities to the underwriter(s) whose bid results in the lowest net interest cost to the issuer.

7. 5 TYPES OF UNDERWRITING COMMITMENTS

Different types of underwriting agreements require different levels of commitment from underwriters. This results in different levels of risk.

7. 5. 1   FIRM COMMITMENT

The **firm commitment** is a widely used type of underwriting contract. Under its terms, the underwriter contracts with the issuer, selling investors, or both to buy the securities described in the contract at a specified price and quantity range on or about a given date. The terms are detailed in a **letter of intent (LOI)** signed by the underwriter and the issuer during the early stages of negotiation.

Although this LOI is conditional for all practical purposes, the underwriter is committing to buy securities from the issuer and paying the underwriting proceeds to the company. Under a firm commitment contract, any losses incurred due to unsold securities are prorated among the underwriting firms according to their participation.

7. 5. 1. 1   Market-Out Clause

In a firm commitment underwriting, the underwriter assumes substantial financial risk for the underwriting. To limit its risks, a **market-out clause** in the underwriting agreement specifies conditions under which the offering may be canceled.

7. 5. 1. 2   Risks Beyond the Underwriter's Control

Underwriters may suspend or abort an offering if a material, adverse event occurs that affects the issuing corporation and impairs the investment quality of the securities being offered. An example of such an event would be the sudden death of the company president.

7. 5. 1. 3   Risks That the Underwriter Must Assume

Underwriters may not exercise market-out provisions if a nonmaterial, adverse event occurs that affects the issuing company but does not impair the securities' investment quality. A nonmaterial adverse event could be a Federal Reserve policy shift that leads to a general market decline before the offering. This would not qualify as a material event for this purpose.

7. 5. 2   STANDBY

When a company's current stockholders do not exercise their preemptive rights in an additional offering, a corporation has an underwriter **standing by** to purchase whatever shares remain unsold as a result of rights expiring.

Because the standby underwriter unconditionally agrees to buy all shares that current stockholders do not subscribe to at the subscription price, the offering is a firm commitment.

TAKE NOTE   By engaging a standby underwriter, an issuer is assured of selling all of the shares being offered.

7. 5. 3 BEST EFFORTS

A **best efforts underwriting** calls for the broker to buy securities from the issuer as agent, not as principal. This means that the underwriter is not committed and is therefore not at risk. The underwriter acts as agent contingent on the underwriter's ability to sell shares in either a public offering or a private placement.

7. 5. 3. 1 All or None

In an **all-or-none (AON) underwriting**, the issuing corporation has determined that it wants an agreement outlining that the underwriter must either sell all of the shares or cancel the underwriting. Because of the uncertainty over the outcome of an AON offering, any funds collected from investors during the offering period must be held in escrow pending final disposition of the underwriting.

Brokers engaged in an AON distribution are prohibited from deceiving investors by stating that all of the securities in the underwriting have been sold if it is not the case.

7. 5. 3. 2 Mini-Max

A **mini-max offering** is a best efforts underwriting setting a floor or minimum, which is the least amount the issuer needs to raise in order to move forward with the underwriting, and a ceiling or maximum on the dollar amount of securities the issuer is willing to sell. The underwriter must locate enough interested buyers to support the minimum (floor) issuance requirement. Once the minimum is met, the underwriter can expand the offering up to the maximum (ceiling) amount of shares the issuer specified. Mini-max underwriting terms are most frequently found in limited partnership program offerings, and funds collected from investors during the offering period must be held in escrow pending final disposition of the underwriting.

TEST TOPIC ALERT

Be prepared for a question that requires an understanding of underwriter risk in firm commitment and best efforts underwriting.

In a firm commitment underwriting, the underwriter takes on the financial risk because the securities are purchased from the issuer. Because of this risk, the underwriter is acting in a principal capacity.

In a best efforts underwriting, the underwriter sells as much as possible, without liability for what cannot be sold. The underwriter is acting in an agent capacity with no financial risk.

For example, if a corporation plans to sell 100,000 shares of common stock, but after exerting its best efforts, the underwriter can only sell 80,000 shares, the underwriter has no liability for the remaining 20,000 shares.

■ Firm commitment = principal capacity, underwriter has risk

■ Best efforts = agency capacity, underwriter has no risk

Remember that a standby offering is a firm commitment offering involving unexercised preemptive rights.

7. 5. 4   UNDERWRITING COMPENSATION

The price at which underwriters buy stock from issuers always differs from the price at which they offer the shares to the public. The price the issuer receives is known as the **underwriting proceeds**, and the price investors pay is the **public offering price (POP)**. The **underwriting spread**, the difference between the two prices, consists of the:

- **manager's fee**, for negotiating the deal and managing the underwriting and distribution process;
- **underwriting fee**, for assuming the risk of buying securities from the issuer without assurance that the securities can be resold; and
- **selling concession**, for placing the securities with investors.

TAKE NOTE
A member can grant discounts and other concessions only to other FINRA member firms. The only exception is that a member firm can grant concessions to a foreign nonmember firm that is ineligible for FINRA membership.

---

7. 5. 4. 1   Industry Standard Practices

The industry norm for allocating the spread for corporate equity issues is as follows.

Spread Allocation

Underwriting Component	Fee Range
Syndicate manager's fee	10–20%
Underwriting syndicate fee	20–30%
Selling concession	50–60%

EXAMPLE
Assume a 1 million share initial public offering of common stock. Shares will be sold to the public for $10.00, and the underwriting spread is $.65 per share. The following illustration depicts the distribution of the spread and proceeds of the underwriting. The $.65 spread is allocated as follows.

- Syndicate manager's fee: compensation for the manager's role in the underwriting—in this case, $.12 per share, or $120,000 for 1 million shares. The manager's fee is typically the smallest portion of the spread.

- Underwriting fee: this portion of the spread compensates syndicate members for the risk they assume in the underwriting. The underwriting fee—in this case, $.13 per share—is allocated to syndicate members on the basis of their participation.

- Selling concession: the largest portion of the spread is the selling concession, the amount received by any member that sells the shares. In this case, the concession is $.40 per share.

Who Gets What in an Underwriting

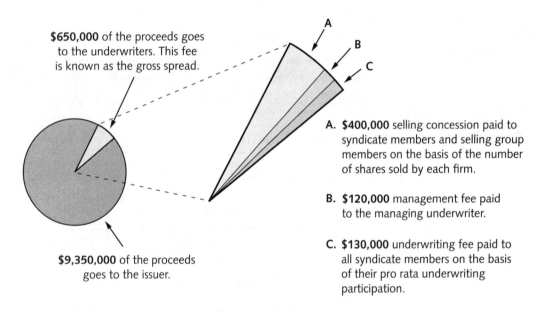

**New Issue
Incorporated
Common Stocks
1 Million Shares
Price $10**

$10 million gross from the sale
of the issue to the public.
(1 million shares × $10 = $10 million)

$650,000 of the proceeds goes
to the underwriters. This fee
is known as the gross spread.

A. **$400,000** selling concession paid to
syndicate members and selling group
members on the basis of the number
of shares sold by each firm.

B. **$120,000** management fee paid
to the managing underwriter.

C. **$130,000** underwriting fee paid to
all syndicate members on the basis
of their pro rata underwriting
participation.

$9,350,000 of the proceeds
goes to the issuer.

The amount of the spread varies by issue and can be influenced by any of the following.

■ Type of commitment: A firm commitment earns a larger spread than a best efforts agreement because of the risks the underwriter assumes.

■ Security's marketability: A bond rated AAA has a smaller spread than a speculative stock.

■ Issuer's business: A stable utility stock usually has a smaller spread than a more volatile stock.

■ Offering size: In a very large offering, the underwriter can spread costs over a larger number of shares; thus, the per-share cost may be lower.

QUICK QUIZ 7.B   Match the items below with the best definition or description.

A. Cooling-off period
B. Securities Act of 1933
C. Red herring
D. Split (combined) offering
E. Indication of interest

_____ 1. Has aspects of both a primary and secondary offering

_____ 2. An investor's expression of a conditional wish to purchase a new security after that investor has read a preliminary prospectus

_____ 3. Interval between the filing date of a registration statement and the date on which the security becomes effective

_____ 4. Abbreviated prospectus distributed while an issuer's registration statement is reviewed by the SEC

_____ 5. Federal securities legislation mandating full and fair disclosure about new issues

7. 6 EXEMPTIONS FROM THE SECURITIES ACT OF 1933

7. 6. 1 EXEMPT ISSUERS AND SECURITIES

Certain securities are exempt from the registration statement and prospectus requirements of the 1933 Act, either because of the issuer's level of creditworthiness or because another government regulatory agency has jurisdiction over the issuer.

These exempt securities include:

- U.S. government securities;
- municipal bonds;
- commercial paper and banker's acceptances that have maturities of less than 270 days;
- insurance policies and fixed annuity contracts (but not variable annuities);
- national and state bank (not bank holding company) securities;
- building and loan (S&L) securities;
- charitable, religious, educational, and nonprofit association issues; and
- interests in railroad equipment certificates.

Banks are exempted from SEC registration of their securities because they file information on new issues with bank regulators and make it available to investors.

TAKE NOTE   This exemption applies only to the securities of banks, not to the securities of bank holding companies.

Insurance policies are not included in the definition of *security*; however, variable annuities, variable life insurance, and variable universal life insurance are funded by separate accounts and must be registered as securities with the SEC.

7. 6. 2 EXEMPT TRANSACTIONS

Securities offered by industrial, financial, and other corporations may qualify for exemption from the registration statement and prospectus requirements of the 1933 Act under one of the following exclusionary provisions:

■ Regulation A+: small and medium corporate offerings

■ Regulation D: private placements

■ Rule 147: securities offered and sold exclusively intrastate

■ Regulation S: offers and sales made outside the United States by U.S. issuers

■ Other exempt transactions, including Rule 144, Rule 144a, and Rule 145

7. 6. 2. 1 Regulation A+: Small and Medium Offerings

With the passage of the JOBs Act, a capital formation scheme was called for that would further ease the requirements for small- and medium-sized companies to raise capital. Previously known as Regulation A, the new rule is Regulation A+.

Regulation A+ provides two offering tiers for small- and medium-sized companies that will allow the companies to raise capital in amounts substantially more than the $5 million previously allowed under Regulation A.

■ **Tier 1:** Securities offerings up to $20 million in a 12-month period will be allowed. Of the $20 million, no more than $6 million can be sold on behalf of existing selling shareholders. The offering would be subject to a coordinated review by individual states and the SEC.

■ **Tier 2:** Securities offerings up to $50 million in a 12-month period will be allowed. Of the $50 million, no more than $15 million can be sold on behalf of existing selling shareholders. These offerings are subject to SEC review only and none at the state level. Tier 2 offerings are still subject to rigorous disclosure requirements to the SEC including audited financial statements, annual, semi-annual and current reports.

Offerings under both tiers are open to the public and general solicitation is permitted for both tiers. However, Tier 2 investors must be "qualified" investors, and there are two ways to qualify:

1. Be an accredited investor as defined in Rule 501 of Regulation D

2. Limit the investment to a maximum of the greater of 10% of the investor's net worth or 10% of the investor's net income per offering. Note that self-certification for Tier 2 as to net worth and income is all that is required with no burdensome filings. Tier 1 has no investment limits.

Finally, remembering that the new Regulation A+ is intended for small- and medium-sized companies, the regulation specifically excludes investment companies (i.e., private equity funds, venture capital funds, and hedge funds).

In a Regulation A+ offering, the issuer files an abbreviated **notice of sale**, or **offering circular**, with the regional SEC office. Investors are provided with this offering circular rather than a full prospectus.

The cooling-off period is 20 days between the filing date and effective date, and the issuer need not provide audited financial information. Individuals buying securities in a Regulation A+ offering must receive a final offering circular at least 48 hours before confirmation of sale.

7. 6. 2. 2   Regulation D: Private Placements

The SEC does not require registration of an offering if it is privately placed with:

- accredited investors that do not need SEC protection; or
- a maximum of 35 individual (nonaccredited) investors.

An **accredited investor** is defined as one who:

- has a net worth of $1 million or more, not including net equity in a primary residence; or
- has had an annual income of $200,000 or more in each of the two most recent years (or $300,000 jointly with a spouse) and who has a reasonable expectation of reaching the same income level during the current year.

Officers and directors of the issuer are also accredited.

Purchasers must have access to the same type of information they would receive if the securities were being sold under prospectus in a registered offering. The amount of capital that can be raised is unlimited.

A private placement investor must sign a letter stating that he intends to hold the stock for investment purposes only. Private placement stock is referred to as **lettered stock** due to this investment letter. The certificate may bear a legend indicating that it cannot be transferred without registration or exemption; therefore, private placement stock is also referred to as **legend stock**.

The SEC requires that all companies raising capital in a non-public offering that qualify under the Regulation D exemption file the information on Form D electronically via the internet. The SEC also specifies the instances when an amended Form D be filed, such as to correct a mistake of fact or error or to reflect a change in information.

7. 6. 2. 2. 1   General Solicitations and Advertising Private Placements

In order to solicit or advertise private securities offerings (private placements) a business will need to meet certain requirements regarding the intended investors. First, meeting the requirements assumes that the securities are in fact being offered under the Regulation D registration exemption. Beyond that assumption the requirements are as follows:

- All purchasers of the advertised securities must be accredited investors or the business must reasonably believe that the investors are accredited investors at the time of the sale. In other words, while businesses may sell to up to 35 nonaccreditied investors, in order to solicit or advertise, all purchasers must be accredited.
- The business must take reasonable steps to verify that all purchasers are accredited, considering background, relevant facts (such as reported income), and particular circumstances of each purchaser.

TEST TOPIC ALERT   Sometimes it is difficult to identify private placement stock in a question because of the many terms that can be used to describe it. Recognize all of the following terms as synonymous with private placement stock:

- Restricted (because it must be held for a six-month period)

- Unregistered (no registration statement on file with the SEC)

- Letter stock (investor agreed to terms by signing an investment letter)

- Legend stock (a special inscription on the stock certificate indicates restricted transfer)

7. 6. 2. 3   Rule 147: Intrastate Offerings

Under **Rule 147**, offerings that take place entirely in one state are exempt from registration when:

- the issuer has its principal office and receives at least 80% of its income in the state;
- at least 80% of the issuer's assets are located within the state;
- at least 80% of the offering proceeds are used within the state;
- the broker-dealer acting as underwriter is a resident of the state and has an office in the state; and
- all purchasers are residents of the state.

TAKE NOTE   To qualify under the Rule 147 exemption, only one of the three 80% tests noted above must be met.

Purchasers of an intrastate issue may not resell the stock to any resident of another state for at least six months after the purchase.

7. 6. 2. 4   Rule 144

Rule 144 regulates the sale of control and restricted securities, stipulating the holding period, quantity limitations, manner of sale, and filing procedures.

Control securities are those owned by directors, officers, or persons who own or control more than 10% of the issuer's voting stock.

TAKE NOTE   If an unaffiliated individual owns 7% of the voting stock of XYZ, that person is not a control person. However, if that person's spouse owns 4% of the voting stock, then both would be considered control persons. In other words, if there is a 10% or more interest held by immediate family members, then all those family members owning voting stock are control persons.

Restricted securities are those acquired through some means other than a registered public offering. A security purchased in a private placement is a restricted security. Restricted securities may not be sold until they have been held fully paid for six months. According to Rule 144, after holding restricted stock fully paid for six months, an affiliate may begin selling shares but is subject to the volume restriction rules as enumerated below. In any 90-day period, an investor may sell the greater of:

- 1% of the total outstanding shares of the same class at the time of sale; or

- the average weekly trading volume in the stock over the past four weeks on all exchanges or as reported through Nasdaq.

After the six-month holding period, affiliated persons are subject to the volume restrictions for as long as they are affiliates. For unaffiliated investors, the stock may be sold completely unrestricted after the six-month holding period has been satisfied.

Selling shares under Rule 144 effectively registers the shares. In other words, buyers of stock being sold subject to Rule 144 are not subject to any restrictions if they choose to resell.

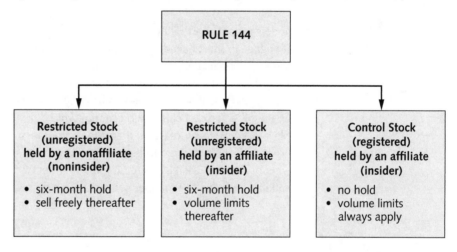

TEST TOPIC ALERT

When you encounter a Rule 144 question, always look for two things:

What kind of stock is being sold? (Restricted or control)
Who is selling it? (Insider or noninsider)

Only restricted stock has a holding period. Control stock, unless it is restricted, can be sold immediately, but volume limits always apply.

Which of the following is subject to the holding period provisions of Rule 144?

A. A corporate insider who has held restricted stock for 2 years.

B. A nonaffiliate who has held registered stock for 3 years.

C. A nonaffiliate who has held control stock for 6 months.

D. A nonaffiliate who has held restricted stock for 3 months.

Answer: D. Only restricted stock is subject to the six-month holding period for both affiliates and nonaffiliate; registered shares are not and control stock is not. The nonaffiliate in choice D, who has only held the shares for 3 months, will still be subject to the holding period until the six-month requirement is met.

When required, Form 144 must be filed no later than concurrently with the sale of the stock, and the filing is good for 90 days. If the intended sale during any 90-day period for an affiliate is small, the filing requirement is waived. This is known as the *de minimis filing threshold* for affiliates. Sales in amounts not exceeding 5,000 shares or $50,000 in sale proceeds are permitted without filing Form 144.

Current information about the company must be made available to the buyer. This can be accomplished by verifying that the company is a reporting company that regularly files 10K and 10Q reports with the SEC.

Insiders defined under Rule 144 are not allowed to enter short sales in the securities of companies in which they are insiders. They are also restricted from participating in speculative options transactions. If an insider profits from the sale of securities held for less than six months, these short-swing profits are required to be disgorged (returned) to the company. Any trading of insider-owned securities must be reported to the SEC within two business days of the transaction.

TAKE NOTE

Insiders cannot short. They are prohibited from taking short-swing profits and cannot engage in short naked options positions or short sales.

However, insiders are permitted to write calls against a long stock position but only if the shares held are unrestricted. If the shares held were restricted, the resale restriction would not allow the shares to be delivered should the calls be exercised.

On the other hand, a corporation cannot write calls against its own stock; for example, stock held in its treasury (shares the corporation has purchased back from shareholders). If the calls were to be exercised, the company must deliver shares to the owner of the calls, thereby increasing the number of outstanding shares for the corporation. Increasing the number of outstanding shares would require shareholder approval.

7. 6. 2. 5   Rule 144a

Rule 144a allows nonregistered foreign and domestic securities to be sold to certain institutional investors in the United States without holding period requirements. To qualify for this exemption, the buyer must be a **qualified institutional buyer (QIB)**. One requirement of a QIB is a minimum of $100 million in assets.

7. 6. 2. 6   Rule 145

Rule 145 of the 1933 Act is intended to protect stockholders of any company that proposes to reorganize its ownership structure, acquire another company, or merge with another company. Any such proposition requires stockholder approval. Rule 145 requires that stockholders be sent a full disclosure document (a proxy statement) to inform them of the proposition.

7. 6. 2. 6. 1   Transactions Covered by Rule 145

Transactions that Rule 145 covers are reclassifications, mergers or consolidations, and transfers of assets, defined as follows:

■ **Reclassification**—when one class of securities is to be exchanged internally for another class in a way that shifts ownership control

- **Merger or consolidation**—when stockholders in a target company are offered securities in another company in exchange for the surrender of their stock

- **Transfer of assets**—when all or some of one company's business assets are exchanged for another company's securities; stockholders thus solicited are being asked to approve their company's dissolution

---

TAKE NOTE   Rule 145 specifically excludes shares resulting from a stock split or a stock dividend from having to be registered with the SEC.

7. 6. 3   ANTIFRAUD REGULATIONS OF THE ACTS OF 1933 AND 1934

Although a security may be exempt from the registration and prospectus requirements, no offering is exempt from the antifraud provisions of the Securities Act of 1933 or any other securities act, including the Securities Exchange Act of 1934. The antifraud provisions of the Act of 1933 apply to all new securities offerings, whether exempt from registration or not. Issuers must provide accurate information regarding any securities offered to the public.

7. 6. 3. 1   Protecting the Public and Restricted Persons Prohibitions (FINRA Rule 5130)

The rule is designed to protect the integrity of the public offering process by ensuring that:

- members make a bona fide public offering of securities at the public offering price;

- members do not withhold securities in a public offering for their own benefit or use such securities to reward persons who are in a position to direct future business to the member; and

- industry insiders, such as members and their associated persons, do not take advantage of their insider status to gain access to new issues for their own benefit at the expense of public customers.

The rule applies only to a new issue, which is defined to mean any initial public offering of equity securities. The rule does not apply to additional issue offerings, debt securities, restricted or exempt securities, convertible securities, preferred stock, investment company securities, offerings of business development companies, direct participation companies, and real estate investment trusts. Essentially, the rule applies to IPOs of common stock.

The rule prohibits member firms from selling a new issue to any account where restricted persons are beneficial owners. Restricted persons are defined as follows:

1. Member firms.

2. Employees of member firms.

3. Finders and fiduciaries acting on behalf of the managing underwriter, including attorneys, accountants, financial consultants, and so on.

4. Portfolio managers, including any person who has the authority to buy or sell securities for a bank, savings and loan association, insurance company, or investment company.

5. Any person owning 10% or more of a member firm.

Furthermore, any immediate family member of any person in 2–5 above is also restricted. Immediate family includes parents, in-laws, spouses, siblings, children, or any other individual to whom the person provides material support.

E X A M P L E
Aunts and uncles as well as grandparents are not considered immediate family. If, however, one of these individuals lives in the same household as a restricted person, that individual would be a restricted person.

Finally, there is a de minimis exemption. If the beneficial interests of restricted persons do not exceed 10% of an account, the account may purchase a new equity issue. In other words, restricted persons will be able to have an interest in an account that purchases new equity issues as long as no more than 10% of the account's beneficial owners are restricted persons.

Spinning is the practice of allocating highly sought after IPO shares to individuals who are in a position to direct securities business to the firm. This is why portfolio managers are categorized as restricted persons. These individuals are in a position to direct business to a firm and may be willing to do so on the basis of the size of their allocation.

Before selling an IPO to any account, representatives are required to obtain a written representation from the account owner(s) that the account is eligible to purchase a new common stock issue at the public offering price. All representations must be obtained within the 12-month period before the sale of the new issue and must be retained for at least three years following the new issue sale.

UNIT TEST

1. ABC is preparing a registration statement for a new issue consisting of 300,000 new shares and 200,000 existing shares held by officers. The offering price is $30 per share, and the spread taken by the underwriters is $2 per share. After the offering is complete, ABC will receive
   A. $8.4 million
   B. $9 million
   C. $14 million
   D. $15 million

2. An offering of securities in compliance with Rule 144a is sold primarily to
   A. American individual investors
   B. qualified institutional buyers
   C. foreign individual investors
   D. all of the above

3. An underwriting spread is
   A. the amount a managing underwriter receives
   B. the amount a selling group receives
   C. the amount a syndicate receives
   D. the difference between an offering price and the proceeds to an issuer

4. A company has filed a registration statement for an initial public offering of its common stock with the SEC. As a registered representative, you can
   I. send out a research report on the company to your customers
   II. take indications of interest from your customers
   III. send a preliminary prospectus to each of your customers
   IV. take orders for the stock from customers in cash accounts only
   A. I and II
   B. I and III
   C. II and III
   D. III and IV

5. The principal functions of an investment banker are to
   I. distribute securities to the public
   II. provide a secondary market
   III. provide financing for an individual
   IV. advise the issuer about alternatives in raising capital
   A. I and II
   B. I and IV
   C. II and III
   D. III and IV

6. A Regulation A+ exemption covers
   A. an offering of $50 million or less in 12 months
   B. an offering of letter stock
   C. a private offering
   D. an offering of $50 million or more in 12 months

7. Which of the following are characteristics of the Securities Act of 1933?
   I. Requires registration of exchanges
   II. Called the Truth in Securities Act
   III. Requires full and fair disclosure of material facts
   IV. Requires that all debt securities be issued with a trust indenture
   A. I and II
   B. II and III
   C. II and IV
   D. III and IV

8. A final prospectus must include all of the following EXCEPT
   A. the effective date of the registration
   B. whether the underwriter intends to stabilize the issue
   C. a statement indicating that the SEC has approved the issue
   D. disclosure of material information concerning the issuer's financial condition

9. Which of the following are considered to be non-exempt offerings according to the Securities Act of 1933?

   I.   Government securities
   II. Private placements
   III. Public offering of $60 million by a brokerage firm
   IV. Sales of corporate bonds of $52 million

   A. I and II
   B. I and III
   C. II and IV
   D. III and IV

10. The largest portion of an underwriting spread is

   A. the manager's fee
   B. the underwriting fee
   C. the concession
   D. the stabilizing bid

11. Under the intrastate offering rule (Rule 147), when may a resident purchaser of securities resell them to a nonresident?

   A. 3 months after the first sale made in that state
   B. 6 months after the last sale made in that state
   C. At least 6 months after the date of purchase
   D. None of the above

12. Which of the following statements regarding a Rule 144 sale of restricted stock are TRUE?

   I.   Stock sold through a 144 sale is considered registered stock after the sale.
   II. After holding the stock for 6 months, the holding period is satisfied for nonaffiliates.
   III. After holding the stock for 2 years, there are no volume restrictions for affiliates.
   IV. Form 144 must be filed with the SEC at least 10 business days before a 144 sale.

   A. I and II
   B. I and III
   C. II and III
   D. III and IV

13. An affiliate holding restricted stock wishes to sell under Rule 144. The shares have been held fully paid for one year. The issuer has outstanding 2.4 million shares. Form 144 is filed on Monday, April 10, and the weekly trading volume for the stock is shown below.

Week Ending	Trading Volume
April 7	23,000
March 31	25,000
March 24	26,000
March 17	24,000
March 10	22,000

The maximum number of shares the customer can sell with this filing is

   A. 23,000
   B. 24,000
   C. 24,250
   D. 24,500

14. The group of investment bankers that actually purchases the stocks to be resold to the investing public is called

   A. the standby group
   B. the syndicate
   C. the selling group
   D. the underwriting manager

15. If an underwriter purchases what is left of a rights issue from the issuer, under what terms is he buying?

   A. Firm commitment
   B. Best efforts
   C. All or none
   D. Standby

16. When a corporation issues a portion of the stock offered, and existing shareholders offer the balance of the shares offered, this is known as

   A. a split offering
   B. a secondary offering
   C. a primary offering
   D. a combination offering

17. The underwriting agreement is signed by
    A. the issuer and the SEC
    B. the issuer and the managing underwriter
    C. the managing underwriter and the syndicate members
    D. the selling group members and the syndicate members

18. All of the following would be defined by FINRA as a restricted person EXCEPT
    A. member firms
    B. employees of member firms
    C. the aunt of a member firm employee
    D. the sibling of a member firm employee

19. Regarding the antifraud provisions of the Securities Acts of 1933 and 1934, which of the following statements is TRUE?
    A. Exempt issuers, like the federal government, are exempt from the provisions.
    B. Exempt securities, like those issued by municipalities, are exempt from the provisions.
    C. Exempt transactions, like those offered under Regulation A+, are exempt from the provisions.
    D. No securities, issuers, or transactions are exempt from the antifraud provisions of these acts.

20. Regulation D. mandates all of the following EXCEPT
    A. if the offering is advertised, all purchasers must be accredited
    B. under no circumstances can more than 20 nonaccredited investors participate in the purchase of shares
    C. investors agree to terms by signing an investment letter
    D. a special inscription or legend on the stock certificate indicates that its transfer is restricted

ANSWERS AND RATIONALES

1. **A.** ABC Corporation will receive $28 per share for each of the 300,000 new shares being issued ($30 per share price less $2 spread). The proceeds from the 200,000 shares sold by the officers will benefit the officers themselves, not ABC Corporation.

2. **B.** Rule 144a allows securities to be sold to institutional buyers (qualified institutional buyers) without having to meet the holding period or volume requirements of Rule 144.

3. **D.** A spread is the difference between the public offering price and the price an underwriter pays an issuer.

4. **C.** New issues can be sold only by prospectus, and indications of interest can be taken when the issue is in registration. During the registration period, only the preliminary prospectus may be sent to clients. Sales literature, such as research reports, may not be distributed nor may orders be taken while the IPO is in registration.

5. **B.** The principal functions of the underwriter are to advise the issuer about the financial alternatives and to sell securities to the public.

6. **A.** A Regulation A+ filing under the Securities Act of 1933 exempts the security from registration and limits offerings to $50 million or less within a 12-month period.

7. **B.** The Securities Act of 1933 regulates new issues of corporate securities sold to the public. The act is also referred to as the Full Disclosure Act, the Paper Act, the Truth in Securities Act, and the Prospectus Act. The purpose of the act is to require full, written disclosure about a new issue. The Securities Exchange Act of 1934 requires exchanges to register with the SEC, and the Trust Indenture Act of 1939 requires corporations issuing more than $50 million in bonds to have a trust indenture.

8. **C.** If the underwriter intends to engage in activities designed to stabilize the security's market price, disclosure in the prospectus is required. The SEC disclaimer must appear on every prospectus and state that the SEC has neither approved nor disapproved the issue. The effective date must be printed on the final prospectus. Its purpose is full disclosure about the issuer and security being issued.

9. **D.** The Securities Act of 1933 exempts U.S. government bonds and private placements from registration. Public offerings of less than $50 million, and in some cases $20 million, are also exempt (under Regulation A+), so an offering of $60 million and sales of corporate bonds are not exempt; they must be registered with the SEC.

10. **C.** The largest portion of the spread is the concession.

11. **C.** In an intrastate offering, a purchaser of the issue may not sell the securities to a resident of another state for at least 6 months from the date of purchase.

12. **A.** After stock is sold by an affiliate or a nonaffiliate, it is considered registered stock, and affiliates are always subject to volume restrictions. Form 144 must be filed with the SEC on or before date of sale. After holding the stock fully paid for a total of 6 months, nonaffiliates may sell the stock completely unrestricted.

13. **D.** Under Rule 144, having held the fully paid restricted shares for at least 6 months, the affiliate can begin selling subject to the volume restrictions of Rule 144. The affiliate can sell the greater of 1% of the total shares outstanding or the weekly average of the prior 4 weeks' trading volume (the 4 weeks preceding the Form 144 filing). In this case, 1% of the total shares outstanding equals 24,000, (1% × 2.4 million). The weekly average of the prior 4 weeks' trading volume is 24,500. Therefore, the most the affiliate can sell during the 90 days following the form filing is 24,500 shares.

14. **B.** It is the syndicate members who purchase the securities issue being offered and are responsible for reselling to the public. The underwriting manager is the manager of that syndicate. Selling group members work on behalf of syndicate members as agents trying their best to sell for the benefit of the syndicate.

15. **D.** This is the definition of standby underwriting. It will also be important for you to know that in both firm commitment and standby commitment, the underwriter actually purchases the securities for resale. He is a principal in the deal. In a best efforts or all-or-none underwriting, the underwriter is acting as an agent. He does not have the financial liability of ownership.

16. **A.** When a corporation issues a portion of the stock offered, and existing shareholders offer the balance of the shares offered, this is known as a split offering.

17. **B.** The underwriting manager directs the entire underwriting process, including signing the underwriting agreement with the issuer. The agreement among underwriters is signed by the managing underwriter and all syndicate members. The selling group members have no formal agreement with the underwriters to be signed.

18. **C.** While immediate family members are considered restricted persons, aunts, uncles and grandparents are not considered immediate family unless they live in the same household as a restricted person.

19. **D.** No securities, issuers, or transactions are exempt from the antifraud provisions of these acts.

20. **B.** A maximum of 35 nonaccredited investors may participate in the purchase of securities offered under a Regulation D exempt offering.

Securities Act 33
Securities exchange Act 34
trust indenture Act 39

QUICK QUIZ ANSWERS

Quick Quiz 7.A

1. **C.** A preliminary prospectus is issued before the price is established, and it does not include the eventual offering date or the spread.

2. **D.** A registered representative is prohibited from sending a research report with either a preliminary or final prospectus.

3. **A.** A preliminary prospectus is used to obtain indications of interest from investors.

4. **B.** The SEC does not approve, endorse, or guarantee the accuracy of a registration statement.

Quick Quiz 7.B

1. **D.**

2. **E.**

3. **A.**

4. **C.**

5. **B.**

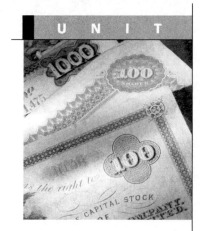

8

Trading Securities

This Unit will examine trading activities both on the exchanges and OTC. It presents many terms and rules that are used by the industry and are critical for exam success.

The trading of securities in the secondary market is regulated by the Securities Exchange Act of 1934. The Act of 1934 created the Securities and Exchange Commission and gave it the authority to regulate securities exchanges and the OTC market.

Exchanges, such as the NYSE, operate as double-auction markets where stocks listed on the exchange are traded. The OTC market is an interdealer computer and telephone network where market makers in stocks show the bid and ask price for stocks in which they make a market.

The Series 7 exam is likely to include approximately 20–25 trading questions on the information covered in this Unit. ■

When you have completed this Unit, you should be able to:

■ **explain** the impact of the Securities Exchange Act of 1934 on trading activities;

■ **describe** the four markets of the secondary marketplace;

■ **identify** the different types of exchange members and explain their roles;

■ **compare** the types of orders available to customers;

■ **identify** unique concepts of OTC trading and the securities included; and

■ **explain** the 5% markup policy and identify the transactions subject to it.

8. 1 THE REGULATION OF TRADING

The Securities Act of 1933 regulates primary issues of securities, and the Securities Exchange Act of 1934 regulates secondary trading.

8. 1. 1 THE SECURITIES EXCHANGE ACT OF 1934

The 1934 Act, known as the *Exchange Act*, established the Securities and Exchange Commission (SEC) and gave it the authority to regulate, in part, broker-dealers, the securities exchanges, and the over-the-counter (OTC) markets to maintain a fair and orderly market for the investing public.

The Securities Exchange Act of 1934 requires exchange members, broker-dealers that trade securities OTC, on exchanges, or both, and individuals who make securities trades for the public to be registered with the SEC.

The Securities Exchange Act of 1934 provides for:

- the creation of the SEC;
- the regulation of exchanges;
- the regulation of the OTC market;
- the regulation of credit by the Federal Reserve Board (FRB);
- the registration of broker-dealers;
- the net capital rules;
- the regulation of insider transactions, short sales, and proxies;
- the regulation of trading activities;
- the regulation of client accounts;
- the customer protection rule;
- the filing of 10-Qs, 10-Ks, and other financial statements by companies that are required to report; and
- the regulation of officers, directors, and principal shareholders.

8. 1. 1. 1 The Securities and Exchange Commission (SEC)

Composed of five commissioners appointed by the President of the United States and approved by the Senate, the SEC enforces the 1934 Act by regulating the securities markets and the behavior of market participants.

8. 1. 1. 2 Registration of Exchanges and Firms

The 1934 Act requires national securities exchanges to file registration statements with the SEC. By registering, exchanges agree to comply with and help enforce the rules of this act. Each exchange gives the SEC copies of its bylaws, constitution, and articles of incorporation. An exchange must disclose to the SEC any amendment to exchange rules as soon as it is adopted.

The Act of 1934 also requires companies that list their securities on the exchanges and certain firms traded OTC to register with the SEC. An SEC-registered company must file both quarterly and annual reports (Forms 10-Q and 10-K, respectively) informing the SEC of its financial status and providing other information.

8. 2 SECURITIES MARKETS AND BROKER-DEALERS

8. 2. 1 SECURITIES MARKETS

The market in which securities are bought and sold is also known as the **secondary market**, as opposed to the primary market for new issues. All securities transactions take place in one of four trading markets.

8. 2. 1. 1 Exchange Market (Auction Market)

The **exchange market** is composed of the NYSE and other exchanges on which listed securities are traded. This market is also known as an **auction market**. The term **listed security** refers to any security listed for trading on an exchange.

8. 2. 1. 2 Over-the-Counter (OTC) Market (Second Market)

The **OTC market** is an inter-dealer market in which **unlisted securities**—that is, securities not listed on any exchange—trade. It is also known as the **second market**. In the OTC market, securities dealers across the country are connected by computer and telephone. Thousands of securities are traded OTC, including stocks, bonds, and all municipal and U.S. government securities.

As far as equities are concerned, the OTC market is divided into Nasdaq and non-Nasdaq. Nasdaq consists of three markets: Global Select Market, Global Market, and Capital Market. Non-Nasdaq consists of stock on the OTC *Pink* or on the OTC Bulletin Board.

8. 2. 1. 3 Third Market (OTC Listed)

The **third market**, or **Nasdaq Intermarket,** is a trading market in which exchange-listed securities are traded in the OTC market. Broker-dealers registered as OTC **market makers** in listed securities can do transactions in the third-market. All securities listed on the NYSE and most securities listed on the regional exchanges are eligible for OTC trading as long as the trades are reported to the **Consolidated Tape** within 10 seconds of execution.

8. 2. 1. 4 Fourth Market

The **fourth market** is a market for institutional investors in which large blocks of stock, both listed and unlisted, trade in transactions unassisted by broker-dealers. These transactions take place through **electronic communications networks (ECNs)**. ECNs are open 24 hours a day and act solely as agents.

8. 2. 1. 5 Trading Hours

The NYSE trades between 9:30 am and 4:00 pm ET each business day. Normal hours for retail OTC trading are the same as those of the NYSE, although many market makers remain open until 6:30 pm in extended hours trading. The after-hours market is much less liquid because order flow is limited. As a result, the spreads between bid and ask prices are wider and there is greater price volatility.

8. 2. 2   COMPARISON OF LISTED AND OTC MARKETS

8. 2. 2. 1   Listed Markets

Each stock exchange requires companies to meet certain criteria before it will allow their stock to be listed for trading on the exchange.

Location. Listed markets, such as the NYSE and other exchanges, have central market-places and trading floor facilities.

Pricing System. Listed markets operate as **double-auction** markets. Floor participants compete among themselves to execute trades at prices most favorable to the public.

8. 2. 2. 2   OTC Markets

OTC markets also have criteria that a company must meet to be traded on a particular OTC venue just as exchanges do. While historically these criteria were not as stringent as those imposed by the exchanges, over time the quality of issues-traded OTC closed the gap and today equal exchange-traded issues.

Location. No central marketplace facilitates OTC trading. Trading takes place over the phone, over computer networks, and in trading rooms across the country.

Pricing System. The OTC market works through an **interdealer network**. Registered market makers compete among themselves to post the best bid and ask prices. The OTC market is a negotiated market.

8. 2. 2. 3   Quotes

Quotes are in terms of bid and ask. The ask price is the price at which dealers are willing to sell. The bid price is the price at which dealers are willing to buy. To make a profit, the ask is always higher than the bid. The difference between bid and ask is called the **spread**.

EXAMPLE   A dealer is quoting a stock at 21.50 bid–21.55 ask. The dealer is offering stock to any buyer at 21.55. The dealer is willing to buy stock from any seller at 21.50. The spread, the dealer's gross profit, is $.05 per share. The size of the market is expressed by two numbers: If the quote is 21.50–21.55 19 × 7, it means that the dealer is willing to buy up to 1,900 shares at 21.50 and is willing to sell up to 700 shares at 21.55.

8. 2. 2. 4   Dark Pools of Liquidity

Dark pools, sometimes referred to as dark pools of liquidity or simply dark liquidity, is trading volume that occurs or liquidity that is not openly available to the public. The bulk of this volume represents trades engaged in by institutional traders and trading desks away from the exchange markets. Generally, these are large volume transactions that occur on crossing networks or alternative trading systems (ATS) that match buy and sell orders electronically for execution without routing the order to an exchange or other market where quote, last sale price, and volume information is displayed.

Institutional trading desks who choose to utilize dark pools are able to execute large block orders without impacting public quotes or price, or revealing their investment strategy regarding any of their holding accumulations or divestitures. Additionally, orders can be placed anonymously so that the identity of the entity placing the order is unknown to the general investing public along with the volume and price for the transaction. The concern with dark pools is that some market participants are left disadvantaged because they cannot see the trades, volume, or prices agreed upon within the pools, and thus market transparency is darkened.

8. 2. 2. 5   Trade Reporting Facility (TRF)

The FINRA Trade Reporting Facility (TRF) is an automated trade reporting and reconciliation service that is operated on the Automated Confirmation Transaction (ACT) service platform. TRF electronically facilitates all of the data reporting, such as price and volume, after a trade has taken place, as well as trade comparison and clearing functions. It is used to report data for trades in Nasdaq-listed securities as well as trades that take place in NYSE-listed and other exchange-listed securities that occur off of the exchange trading floors. In this light, the system handles trades that are negotiated between brokers.

8. 2. 3   ROLE OF THE BROKER-DEALER

Firms engaged in buying and selling securities for the public must register as **broker-dealers**. Most firms act both as brokers and dealers, but not in the same transaction.

8. 2. 3. 1   Brokers

Brokers are agents that arrange trades for clients and charge commissions. Brokers do not effect trades as principal but arrange trades between buyers and sellers.

8. 2. 3. 2   Dealers

Dealers, or **principals**, buy and sell securities for their own accounts, often called **position trading**. When selling from their inventories, dealers charge their clients markups rather than commissions. A **markup** is the difference between the current interdealer offering price and the actual price charged to the client. When a price to a client includes a dealer's markup, it is called a **net price**.

TAKE NOTE

To clarify the role of dealers in the securities marketplace, try thinking of dealers as a car dealer. If you were a car dealer, you would maintain an inventory, or lot, of cars. If someone bought a car from you, you would not sell it at the wholesale price. Instead, you mark up the price to make a profit.

If someone wanted to sell you his used car, you would not offer him top dollar. Instead, you would mark down the price to make a profit. Securities dealers hold inventories of securities and buy and sell from inventory. They profit on transactions by charging markups and markdowns.

8. 2. 3. 3   Filling an Order

A broker-dealer may fill a customer's order to buy securities in any of the following ways.

- A firm may act as the client's agent by finding a seller of the securities and arranging a trade.
- A firm may buy the securities from a market maker, mark up the price, and resell them to the client.
- If it has the securities in its own inventory, the firm may sell the shares to the client from that inventory.

8. 2. 3. 4   Broker-Dealer Role in Transactions

A firm cannot act as both a broker and a dealer in the same transaction.

A broker:	**A dealer:**
- acts as an agent, transacting orders on the client's behalf;	- acts as a principal, dealing in securities for its own account and at its own risk;
- charges a commission;	- charges a markup or markdown;
- is not a market maker; and	- may make markets and take positions (long or short) in securities; and
- must disclose its role to the client and the amount of its commission.	- must disclose its role to the client and the markup or markdown if a Nasdaq security.

8. 3 NYSE EURONEXT

The **NYSE** is the most widely known stock exchange. Although exchanges are called stock markets, other securities may trade there as well. Often called the **Big Board**, the NYSE is the largest of all U.S. listed exchanges. Stocks listed on the NYSE can also be listed on regional exchanges, such as the Chicago Stock Exchange. It should be noted that the exchange does not influence or determine price.

8. 3. 1   EXCHANGE LISTING REQUIREMENTS

Securities traded on the NYSE, known as **listed securities**, must satisfy the exchange's listing requirements. Generally, a corporation that wants its securities listed must have a minimum number of publicly held shares and a minimum number of shareholders, each holding 100 shares or more. Although the minimum numerical criteria are not tested, it is important that you recognize that only companies of significant size and public ownership qualify for listing on the NYSE.

8. 3. 1. 1   Delisting

The NYSE reserves the right to **delist** issuers for a number of reasons, including failure to meet the minimum maintenance criteria. In addition, bankruptcy, abnormally low share price or share volume, and corporate actions not deemed to be in the public interest will result in delisting.

If an issuer wants to voluntarily delist from the NYSE, its board of directors must approve the action.

8. 3. 2   FLOOR PERSONNEL

Only NYSE members (individual seat owners) can trade on the floor. There are four types of traders.

8. 3. 2. 1   Commission House Broker (CHB)

Also called **floor brokers, commission house brokers (CHBs)** execute orders for clients and for their firms' accounts.

8. 3. 2. 2   Two-Dollar Broker

When commission brokers are too busy to execute all of their firms' orders, they call on **two-dollar brokers** to execute orders for them. Two-dollar brokers charge commissions for their services.

8. 3. 2. 3   Registered Trader

Registered traders are members of the Exchange who trade primarily for their own accounts. If they accept a public customer's order from a floor broker, they must give that order priority. They may not execute their own trades while holding an unfilled public order.

8. 3. 2. 4   Specialist or Designated Market Maker (DMM)

Specialists (DMMs) facilitate trading in specific stocks, and their chief function is to maintain a fair and orderly market in those stocks. In fulfilling this function, they act as both brokers and dealers; they act as dealers when they execute trades for their own accounts and as brokers when they execute orders other members leave with them. The specialist (DMM) acts as an auctioneer. In return for providing this service to the exchange, DMMs receive rebates on fees charged by the exchange whenever their quotes result in trades.

T A K E   N O T E   The New York Stock Exchange now allows floor traders to handle non-NYSE-listed stocks. NYSE floor traders can now transmit orders to and access liquidity from other exchanges without leaving the NYSE trading floor.

8. 3. 3   AUCTION MARKET

Exchange securities are bought and sold in an **auction market.** Exchange markets are also sometimes referred to as **double auction markets** because both buyers and sellers call out their best bids and offers in an attempt to transact business at the best possible price.

To establish the best bid, a buying broker-dealer must initiate a bid at least $.01 higher than the current best bid. The best offer by a selling broker-dealer must be at least $.01 lower than the current best offer.

E X A M P L E

A quote might look like this:

Last	Bid	Ask	Size
$46.71	$46.66	$46.74	30 × 14

Several bids at the same price and several offers at the same price may occur. To provide for the orderly transaction of business on the floor, the highest bids and lowest offers always receive first consideration.

8. 3. 3. 1   Priority, Precedence, and Parity

When more than one broker enters the same bid or offer, the specialist (DMM) awards the trade in the following order.

1. **Priority**—first order in
2. **Precedence**—largest order of those submitted
3. **Parity**—random drawing

8. 3. 4   VOLATILE MARKET CONDITIONS

Rules known as the market-wide circuit breaker rules (MWCB) protect against rapid, uncontrolled drops in the market. Based on the S&P 500 index (recalculated daily) the circuit breakers work as follows:

Level 1 Halt = 7% decline in S&P 500
Before 3:25 pm—15 minutes;
At or after 3:25 pm—trading shall continue, unless there is a Level 3 halt.

Level 2 Halt = 13% decline in S&P 500
Before 3:25 pm—15 minutes;
At or after 3:25 pm—trading shall continue, unless there is a Level 3 halt.

Level 3 Halt = 20% decline in S&P 500
At any time—trading shall halt and not resume for the rest of the day.

A level 1 or 2 halt cannot occur more than one time per day. In other words, if a level 1 halt has already occurred, it would take a level 2 halt to stop trading again.

Lastly, trading halts for listed securities trading on an exchange will generally be initiated by the exchange itself or by the SEC. For OTC stocks, either the specific trading venue such as Nasdaq or FINRA can initiate a trading halt.

TAKE NOTE
During a market halt, while no trading can occur, investors can still cancel existing (open) orders that had been entered previously.

TEST TOPIC ALERT
In conjunction with the market-wide circuit breaker rules there is the limit up/limit down rule. This is covered in a later unit under Regulation NMS.

8. 3. 5   ARBITRAGE

Arbitrage is a trading strategy that specialized traders, called **arbitrageurs,** use to profit from temporary price differences between markets or securities. In general, arbitrageurs look for ways to profit from temporary price disparities in the same or equivalent securities.

8. 3. 5. 1   Market Arbitrage

Some securities trade in more than one market—on two exchanges, for instance—creating the possibility that one security may sell for two different prices at the same time. When that happens, arbitrageurs buy at the lower price in one market and sell at the higher price in the other.

8. 3. 5. 2   Convertible Security Arbitrage

Arbitrage trades are also possible in equivalent securities—convertible bonds and the underlying stock, for instance. If conditions are right, an arbitrageur may be able to convert bonds to stock and sell the stock for a profit.

8. 3. 5. 3   Risk Arbitrage

Risk arbitrage becomes possible in proposed corporate takeovers. Arbitrageurs buy the stock in the company being acquired and sell short the acquiring company's stock, believing that the merger will raise the acquisition's stock price and lower the acquirer's stock price.

8. 4   FLOOR STRUCTURE AND ORDER TYPES

NYSE Euronext has adopted a multi-dealer structure for the NYSE. Following is a discussion of that market maker structure and the different order types commonly entered.

8. 4. 1   ROLE OF THE SPECIALIST OR DESIGNATED MARKET MAKER (DMM)

In addition to maintaining an orderly market, a secondary function of the specialist (DMM) is to minimize price disparities that may occur at the opening of daily trading. He does this by buying or selling (as a dealer) stock from his own inventory only when a need for such intervention exists. Otherwise, the specialist (DMM) lets public supply and demand set the market's course.

8. 4. 1. 1   Market Maker

Maintaining a market in a stock requires considerable financial resources. Therefore, the specialist (DMM) must have enough capital to maintain a substantial position in the security.

8. 4. 1. 1. 1   Supplemental Liquidity Providers (SLPs)

Under the multi-dealer market maker structure, an off-floor market maker, known as a Supplemental Liquidity Provider (SLP), may operate and compete with the on-floor Designated Market Maker. The SLP must maintain a bid or an offer in an assigned stock at least 10% of the trading day, unlike a DMM who is required to maintain a two-sided market at all times. Like the DMM, the SLP will receive rebates from the exchange for the SLP's quotes that result in trades, but the rebates are not as large as those received by the DMMs. Finally, SLPs will trade only for their proprietary accounts, not for public customers or on an agency basis.

8. 4. 1. 2   Agent and Principal

The specialist (DMM) is both agent and principal. On the Exchange floor, they can act in the following ways.

As **agents**, or brokers' brokers, they execute all orders other brokers leave with them. They accept certain kinds of orders from members, such as limit and stop orders, and execute these as conditions permit.

As **principals**, or dealers, they buy and sell in their own accounts to make markets in assigned stocks. They are expected to maintain continuous, fair, and orderly markets—that is, markets with reasonable price variations. A specialist, however, may not buy stock for his own account at a price that would compete with the current market. In other words, a specialist cannot buy, as principal, at a price that would satisfy a customer order to buy.

8. 4. 1. 3   Responsibilities of the Designated Market Maker

A specialist (DMM) must abide by certain NYSE floor rules in the daily conduct of his business. The specialist:

- must maintain a fair and orderly market;
- must stand ready to buy and sell for his own account, if necessary, to maintain a fair and orderly market;
- is expected to transact business for his own account in such a way as to maintain price continuity and minimize temporary price disparities attributable to supply and demand differences;

- must avoid transacting business for his own account at the opening or reopening of trading in a stock if this would upset the public balance of supply and demand;
- must file the reports and keep the books and records the Exchange requires; and
- may trade for his own account in between the current bid and ask quotes in his book.

8. 4. 2   TYPES OF ORDERS

8. 4. 2. 1   Price-Restricted Orders

Many types of orders are available to customers. Some orders, such as limit and stop limit, restrict the price of the transaction. Typical orders include the following:

- **Market**—executed immediately at the market price
- **Limit**—limits the amount paid or received for securities
- **Stop**—becomes a market order if the stock reaches or goes through the stop (trigger or election) price
- **Stop limit**—entered as a stop order and changed to a limit order if the stock hits or goes through the stop (trigger or election) price

8. 4. 2. 2   Market Orders

A **market order** is sent immediately to the floor for execution without restrictions or limits. It is executed immediately at the current market price and has priority over all other types of orders. A market order to buy is executed at the lowest offering price available; a market order to sell is executed at the highest bid price available. As long as the security is trading, a market order guarantees execution.

8. 4. 2. 3   Limit Orders

In a **limit order**, a customer limits the acceptable purchase or selling price. A limit order can be executed only at the specified price or better. If the order cannot be executed at the market, it is placed on the book and executed if and when the market price meets the order limit price. Buy limit orders are placed below the current market, whereas sell limit orders are placed above the current market.

8. 4. 2. 3. 1   Risks of Limit Orders

A customer who enters a limit order risks missing the chance to buy or sell, especially if the market moves away from the limit price. The market may never go as low as the buy limit price or as high as the sell limit price. Sometimes limit orders are not executed, even if the stock trades at the limit price.

Stock Ahead. Limit orders on the DMM's book for the same price are arranged according to when they were received. If a limit order at a specific price was not filled, chances are another order at the same price took precedence; that is, there was stock ahead.

Limit orders stand in time priority. There may be multiple orders to buy stock at a particular price. Once the stock begins trading at that price, those limit orders that were entered first will be filled first.

8. 4. 2. 3. 2   Order Protection Rule

SEC regulation NMS (National Market System) requires that firms holding customer limit orders not trade through or ahead of orders.

For example, if a firm accepts a customer limit order to buy 500 shares at 31.60 and in its market making capacity buys 200 shares at that price, it must fill that customer's order for 200 shares at 31.60 and protect the remaining 300 shares.

The firm cannot, as principal, buy or sell stock at a price that would satisfy a customer limit order without filling that order.

In the above example, the firm could, as principal, buy stock at 31.61 without creating an obligation to fill the customer limit order.

8. 4. 2. 4   Stop Orders

A **stop order**, also known as a **stop loss order**, is designed to protect a profit or prevent a loss if the stock begins to move in the wrong direction.

The stop order becomes a market order once the stock trades at or moves through a certain price, known as the stop price. Stop orders are left with and executed by the DMM. No guarantee exists that the executed price will be the stop price, unlike the price on a limit order. Buy stop orders are entered above the current market, whereas sell stop orders are entered below the current market.

A trade at the stop price triggers the order, which then becomes a market order. A stop order takes two trades to execute, which are:

■ **trigger**—the trigger transaction at or through the stop price activates the trade; and then

■ **execution**—the stop order becomes a market order and is executed at the next price, completing the trade.

8. 4. 2. 4. 1   Buy Stop Order

A **buy stop order** protects a profit or limits a loss in a short stock position. The buy stop is entered at a price above the current market and is triggered when the market price touches or goes through the buy stop price.

A customer has shorted 1,000 shares of XYZ stock at $55, and the stock is now at $48. The customer would like to hang on for more gain but is concerned the stock will reverse itself and begin to rise, eroding some of the unrealized profit. To deal with this, the customer could place the following order: buy 1,000 XYZ 49 stop. If the stock does start to head north, once it trades at or through the stop price of 49, the order becomes a market order to buy 1,000 XYZ.

Buy stop orders are also used by technical traders who track support and resistance levels for stocks. For instance, COD stock trades between 38 and 42. It never seems to go above 42 or below 38. Technicians believe that if the stock breaks through resistance, it will continue to move upward at a rapid pace. Therefore, they will not buy at 40 because there is little upside potential. However, they may place a buy stop order above the resistance level knowing that if the stock breaks resistance and begins to move up, they will buy the stock before it develops upward momentum.

An investor might place a stop order to buy 100 COD at 42.25 stop when the market is at 40 if he believes 42 represents a technical resistance point, above which the stock price will continue to rise.

COD Buy Stop Order

8. 4. 2. 4. 2 Sell Stop Order

A **sell stop order** protects a profit or limits a loss in a long stock position and is entered at a price below the current market.

EXAMPLE A customer is long 1,000 shares of XYZ at $32, and the stock is now at $41. The customer would like to hang on for more gain but is concerned the stock will reverse itself and begin to fall, eroding some of the unrealized profit. To deal with this, the customer could place the following order: sell 1,000 XYZ 40 stop. If the stock does start to head south, once it trades at or through the stop price of 40, the order becomes a market order to sell 1,000 XYZ.

Sell stop orders are also used by technical traders. Technicians believe that if a stock breaks through support, it will fall like a rock. Therefore, they will not short the stock at 40 because there is little downside potential. Historically, the stock has not traded below 38. However, they may place a sell stop order just below the support level knowing that if the stock breaks through support and begins to move down, they will short the stock before it develops downward momentum.

An investor who is long stock might place a stop order to sell 100 COD at 37.75 stop when the market is at 40 if he believes 38 represents a technical support point below which the stock will continue to fall.

COD Sell Stop Order

If a large number of stop orders are triggered at the same price, a flurry of trading activity takes place as they become market orders. This activity will accelerate the advance or decline of the stock price.

8. 4. 2. 4. 3   Stop Limit Order

A **stop limit order** is a stop order that, once triggered, becomes a limit order instead of a market order.

EXAMPLE
A customer calls you and says, "I want to sell my ABC stock if it falls to $30, but I don't want less than $29.95 for my shares." So you enter the following order: sell 1,000 ABC 30 stop 29.95. Once ABC trades at or below 30, the order becomes a limit order to sell at 29.95 or better. The problem here is that the market could leapfrog between the stop price and the limit price. As a result, the customer will not get an execution.

Assume once the order is entered, the stock trades as follows: 30.01, 29.97, 29.94, 29.92, and so on. The trade at 29.97 triggers the order at which point the order becomes a limit order to sell at 29.95 or better (higher). In the above scenario, the customer does not sell. The moral of this example is if you are concerned that a stock is heading south, place a market order to sell or a stop order. A stop limit may leave you without an execution.

Stop and Limit Orders

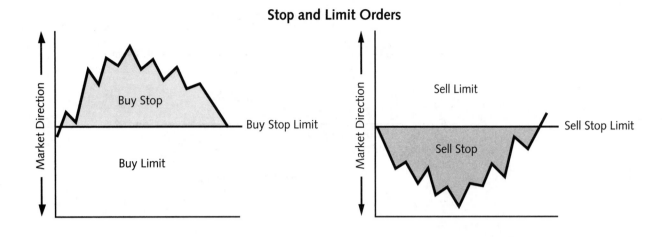

TEST TOPIC ALERT

Be prepared for two to four questions regarding limit and stop orders. Use the chart to solve some problems, starting with limit orders.

XYZ is currently trading at 52. Where would a customer enter a buy limit order?

Refer to the chart. Think of the horizontal middle line as the current price. The buy limit would be entered somewhere below 52. The investor wants to buy at a better price—a lower price for a buyer. The order would be filled at or below the order price.

A sell limit order for XYZ would be entered above the market price. The seller is waiting for a price that is better than 52. The order would be filled at a price equal to or higher (better for a seller) than the order price.

Stop orders are a little more tricky because they have two parts: trigger (election) and execution. Consider a buy stop at 52 entered when the market is 51. Based on the ticks below, at what price would this order be executed?

51.88   51.99   52.13   52.13   51.88

Look at the chart. The chart shows you that a buy stop is entered above the market price. This reminds you that it is only elected or triggered at the first price where the market is at or above the order price. Stops become market orders when triggered, so it executes at the price immediately following the trigger. Based on this example, this buy stop triggers at 52.13 and could execute at 52.13.

If this had been a buy stop limit at 52, the trigger would still be 52.13. Just as before, it triggers at or above the order price. When a stop limit is triggered, it becomes a limit order, which means it will execute only at a price at or below the stated price (lower is better for a buyer).

Based on this example, this buy stop limit triggers at 52.13 and could execute at 51.88.

Consider a sell stop at 52 entered when the market is 53. Based on the ticks shown below, at what price could this order be executed?

52.50   51.88   51.50   51.75   52.25

The chart shows you that a sell stop is entered below the market price. This reminds you that it is only elected or triggered when the market is at or below the order price. Stops become market orders when triggered, so it executes at the next available price immediately following the trigger. Based on this example, this sell stop triggers at 51.88 and executes at 51.50.

If this had been a sell stop limit at 52, the trigger would still be 51.88. Just as before, it triggers at or below the order price. When a stop limit is triggered, it becomes a limit order, which means it will execute only at a price at or above the stated price (higher is better for a seller). This sell stop limit triggers at 51.88 and could execute at 52.25.

When drawing your order reference chart, think of the word BLISS. It stands for Buy Limits and Sell Stops. These are the orders that are placed below the market price. ("B" in BLISS reminds you of "B" in below.)

Why use stop orders?

Buy stop orders:	**Sell stop orders:**
■ protect against loss in a short stock position;	■ protect against loss in a long stock position;
■ protect a gain from a short stock position; and	■ protect a gain from a long stock position; and
■ establish a long position when a breakout occurs above the line of resistance.	■ establish a short position when a breakout occurs below the line of support.

TAKE NOTE

There is no guarantee that if a stop order is elected (triggered), the investor will pay or receive the stop price.

8. 4. 2. 5   Specialist (Designated Market Maker) Display Book

Orders that cannot be immediately executed are placed on the (DMM's) display book. Orders placed on the display book are those to buy or sell at prices away from the current market. Note that although the display book will accept and execute any size market order, only round lots (units of 100 shares) are placed on the book.

When any specification on an order is changed, it will lose its original order priority on the book. When an order specification is changed, it is done through a cancel and replace process, whereby the original order is considered to be cancelled and replaced with the new order.

QUICK QUIZ 8.A

1. An order to sell at 38.63 stop, 38.63 limit is entered before the opening. The subsequent trades are 38.88, 38.50, 38.38. The order

   A. was executed at 38.50
   B. was executed at 38.63
   C. was executed at 38.88
   D. has not yet been executed

2. A sell stop order is entered

   A. above the current market price
   B. below the current market price
   C. either above or below the current market price
   D. at the current market price

3. All of the following are true of stop orders EXCEPT

   A. they can limit a loss in a declining stock
   B. they become market orders when there is a trade at, or the market passes through, a specific price
   C. they are the same as limit orders
   D. they can affect the price of the stock when the specific stop price is reached

4. A client bought 100 shares of MCS at 20. The stock rose to 30, and the client wants to protect his gain. Which of the following orders should be entered?

   A. Sell stop at 29
   B. Sell limit at 30
   C. Sell limit at 30.13
   D. Sell stop at 30.13

5. A customer sold 100 shares of QRS short when the stock was trading at 19. QRS is now trading at 14, and the customer wants to protect his gain. Which of the following orders should he place?

   A. Sell stop at 13.88
   B. Sell limit at 14
   C. Buy limit at 14
   D. Buy stop at 14.38

6. ZOO is trading at 50.63. Your customer, who owns 100 shares of the stock, places an order to sell ZOO at 50.25 stop limit. The Tape subsequently reports the following trades:

   ZOO   50.63   50.75   50.13   50.13   50.25

   Your customer's order could first be executed at

   A. 50.13
   B. 50.25
   C. 50.63
   D. 50.75

Quick Quiz answers can be found at the end of the Unit.

Comparison of Order Characteristics

Order Type	Description	Exchange Orders	OTC Orders
Market	Buy or sell at the best available market price	Most common order type on all exchanges	Most common OTC order type
Limit	Minimum price for sell orders; maximum price for buy orders	Can be handled by a specialist (DMM) or floor broker as a day order. GTCs may not be acceptable depending on the exchange.	Acceptable on either a day or GTC basis if GTCs are accepted
Stop	Buy orders entered above the market; sell orders entered below the market	May or may not be acceptable depending on the exchange	Acceptable by some dealers
Stop Limit	Stop order that becomes a limit order once the stop price has been reached or exceeded	May or may not be acceptable depending on the exchange	Acceptable by some dealers

8. 4. 2. 6   Reducing Orders

Certain orders on the order book are reduced when a stock goes ex-dividend. All orders entered below the market are reduced on the **ex-dividend date** (or **ex-date**), the first date on which the new owner of stock does not qualify for the current dividend. On the ex-date, the stock price opens lower by the amount of the distribution. Orders reduced include buy limits, sell stops, and sell stop limits. These orders are reduced by the dividend amount. Without this reduction, trading at the lower price on the ex-dividend date could cause an inadvertent execution.

EXAMPLE   ABC closes at 35.00. The following day is the ex-date for a $.31 cash dividend. ABC stock should open at 34.69.

8. 4. 2. 6. 1   Do Not Reduce (DNR)

A DNR order is not reduced by an ordinary cash dividend. In this case, the customer does not care if there is an execution due solely to the ex-date reduction.

TEST TOPIC ALERT   You are likely to be asked which orders are reduced for cash dividends. Only those placed below the market price are automatically reduced. Remember that BLISS (buy limits and sell stops) orders are placed below the market price and are reduced for cash dividend distributions. All orders are adjusted for stock dividends and stock splits, whether placed above or below the market.

1. An order that instructs the specialist (DMM) not to adjust the limit (or stop) price when a stock goes ex-dividend is designated

    A. DNA
    B. DNR
    C. FOK
    D. EX

2. Which of the following orders would be reduced by the specialist (DMM) on the ex-dividend date?

    I.   Buy limit order
    II.   Sell stop order
    III. Buy stop order
    IV.   Sell limit order

    A. I and II
    B. I and IV
    C. II, III and IV
    D. III and IV

3. A company is about to pay a dividend of $.70. On the ex-dividend date, an open order to sell at 46 stop would

    A. be automatically adjusted to 45.30 stop
    B. be automatically adjusted to 45.38 stop
    C. be automatically adjusted to 45.50 stop
    D. remain 46 stop

8. 4. 2. 6. 2   Reductions for Stock Splits

If there is a stock dividend or stock split, the specialist (DMM) will adjust all open orders.

EXAMPLE

There is an open order to sell 100 XYZ at 50 stop. If there is a 2-for-1 split, the order becomes sell 200 XYZ at 25 stop.

EXAMPLE

There is an open order to buy 500 XYZ at 30. If there is a 20% stock dividend, the order becomes buy 600 XYZ at 25.

EXAMPLE

There is an open order to buy 100 XYZ at 30. If there is a 20% stock dividend, the order becomes buy 100 XYZ at 25. Common sense says the order size should be 120 shares. However, only round lots are allowed on the order book. The additional 20 shares are in the customer's account but cannot be part of an open order.

For reverse splits, all open orders are canceled.

8. 4. 3   TIME-SENSITIVE ORDERS

Orders based on time considerations include the following:

- Day
- Good till canceled
- At the open and market on close
- Not held
- Fill or kill
- Immediate or cancel
- All or none
- Alternative, which provides two alternatives, such as sell a stock at a limit or sell it on stop

8. 4. 3. 1   Day Orders

Unless marked to the contrary, an open order (stop or limit) is assumed to be a day order, valid only until the close of trading on the day it is entered. If the order has not been filled, it is canceled at the close of the day's trading.

8. 4. 3. 2   Good Til Canceled (GTC) Orders

GTC orders are valid until executed or cancelled. However, all GTC orders are automatically cancelled if unexecuted on the last business day of April and the last business day of October. If the customer wishes to have the order remain working beyond those specific days, the customer must reentered the order.

8. 4. 3. 3   At-the-Open and Market-on-Close Orders

At-the-open orders are executed at the opening of the market. Partial executions are allowable. They must reach the post by the open of trading in that security or else they are canceled. Market-on-close orders are executed at or as near as possible to the closing price in the OTC market. On the NYSE, however, a market-on-close order must be entered before 3:40 pm and will be executed at the closing price.

8. 4. 3. 4   Not Held (NH) Orders

A market order coded **NH** indicates that the customer agrees not to hold the floor broker or broker-dealer to a particular time and price of execution. This provides the floor broker with authority to decide the best time and price at which to execute the trade. Market not held orders may not be placed with the specialist (DMM).

TAKE NOTE   Market not held orders in which a retail customer gives you authority over price or timing are limited to the day the order is given. In other words, they are day orders. An exception is granted if the customer, in writing, states that the order is GTC.

8. 4. 3. 5   Fill-or-Kill (FOK) Orders

The commission house broker is instructed to fill an entire FOK order immediately at the limit price or better. A broker that cannot fill the entire order immediately cancels it and notifies the originating branch office.

8. 4. 3. 6   Immediate-or-Cancel (IOC) Orders

IOC orders are like FOK orders except that a partial execution is acceptable. The portion not executed is canceled.

8. 4. 3. 7   All-or-None (AON) Orders

AON orders must be executed in their entirety or not at all. AON orders can be day or GTC orders. They differ from the FOKs in that they do not have to be filled immediately.

8. 4. 3. 8   Alternative Orders (OCO)

Assume a customer is long stock at $50 that was purchased six months earlier at $30. To protect his unrealized gain, the customer might enter a sell stop at $48. Alternatively, if the stock continues to rise, he wants out at $53. What he might do is enter both orders with the notation "one cancels the other" (OCO). If one of the orders is executed, the other is immediately canceled.

TAKE NOTE   Exchanges can limit the order types they will accept. For instance, the NYSE does not accept GTC or stop orders (stop loss or stop limit) or all-or-none (AON) or fill-or-kill (FOK) orders to be entered in its equity market. Because these different order types are also used in the bond market and Nasdaq, students should still be familiar with them and be able to distinguish them from other order types. Additionally, though an exchange might not accept them, a broker-dealer is still able to do so if they wish to, but would need to manually monitor the status of the order if entered on an exchange that does not accept them.

QUICK QUIZ 8.C   Match each of the following items with the appropriate description below.

A. Fill or kill
B. All or none
C. Immediate or cancel
D. Not held

_____ 1. Executed by the floor broker, who is given authority to select time and price

_____ 2. Execute immediately, in its entirety, or cancel

_____ 3. Execute in its entirety but not necessarily immediately

_____ 4. Execute as much as possible immediately; cancel the rest

8. 4. 4   SHORT SALE RULES

The SEC has rescinded rules previously in place to limit how and when short sales could be done. This process to eliminate what were previously known as the "up-tick" rules began in 2004 with Regulation SHO and was completed in 2008. Short sales may now occur anytime during the trading day including at the opening and closing of the day.

8. 4. 4. 1   Regulation SHO

In 2004, the SEC initiated a pilot program suspending the tick rule and the bid test rule for a select group of both exchange-listed and Nasdaq stocks. In 2007, the SEC voted to end price restrictions on short selling permanently for all equity securities. This means that the up-tick rule for exchange-listed stocks and the bid test rule for Nasdaq Global Select and Nasdaq Global Market stocks have been rescinded and will no longer be applicable to short sellers.

In addition, Regulation SHO also mandates a **locate requirement**, which means that before the short sale of any equity security, firms must locate the securities for borrowing to ensure that delivery will be made on settlement date. Not doing so is known as **naked short selling** and is not permitted.

8. 4. 4. 2   Insider Short Sale Regulations

The Securities Exchange Act of 1934 prohibits directors, officers, and principal stockholders (insiders) from selling short stock in their own companies.

8. 4. 4. 3   Sell Order Tickets

8. 4. 4. 3. 1   Sell Orders Must Be Identified

The SEC requires that all sell orders be identified as either long or short. No sale can be marked long unless the security to be delivered is in the customer's account or is owned by the customer and will be delivered to the broker by the settlement date.

A person is long a security if he:

- has title to it;
- has purchased the security or has entered into an unconditional contract to purchase the security but has not yet received it;
- owns a security convertible into or exchangeable for the security and has tendered such security for conversion or exchange; or
- has an option to purchase the security and has exercised that option.

Unless one or more of these conditions are met, the SEC considers any sale of securities a short sale.

TAKE NOTE
When a customer is both long and short shares of the same stock simultaneously, the positions must be netted out to determine if the customer is net long or net short. For example, if a customer is long 500 shares of XYZ and short 200 shares of XYZ, the net position is long 300 shares. In this case, if the customer wished to sell 400 shares of XYZ, the sell order ticket must read: SELL 300 shares long and 100 shares short because the customer is only long 300 shares (net).

8. 4. 4. 4   Shorting Bonds

Securities, such as listed stocks, have many equivalent securities trading at any time. For instance, it is easy to short 100 shares of GM because an equivalent 100 shares of GM can be purchased on the NYSE at any time. It is not easy to cover shorts for most municipal bonds because the limited number of bonds available in each issue could make it difficult to buy in the short position. In other words, the municipal market is too thin.

8. 5   OTHER DOMESTIC AND REGIONAL EXCHANGES

In addition to the national stock exchanges, other stock exchanges serve the financial communities in different regions of the country.

8. 5. 1   REGIONAL EXCHANGES

Regional exchanges tend to focus on the securities of companies within their regions, although they also offer trading in many securities listed on the NYSE. This is known as dual listing. Listing requirements on regional exchanges are often less stringent than those of the national exchanges, and the companies they list are usually among the smallest and newest in their industries.

8. 5. 1. 1   NASDAQ OMX PHLX

The NASDAQ OMX PHLX was formed when Nasdaq took over operations of the Philadelphia Stock Exchange, which had previously operated as a regional exchange. Operations continue to be maintained at the Philadelphia Stock Exchange, including the options trading floor. The Nasdaq OMX PHLX offers customers a unique hybrid of both electronic and floor-based trading in equity, index, and U.S. dollar settled currency options.

8. 6   COMPUTERIZED ORDER ROUTING

A large percentage of the orders the NYSE receives each day are processed through a computerized trading and execution system called **Super Display Book (SDBK)**.

8. 6. 1   SUPER DISPLAY BOOK (SDBK)

Broker-dealers use this computerized order routing system to route an order directly to the appropriate equity post on the trading floor.

Orders can be sent through the system either preopening or postopening. The computer automatically pairs preopening orders received before the opening of trading with other orders and executes them at the opening price. Any order that cannot be matched before the opening is left on the Display Book for the Designated Market Maker to handle. If an order is received postopening, it is sent directly to the Display Book and presented to the crowd. All NYSE-listed stocks are eligible for order entry over the Super Display Book (SDBK).

8. 7   THE CONSOLIDATED TAPE

The **Consolidated Tape System (CTS)** receives, validates, and sequences the last sale price and size of all equity transactions in listed securities from all U.S. Stock Exchanges and the Financial Industry Regulatory Authority. Information is made available via computer-to-computer linkages and ticker networks to subscribers within the financial community in the United States and abroad.

8. 7. 0. 1   How the Tape Works

The Tape reports are distributed over two networks. **Network A** reports transactions in NYSE-listed securities wherever they are traded. This includes trades on the NYSE floor, regional exchanges, the third market, and the ECN market. As an example, a trade involving NYSE-listed IBM on the Pacific Stock Exchange would be reported on Network A. **Network B** represents last sales for securities that are listed on the NYSE AMEX, securities eligible for the NYSE AMEX listing but traded solely by Regional Exchanges, Local Issues, and Bonds.

8. 7. 0. 2   How to Read the Consolidated Tape

The Tape prints volumes and prices of securities transactions within seconds of their execution. On the high-speed line, the transactions are reported with market identifiers, letters identifying the security traded, its price, and the number of shares. On the low-speed ticker (LST), the traditional horizontal tape where stock symbols and prices move right to left, some information such as volume has been omitted over time.

Lastly, transaction prices reported to and printed on the tape over either network do not include commissions, mark-ups, or mark-downs.

8. 7. 0. 3 Active Markets

At times, the market and exchanges can be so active that trade information can be inaccurate or out of sequence. Several delete information modes have been established to abbreviate reports and keep the Tape from running late. The following notations indicate information will be omitted.

- **DIGITS & VOL DELETED.** When this message appears, both the first digit of the price and the volume will be dropped. A trade for 200 shares of IBM at 92.50 will appear as IBM2.50. DIGITS & VOL RESUMED appears when trading activity slows.

- **REPEAT PRICES OMITTED.** This indicates that the Tape will show only transactions that differ in price from the previous reports.

8. 7. 0. 3. 1 Other Messages

Other messages that might appear on the Tape follow.

- **SLD** indicates that the exchange did not report a sale on time, so it is out of sequence on the Tape. For example, a customer who sees AEP25 on the Tape followed by AEP.SLD 25.13 might believe that AEP's price is going up. In reality, the price may be going down: the 25.13 is out of sequence and should have appeared before the 25.

- **OPD** announces the initial transaction in a security for which the opening has been delayed. As an example, the delayed opening of DWQ at 42 would appear as DWQ.OPD 42.

- **HALT** means that trading in a security has been halted.

TAKE NOTE

If a trade is being reported late (SLD), it is not considered to be in the trade sequence that it occurred. Consider the following trades in ABC:

24.00   24.03   23.99   24.13 SLD   24.10

The trade reported as 24.13 SLD indicates to those viewing the consolidated tape that this trade occurred sometime earlier in the trade sequence.

QUICK QUIZ 8.D

1. Under the Consolidated Tape System (CTS) the symbol SLD indicates that
   A. the transaction is appearing out of sequence in the system
   B. a large block of stock was sold
   C. the transaction is for an odd-lot (less than 100 shares)
   D. the transaction was reported to the system by the seller

8. 8 THE OVER-THE-COUNTER MARKET

The largest securities market (in terms of number of issues) is the over-the-counter (OTC) market, in which brokers/dealers negotiate trades directly with one another. When we say that the OTC market is a negotiated market, we mean that it is one in which market makers may bargain during a trade. A negotiated market is competitive: a firm competes against other brokerage firms, each trading for its own inventory.

The OTC market is a highly sophisticated telecommunications and computer network connecting brokers/dealers across the country. Securities that can be traded in the OTC market include, but are not limited to:

- American depositary receipts (ADRs);
- common stocks, especially of banks and insurance and technology companies;
- most corporate bonds (typically convertibles);
- municipal bonds;
- U.S. government securities;
- preferred stock;
- equipment trust certificates;
- closed-end investment companies; and
- warrants.

The OTC market is historically associated with unlisted securities; those not listed on U.S. exchanges. However, in recent years some traditional OTC market participants such as Nasdaq have purchased U.S. exchanges (for example, the Philadelphia Stock Exchange was purchased by and is now a part of the Nasdaq OMX Group).

OTC Versus NYSE Markets

OTC	NYSE
Securities' prices determined through negotiation	Securities' prices determined through auction bidding
Regulated by FINRA	Regulated by FINRA
Market Makers must register with both the SEC and FINRA	Designated Market Makers must be registered with the SEC and must be Exchange members
Traded at many locations across the country	Traded only on the NYSE floor

TAKE NOTE OTC trading is regulated by both the SEC and FINRA, the **self-regulatory organization (SRO)** for the OTC market.

8. 8. 1 NASDAQ

The computerized information system that tracks OTC equities trading is called the **National Association of Securities Dealers Automated Quotation** service (Nasdaq).

TAKE NOTE   Not all OTC securities are listed on Nasdaq. For instance, government securities, while traded OTC, are not listed on Nasdaq.

8. 8. 1. 1   Order Audit Trail System (OATS)

The Order Audit Trail System (OATS) is an automated computer system created to record information relating to orders, quotes, and other trade information from all equities that are traded on Nasdaq. OATS helps to ensure that all of the time-sensitive information relating to the sequence of events throughout the order execution process is recorded accurately. OATS tracks orders from the time of order entry until execution or cancellation, and in doing so provides an accurate audit trail. For example, one detail required by the system is that all computer clocks and time stamps be coordinated and capable of providing time to the hour, minute, and second. OATS reports are made on an order-by-order basis to FINRA.

8. 8. 2   OTC MARKET MAKERS

Specialists (Designated Market Makers) on an exchange stand ready to trade in specified securities. The OTC market has no specialists. Rather, firms wishing to make a market in a particular security must register with, and receive approval from, FINRA. They buy and sell for their own inventories, for their own profit, and at their own risk. A broker-dealer acting as a market maker, buying and selling for its own account rather than arranging trades, acts as a principal, not an agent.

8. 9   QUOTATIONS

A full quote consists of a bid price and an offer (ask) price.

8. 9. 1   BIDS, OFFERS, AND QUOTES

The **current bid** is the highest price at which the dealer will buy, and the **current offer** is the lowest price at which the dealer will sell. The difference between the bid and ask is known as the **spread**.

A typical quote might be expressed as bid 63–offered 63.07. The highest price the dealer will pay is 63, and the lowest price the dealer will accept is 63.07. The spread is .07 of a point between the bid and ask. The broker could also say 63 bid–63.07 ask or 63 to .07.

The Customer's and the Market Maker's Relationship to the Quote

	Bid-63	Ask/Offer-63.07
Quoting dealer	Buys	Sells
Customer	Sells	Buys

When a customer buys a stock from a firm acting as principal, the broker marks up the ask price to reach the net price to the customer. Likewise, when a customer sells stock to a firm acting as principal, the dealer marks down from the bid price to reach the net proceeds to the customer.

EXAMPLE   If WXYZ is quoted as 43.25 to .50, (short hand for 43.25 bid / 43.50 ask or offer), and the dealer wants a half-point for the trade, a customer buying would pay 44 net, and a customer selling would receive 42.75 net. The additional half point (added to the ask or offer, or subtracted from the bid) is the dealer's markup and markdown, respectively.

8. 9. 1. 1   Firm Quote

A **firm quotation** is the price at which a market maker stands ready to buy or sell at least one trading unit—100 shares of stock or five bonds—at the quoted price with other member firms. When an OTC firm makes a market in a security, the broker-dealer must be willing to buy or sell at least one trading unit of the security at its firm quote. All quotes are firm quotes unless otherwise indicated.

As is true of market order executions on an exchange floor, an OTC trader may attempt to negotiate a better price with a market maker by making a **counter offer** or a **counter bid**, especially if the spread between the market maker's bid and ask is fairly wide. However, the only way to guarantee an immediate execution is to buy stock at the market maker's ask price or sell at the bid price.

In a typical bond transaction, a trader at one broker-dealer calls a trader at another broker-dealer (a market maker) to buy a specific bond. A market maker might give another broker-dealer a quote that is firm for an hour with five-minute recall. This is a firm quote that remains good for an hour. If, within that hour, the market maker receives another order for the same security, the trader calls the broker-dealer back and gives it five minutes to confirm its order or lose its right to buy that security at the price quoted.

8. 9. 1. 1. 1   Backing Away

A market maker can revise a firm quote in response to market conditions and trading activity, but a market maker that refuses to do business at the price(s) quoted is **backing away** from the quote. Backing away is a violation of trading rules.

8. 9. 1. 2   Recognized Quotation

A recognized quotation under FINRA rules is any public bid or offer for one or more round lots or other normal trading units. Any bid for less than a round lot must state the amount of the security for which it is good. If the bid or offer is made for multiple round lots, it must also be good for a smaller number of units.

EXAMPLE   If the bid is for 1,000 shares of stock, the bidder must buy any round lots offered of 100 or more at the same price.

8. 9. 1. 3 Subject Quote

A **subject quote** is one in which the price is tentative, subject to reconfirmation by the market maker. When a market maker knows the transaction size, the broker-dealer firms up the subject quote or gives a replacement quote. Some typical expressions used to denote subject and firm quotes are shown below. Firm quotes are absolute statements, but subject quotes are hedged.

8. 9. 1. 4 Qualified Quotes

A quote will often be given with **qualifiers** intended to allow the broker-dealer to back away if market conditions change.

8. 9. 1. 4. 1 Workout Quote

This term is usually reserved for situations in which a market maker knows that special handling will be required to accommodate a particular trade. Either the order size is too big for the market to absorb without disruption or the market is too thin or temporarily unstable.

A **workout quote** is an approximate figure used to provide the buyer or seller with an indication of price, not a firm quote. Block positioners use workout quotes frequently.

Subject or Workout Market	Firm Market
"It is around 40–41."	"The market is 40–41."
"Last I saw, it was 40–41."	"It is currently 40–41."
"It is 40–41 subject."	
"40–42.50 workout."	

8. 9. 1. 4. 2 Nominal Quote

A **nominal quote** is someone's assessment of where a stock might trade in an active market. Nominal quotes may be used to give customers an idea of the market value of an inactively traded security, but they are not firm quotes. Nominal quotes in print must be clearly labeled as such.

8. 9. 2 QUOTATION SPREAD AND SIZE

The difference between a security's bid and offer (ask) price is known as the spread. The size of the quote tells you how many shares are bid for or offered.

8. 9. 2. 1 Spread

Many factors influence a spread's size, including the:

- issue's size;
- issuer's financial condition;
- amount of market activity in the issue; and
- market conditions.

8. 9. 2. 2   Size

Unless otherwise specified, a firm quote is always good for one round lot (100 shares).

EXAMPLE   A firm quote of 8.25–.50 means the market maker stands ready to buy 100 shares of stock from another broker-dealer at the 8.25 bid price or sell 100 shares at the 8.50 ask price.

8. 9. 2. 3   Non-Nasdaq

For securities quoted on either the OTC *Pink* or the over-the-counter bulletin board (OTCBB), the three-quote rule often applies. Unless there are at least two market makers displaying quotes, broker-dealers receiving orders to buy or sell non-Nasdaq securities must contact a minimum of three dealers to determine the prevailing price.

TAKE NOTE   Quotes disseminated in this fashion are not considered to be firm quotes because they are generally updated on a basis too infrequent to be considered current. Therefore, in order to obtain a current and firm quote, the dealers listed as making quotes for a particular security must be contacted. Once a firm quote is gotten a transaction can occur if both parties agree to a price.

8. 9. 2. 4   Manipulative and Deceptive Practices

The Conduct Rules mandate that any quote given must represent a real bid or offer. No fictitious quotes are allowed.

TEST TOPIC ALERT   Following is a list of important test points about OTC quotes.

- Markups and markdowns are charged when a market maker is acting as a principal (dealing from inventory with financial risk).

- Firm quotes are good for a round lot only, unless otherwise stated. A quote of 11–11.50 3 × 5 is firm between dealers for 300 shares at the bid of 11 and 500 shares at the asked of 11.50.

- Nominal quotes can be given for informational purposes, and can be printed only if clearly labeled as such.

- A relatively wide spread indicates a thin trading market for the security.

8. 10   5% MARKUP POLICY

The **5% markup policy** was adopted to ensure that the investing public receives fair treatment and pays reasonable rates for brokerage services in both exchange and OTC markets. It is considered a guideline only and is not a firm rule for markups and markdowns. A firm charging a customer more or less than a 5% markup may or may not be in violation of fair and equitable trade practices. The markup may be considered excessive once all of the relevant factors are taken into account.

A broker-dealer can fill a customer order in the following three ways.

- If the broker-dealer is a market maker in the security, it will (as principal) buy from or sell to the customer, charging a markup or markdown.

- If the firm is not a market maker in the security, it can fill the order as agent, without taking a position in the security, and charge a commission for its execution services.

- An order can be filled as a riskless and simultaneous transaction.

8. 10. 2. 1   Markup Based on Representative Market Prices

The 5% markup is based on the price representative of prevailing (inside) market prices at the time of a customer transaction. The 5% markup policy applies to all transactions in nonexempt listed or unlisted securities traded on an exchange or OTC regardless of whether the transactions are executed as agency or principal trades.

TAKE NOTE   The 5% policy applies to markups, markdowns, and commissions.

---

8. 10. 2. 2   Fixed Public Offering Price Securities

The 5% markup policy does not apply to mutual funds, variable annuity contracts, or securities sold in public offerings, all of which are sold by a prospectus, nor does it apply to municipal securities.

8. 10. 2. 3   Dealer's Inventory Costs

If a customer's buy order is filled from a broker-dealer's inventory, the net price to the customer is based on the prevailing market price, regardless of whether the broker-dealer selling to the customer is also making a market in the stock and what the firm's quote might be.

The price at which the broker-dealer acquired the stock being sold to the customer has no bearing on the net price to the customer; the price to the customer must be reasonably related to the current market.

8. 10. 2. 4   Riskless and Simultaneous Transactions

A **riskless and simultaneous transaction** is an order to buy or sell stock in which the firm receiving the order is not a market maker. The dealer has the following two options for filling the order.

- As agent for the customer, it could buy or sell on the customer's behalf and charge a commission, subject to the 5% policy.

- It could buy or sell for its riskless principal account, then buy or sell to the customer as principal, charging a markup or markdown subject to the 5% policy.

When the order is filled as a principal transaction, the broker-dealer must disclose the markup to the customer.

8. 10. 2. 5 Proceeds Transactions

When a customer sells securities and uses the proceeds to purchase other securities in a proceeds transaction, the broker-dealer's combined commissions and markups must be consistent with the 5% markup policy. In other words, member firms must treat proceeds transactions as one transaction for markup and markdown purposes.

8. 10. 2. 6 Markup Policy Considerations

While the policy is applicable to all account types, in assessing the fairness of a broker-dealer's commission and markup practices, the following factors are considered.

Type of Security. In general, more market risk is associated with making markets and trading common stocks than is associated with dealing in bonds. The policy gives guidance to markups specific to both stock and bond transactions, including government securities. The more risk a broker-dealer assumes, the greater the justification for higher markups.

Inactively Traded Stocks. The thinner the market for a security, the more volatile the stock and the greater the market risk to anyone dealing in the stock. Thus, a broker-dealer is justified in charging higher markups on inactively traded stocks.

Selling Price of Security. Commission and markup rates should decrease as a stock's price increases.

Dollar Amount of Transaction. Transactions of relatively small dollar amounts generally warrant higher percentage markups than large-dollar transactions.

Nature of the Broker-Dealer's Business. This standard pertains to full-service brokers versus discount brokers. In most cases, a general securities firm has higher operating costs than does a discount broker and thus may justify higher commissions and markups.

Pattern of Markups. Although the regulators are concerned primarily with detecting cases where broker-dealers have established patterns of excessive markups, a single incident could still be considered an unfair markup.

Markups on Inactive Stocks (Contemporaneous Cost). For inactive stocks and situations where no prevailing market quotes are available, a broker-dealer may base a markup on its cost in the stock.

TEST TOPIC ALERT   The 5% markup policy is peculiarly named for two reasons:

1.   It applies to markups, markdowns, and commissions, meaning it is applicable to principal and agency transactions.
2.   Five percent is not the limit. A transaction charge of more than 5% might be fine if it is reasonably based on the circumstances of the trade.

Examples of subject transactions are REITS, closed-end company shares, ADRs, third market trades, listed and unlisted stocks, bonds, and government securities.

New issues sold by prospectus and municipal securities are not subject to this policy.

Remember that all computations must be based on the inside quote (the best available from all the market makers), not the firm's quote.

QUICK QUIZ 8.E

1. A member firm is selling stock to a customer from inventory. The broker-dealer has held the shares sold for several months. What price should the dealer use as a basis for a markup?

   A. Price at which it purchased the securities
   B. Offer price shown on the OTC *Pink* on the day of the current sale
   C. Broker-dealer's own current offer price
   D. Best offering price quoted in the interdealer market

2. The 5% markup policy applies to

   I. commissions charged when executing customer agency (broker) transactions
   II. markups and markdowns on principal (dealer) transactions filled for customers from a firm's trading inventory
   III. markups on stocks or bonds bought for inventory, then immediately resold to customers
   IV. markdowns on stocks or bonds bought from customers for inventory, then immediately resold to another broker-dealer

   A. I and II
   B. II only
   C. III and IV
   D. I, II, III and IV

3. Which of the following transactions are NOT subject to the 5% policy on markups and markdowns?

   I. New issue corporate equity securities sold in a public offering
   II. Mutual fund shares sold to the public
   III. Municipal bonds
   IV. NYSE-listed stock traded in the third market

   A. I and II
   B. I, II and III
   C. III and IV
   D. I, II, III and IV

4. The 5% markup policy

   A. allows a member to determine fair markups on the basis of the firm's actual acquisition costs
   B. is a guide to fairness, not a rule
   C. automatically judges any markup or markdown exceeding 5% to be unfair
   D. applies only to common stock transactions

5. Which of the following is NOT relevant in applying the 5% markup policy?

   A. Amount of money involved
   B. Type of security
   C. Current price of the security
   D. Type of account

8. 11   AUTOMATED QUOTATION SYSTEM

Nasdaq provides a computer link between broker-dealers that trade OTC.

8. 11. 1   NASDAQ QUOTATION SERVICE

The system provides three levels of stock quotation service to the securities industry.

- **Nasdaq Level 1** is available to registered representatives through a variety of public vendors. Level 1 displays the inside market only, the highest bids and the lowest asks for securities included in the system, and other basic information such as last sale and volume. Normal market price fluctuations prevent a registered representative from guaranteeing a Level 1 price to a client.

- **Nasdaq Level 2** is available to approved subscribers only. Level 2 provides the current quote and quote size available from each market maker in a security in the system. To list a quote on Level 2, a market maker must guarantee that the quote is firm for at least 100 shares.

- **Nasdaq Level 3** provides subscribers with all of the services of levels 1 and 2 and allows registered market makers to input and update their quotes on any securities in which they make a market.

Levels of Nasdaq Service

DWAQ 35 – 35.13

Level 1: The inside quote

DWAQ 35 – 35.13		
DWAQ	Bid	Ask
Serendip	35	35.25
Tippec	34.88	35.13
Cheath	35	35.13

Level 2: The inside quote plus quotes from all market makers

DWAQ 35 – 35.13		
DWAQ	Bid	Ask
Serendip	35	35.25
Tippec	34.88	35.13
Cheath	35	35.13
Enter	BID:	ASK:

Level 3: The inside quote, all other quotes, plus ability to enter or change your own quote

UNIT TEST

1. The Securities Exchange Act of 1934 regulates or mandates all of the following EXCEPT

   A. full and fair disclosure on new offerings
   B. creation of the SEC
   C. manipulation of the market
   D. margin requirements on securities

2. All of the following statements regarding the short sale of a listed security are true EXCEPT

   A. the order ticket must indicate that the sale is short
   B. short sales may take place at the opening
   C. the buyer must be advised that he is purchasing borrowed shares
   D. short sales may take place at the closing

3. XYZ stock is quoted as 15.11 bid and offered at 15.22. If the specialist (designated market maker) increases the bid by the minimum amount, the bid would now be

   A. 15.12
   B. 15.13
   C. 15.16
   D. 15.20

4. Each of the following types of orders remains open on the NYSE until certain conditions are met EXCEPT

   A. stop orders
   B. good til canceled orders
   C. all-or-none orders
   D. market orders

5. The SEC regulates the trading of all of the following EXCEPT

   A. commodity futures
   B. options
   C. preferred stock
   D. corporate bonds

6. Which of the following statements regarding the third market is TRUE?

   A. It is composed of listed securities traded OTC.
   B. It is composed only of unlisted securities.
   C. The services of a brokerage firm are not used.
   D. It refers to the block trading of unlisted securities.

7. A large volume transaction for an institutional investor has occurred on an alternative trading system or network. Entered anonymously, the general public will see no information regarding the volume, price, or who the institutional investor was. This transaction scenario is generally referred to as having occurred

   A. on a U.S. exchange
   B. in a dark pool
   C. in the over-the-counter (OTC) market
   D. in the third market

8. During a trading halt, an investor can

   A. cancel an order that was placed before the halt
   B. execute a market order
   C. execute a limit order
   D. close an existing position

9. Which of the following orders are entered above the current market?

   I. Buy stop
   II. Sell stop
   III. Buy limit
   IV. Sell limit

   A. I and II
   B. I and IV
   C. II and III
   D. II and IV

10. An order designated GTC is

    A. good only until the end of the day on which the order was entered
    B. good until executed with no time restriction
    C. good until it is executed or canceled with no time restriction
    D. good until either executed, canceled, or the last trading day of April or the last trading day of October when it will be automatically canceled

11. Which of the following activities is NOT a function of a specialist (designated market maker) on the NYSE?

    A. Setting strike prices for options on the securities he works
    B. Keeping a book of public orders
    C. Maintaining a bid and offer at all times
    D. Buying and selling stock for his own account

12. An immediate-or-cancel (IOC) order

    I. must be executed in its entirety
    II. may be executed in part or in full
    III. must be executed in one attempt
    IV. may be executed after several attempts
    A. I and III
    B. I and IV
    C. II and III
    D. II and IV

13. The over-the-counter market could be characterized as what type of market?

    A. Auction
    B. First
    C. Negotiated
    D. Primary

14. All of the following statements regarding the 5% markup policy are true EXCEPT

    A. it applies to markups on stocks or bonds sold from inventory
    B. it only applies to markups and markdowns on principal transactions and not to commissions on agency transactions
    C. it applies to markdowns on stocks or bonds bought for inventory
    D. it applies to riskless and simultaneous transactions

15. An open-end investment company bought preferred stock from a bank through an ECN. This trade took place in which of the following markets?

    A. Primary
    B. Secondary
    C. Third
    D. Fourth

16. The market-wide circuit breaker (MWCB) rules used to prevent rapid uncontrolled drops in the market use which of the following as a price reference to measure declines?

    A. The Dow Jones Industrial Average (DJIA) recalculated quarterly.
    B. The Dow Jones Industrial Average (DJIA) recalculated weekly.
    C. The S&P 500 Index recalculated daily.
    D. The Volatility Index (VIX) recalculated monthly.

17. A market maker buys 100 shares of LMN at $14 per share for inventory. Two weeks later, the stock is being quoted at 14.50–15, and the firm sells 100 shares of LMN to a customer. Which of the following prices is the basis for the firm's markup?

    A. 14
    B. 14.50
    C. 14.75
    D. 15

18. Your client, who has sold 100 shares of GGZ short, places a buy stop order at 80. The order is activated when the price of GGZ

    A. falls to 80 or below
    B. falls below 80
    C. rises to 80 or above
    D. rises above 80

19. A customer places an order to sell 100 DEF 52.25 stop. After placing the order, DEF trades as follows: 53, 52.60, 52.20, 52.10, 52.25. Which trade elects or triggers the order?

    A. 52.10
    B. 52.25
    C. 52.20
    D. 52.60

20. Under the locate requirement of Regulation SHO, naked short selling of an equity security is

    A. permitted without restriction
    B. permitted on a plus tick
    C. permitted on an up bid
    D. prohibited

21. Which of the following would be the usual use of a stop order?

    I. To protect the profit on a long position
    II. To prevent loss on a short position
    III. To buy at a specific price only
    IV. To guarantee execution at or near the close

    A. I and II
    B. I and III
    C. II and III
    D. II and IV

22. A fill-or-kill (FOK) order

    I. must be executed in its entirety
    II. may be executed in part or in full
    III. must be executed in one attempt
    IV. may be executed after several attempts

    A. I and III
    B. I and IV
    C. II and III
    D. II and IV

23. Which of the following orders would be executed in a rising market?

    I. Buy stops
    II. Buy limits
    III. Sell limits
    IV. Sell stops

    A. I and III
    B. I and IV
    C. II and III
    D. II and IV

24. Trades are reported to the Consolidated Tape System (CTS) by

    A. the SEC
    B. exchanges and FINRA
    C. buyers
    D. sellers

25. A customer asks you to sell 1,000 shares of XYZ stock and instructs you to use the money generated by the sale to purchase as many shares of ABCD stock as you can at the market. This is known as

    A. a short sale
    B. a proceeds transaction
    C. a riskless and simultaneous transaction
    D. backing away

ANSWERS AND RATIONALES

1. **A.** The Securities Exchange Act of 1934 set up the SEC and regulates the secondary market. The Securities Exchange Act of 1934 does not address full and fair disclosure for new issues; the Act of 1933 addresses such issues. This act gave the Federal Reserve Board the authority to determine margin requirements.

2. **C.** A buyer need not be advised that shares purchased were sold short, but the order ticket prepared by the brokerage firm representing the seller must indicate that the sale is short. Short sales may be executed at any time during the trading day including the opening and closing.

3. **A.** The minimum trading increment is .01. If the specialist (designated market maker) increases a 15.11 bid by the minimum amount, the bid is now 15.12.

4. **D.** A market order is executed immediately at the prevailing market price. A stop order is not triggered until a set price is hit or passed through. A good til canceled order remains open until executed or canceled. An all-or-none order is not filled until the total number of shares specified is bought or sold.

5. **A.** The SEC regulates the trading of all nonexempt securities. Commodity futures, which are not considered securities, are regulated by the Commodities Futures Trading Commission (CFTC).

6. **A.** The third market refers to the trading of listed securities in the over-the-counter market.

7. **B.** Transactions such as the one described are generally known to have occurred in a dark pool. They occur away from exchanges on alternative trading systems and networks. Primarily used by institutional traders for large volume transactions they allow traders to be anonymous, not revealing the full extent of their market positions or their tendency to be a buyer or seller at any particular time. Though market transparency is of concern, dark pool transactions violate no industry rules.

8. **A.** If trading is halted in a security, investors cannot buy or sell the security. An open order can be canceled during a trading halt.

9. **B.** A limit order is an order to buy or sell at a specific price or better. Therefore, buy limits are entered below the current market and sell limits are entered above the current market. Stop orders have several uses. The most common of these is to protect gains on both long and short positions. For example, if a customer were to buy stock at $30 a share and the stock is now trading at $50, the customer could enter a sell stop order below the current market to protect the unrealized gain. If the market falls, the stop order will be elected once the stock trades at or through the stop price. Similarly, a customer with an unrealized gain on a short stock position could enter a buy stop above the prevailing market in order to protect the gain.

10. **D.** GTC stands for "good til canceled." GTC orders remain working day to day until they are either executed, canceled, or will be automatically canceled on the last trading day of April or October.

11. **A.** A specialist (designated market maker) keeps a book of public orders, must maintain a bid and offer at all times, and will buy or sell stock for his own account. He may not set option strike prices. That is the prerogative of the Options Clearing Corporation (OCC).

12. **C.** An immediate-or-cancel order is one in which the firm handling the order has one attempt to fill the order but a partial execution is binding on the customer.

13. **C.** The New York Stock Exchange is an auction market, and the OTC market is a negotiated market.

14. **B.** The 5% markup policy applies both to commission charges on agency transactions and to markups and markdowns on principal transactions, including riskless principal trades.

15. **D.** The fourth market consists of direct trades between institutions, pension funds, broker-dealers, and others. In theory, there are no brokers involved in these transactions. The fourth market is the ECN market.

16. **C.** The market-wide circuit breaker (MWCB) rules used to prevent rapid uncontrolled drops in the market use the S&P 500 Index recalculated daily as a price reference to measure declines in the market.

17. **D.** The basis for the markup is the current interdealer offering price, which is, in this case, $15 per share.

18. **C.** A buy stop order is always entered at a price above the current offering price. A buy stop order at 80 means that if the market price rises to 80 or above, the order becomes a market order to buy and is filled immediately.

19. **C.** Sell stop orders are elected or triggered as soon as the stock trades at or through the stop price. The trade at 52.20 represents the first such transaction after the order is placed.

20. **D.** The short sale of any equity security requires that the short seller meet the locate requirement of Regulation SHO before effecting the sale. Failure to meet the locate requirement on a short sale transaction is considered a naked short sale and is not permitted.

21. **A.** A buy stop could be used to protect an investor who is short, and a sell stop could be used to protect an investor who is long. Stop orders never guarantee execution price.

22. **A.** A fill-or-kill order is one in which the firm handling the order can make one attempt to fill the order in its entirety. If unable to do so, the order is canceled.

23. **A.** Buy limits and sell stops are entered below the current market and will be executed if the market is falling. On the other hand, sell limits and buy stops are entered above the current market and would be executed if the market is rising.

24. **B.** Exchanges and FINRA report last sale transaction prices to the Consolidated Tape System (CTS).

25. **B.** The use of the sale proceeds from one transaction to make another purchase is known as a proceeds transaction. One key element of a proceeds transaction is that for commission or markup purposes, the two transactions must be treated as one and would have to be consistent with the markup policy.

QUICK QUIZ ANSWERS

Quick Quiz 8.A

1. **D.** A stop limit order is a stop order that becomes a limit order once the stop price has been triggered. When the limit price is the same as the stop price on a stop limit order, the order can be executed only at or better than the limit price. In this case, the order has not yet been executed because no transaction has occurred at or above 38.63 since the stop was triggered at 38.50.

2. **B.** Sell stop orders are always entered below the market price. A sell stop order is triggered when a transaction occurs at or below the price specified on the order. A buy stop order is always entered at a price above the current offering price. Once elected, stop orders become market orders.

3. **C.** A stop order becomes a market order once the market price reaches or passes the specific stop price. An investor in a long position can use the sell stop order for protection against a market decline. When a large number of stop orders are triggered at a particular price, the advance or decline of the market at that point can be magnified. Stop orders are not the same as limit orders because there is no guarantee of a specific execution price for a stop order.

4. **A.** A sell limit order is used to sell out a long position at a higher price (when the market moves up). A sell stop order is used to sell out a long position at a lower price (when the market moves down). To protect against erosion of the gain, a sell stop order would be placed just below where the stock is currently trading.

5. **D.** A buy limit order is used to buy in a short position at a lower price (when the market moves down). A buy stop order is used to buy in a short position at a higher price (when the market moves up). To protect against a loss of the gain, a buy stop order would be placed just above where the stock is currently trading.

6. **B.** The sell stop limit order is elected (triggered) at the first trade of 50.13, when the stock trades at or below the stop price of 50.25. The order becomes a sell limit order at 50.25. The order can be executed at that price or higher (the limit placed by the customer). The next trade reported after the trigger is reached is below the limit price. The order could be executed at the next trade of 50.25.

Quick Quiz 8.B

1. **B.** The qualifying price on a do-not-reduce (DNR) order will not be reduced by ordinary cash dividends on the ex-dividend date.

2. **A.** When a stock goes ex-dividend, the specialist (designated market maker) will reduce open buy limit orders and open sell stop orders because they are placed below the market price and could be triggered when the market price is reduced for the loss of dividend. The specialist will not reduce open sell limit orders and open buy stop orders.

3. **A.** When a stock goes ex-dividend, the price of the stock falls by the amount of the dividend. A dividend of $.70 would reduce the stop price by that amount.

Quick Quiz 8.C

1. **D.**

2. **A.**

3. **B.**

4. **C.**

Quick Quiz 8.D

1. **A.** When the symbol SLD appears it is because the transaction was reported to the Consolidated Tape System (CTS) by an exchange or FINRA late. Because it was reported late, it indicates that the transaction is appearing out of sequence in the system.

Quick Quiz 8.E

1. **D.** Rules require that a dealer's markup to a customer be based on the current market rather than the dealer's cost. The dealer's potential loss on inventory is considered to be the risk of making a market.

2. **D.** The 5% policy applies both to commission charges on agency transactions and to markups and markdowns on principal transactions with customers.

3. **B.** The 5% markup policy does not apply to new issues sold with a prospectus, mutual funds or municipal bonds.

4. **B.** The 5% policy is only a guide to fair markups and commissions; it is not a strict rule. Markups or markdowns that amount to more than 5% may very well be justified; by the same token, a markup of only 1% or 2% could be excessive, depending on the security type, the transaction size, and the dollar amount of the markup or commission charge.

5. **D.** The type of account is not relevant in deciding the 5% policy because the markup policy is used as a guide in all types of accounts.

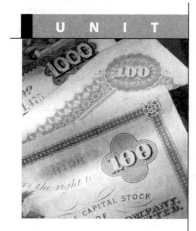

9

Brokerage Support Services

Brokerage firms are required to follow strict procedures for maintaining accurate and thorough client information. This Unit discusses the Uniform Practice Code and the standardized procedures that apply to member firms.

It is important to know the general roles of the various departments involved in processing customer orders.

Most records must be maintained for three years, and it is the principal's responsibility to ensure that records are accurate. The Regulation T settlement date and regular way settlement dates are different. Unless specified otherwise, always assume regular way settlement.

The Series 7 exam will have approximately 15–20 questions on the material presented in this Unit. ■

After you have completed this Unit, you should be able to:

■ **list** the steps and departments involved in processing an order;

■ **identify** the required documentation of customer transactions;

■ **identify** the standard transaction settlement dates; and

■ **identify** critical elements for good delivery of securities.

9. 1 PROCESSING AN ORDER

Several steps are involved in processing a securities transaction. The process begins when a client places an order with a registered representative. The registered representative enters the transaction on a computer or writes an order ticket. The order is routed through the following departments.

- **The order department (wire room, order room)** transmits orders to the proper markets for execution. Completed trade tickets are sent to the registered representatives who initiated the trades and to the purchases and sales department.

- **The purchases and sales (P&S) department** records all transactions in a client's account and handles all billing. It mails trade confirmations, which specify commission and total cost.

- **The margin,** or **credit department,** handles activities involving credit for cash and margin accounts. It computes the dates on which clients must deposit money and the deposit amount.

- **The cashiering department (cage)** is responsible for receiving and delivering securities and money. It issues payment only if the margin department instructs it to do so. It sends certificates to transfer agents to be transferred and registered and then forwards the certificates to clients.

A clearing corporation, such as the **National Securities Clearing Corporation (NSCC),** can simplify this process by providing specialized comparison clearance and settlement services.

Other departments involved in customer transactions follow.

- **The reorganization department** handles any transaction that represents a change in the securities outstanding. This includes exchanging or transmitting customer securities involved in tender offers, bond calls, redemptions of preferred stock, mergers, and acquisitions.

- **The dividend department** credits customer accounts with dividends and interest payments for securities held in the firm's name.

- **The proxy department** sends proxy statements to customers whose securities are held in the firm's name. It also sends out financial reports and other publications received from the issuer for its stockholders.

- **The stock record department** maintains the ledger that lists each stock owner and the certificate's location.

TEST TOPIC ALERT   Be ready for a question that asks you to identify the flow of an order through a brokerage firm: an easy way to remember this process is **O**ther **P**eople **M**ight **C**are.

OPMC reminds you that an order starts with the **O**rder department, then goes to the **P**&S department, the **M**argin department, and finally the **C**ashiering department. Sometimes the order department is referred to as the wire room, so you might see **WPMC** instead.

Route of an Order

(1) Customer places order with registered representative.

(2) Registered representative sends order to order department (wire room).

(3) Order department sends order to appropriate market for execution.

(4) Market sends wire report of execution back to order department.

(5) Order department sends report of execution to registered representative.

(6) Registered representative calls customer to report execution of order.

(7) Order department sends report of trade to P&S department.

(8) P&S department sends confirmation to customer and a copy to registered representative.

(9) P&S department processes trade for settlement through the:

a. margin department, customer credit area; or
b. cashiering department, which delivers or receives securities from buyer or seller and exchanges monies.

Customer

Cashiering Department

Registered Representative

Purchases and Sales Department

Order Department (Wire Room)

Margin Department

Market

9. 1. 1   TRANSACTIONS AND TRADE SETTLEMENT

Processes must be in place in order to accept an order from a customer, report the execution back to the customer, and ultimately have the transaction settle.

9. 1. 1. 1   Receipt and Delivery of Securities

When a representative accepts a buy or sell order from a customer, the representative must be assured that the customer can pay for or deliver the securities. If the customer claims the securities are being held in street name at another firm, the representative must verify this before executing a sale for the customer.

9. 1. 1. 2   Order Memorandum

To enter a customer order, the registered representative traditionally has filled out an **order ticket**. Increasingly, representatives are entering orders electronically.

After the representative prepares the order ticket it is sent to the wire room or desk where the order is routed to the proper market for execution. A registered principal must approve the order promptly after execution. Promptly after execution is interpreted as meaning no later than the end of the trading day.

A customer order is most susceptible to error at two points: communication of the order between customer and broker and transmission of the order from broker to wire operator. Breakdowns in communication in the ordering process most often occur because of inaccurate information on a ticket.

The information required on the order ticket includes:

- customer account number;
- registered representative identification number;
- whether the order is solicited or unsolicited;
- whether the order is subject to discretionary authority;
- description of the security (symbol);
- number of shares or bonds to be traded;
- action (buy, sell long, or sell short);
- options (buy, write, covered, uncovered, opening, or closing);
- order restrictions and price qualifications (e.g., market, GTC, or day order);
- type of account (cash or margin); and
- the time the order was received, the time of entry, and the price at which it was executed.

TAKE NOTE   The account name or number must be on an order ticket before order execution. If a mistake is made (e.g., a wrong account number), no change to the order can be made without the approval of a principal or the branch manager. All of the facts surrounding the change must be put in writing and retained for three years.

9. 1. 1. 3   Report of Execution

The registered representative receives a report after a trade is executed. He first checks the execution report against the order ticket to make sure that everything was done as the customer requested. If everything is in order, he reports the execution to the customer. If an error exists, the representative must report it to the branch office manager (BOM) or principal immediately. Changing an account number on an order ticket (cancel and rebill) requires manager approval.

9. 1. 1. 3. 1   Incorrect Trade Reports

Sometimes the details of a trade are reported to a customer incorrectly. Despite the mistaken report, the actual trade is binding on the customer. However, if an order is executed outside the customer's instructions, the trade is not binding.

9. 1. 1. 3. 2   Reporting an Error

FINRA rules require that a record of any errors made be reported to the person designated to receive such error reports by the firm. At a broker-dealer, that individual would always be a manager or someone who holds a principal's license. All such reports should be made immediately in writing and retained for three years under the general record retention rules. These reports may be referred to as error reports, error records, trade correction reports, or any number of generic names a firm might assign to such records.

9. 1. 1. 4 Trade Confirmations

A **trade confirmation** is a printed document that confirms a trade, its settlement date, and the amount of money due from or owed to the customer. For each transaction, a customer must be sent or given a written confirmation of the trade at or before the completion of the transaction, the **settlement date**.

The trade confirmation includes the following information:

- **Trade date**—day on which the transaction is executed (the settlement date is usually the second business day after the trade date)
- **Account number**—branch office number followed by an account number
- **Registered representative internal ID number** (or **AE number**)—account executive's identification number
- **BOT** (bought) or **SLD** (sold)—indicates a customer's role in a trade
- **Number** (or **Quantity**)—number of shares of stock or the par value of bonds bought or sold for the customer
- **Description**—specific security bought or sold for the customer
- **Yield**—indicates that the yield for callable bonds may be affected by the exercise of a call provision
- **CUSIP number**—applicable Committee on Uniform Securities Identification Procedures (CUSIP) number, if any
- **Price**—price per share for stock or bonds before a charge or deduction
- **Amount**—price paid or received before commissions and other charges, also referred to as **extended principal** for municipal securities transactions
- **Commission**—added to buy transactions; subtracted from sell transactions completed on an agency basis; a commission will not appear on the confirmation if a markup has been charged in a principal transaction
- **Net amount**—obtained on purchases by adding expenses (commissions and postage) to the principal amount (whether the transaction is a purchase or sale, interest is always added whenever bonds are traded with accrued interest)

9. 1. 1. 4. 1 Disclosure of Capacity

The confirmation must also show the capacity in which the broker-dealer acts (agency or principal) and the commission in cases where the broker-dealer acts as an agent. Markups or markdowns are disclosed for Nasdaq securities.

TAKE ✓ **NOTE**

All firms can act in one of two capacities in a customer transaction. If the firm acts as an agent, it is the broker between the buying and selling parties. Agents receive commissions for transactions they perform, and commissions must be disclosed on confirmations.

If the firm acts as a dealer and transacts business for or from its inventory, it acts in a principal capacity and is compensated by a markup or markdown.

Additionally, confirmations must disclose markups or markdowns for Nasdaq securities, and a firm can never act as both agent and principal in the same transaction.

9. 1. 1. 4. 2   *Timely Mailing of Confirmations*

Customer confirmations must be sent no later than at or before the completion of the transaction.

9. 1. 1. 5   Customer Account Statements

At a minimum, firms must send each customer a quarterly statement, but most firms send customers monthly statements. A statement shows:

■ all activity in the account since the previous statement;

■ securities positions, long or short; and

■ account balances, debit or credit.

If a customer's account has a cash balance, the firm may hold it in the account. However, the statement must advise the customer that these funds are available on request.

TAKE NOTE   If there is activity in an account or if penny stocks are held in the account, statements are sent monthly. If neither of these conditions exists, there is no activity, and penny stocks are not being held, then statements may be sent quarterly.

9. 1. 1. 6   Disclosure of Financial Condition

Upon written request, a member firm must deliver a copy of its most recently prepared balance sheet to:

■ any customer with securities or cash held by the member; or

■ a member firm with cash or securities on deposit or transacting business with the member.

9. 1. 1. 7   Charges for Services Performed

A member broker-dealer's fees and charges must:

■ be reasonable;

■ relate to the work performed, transaction entered, or advisory services given; and

■ not be unfairly discriminatory among customers.

A **reasonable fee** is one that is not excessive, compared with the fees charged by other broker-dealers or investment advisers charge for similar services.

TEST TOPIC ALERT   True or False? If a customer of a broker-dealer requests a copy of the firm's most recent income statement in writing, the broker-dealer must comply.

Answer: False. Upon request, the customer is entitled to the most recent balance sheet, not income statement.

Order Process Diagram

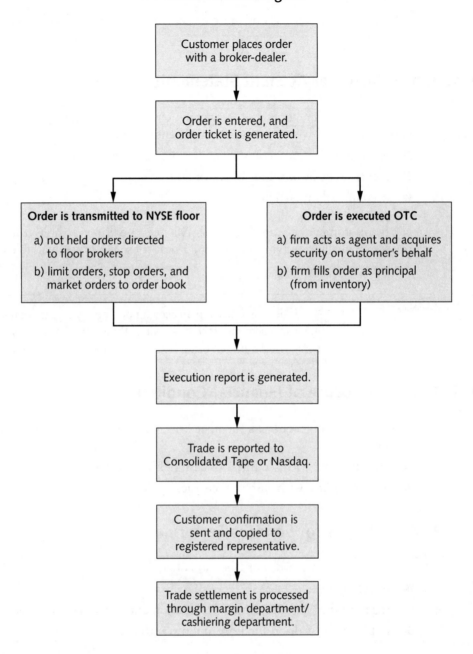

1. Which department in a brokerage firm handles all credit transactions for a customer?

   A. Margin
   B. Cashiering
   C. Purchases and sales
   D. Reorganization

2. Once orders are received, in which sequence do they flow through a brokerage firm?

   I.   Order or wire room
   II. Purchases and sales department
   III. Margin department
   IV. Cashiering department

   A. I, II, III, IV
   B. I, IV, II, III
   C. II, I, IV, III
   D. III, IV, II, I

3. Rules require that a statement for an inactive account should be sent to each customer

   A. weekly
   B. monthly
   C. quarterly
   D. immediately after each trade

Quick Quiz answers can be found at the end of the Unit.

9. 1. 2   TRANSACTION SETTLEMENT DATES AND TERMS

Settlement date is the date on which ownership changes between buyer and seller. It is the date on which broker-dealers are required to exchange the securities and funds involved in a transaction and customers are requested to pay for securities bought and to deliver securities sold.

The **Uniform Practice Code (UPC)** standardizes the dates and times for each type of settlement.

9. 1. 2. 1   Regular Way Settlement

Regular way settlement for most securities transactions is the second business day following the trade date, known as T+2.

EXAMPLE   If a trade occurs on a Tuesday (trade date), it will settle regular way on Thursday. If a trade takes place on a Thursday, it will settle the following Monday.

Knowing that not all securities settle T+2 is equally important, and a summary of settlement rules is included later in this section. Briefly, corporate securities, municipals, and government agency securities settle T+2. U.S. government T-bills, T-notes, T-bonds, and options settle next business day, T+1. Money market securities transactions settle the same day.

In trades between dealers, if the seller delivers before the settlement date, the buyer may either accept the security or refuse it without prejudice.

TAKE NOTE   Interdealer trades in government securities settle in federal funds. Interdealer trades in all other securities settle in clearinghouse funds.

9. 1. 2. 2   Cash Settlement

Cash settlement, or **same day settlement**, requires delivery of securities from the seller and payment from the buyer on the same day a trade is executed. Stocks or bonds sold for cash settlement must be available on the spot for delivery to the buyer.

Cash trade settlement occurs no later than 2:30 pm ET if the trade is executed before 2:00 pm. If the trade occurs after 2:00 pm, settlement is due within 30 minutes.

9. 1. 2. 3   Seller's Option Contracts

This form of settlement is available to customers who want to sell securities but cannot deliver the physical securities in time for regular way settlement. A **seller's option contract** lets a customer lock in a selling price for securities without having to make delivery on the second business day. Instead, the seller can settle the trade as specified in the contract. Or, if the seller elects to settle earlier than originally specified, the trade can be settled on any date from the third business day through the contract date, provided the buyer is given a one-day written notice.

A buyer's option contract works the same way, with the buyer specifying when settlement will take place.

9. 1. 2. 4   When-, As-, and If-Issued Contracts (When-Issued Trades)

Typically, new municipal bond issues are sold to investors before the bonds are issued. An investor receives a when-issued confirmation describing the bonds. The confirmation does not include a total dollar amount or settlement date because, until the settlement date is known, the accrued interest cannot be calculated to determine the total dollar amount. Once the bonds are issued, the investor receives a new confirmation stating the purchase price and settlement date.

A when-issued transaction confirmation must include:

- a description of the security, with the contract price (yield); and
- trade date.

Because the settlement date is unknown, a when-issued confirmation for municipal bonds cannot include accrued interest.

9. 1. 2. 5   Regulation T Payment

Regulation T specifies the date customers are required to pay for purchase transactions. The **settlement date**, however, is the date customers are requested to deliver cash or securities involved in transactions. Under Regulation T, payment is due two business days after regular way settlement.

9. 1. 2. 5. 1 Extensions

If a buyer cannot pay for a trade within four business days from the trade date as allowed under Regulation T, the broker-dealer may request an extension from its designated examining authority (DEA) before the fourth business day. In the case of introducing broker-dealers, those that do not clear their own trades, the extension request is made by the clearing firm. The broker-dealer has the option of ignoring amounts of $1,000 or less without violating Regulation T requirements.

If the customer cannot pay by the end of the extension, the broker-dealer has the option to either request an additional extension from its DEA or sell the securities in a closeout transaction. Broker-dealers are not likely to request too many extensions as a firm and are generally reluctant to request many for the same customer repeatedly unless severe circumstances warrant the request.

If the option to close out the position is chosen, the account is frozen for 90 days. A **frozen account** must have sufficient cash in it before a buy transaction can be executed.

TAKE NOTE   Regulation T deals with the extension of credit for regular security trades. If a broker-dealer must close out a transaction and freeze the account, the customer may not be extended credit.

9. 1. 2. 5. 2 Frozen Accounts

If a customer buys securities in a cash account and sells them before paying for the buy side by the fourth business day, the account is frozen. Any additional buy transactions require full payment in the account, and sell transactions need securities on deposit. Frozen account status continues for 90 calendar days. Frozen account status is lifted if the customer pays by the fourth business day.

TEST TOPIC ALERT   The following table gives a summary of the trade settlements and delivery times for different securities and different types of settlement choices.

Summary of Settlement Rules

Regular way—Equity	2 business days
Regular way—Corporate and municipal bonds	2 business days
Regular way—Equity options	Next business day
Regular way—Index options	Next business day
Regular way—T-bills, T-notes, and T-bonds	Next business day
Regular way—U.S. government agency	2 business days
Seller's option	No sooner than T+3
Cash settlement	Same day
Regulation T	2 days after regular way

Assume a question is asking about the normal customer settlement terms, regular way, unless the question specifically mentions Regulation T.

Also, here's a hint on municipal when-issued settlements. A probable question will ask either what is not included or what is included on a when-issued confirmation. To discern the correct answer, remember **SAT**, which identifies what is not included:

- **S**ettlement date

- **A**ccrued interest

- **T**otal dollar amount due at settlement

If a question asks when customer confirmations must be sent, the answer is no later than the settlement date. But if the question asks when broker-to-broker confirmations must be sent, the answer is no later than the business day following the trade date (T+1).

9. 1. 3 PROXY DEPARTMENT

The proxy department sends proxy material to customers who have securities held in the broker-dealer's name (street name). In addition, other materials received from the issuer such as financial reports are also forwarded to the customer by the proxy department.

9. 1. 3. 1 The Proxy

A corporation's stockholders usually vote by means of a **proxy**, like an absentee ballot. A **proxy** is a limited power of attorney that a stockholder gives to another person, transferring the right to vote on the stockholder's behalf. A proxy is automatically revoked if the stockholder attends the shareholder meeting or, if the proxy is replaced by another proxy, the stockholder executes at a later date.

9. 1. 3. 2 Proxy Solicitation

Stockholders can receive multiple **proxy solicitations** for controversial company proposals. If proxies are solicited, the SEC requires a company to give stockholders information about the items to be voted on and allow the SEC to review this information before it sends the proxies to stockholders. In a **proxy contest**, everyone who participates must register with the SEC. Also, anyone who is not a direct participant but who provides stockholders with unsolicited advice must register as a participant.

9. 1. 3. 3 Forwarding Proxies and Other Materials

Member firms must cooperate with issuers by ensuring that customers whose stock is held in street name are alerted to all financial matters concerning issuers (e.g., quarterly reports and proxy statements). To do so, members act as forwarding agents for all proxies and other corporate materials received from an issuer for street name stock.

Member firms that are nominal owners of record must vote street name stock in accordance with the wishes of the beneficial owners. If a customer signs and returns a proxy statement and fails to indicate how the shares are to be voted, the member must vote the shares as recommended by management.

If a customer does not return the proxy by the 10th day before the annual shareholders' meeting, the member may vote the shares as it sees fit as long as the matters to be voted on are of minor importance. If the matters to be voted on are of major importance (e.g., merger or issuance of additional securities), the member may never vote the shares as it sees fit. In this case, if the proxy is not returned, the shares are not voted.

Member firms are reimbursed by issuers for all costs relating to the forwarding of proxy materials. Such costs include postage and related clerical expenses.

9. 1. 4   DON'T KNOW (DK)

In an interdealer trade, each side electronically submits its version of the transaction to ACT (Automated Confirmation Transaction System). If one side does not recognize the other side's details of the transaction (e.g., the number of shares is wrong or the price is wrong), it will electronically DK (Don't Know) the trade.

TAKE NOTE

DKs are used in interdealer trades for which one party to the transaction does not recognize the trade or, if it does, disagrees with the terms of the trade as submitted by the other party.

The term can also be used within a broker-dealer when an order or wire room does not recognize the account number or other information on an order ticket.

9. 1. 4. 1   Due Bills

If one of your customers buys stock before the ex-date, your customer is entitled to the dividend. However, if the trade is somehow mishandled and does not settle until after the record date, the seller will receive the dividend in error. In this case, your firm will send a due bill to the seller's firm stating, "Our customer is due the dividend—kindly remit."

TAKE NOTE

Due bills are sent when the wrong party receives a dividend from the issuer.

QUICK QUIZ 9.B

1. In a contested proxy solicitation, all those soliciting proxies from shareholders must register with

    A. SEC
    B. FINRA
    C. FRB
    D. NSCC

2. If a broker-dealer chooses to close out a customer's position rather than request an extension, the account will be frozen for

    A. 20 days
    B. 30 days
    C. 90 days
    D. 120 days

3. Broker-to-broker confirmations are sent no later than
   A. the regular way settlement date
   B. the next business day
   C. the same day as the transaction
   D. the trade date plus three business days

9. 2 RULES OF GOOD DELIVERY

A security must be in **good delivery form** before it can be delivered to a buyer. It is the registered representative's responsibility to ensure that a security is in good deliverable form when a customer sells it.

9. 2. 1 PHYSICAL REQUIREMENTS

Good delivery describes the physical condition of, signatures on, attachments to, and denomination of the certificates involved in a securities transaction. Good delivery is normally a back-office consideration between buying and selling brokers. In any broker-to-broker transaction, the delivered securities must be accompanied by a properly executed uniform delivery ticket. The transfer agent is the final arbiter of whether a security meets the requirements of good delivery.

9. 2. 1. 1 Overdelivery and Underdelivery

In settling customer sell transactions in which the securities delivery matches the exact number of shares or bonds sold, the first rule of good delivery is met. But if the customer overdelivers or underdelivers, the transaction is not good delivery.

EXAMPLE

Overdelivery:
A customer sells 300 shares and brings in one certificate for 325 shares.

Underdelivery:
A customer sells 100 shares and brings in one certificate for 80 shares.

9. 2. 1. 2 Partial Delivery

A broker-to-broker **partial delivery** must be accepted if the remainder of the delivery constitutes a round lot or multiple thereof.

9. 2. 1. 3 Good Delivery Clearing Rule (100-Share Uniform Units)

When one broker-dealer delivers stock to another broker-dealer, single round lots and odd lots are cleared separately. However, odd-lot certificates can be used to clear round-lot trades provided the odd lot certificates add up to single round lots (100 shares).

EXAMPLE

For a 300-share sale, the seller could deliver:

- one 300-share certificate;

- three 100-share certificates;

- six 50-share certificates;

- two 100-share certificates, one 60 share certificate, and one 40 share certificate; or

- three 60-share certificates and three 40-share certificates.

Each of the above deliveries meets the requirements of the rule. However, delivering four 75-share certificates would not be good delivery. Think of it this way: can you take the certificates and make piles of 100 shares? If the answer is *yes*, it is good delivery.

9. 2. 1. 4   Good Delivery for Bonds

Delivery of bonds in coupon or bearer form should be made in denominations of $1,000 or $5,000. Fully registered bonds are delivered in denominations of $1,000 or multiples of $1,000, but in no case larger than $100,000. Municipal bonds may settle in bearer or registered form and be delivered in the denominations stated above.

9. 2. 1. 5   Missing Coupons

If coupons are missing from a bond, it is not good delivery. If an issuer is in default on a coupon bond, all of the unpaid coupons must be attached for it to be good delivery.

9. 2. 2   CERTIFICATE NEGOTIABILITY

In order for ownership to change hands, the certificate representing ownership must be negotiable. Following are the criteria that determine negotiability.

9. 2. 2. 1   Assignment

Each stock and bond certificate must be **assigned** (endorsed by signature) by the owner(s) whose name is registered on the certificate's face. Certificates registered in joint name require all owners' signatures.

Endorsement by a customer may be made on the back of a certificate on the signature line or on a separate **stock or bond power of substitution**. One stock or bond power can be used with any number of certificates for one security, but a separate power is required for each security.

9. 2. 2. 1. 1   Alteration

If an **alteration** or a correction has been made to an assignment, a full explanation of the change signed by the person or firm who executed the correction must be attached.

9. 2. 2. 2   Signature Guarantee

All customer signatures must be **guaranteed** by a party acceptable to the transfer agent (e.g., an exchange member or a national bank).

9. 2. 2. 3   Signature Requirements

A customer's signature must match exactly the name registered on the face of a security.

TAKE NOTE Regarding signature requirements for purposes of good delivery the only two acceptable abbreviations within a signature are "Co." for the word company and "&" for the word and. No other abbreviations such as Inc. or Corp. are permitted.

9. 2. 2. 4   Legal Transfer Items

Any form of registration other than individual or joint ownership may require supporting guarantees or documentation to render a certificate negotiable.

For business registrations involving sole proprietorships or partnerships, a simple guarantee by a broker-dealer is usually sufficient. For corporate registrations and certificates in the names of fiduciaries, a transfer agent may require a corporate resolution naming the person signing a certificate as authorized to do so. Fiduciaries must supply either a certified copy of a trust agreement or a copy of a court appointment, depending on the type of fiduciary involved.

9. 2. 2. 5   Invalid Signatures

If a broker-dealer guarantees a forged signature, such as that of a deceased person, the firm becomes liable. The executor or administrator of the estate must endorse the certificate or furnish a stock power and transfer the securities to the name of the estate before they can be sold.

Minors' signatures are invalid for securities registration purposes.

9. 2. 2. 6   Good Condition of Security

If a certificate is mutilated or appears to be counterfeit, appropriate authentication must be obtained before a transfer agent can accept the security for replacement. If the damage is so extensive that the transfer agent doubts the certificate's authenticity, it will require a surety bond.

9. 2. 3   CUSIP REGULATIONS

Committee on Uniform Securities Identification Procedures (CUSIP) numbers are used in all trade confirmations and correspondence regarding specific securities. A separate CUSIP number is assigned to each issue of securities; if an issue is subdivided into classes with differing characteristics, each class is assigned a separate CUSIP number. In general, a CUSIP number will aid in identifying and tracking a security throughout its life.

9. 2. 4 LEGAL OPINION: MUNICIPAL SECURITIES

Unless a municipal bond is traded and stamped *ex-legal* (without a legal opinion), the legal opinion must be printed on or attached to the bond as evidence of the bond's validity. Securities traded ex-legal are in good delivery condition without the legal opinion.

9. 2. 5 FAIL TO DELIVER

A **fail to deliver** situation occurs when the broker-dealer on the sell side of a contract does not deliver the securities in good delivery form to the broker-dealer on the buy side on settlement. As long as a fail to deliver exists, the seller will not receive payment.

In a fail to deliver situation, the buying broker-dealer may buy in the securities to close the contract and may charge the seller for any loss caused by changes in the market. If a customer fails to deliver securities to satisfy a sale, the firm representing the seller must buy in the securities after 10 business days from settlement date.

9. 2. 6 RECLAMATION

Reclamation occurs when a buying broker-dealer, after accepting securities as good delivery, later discovers that the certificates were not in good deliverable form (e.g., certificates are mutilated). The securities can be sent back to the selling broker-dealer with a Uniform Reclamation Form attached within specific time frames, depending on the reason reclamation is being made.

- If the certificates delivered have minor irregularities, the time frame for reclamation is 15 days from delivery date.
- If the certificates delivered are refused by the transfer agent (for whatever reason) or if the certificates are stolen or counterfeit, the time frame is 30 months from delivery date.
- If the certificates (bonds) are subject to partial call, there is no time limit for reclamation.

There are two types of bond deliveries that are never subject to reclamation: (1) bond certificates subject to an in-whole call and (2) bonds where the issuer goes into default after trade date.

QUICK QUIZ 9.C

1. To be considered in good delivery form, certificates must be

   A. accompanied by a preliminary prospectus
   B. called for redemption by the issuing body
   C. accompanied by an assignment or a stock power
   D. in the name of the deceased person if the person died after the trade date

2. Which of the following would be considered good delivery for a sale of 600 shares of MCS?

   A. 3 certificates for 100 shares each and 8 certificates for 25 shares each
   B. 2 certificates for 100 shares each and 4 certificates for 50 shares each
   C. 6 certificates for 75 shares each and 6 certificates for 25 shares each
   D. 8 certificates for 75 shares each

3. As long as a fail to deliver situation exists, the seller
    A. will have all accounts frozen
    B. must conduct all transactions on a cash basis
    C. will not receive payment
    D. will not receive accrued interest on bonds

UNIT TEST

1. Which of the following statements regarding trade settlements are TRUE?

   I. Trades in a cash account normally settle on the same day.
   II. Trades in a cash account normally settle regular way.
   III. Cash transactions settle on the same day.
   IV. Cash transactions settle regular way.

   A. I and II
   B. I and IV
   C. II and III
   D. II and IV

2. All of the following would be good delivery for 470 shares EXCEPT

   A. 2 100-share certificates and 3 90-share certificates
   B. 4 100-share certificates and 1 70-share certificate
   C. 8 50-share certificates, 1 40-share certificate, and 1 30-share certificate
   D. 47 10-share certificates

3. In a seller's option, securities may be delivered before the date specified if the seller

   A. gives 1 day's written notice to the buyer
   B. gives notice to the buyer on the day of delivery
   C. cannot deliver on the specified date
   D. wishes to be paid earlier

4. Account service charges (other than commissions) must be

   A. limited to less than 1% a year
   B. based on the size and the amount of activity in a client's account
   C. standardized across the board at 5% a year
   D. reasonable and not unfairly discriminatory among clients

5. All of the following transactions must settle on the second business day after the trade date EXCEPT

   A. a broker-dealer buying a corporate bond from another dealer
   B. a customer selling a municipal bond through a broker-dealer
   C. a broker-dealer buying a Treasury bond for its own account
   D. a customer buying closed-end fund shares through a broker-dealer

6. Customer statements must be sent out at least

   A. daily
   B. weekly
   C. monthly
   D. quarterly

7. When a client's cash account is frozen, the client

   A. must deposit the full purchase price no later than the settlement date for a purchase
   B. must deposit the full purchase price before a purchase order may be executed
   C. may make sales with the firm's permission
   D. may not trade under any circumstances

8. After execution, orders flow through a brokerage firm in which sequence?

   I. Order or wire room
   II. Purchases and sales department
   III. Margin department
   IV. Cashiering department

   A. I, II, III, IV
   B. I, IV, II, III
   C. II, I, IV, III
   D. III, IV, II, I

9. A confirmation of each customer trade must be given or sent

   A. on the trade date
   B. before the trade date
   C. on or before the settlement date
   D. before the settlement date

10. Which of the following appears on the confirmation statement for a when-issued trade of municipal bonds?

    A. Settlement date
    B. Total contract price
    C. Accrued interest
    D. Principal or agency trade

11. A customer's order to buy 500 shares of QRS at $60 per share is executed, and the registered representative reports the trade execution to the customer. One hour later, the customer notices that QRS is down 2 points and informs the representative that he no longer wants the stock and is not planning to pay for it. The representative should tell the customer that

    A. the customer owns the stock and must submit payment
    B. the customer may sell the stock at the purchase price in the open market
    C. the firm will repurchase the securities from the customer for the price paid
    D. he personally will repurchase the securities from the customer for the price paid

12. Your customer owns 100 shares of ABC Corporation, which are being held in street name. What procedure will apply regarding your customer's proxy?

    A. ABC Corporation must send a proxy to your customer.
    B. The brokerage firm holding the shares must vote the proxy.
    C. The customer is required to sign one proxy card for his 100 shares.
    D. The brokerage firm must forward the proxy to your customer.

13. The certificate that supplies the customer with all the details of the trade and is sent out by the completion of the trade is known as

    A. the broker's order
    B. the comparison form
    C. the customer's exchange order
    D. the customer's confirmation

14. For a registered security to be good delivery, it must bear or be accompanied by

    A. an assignment or a power of substitution
    B. a written confirmation of the trade giving an adequate description of the security and the price at which the transaction was made
    C. a currently effective prospectus
    D. a certificate of clear title designation from the Secretary of State in which the issuer is incorporated

15. Instead of signing on the back of a security sold, the registered owner could sign on a separate paper called

    A. an endorsement
    B. a stock (or bond) power
    C. a proxy
    D. a stock split

ANSWERS AND RATIONALES

1. **C.** Cash settlement transactions may take place in any type of account and settle on the same day. Regular way settlement for most securities is T+2, regardless of the type of account in which the order is executed.

2. **A.** Shares must add up to 100 or be in multiples of 100, with the exception of odd lots.

3. **A.** In a seller's option trade, the seller may deliver (at his option) by giving the buyer written notice one day before making delivery.

4. **D.** According to the Conduct Rules, charges for services performed (e.g., the collection of dividends or safekeeping of securities held in street name) must be reasonable and not unfairly discriminatory among clients.

5. **C.** Regular way settlement for U.S. government bonds is the business day after the trade date. Corporate bonds and closed-end funds fall under the SEC's settlement rule (T+2), and MSRB rules require a 2-day settlement of municipal bond secondary transactions.

6. **D.** Member firms are required to send out customer account statements at least once per calendar quarter.

7. **B.** When an account is frozen, the client must deposit the full purchase price before any subsequent orders.

8. **A.** After execution, the order flows from where it was executed back to the order department (wire room), to purchases and sales, to the margin department, and then to the cashiering department.

9. **C.** A confirmation must be given or sent to a customer at or before the completion of the transaction (the settlement date).

10. **D.** A when-issued trade establishes the contract price but not the settlement date. Because the settlement date will not be established until the securities become available, the amount of accrued interest and the total amount due cannot be calculated at the time of the trade. Trade date and price are included on when-issued confirmations.

11. **A.** The customer has entered into a contract to purchase a security as soon as the buy order is executed and must pay regardless of any subsequent change in the market price. The firm and the representative are prohibited from offering to repurchase the securities at the original price.

12. **D.** The broker-dealer must forward the proxy to the beneficial owner.

13. **D.** The Conduct Rules require a member at or before the completion of each transaction with a customer to give or send that customer a written confirmation that confirms all of the details of the trade, including whether the firm acted as a broker or as a dealer.

14. **A.** The term *registered security* refers to a security with someone's name on it (as compared to a bearer security). It should be obvious that the most important requirement to be able to transfer something with an owner's name is the signature or assignment of that owner. A power of substitution is a form of a power of attorney.

15. **B.** If the client were to assign the back of the certificate, that security would now be completely negotiable. If lost, it would be the same as losing an endorsed check. To minimize problems, make the assignment on a stock power, which is a separate piece of paper, and when it is put together with the actual certificate, it is treated as if the certificate itself had been signed.

QUICK QUIZ ANSWERS

Quick Quiz 9.A

1. **A.** The credit that a broker-dealer extends to its customers is handled by its margin department.

2. **A.** Orders are received by the wire room and then are sent to the appropriate market. When the wire room gets the transaction report back, it sends it to the purchases and sales department. The P&S department sends a confirmation to the customer and then sends notice of the trade to the margin department. Margin then notifies the cashier of any balance due to or from the customer.

3. **C.** Broker-dealers must send quarterly statements to customers with inactive accounts.

Quick Quiz 9.B

1. **A.** In a contested proxy solicitation, all those soliciting proxies from shareholders must register with the Securities Exchange Commission (SEC).

2. **C.** When a broker-dealer chooses to close out a customer's position rather than request an extension, the customer's account will be frozen for 90 days.

3. **B.** Confirmations between brokers (broker-to-broker confirmations) are sent no later than the next business day (T+1).

Quick Quiz 9.C

1. **C.** To be considered in good delivery form, certificates must be accompanied by an assignment or a stock power.

2. **C.** Each certificate for 25 shares can be matched to a certificate for 75 shares to make a round lot; with 6 round lots, these certificates would be considered good delivery. Choice A is only 500 shares; choice B includes only 400 shares; and choice D cannot be bunched into round lots.

3. **C.** Until the seller delivers the securities sold, he will not receive payment for them.

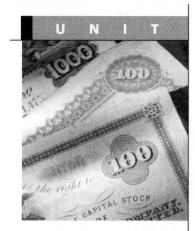

10

Investment Company Products

Investment company products offer a diversified portfolio of securities and reduced transaction costs. Because of these features, they are very popular with investors. Mutual funds (one form of investment company) currently manage trillions of dollars for investors.

The Series 7 exam will ask you approximately 17–20 questions on these products and their features. ∎

When you have completed this Unit, you should be able to:

■ **list** and describe the three types of investment companies defined by the Investment Company Act of 1940;

■ **contrast** characteristics of open- and closed-end management companies;

■ **describe** the registration requirements imposed by the Investment Company Act of 1940;

■ **list** several situations that require a majority vote of the outstanding shares;

■ **list** and describe the unique characteristics of mutual fund shares;

■ **calculate** the POP and the sales charge percentage;

■ **compare** and contrast three different methods for collecting fees for the sale of shares;

■ **identify** three ways to qualify for sales charge reductions;

■ **discuss** tax consequences of mutual fund distributions to shareholders; and

■ **assess** customer goals and risk tolerance and make suitable recommendations.

10. 1   INVESTMENT COMPANY PURPOSE

An **investment company** pools investors' money and invests in securities on their behalf. Investment company management attempts to invest funds for people more efficiently than the individual investors could themselves. They operate and invest these pooled funds as a single large account jointly owned by every investor in the company.

Like corporate issuers, investment companies raise capital by selling shares to the public. Investment companies must abide by the same registration and prospectus requirements imposed on every other issuer by the Securities Act of 1933 and are also subject to regulations regarding how their shares are sold to the public. The Investment Company Act of 1940 provides for SEC regulation of investment companies and their activities.

10. 1. 1   TYPES OF INVESTMENT COMPANIES

The Investment Company Act of 1940 classifies investment companies into three broad types: **face-amount certificate companies (FACs)**, **unit investment trusts (UITs)**, and **management investment companies**.

10. 1. 1. 1   Face-Amount Certificate Companies

A **face-amount certificate** is a contract between an investor and an issuer in which the issuer guarantees payment of a stated (or fixed) sum to the investor at some set date in the future. In return for this future payment, the investor agrees to pay the issuer a set amount of money either as a lump sum or in periodic installments. Issuers of these investments are called **face-amount certificate companies**. If the investor pays for the certificate in a lump sum, the investment is known as a fully paid face-amount certificate. Very few face-amount certificate companies operate today because tax law changes have eliminated their tax advantages.

10. 1. 1. 2   Unit Investment Trusts (UITs)

A **unit investment trust** is an investment company organized under a trust indenture and identified by several characteristics.

UITs do not have boards of directors, employ investment advisers, or actively manage their own portfolios (or trade securities).

A UIT functions as a holding company for its investors. UITs typically purchase other investment company shares or government and municipal bonds. They then issue redeemable shares, also known as **units** or **shares of beneficial interest**, in its portfolio of securities. Each share is an undivided interest in the entire underlying portfolio. Because UITs are not managed, when any securities in the portfolio are liquidated, the proceeds must be distributed pro rata to the unit holders.

A UIT may be fixed or nonfixed. A **fixed** UIT typically purchases a portfolio of bonds and terminates when the bonds in the portfolio mature. A **nonfixed** UIT purchases shares of an underlying mutual fund. Under the Act of 1940, the trustees of both fixed and nonfixed UITs must stand ready to redeem the units, thus providing liquidity to shareholders. Like other investment company products, UITs can be structured to meet different investment objectives, such as growth, income, balanced, or international diversification.

Classification of Investment Companies

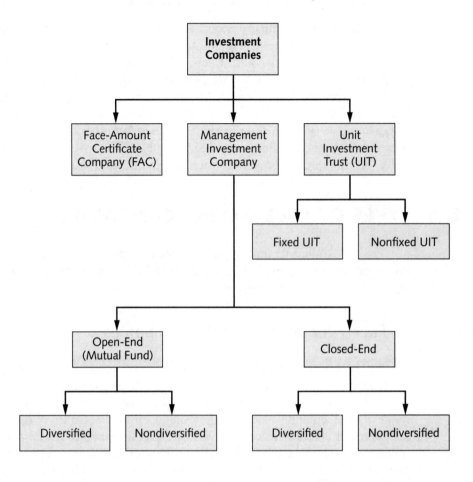

Think of a unit investment trust like a mutual fund (to be discussed in the following sections)—up to a point. Both fixed UITs and mutual funds are composed of a pool of securities in which investors own a proportionate share.

The major difference is that mutual funds actively trade their portfolios; a portfolio manager gets paid a fee to buy and sell as needed to meet the objectives of the fund. UIT portfolios usually are not traded; they are fixed trusts. The advantage to investors in UITs is that they own a diversified interest, but they do not have to pay a management fee—the biggest expense of mutual fund ownership. The downside is that the UIT portfolio cannot be traded in response to market conditions.

Expect to see no more than one question related to UITs. Know the following.

■ UITs are not actively managed; there is no BOD or investment adviser.

■ UIT shares (units) are not traded in the secondary market; they must be redeemed by the trust.

■ UITs are investment companies as defined under the Investment Company Act of 1940.

10. 1. 1. 3 Management Investment Companies

The most familiar type of investment company is the **management investment company**, which actively manages a securities portfolio to achieve a stated investment objective. A management investment company is either **closed end** or **open end**. Initially, both closed- and open-end companies sell shares to the public; the difference between them lies in the type of securities they market and where investors buy and sell shares.

10. 1. 1. 3. 1 Closed-End Investment Companies

When a closed-end investment company wants to raise capital for its portfolio, it conducts a **common stock offering**. For the initial offering, the company registers a fixed number of shares with the SEC and offers them to the public for a limited time through underwriters. The fund's capitalization is fixed unless an additional public offering is made at some future time. Closed-end investment companies can also issue bonds and preferred stock.

Closed-end shares are not redeemed by the issuer. Investors wishing to liquidate their shares must sell them in the secondary market either on an exchange or over the counter (OTC) at the prevailing market price. Supply and demand determine the **bid price** (price at which an investor can sell) and the **ask price** (price at which an investor can buy). Because the price is determined by supply and demand, closed-end fund shares may trade at a premium or discount to the shares' underlying value.

TEST TOPIC ALERT An easy way to remember the features of a closed-end company is to think about what would be true for any corporate security.

- Where do shares of closed-end companies trade? Like corporates, in the secondary market.

- What types of securities can closed-ends issue? Like corporates, common, preferred, and bonds.

- Can fractional shares be purchased? Like corporates, only full shares can be purchased.

- When must a prospectus be used? Like corporates, only in the IPO.

No prospectus is given when the shares are purchased in a secondary market transaction.

10. 1. 1. 3. 2 Open-End Investment Companies

An open-end investment company, or **mutual fund**, does not specify the exact number of shares it intends to issue; it registers an open offering with the SEC. With this registration type, the open-end investment company can raise an unlimited amount of investment capital by continuously issuing new shares. Conversely, when investors liquidate holdings in a mutual fund, the fund's capital shrinks because the fund redeems shares. The offering never closes because the number of shares the company can offer is unlimited.

Any person who wants to invest in the company buys shares directly from the company or its underwriters at the **public offering price** (**POP**). A mutual fund's POP is the **net asset value** (**NAV**) per share plus a sales charge.

Comparison of Open-End and Closed-End Investment Companies

	Open-End	Closed-End
Capitalization	Unlimited; continuous offering of shares	Fixed; single offering of shares
Issues	Common stock only; no debt securities; permitted to borrow	Common and preferred stock, debt securities
Shares	Full or fractional	Full only
Offerings and Trading	Sold and redeemed by fund only Continuous primary offering Must redeem shares	Initial primary offering Secondary trading OTC or on an exchange Does not redeem shares
Pricing	NAV + sales charge Selling price determined by formula in the prospectus	CMV + commission Price determined by supply and demand
Shareholder Rights	Dividends (when declared), voting	Dividends (when declared), voting, preemptive
Ex-date	Set by BOD	Set by the exchange or FINRA

10. 1. 1. 3. 3 Diversified and Nondiversified

Diversification provides risk management that makes mutual funds popular with many investors. However, not all investment companies feature diversified portfolios.

Diversified. Under the Investment Company Act of 1940, an investment company qualifies as a **diversified investment company** if it meets the following **75-5-10** test.

75% of total assets must be invested in securities issued by companies other than the investment company or its affiliates. Cash on hand and cash equivalent investments (short-term government and money market securities) are counted as part of the 75% required investment in outside companies.

The 75% must be invested in such a way that:

- within the 75%, no more than 5% of the fund's total assets are invested in the securities of any one issuer; and

- within the 75%, the fund does not own more than 10% of the outstanding voting securities of any one issuer.

Because the remaining 25% of the fund's assets does not have to be diversified in this manner, a fund could have as much as 30% of its assets invested in one company (25 + 5) and own more than 10% of a company and still call itself diversified.

EXAMPLE

Assume a mutual fund has $200,000 total assets. To call itself diversified, at least $150,000 must be invested (75%). That $150,000 must be invested so that no more than $10,000 may be invested in the securities of any one company (5% of the total $200,000); if a target company has $100,000 of outstanding common stock, the mutual fund could own no more than $10,000 of that stock (10% of $100,000).

Nondiversified. A **nondiversified investment company** fails to meet the 75-5-10 test. An investment company that specializes in a single industry is not necessarily a nondiversified company. Some investment companies choose to concentrate their assets in an industry or a geographic area, such as health care, technology stocks, or northeast coast company stocks. These are known as **specialized** or **sector funds**. An investment company that invests in a single industry may still be considered diversified as long as it meets the 75-5-10 test.

TAKE NOTE   Both open- and closed-end companies can be diversified or nondiversified.

---

10. 1. 1. 3. 4 Exchange-Traded Funds (ETFs)

Exchange-traded funds, or ETFs, are investment companies that are legally classified as open-end companies or Unit Investment Trusts (UITs), but differ from traditional open-end companies and UITs. ETFs issue their shares in large blocks (blocks of 50,000 shares, for example) that are known as Creation Units. Those who purchase Creation Units are frequently large institutional traders or investors. The Creation Units can then be split up and sold as individual shares in the secondary markets. This permits individual investors to purchase individual shares (instead of Creation Units).

Investors who want to sell their ETF shares have two options: (1) they can sell individual shares to other investors in the secondary market, or (2) if they own Creation Units they can sell the Creation Units back to the ETF. In addition, ETFs generally will redeem Creation Units by giving investors the securities that comprise the portfolio instead of cash. It is important to remember that because of the limited redeemability of ETF shares, ETFs are not considered to be, nor may they call themselves, mutual funds.

For purposes of Series 7 testing we will consider individual investors who own exchange-traded fund shares (not Creation Units) purchased in the secondary market. Understanding that exchange-traded fund shares are not mutual fund shares, it should be expected and is common that they are often compared to mutual fund shares. In that light exchange-traded funds have some advantages and disadvantages to be considered when compared to open-end (mutual funds).

Following are some advantages of exchange-traded funds when compared to open-end (mutual funds).

- Pricing and ease of trading—since individual ETF shares are traded on exchanges, they can be bought or sold anytime during the trading day at the price they are currently trading at as opposed to mutual funds which use forward pricing and are generally priced once at the end of the trading day.

- Margin—ETFs can be bought and sold short on margin like other exchange-traded products. Mutual funds cannot be bought on margin nor can they be sold short.

- Operating costs—ETFs traditionally have operating costs and expenses that are lower than most mutual funds.

- Tax efficiency—ETFs can and sometimes do distribute capital gains to shareholders like mutual funds do but this is rare. Understanding that these capital gains distributions are not likely, there are no further tax consequences with ETF shares until investors sell their shares. This may be the single greatest advantage associated with ETFs.

Following are some disadvantages of exchange-traded funds when compared to open-end (mutual funds).

- Commissions—the purchase or sale of ETF shares is a commissionable transaction. The commissions paid can erode the low expense advantage of ETFs. This would have the greatest impact when trading in and out of ETF shares frequently or when investing smaller sums of money.

■ Over trading—given the ability to trade in and out of ETFs easily, the temptation to do so is possible. Excessive trading can eliminate the advantages associated with investing in a diversified portfolio and add to overall commissions being paid by the investor, further eroding any of the other expense and operating advantages associated with ETFs.

QUICK QUIZ 10.A

1. Which of the following are covered under the Investment Company Act of 1940?

   I. Unit investment trusts
   II. Face-amount companies
   III. Open-end management companies
   IV. Closed-end management companies

   A. I and II
   B. I, III and IV
   C. III and IV
   D. I, II, III and IV

2. What kind of investment company has no provision for redemption of outstanding shares?

   A. Open-end company
   B. Closed-end company
   C. Unit investment trust
   D. Mutual fund

3. Diversified management companies must be invested so that within the minimum 75% of assets invested in securities other than those of the investment company

   I. they own no more than 5% of the voting stock of a single company
   II. no more than 5% is invested in any one company
   III. they own no more than 10% of the voting stock of any one company
   IV. if they own more than 25% of a target company, they do not vote the stock

   A. I and II
   B. I and IV
   C. II and III
   D. II and IV

4. According to the Investment Company Act of 1940, an investment company with a fixed portfolio, redeemable shares, and no management fee is

   A. a face-amount certificate company
   B. a management company
   C. a unit investment trust
   D. a closed-end investment company

5. Open-end investment companies, but not closed-end investment companies

    I.   may make continuous offerings of shares, provided the original registration statement and prospectus are periodically updated

    II.   may be listed on registered national exchanges

    III. always redeem their shares

    IV. may issue only common stock

    A. I, II and III

    B. I and III

    C. I, III and IV

    D. II and IV

6. Exchange-traded funds (ETFs) are

    A. closed-end fund companies

    B. open-end fund companies

    C. mutual funds

    D. priced no more than once per trading day

7. Which of the following statements are accurate regarding exchange-traded fund (ETF) shares purchased in the secondary market?

    A. The shares are priced continuously throughout the trading day and can be purchased on margin.

    B. The shares are priced continuously throughout the trading day and can not be purchased on margin.

    C. The shares use a forward pricing model like mutual funds and can not be purchased on margin.

    D. The shares use a forward pricing model like mutual funds and can be purchased on margin.

Quick Quiz answers can be found at the end of the Unit.

10. 2   INVESTMENT COMPANY REGISTRATION

Investment companies are required to register with the securities exchange commission if they are engaged in certain types of business and then, in order to do so, must meet minimum criteria.

10. 2. 1 REGISTRATION WITH THE SEC

A company must register with the SEC as an investment company if it:

- is in the business of investing in, reinvesting in, owning, holding, or trading securities; or
- has 40% or more of its assets invested in securities (government securities and securities of majority-owned subsidiaries are not used in calculating the 40% limitation).

A company must meet certain minimum requirements before it may register as an investment company with the SEC. An investment company may not issue securities to the public unless it has:

- private capitalization (seed money) of at least $100,000 of net assets;
- 100 investors; and
- clearly defined investment objectives.

If the investment company does not have 100 shareholders and $100,000 in net assets, it may still register a public offering with the SEC if it can meet these requirements within 90 days of registration.

The company must clearly define an **investment objective** under which it plans to operate. Once defined, the objective may be changed only by a majority vote of the company's outstanding shares.

10. 2. 1. 1 Open-End Companies

In addition, the Act of 1940 requires open-end companies, also called mutual funds, to have no more than one class of security issued and a minimum asset-to-debt ratio of 300%. Open-end investment companies may issue only one class of security (common stock) because they are permitted to borrow from banks as long as a company's asset-to-debt ratio is not less than 3:1—that is, debt coverage by assets of at least 300%, or no more than one-third of assets from borrowed money.

10. 2. 1. 2 SEC Registration and Public Offering Requirements

Investment companies must file registration statements with the SEC, provide full disclosure, and generally follow the same public offering procedures required of other corporations when issuing securities. In filing for registration, an investment company must identify:

- the type of investment company it intends to be (i.e., open-end or closed-end);
- plans the company has to raise money by borrowing;
- the company's intention, if any, to concentrate its investments in a single industry;
- plans for investing in real estate or commodities;
- conditions under which investment policies may be changed by a vote of the shares;
- the full name and address of each affiliated person; and
- a description of the business experience of each officer and director during the preceding five years.

In filing for registration, an investment company must identify the overall investment intentions of the fund and background information on affiliated persons, officers, and directors.

10. 2. 1. 3 Registration Statement and Prospectus

The **registration statement** an investment company must file consists of two parts. **Part 1** is the prospectus that must be furnished to every person to whom the company offers the securities. Part 1 is also called an **N1-A prospectus** or a **summary prospectus. Part 2** is the document containing information that need not be furnished to every purchaser but must be made available for public inspection. Part 2 is called the **statement of additional information (SAI)**.

The prospectus must contain any disclosure that the SEC requires. The fact that all publicly issued securities must be registered with the SEC does not mean that the SEC in any way approves the securities. For that reason, every prospectus must contain a disclaimer.

EXAMPLE

These securities have not been approved or disapproved by the Securities and Exchange Commission, nor has the Commission passed on the accuracy or adequacy of this prospectus. No state has approved or disapproved this offering. Any representation to the contrary is a criminal offense.

In addition, open-end management investment companies (mutual funds) are required to provide enhanced disclosure in their prospectuses in the form of a "summary section." The SEC mandates that the key information be written in plain English and specifies the following items and the order they must appear in:

1. Investment objectives
2. Costs of investing
3. Principal investment strategies, risks, and performance
4. Investment advisers and portfolio managers
5. Brief purchase, sale, and tax information
6. Financial intermediary compensation

10. 2. 1. 3. 1 Statement of Additional Information (SAI)

Although a prospectus is always sufficient for the purpose of selling shares, some investors may wish to have additional information not found in the prospectus. This additional information is not necessarily needed to make an informed investment decision but may be useful to the investor.

Mutual funds and closed-end funds are required to have an SAI available to investors upon request without charge. Investors can obtain a copy by calling or writing to the investment company, via a company website, contacting a broker that sells the investment company shares, or contacting the SEC.

The SAI affords the fund an opportunity to have expanded discussions on such matters as the fund's history and policies. It will also typically contain the fund's consolidated financial statements.

10. 2. 1. 4 Continuous Public Offering Securities

The SEC treats the sale of open-end investment company shares as a continuous public offering of shares, which means all sales must be accompanied by a prospectus. The financial information (statements) in the prospectus must be dated not more than 16 months before the sale. With closed-end funds, only the initial public offering of stock is sold with a prospectus.

10. 2. 1. 4. 1 Purchasing Mutual Fund Shares on Margin

Because a mutual fund is considered a continuous primary offering, Regulation T of the Federal Reserve Board prohibits the purchase of mutual fund shares on margin. **Margin** is the use of money borrowed from a brokerage firm to buy securities. However, mutual fund shares may be used as collateral in a margin account if they have been held fully paid for more than 30 days.

10. 2. 2 RESTRICTIONS ON OPERATIONS

The SEC prohibits a mutual fund from engaging in certain activities unless the fund meets stringent disclosure and financial requirements. The fund must specifically disclose the following activities—and the extent to which it plans to engage in these activities—in its prospectus:

- Purchasing securities on margin
- Selling securities short
- Participating in joint investment or trading accounts or acting as distributor of its own securities, except through an underwriter

10. 2. 2. 1 Shareholders' Right to Vote

Before any change can be made to a fund's published bylaws or objectives, shareholder approval is mandatory. In voting matters, it is the majority of shares voted for or against a proposition that counts, not the majority of people voting. Thus, one shareholder holding 51% of all the shares outstanding can determine a vote's outcome.

TAKE NOTE

Among the changes requiring a majority vote of the shares outstanding are:

- changes in borrowing by open-end companies;
- issuing or underwriting other securities;
- purchasing or underwriting real estate;
- making loans;
- changing subclassification (e.g., from open-end to closed-end or from diversified to nondiversified);
- changing sales load policy (e.g., from a no-load fund to a load fund);
- changing the nature of the business (e.g., ceasing business as an investment company); and
- changing investment policy (e.g., from income to growth or from bonds to small capitalization stocks).

In addition to the right to vote on these items, shareholders retain all rights that stockholders normally possess.

10. 3   MANAGEMENT OF INVESTMENT COMPANIES

Five parties work together to operate an investment company: the board of directors, investment adviser, custodian, transfer agent, and underwriter.

10. 3. 1   BOARD OF DIRECTORS

Like publicly owned corporations in general, a management investment company has a chief executive officer (CEO), a team of officers, and a board of directors (BOD) to serve the interests of its investors. The officers and directors concern themselves with policy and administrative matters; they do not manage the investment portfolio. As with other types of corporations, the shareholders of an investment company elect the BOD to make decisions and oversee operations.

A management investment company's BOD coordinates the different functions of a mutual fund.

The BOD:

■ defines the type of fund(s) to offer (e.g., growth, income, or sector);

■ defines the fund's objective; and

■ approves and hires the transfer agent, custodian, and investment adviser.

The Act of 1940 restricts who may sit on an investment company's board of directors. A majority of the directors must be independent or noninterested persons. **Noninterested** persons are connected with the investment company only in their capacity as directors. A noninterested person is not connected with the investment company's investment adviser, transfer agent, or custodian bank.

TAKE NOTE   Investment company board members must serve terms that are no less than one year but not longer than five years.

10. 3. 2   INVESTMENT ADVISER

An investment company's BOD contracts with an outside **investment adviser** or **portfolio manager** to:

■ invest the cash and securities in the fund's portfolio;

■ implement investment strategy;

■ identify the tax status of distributions made to shareholders; and

■ manage the portfolio's day-to-day trading.

Naturally, the adviser must adhere to the objective stated in the fund's prospectus and may not transfer the responsibility of portfolio management to anyone else. An investment company may not contract with an investment adviser who has been convicted of a securities-related felony (unless the SEC has granted an exemption). In addition, an investment company may not lend money to its investment adviser.

Because the investment adviser of a mutual fund is paid a fee for investment advice, the adviser must be registered under the Investment Advisers Act of 1940.

The investment adviser's contract is for a maximum of two years but is subject to annual shareholder approval.

The investment adviser earns a management fee, typically a set annual percentage of the portfolio's value, paid from the fund's net assets. This fee tends to be a fund portfolio's single greatest expense. In addition, if the investment adviser consistently outperforms a specified market performance benchmark, he usually earns an incentive bonus.

10. 3. 3 CUSTODIAN

To protect investor assets, the Act of 1940 requires each investment company to place its portfolio securities in the custody of a bank or a stock exchange member broker-dealer. The bank or broker-dealer performs an important safekeeping role as **custodian** of the company's securities and cash. Often, the custodian handles most of the investment company's clerical functions.

The custodian may, with the consent of the investment company, deposit the securities it is entrusted to hold in one of the systems for the central handling of securities. These systems make it easier to transfer or pledge securities. Once securities are placed in the system, most such transfers can be accomplished with a bookkeeping entry rather than physical delivery of the securities.

Once an investment company designates a custodian and transfers its assets into the custodian's safekeeping, the custodian must:

- keep the investment company's assets physically segregated at all times; and
- restrict access to the account to certain officers and employees of the investment company.

The custodian receives a fee for its services.

10. 3. 4 TRANSFER AGENT (CUSTOMER SERVICES AGENT)

The **transfer agent's** functions include:

- issuing, redeeming, and canceling fund shares;
- handling name changes for the fund;
- sending customer confirmations and fund distributions; and
- recording outstanding shares so distributions are properly made.

The transfer agent may be the fund custodian or a separate service company. The fund pays the transfer agent a fee for its services.

10. 3. 5 UNDERWRITER

A mutual fund's **underwriter**, often called the **sponsor** or **distributor**, is appointed by the BOD and receives a fee for selling and marketing the fund shares to the public. The open-end investment company sells its shares to the underwriter at the current NAV, but only as the underwriter needs the shares to fill customer orders. The underwriter is prohibited from maintaining an inventory of open-end company shares and is compensated by adding a sales charge to the share's NAV when it makes sales to the public.

In general, a mutual fund may not act as its own distributor or underwriter. An exception exists for no-load and 12b-1 funds.

TAKE NOTE

A fund is allowed to act as its own underwriter under Section 12b-1 of the Act of 1940. Many funds today follow this section, and 12b-1 distribution fees are very common.

Investment Company Operators and Their Functions

Board of Directors	Investment Adviser	Custodian	Transfer Agent	Underwriter
Administrative matters	Makes investment decisions	Holds assets	Issues and redeems shares	Distributes shares
Elected by shareholders	Paid a percentage of assets	Paid a fee by the fund	Paid a fee by the fund	Paid from sales charges
—	—	Clerical duties	—	—

10. 4   INFORMATION DISTRIBUTED TO INVESTORS

Investors must be provided with specific information when purchasing and tracking mutual funds.

10. 4. 1 PROSPECTUS

The **prospectus** must be distributed to an investor before or during any solicitation for sale. The prospectus contains information on the fund's objective, investment policies, sales charges, management expenses, and services offered. It also discloses 1-, 5-, and 10-year performance histories.

The SAI typically contains the fund's consolidated financial statements, including:

- balance sheet;
- statement of operations;
- income statement; and
- portfolio list at the time the statement was compiled.

10. 4. 2 FINANCIAL REPORTS

The Act of 1940 requires that shareholders receive financial reports at least semiannually. One of these must be an audited annual report. The reports must contain:

- the investment company's balance sheet;
- a valuation of all securities in the investment company's portfolio as of the date of the balance sheet (a portfolio list);
- the investment company's income statement;
- a complete statement of all compensation paid to the BOD and to the advisory board; and
- a statement of the total dollar amount of securities purchased and sold during the period.

In addition, the company must send a copy of its balance sheet to any shareholder who requests one in writing between semiannual reports.

10. 4. 3 ADDITIONAL DISCLOSURES

The SEC also requires the fund to include in its prospectus or annual reports the following:

- A discussion of those factors and strategies that materially affected its performance during its most recently completed fiscal year
- A line graph comparing its performance to that of an appropriate broad-based securities market index
- The name(s) and title(s) of the person(s) primarily responsible for the fund portfolio's day-to-day management

---

QUICK QUIZ 10.B

1. The custodian of a mutual fund usually

   A. approves changes in investment policy
   B. holds the cash and securities of the fund and performs clerical functions
   C. manages the fund
   D. provides accounting services for companies whose securities are in the fund

2. Investment company financial statements are sent to shareholders

   A. monthly
   B. quarterly
   C. semiannually
   D. annually

3. The role of a mutual fund's underwriter is to

   A. hold the fund's assets and perform clerical responsibilities
   B. administer and supervise the investment portfolio
   C. market shares
   D. provide investment advisory services

4. When a bank is serving as the custodian of a mutual fund, it

   A. manages the portfolio
   B. signs all margin agreements
   C. holds the cash and securities and performs other clerical functions
   D. serves as the distributor of the fund and manages interactions with other underwriters

5. Typically, the largest single expense of a mutual fund is the

    A. custodian fee
    B. registration fee
    C. management fee
    D. brokerage fee

10. 5   CHARACTERISTICS OF MUTUAL FUNDS AND THE MUTUAL FUND CONCEPT

Mutual funds have several unique characteristics. For instance, a mutual fund must redeem shares at the net asset value. Unlike other securities, mutual funds offer guaranteed marketability: there is always a willing buyer for the shares—the fund itself.

Each investor in the mutual fund's portfolio owns an undivided interest in the portfolio, and all investors in an open-end fund are mutual participants. No one investor has a preferred status over any other investor because mutual funds issue only one class of common stock. Each investor shares mutually with other investors in gains and distributions derived from the investment company portfolio.

Each investor's interest in the fund's performance is based on the number of shares owned. Mutual fund shares may be purchased in either full or fractional units (unlike corporate stock, which must be purchased in full units).

An investment company portfolio is elastic. Money is constantly being invested or paid out when shares are redeemed. The mutual fund portfolio's value and holdings fluctuate as money is invested or redeemed and as the value of the securities held by the portfolio rises and falls. The investor's account value fluctuates proportionately with the mutual fund portfolio's value.

TEST TOPIC ALERT

Characteristics:

■   A professional investment adviser manages the portfolio for investors.

■   Mutual funds provide diversification by investing in many different companies.

■   A custodian holds a mutual fund's shares to ensure safekeeping.

■   An investor may liquidate a portion of his holdings without disturbing the portfolio's balance or diversification.

■   An investor retains voting rights similar to those extended to common stockholders, such as the right to vote for changes in the board of directors, approval of the investment adviser, changes in the fund's investment objective, changes in sales charges, and liquidation of the fund.

■   Tax liabilities for an investor are simplified because each year the fund distributes a 1099 form explaining taxability of distributions.

Features Offered:

■   Most funds allow a minimum investment, often $500 or less, to open an account, and they allow additional investment for as little as $25.

- Many funds offer automatic reinvestment of capital gains and dividend distributions without a sales charge.

- An investment company may allow investments at reduced sales charges by offering breakpoints—for example, through larger deposits, a letter of intent, or rights of accumulation.

- A fund may offer various withdrawal plans that allow different payment methods at redemption.

- Funds may offer reinstatement provisions that allow investors that withdraw funds to reinvest up to the amount withdrawn within 30 days with no new sales charge. This provision must be disclosed in the prospectus and is available one time only.

10. 5. 1 INVESTMENT OBJECTIVES

Once a mutual fund defines its objective, the portfolio is invested to match it. The objective must be clearly stated in the mutual fund's prospectus and may be changed only by a majority vote of the fund's outstanding shares.

TAKE NOTE It is important to know the different types of funds available and the suitability characteristics of each.

Common stock is normally the growth component of any mutual fund that has growth as a primary or secondary objective. Bonds, preferred stock, and blue-chip stocks are typically used to provide the income component of any mutual fund that has income as a primary or secondary objective.

10. 5. 1. 1 Stock Funds

10. 5. 1. 1. 1 Growth Funds

Growth funds invest in stocks of companies whose businesses are growing rapidly. Growth companies tend to reinvest all or most of their profits for research and development rather than pay dividends; therefore, growth funds are focused on generating capital gains rather than income.

10. 5. 1. 1. 2 Income Funds

An income fund stresses current income over growth. The fund's objective may be accomplished by investing in the stocks of companies with long histories of dividend payments, such as utility company stocks, blue-chip stocks, and preferred stocks.

10. 5. 1. 1. 3 Combination Funds

A combination fund, also called a **growth and income fund**, may attempt to combine the objectives of growth and current yield by diversifying its portfolio among companies showing long-term growth potential and companies paying high dividends.

10. 5. 1. 1. 4 Specialized (Sector) Funds

Many funds attempt to specialize in particular economic sectors or industries. Examples include gold funds (gold mining stock), technology funds, and low-grade (noninvestment-grade) bond funds, among others. Sector funds offer high appreciation potential but may also pose higher risks to the investor.

10. 5. 1. 1. 5 Special Situation Funds

Special situation funds buy securities of companies that may benefit from a change within the companies or in the economy. Takeover candidates, companies with patents pending, and turnaround situations are common investments for these funds.

10. 5. 1. 1. 6 Index Funds

Index funds invest in securities to mirror a market index, such as the S&P 500. An index fund buys and sells securities in a manner that mirrors the composition of the selected index. The fund's performance tracks the underlying index's performance. Turnover of securities in an index fund's portfolio is minimal. As a result, an index fund generally has lower management costs than other types of funds.

10. 5. 1. 1. 7 Foreign Stock Funds

Foreign stock funds invest mostly in the securities of companies that have their principal business activities outside the United States. Long-term capital appreciation is their primary objective, although some funds also seek current income.

Comparison of Common Stock and Mutual Fund Shares

Common Stock	Mutual Fund Shares
Dividends from corporate profits	Dividends from net investment income
Price of stock determined by supply and demand	Price of share determined by forward pricing—the next NAV per share calculated as determined by the fund's pricing policy
Traded on an exchange or the OTC market	Purchased from and redeemed by the investment company; no secondary trading
Sold in full shares only	Can purchase full or fractional shares
First security issued by a public corporation	Only security issued by a mutual fund
Carries voting rights	Carries voting rights
May carry preemptive rights	Does not carry preemptive rights
Ex-dividend: one business day	Ex-dividend: typically the day after record date as set by the BOD

10. 5. 1. 2 Balanced Funds

Balanced funds invest in stocks (equities) for appreciation and bonds (debt) for income. The debt securities offer some downside protection when equity markets are faltering or underperforming. In a balanced fund, the different types of securities are purchased according to a formula that the manager may adjust to reflect market conditions, adding more equities or more debt when appropriate.

EXAMPLE   A balanced fund's portfolio may contain 60% stocks and 40% bonds.

10. 5. 1. 3 Asset Allocation Funds

Asset allocation funds split investments between stocks for growth, bonds for income, and money market instruments or cash for stability. Fund advisers switch the percentage of holdings in each asset category according to the performance, or expected performance, of that group.

EXAMPLE   A fund may have 60% of its investments in stock, 20% in bonds, and the remaining 20% in cash. If the stock market is expected to do well, the adviser may switch from cash and bonds into stock. The result may be a portfolio of 80% in stock, 10% in bonds, and 10% in cash. Conversely, if the stock market is expected to decline, the fund may invest heavily in cash and sell stocks.

10. 5. 1. 4 Bond Funds

Bond funds have income as their main investment objective. Some funds invest solely in investment-grade corporate bonds. Others, seeking enhanced safety, invest in government issues only. Still others pursue capital appreciation by investing in lower-rated bonds for higher yields.

10. 5. 1. 4. 1 Tax-Free (Tax-Exempt) Bond Funds

Tax-exempt funds invest in municipal bonds or notes that produce income exempt from federal income tax. Tax-free funds can invest in municipal bonds and tax-exempt money market instruments.

10. 5. 1. 4. 2 U.S. Government and Agency Security Funds

U.S. government funds purchase securities issued by the U.S. Treasury or an agency of the U.S. government, such as Ginnie Mae. Investors in these funds seek current income and maximum safety.

10. 5. 1. 5 Dual-Purpose Funds

Dual-purpose funds are closed-end funds that meet two objectives: investors seeking income purchase income shares and receive all the interest and dividends the fund's portfolio earns, and investors interested in capital gains purchase the gains shares and receive all gains on portfolio holdings. The two types of shares in a dual fund are listed separately in the financial pages of major newspapers.

10. 5. 1. 6 Money Market Funds

Money market funds are usually no-load, open-end mutual funds that serve as temporary holding tanks for investors who are most concerned with liquidity. **No load** means investors pay no sales or liquidation fees. A fund manager invests the fund's capital in money market instruments that pay interest and have short maturities.

Interest rates on money market funds are not fixed or guaranteed and change often. The interest these funds earn is computed daily and credited to customers' accounts monthly.

The NAV of money market funds is set at $1 per share. Although this price is not guaranteed, a fund is managed in order not to "break the buck" regardless of market changes. Thus, the price of money market shares does not fluctuate in response to changing market conditions.

Money market funds and other no-load funds are both purchased and redeemed at their NAV.

10. 5. 1. 6. 1 Restrictions on Money Market Funds

SEC rules limit the investments available to money market funds and require certain disclosures to investors.

Restrictions include the following.

- The front cover of every prospectus must prominently disclose that an investment in a money market fund is neither insured nor guaranteed by the U.S. government and that an investor has no assurance the fund will be able to maintain a stable NAV. This statement must also appear in all literature used to market the fund.

- Investments are limited to securities with remaining maturities of not more than 13 months, with the average portfolio maturity not exceeding 90 days.
- Investments include T-bills, commercial paper, repurchase agreements, and banker's acceptances.

10. 5. 1. 7 Lifecycle Funds

Lifecycle funds use a predetermined asset mix that is tailored to meet investment objectives based on various time horizons or target dates. The target date is generally an investor's expected retirement date. The objective is to strike an optimal balance between risk and return, as is appropriate for an investor, as they age and near retirement. The strategy assumes that the longer investors have before retirement, the more willing and able they will be to tolerate risk and endure price fluctuations. Generally, the investment mix within the fund portfolio becomes more conservative as the target date approaches and will be adjusted quarterly or on some other predetermined schedule.

Lifecycle funds are structured as "funds of funds" so that investing in one generally means that you are invested in a number of funds offered by the same fund family. Companies offering lifecycle funds add new ones for distant target dates as they are needed and some are set up to have the lifecycle fund automatically roll into one of the fund families' more conservative funds, such as an income fund, when the target date is reached.

10. 5. 1. 8 Funds of Hedge Funds

Though hedge funds discussed later in this unit are generally available to and suitable for highly qualified or sophisticated (accredited) investors, there are registered mutual funds available to all investors that invest primarily in unregistered hedge funds known as **funds of hedge funds**. They can target and diversify among several hedge funds and, in this way, give non-accredited investors access to hedge funds. These funds share some of the benefits and risks associated with hedge funds. One benefit could be that lower initial investments might be required than when investing directly in a hedge fund. In contrast, one risk to note is that like all mutual funds, the shares are not traded and that divesting of them can only occur if the mutual fund company redeems them. Recommendations of funds of hedge funds would need to include the specific risks associated with hedge funds and the transfer of those risks that occurs when mutual funds invest in hedge funds.

10. 6   COMPARING MUTUAL FUNDS

When comparing mutual funds, investors should select funds that match their personal objectives. When comparing funds with similar objectives, the investor should review information regarding their:

- performance;
- costs;
- portfolio turnover; and
- services offered.

10. 6. 1   PERFORMANCE

Securities law requires that each fund disclose the average annual total returns for 1, 5, and 10 years, or since inception. Performance must reflect full sales loads with no discounts. The manager's track record in keeping with the fund's objectives as stated in the prospectus is important as well.

10. 6. 2   COSTS

Sales loads, management fees, and operating expenses reduce an investor's returns because they diminish the amount of money invested in a fund.

10. 6. 2. 1   Sales Loads

Historically, mutual funds have charged front-end loads of up to 8.5% of the money invested. This percentage compensates the sales force. Many low-load funds charge between 2 and 5%. Other funds may charge a back-end load when funds are withdrawn. Some funds charge ongoing fees under Section 12b-1 of the Investment Company Act of 1940. These funds deduct annual fees to pay for marketing and distribution costs. Sales loads are covered in detail later in this Unit.

10. 6. 2. 2   Expense Ratio

A fund's **expense ratio** compares the management fees and operating expenses, including any 12b-1 fees, with the fund's net assets. All mutual funds, both load and no load, have expense ratios. The expense ratio is calculated by dividing a fund's expenses by its average net assets.

EXAMPLE   An expense ratio of 1.72% means that the fund charges $1.72 per year for every $100 invested.

Stock funds generally have expense ratios between 1 and 1.5% of a fund's average net assets. Typically, more aggressive funds have higher expense ratios. For bond funds, the ratio is typically between .5 and 1%.

10. 6. 3   PORTFOLIO TURNOVER

The costs of buying and selling securities, including commissions or markups and mark-downs, are reflected in the **portfolio turnover ratio**.

The portfolio turnover rate reflects a fund's holding period. If a fund has a turnover rate of 100%, it holds its securities, on average, for less than one year. Therefore, all gains are likely to be short term and subject to the maximum tax rate. On the other hand, a portfolio with a turnover rate of 25% has an average holding period of four years, and gains are likely taxed at the long-term rate.

It is not uncommon for an aggressive growth fund to reflect an **annual turnover rate** of 100% or more. A 100% turnover rate means the fund replaces its portfolio annually. If the fund achieves superior returns, the strategy is working; if not, the strategy is subjecting investors to undue costs.

10. 6. 4   SERVICES OFFERED

The services mutual funds offer may include retirement account custodianship, investment plans, check-writing privileges, telephone transfers, conversion privileges, combination investment privileges, withdrawal plans, and others. However, an investor should always weigh the cost of services provided against the value of the services to the investor.

10. 7   MUTUAL FUND MARKETING AND PRICING

Mutual fund shares may be marketed in several ways, but mutual fund shares are priced according to a set formula.

10. 7. 1   MARKETING MUTUAL FUND SHARES

A fund may use any number of methods to market its shares to the public. A discussion of some of the marketing methods various firms use follows.

10. 7. 1. 1   Fund to Underwriter to Dealer to Investor

An investor gives an order for fund shares to a dealer. The dealer then places the order with the underwriter. To fill the order, the fund sells shares to the underwriter at the current NAV. The underwriter sells the shares to the dealer at the NAV plus the underwriter's concession (the public offering price less the dealer's reallowance or discount). The dealer sells the shares to the investor at the full POP.

10. 7. 1. 2   Fund to Underwriter to Investor

The underwriter acts as dealer and uses its own sales force to sell shares to the public. An investor gives an order for fund shares to the underwriter. To fill the order, the fund sells shares to the underwriter at the current NAV. The underwriter then adds the sales charge and sells the shares to the investor at the POP. The sales charge is split among the various salespeople.

10. 7. 1. 3   Fund to Investor

Some funds sell directly to the public without using an underwriter or a sales force and without assessing a sales charge. If an open-end investment company distributes shares to the public directly—that is, without the services of a distributor—and the fund offers its shares with no sales charge, the fund is called a no-load fund. The fund pays all sales expenses.

TAKE NOTE   Funds that offer shares with a 12b-1 fee of less than .25% may also be referred to as no-load funds.

10. 7. 2   SALES AT THE POP

Any sale of fund shares to a customer must be made at the public offering price (POP). A **customer** is anyone who is not a member. The route the sale takes is not important—the non-member customer must be charged the public offering price. Only a member acting as a dealer or an underwriter may purchase the fund shares at a discount from the issuer.

10. 7. 3   DETERMINING THE VALUE OF MUTUAL FUND SHARES

Mutual fund shares do not trade in the open market. Instead, they are purchased from the investment company; when a shareholder wishes to sell shares, the shares are redeemed by the investment company. Therefore, they are not priced by supply and demand like shares traded in the open market, but are instead priced by formula using net asset value.

10. 7. 3. 1   NAV and Forward Pricing

Mutual funds must calculate the NAV of fund shares at least once per business day because purchase and redemption prices are based on the NAV. Most funds wait until after the NYSE closes (4:00 pm ET) before making their NAV calculations. The price of purchase or redemption for mutual fund shares is determined at the next NAV calculation after an order is entered. This is known as **forward pricing**.

To determine the fund's total NAV, the custodian totals the value of all assets and subtracts all liabilities.

Assets (cash + current value of securities) – liabilities = fund's NAV

The NAV per share is determined by dividing the net asset value by the number of shares outstanding.

$$\frac{\text{Fund's NAV}}{\text{Number of shares outstanding}} = \text{NAV per share}$$

In working with NAV calculations, a fund's total assets include everything of value the fund owns, not just the investment portfolio.

10. 7. 3. 2   Changes in NAV

The NAV can change daily as follows.

- NAV per share increases when portfolio securities increase in value or when the portfolio receives investment income.

- NAV per share decreases when portfolio securities decrease in value or when portfolio income and gains are paid to shareholders.
- NAV per share does not change when shares are sold or redeemed or when portfolio securities are bought or sold. In these circumstances, the fund exchanges securities for cash so that the NAV per share remains unchanged.

10. 7. 3. 3   Net Asset Value per Share

Customers who buy mutual fund shares are charged the **public offering price**. The POP equals the NAV per share plus the sales charge. When a customer sells, the liquidation price is the current NAV.

10. 7. 4   SALES CHARGES

Rules prohibit members from assessing sales charges in excess of 8.5% of the POP on customer mutual fund purchases. Mutual funds may charge lower rates if they specify these rates in the prospectus. Typically, mutual fund sales loads today are substantially lower than the maximum allowed.

10. 7. 4. 1   Closed-End Funds

Closed-end funds do not have sales charges. An investor pays a **brokerage commission** in an agency transaction or pays a **markup** or **markdown** in a principal transaction.

10. 7. 4. 2   Open-End Funds

All **sales commissions** and **expenses** are paid from the sales charges collected. Sales expenses include commissions for the managing underwriter, dealers, brokers, and registered representatives, as well as all advertising and sales literature expenses.

Mutual fund distributors use three different methods to collect the fees for the sale of shares:

- Front-end loads (difference between POP and net NAV)
- Back-end loads (contingent deferred sales loads)
- 12b-1 sales charges (asset-based fees)

10. 7. 4. 3   Front-End Loads

Front-end sales loads are the charges included in a fund's public offering price. The charges are added to the NAV at the time an investor buys shares. Front-end loads are the most common way of paying for the distribution services a fund's underwriter provides.

TAKE NOTE   This is how a front-end load operates: An investor deposits $10,000 with a mutual fund that has a 5% front-end load. The 5% load amounts to $500, which is deducted from the invested amount. A total of $9,500 would be invested in the fund's portfolio on the investor's behalf.

10. 7. 4. 4   Back-End Loads

A **back-end sales load**, also called a **contingent deferred load**, is charged at the time an investor redeems mutual fund shares. The sales load, a declining percentage charge reduced annually (e.g., 8% the first year, 7% the second, 6% the third, etc.), is applied to the proceeds of any shares sold in that year. The back-end load is usually structured so that it drops to zero after an extended holding period. The sales load schedule is specified in a fund's prospectus.

10. 7. 4. 5   12b-1 Asset-Based Fees

Mutual funds cannot act as distributors for their own fund shares except under **Section 12b-1** of the Investment Company Act of 1940. This section permits a mutual fund to collect a fee for promoting, selling, or undertaking activity in connection with the distribution of its shares. The fee is determined annually as a flat dollar amount or as a percentage of the fund's average total NAV during the year and is charged quarterly. The fee is disclosed in the fund's prospectus. Requirements include the following.

- 12b-1 fees can have different norms depending on share class. The maximum allowed under any share class condition is 1% of a fund's net assets.
- The fee must reflect the anticipated level of distribution services.

The payments represent fees that would have been paid to an underwriter if sales charges had been negotiated for sales, promotion, and related activities. The following 12b-1 restrictions also exist.

- **Approval**: The 12b-1 plan must be approved initially and reapproved at least annually by a majority of the outstanding shares, the BOD, and those directors who are noninterested persons.
- **Termination**: The 12b-1 plan may be terminated at any time by a majority vote of the noninterested directors or by a majority vote of outstanding shares.
- **Misuse of no-load terminology**: A fund with a deferred sales charge or an asset-based 12b-1 fee of more than .25% of average net assets may not be described as a no-load fund.

10. 7. 4. 6   Computing the Sales Charge Percentage

When the NAV and the POP are known, the sales charge percentage can be determined as shown:

$$POP - NAV = \text{sales charge (\$ amount)}$$

$$\frac{\text{Sales charge (\$ amount)}}{POP} = \text{sales charge \%}$$

If the dollar amounts for the NAV and sales charges are specified, the formula for determining the POP of mutual fund shares is:

$$NAV + \text{sales charge (\$)} = POP \text{ (\$)}$$

A mutual fund prospectus must contain a formula that explains how the fund computes the NAV and how the sales charge is added. The sales charge is always based on the POP, not on the NAV.

To determine the POP, divide the NAV by 100% and subtract the sales charge. The formula follows:

$$\frac{NAV}{100\% - \text{sales charge } \%} = POP$$

TAKE NOTE   Because of the possible high front-end sales charge, mutual funds should be recommended for long-term investing.

TEST TOPIC ALERT   A review of the two calculations just covered:
With NAV of $10 and POP of $10.50, what is the sales charge percentage?
The sales charge percentage is calculated by finding the sales charge amount ($10.50 – $10.00) and dividing by the POP.
Remember, sales charge is a percentage of the POP—not the NAV.

$$\$.50 \div \$10.50 = 4.8\% \text{ (when rounded)}$$

Assume an NAV of $10 and a sales charge of 5%. What is the POP?
The POP is found by dividing the NAV by the difference between 100% and the sales charge: NAV / (100% – sales charge). In this example, $10 ÷ 0.95 = $10.53.

10. 7. 5   REDUCTIONS IN SALES CHARGES

The maximum permitted sales charge is reduced from 8½% to 6¼% if an investment company does not offer certain features. To qualify for the maximum 8½% sales charge, the investment company must offer:

■ breakpoints—a scale of declining sales charges based on the amount invested;
■ rights of accumulation; and
■ automatic reinvestment of distributions at NAV.

TAKE NOTE   All newly formed mutual funds offer automatic reinvestment of distributions at NAV.

10. 7. 5. 1   Breakpoints

The schedule of quantity purchase discounts a mutual fund offers is called the fund's **breakpoints**. Breakpoints are available to any person. For a breakpoint qualification, *person* includes married couples, parents and their minor children, corporations, and certain other entities. Investment clubs or associations formed for the purpose of investing do not qualify for breakpoints. The following table is an example of a breakpoint schedule:

Purchase	Sales Charge
$1 to $9,999	8½%
$10,000 to $24,999	6½%
$25,000 to $49,999	4%
$50,000 +	2%

Here are some important breakpoint considerations.

■ Breakpoint rules vary across mutual fund families. There is no industry standardized breakpoint schedule.

■ Mutual funds that offer breakpoints must disclose their breakpoint schedule in the prospectus and how an account is valued for breakpoint purposes.

■ Purchases made by the same investor in various accounts may be aggregated to qualify for a breakpoint discount. Eligible accounts include traditional brokerage, accounts held directly with a fund company, 401(k), IRA, and 529 college savings.

■ Shares purchased in the same fund family, other than money market accounts, are eligible to be aggregated together to qualify for a breakpoint discount, including those held at separate broker-dealers.

■ A large, lump-sum investment is one method to qualify for a breakpoint. Mutual funds offer additional incentives for an investor to continue to invest and qualify for breakpoints using a letter of intent or rights of accumulation.

10. 7. 5. 1. 1 Letter of Intent (LOI)

A person who plans to invest more money with the same mutual fund company may immediately decrease the overall sales charges by signing a **letter of intent (LOI)**. In the LOI, the investor informs the investment company of the intention to invest the additional funds necessary to reach the breakpoint within 13 months.

The LOI is a one-sided contract binding on the fund only. However, the customer must complete the investment to qualify for the reduced sales charge. The fund holds the extra shares purchased from the reduced sales charge in escrow. A customer who deposits the money to complete the LOI receives the escrowed shares. Appreciation and reinvested dividends do not count toward the LOI.

EXAMPLE   Referring back to the sample breakpoint schedule, a customer investing $9,000 is just short of the $10,000 breakpoint. In this situation, the customer might sign an LOI promising an amount that will qualify for the breakpoint within 13 months from the date of the letter. An additional $1,000 within 13 months qualifies the customer for the reduced sales charge.

If a customer has not completed the investment within 13 months, he will be given the choice of sending a check for the difference in sales charges or cashing in escrowed shares to pay the difference.

Backdating the Letter. A fund often permits a customer to sign a letter of intent as late as the 90th day after an initial purchase. The LOI may be backdated by up to 90 days to include prior purchases but may not cover more than 13 months in total.

10. 7. 5. 1. 2 Breakpoint Sales

Rules prohibit registered representatives from making or seeking higher commissions by selling investment company shares in a dollar amount just below the point at which the sales charge is reduced. This violation is known as a **breakpoint sale**.

10. 7. 5. 2   Rights of Accumulation

Rights of accumulation, like breakpoints, allow an investor to qualify for reduced sales charges. The major differences are that rights of accumulation:

- are available for subsequent investments and do not apply to initial transactions;
- allow the investor to use prior share appreciation to qualify for breakpoints; and
- do not impose time limits.

The customer may qualify for reduced charges when the total value of shares previously purchased and shares currently being purchased exceed a certain dollar amount. For the purpose of qualifying customers for rights of accumulation, the mutual fund bases the quantity of securities owned on the higher of current NAV or the total of purchases made to date.

Rights of accumulation allow an investor to combine prior investments in the fund with today's investment to determine today's sales charge. Referring back to the sample breakpoint schedule, once an investor accumulates $50,000 in the fund, each additional investment, no matter how small, qualifies for the lowest sales charge—in this case, 2%.

10. 7. 5. 3   Automatic Reinvestment of Distributions

Dividends and capital gains are distributed in cash. However, a shareholder may elect to reinvest distributions in additional mutual fund shares. The automatic reinvestment of distributions is similar to compounding interest.

Typically, customers may systematically reinvest dividends and capital gains at NAV and may use them to buy full and fractional shares only if:

- shareholders who are not already participants in the reinvestment plan are given a separate opportunity to reinvest each dividend;
- the plan is described in the prospectus;
- the securities issuer bears no additional costs beyond those that it would have incurred in the normal payout of dividends; and
- shareholders are notified of the availability of the dividend reinvestment plan at least once every year.

10. 7. 5. 4   Combination Privilege

A mutual fund sponsor frequently offers more than one fund and refers to these multiple offerings as its *family of funds*. An investor seeking a reduced sales charge may be allowed to combine separate investments in two or more funds within the same family to reach a breakpoint.

10. 7. 5. 4. 1 Exchanges Within a Family of Funds

Many sponsors offer **exchange** or **conversion privileges** within their families of funds. Exchange privileges allow an investor to convert an investment in one fund for an equal investment in another fund in the same family, often without incurring an additional sales charge. This exchange is considered a taxable event, and there may be tax consequences.

10. 7. 5. 5   Classes of Shares

Investors can purchase the same underlying mutual fund shares in several ways. Generally, investors can purchase Class A shares, Class B shares, Class C shares, or Class D shares. The differences among these shares is how much and in what way investors will pay sales charges and related expenses.

- Class A—front-end load that can be reduced or eliminated by breakpoints
- Class B—back-end load that declines over time combined with 12b-1 fees
- Class C—12b-1 fees charged quarterly with small back-end load in first year
- Class D—level load plus a redemption fee

A key point is that Class B, C, and D shares cannot take advantage of breakpoint reductions that are available on large purchases of Class A shares. Therefore, a long-term investor contemplating a large investment in a mutual fund should carefully consider the advantages of Class A shares before making a decision, but for smaller investments, B shares might still be appropriate.

10. 7. 6   REDEMPTION OF FUND SHARES

A mutual fund must redeem shares within seven calendar days of receiving a written request for redemption. If the customer holds the fund certificates, the mutual fund must redeem shares within seven days of the date that the certificates and instructions to liquidate arrive at the custodian bank. The customer's signature on the written request must be guaranteed.

The price at which shares are redeemed is the NAV (calculated at least once per business day).

The redemption requirement may be suspended only when:

- the NYSE is closed other than for a customary weekend or holiday closing;
- trading on the NYSE has been restricted; or
- the SEC has ordered the suspension of redemptions for the protection of the company's securities holders.

Otherwise, the fund must redeem shares upon request.

TAKE NOTE   Some mutual funds charge redemption fees. If redemption fees are charged, all fees and sales loads may not exceed a maximum of 8.5%. For example, a fund that charges a front-end load of 8% could charge a redemption fee of .5%.

10. 7. 6. 1   Cancelation of Fund Shares

Because an open-end mutual fund makes a continuous public offering, a share is destroyed once a mutual fund share has been redeemed. Unlike other corporate securities, mutual fund shares may not be sold to other owners. An investor purchasing mutual fund shares receives new shares.

TEST TOPIC ALERT

■ The maximum sales charge allowed is 8.5% of the POP.

■ An investor buys and redeems shares at the price next calculated (forward pricing).

■ Only member firms may buy below the POP—not the public or nonmembers.

■ The NAV per share does not change when new shares are issued or when shares are redeemed.

■ 12b-1 fees are charged quarterly but must be approved annually.

■ Breakpoints are not allowed for investment clubs or a parent and child above the age of majority. They are allowed for corporations, husband and wife, and a parent and child below the age of majority.

■ A fund can charge an 8½% sales load only if it offers breakpoints, rights of accumulation, and reinvestment at NAV. (Remember, all newly formed funds offer reinvestment at NAV.)

■ Mutual fund shares that have been redeemed are canceled. They are never reissued.

If a customer redeems mutual fund shares within seven business days of purchase, any fees or concessions earned by the firm for selling the shares must be returned to the underwriter. This includes the portion payable to the representative who sold shares to the customer.

QUICK QUIZ 10.C

1. For a company to charge the maximum sales charge of 8½%, it must offer all of the following EXCEPT
   A. automatic reinvestment of dividends and capital gains at NAV
   B. breakpoints
   C. automatic reinvestment at POP
   D. rights of accumulation

2. A mutual fund is quoted at $16.56 NAV and $18.00 POP. The sales charge is
   A. 7%
   B. 7½%
   C. 8%
   D. 8½%

3. Redemption of a no-load fund may be made at the

   A. NAV minus the sales charge
   B. POP minus the sales charge
   C. NAV plus the sales charge
   D. NAV

4. A customer purchased mutual fund shares with a net asset value of $7.82 and an 8% sales charge. The sales charge is

   A. $.68
   B. $.74
   C. $.80
   D. $.87

5. Which of the following statements regarding a letter of intent and breakpoints are TRUE?

   I.   The letter of intent can be backdated a maximum of 30 days.
   II. The letter of intent is valid for 13 months.
   III. The investor is legally bound to meet the terms of the agreement.
   IV. The fund holds the additional shares in escrow.

   A. I and II
   B. II and III
   C. II and IV
   D. III and IV

6. All of the following investors can take advantage of breakpoints EXCEPT

   A. an individual
   B. an investment club
   C. a trust
   D. a corporation

10. 8   MUTUAL FUND DISTRIBUTIONS AND TAXATION

Distributions from mutual funds are derived from income received from portfolio securities or gains from the sale of portfolio securities. Whether taken in cash or reinvested, distributions are taxable.

10. 8. 1   DISTRIBUTIONS FROM MUTUAL FUNDS

Many mutual fund distributions are taxed according to the conduit theory, as described in this section.

10. 8. 1. 1   Dividend Distributions

A mutual fund may pay dividends to each shareholder in the same way that corporations pay dividends to stockholders. Dividends are paid from the mutual fund's net investment income.

Net investment income includes gross investment income—dividend and interest income from securities held in the portfolio—minus operating expenses. Advertising and sales expenses are not included in a fund's operating expenses when calculating net investment income. Depending on an individual's ordinary income tax bracket, qualified dividends can be taxed at 0% up to a maximum percentage as determined by the IRS tax code.

TAKE NOTE   Dividends from municipal bond funds, which represent the flow-through of municipal bond interest, are not taxable.

10. 8. 1. 2 The Conduit Theory

Because an investment company is organized as a corporation or trust, one might assume its earnings are subject to tax. Consider, however, how an additional level of taxation shrinks a dividend distribution's value.

EXAMPLE   ABC Fund owns shares of XYZ Co. First, XYZ is taxed on its earnings before it pays a dividend; second, ABC pays tax on the amount of the dividend it receives; and finally, the investor pays income tax on the distribution from the fund.

Triple taxation of investment income may be avoided if the mutual fund qualifies under Subchapter M of the Internal Revenue Code (IRC). If a mutual fund acts as a conduit, or pipeline, for the distribution of net investment income, the fund may qualify as a regulated investment company, subject to tax only on the amount of investment income the fund retains. The investment income distributed to shareholders escapes taxation at the mutual fund level.

Subchapter M requires a fund to distribute at least 90% of its net investment income to shareholders. The fund then pays taxes only on the undistributed 10%. If the fund distributes 89%, it pays taxes on 100% of net investment income.

10. 8. 1. 3 Capital Gains Distributions

The appreciation or depreciation of portfolio securities is an **unrealized capital gain or loss**. If the fund does not sell, the fund shareholders experience no tax consequences. When the fund sells the securities, the gain or loss is **realized** and affects shareholder taxes. Distributions of these realized gains to shareholders are taxable.

If the fund has held the securities for more than one year, the gain is a **long-term capital gain**, taxed as determined by the IRS tax code. A long-term capital gains distribution may not be made more often than once per year.

A **short-term gain** is identified, distributed, and taxed at ordinary income tax rates.

TAKE NOTE   Only realized gains are taxable to shareholders. Unrealized gains result in an increased NAV only.

10. 8. 1. 3. 1 Calculating Fund Yield

To calculate fund yield, divide the annual dividend paid from net investment income by the current offering price. Yield quotations must disclose the:

■ general direction of the stock market for the period in question;

■ fund's NAV at the beginning and the end of the period; and

■ percentage change in the fund's price during the period.

Current yield calculations may be based only on income distributions for the preceding 12 months. Gains distributions may not be included in yield calculations. Most mutual funds distribute dividends quarterly. A mutual fund must disclose the source of a dividend payment if it is from other than retained or current income.

10. 8. 1. 3. 2 Ex-Dividend Date

Unlike the ex-dividend date for other corporate securities, the ex-dividend date for mutual funds is set by the BOD. Normally, the ex-dividend date for mutual funds is the day after the record date.

10. 8. 1. 3. 3 Selling Dividends

If an investor purchases fund shares just before the ex-dividend date, the fund shares' market value decreases by the distribution amount. The investor is also taxed on the distribution. A registered representative may not encourage investors to purchase fund shares before a distribution because of this tax liability. Doing so is **selling dividends**, a violation of FINRA rules.

10. 8. 1. 3. 4 Taxation of Reinvested Distributions

Distributions are taxable to shareholders whether the distributions are received in cash or reinvested. The fund must disclose whether each distribution is from income or capital tax transactions. **Form 1099**, which is sent to shareholders after the close of the year, details tax information related to distributions for the year.

10. 8. 1. 4 Fund Share Liquidations to the Investor

When an investor sells mutual fund shares, he must establish his cost base, or basis, in the shares to calculate the tax liability. A simple definition of cost base is the amount of money invested. Upon liquidation, cost base represents a return of capital and is not taxed again.

10. 8. 1. 4. 1 Valuing Fund Shares

The cost base of mutual fund shares includes the shares' total cost, including sales charges plus any reinvested dividend and capital gains distributions. For tax purposes, the investor compares cost base to the amount of money received from selling the shares. If the amount received is greater than the cost base, the investor reports a taxable gain. If the amount received is less than the cost base, the investor reports a loss.

10. 8. 1. 5 Accounting Methods

If an investor decides to liquidate shares, he determines the cost base by electing one of three accounting methods: **first in, first out (FIFO)**; **share identification**; or **average basis**. If the investor fails to choose, the IRS assumes the investor liquidates shares on a FIFO basis.

10. 8. 1. 5. 1 First In, First Out

When FIFO shares are sold, the cost of the shares held the longest is used to calculate the gain or loss. In a rising market, this method normally creates adverse tax consequences.

10. 8. 1. 5. 2 Share Identification

When using the share identification accounting method, the investor keeps track of the cost of each share purchased and uses this information when deciding which shares to liquidate. He then liquidates the shares that provide the desired tax benefits.

10. 8. 1. 5. 3 Average Basis

The shareholder may elect to use an average cost basis when redeeming fund shares. The shareholder calculates average basis by dividing the total cost of all shares owned by the total number of shares.

10. 8. 1. 6 Other Mutual Fund Tax Considerations

Mutual fund investors must consider many tax factors when buying and selling mutual fund shares.

10. 8. 1. 6. 1 Withholding Tax

If an investor neglects or fails to include a Social Security number or tax ID number when purchasing mutual fund shares, the fund must withhold a percentage of the distributions to the investor as a withholding tax.

10. 8. 1. 6. 2 Taxation of Investment Returns

The taxation of investment returns may be summarized as follows.

- Qualified dividends are taxed at a percentage as determined by the IRS tax code depending on the investor's ordinary income tax bracket.
- Long-term capital gains distributions are taxed at a percentage as determined by the IRS tax code depending on the investor's ordinary income tax bracket.
- Short-term capital gains distributions are taxed as ordinary income.

10. 8. 1. 6. 3 Exchanges Within a Family of Funds

Even though exchange within a fund family incurs no sales charge, the IRS considers a sale to have taken place, and if a gain occurs, the customer is taxed. This tax liability can be significant, and shareholders should be aware of this potential conversion cost.

TEST TOPIC ALERT   Below are testable points about mutual fund distributions and taxation.

- Funds that comply with Subchapter M (conduit theory) are known as regulated investment companies.

- Mutual fund yield is calculated by dividing the annual dividend by the POP. Capital gains distributions are not included.

- When is the ex-date of a mutual fund? The best answer is as determined by the BOD, but if that choice is not given, choose the business day after the record date.

- Dividends and capital gains are taxable whether reinvested or taken in cash.

- An investor's cost basis in mutual fund shares is what was paid to buy the share plus reinvested dividends and capital gains distributions.

- The IRS always assigns FIFO for share liquidation unless the investor chooses a different method.

- Although an exchange from one fund to another within the same family is not subject to a sales charge, it is a taxable event. Any gain or loss on the shares sold is reportable at the time of the exchange.

10. 9   MUTUAL FUND PURCHASE AND WITHDRAWAL PLANS

Mutual fund investors may select from among several methods by which to buy mutual fund shares or withdraw money from their mutual fund accounts.

10. 9. 1   TYPES OF MUTUAL FUND ACCOUNTS

When a customer opens an account with a mutual fund, he makes an initial deposit and specifies whether fund share distributions are to be made in cash or reinvested. If the customer elects to receive distributions in cash rather than reinvesting them, his proportionate interest in the fund is reduced each time a distribution is made. A customer may make additional investments in an open account at any time and in any dollar amount—the law sets no minimum requirement, although each fund may set its own.

10. 9. 1. 1   Accumulation Plans

Mutual funds have established several accumulation plans that allow investors to use the dollar cost averaging strategy.

10. 9. 1. 1. 1   Voluntary Accumulation Plan

A **voluntary accumulation plan** allows a customer to deposit regular periodic investments on a voluntary basis. The plan is designed to help the customer form regular investment habits while still offering some flexibility.

Voluntary accumulation plans may require a minimum initial purchase and minimum additional purchase amounts. Many funds offer automatic withdrawal from customer checking accounts to simplify contributions. If a customer misses a payment, the fund does not penalize him because the plan is voluntary. The customer may discontinue the plan at any time.

Dollar Cost Averaging. One method of purchasing mutual fund shares is called **dollar cost averaging**, whereby a person invests identical amounts at regular intervals. This form of investing allows the individual to purchase more shares when prices are low and fewer shares when prices are high. In a fluctuating market and over time, the average cost per share is lower than the average price of the shares. However, dollar cost averaging does not guarantee profits in a declining market because prices may continue to decline for some time. In this case, the investor buys more shares of a sinking investment.

The following example illustrates how average price and average cost may vary with dollar cost averaging.

Month	Amount Invested	Price Per Share	No. of Shares
January	$600	$20	30
February	$600	$24	25
March	$600	$30	20
April	$600	$40	15
Total	$2,400	$114	90

The average cost per share equals $2,400 (the total investment) ÷ 90 (the total number of shares purchased), or $26.67 per share, whereas the average price per share is $28.50 ($114 ÷ 4).

TAKE NOTE   Dollar cost averaging is effective if the average cost per share is less than the average price per share.

10. 9. 1. 2   Withdrawal Plans

In addition to **lump-sum withdrawals**, whereby customers sell all of their shares, mutual funds offer **systematic withdrawal plans**. Withdrawal plans are normally a free service. Not all mutual funds offer withdrawal plans, but those that do may offer the plan alternatives described here.

10. 9. 1. 2. 1 Fixed Dollar

A customer may request the periodic withdrawal of a **fixed dollar amount**. Thus, the fund liquidates enough shares each period to send that sum. The amount of money liquidated may be more or less than the account earnings during the period.

10. 9. 1. 2. 2 Fixed Percentage or Fixed Share

Under a **fixed-percentage** or **fixed-share withdrawal plan**, either a fixed number of shares or a fixed percentage of the account is liquidated each period.

10. 9. 1. 2. 3 Fixed Time

Under a **fixed-time withdrawal plan**, customers liquidate their holdings over a fixed period. Most mutual funds require a customer's account to be worth a minimum amount of money before a withdrawal plan may begin. Additionally, most funds discourage continued investment once withdrawals start.

10. 9. 1. 2. 4 Withdrawal Plan Disclosures

Withdrawal plans are not guaranteed. With fixed-dollar plans, only the dollar amount to be received each period is fixed. All other factors, including the number of shares liquidated and a plan's length, are variable. For a fixed-time plan, only the time is fixed; the amount of money the investor receives varies each period.

Because withdrawal plans are not guaranteed, the registered representative must:

- never promise an investor a guaranteed rate of return;
- stress to the investor that it is possible to exhaust the account by overwithdrawing;
- state that during a down market it is possible that the account will be exhausted if the investor withdraws even a small amount; and
- never use charts or tables unless the SEC specifically clears their use.

TAKE NOTE

Mutual fund withdrawal plans are not guaranteed in any way. All charts and tables regarding withdrawal plans must be cleared by the SEC before use.

QUICK QUIZ 10.D

1. Under which of the following circumstances will dollar cost averaging result in an average cost per share lower than the average price per share?

   I. The price of the stock fluctuates over time.
   II. A fixed number of shares is purchased regularly.
   III. A fixed dollar amount is invested regularly.
   IV. A constant dollar plan is maintained.

   A. I and II
   B. I and III
   C. I, III and IV
   D. II and III

2. All of the following statements regarding dollar cost averaging are true EXCEPT

   A. dollar cost averaging results in a lower average cost per share
   B. dollar cost averaging is not available to large investors
   C. more shares are purchased when prices are lower
   D. in sales literature, dollar cost averaging cannot be referred to as averaging the dollar

3. Which of the following is a risk of a withdrawal plan?

   A. The sales charge for the service is high.
   B. The cost basis of the shares is high.
   C. The plan is illegal in many states.
   D. The investor may outlive his income.

4. An investor has requested a withdrawal plan from his mutual fund and currently receives $600 per month. This is an example of what type of plan?

   A. Variable withdrawal
   B. Fixed-share periodic withdrawal
   C. Fixed-dollar periodic withdrawal
   D. Fixed-percentage withdrawal

10. 10 TRACKING INVESTMENT COMPANY SECURITIES

Investment company prices, like those for individual securities, are quoted daily in the financial press. However, because various methods are used to calculate sales charges (as described here), the financial press provides several footnotes to explain the type of sales charge a mutual fund issuer uses. A registered representative must understand the presentation and meaning of the footnotes associated with investment company quotes so as to accurately describe the quotes to the investing public.

Most newspapers carry daily quotes of the NAVs and offer prices for major mutual funds. A mutual fund's NAV is its bid price. The **offer price** (also called the public offering price or POP) is the ask price; it is the NAV plus the maximum sales charge applicable to the fund. The NAV Chg column reflects the change in NAV from the previous day's quote.

EXAMPLE

Look at the family of funds called ArGood Mutual Funds. ArGood Growth Fund is a part of this group; its net asset value, offering price, and the change in its NAV per share are listed. As stated previously, when a difference exists between the NAV and the offering price, the fund is a load fund. A no-load fund is usually identified by the letters NL in the Offer Price column. This is illustrated by the Best Mutual funds, a family of no-load funds.

Mutual Fund Quotations

Price ranges for investment companies. NAV stands for net asset value per share. The offering price includes net asset value plus maximum sales charge, if any.

	NAV	Offer Price	NAV Chg		NAV	Offer Price	NAV Chg
ArGood Mutual Funds				**FastTrak Funds**			
CapApp	4.80	5.04	+ .02	App	13.79	14.44	− .01
Grwth	6.87	7.21	+ .02	CapAp	22.13	23.17	+ .15
HiYld	10.28	10.79	+ .01	Grwth	18.33	19.24	− .10
TaxEx	11.62	12.20	− .04	**Z Best Invest**			
Best Mutual				Grth p	14.81	15.59	− .03
Balan	12.32	NL	− .06	HiYld p	9.25	9.74	+ .03
Canada	10.59	NL	− .04	Inco p	7.95	8.37	− .04
US Gov	10.49	NL	− .02	MuniB p	8.11	8.54	− .03

e: Ex-distribution. **f:** Previous day's quote. **s:** Stock split or div. **x:** Ex-dividend. **NL:** No load. **p:** Distribution costs apply, 12b-1 plan. **r:** Redemption charge may apply.

*This sample comprises formats, styles, and abbreviations from a variety of currently available sources and has been created for educational purposes.

The final column shows the change in a share's NAV since the last trading date. A plus (+) indicates an upward move, and a minus (–) indicates a downward turn.

From this information, you can calculate any mutual fund's sales charge. For example, find the FastTrak group of funds. The first entry is "App."

Remember the formula for calculating the sales charge.

$$\text{Public offering price} - \text{NAV} = \text{sales charge}$$

Therefore, in this case, the calculation is: $14.44 - $13.79 = $.65.
To calculate the sales charge percentage, use the following formula:

$$\text{Sales charge} \div \text{public offering price} = \text{sales charge \%}$$

In this case, the calculation is as follows: $.65 \div $14.44 = 4.5%.
You can also watch the movements of the fund's share value.

10. 10. 1 INDEX TRACKING FUNDS

Some funds are designed to track the performance of an underlying investment portfolio or index.

These funds are known as index funds. While they are not investment company products, they do have characteristics similar to both open-end and closed-end funds.

Like closed-end funds, index fund shares trade and are priced like shares of stock. Like open-end funds, they can create (issue) additional shares.

TAKE NOTE   Index tracking funds have low portfolio turnover, which is a contributing factor to having low expense ratios.

Investors use index funds for:
- asset allocation;
- following industry trends;
- balancing a portfolio;
- speculative trading; and
- hedging.

Remember that index funds are different from mutual funds in the following ways.
- **Intraday trading**—Investors do not have to wait until the end of a trading day to purchase or sell shares. Shares trade and are priced continuously throughout the day, making it easier for investors to react to market changes.
- **Margin eligibility**—index fund shares can be purchased on margin, subject to the same terms that apply to common stock.
- **Short selling**—index funds can be sold short at any time during trading hours.

Popular index funds include one that tracks the S&P 500 index; Spiders. There are also Spiders on various components of the S&P 500. There are nine Select Sector index funds (e.g., consumer services, energy, and technology), and each of the 500 stocks in the S&P

index is allocated to only one Select Sector index fund. These funds generally pay quarterly cash dividends that represent, after expenses, dividends accumulated on the underlying stock portfolio.

Lastly it should be noted that many index tracking funds are exchange-traded funds (ETFs) offered by a variety of different issuers. One popular exchange-traded index fund is the **Q's (QQQQ)**, which tracks the price performance of the Nasdaq 100 Trust. This index tracking ETF trades on Nasdaq.

10. 10. 2 LEVERAGED FUNDS

These funds attempt to deliver a multiple of the return of the benchmark index they are designated to track. For instance, a 2X leveraged fund would try to deliver two times the return of whatever index it is tracking. With leveraged funds, there are no limits by rule or regulation as to the amount of leverage that could be applied to a portfolio. Currently there are numerous 2X and 3X leveraged funds available to investors.

The risk associated with leverage is that it is always a "double edged" sword. Therefore, the risk to be recognized regarding this fund strategy is that if the benchmark index is falling, then the fund's returns will be, in theory, the designated leverage amount (perhaps 2 or 3) times the loss. In addition, most of these funds use derivatives products such as options, futures, and swaps to enable them to achieve the stated goal. As these products are not suitable for all investors, so too can it be said of the leverage fund portfolio containing them. Ultimately, as always, suitability becomes an issue when recommending these products.

10. 10. 3 INVERSE (REVERSE) FUNDS

Inverse funds, sometimes referred to as reverse or short funds, attempt to deliver returns that are the opposite of the benchmark index they are tracking. For example, if the benchmark is down 2%, the fund's goal is to be up 2%. In addition, inverse funds can also be leveraged funds, or said another way, 2 or 3 times the opposite of the indices return.

TAKE NOTE   Both leveraged and inverse index funds (leveraged or not) can be traded on an exchange. When they are, they are known as exchange-traded funds (ETFs). If the shares are exchange-traded, they are priced by supply and demand, can be purchased on margin, and bought and sold throughout the trading day, like all exchange-traded products. For those that are not exchange-traded, they would be priced, purchased, and redeemed like all investment company shares. Neither of these fund types carry any guarantee that they will achieve the stated goal or objective.

10. 11   HEDGE FUNDS

Hedge funds are similar to mutual funds in that investments are pooled and professionally managed, but they differ in that the fund has more flexibility in the investment strategies employed and are unregulated by U.S. securities laws. They are aggressively managed portfolios of investments that use advanced investment strategies. Generally these investment vehicles are considered suitable for sophisticated investors—those meeting the standard of accredited investors. While hedging is the practice of attempting to limit risk, most hedge funds specify generating high returns as their primary investment objective. Some of the more common strategies employed by hedge funds are:

- highly leveraged portfolios;
- the use of short positions;
- utilizing derivative products such as options and futures;
- currency speculation;
- commodity speculation; and
- investing in politically unstable international markets.

Because hedge funds, unlike mutual funds or investment companies, are unregulated, the very nature of the investment is almost always considered speculative. Most hedge funds are organized as private investment partnerships, allowing them to limit the number of investors or require large initial or minimum investments if they so desire. Some also require that investors maintain the investment for a minimum length of time (e.g., one year) and to that extent they can be considered illiquid. These requirements are known as lock-up provisions.

TAKE NOTE   While hedge funds are unregulated, U.S. laws do require that the majority of investors meet the test of a sophisticated investor. They should be considered "accredited" investors, having a minimum annual income and net worth, and have considerable investment knowledge.

10. 11. 1 HEDGE FUND LOCK-UP PROVISIONS

This provision provides that during a certain initial period, an investor may not make a withdrawal from the fund. The period when the investor cannot withdraw investment dollars is known as the actual lock-up period. Generally recognized as one way the manager of the hedge fund portfolio can have capital retained in the fund, it is also seen to be another factor adding to the unique risk of hedge funds—in this case, shares being illiquid for that specified length of time.

Lock-up periods are generally associated with new or start-up hedge funds and can differ in length from one fund to another. The length of the lock-up period will largely be dependent on what the investment strategy of the fund is and how long the portfolio manager anticipates it will take to implement the strategy and then see results of that implementation.

10. 11. 2 BLANK-CHECK OR BLIND-POOL HEDGE FUND

Some hedge funds target blank-check companies to invest in. Blank-check companies, sometimes known as special purpose acquisition companies (SPACS), carry their own unique risks. Blank-check companies are companies without business operations that raise money through IPOs in order to have their shares publicly traded for the sole purpose of seeking out a business or combination of businesses. When a business is located, they will present proposals to holders of their shares for approval.

Some hedge funds target blind-pool companies. Similar to blank-check companies, these issuers raise capital by selling securities to the public without telling investors what the specific use of the proceeds will be, but might target a particular industry or sector.

Some characterize blank-check companies as a type of blind-pool, with one discernable difference. While the blind-pool company will usually provide at least some indication of what general industry the funds will be invested in, blank-check offerings do not identify any proposed investment intent.

While some hedge funds target these types of holdings for their portfolios, it should be noted that they might be included within any hedge fund portfolio, and in both cases should be considered when assessing risk and determining suitability.

QUICK QUIZ 10.E

True or False?

_____ 1. An index fund trading on an exchange is priced at the end of the day.

_____ 2. Index fund shares trading on exchanges can be purchased on margin.

_____ 3. Exchange-traded funds are priced by formula recalculating NAV at least once per day.

_____ 4. Hedge funds are conservatively managed portfolios suitable for most investors to hedge existing portfolios.

_____ 5. Inverse or reverse funds attempt to deliver returns opposite of a benchmark index.

UNIT TEST

1. According to investment company rules, open-end investment companies may not distribute capital gains to their shareholders more frequently than
   A. monthly
   B. quarterly
   C. semiannually
   D. annually

2. Under the definition of a management company, which of the following would qualify?
   I. Face-amount certificate companies
   II. Unit investment trusts
   III. Closed-end investment companies
   IV. Open-end investment companies
   A. I and II
   B. I and III
   C. II and III
   D. III and IV

3. If a customer purchases shares in a municipal bond fund, which of the following statements are TRUE?
   I. Dividends are taxable.
   II. Dividends are not taxable.
   III. Capital gains distributions are taxable.
   IV. Capital gains distributions are not taxable.
   A. I and III
   B. I and IV
   C. II and III
   D. II and IV

4. When a customer transfers the proceeds of a sale from one fund to another within the same family of funds, what are the tax consequences?
   A. No gains or losses are recognized until the final redemption.
   B. Gains are taxed at the time of the transfer, but losses are deferred until the final redemption.
   C. Losses are deducted at the time of the transfer, but gains are deferred until the final redemption.
   D. All gains and losses are recognized on the transfer date.

5. For an open-end investment company registered as a mutual fund, all of the following are true EXCEPT
   A. fund shares may be purchased or sold during normal trading hours at the current market value when an order is entered
   B. the fund can sell new shares in any quantity at any time
   C. the fund must redeem shares in any quantity within 7 days of request
   D. the investment in fund shares provides for mutual ownership of portfolio assets by shareholders

6. According to the Investment Company Act of 1940, a diversified mutual fund may hold, at most, what percentage of a corporation's voting securities?
   A. 5%
   B. 10%
   C. 50%
   D. 75%

7. All of the following statements are TRUE of mutual fund dividend distributions EXCEPT
   A. the fund pays dividends from net investment income
   B. dividend distributions are not guaranteed
   C. an investor is liable for taxes on distributions whether a dividend is a cash distribution or is reinvested in the fund
   D. an investor is not liable for taxes if he automatically reinvests distributions

8. A certain mutual fund has a bid price of $9.15 and a sales charge of 8.5%. What is the price an investor will pay (rounded to the nearest cent) for each share of this fund?
   A. $8.37
   B. $9.93
   C. $10.00
   D. $10.76

9. XYZ Technology Fund permits rights of accumulation. A shareholder has invested $9,000 and has signed a letter of intent for a $15,000 investment. Her reinvested dividends during the 13 months total $720. How much money must she contribute to fulfill the letter of intent?

   A. $5,280
   B. $6,000
   C. $9,000
   D. $15,000

10. Net asset value per share for a mutual fund can be expected to decrease if

   A. the securities in the portfolio have appreciated in value
   B. the issuers of securities in the portfolio have made dividend distributions
   C. the fund has experienced net redemption of shares
   D. the fund has made dividend distributions to shareholders

11. All of the following events will affect the NAV per share of a mutual fund EXCEPT

   A. wholesale redemption of fund shares
   B. changes in the market value of the fund's portfolio of securities
   C. the fund receives cash dividends on the securities in its portfolio
   D. the fund pays dividends to its shareholders

12. The redemption price of a mutual fund is equal to

   A. its offering price
   B. its net asset value
   C. its bid price plus the sales charge
   D. its asked price plus the sales charge

13. If a relatively high rate of current return is the stated objective of an open-end investment company, it would be known as

   A. a specialized common stock fund
   B. a special situation fund
   C. a growth fund
   D. an income fund

14. An open-end investment company may change its basic investment policies only if this change has been

   A. recommended by the investment adviser of the fund
   B. approved by the SEC
   C. approved by the directors and a majority vote of the shareholders
   D. made by the principal underwriter in an effort to increase lagging sales of new fund shares

15. The major difference between an open-end and a closed-end investment company is that

   A. the closed-end shares are sold on a registered stock exchange
   B. the open-end company is regulated by the SEC
   C. the shares of open-end companies are sold at NAV plus a sales commission
   D. the open-end companies continuously offer their shares, whereas closed-end companies have a limited number of shares outstanding

A N S W E R S   A N D   R A T I O N A L E S

1. **D.** Under the Act of 1940, investment companies cannot distribute capital gains more frequently than once per year.

2. **D.** As defined in the Act of 1940, closed- and open-end funds are subclassifications of management companies (actively managed portfolios). Face-amount certificate companies and unit trusts are separate investment company classifications under the act.

3. **C.** Municipal bond funds distribute federally tax-free dividends, but any capital gains distribution is subject to taxation. The tax preferential treatment of municipals is limited to the income earned, not the gains.

4. **D.** Although a transfer within a family of funds is generally not subject to a sales charge, there is liability for any taxes due. The IRS considers this transaction a sale and a purchase. Any losses or gains must be declared on that year's tax form.

5. **A.** An open-end investment company registered as a mutual fund may sell any quantity of new shares, redeem shares within 7 days, and provide for mutual ownership of portfolio assets by shareholders. For purchases and redemptions, mutual funds use forward pricing which means that all transactions will be done at the next calculated net asset value (NAV) after an order is received.

6. **B.** To be considered a diversified investment company, a mutual fund may own no more than 10% of a target company's voting securities. Additionally, no diversified investment company may invest more than 5% of its portfolio in a single company's securities.

7. **D.** Mutual funds pay dividends from net investment income, and shareholders are liable for taxes on all distributions, whether reinvested or taken in cash. Dividend distributions from mutual funds, like individual corporate dividend distributions, are not guaranteed.

8. **C.** To calculate the offering price when you know the bid price (the NAV) and the percentage of sales charge, divide the bid price ($9.15) by the complement of the sales charge (.915). This equals $10, the offering price.

9. **B.** The shareholder must put in the full $15,000, so she owes an additional $6,000. Reinvested dividends and changes in the NAV do not affect the amount required to fulfill a letter of intent.

10. **D.** The NAV per share will rise or fall relative to the value of the underlying portfolio. If dividends are distributed to shareholders, the fund's assets decrease, and per share value will decline accordingly. Appreciation of the portfolio and dividends received will increase the value. Redemption of shares will have no impact on the NAV per share because the money paid out is offset by a reduced number of shares outstanding.

11. **A.** Dividends paid and received by the fund directly affect NAV. Changes in the portfolio value affect NAV because the securities are marked to market daily. Although share redemption will reduce total net asset value, the number of shares outstanding decreases in proportion, so the NAV per share stays the same.

12. **B.** Mutual funds are redeemed at the net asset value. The net asset value is also known as the bid price (not the bid price plus the sales charge). Some mutual funds charge a redemption charge. That is merely a fee to be subtracted from the net asset value upon redemption.

13. **D.** Current return is synonymous with income.

14. **C.** Only the directors and shareholders can approve a change of this major significance.

15. **D.** Capitalization represents the major difference between these two types of investment companies. Open-end companies use a continuous primary offering for which every share issued is a new share. Closed-end companies issue a fixed number of shares, which are traded in the secondary market after the initial offering much like common stock.

QUICK QUIZ ANSWERS

Quick Quiz 10.A

1. **D.** All are covered under the Act of 1940. Unit investment trusts, face-amount companies, and management companies are all mentioned in this act. Both open-end and closed-end management companies are subclassifications of management investment companies.

2. **B.** The closed-end company does not redeem the shares that it issues. The closed-end company has a fixed capitalization and, like regular corporations, outstanding shares trade on the open market.

3. **C.** A diversified investment company must have at least 75% of its assets invested in cash and/or securities, may have no more than 5% invested in one company, and may own no more than 10% of the voting stock of a company.

4. **C.** Unlike unit investment trusts, which issue redeemable securities, face-amount certificate companies issue installment certificates with guaranteed principal and interest. A unit investment trust has a diversified portfolio that, once established, does not change. Therefore, it cannot be called a management company. A closed-end investment company is a type of management company.

5. **C.** Open-end investment companies, but not closed-end investment companies, can make continuous offerings of shares, redeem their shares, and issue only common stock.

6. **B** Exchange-traded funds (ETFs) are classified as open-end fund companies. Individual shares traded in the secondary market are priced continuously throughout the trading day like other exchange-traded product shares.

7. **A.** Exchange-traded fund (ETF) shares are priced continuously throughout the trading day like other exchange-traded product shares. Additionally, they can be purchased on margin. Each of these features distinguishes them from mutual fund shares which use a forward pricing model and can not be purchased on margin.

Quick Quiz 10.B

1. **B.** The main functions of the custodian, usually a commercial bank, are to hold the fund's cash and assets for safekeeping and to perform related clerical duties. The custodian may also issue and redeem customer shares, send out customer confirmations, and hold customer shares.

2. **C.** Investment company financial statements must be sent to shareholders at least semiannually.

3. **C.** The underwriter markets the fund's shares. Choice A is the responsibility of the custodian, Choice B is the responsibility of the fund, and Choice D is the manager's responsibility.

4. **C.** The primary function of a mutual fund's custodian bank is to safeguard the physical assets of the fund, hold the cash and securities, and perform other purely clerical functions. It does not manage the portfolio or serve in a selling capacity for the fund.

5. **C.** Typically, the largest single expense for a mutual fund is the management fee—the fee paid to the management company for buying and selling securities and managing the portfolio. A typical annual fee is ½ of 1% of the portfolio's asset value.

Quick Quiz 10.C

1. **C.** The maximum sales load is 8½% only if the company offers rights of accumulation, breakpoints, and automatic reinvestment at NAV, not at POP.

2. **C.** The formula is sales cost divided by public offering price. The sales cost is the difference between NAV and POP, or $1.44 per share ($1.44 ÷ $18 = 8%).

3. **D.** No-load funds are redeemed at NAV.

4. **A.** To find the dollar amount of the sales charge when the NAV and the sales charge percentage are provided, calculate the complement of the sales charge by subtracting the sales charge from 100% (100% − 8% = 92%). Then divide the NAV by complement of the sales charge to find the offering price ($7.82 ÷ .92 = $8.50, the offering price). The dollar amount of the sales charge is the offering price minus the NAV ($8.50 − $7.82 = $.68, the sales charge).

5. **C.** The letter of intent may be backdated 90 days. The investor is not required by law to satisfy the letter of intent, although in the case of default, he will pay a higher sales charge.

6. **B.** Breakpoint advantages are available only to individuals. An investment club is not considered an individual, but trusts and corporations are.

Quick Quiz 10.D

1. **B.** Dollar cost averaging benefits the investor if the same amount is invested on a regular basis over a substantial period, during which the price of the stock fluctuates. A constant dollar plan is one in which the investor maintains a constant dollar value of securities in the investment portfolio.

2. **B.** Dollar cost averaging is available to both small and large investors.

3. **D.** Mutual fund withdrawal plans are not guaranteed. Because principal values fluctuate, investors may not have sufficient income for their entire lives.

4. **C.** If the investor receives $600 a month, the dollar amount of the withdrawal is fixed; therefore, this must be a fixed-dollar plan.

Quick Quiz 10.E

1. **F.** An index fund trading on an exchange is priced intraday, just as all exchange trading products are.

2. **T.** Index fund shares trading on exchanges can be purchased on margin. This is one feature that makes them different from mutual funds.

3. **F.** Exchange-traded funds are priced by supply and demand throughout the trading day.

4. **F.** Hedge funds employ aggressive management using risky investment techniques making them unsuitable for all but the most sophisticated investors.

5. **T.** Inverse or reverse funds attempt to deliver returns opposite of a benchmark index. The portfolio is managed in such a way that it will gain when the index is down but lose when the index is up.

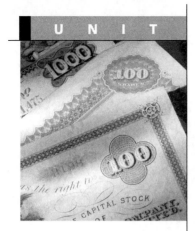

11

Retirement Plans

Providing income for retirement is one of the most important financial goals for many investors, but many regulations accompany the different retirement plan options. Qualified retirement plans allow employer contributions of tax-deductible dollars to an investment account. Contributions to nonqualified retirement plans are not tax deductible, but the income and gains generated by the investments in the plan are not taxed until funds are withdrawn.

Retirement plans may be established by individuals in an IRA; by a company on behalf of its employees through 401(k), SEP, or Keogh (HR-10) plans; or through tax-sheltered annuities. Corporate qualified retirement plans are either defined contribution or defined benefit plans. A defined contribution plan provides for a specific contribution amount and may permit employee contributions. A defined benefit plan provides a specific retirement benefit (based on a formula) for the participant, and the plan sponsor assumes the investment risk.

The Series 7 exam will ask approximately 5–10 questions on this topic, but most of these are concerned with fairly basic rules. ■

When you have completed this Unit, you should be able to:

- **compare** and contrast the features of qualified and nonqualified plans;

- **identify** eligibility and contribution rules for IRAs and Keogh plans;

- **identify** eligibility rules and requirements for tax-sheltered annuities;

- **describe** basic features of pension and profit-sharing plans;

- **list** penalties that affect retirement plan investors; and

- **understand** ERISA guidelines for the regulation of retirement plans.

11. 1   RETIREMENT PLANS

Retirement plans are categorized as **qualified** or **nonqualified**. Both plans allow tax-deferred growth on earnings attributable to plan contributions. But there are differences, one of which is whether the contributions made to the plan are tax deductible. Below is a comparison of the two plans' features.

Qualified Plans vs. Nonqualified Plans

Qualified Plans	Nonqualified Plans
Contributions tax deductible	Contributions not tax deductible
Plan approved by the IRS	Plan does not need IRS approval
Plan cannot discriminate	Plan can discriminate
Tax on accumulation is deferred	Tax on accumulation is deferred
All withdrawals taxed	Excess over cost base taxed
Plan is a trust	Plan is not a trust

11. 1. 1   RETIREMENT PLAN CONTRIBUTION LIMITS

As you proceed with studying the information in this Unit, you will learn many features of retirement plans, including contribution limits. Tax law changes and updates cause periodic changes to these limits, and it is our editorial policy to provide plan contribution limits for the current year and the next year if this information is available.

Although exam questions generally focus on features of retirement plans other than contribution limits, we suggest that you include a review of these limits in your preparation. You should always choose the answer choice that reflects current information if it is available.

11. 1. 2   NONQUALIFIED RETIREMENT PLANS

Deferred compensation and payroll deduction plans are two types of nonqualified retirement plans. Both plans may be used to favor certain employees (typically executives) because nondiscrimination rules are not applicable to nonqualified plans.

11. 1. 2. 1   Deferred Compensation Plans

A **nonqualified deferred compensation plan** is an agreement between a company and an employee in which the employee agrees to defer receipt of current income in favor of payout at retirement. It is assumed that the employee will be in a lower tax bracket at retirement age (persons affiliated with the company solely as board members are not eligible for these plans because they are not considered employees for retirement planning purposes).

Deferred compensation plans may be somewhat risky because the employee covered by the plan has no right to plan benefits if the business fails. In this situation, the employee becomes a general creditor of the firm. Covered employees may also forfeit benefits if they leave the firm before retirement.

When the benefit is payable at the employee's retirement, it is taxable as ordinary income to the employee. The employer is entitled to the tax deduction at the time the benefit is paid out.

11. 1. 2. 2 Payroll Deduction Plans

Payroll deduction plans allow employees to authorize their employer to deduct a specified amount for retirement savings from their paychecks. The money is deducted after taxes are paid and may be invested in any number of retirement vehicles at the employee's option.

TEST TOPIC ALERT   You might think of a 401(k) plan as a payroll deduction plan. For the FINRA exams, 401(k) plans are considered salary reduction plans, not payroll deduction plans. In exam questions, assume that payroll deduction plans are nonqualified. Also note that 401(k) plans are qualified plans, whereas payroll deduction plans are not.

---

11. 2   INDIVIDUAL RETIREMENT ACCOUNTS (IRAs)

Individual retirement accounts (IRAs) were created to encourage people to save for retirement in addition to any other retirement plans. Those with earned income are eligible to make annual contributions up to a specified percentage as determined by the IRS tax code or 100% of earned income, whichever is less.

TAKE NOTE   For individuals age 50 or older, a catch-up contribution is allowed in an amount as determined by the IRS tax code.

Earned income is defined as income from work, such as wages, salaries, bonuses, commissions, tips, and so forth. Income from investments is not considered earned income. If the contribution limit is exceeded, a 6% excess contribution penalty applies to the amount over the allowable portion.

11. 2. 1   CONTRIBUTIONS

An eligible individual may make contributions up to a maximum dollar amount that can change from year to year (as determined by the IRS tax code), provided that the contribution does not exceed earned income (normally compensation and income from self-employment) for the year. The dollar cap is increased by a catch-up amount for individuals age 50 and older.

Contributions to IRAs may or may not be tax deductible. Contributions are fully deductible, regardless of income, if the investor is ineligible to participate in any other qualified plan. If the investor is eligible to participate in a qualified plan, contributions are deductible (or partially deductible) if the taxpayer's AGI falls within established income guidelines.

How much of the annual contribution is deductible is determined by the IRS phase-out schedule tied to the individual's AGI. The allowable deductible amount gradually phases out from the low end of the phase-out scale until the high end of the scale, above which one's contribution would no longer be deductible at all. Consider, however, that while the phase-out schedule may not allow a high-earning individual to take a tax deduction for an IRA contribution, they may still make a contribution.

Individuals with nonworking spouses are allowed to contribute twice the allowable maximum contribution split between two accounts. This benefit is known as the **spousal IRA** and is only available to couples filing joint tax returns.

Contributions to IRAs must be made by April 15 of the year following the tax year. Individuals may contribute until age 70½, provided they have earned income.

TEST TOPIC ALERT   Current IRA contribution limits and catch-up contribution limits for those age 50 and older may be tested. These limits may change, sometimes annually. Current contribution limits can be found on www.irs.gov/retirement-plans.

TAKE NOTE   FDIC insurance on retirement accounts held at banks is $250,000.

11. 2. 1. 1 Ineligible Funding and Practices

Certain investments are not permitted for funding IRAs. Collectibles, such as antiques, gems, rare coins, works of art, and stamps, are not acceptable. Life insurance contracts cannot be purchased within an IRA. Municipal bonds are considered inappropriate because of their low yields and tax-exempt status. Why buy tax-free interest income that will be fully taxable on withdrawal?

Certain investment practices are also considered inappropriate. No short sales of stock, speculative option strategies, or margin account trading are permitted within IRAs or any other retirement plan. However, covered call writing is permissible because it does not increase risk.

Ineligible Investments and Ineligible Investment Practices

Ineligible Investments	Ineligible Investment Practices
Collectibles	Short sales of stock
Life insurance	Speculative option strategies
	Margin account trading

TAKE NOTE   Although life insurance is not allowed within IRAs, other life insurance company products (like annuities) are. Annuities are frequently used as funding vehicles for IRAs. Following is a partial list of investments appropriate for IRAs:

- Stocks

- Bonds

- Mutual funds

- UITs

- Government securities

- U.S. government-issued gold and silver coins

- Annuities

11. 2. 2 DISTRIBUTIONS

Distributions may begin without penalty after age 59½ and must begin by April 1 of the year after the individual turns 70½. Distributions before age 59½ are subject to a 10% penalty as well as regular income tax, except in the event of:

- death;
- disability;
- first-time homebuyer for purchase of a principal residence;
- education expenses for the taxpayer, spouse, child, or grandchild;
- medical premiums for unemployed individuals; and
- medical expenses in excess of defined adjusted gross income (AGI) limits.

If distributions do not begin by April 1 of the year after the individual turns 70½, a 50% **insufficient distribution penalty** applies. It is applicable to the amount that should have been withdrawn on the basis of IRS life expectancy tables. These are known as the IRA holder's annual "required minimum distribution" (RMD) and "required beginning date" (RBD). Ordinary income taxes also apply to the full amount.

11. 2. 3 ROLLOVERS AND TRANSFERS

Individuals may move their investments from one IRA to another IRA or from a qualified plan to an IRA. These movements are known as rollovers or transfers.

11. 2. 3. 1 IRA Rollovers

Individuals may take possession of the funds and investments in a qualified plan to move them to another qualified plan but may do so not more than once a year. Such a **rollover** into another account must be completed within 60 calendar days of withdrawal.

EXAMPLE   If an individual changes employers, the amount in her pension plan may be
distributed to her in a lump-sum payment. She may then deposit the distribution in an
IRA rollover account, where the amount deposited retains its tax-deferred status.

If an individual receives a distribution of assets from an employer-sponsored qualified plan, the payor of the distribution must retain 20% of the distribution as a **withholding tax**. The option to forgo withholding is not available to the participant. This 20% withholding tax does not apply to rollovers made from individual IRAs. If the individual elects a **direct transfer**, there is no withholding on the amount directly transferred.

11. 2. 3. 2 Transfers

IRA assets may be directly transferred from an IRA or qualified plan. A **transfer** occurs when the account assets are sent directly from one custodian to another, and the account owner never takes possession of the funds. There is no limit on the number of transfers that may be made during a 12-month period.

11. 2. 3. 3 Health Savings Account One Time Funding Distribution

Health Savings Accounts are qualified employer sponsored plans that allow before-tax contributions to a savings account to be used for medical expenses. The IRS allows a one-time funding distribution from an individual retirement account (IRA) to a qualified HSA without paying federal income taxes or penalties on the IRA distribution.

11. 2. 4 ROTH IRA

Roth IRAs allow after-tax contributions up to a maximum annual allowable limit per individual per year. Contributions to other IRAs when combined with contributions to a Roth may not exceed the maximum annual allowable limit.

Contributions to Roth IRAs are not deductible on one's tax return. Therefore, there is no phase-out schedule regarding a contribution being deductible as there is with a traditional IRA. However, there is a phase-out schedule regarding the contribution that can be made to a Roth IRA, and again the schedule is tied to an individual's AGI. The contribution limit is phased out from the low end of the phase-out scale until the high end, above which no contribution to a Roth IRA would be allowed.

Earnings are not taxed as they accrue or when they are distributed from an account as long as the money has been in an account for five taxable years and the IRA owner has reached age 59½.

Required minimum distributions at age 70½ do not apply to Roth IRAs. The 10% penalty for distributions before age 59½ is waived for first-time homebuyers if they use the funds to purchase a principal residence.

11. 2. 4. 1 Conversions and Re-Characterization

The IRS, during specified periods of time, has allowed investors to convert one type of IRA to another. In addition, the IRS has allowed, under current tax code, investors the opportunity to treat a contribution allocated to one type of IRA as if it had been made to a different type of IRA. It is known as re-characterizing the contribution.

The most common case of re-characterization is when a traditional IRA has been converted into a Roth IRA, and the participant wishes to go back to the traditional IRA instead of remaining in the Roth. This would be accomplished by having the contribution transferred from the Roth IRA back to the traditional IRA in a trustee-to-trustee transfer. If the transfer is made by the due date (including extensions) for the individual's tax return for the year during which the contribution is made, the individual can treat the original conversion as if it never happened.

There are several reasons why an individual might choose to re-characterize their contributions, but here are two of the most common:

- Exceeding the earnings limitation on contributing to a Roth IRA. Example: A Roth contribution might have been made early in the year. Due to larger than expected earnings by year end, the investor's adjusted gross income exceeds the allowable limit. Re-characterization is a way to "undo" the Roth IRA contribution and put the money into a traditional IRA.

- A significant decrease in the value of the account since the original conversion. Example: A conversion of $100,000 in a traditional IRA to a Roth IRA takes place. The investor has until April 15, or any available extension time for filing, to decide what to do. If on that date, the value of the Roth is less than the original amount converted, the investor will still owe ordinary income taxes on the $100,000 converted. But, if the individual were to re-characterize the entire account (worth less than the amount originally converted), the funds would be back in a traditional IRA, and no taxes would be due until the money is withdrawn.

Be aware of the rules regarding conversions and re-characterizations. You cannot convert and reconvert an amount during the same tax year or, if later, during the 30-day period following a re-characterization. If you reconvert during either of these periods, it will be a failed conversion.

11. 2. 5   EDUCATION SAVINGS ACCOUNTS

Just as there are tax-advantaged savings plans for retirement, there are also such plans for education.

11. 2. 5. 1   Coverdell (Education IRA)

Coverdell Education IRAs allow after-tax contributions of up to $2,000 per student per year for children younger than age 18. Contribution limits may be reduced or eliminated for higher-income tax payers. Distributions are tax free as long as the funds are used for qualified education expenses. These expenses include those for college, secondary, or elementary school. If a student's account is not depleted by age 30, the funds must be distributed to the individual subject to income tax and 10% penalty or rolled into an education IRA for another family member beneficiary.

11. 2. 5. 2   Section 529 Plans

There are two basic types of 529 plans: prepaid tuition plans for state residents and college savings plans for residents and nonresidents. Prepaid plans allow resident donors to lock in current tuition rates by paying now for future education costs. The more popular option is the college savings plan, which allows donors to save money to be used later for college tuition.

Any adult can open a 529 plan for a future college student. The donor does not have to be related to the student. With a 529 plan, the donor can invest a lump sum or make periodic payments. When the student is ready for college, the donor withdraws the amount needed to pay for qualified education expenses (e.g., tuition, room and board, and books).

Contributions, which are considered gifts under federal tax law, are made with after-tax dollars, and earnings accumulate on a tax-deferred basis. Withdrawals are tax free at the federal level if they are used for qualified education expenses. Most states permit tax-free withdrawals as long as the donor has opened an in-state plan. In addition, many states allow contributions into in-state plans to be tax deductible. Therefore, if one of your customers wishes to open an out-of-state plan, you must advise the customer that certain tax advantages may not be available.

Other relevant points regarding Section 529 plans are as follows.

■   Overall contribution levels vary from state to state but generally allow greater contributions than Coverdell plans.

■   Assets in the account remain under the donor's control even after the student becomes of legal age.

■   There are no income limitations on making contributions to a 529 plan.

- Plans allow for monthly payments if desired by the account owner.
- Account balances may be transferred to a related beneficiary.
- A rollover from one state's plan to another state's plan is permitted no more than once every twelve months.

11. 2. 6   SIMPLIFIED EMPLOYEE PENSIONS (SEP IRAs)

Simplified employee pension plans (SEPs) are qualified individual retirement plans that offer self-employed persons and small businesses easy-to-administer pension plans. SEPs allow an employer to contribute money to SEP IRAs that its employees set up to receive employer contributions.

Self-employed individuals may contribute up to a maximum amount each year to a SEP IRA for themselves or employees. Catch-up contributions are generally not allowed for the self-employed person. However, if an employee is enrolled in a SEP and the SEP permits non SEP-IRA contributions be made to the SEP account, they may also make additional catch-up contributions to the SEP account if they are age 50 or older.

Generally, an employer can take an income tax deduction for contributions made each year to each employee's SEP. Also, the amounts contributed to a SEP by an employer on behalf of an employee are excludable from the employee's gross income.

QUICK QUIZ 11.A

1. An individual less than age 70½ may contribute to an IRA
   A. if he has earned income
   B. provided he is not covered by a pension plan through an employer
   C. provided he does not own a Keogh plan
   D. provided his income is between $40,000 and $50,000 if married and $25,000 and $35,000 if single

2. A 50-year-old wants to withdraw funds from her IRA. The withdrawal will be taxed as
   A. ordinary income
   B. ordinary income plus a 10% penalty
   C. capital gains
   D. capital gains plus a 10% penalty

3. Premature distribution from an IRA is subject to
   A. a 5% penalty plus tax
   B. a 6% penalty plus tax
   C. a 10% penalty plus tax
   D. a 50% penalty plus tax

4. Which of the following will not incur a penalty on an IRA withdrawal?

    A. Man who has just become totally disabled
    B. Woman who turned 59 a month before the withdrawal
    C. Woman, age 50, who decides on early retirement
    D. Man in his early 40s who uses the money to buy a second home

5. Which of the following statements regarding IRAs is NOT true?

    A. IRA rollovers must be completed within 60 days of receipt of the distribution.
    B. Cash-value life insurance is a permissible IRA investment, but term insurance is not.
    C. The investor must be under age 70½ to open and contribute to an IRA.
    D. Distributions may begin at age 59½ and must begin by the year after the year in which the investor turns 70½.

6. Which of the following statements regarding SEP IRAs is TRUE?

    A. They are used primarily by large corporations.
    B. They are used primarily by small businesses.
    C. Annual contributions are unlimited.
    D. They cannot be set up by self-employed persons.

7. Which of the following statements regarding traditional IRAs and Roth IRAs is TRUE?

    A. Contributions are deductible.
    B. Withdrawals at retirement are tax free.
    C. Earnings on investments are not taxed immediately.
    D. To avoid penalty, distributions must begin the year after the year the owner reaches age 70½.

8. The maximum amount that may be invested in an education IRA in 1 year is

    A. $500 per parent
    B. $2,000 per child
    C. $500 per couple
    D. $2,000 per couple

Quick Quiz answers can be found at the end of the Unit.

11. 3   KEOGH (HR-10) PLANS

Keogh plans, also known as **HR-10 plans**, are qualified plans intended for self-employed persons and owner-employees of unincorporated businesses or professional practices. Self employed individuals who want to establish such a plan would most likely now ask about defined benefit or defined contribution plans for the self employed. While the term Keogh is rarely used by financial institutions currently we must acknowledge that plans originally set up as Keogh plans still exist.

11. 3. 1 CONTRIBUTIONS

The planholder is permitted to make tax-deductible cash contributions each year up to a maximum amount. The plans can be set up as either defined-contribution plans or defined-benefit plans. With a defined-contribution plan, a contribution up to 25% of taxable income after the contribution is made is allowed. With a defined-benefit plan, contributions must be calibrated to ensure that the plan will be able to provide the benefit. This would generally require an actuary. As with IRAs, a person may make contributions until age 70.

In addition, employers must make contributions into the plans of eligible employees. The contribution rate for eligible employees can be complicated. To simplify, a high-income employer making the maximum contribution to his own plan must contribute to the Keogh of an eligible employee at a rate of 25%.

EXAMPLE   A self-employed writer earns $300,000 per year and makes the maximum contribution into his Keogh. If the writer has a full-time editor earning $50,000 per year, the writer will have to contribute $12,500 (25% of $50,000) to the editor's Keogh. The writer gets a tax deduction for the contribution.

Employees are eligible if they:

- have worked at least 1,000 hours in the year;
- have completed one or more years of continuous employment; and
- are at least 21 years of age.

Differences Between Keogh Plans and IRAs

Characteristic	Keogh Plans	IRAs
Source of contributions	Employer; employee may also make nondeductible contributions	Employee
Permissible investments	Most equity and debt securities, U.S. government-minted precious metal coins, annuities, cash-value life insurance	Most equity and debt securities, U.S. government-minted precious metal coins, annuities
Nonpermissible investments	Term insurance, collectibles	Term insurance, collectibles, cash-value life insurance
Change of employer	Lump-sum distribution may be rolled over into an IRA within 60 days	Does not apply
Penalty for excess contribution	10% penalty	6% penalty
Taxation of distributions	Taxed as ordinary income	Taxed as ordinary income

11. 4   TAX-SHELTERED ANNUITIES (403(b) PLANS)

Tax-sheltered annuities (TSAs) are available to employees of:

■ public educational institutions;

■ tax-exempt organizations (501(c)(3) organizations); and

■ religious organizations.

In general, the clergy and employees of charitable institutions, private hospitals, colleges and universities, elementary and secondary schools, and zoos and museums are eligible to participate if they are at least 21 years old and have completed one year of service.

TSAs are funded by elective employee deferrals. The deferred amount is excluded from the employee's gross income, and earnings accumulate tax free until distribution. A written salary reduction agreement must be executed between the employer and the employee.

As with other qualified plans, distributions are 100% taxable, and a 10% penalty is applied to distributions before age 59½.

TEST TOPIC ALERT   You might see a question that asks if a student can be a participant in an educational institution's TSA. The answer is no because the plan is only available to employees.

11. 5   CORPORATE RETIREMENT PLANS

Corporate pension plans fall into one of two categories: defined benefit or defined contribution.

11. 5. 1 DEFINED BENEFIT PLAN

A **defined benefit plan** promises a specific benefit at retirement determined by a formula involving retirement age, years of service, and compensation. The amount of the contribution must be determined by actuarial calculation because it involves complex assumptions about investment returns, future interest rates, and other matters. This type of plan may be used by firms who wish to favor older key employees because a much greater amount may be contributed for those with only a short time until retirement.

11. 5. 1. 1. 1 Unfunded Pension Liability

A **pension liability** is a legal obligation to pay retirement benefits to future retirees. An **unfunded pension liability** is one where adequate reserves have not been set aside to meet this future obligation. Governmental units such as cities and towns as well as corporations may be affected. Although pension plans may be either defined benefit or defined contribution, an unfunded liability will generally arise in defined benefit plans, which require the use of an actuary to determine the necessary contribution levels needed today to meet tomorrow's liability. Poor investment performance of the monies set aside today can lead to an unfunded liability.

11. 5. 2 DEFINED CONTRIBUTION PLAN

Defined contribution plans are much easier to administer. The contribution amount is specified by the plan (trust agreement); however, the benefit that will be paid at retirement is unknown. A typical defined contribution formula might be expressed as a percentage of income.

11. 5. 2. 1 Profit Sharing

Profit-sharing plans are a popular form of defined contribution plan. These plans do not require a fixed contribution formula and allow contributions to be skipped during years of low profits. Their flexibility and ease of administration has made them a popular retirement plan option for employers.

11. 5. 2. 2 Savings Incentive Match Plans for Employees (SIMPLEs)

These are retirement plans for businesses with fewer than 100 employees that have no other retirement plan in place. The employee makes pretax contributions into a SIMPLE up to an annual contribution limit. The employer makes matching contributions. Matching contribution requirements and limits for employers are specified by the IRS and include catch-up contributions for those age 50 and older.

11. 5. 2. 3 401(k) Plans

401(k) plans, also known as **thrift plans**, are a type of defined contribution plan that allows an employee to elect to contribute a percentage of salary up to a maximum dollar limit to a retirement account. Catch-up contributions for those age 50 and older are also allowed. Contributions are excluded from the employee's gross income and accumulate tax deferred. Employers are permitted to make matching contributions up to a specified percentage of the employee's contributions. In addition, 401(k) plans permit hardship withdrawals.

11. 5. 2. 3. 1 Self-Employed 401(k) Plan

A self-employed 401(k) plan can be set up by a business with no full-time employees—only the owner(s), spouse(s), and part-time employees. Such plans offer higher contribution limits than other plans, greater flexibility as to when and how often contributions will be made, and penalty-free loans from the plan's funding, provided the loan is paid back on time. The business can be a sole proprietorship, a partnership, or a C corporation, S corporation, or limited liability company.

TEST TOPIC ALERT   All corporate retirement plan administrators have fiduciary responsibility. Risk must be the first consideration in investment of plan assets. Short sales, uncovered options, and margin account transactions are not suitable within corporate retirement plans.

11. 6 THE EMPLOYEE RETIREMENT INCOME SECURITY ACT OF 1974 (ERISA)

ERISA was established to prevent abuse and misuse of pension funds. ERISA guidelines apply to private sector (corporate) retirement plans and certain union plans—not public plans like those for government workers.

Significant ERISA provisions include the following.

■ **Participation**—ERISA identifies eligibility rules for employees and states that all employees must be covered if they are 21 years or older and have performed one year of full-time service (which ERISA defines as 1,000 hours).

■ **Funding**—ERISA requires that funds contributed to the plan be segregated from other corporate assets. Plan trustees have the responsibility to administer and invest the assets prudently and in the best interest of all participants. IRS contribution limits must be observed.

■ **Vesting**—Employees are entitled to their entire retirement benefit within a certain number of years of service, even if they leave the company.

■ **Communication**—The plan document must be in writing, and employees must be given annual statements of account and updates of plan benefits.

■ **Nondiscrimination**—All eligible employees must be impartially treated through a uniformly applied formula.

■ **Beneficiaries**—Beneficiaries must be named to receive an employee's benefits at his death.

QUICK QUIZ 11.B

1. Regulations regarding how contributions are made to tax-qualified plans relate to which of the following ERISA requirements?

   A. Vesting
   B. Funding
   C. Nondiscrimination
   D. Reporting and disclosure

2. Which of the following determines the amount paid into a defined contribution plan?

   A. ERISA-defined contribution requirements
   B. Trust agreement
   C. Employer's age
   D. Employee's retirement age

3. Your customer works as a nurse in a public school. He wants to know more about participating in the school's TSA plan. Which of the following statements are TRUE?

   I. Contributions are made with before-tax dollars.
   II. He is not eligible to participate.
   III. Distributions before age 59½ are normally subject to penalty tax.
   IV. Mutual funds and CDs are available investment vehicles.

   A. I and II
   B. I and III
   C. I, III and IV
   D. II and III

4. Which of the following statements regarding a defined benefit plan is TRUE?

    A. All employees receive the same benefits at retirement.
    B. All participating employees are immediately vested.
    C. High-income employees near retirement may receive much larger contributions than younger employees with the same salary.
    D. The same amount must be contributed for each eligible employee.

5. The requirements of ERISA apply to pension plans established by

    A. U.S. government workers
    B. only public entities, such as the City of New York
    C. only private organizations, such as Exxon
    D. both public and private organizations

UNIT TEST

1. Distribution from a traditional IRA may begin at age 59½ and must begin no later than

   A. age 65
   B. age 68
   C. age 70½
   D. 15 years from the individual's date of retirement

2. ERISA regulations cover

   I. public sector retirement plans
   II. private sector retirement plans
   III. federal government employee retirement plans

   A. I and II
   B. II only
   C. II and III
   D. I, II and III

3. Which of the following plans requires an actuary's services?

   A. Profit-sharing
   B. Defined benefit
   C. Defined contribution
   D. 401(k)

4. The amount paid into a defined contribution plan is set by the

   A. ERISA-defined contribution requirements
   B. trust agreement
   C. employer's age
   D. employer's profits

5. Which of the following is not eligible to open a Keogh but is eligible to open an IRA?

   A. College professor who makes $10,000 on the sale of a book and several articles
   B. Corporate officer who earns $40,000 plus an additional $10,000 as a part-time speaker
   C. Doctor who receives $10,000 from a restaurant he owns
   D. Corporate officer who receives a $5,000 bonus

6. A self-employed attorney has an income of $110,000 per year. He has no other retirement plans and makes the maximum allowable contribution to his IRA. His contribution is

   A. fully tax deductible
   B. partially tax deductible
   C. not tax deductible
   D. not permitted

7. Which of the following securities is the least suitable recommendation for a qualified plan?

   A. Blue-chip common stock
   B. Investment-grade municipal bond
   C. Treasury bill
   D. A rated corporate bond

8. Which of the following statements regarding Roth IRAs are TRUE?

   I. Contributions are made with pretax dollars.
   II. Earnings accumulate tax free.
   III. Distributions are not taxable if a holding period is satisfied.
   IV. Only cost basis is taxable at the time of distribution.

   A. I and II
   B. I and III
   C. II and III
   D. II and IV

9. Which of the following individuals would NOT be permitted to open an IRA?

   A. An individual whose sole income consists of dividends and capital gains
   B. A divorced mother whose sole income is alimony and child support
   C. A self-employed attorney who has a Keogh plan
   D. A corporate officer covered by a 401(k) plan

10. Payments received by the owner of a 403(b) plan are

    A. 100% taxable
    B. taxable only to extent of earnings
    C. taxable only to extent of the owner's cost basis
    D. not taxable

ANSWERS AND RATIONALES

1. **C.** As a result of the Tax Reform Act of 1986, the owner of a traditional IRA or a Keogh retirement plan has until April 1 of the year after the year in which he turns 70½ to begin withdrawing from the account.

2. **B.** ERISA regulations pertain only to corporate and certain union-sponsored pension plans, which are retirement plans for the private sector.

3. **B.** In a defined benefit plan, the payout is established, and employers must contribute annually to ensure payment of the benefit amount. An actuary must calculate the annual contribution amount necessary to meet the benefit requirement.

4. **B.** A defined contribution plan's trust agreement contains a section explaining the formula(s) used to determine the contributions to the retirement plan.

5. **D.** Anyone with earned income can open an IRA; the tax deductibility of a person's contributions depends on eligibility to participate in an employer-sponsored qualified retirement plan and on the person's income. Each of the listed individuals had income earned from self-employment, and therefore could open a Keogh plan, except for the corporate officer receiving a bonus.

6. **A.** IRA contributions are fully deductible, regardless of income, if the taxpayer is not covered by any other qualified plans.

7. **B.** Municipal bonds provide tax-exempt interest payments and, consequently, offer lower yields. Because earnings in a qualified retirement plan account grow tax deferred, the lower-yielding municipal bond is not a suitable investment. In addition, they will be fully taxed on withdrawal.

8. **C.** Contributions to Roth IRAs are made with after-tax dollars, and distributions are received tax free (both cost basis and earnings) if holding period requirements are met.

9. **A.** An IRA contribution may be made only from earned income. Dividends and interest are investment income, but alimony is considered earned income. Individuals may contribute to an IRA even if they are already covered by a corporate pension plan or Keogh plan. However, although a contribution can be made, it may or may not be deductible, depending on the individual's income.

10. **A.** When TSA funds are withdrawn, they are fully taxed at ordinary income rates. Funds were contributed pretax, and earnings accumulate tax deferred. Because no taxes were ever paid, the full withdrawal is taxable.

QUICK QUIZ ANSWERS

Quick Quiz 11.A

1. **A.** Any individual under age 70½ with earned income may contribute to an IRA. The deductibility of those contributions will be determined by that person's coverage under other qualified plans and by his level of income.

2. **B.** All withdrawals from IRAs are taxed at the individual's ordinary income tax rate at the time of withdrawal. Distributions taken before age 59½ will incur an additional 10% penalty.

3. **C.** The penalty for premature withdrawals from an IRA or a Keogh account is 10%.

4. **A.** Early withdrawals, without penalty, are permitted only for death or disability.

5. **B.** Cash-value life insurance, term insurance, and collectibles are not permissible investments in an IRA.

6. **B.** Small businesses and self-employed persons typically establish SEP IRAs because they are much easier and less expensive than other plans for an employer to set up and administer.

7. **C.** The common factor for both traditional and Roth IRAs is that investment earnings are not taxed when earned. Traditional IRAs offer tax-deductible contributions, but withdrawals are taxed. Roth IRAs do not offer tax-deductible contributions, but qualified withdrawals are tax free. Traditional IRAs require distributions to begin in the year after the year an owner reaches age 70½, but this is not true for Roth IRAs.

8. **B.** Only $2,000 may be invested in each child's education IRA every year. If a couple has 3 children, they may contribute $6,000 in total, or $2,000 for each child.

Quick Quiz 11.B

1. **B.** Funding covers how an employer contributes to or funds a plan. Vesting describes how quickly rights to a retirement account turn over to the employee. Nondiscrimination refers to broad employee coverage by a plan. All retirement plans must meet ERISA's reporting and disclosure requirements.

2. **B.** The retirement plan's trust agreement contains a section explaining the formula(s) used to determine the contributions to a defined contribution plan.

3. **C.** Because he is employed by a public school system, your customer is eligible to participate in the tax-sheltered annuity plan. Employee contributions to a TSA plan are excluded from gross income during the year when they are made. As other retirement plans, a penalty tax is assessed on distributions received before age 59½. Mutual funds, CDs, and annuity contracts are among the investment choices available for TSA plans.

4. **C.** The rules regarding the maximum amount of contributions differ for defined contribution plans and defined benefit plans. Defined benefit plans set the amount of retirement benefits that a retiree receives as a percentage of the previous several years' salaries. For the highly paid individual nearing retirement, the defined benefit plan allows a larger contribution in a shorter time. Choice D describes a defined contribution plan rather than a defined benefit plan.

5. **C.** ERISA was established to protect the retirement funds of employees working in the private sector only. It does not apply to self-employed persons or public organizations.

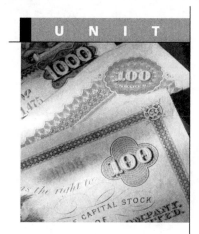

12

Variable Annuities

Variable annuities have become a very popular retirement planning product. Tax-deferred growth and lifetime payout options are among the factors that make variable annuities very popular with investors.

A variable annuity is a contract with an insurance company, with many similarities to a mutual fund. Annuities and mutual funds are subject to many of the same regulations. Like any retirement account, an annuity is most often used to accumulate funds for retirement. Taxes on income and capital gains are deferred until the funds are withdrawn. Unlike a qualified retirement account, however, an annuity does not restrict the amount of funds that may be invested, and the funds invested are not tax deductible.

The Series 7 exam is likely to ask 5–10 questions on this topic. ■

When you have completed this Unit, you should be able to:

- **list** the similarities between variable annuities and mutual funds;

- **identify** the unique features and guarantees associated with variable annuities;

- **describe** the phases of the annuity contract;

- **determine** fluctuations in monthly payouts based on comparison of the assumed interest rate (AIR) and separate account rate of return;

- **calculate** the taxation of withdrawals;

- **compare** and contrast various payout options; and

- **explain** the risks associated with ownership of variable annuities.

12. 1   TYPES OF ANNUITY CONTRACTS

An **annuity** is a life insurance company product designed to provide supplemental retirement income. The term *annuity* specifically refers to a stream of income payments guaranteed for life. This product is unique from other securities products that have been discussed because of the guarantee it offers.

Life insurance companies offer two basic annuity products: fixed annuities and variable annuities. Both products require that the purchaser make deposits to the insurance company, either in a lump sum or over time, and then at some point begin to withdraw the funds. Although designed to provide monthly income for the life of the annuitant, withdrawals are frequently taken in lump sums or random withdrawals.

12. 1. 1   FIXED ANNUITY

In a **fixed annuity**, investors pay premiums to the insurance company that are invested in the company's general account. The insurance company is then obligated to pay a guaranteed amount of payout (typically monthly) to the annuitant based on how much was paid in.

The insurer guarantees a rate of return and as such bears the investment risk. Because the insurer is at risk, this product is not a security; an insurance license (but not a securities registration) is required to sell fixed annuities.

A significant risk is associated with fixed annuities: **purchasing power risk**. The fixed payment that the annuitant receives loses buying power over time as a result of inflation.

EXAMPLE

To understand the risk of a fixed annuity, consider the following.

An individual who purchased a fixed annuity in 1980 began to receive monthly income of $3,100 in 2000. Years later, this amount, which seemed a sufficient monthly income in 2000, is no longer enough income to live on.

Fixed Annuity

---

12. 1. 2   VARIABLE ANNUITY

Insurance companies introduced the **variable annuity** as an opportunity to keep pace with inflation. For this potential advantage, the investor, rather than the insurance company, assumes the investment risk. Because the investor takes on this risk, the product is considered a security. It must be sold with a prospectus and may be sold only by individuals who are both insurance licensed and securities licensed.

Variable Annuity

Fixed vs. Variable Annuity

Fixed Annuity	Variable Annuity
Payments made with after-tax dollars	Payments made with after-tax dollars
Payments are invested in the general account	Payments are invested in the separate account
Portfolio of fixed-income securities/real estate	Portfolio of equity, debt, or mutual funds
Insurer assumes investment risk	Annuitant assumes investment risk
Not a security	Is a security
Guaranteed rate of return	Return depends on separate account performance
Fixed administrative expenses	Fixed administrative expenses
Income guaranteed for life	Income guaranteed for life
Monthly payment never falls below guaranteed minimum	Monthly payments may fluctuate up or down
Purchasing power risk	Typically protects against purchasing power risk
Subject to insurance regulation	Subject to registration with the state insurance commission and the securities exchange commission (SEC)

12. 1. 2. 1. 1   Separate Account

As with a fixed annuity, the purchaser makes payments to the insurer. However, the premium payments for variable annuities are invested in the **separate account** of the insurer. This account is separated from the general funds of the insurer because it is invested differently. Investments include common stock, bonds, and mutual funds, with the objective of achieving growth that will match or exceed the rate of inflation.

Although annuitants are guaranteed monthly income for life, the amount of monthly income received is dependent on the performance of the separate account. Monthly income either increases or decreases, as determined by the separate account's performance.

Investing Variable Annuity Premium Dollars

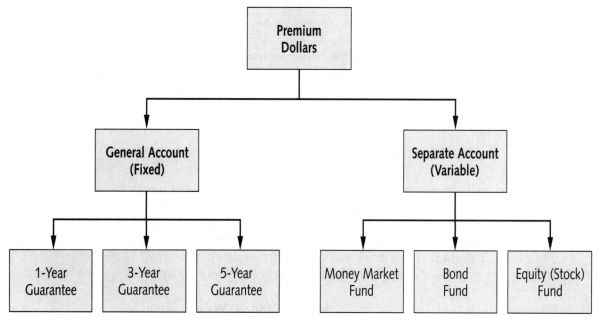

12. 1. 2. 1. 2 *Death Benefit Provision*

If an annuitant dies during the accumulation period, most contracts call for a death benefit to be paid to the variable annuitant's beneficiary in an amount equal to the total of all the investments made plus any earnings that have accrued. If the separate account has lost money, the annuitant's beneficiary is guaranteed the return of the total invested money at a minimum. Upon the death of the annuitant, the beneficiary will be liable for the ordinary income taxes on the earnings received just as if the annuitant had surrendered the annuity during the accumulation period. Finally, there is no penalty for early withdrawal even if the beneficiary is younger than age 59½.

12. 1. 3 COMBINATION ANNUITY

Investors may purchase a **combination annuity** to receive the advantages of both the fixed and variable annuities. In a combination annuity, the investor contributes to both the general and separate accounts, which provides for guaranteed payments as well as inflation protection.

12. 1. 4 SIMILARITY OF VARIABLE ANNUITIES TO MUTUAL FUNDS

12. 1. 4. 1 Separate Account

As described previously, the separate account of the variable annuity consists of the purchasers' funds pooled together and invested in a diversified portfolio of stocks, bonds, and mutual funds. Investors own a proportionate share of these securities, and the value of their investment rises and falls based on the performance of the securities in the pool. This is precisely how mutual funds perform: the separate account of a variable annuity is operated and regulated just like a mutual fund.

TAKE NOTE

Variable universal life policies are also insurance company products that have a separate account. The investor assumes the investment risk of the separate account. Because of the investment risk associated with them, they can only be sold by those with both a securities and life insurance license. It is important to remember that these products should only be represented as insurance products and not as investments and should be purchased primarily for the insurance feature of the contract.

12. 1. 4. 2 Management and Registration

If the investment manager of an insurance company is responsible for selecting the securities to be held within the separate account, the separate account is directly managed and must be registered under the Investment Company Act of 1940 as an open-end management investment company. However, if the investment manager of the insurance company passes the portfolio management responsibility to another party, the separate account is indirectly managed and must be registered as a unit investment trust under the Act of 1940.

Mutual Fund vs. Variable Annuity

	Mutual Fund	**Variable Annuity**
Sales load:	8½% maximum	No maximum
Pricing:	NAV calculated once per business day	Unit value calculated once per business day
Share value:	Depends on performance of fund	Depends on performance of securities held in the separate account
Regulated by:	Act of 1933	Act of 1933
	Act of 1934	Act of 1934
	Investment Company Act of 1940	Investment Company Act of 1940
	Investment Advisers Act of 1940	Investment Advisers Act of 1940
	(Portfolio manager receives fee)	(Separate account manager receives fee)
Voting rights:	Shareholders may vote for changes in investment policy and investment adviser	Investors may vote for changes in investment policy and investment adviser

Although there are many similarities between mutual funds and variable annuities, there are two extremely significant features that differentiate these products.

■ **The earnings on dollars invested into a variable annuity accumulate tax deferred.** Mutual funds periodically distribute dividends and capital gains, and all of these distributions are taxable upon receipt or reinvestment. Such distributions are never paid directly to owners of annuities; instead, they increase the value of units in the separate account. Tax liability is postponed until withdrawals take place. This feature of tax-deferred growth has established the annuity as a popular product for retirement accumulation. If withdrawals are made before age 59½, a 10% penalty is applied to the earnings.

■ **Variable annuities offer the advantage of income guaranteed to some extent depending on how the contract is set up.** Mutual fund shareholders are offered no guarantees on income provided.

QUICK QUIZ 12.A

1. Which of the following represent rights of an investor who has purchased a variable annuity?

   I.   Right to vote on proposed changes in investment policy
   II. Right to approve changes in the plan portfolio
   III. Right to vote for the investment adviser
   IV. Right to make additional purchases at no sales charge

   A. I and III
   B. I and IV
   C. II and III
   D. II and IV

2. Which of the following statements are TRUE for both variable annuities and mutual funds?

   I.   They contain managed portfolios.
   II. An owner's account value typically passes to his estate at the time of his death.
   III. They are regulated by the Investment Company Act of 1940.
   IV. All investment income and realized capital gains are taxable to the owner in the year they are generated.

   A. I and III
   B. I and IV
   C. II and III
   D. II and IV

3. Which of the following has the greatest effect on the value of annuity units in a variable annuity?

   A. Changes in the Standard & Poor's index
   B. Changes in cost-of-living index
   C. Fluctuations in the securities held in the separate account
   D. Changes in stock market prices

4. A variable annuity contract guarantees

   I.   a rate of return
   II. a fixed mortality expense
   III. a fixed administrative expense

   A. I and II
   B. I and III
   C. II and III
   D. I, II and III

5. Separate accounts are similar to mutual funds in that both
   I. may have diversified portfolios of common stock
   II. are managed by full-time professionals
   III. give investors voting rights

   A. I and II
   B. I and III
   C. II and III
   D. I, II and III

Quick Quiz answers can be found at the end of the Unit.

12. 2   PURCHASING ANNUITIES

An investor is offered a number of options when purchasing an annuity. Payments to the insurance company may be made either with a single lump-sum investment or periodically on a monthly, quarterly, or annual basis.

■ A **single premium deferred annuity** is purchased with a lump sum, but payment of benefits is delayed until a later date selected by the annuitant.

■ A **periodic payment deferred annuity** allows investments over time. Payments of benefits on this type of annuity are always deferred until a later date selected by the annuitant.

■ An **immediate annuity** is purchased with a lump sum, and the payout of benefits usually commences within 30 days.

TEST TOPIC ALERT   There is no such thing as an immediate deferred annuity; deferred annuities have delayed payouts.

12. 2. 1 THE TWO PHASES OF VARIABLE ANNUITIES

The variable annuity has two distinct phases. The growth phase is its **accumulation phase**, whereas the payout phase is its **annuity phase**. A contract owner's interest in the separate account is known as either **accumulation units** or **annuity units,** depending on the contract phase. Both accumulation units and annuity units vary in value based on the separate account's performance.

At some point, the annuitant will begin to take income from the account. This is known as the **annuitization** of the contract. Technically, the value of the accumulation units is converted into a fixed number of annuity units. These annuity units are then liquidated to provide monthly income guaranteed for the life of the annuitant.

Annuitization

↓

Accumulation Phase	Annuity Phase
Accumulation Units	Annuity Units

TAKE NOTE

The value of both accumulation units and annuity units will vary based on the performance of the separate account. The number of accumulation units varies as additional investments purchase additional units. However, once the contract is annuitized, the number of annuity units received is fixed.

12. 3 RECEIVING DISTRIBUTION FROM ANNUITIES

An annuity offers several payment options for money accumulated in the separate account. The investor can withdraw the funds randomly, in a lump sum, or annuitize the contract (receive monthly income).

12. 3. 1 PAYOUT AND ASSUMED INTEREST RATE (AIR)

If **annuitization** is chosen, the actuarial department of the insurance company determines the initial value for the annuity units and the amount of the first month's annuity payment. At this time, an **assumed interest rate (AIR)** is established. The AIR is a conservative projection of the performance of the separate account over the estimated life of the contract. It is only relevant during the annuity phase of the contract.

The value of each annuity unit and the annuitant's subsequent monthly income will vary, depending on separate account performance, compared with the AIR. To determine whether the monthly income will increase, decrease, or stay the same as in the previous month, the following rules are applied.

- If separate account performance is greater than the AIR, the monthly income is more than the previous month's payment.

- If separate account performance is equal to the AIR, the monthly income stays the same as the previous month's payment.

- If separate account performance is less than the AIR, the monthly income is less than the previous month's payment.

TAKE NOTE

Review the following for mastery of the AIR concept.

Month 1: AIR of 4%. The actuaries have determined the first month's payment to be $1,000.

Month 2: Separate account performance is 8%. Does monthly income go up, go down, or stay the same?

It goes up. Remember, you must compare the 8% rate of the separate account with the AIR. Since 8% is greater than 4%, the payment increases. The amount of the increase is actuarially determined.

Month 3: Separate account performance drops to 6%. Does monthly income go up, go down, or stay the same?

Although you might be tempted to say "goes down," the payment still increases even though the separate account performance fell. The separate account return is greater than the 4% AIR.

Month 4: Separate account performance is 4%. What happens to monthly income?

According to the rules, when separate account performance equals the AIR, the monthly income does not change. The monthly income amount is the same as the previous month's.

Month 5: Separate account performance is 3%. What happens to monthly income?

It falls. When the separate account return is less than the AIR, the monthly income is lower than the previous month.

Month 6: Separate account performance is 3% again. What happens to monthly income?

Because the separate account return is less than the AIR, the monthly income decreases, even though the separate account performance did not change.

AIR/Separate Account Return/Effect on Income

	Month 2	Month 3	Month 4	Month 5	Month 6
AIR	4%	4%	4%	4%	4%
Separate Account Return	8%	6%	4%	3%	3%
Effect on Income	Up	Up	Equal to previous month	Down	Down

QUICK QUIZ 12.B

1. Your customer invests in a variable annuity. At age 65, she chooses to annuitize. Under these circumstances, which of the following are TRUE?

   I. She will receive the annuity's entire value in a lump-sum payment.
   II. She may choose to receive monthly payments for the rest of her life.
   III. The accumulation units' value is used to calculate the total number of annuity units.
   IV. The accumulation units' value is used to calculate the annuity unit's value.

   A. I and III
   B. I and IV
   C. II and III
   D. II and IV

2. An investor is in the annuity period of a variable annuity he purchased 15 years ago. During the present month, the annuitant receives a check for an amount less than the previous month's payment. Which of the following events caused the annuitant to receive the smaller check?

   A. Account performance was less than the previous month's performance.
   B. Account performance was greater than the previous month's performance.
   C. Account performance was less than the assumed interest rate.
   D. Account performance was greater than the assumed interest rate.

3. An insurance company offering a variable annuity makes payments to annuitants at the end of each month. The contract has an assumed interest rate of 3%. In July of this year, the contract earned 4%. In August, the account earned 6%. If the contract earns 3% in September, the payments to annuitants will be

   A. greater than the payments in August
   B. less than the payments in August
   C. the same as the payments in August
   D. less than the payments in July

12. 3. 2 PAYOUT OPTIONS

At the time of annuitization, the annuitant is required to select an annuity payout option. The choices that you must understand for Series 7 are:

- life income (also called life only or straight life);
- life with period certain; and
- joint life with last survivor.

12. 3. 2. 1 Life Income

If an annuitant selects the **life income (life-only annuity)** option, the insurance company will pay the annuitant for life. When the annuitant dies, there are no continuing payments to a beneficiary.

TEST TOPIC ALERT
Generally, this option will give the annuitant the largest monthly payment because all calculations are based on the payments ceasing upon the annuitant's death.

12. 3. 2. 2 Life with Period Certain

To guarantee that a minimum number of payments are made even if the annuitant dies, the **life with period certain** option may be chosen. The contract will specifically allow the choice of a period of 10 or 20 years, for example. The annuitant is guaranteed monthly income for life with this option, but if death occurs within the period certain, a named beneficiary receives payments for the remainder of the period.

EXAMPLE
A client selects a life annuity with a 10-year period certain. If the annuitant lives to be 100 years old, annuity payments are still made by the insurer. But, if the annuitant dies after receiving payments for two years, the beneficiary will receive payments for eight more years.

12. 3. 2. 3 Joint Life with Last Survivor

The **joint life with last survivor** option guarantees payments over two lives. It is often used for husbands and wives. If the husband were to die first, his spouse would continue to receive payments for as long as she lives. If the wife were to die first, her spouse would receive payments for as long as he lives.

12. 3. 2. 4 Contract Payout Specifications and Riders

Variable annuity contracts can be set up a number of ways regarding how the periodic payments will be made. Insurance company names for these different contract specifications can also differ from one issuer to the next. Here are some specifications to consider.

■ Guaranteed Minimum Withdrawal Benefits (GMWBs)—This benefit guarantees a regular periodic payment (monthly, quarterly, or annually) but only until the insurance company has paid back the annuitant an amount equal to the principal account value, or until the end of the contract term. Therefore, it should be noted that a "lifetime" of periodic payments is not guaranteed.

■ Lifetime Withdrawal Benefit (LWB) or Lifetime Income—This benefit generally comes in the form of a rider that an annuitant can attach to the annuity contract. With this rider, the insurance company guarantees a regular periodic payment for the lifetime of the annuitant even if the account balance goes to zero. Such riders come at a cost. One such cost is that in many policies the amount the investment grows to is not accessible to the annuitant under any circumstances. Therefore, cashing out the annuity contract is simply not possible. Different issuers might apply different formulas to determine if any portion of the growth might be available to withdraw and this can add to the complexity of the contract. These riders would not be suitable for anyone who isn't planning for or anticipates a lengthy retirement. For those who can, the costs of such a rider might be palatable to gain the peace of mind that comes with knowing that the income stream is guaranteed for as long as one lives.

TEST TOPIC ALERT   There is a risk-reward trade-off with annuity payout options.

1. Which of the following annuity options typically pays the largest monthly income?

    A. Life only
    B. Joint life with last survivor
    C. Life with 10-year period certain
    D. Contingent deferred option

    Answer: A. Remember that there is no beneficiary with this option. Greater risk means greater reward.

2. Which of the following annuity options is likely to provide the smallest monthly income?

    A. Life only
    B. Joint life with last survivor
    C. Life with 10-year period certain
    D. Life with 20-year period certain

    Answer: B. There is a cost in monthly income amount for the guarantee on two lives.

Match each of the following terms found thus far in this unit with the appropriate description below.

A.   Accumulation unit
B.   Joint life with last survivor annuity
C.   Deferred annuity
D.   Variable annuity
E.   Assumed interest rate
F.   Immediate annuity
G.   Life income with period certain
H.   Separate account

_____ 1.   Delays distributions until the owner elects to receive them

_____ 2.   Determines an annuitant's interest in the insurer's separate account during accumulation stage of an annuity

_____ 3.   Performance of a separate account determines value

_____ 4.   Annuity payments continue as long as one of the annuitants remains alive

_____ 5.   Contract starts to pay the annuitant immediately following its purchase

_____ 6.   Forms the basis for projected annuity payments but is not guaranteed

_____ 7.   Holds funds paid by variable annuity contract holders

_____ 8.   If the annuitant dies before a specified time expires, payments go to the annuitant's named beneficiary

12. 3. 3   TAXATION OF ANNUITIES

All contributions to annuities are made with after-tax dollars, unless the annuity is part of an employer-sponsored (qualified) retirement plan or held in an IRA.

TEST TOPIC ALERT   Assume an annuity is nonqualified unless a question specifically states otherwise.

When contributions are made with after-tax dollars, these already-taxed dollars are considered the investor's cost basis and are not taxed when withdrawn. The earnings in excess of the cost basis are taxed as ordinary income when withdrawn.

EXAMPLE   An investor has contributed $100,000 to a variable annuity. The annuity is now worth $150,000. What is the investor's cost basis, and what amount is taxable upon withdrawal?

The cost basis is equal to the contributions, or $100,000. The taxable amount at withdrawal will be the earnings of $50,000.

Because annuities are designed to supplement retirement income and provide tax-deferred growth, withdrawals before age 59½ are subject to the 10% early withdrawal penalty and ordinary income tax on the earnings portion of the withdrawal.

When an investor chooses to annuitize and selects a monthly income payout option, each month's payment is considered partly a return of cost basis and partly earnings. Only the earnings portion is taxable.

Many contract owners choose random withdrawals over the annuity option. If this choice is made, last in, first out (LIFO) taxation applies. The IRS requires that all earnings are withdrawn first and are taxed at ordinary income rates. After earnings are completely withdrawn, there is no additional taxation because the cost basis has already been taxed.

TAKE NOTE

Assume the following:

$100,000	after-tax contributions (cost basis)
+ 50,000	earnings
$150,000	total account value

If the investor makes a random withdrawal of $60,000, what are the tax consequences?

Remember that LIFO applies—the IRS chooses tax revenue as early as possible. Those earnings that accumulated tax deferred are now fully taxable. The investor must pay ordinary income taxes on the first $50,000 withdrawn because that is the amount of earnings. Furthermore, if the investor is under age 59½, an extra 10% early withdrawal tax applies. The remaining $10,000 is a return of the cost basis and is not taxed.

Any answer choice that mentions capital gains taxation on annuities or retirement plans is wrong. There is only ordinary income tax on distributions from annuities and retirement plans.

12. 3. 4   SUITABILITY

A variable annuity can be a very important part of one's financial well being if utilized correctly. However, there are suitability issues to consider. Variable annuities are meant to bring supplemental income into the household at a time in one's life when the income is needed. Therefore, supplemental income for retirement, not preservation of capital, should be the catalyst to consider a VA. Here are some general rules of thumb regarding the suitability of variable annuities.

■ Variable contracts are considered most suitable for someone who can fund the contract with cash. In other words, enticements to cash out a life insurance policy or an existing annuity (either of which might come with high surrender charges) is considered abusive and not a suitable recommendation. Refinancing a home or withdrawing equity from a home to fund a purchase could never be considered suitable.

■ Variable contracts are not suitable for anyone who might need the lump sum of cash invested in the VA at a later time for any reason. Anticipating buying a home, needing cash for your children's college education, or any other upcoming expense would need to be considered outside the variable annuity investment.

■ Because earnings in a VA are tax deferred (not taxed until withdrawn) there is no reason to place a VA in a tax-favored account like an IRA.

■ Variable annuity contracts are insurance company products that invest in a portfolio of securities via their separate account. If someone has a low risk tolerance or is wary of the stock market, a VA is not likely a very suitable recommendation for that individual.

■ Maximum contributions to all other retirement savings vehicles available to an individual should be made before a VA is considered a suitable recommendation. In other words, they are best considered supplements to retirement income one can already anticipate like pensions and IRA or 401(k) distributions.

12. 4   VARIABLE LIFE

Variable life insurance is a form of permanent life insurance that provides protection for the beneficiary in the event of the policy holders' death. Variable life insurance contracts invest the premiums paid in both the insurance company's general account as well as their separate account. Investment in the separate account gives the insured some investment choices such as common stock, bonds, or money market instruments, which in turn enables the insured to assume some investment risk in order to achieve some inflation protection for their death benefit.

Cash value fluctuates with the performance of the separate account and is not guaranteed. Instead, what is provided is a minimum guaranteed death benefit, which may increase above the minimum guaranteed amount depending on the separate account performance but never fall below. Any policy benefit that is guaranteed, such as the minimum guaranteed death benefit, is funded by that portion of the premium invested in the insurance company's general account. Any portion of the premium above what is necessary to pay for the minimum death benefit is invested in the separate account. In this way, the death benefit will never be less than the minimum guaranteed death benefit even if the separate account performs poorly.

12. 4. 1 WAIVER OF PREMIUM

Different riders to a policy can account for a number of different conditions. One to be aware of is "waiver of premium," which states that the premium will be forgiven or waived under conditions relating to an insured becoming totally disabled. Under a qualified plan, contributions used to purchase waiver of premium benefits are taxable to the plan participant and must be included in gross income in the year in which they were paid.

QUICK QUIZ 12.D

1. Cost basis for a nonqualified variable annuity is calculated using
   A. pretax dollars contributed
   B. after-tax dollars contributed
   C. dollars contributed minus any gains at the time of payout
   D. earnings in excess of dollars contributed

2. Annuitized payments from a variable annuity are viewed for tax purposes as
   A. all earnings
   B. all return of cost basis
   C. part earnings and part cost basis
   D. all tax free

3. Which of the following are TRUE for both variable life and variable annuity contracts?

 I. Both are insurance company products
 II. Both eliminate investment risk for the contract holder
 III. Both have a separate account containing securities investments
 IV. Both have a guaranteed death benefit

 A. I and III
 B. I and IV
 C. II and III
 D. II and IV

4. All of the following are true EXCEPT

 A. variable annuities are best considered supplements to retirement income one can already anticipate, like pensions and IRA or 401(k) distributions
 B. recommendations to fund a variable annuity by liquidating other investments are generally not considered suitable
 C. availability of funds in the future for life expenses such as college tuition or a home should be considered when recommending variable annuities
 D. variable annuities are most suitable for those with low risk tolerance

UNIT TEST

1. Which of the following is NOT a characteristic shared by both a mutual fund and a variable annuity's separate account?

   A. The investment portfolio is professionally managed.
   B. The client may vote for the board of directors or board of managers.
   C. The client assumes the investment risk.
   D. The payout plans guarantee the client income for life.

2. A joint life with last survivor annuity

   I. covers more than 1 person
   II. continues payments as long as 1 annuitant is alive
   III. continues payments as long as all annuitants are alive
   IV. guarantees payments for a certain period of time

   A. I and II
   B. I and III
   C. I and IV
   D. II and IV

3. A customer is about to buy a variable annuity contract. He wants to select an annuity that will give him the largest possible monthly payment. Which of the following payout options would be most suitable?

   A. Life annuity with period certain
   B. Unit refund life option
   C. Life annuity with 10-year period certain
   D. Life-only annuity

4. Your 65-year-old client owns a nonqualified variable annuity. He originally invested $29,000 4 years ago; it now has a value of $39,000. Your client, who is in the 28% tax bracket, makes a lump-sum withdrawal of $15,000. What tax liability results from the withdrawal?

   A. $0
   B. $2,800
   C. $3,800
   D. $4,200

5. Regarding a variable annuity's separate account, all of the following are true EXCEPT

   A. the separate account is used for the investment of monies paid by variable annuity contract holders
   B. the account is separate from the insurance company's general investments
   C. the account is operated in a manner similar to an investment company portfolio
   D. the separate account is considered an insurance product, not a security

6. Variable annuities must be registered with the

   I. state banking commission
   II. state insurance commission
   III. SEC
   IV. FDIC

   A. I and II
   B. II and III
   C. II and IV
   D. III and IV

7. A customer has a nonqualified variable annuity. Once the contract is annuitized, monthly payments to the customer are
   A. 100% taxable
   B. partially a tax-free return of capital and partially taxable
   C. 100% tax free
   D. 100% tax deferred

8. An accumulation unit in a variable annuity contract is
   A. an accounting measure used to determine the contract owner's interest in the separate account
   B. an accounting measure used to determine payments to the owner of the variable annuity
   C. exactly the same as a shareholder's ownership interest in a mutual fund
   D. none of the above

9. Your client has just retired and has a large sum of money to invest from the sale of his home. If he wants to purchase an annuity and start receiving payments now, what would you suggest?
   A. Single payment immediate annuity
   B. Single payment deferred annuity
   C. Periodic payment deferred annuity
   D. Any of the above

10. An annuitant has taken a 10-year certain payout and dies at age 64 after having retired at age 60. The named beneficiary will receive a monthly payment
    A. for 6 years
    B. for 10 years, unless death occurs
    C. until death
    D. none of the above

ANSWERS AND RATIONALES

1. **D.** Both a mutual fund portfolio and a variable annuity's separate account offer professional management and a board of managers or directors that shareholders have the right to vote for. Additionally, the client assumes the investment risk with each. Only variable annuities have payout plans that guarantee the client income for life.

2. **A.** A joint life with last survivor contract covers multiple annuitants and ceases payments at the death of the last surviving annuitant. A period certain contract guarantees payments for a certain amount of time.

3. **D.** Generally, a life-only contract pays the most per month because payments cease at the annuitant's death.

4. **B.** This annuity is nonqualified, which means the client has paid for it with after-tax dollars and therefore has a basis equal to the original $29,000 investment. Consequently, the client pays taxes only on the growth portion of the withdrawal ($10,000). The tax on this is $2,800 ($10,000 × 28%). Because the client is older than age 59½, he pays no 10% premature distribution penalty tax. However, had the client been younger than age 59½, he would have paid a $1,000 penalty tax ($10,000 × 10%) in addition to the $2,800 income tax.

5. **D.** The separate account is used for the monies invested in variable annuities. It is kept separate from the general account of the insurance company and operated much like an investment company mutual fund portfolio. It is considered both an insurance product and an investment product.

6. **B.** A variable annuity is a combination of two products: an insurance contract and a mutual fund. Therefore, variable annuities must be registered with the state insurance commission and the SEC.

7. **B.** The investor has already paid tax on the contributions, but the earnings have grown tax deferred. When the annuitization option is selected, each payment represents both capital and earnings. The money paid in will be returned tax free, but the earnings portion will be taxed as ordinary income.

8. **A.** When money is being deposited into the annuity, it is purchasing accumulation units.

9. **A.** The single payment annuity uses a lump-sum investment, such as from the sale of a home. In an immediate annuity, payout generally begins within 30 days.

10. **A.** A 10-year certain guarantees a lifetime payout (to the primary annuitant), subject to a minimum of 10 years. After death, having received 4 years of monthly payments, the remainder of the minimum guaranteed 10 years will be paid to the designated beneficiary.

QUICK QUIZ ANSWERS

Quick Quiz 12.A

1. **A.** Owners of variable annuities, like owners of mutual fund shares, have the right to vote on changes in investment policy and the right to vote for an investment adviser.

2. **A.** The Act of 1940 regulates both mutual funds and variable annuities. Mutual funds owned in a single name typically pass to the owner's estate at death. Variable annuity proceeds, however, usually pass directly to the owner's designated beneficiary at death, like a typical insurance policy. Investment income and capital gains realized generate current income to the owner of mutual funds, but in variable annuities, income is deferred until withdrawal begins.

3. **C.** Annuity unit price changes are based on changes of value of securities held in the separate account. This price change is a risk that is passed on to the investor in a variable annuity.

4. **C.** A variable annuity does not guarantee an earnings rate, but it does guarantee payments for life (mortality) and normally guarantees that expenses will not increase above a specified level.

5. **D.** Separate accounts as well as mutual funds may contain diversified portfolios of securities and may be managed by professional investment advisers. Voting rights for policy and management elections are available.

Quick Quiz 12.B

1. **C.** When a variable contract is annuitized, the number of accumulation units is multiplied by the unit value to arrive at the total annuitization value. An annuity factor has been actuarially determined by considering the investor's gender, age, mortality, and payout option selected, for example. This factor is used to establish the dollar amount of the first annuity payment. Future annuity payments will vary according to the separate account's value.

2. **C.** In the annuity period of a variable annuity, the amount received depends on the account performance, compared with the assumed interest rate. If actual performance is less than the AIR, the payout's value declines.

3. **C.** The contract earned 3% in September. The AIR for the contract is 3%. Payment size will not change from the payment made the previous month.

Quick Quiz 12.C

1. **C.**

2. **A.**

3. **D.**

4. **B.**

5. **F.**

6. **E.**

7. **H.**

8. **G.**

Quick Quiz 12.D

1. **B.** For a nonqualified variable annuity cost, basis for the annuitant would be the after-tax dollars contributed.

2. **C.**   Annuitized payments from a variable annuity are viewed for tax purposes as part earnings and part cost basis. The earnings are taxable, but the cost basis is returned tax-free.

3. **A.**   Both variable life contracts and variable annuities are insurance company products with an investment component in the separate account. The investment component means that the contract holder assumes investment risk. Only the life contract has a guaranteed death benefit.

4. **D.**   Because of the investment component within the separate account, VAs are not suitable for those with low risk tolerances. These investments are best considered supplements to retirement income one can already anticipate, like pensions and IRA or 401(k) distributions, and they should ideally be funded with available cash rather than liquidating existing investments. Because of potentially high surrender charges, future needs for funds must always be considered before purchasing a VA contract.

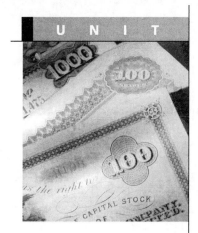

13

Direct Participation Programs

Direct participation programs (DPPs) are illiquid investments that pass income, gains, losses, and tax benefits (such as depreciation, depletion, and tax credits) directly to the limited partners. There are some unique tax concepts and suitability issues involving DPPs. Limited Partnerships (LPs) are one of the most common types of direct participation programs.

A general partner (GP) runs the partnership business and assumes certain liabilities with regard to the partnership's commitments. Limited partners are not allowed to be actively involved in business decisions and have limited liability in the event of a business failure. Most limited partnerships invest in real estate or oil and gas programs.

Limited partnership programs are either private placements (offered to wealthy accredited investors who make substantial investments) or public programs requiring much smaller investments. Under current tax law, limited partnerships generate passive income and losses. Passive losses may be used to shelter passive income only.

DPPs account for about 5–12 questions on the Series 7 exam. ∎

When you have completed this Unit, you should be able to:

■ **outline** the structure of DPPs as flow-through vehicles;

■ **list** the rights and responsibilities of DPP participants;

■ **name** and define the critical documents in the administration of limited partnerships;

■ **list** the payment order priority at dissolution;

■ **identify** the unique tax concepts related to DPP interests;

■ **compare** and contrast the features of various real estate programs as well as oil and gas programs; and

■ **describe** methods of analysis of DPP performance.

13. 1   CHARACTERISTICS OF LIMITED PARTNERSHIPS

Limited partnerships (LPs) are unique investment opportunities that permit the economic consequences of a business to flow through to investors. These programs offer investors a share in the income, gains, losses, deductions, and tax credits of the business entity.

Limited partners in DPPs enjoy several advantages:

- An investment managed by others
- Limited liability
- Flow-through of income and certain expenses

The greatest disadvantage to limited partners is their lack of liquidity. The secondary market for limited partnership interests is extremely limited; investors who wish to sell their interests frequently cannot locate buyers (i.e., the shareholder's interest is not freely transferable).

TAKE NOTE   A small number of limited partnership interests are negotiable and trade on the OTC and exchanges. These partnerships are known as **master limited partnerships (MLPs)**.

13. 1. 1   TAX REPORTING FOR PARTNERSHIPS

DPPs are generally structured as **limited partnerships** or **subchapter S corporations**. These business forms are not tax-paying entities like corporations; instead, they only report income and losses to the IRS, and then the **partners** (in a limited partnership) or **shareholders** (in a subchapter S corporation) have the responsibility to report income and losses individually and pay the taxes due.

By contrast, in a typical corporation, taxes must be paid on the earnings of the corporation before a dividend is distributed. Then the shareholder is taxed again on the dividend received.

Since an investment in a DPP is not taxed first at the level of the business, double taxation is avoided. The term *flow-through* (or pass-through) means that all the income and losses and corresponding tax responsibilities go directly to the investors with no taxation to the business entity.

Features of Corporations and DPPs

Corporation	Direct Participation Program
Tax-paying entity	Tax-reporting entity (entity does not pay taxes)
Shareholders receive dividend distributions	Investors receive a share of all income and losses of the business reported on Form K-1
Dividend distributions are subject to double taxation	No double taxation on distributions

---

TEST TOPIC ALERT   DPPs (limited partnerships) are the only investment opportunity that you will study that offer a pass-through of losses to the investor. Also, DPP passive losses shelter passive income, not ordinary income.

13. 1. 1. 1 Profit Motive

Any DPP established without a profit motive or with the intention of only generating tax losses for investors may be determined abusive. Investors in abusive DPPs may be subject to:

- back taxes;
- recapture of tax credits;
- interest penalties; or
- prosecution for fraud.

13. 1. 1. 2 Organizations Classified as Partnerships

An unincorporated organization with two or more members is generally classified as a partnership for federal tax purposes if its members engage in a trade, business, financial operation, or venture and divide its profits. However, a joint undertaking merely to share expenses is not a partnership. For example, co-ownership of property maintained and rented or leased is not a partnership unless the co-owners provide services to the tenants.

An organization is classified as a **partnership** for federal tax purposes if it has two or more members and is none of the following:

- An organization formed under a federal or state law that refers to it as incorporated or as a corporation, body corporate, or body politic
- An organization formed under a state law that refers to it as a joint-stock company or joint-stock association
- An insurance company
- Certain banks
- An organization wholly owned by a state or local government
- An organization specifically required to be taxed as a corporation by the Internal Revenue Code (e.g., certain publicly traded partnerships)
- Certain foreign organizations
- A tax-exempt organization
- A real estate investment trust
- An organization classified as a trust or otherwise subject to special treatment under the Internal Revenue Code
- Any other organization that elects to be classified as a corporation by filing Form 8832

A partnership must avoid corporate characteristics. The easiest of the corporate characteristics to avoid is continuity of life. Typically, partnerships have a predetermined date of dissolution when they are established.

TEST TOPIC ALERT   Several exam questions are possible from the list of corporate characteristics.

1. Which of these characteristics is the most difficult to avoid?

    Centralized management—no business can function without it.

2. Which of these characteristics is the easiest to avoid?

    Continuity of life—there is a predetermined time at which the partnership interest is dissolved.

3. Which two corporate characteristics are most likely to be avoided by a DPP?

    Continuity of life and freely transferable interests—interests cannot be freely transferred; general partner approval is required to transfer shares.

Other important tax concepts of DPPs include the following.

- DPPs were formerly known as tax shelters because investors used losses to reduce or shelter ordinary income (by writing off passive losses against ordinary income).

- Tax law revisions now classify income and loss from these investments as passive income and loss. Current law allows passive losses to shelter only passive income, not all ordinary income as before. Many programs lost their appeal because of this critical change in tax law.

- Investors should not purchase DPPs primarily for tax shelter; they should be economically viable and offer investors the potential of cash distributions and capital gains.

TEST TOPIC ALERT   1.   When considering the purchase of a limited partnership interest, an investor should be most concerned with

    A.   loss pass-through
    B.   potential tax shelter
    C.   economic viability
    D.   short-term trading opportunities

    Answer: C. Economic viability is the number one reason for the purchase of an interest in a limited partnership. Tax sheltering and loss pass-through are also considerations but should not be the primary motive to invest. Short-term trading opportunities do not exist. The investor should expect to hold the interest until the partnership is dissolved or liquidated.

13. 1. 2   FORMING A LIMITED PARTNERSHIP

LPs may be sold through private placements or public offerings. If sold privately, investors receive a **private placement memorandum** for disclosure. Generally, such private placements involve a small group of limited partners, each contributing a large sum of money. These investors must be **accredited investors**—that is, they must have substantial investment experience. The general public does not meet this description.

In a public offering, limited partnerships are sold with prospectus to a larger number of limited partners, each making a relatively small capital contribution, such as $1,000 to $5,000.

The **syndicator** oversees the selling and promotion of the partnership. The syndicator is responsible for the preparation of any paperwork necessary for the registration of the partnership. Syndication or "finders" fees are limited to 10% of the gross dollar amount of securities sold.

13. 1. 2. 1 Required Documentation

Three important documents are required for a limited partnership to exist:
- The certificate of limited partnership
- The partnership agreement
- The subscription agreement

13. 1. 2. 1. 1 Certificate of Limited Partnership

For legal recognition, this document must be filed in the home state of the partnership. It includes the:
- partnership's name;
- partnership's business;
- principal place of business;
- amount of time the partnership expects to be in business;
- size of each LP's current and future expected investments;
- contribution return date, if set;
- share of profits or other compensation to each LP;
- conditions for LP assignment of ownership interests;
- whether LPs may admit other LPs; and
- whether business can be continued by remaining general partners (GPs) at death or incapacity of a GP.

If any material information on the certificate has changed, an update must be made within 30 days of the event.

13. 1. 2. 1. 2 Partnership Agreement

Each partner receives a copy of this agreement. It describes the roles of the general and limited partners and guidelines for the partnership's operation.

TAKE NOTE

Rights of the GP as defined in the partnership agreement include the:
- right to charge a management fee for making business decisions for the partnership;
- authority to bind the partnership into contracts;
- right to determine which partners should be included in the partnership; and
- right to determine whether cash distributions will be made.

13. 1. 2. 1. 3 Subscription Agreement

All investors interested in becoming limited partners must complete a subscription agreement. The agreement appoints one or more GPs to act on behalf of the limited partners and is only effective when the GPs sign it. Along with the subscriber's money, the subscription agreement must include:

■ the investor's net worth;

■ the investor's annual income;

■ a statement attesting that the investor understands the risk involved; and

■ a power of attorney appointing the GP as the agent of the partnership.

In addition to a cash contribution, subscribers may assume responsibility for the repayment of a portion of a loan made to the partnership. This type of loan is called a **recourse loan**. Frequently, partnerships borrow money through **nonrecourse loans**; the GPs have responsibility for repayment of nonrecourse loans (not the LPs).

TEST TOPIC ALERT   LPs are liable for a proportionate share of recourse loans assumed by partnerships. LPs have no liability for nonrecourse loans, except in real estate partnerships.

13. 1. 3   DISSOLVING A LIMITED PARTNERSHIP

Generally, limited partnerships are liquidated on the date specified in the partnership agreement. Early shutdown may occur if the partnership sells or disposes of its assets or if a decision is made to dissolve the partnership by the LPs holding a majority interest. When **dissolution** occurs, the GP must cancel the certificate of limited partnership and settle accounts in the following order:

■ Secured lenders

■ Other creditors

■ Limited partners

— First, for their claims to shares of profits

— Second, for their claims to a return of contributed capital

■ General partners

— First, for fees and other claims not involving profits

— Second, for a share of profits

— Third, for capital return

DPP Life Cycle Diagram

Limited partnership

Requires at least one GP and one LP

↓

Syndicator (GP) promotes and offers partnership interests to potential LPs

↓

Interested parties complete subscription agreement

Submit cash and/or interest in recourse/nonrecourse loans as payment

↓

GP approves or disapproves completed subscription agreements

Approval required for completion of sale

↓

Partnership passes through income and losses to partners

↓

Partnership is dissolved or sold and gains/losses are distributed

---

QUICK QUIZ 13.A

1. DPP stands for

   A. direct placement program
   B. directed profits program
   C. direct participation program
   D. directors' and principals' program

2. The person who organizes and registers a partnership is known as

   A. a syndicator
   B. a property manager
   C. a program manager
   D. an underwriter

3. A limited partnership becomes effective when

    A. the certificate is filed with the proper authorities
    B. all limited partnership interests are sold
    C. all LPs are notified that all units are sold
    D. the limited partnership registration is filed

4. When a certificate of limited partnership must be rerecorded, it must be filed

    A. before the change
    B. within 5 business days of the change
    C. within 30 days of the change
    D. within 60 days of the change

5. The rights and liabilities of general and limited partners are listed in

    A. the certificate of partnership
    B. the Uniform Limited Partnership Act
    C. the agreement of limited partnership
    D. the partnership title

6. Which of the following corporate characteristics do most limited partnerships avoid?

    I.   Continuity of life
    II.   Limited liability
    III. Centralized management
    IV.   Free transferability of interest

    A. I and II
    B. I and IV
    C. II and III
    D. II and IV

7. A subscription for a limited partnership is accepted when

    A. the proposed LP signs the partnership agreement
    B. the LP's check is cashed
    C. the GP signs the subscription agreement
    D. the certificate of limited partnership is filed

8. All of the following statements are true with respect to a limited partnership subscription agreement EXCEPT

    A. the investor's registered representative must verify that the investor has provided accurate information
    B. the general partner endorses the subscription agreement, signifying that a limited partner is suitable
    C. the investor's signature indicates that he has read the prospectus
    D. the general partner's signature grants the limited partners power of attorney to conduct the partnership's affairs

Quick Quiz answers can be found at the end of the Unit.

13. 1. 4 INVESTORS IN A LIMITED PARTNERSHIP

The limited partnership form of DPP involves two types of partners: the GP(s) and the LP(s). A limited partnership must have at least one of each.

General Partners vs. Limited Partners

General Partners	Limited Partners
Unlimited liability: personal liability for all partnership business losses and debts	Limited liability: can lose no more than their investment and proportionate interest in recourse notes
Management responsibility: assumes responsibility for all aspects of the partnership's operation	No management responsibility: provides capital for the business but may not participate in its management; known as a passive investor
	Attempting to take part in a management role jeopardizes limited liability status
Fiduciary responsibility: morally and legally bound to use invested capital in the best interest of the investors	May sue the GP: lawsuits may recover damages if the GP does not act in the best interest of the investors or uses assets improperly

The following tables compare other activities of GPs and LPs.

General Partners and Limited Partners: Allowed Activities

General partners can:	Limited partners can:
make decisions that legally bind the partnership	vote on changes to partnership investment objectives or the admission of a new GP
buy and sell property for the partnership	vote on sale or refinancing of partnership property
maintain a financial interest in the partnership (must be a minimum of 1%)	receive cash distributions, capital gains, and tax deductions from partnership activities
receive compensation as specified in the partnership agreement	inspect books and records of the partnership
	exercise the partnership democracy (vote under special circumstances, such as permitting the GP to act contrary to the agreement, to contest a judgment against the partnership, or admit a new GP)

General Partners and Limited Partners Cannot: Prohibited Activities

General partners cannot:	Limited partners cannot:
compete against the partnership for personal gain	act on behalf of the partnership or participate in its management
borrow from the partnership	knowingly sign a certificate containing false information
commingle partnership funds with personal assets or assets of other partnerships	have their names appear as part of the partnership's name
admit new GPs or LPs or continue the partnership after the loss of a GP unless specified in the partnership agreement	

QUICK QUIZ 13.B   Match each of the following descriptions of terms discussed thus far in this unit with the appropriate items below.

A. Provides creditors with information regarding an LP's term and member contributions

B. Allows LPs to vote on major decisions, but not on day-to-day operations

C. Passive investors only

D. Outlines roles of both general and limited partners

_____ 1. Partnership agreement

_____ 2. Subscription agreement

_____ 3. Certificate of limited partnership

_____ 4. Partnership democracy

13. 2   TYPES OF LIMITED PARTNERSHIP PROGRAMS

Limited partnerships can be formed to run any type of business. The most common types are real estate, oil and gas, and equipment-leasing businesses.

13. 2. 1   REAL ESTATE PARTNERSHIPS

Real estate limited partnerships provide investors with the following benefits:

■ **Capital growth potential**—achieved through appreciation of property

■ **Cash flow (income)**—collected from rents

■ **Tax deductions**—from mortgage interest expense and depreciation allowances for "wearing out the building" and capital improvements

■ **Tax credits**—for government-assisted housing and historic rehabilitation (reduce tax liability dollar for dollar but are subject to recapture)

Five types of real estate programs and their features follow.

Raw Land	
Partnership Objective	Purchase undeveloped land for its appreciation potential
Advantages	Appreciation potential of the property
Disadvantages	Offers no income distributions or tax deductions
Tax Features	No income or depreciation deductions
	Not considered a tax shelter
Degree of Risk	Most speculative real estate partnership

New Construction	
Partnership Objective	Build new property for potential appreciation
Advantages	Appreciation potential of the property and structure; minimal maintenance costs in the early years
Disadvantages	Potential cost overruns; no established track record; difficulty of finding permanent financing; inability to deduct current expenses during construction period
Tax Features	Depreciation and expense deductions after construction is completed and income is generated
Degree of Risk	Less risky than new land; more risky than existing property

Existing Property	
Partnership Objective	Generate an income stream from existing structures
Advantages	Immediate cash flow; known history of income and expenses
Disadvantages	Greater maintenance or repair expenses than for new construction; expiring leases that may not be renewed; less than favorable rental arrangements
Tax Features	Deductions for mortgage interest and depreciation
Degree of Risk	Relatively low risk

Government-Assisted Housing Programs	
Partnership Objective	Develop low-income and retirement housing
Advantages	Tax credits and rent subsidies
Disadvantages	Low appreciation potential; risk of changing government programs; high maintenance costs
Tax Features	Tax credits and losses
Degree of Risk	Relatively low risk

Historic Rehabilitation	
Partnership Objective	Develop historic sites for commercial use
Advantages	Tax credits for preserving historic structure
Disadvantages	Potential cost overruns; no established track record; difficulty of finding permanent financing; inability to deduct current expenses during construction period
Tax Features	Tax credit and deductions for expenses and depreciation
Degree of Risk	Similar to risk of new construction

13. 2. 2   OIL AND GAS PARTNERSHIPS

Oil and gas programs include speculative drilling programs and income programs that invest in producing wells. Unique tax advantages associated with these programs include intangible drilling costs and depletion allowances.

13. 2. 2. 1 Intangible Drilling Costs (IDCs)

Write-offs for the expenses of drilling are usually 100% deductible in the first year of operation. These include costs associated with drilling such as wages, supplies, fuel costs, and insurance. An **intangible drilling cost** can be defined as any cost that, after being incurred, has no salvage value.

13. 2. 2. 2 Tangible Drilling Costs (TDCs)

Tangible drilling costs are those costs incurred that have salvage value (e.g., storage tanks and wellhead equipment). These costs are not immediately deductible; rather, they are deducted (depreciated) over several years.

13. 2. 2. 3 Depletion Allowances

Tax deductions that compensate the partnership for the decreasing supply of oil or gas (or any other resource or mineral).

Depletion allowances may be taken only once the oil or gas is sold.

Three types of oil and gas programs are exploratory, developmental, and income.

13. 2. 2. 4 (1) Exploratory (Wildcatting)

Partnership Objective	Locate undiscovered reserves of oil and gas
Advantages	High rewards for discovery of new reserves
Disadvantages	Few new wells actually produce
Tax Features	High IDCs for immediate tax sheltering
Degree of Risk	High; most risky oil and gas program

13. 2. 2. 5 (2) Developmental

Partnership Objective	Drill near existing fields to discover new reserves (called step out wells)
Advantages	Less risk of discovery than exploratory
Disadvantages	Few new wells actually produce
Tax Features	Medium IDCs, immediate tax sheltering
Degree of Risk	Medium to high risk

13. 2. 2. 6 (3) Income

Partnership Objective	Provide immediate income from sale of existing oil
Advantages	Immediate cash flow
Disadvantages	Oil prices; well stops producing
Tax Features	Income sheltering from depletion allowances
Degree of Risk	Low

There is a fourth type of oil and gas partner: combination. In this program, the partnership allocates dollars between income and exploratory drilling.

13. 2. 2. 7 Sharing Arrangements

The costs and revenues associated with oil and gas programs are shared in a variety of ways. A description of these arrangements follows.

Overriding Royalty Interest. The holder of this interest receives royalties but has no partnership risk. An example of this arrangement is a landowner that sells mineral rights to a partnership.

Working Interest. This operating interest in a mineral-bearing (oil and gas) partnership entitles a partner to a share of the income or revenues from production but also carries the obligation to bear a corresponding share of all costs to extract the minerals.

Reversionary Working Interest. The GP bears no costs of the program and receives no revenue until LPs have recovered their capital. LPs bear all deductible and nondeductible costs.

Net Operating Profits Interest. The GP bears none of the program's costs but is entitled to a percentage of net profits. The LP bears all deductible and nondeductible costs. This arrangement is available only in private placements.

Disproportionate Sharing. The GP bears a relatively small percentage of expenses but receives a relatively large percentage of the revenues.

Carried Interest. The GP shares tangible drilling costs with the LPs but receives no IDCs. The LP receives the immediate deductions, whereas the GP receives write-offs from depreciation over the life of the property.

Functional Allocation. Under this most common sharing arrangement, the LP receives the IDCs, which allow immediate deductions. The GP receives the tangible drilling costs, which are depreciated over several years. Revenues are shared.

13. 2. 3 EQUIPMENT LEASING PROGRAMS

Equipment leasing programs are created when DPPs purchase equipment leased to other businesses. Investors receive income from lease payments and also a proportional share of write-offs from operating expenses, interest expense, and depreciation. Tax credits were once available through these programs but were discontinued by tax law changes. The primary investment objective of these programs is tax-sheltered income.

13. 2. 4 ANALYSIS OF LIMITED PARTNERSHIPS

In selecting a limited partnership interest, an investor should first consider whether the partnership matches his investment objectives and has economic viability. **Economic viability** means that there is potential for returns from cash distributions and capital gains. Although tax benefits may be attractive, they should not be the first consideration in the purchase of an LP interest.

13. 2. 4. 1 Measuring Economic Viability

How is economic viability measured? Two methods applied to the analysis of DPPs are cash flow analysis and internal rate of return.

- **Cash flow analysis** compares income (revenues) to expenses.
- **Internal rate of return (IRR)** determines the present value of estimated future revenues and sales proceeds to allow comparison to other programs.

13. 2. 4. 2 Tax Features to Consider

As described, limited partnerships distribute income, losses, and gains to limited partners because of their pass-through nature. Limited partners are able to apply certain deductions and/or tax credits to income as described here.

13. 2. 4. 2. 1 Deductions

Expenses of the partnership, such as salaries, interest payments, and management fees, result in deductions in the current year to the LPs. Principal payments on property are not deductible expenses.

Cost recovery systems offer write-offs over a period of years as defined by IRS schedules. **Depreciation write-offs** apply to cost recovery of expenditures for equipment and real estate (land cannot be depreciated). **Depletion allowances** apply to the using up of natural resources, such as oil and gas. Depreciation and depletion allowances may be claimed only when income is being produced by the partnership. Also recognize that some assets are not depreciable nor can they be depleted. For example, farm crops fall into this category and are generally known to be renewable assets.

TAKE NOTE

Depreciation may be taken on a straight line (i.e., the same amount each year) or accelerated basis. Accelerated depreciation, known as modified accelerated cost recovery system (MACRS), increases deductions during the early years and decreases them during the later years.

13. 2. 4. 2. 2 Tax Credits

Tax credits are dollar-for-dollar reductions of taxes due and are the greatest tax benefit available to taxpayers. Currently, there are few available. The limited partnership programs that offer them currently are government-assisted housing programs and historic rehabilitation programs. Formerly, tax credits were available through equipment leasing programs, but tax law changes discontinued this credit. The partnership reports its income and losses to the IRS and then reports to each partner their individual share of income, gains, losses, deductions, and credits.

TAKE NOTE

The **crossover point** is the point at which the program begins to generate taxable income instead of losses. This generally occurs in later years when income increases and deductions decrease.

LPs must keep track of their **tax basis**, or amount at risk, to determine their gain or loss upon the sale of their partnership interest. An investor's basis is subject to adjustment periodically for occurrences such as cash distributions and additional investments.

The tax benefits offered by the partnership should be of secondary importance to the economic viability it offers.

TAKE NOTE

An LP's basis consists of:

■ cash contributions to the partnership;

■ property contributions to the partnership;

■ recourse debt of the partnership; and

■ nonrecourse debt for real estate partnerships only.

Partners must adjust their basis at year end. Any distributions of cash or property and repayments of recourse debt (also nonrecourse debt for real estate only) are reductions to a partner's basis. Partners are allowed deductions up to the amount of their adjusted cost basis.

EXAMPLE

If a partner's basis is $25,000 at year end and the investor has losses of $35,000, only $25,000 of the losses may be used to deduct against passive income. The remaining $10,000 may be carried forward.

13. 2. 4. 3 Other Features to Analyze

Other important factors that investors should consider in their overall analysis of limited partnerships include the following:

■ Management ability and experience of the GP in running other similar programs

■ **Blind pool** or nonspecific program—in a blind pool, less than 75% of the assets are specified as to use; however, in a specified program, more than 75% have been identified

■ Time frame of the partnership

■ Similarity of start-up costs and revenue projections to those of comparable ventures

■ Lack of liquidity of the interest

Limited partnership interests are not for all investors. Careful consideration must be given to the overall safety and lack of liquidity of these programs before investing.

13. 2. 5 CASH FLOW

Cash flow is defined as net income or loss plus noncash changes (such as depreciation).

EXAMPLE

Revenue	$300,000
Costs	
Selling	$50,000
Interest	$70,000
Operating	$160,000
Depreciation	$50,000
	$330,000
Net loss	($30,000)

The above shows a loss of $30,000. However, its cash flow is a positive of $20,000.

Net income or loss	($30,000)
+ Depreciation	$50,000
Cash flow	+$20,000

13. 2. 6 BASIS

In a limited partnership, the term *basis* defines the liability assumed by the LP. An LP can lose no more than his basis, and his basis puts a limit on how much he may deduct on his tax return. This ensures that an LP cannot deduct losses in excess of his basis.

Basis is computed using the following formula:

Investment in partnership + share of recourse debt − cash distribution

It is important to note that any up-front costs incurred by the LP will not affect beginning basis. Assume that an LP invests $50,000 in a partnership unit, and the broker-dealer selling the unit takes a commission of $3,000. Therefore, only $47,000 of the LP's investment goes into the partnership. However, the LP's beginning basis is $50,000, not $47,000.

TEST TOPIC ALERT

1. A customer invests $10,000 in a DPP and signs a recourse note for $40,000. During the first year, the investor receives a cash distribution from the partnership in the amount of $5,000. At year end, he receives a statement showing that his share of partnership losses is $60,000. How much of that $60,000 can he deduct on his tax return?

Answer: The investor cannot deduct losses in excess of his year-end basis, $45,000, computed as follows:

Investment	$10,000
+ Recourse debt	$40,000
	$50,000
− Cash distributions	$5,000
Year-end basis	$45,000

Therefore, the customer can deduct $45,000 on his tax return. The remaining $15,000 is carried forward.

TAKE NOTE
If a partnership interest is sold, the gain or loss is the difference between sales proceeds and adjusted basis at the time of sale. If, at the time of sale, the customer has unused losses, these losses may be added to the cost basis. If a customer has an adjusted cost basis of $22,000 and unused losses of $10,000 and sells his partnership interest for $20,000, his loss on the sale would be $12,000.

13. 2. 6. 1 Depreciation Recapture

When a partnership unit is sold, recapture may apply if the partnership has been depreciating its fixed assets using accelerated depreciation. If, at the time of sale, the limited partner had taken depreciation deductions in excess of what would have been taken had the partnership been using the straight line method, that difference is subject to ordinary income tax. Clearly, depreciation recapture is not a tax advantage.

QUICK QUIZ 13.C

1. All of the following would generally be associated with an existing real estate DPP EXCEPT
   A. immediate income stream
   B. appreciation potential
   C. known history of income and expenses
   D. lower risk than other types of real estate programs

2. Which of the following limited partnership programs provide potential tax credits to partners?
   I.   Rehabilitation of historic properties
   II. Equipment leasing
   III. Developmental oil and gas programs
   IV. Government-assisted housing programs

   A. I and II
   B. I and IV
   C. II and III
   D. III and IV

3. Which of the following sharing arrangements is the most common?
   A. Net operating profits interest
   B. Carried interest
   C. Functional allocation
   D. Overriding royalty interest

4. Cost basis for a limited partner is best defined as
   A. cash contributions + recourse debt – distributions
   B. noncash contribution + nonrecourse debt – recourse debt
   C. cash contributions – distributions
   D. recourse debt – cash contributions

UNIT TEST

1. Which of the following would NOT be a valid use of the partnership democracy?

    A. Deciding which partnership assets should be liquidated to pay creditors

    B. Removing the general partner

    C. Consenting to an action of a general partner that is contrary to the agreement of limited partnership

    D. Consenting to a legal judgment against the partnership

2. Which of the following statements regarding limited partnerships are TRUE?

    I. Maximum commission in selling partnership offerings is 5%.

    II. Maximum commission in selling partnership offerings is 10%.

    III. Commissions taken are deducted from the original investment to determine beginning basis.

    IV. Commissions taken are not deducted from the original investment to determine beginning basis.

    A. I and III

    B. I and IV

    C. II and III

    D. II and IV

3. The rights and liabilities of general and limited partners are listed in

    A. the certificate of partnership

    B. the Uniform Limited Partnership Act

    C. the agreement of limited partnership

    D. the partnership title

4. A client invests $100,000 in a tax shelter as a limited partner, giving him a 10% interest in the program. The general partners cannot meet the expenses of the program. There is a mortgage balance remaining of $3 million. The property of the program is then liquidated for $1 million. How much does the investor get back from his original investment?

    A. $0

    B. $10,000

    C. $33,000

    D. $100,000

5. If an investor expects to have a large amount of passive income over the next 2 years, which of the following programs will most likely lead to the largest amount of shelter?

    A. Equipment leasing

    B. Undeveloped land purchasing

    C. Oil and gas drilling

    D. Real estate income

6. All of the following would be considered tax advantages relating to a DPP investment EXCEPT

    A. depreciation recapture

    B. depletion

    C. intangible drilling costs

    D. accelerated depreciation

7. Which of the following sequences reflects the priority, from first to last, of payments made when a limited partnership is liquidated?

    I. General partners

    II. Limited partners

    III. General creditors

    IV. Secured creditors

    A. I, II, III, IV

    B. I, IV, III, II

    C. IV, III, I, II

    D. IV, III, II, I

8. A customer has an annual income of $38,000 from a fairly secure job and is in the 28% bracket. She has a balanced portfolio of stocks and fixed-income securities and has $10,000 to invest in a limited partnership. She is willing to accept only a moderate amount of risk. Which of the following types of limited partnerships would be the most appropriate recommendation?

A. Oil and gas income program
B. Exploratory oil and gas drilling program
C. New construction real estate limited partnership
D. Blind pool raw land real estate limited partnership

9. Which of the following partnership programs is likely to qualify for tax credits?

A. Oil and gas exploratory
B. Historic rehabilitation real estate
C. Raw land real estate
D. Equipment leasing

10. An investor in a limited partnership generating passive losses can offset these against

I. passive income from other partnerships
II. rental income from direct investments in real estate
III. dividends received from listed securities
IV. capital gains from sale of unlisted securities

A. I and II
B. I and III
C. II and III
D. III and IV

11. A general partner is considered to have a conflict of interest with the business of a limited partnership if he

A. manages the business
B. loans money to the business
C. borrows money from the business
D. acts as agent for the business

12. Which of the following statements describes an oil and gas blind pool offering?

A. The oil exploration occurs in an area that is not adjacent to any known oil reserves.
B. Money is raised without a specific property being stated, and the GP selects the investments.
C. The income from producing wells is purchased at a discount from the present value of the projected future flows.
D. An unknown number of representatives participates in the sale of known partnership units.

13. If a limited partnership interest is sold, the gain or loss in the sale is the difference between the sales proceeds and

A. the original basis
B. the total of the deductible losses taken by the investor
C. the adjusted basis
D. the total of tax preference items allocated to the investor

14. All of the following are types of oil and gas programs EXCEPT

A. Raw land
B. Income
C. Developmental
D. Exploratory

15. Each limited partner's share of partnership losses

A. may be used to reduce ordinary income
B. may be used to offset passive income
C. are deductible up to $3,000 per year
D. cause a dollar-for-dollar decrease in the market value of the limited partnership units

ANSWERS AND RATIONALES

1. **A.** Deciding which partnership assets should be liquidated to pay creditors involves limited partners in the active management of partnership affairs. This would result in their being treated as general partners with respect to liability and possible loss of limited partner status.

2. **D.** Under the rules, the maximum compensation that may be taken by sponsors selling DPPs is 10%. Up-front costs, such as commissions taken, accounting costs, and so forth, do not affect the beginning basis.

3. **C.** The agreement is the contract between the partners and contains each entity's rights and duties.

4. **A.** The limited partner will not receive any return on his investment. In a program that has failed, the creditors of the partnership will be paid first out of any sale proceeds before the limited partners receive any money. Because the limited partners had not signed a recourse agreement, even though the partnership still owes $2 million on the mortgage, the limited partners are not liable for any money beyond their original investments.

5. **C.** Oil and gas drilling programs allocate the majority of investment dollars to drilling. These costs are intangible drilling costs (IDCs), which are 100% deductible when drilling occurs. In equipment-leasing programs, the investment dollars are recovered through depreciation over the lives of the leased assets.

6. **A.** Depreciation recapture can occur when an investor sells his interest in a real estate program. If, at the time of the sale, the amount of accelerated deprecation taken exceeds the straight line depreciation amount, the difference (called recapture) must be reported by the investor as ordinary income.

7. **D.** Creditors are paid first in a liquidation, with priority given to the secured lenders. General partners are the last to get paid.

8. **A.** The customer is not in a high tax bracket and would not be able to take full advantage of the tax benefits produced by an exploratory oil and gas program or by new construction real estate limited partnerships. A raw land real estate partnership is usually speculative. Of the answers listed, the income and moderate risk from an oil and gas income program would probably be of greatest benefit to this investor.

9. **B.** While tax credits available to limited partnerships are few, they would most likely be applicable to historic rehabilitation and government-assisted housing real estate partnerships.

10. **A.** Passive losses can be deducted against passive income and income from certain real estate investments. It cannot be deducted against active or portfolio (investment) income.

11. **C.** The general partner manages the business and acts as agent for the business. The general partner may loan money to the partnership at a reasonable rate of interest but may not borrow from the partnership.

12. **B.** A blind pool offering, also known as a nonspecific program, involves an investment in a program without specific prospects or properties being identified.

13. **C.** The adjusted basis is a limited partner's cost basis at any point in time. Gain or loss on the sale of the partnership is determined by comparing the sales proceeds to the adjusted basis.

14. **A.** Raw land is a type of real estate program—not an oil and gas program. Exploratory drilling programs involve drilling in previously unexplored areas. Developmental drilling involves drilling in areas where oil and gas have already been discovered, and income programs involve purchasing existing oil and gas wells and selling the production.

15. **B.** It is important to remember that passive losses can be used to offset only passive income. An investor with $500,000 worth of passive income could write off up to $500,000 of passive loss (if he had that much loss). Do not confuse this with the $3,000 maximum deduction against income for capital losses. There is no maximum passive loss that can be written against passive income.

QUICK QUIZ ANSWERS

Quick Quiz 13.A

1. **C.** DPP stands for direct participation program.

2. **A.** The individual who organizes and registers the partnership is the syndicator.

3. **A.** The certificate creates the partnership's limited nature; until the document is properly filed, the partnership is a general partnership.

4. **C.** Refiling must occur within 30 days.

5. **C.** The agreement is the contract between the partners and contains each entity's rights and duties.

6. **B.** The 2 corporate characteristics that most limited partnerships avoid are continuity of life and free transferability of interest.

7. **C.** Acceptance of an investor as an LP occurs when the GP signs the subscription agreement. The LP receives confirmation of acceptance when the subscription agreement is returned.

8. **D.** The limited partner's signature on the subscription agreement grants the general partner power of attorney to conduct the partnership's affairs. The subscription agreement for a limited partnership is deemed accepted when the general partner signs the subscription agreement.

Quick Quiz 13.B

1. **D.**

2. **C.**

3. **A.**

4. **B.**

Quick Quiz 13.C

1. **B.** Appreciation potential is generally not associated with existing real estate programs because most appreciation occurs in the earliest years for real estate assets.

2. **B.** Historic rehabilitation and government-assisted housing are the programs discussed that offer potential tax credits. Tax credits were formerly available through equipment leasing, but Congress changed the rules. Developmental oil and gas programs offer high IDCs, not ITCs (investment tax credits).

3. **C.** Functional allocation is most commonly used because it gives the best benefits to both parties. The LPs receive the immediate tax write-offs from the IDCs, whereas the GPs receive continued write-offs from the tangible costs over the course of several years. Both share equally in the revenues.

4. **A.** Cost basis for a limited partner is best defined as cash contributions + recourse debt (debt the LP is responsible for) – distributions. Nonrecourse debt would only be included for real estate programs. These are the only programs where LPs can be responsible for both recourse and nonrecourse debt.

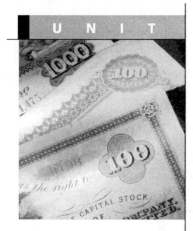

14

Economics and Analysis

The economy has a significant effect on the performance of various industries and corporations. Analysts in firms study economic conditions to make and check predictions about market activity. The Series 7 examination expects you to know fundamental concepts about economic performance and monetary policy.

Analysts also derive information about company performance from the study of financial data in the form of balance sheets and income statements. It is important to be familiar with these statements and the type of ratios that analysts compute.

Expect to see 15–20 questions on economics and analysis on the exam. These questions will typically be concept questions, not mathematical calculations. ■

When you have completed this Unit, you should be able to:

- **describe** the four phases of the business cycle and key characteristics of each;

- **provide** examples of leading, coincident, and lagging indicators;

- **name** three economic theorists and describe the theories they originated;

- **contrast** fiscal and monetary policy;

- **list** and describe the three monetary policy tools of the FRB;

- **contrast** basic theories of fundamental and technical analysis and the type of information important for each study;

- **describe** several technical market theories;

- **identify** the basic components of the balance sheet and key ratios calculated from it; and

- **identify** the basic components of the income statement and key ratios calculated from it.

14. 1   ECONOMICS

Economics is the study of supply and demand. When people want to buy an item that is in short supply, the item's price rises. When people do not want to buy an item that is in plentiful supply, the price declines. This simple notion, the foundation of all economic study, is true for bread, shoes, cars, clothes, stocks, bonds, and money.

The economic climate has an enormous effect on the conditions of individual companies and, therefore, the securities markets. In addition to a company's earnings and business prospects, any changes in business cycles, the money supply, and Federal Reserve Board (FRB) actions affect securities prices and trading.

14. 1. 1   BUSINESS CYCLES

Throughout history, periods of economic expansion have been followed by periods of economic contraction in a pattern called the **business cycle**.

Business cycles go through four stages:

- Expansion
- Peak
- Contraction
- Trough

Expansion is characterized by increased business activity—increasing sales, manufacturing, and wages—throughout the economy. For a variety of reasons, an economy can expand for only so long; when it reaches its upper limit, it has reached its peak. When business activity declines from its peak, the economy is **contracting**. Economists call mild, short-term contractions **recessions**. Longer, more severe contractions are **depressions**. When business activity stops declining and levels off, it is known as a **trough**.

According to the U.S. Commerce Department, the economy is in a recession when a decline in real output of goods and services—the gross domestic product (GDP)—lasts for six months or more. It defines a depression as a severe downturn lasting for six quarters (18 months) or more, with unemployment rates greater than 15%.

The Four Stages of the Business Cycle

In the normal course of events, some industries or corporations prosper as others fail. So, to determine the economy's overall direction, economists consider many aspects of business activity. Expansions are characterized by:

- increased consumer demand for goods and services;
- increases in industrial production;
- rising stock prices;
- rising property values; and
- increasing gross domestic product.

Downturns in the business cycle tend to be characterized by:

- rising numbers of bankruptcies and bond defaults;
- higher consumer debt;
- falling stock prices;
- rising inventories (a sign of slackening consumer demand in hard times); and
- decreasing gross domestic product.

TAKE NOTE   If asked to put the four components of the business cycle in sequence, always start with expansion.

Also remember that while some investments, like stocks, tend to move with the economic cycles, there are investments, such as precious metals (e.g., gold), that historically have been counter cyclical.

14. 1. 1. 1 Gross Domestic Product

A nation's annual economic output—all of the goods and services produced within the nation—is known as its **gross domestic product (GDP)**. The United States' GDP includes personal consumption, government spending, gross private investment, foreign investment, and net exports.

TAKE NOTE   On the exam, you may see the term *GNP (gross national product)* instead of GDP.

14. 1. 1. 2 Price Levels

14. 1. 1. 2. 1 Consumer Price Index

The most prominent measure of general price changes is the **Consumer Price Index (CPI)**. The CPI measures the rate of increase or decrease in a broad range of consumer prices, such as food, housing, transportation, medical care, clothing, electricity, entertainment, and services. The CPI is computed each month.

When comparing the economic output of one period with that of another, analysts must account for changes that have occurred during the intervening time in the relative prices of products. Economists adjust GDP figures to **constant dollars** rather than comparing actual dollars. This allows the economists and others who use GDP figures to compare the actual purchasing power of the dollars rather than the dollars themselves.

14. 1. 1. 2. 2 Inflation

Inflation is a general increase in prices. Mild inflation can encourage economic growth because gradually increasing prices tend to stimulate business investments. High inflation reduces a dollar's buying power, which hurts the economy.

Increased inflation drives up interest rates of fixed-income securities, which drives down bond prices. Decreases in the inflation rate have the opposite effect: as inflation declines, bond yields decline and prices rise.

Inflation is a barometer of the general direction of price levels. As such, it is a measure of the buying power of a dollar. Periods of low inflation have relatively stable prices and low interest rates and, as a result, are positive for business and the stock market. Periods of high inflation have increasing prices and high interest rates and tend to be bad for business and the stock market. In a growing economy, there is always some amount of inflation.

TEST TOPIC ALERT   The consumer price index (CPI) uses a constant dollar adjustment to account for inflation.

14. 1. 1. 2. 3 Deflation

Though rare, **deflation** is a general decline in prices. Deflation usually occurs during severe recessions when unemployment is on the rise.

14. 1. 1. 2. 4 Stagnation

Economic "stagnation" refers to prolonged periods of slow or little economic growth, usually accompanied by high unemployment.

14. 1. 1. 2. 5 Stagflation

"Stagflation" is the term used to describe the unusual combination of inflation (a rise in prices) and high unemployment (stagnation). This generally occurs when the economy isn't growing, there is a lack of consumer demand and business activity, but yet prices for goods are still rising.

14. 1. 1. 3 Economic Indicators

Certain aspects of economic activity serve as barometers, or **indicators**, of business cycle phases.

14. 1. 1. 3. 1 Leading Indicators

Leading indicators are spot checks of business activity that reliably predict trends in the economy. Positive changes in these indicators predict economic improvement. Negative changes predict economic contraction.

Leading indicators used most often include:

- money supply (M2);

- building permits (housing starts);

- average weekly initial claims for state unemployment compensation;

- average work week in manufacturing;

- new orders for consumer goods;

- machine tool orders;

- changes in inventories of durable goods;

- changes in sensitive materials prices;

- stock prices; and

- changes in business and consumer borrowing.

Not all of the indicators move in tandem. Positive changes in a majority of leading indicators point to increased spending, production, and employment. Negative changes in a majority of indicators can forecast a recession.

EXAMPLE   Trends in the stock market, up or down, indicate investor confidence in the economy. These upward or downward trends tend to tell us where the economy is heading—a leading indicator.

14. 1. 1. 3. 2 Coincident Indicators

Leading indicators reflect where the economy is going; coincident indicators confirm where it is. **Coincident indicators** are those measurable factors that vary directly and simultaneously with the business cycle. Widely used coincident indicators include:

- number of hours worked (as a proxy for personal income);

- employment levels;

- nonagricultural employment;

- personal income;

- industrial production;

- manufacturing and trade sales; and

- GDP.

EXAMPLE   Personal income or current job salaries indicate what consumers have to spend at that moment in time. These numbers tell us where the economy currently stands—a coincident indicator.

14. 1. 1. 3. 3 Lagging Indicators

Lagging indicators are those factors that change after the economy has begun a new trend but serve as confirmation of the new trend. Lagging indicators help analysts differentiate long-term trends from short-term reversals that occur in any trend. Lagging indicators include:

- corporate profits;
- average duration of unemployment;
- labor cost per unit of output (manufacturing);
- ratio of inventories to sales;
- commercial and industrial loans outstanding; and
- ratio of consumer installment credit to personal income.

EXAMPLE   The numbers corporations report showing profits or losses generally come at least one quarter after the actual occurrence. These numbers tell us where the company stood at that time—a lagging indicator

---

QUICK QUIZ 14.A   Choose **LE** for leading, **LA** for lagging, and **C** for coincident.

_____   1.   Decrease in number of weekly unemployment claims

_____   2.   Increase in personal income

_____   3.   Decrease in corporate profits

_____   4.   Increase in industrial production

_____   5.   Decrease in building permits

_____   6.   Increase in the S&P 500 Index

_____   7.   Decrease in the duration of unemployment

Quick Quiz answers can be found at the end of the Unit.

TEST TOPIC ALERT   Be able to differentiate between leading, lagging, and coincident indicators. Also recognize that an indicator is not affected by whether there was an increase or decrease in a specific type of economic activity. For instance, an increase in inventories is a leading indicator that signifies a weakening economy. A decrease in inventories is still a leading indicator, but it signifies a strengthening economy.

14. 1. 2 ECONOMIC THEORIES AND THE BUSINESS CYCLE

This section explores some of the theories economists hold to, and how these economists view the economy should be impacted by government.

14. 1. 2. 1 Keynesian Theory

The economist John Maynard Keynes held that active government involvement in the economy was vital to the health and stability of a nation's economy. Keynesians believe that demand for goods ultimately controls employment and prices. Insufficient demand for goods causes unemployment; too much demand causes inflation. Keynes believed that it was the government's right and responsibility to manipulate overall demand (and therefore artificially manipulate the economy) by changing its own levels of spending and taxation.

14. 1. 2. 1. 1 The Government's Role in Keynesian Economics

According to Keynes, a government's fiscal policies determine the country's economic health. Fiscal policy involves adjusting the level of taxation and government spending. The government is expected to intervene in the economy as a major force in creating prosperity by engaging in activities that affect aggregate demand.

Government affects individual levels of spending and saving by adjusting taxes. Increasing taxes removes money from the private sector, which reduces private sector demand and spending. Government spending puts money back into the economy. To increase private sector demand for goods, the government reduces taxes, which increases people's disposable income.

14. 1. 2. 2 Monetarist Theory

Milton Friedman is considered the originator of **monetarist economic theory**. Monetarists believe the quantity of money, the **money supply**, is the major determinant of price levels. Too many dollars chasing too few goods leads to inflation; conversely, too few dollars chasing too many goods leads to deflation.

Monetarists believe a well-controlled, moderately increasing money supply leads to price stability. Price stability allows business managers (considered to be more efficient allocators of resources than the government) to plan and invest, which in turn keeps the economy healthy.

Monetary economic policy is controlled by the Federal Reserve Board. Monetarists believe that the amount of money in the system is the major influence on economic performance. The reserve requirement, discount rate, and open market operations are the tools used by monetarists to regulate the economy.

14. 1. 2. 3 Supply-Side Economics

Supply-side economics holds that government should allow market forces to determine prices of all goods. Supply-siders believe the federal government should reduce government spending as well as taxes. In this way, sellers of goods will price them at a rate that allows them to meet market demand and still sell them profitably.

14. 1. 2. 3. 1 The Laffer Curve

Economist Arthur Laffer studied government revenues as a function of tax rates to find the tax rate that produces the most revenue for the government. The Laffer Curve shows the relationship between tax rates and tax revenue collected by governments. As tax rates increase from low levels, tax revenue would increase. As tax rates continue to rise, there would come a point where people would not work as hard or as much. This lack of incentive would lead to a fall in income and, therefore, a fall in tax revenue. The logical end point is with tax rates at 100%; no one would work, and there would be no tax revenue.

TEST TOPIC ALERT The Series 7 exam may require that you know the originators of fundamental economic theories. Keynesian economists believe in government intervention, whereas Laffer and supply-side economists believe the government should step aside and let market forces take over.

14. 2 ECONOMIC POLICY

In a nutshell, the difference between Keynesians and monetarists is their perspectives toward the government's role in the economy. Keynesians believe the government, through its fiscal policies, should be a driving force in determining the level and allocation of economic resources. Monetarists, on the other hand, believe the private sector allocates resources much more efficiently, and the government's role is to provide a stable monetary environment within which private sector decisions can be made.

14. 2. 1 MONETARY POLICY

14. 2. 1. 1 Definition of Money

Most people think of money as cash in their pockets. An economist takes a much broader view and includes loans, credit, and other liquid instruments. Economists divide money into three categories, as shown here.

The Parts of the Money Supply

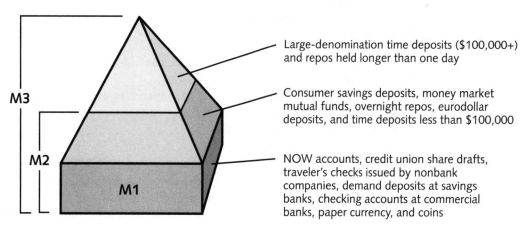

Large-denomination time deposits ($100,000+) and repos held longer than one day

Consumer savings deposits, money market mutual funds, overnight repos, eurodollar deposits, and time deposits less than $100,000

NOW accounts, credit union share drafts, traveler's checks issued by nonbank companies, demand deposits at savings banks, checking accounts at commercial banks, paper currency, and coins

M1. The most readily available type of money, M1 consists of currency in circulation and demand deposits (checking accounts) that can be converted to currency immediately. It is the money consumers use for ordinary purchases of goods and services. Most money (M1) is in demand deposits—that is, checking accounts. M1 is the largest and most liquid component of the money supply.

M2. In addition to M1, M2 includes some time deposits (less than $100,000) that are fairly easy to convert into demand deposits. These time deposits include savings accounts, nonnegotiable CDs, money market funds, and overnight repurchase agreements.

M3. In addition to M1 and M2, M3 includes time deposits of more than $100,000 and repurchase agreements with terms longer than one day.

14. 2. 1. 2 The Federal Reserve Board (FRB)

The **FRB** consists of 12 regional Federal Reserve Banks and hundreds of national and state banks that belong to the system. The FRB determines monetary policy and takes actions to implement its policies, including:

- acting as an agent of the U.S. Treasury;
- regulating the U.S. money supply;
- setting reserve requirements for members;
- supervising the printing of currency;
- clearing fund transfers throughout the system; and
- examining members to ensure compliance with federal regulations.

Because the FRB determines how much money is available for businesses and consumers to spend, its decisions are a critical aspect of the U.S. economy.

The FRB affects the money supply through its use of three policy tools:

- Open-market operations (buying/selling government securities)
- Changes in the discount rate (on loans to member banks)
- Changes in reserve requirements

14. 2. 1. 2. 1 Open-Market Operations

The Fed buys and sells U.S. government securities in the open market to expand and contract the money supply. The **Federal Open Market Committee (FOMC)** meets regularly to direct the government's open-market operations.

When the FOMC buys securities, it increases the supply of money in the banking system, and when it sells securities, it decreases the supply.

When the Fed wants to expand (loosen) the money supply, it buys securities from banks. The banks receive direct credit in their reserve accounts. The increase of reserves allows banks to make more loans and effectively lowers interest rates. Thus, by buying securities, the Fed pumps money into the banking system, expanding the money supply and reducing rates.

When the Fed wants to contract (tighten) the money supply, it sells securities to banks. Each sale is charged against a bank's reserve balance. This reduces the bank's ability to lend money, which tightens credit and effectively raises interest rates. By selling securities, the Fed pulls money out of the system, contracting the money supply and increasing rates.

14. 2. 1. 2. 2 Discount Rate

The Fed can also adjust the money supply by raising or lowering the **discount rate**— that is, the interest rate the Fed charges its members for short-term loans. To compensate for shortfalls in its reserve requirement, a bank may borrow money directly from the Fed at its discount rate or borrow the **excess reserves** (federal funds) from another member bank. The interest rate banks charge each other for such loans is called the **federal funds rate**.

The federal funds rate fluctuates daily and is the most volatile interest rate. A rising rate usually indicates that member banks are more reluctant to lend their funds and want a higher rate of interest in return. A higher rate usually results from a shortage of funds to lend and probably indicates that deposits in general are shrinking. A falling federal funds rate generally means that the lending banks are competing to loan money and are trying to make their loans more attractive by lowering their rates. A lower rate often results from an excess of deposits.

Lowering the discount rate reduces the cost of money to banks, which increases the demand for loans. Raising the discount rate increases the cost of money and reduces the demand for loans.

TAKE NOTE

Short-term rates are more volatile than long-term rates. The federal funds rate, the most volatile rate in the economy, is generally an overnight rate charged in bank-to-bank borrowing. Do not confuse this with the fact that long-term bond prices move more than short-term bond prices in response to interest rate changes.

14. 2. 1. 2. 3 Reserve Requirements and Federal Funds

Commercial banks must deposit a certain percentage of their depositors' money with the Federal Reserve. This is known as the **reserve requirement**. All money commercial banks deposit at Federal Reserve Banks, including money exceeding the reserve requirement, is known as **federal funds**.

When the Fed raises the reserve requirement, banks must deposit more funds with the Fed and thus have less money to lend. Reducing the reserve requirement has the opposite effect.

Federal Reserve Policy Tactics

To expand credit during a recession to stimulate a slow economy:	To tighten credit to slow economic expansion and prevent inflation:
■ Buy U.S. government securities in the open market	■ Sell U.S. government securities in the open market
■ Lower the discount rate	■ Raise the discount rate
■ Lower reserve requirements	■ Raise reserve requirements

14. 3   FISCAL POLICY

Fiscal policy refers to governmental budget decisions, which can include increases or decreases in:

■ federal spending;

■ money raised through taxes; and

■ federal budget deficits or surpluses.

Fiscal policy is based on the assumption that the government can control unemployment levels and inflation by adjusting overall demand for goods and services.

The political process determines fiscal policy. Therefore, it takes time for conditions and solutions to be identified and implemented. Because of the time and negotiations involved, fiscal policy is an inefficient means to solve short-term economic problems.

14. 3. 0. 1 The Stock Market

Fiscal and monetary policies have considerable influence on the stock market. If the FRB eases interest rates, the money supply increases, making credit easier to obtain. This increases overall liquidity.

Similarly, lower tax rates can stimulate spending by leaving more spendable dollars in the hands of individuals and businesses. Like easier credit, lower tax rates are bullish for the stock market. Raising taxes has the opposite effect, reducing the amount of money available to businesses and consumers for spending and investment.

14. 3. 0. 2 Interest Rates

A loan's interest rate is the cost of the money. In large measure, the supply and demand of money determines interest rates. When the money available for loans exceeds demand, interest rates fall. When the FRB tightens the money supply, interest rates rise. The Fed influences the money supply in several ways, which directly or indirectly affect interest rate levels.

14. 3. 1 INTERNATIONAL MONETARY FACTORS

14. 3. 1. 1 Balance of Payments

The flow of money between the United States and other countries is known as the **balance of payments**. The balance of payments may be a **surplus** (more money flowing into the country than out) or a **deficit** (more money flowing out of the country than in). A deficit may occur when interest rates in another country are high because money flows to where it earns the highest return.

The largest component of the balance of payments is the **balance of trade**—the export and import of merchandise.

On the U.S. credit side are sales of American products to foreign countries. On the debit side are American purchases of foreign goods that cause American dollars to flow out of the country. When debits exceed credits, a deficit in the balance of payments occurs; when credits exceed debits, a surplus exists.

Balance of Trade

Debit Items	Credit Items
Imports	Exports
U.S. spending abroad	Foreign spending in the United States
U.S. investments abroad	Foreign investments in the United States
U.S. bank loans abroad	
U.S. foreign aid	

TAKE NOTE

The value of the dollar against foreign currencies affects the balance of trade. If the dollar is weak, foreign currency buys more U.S. goods, so exports increase. When the dollar is strong, foreign currency buys fewer U.S. goods. The dollar buys more foreign goods, so imports increase.

Many European countries, such as France and Germany, converted their home currency to the euro several years ago. Therefore, cross-border transactions between these countries no longer have currency risk. Note, though, that England (British pound) and Switzerland (Swiss franc) did not convert to the euro.

TEST TOPIC ALERT

Know the fundamentals of fiscal and monetary policy.

Fiscal policy:

- Actions of Congress and the president

- Government spending and taxation

Monetary policy:

- Policy of the Federal Reserve Board (FRB)

- Discount rate

- Reserve requirement (most drastic)

- Open-market operations (most frequently used)

Note the following.

- The FRB sets the discount rate, not the federal funds rate.

- A change in the reserve requirement has a multiplier effect on the money supply; it has the most drastic impact of the FRB's tools.

- Open-market operations are the most frequently used tool of the FRB.

QUICK QUIZ 14.B

1. When the FOMC purchases T-bills in the open market, which of the following scenarios are likely to occur?

    I.   Secondary bond prices will rise.
    II. Secondary bond prices will fall.
    III. Interest rates will rise.
    IV. Interest rates will fall.

    A. I and III
    B. I and IV
    C. II and III
    D. II and IV

2. All of the following situations could cause a fall in the value of the U.S. dollar in relation to the Japanese yen EXCEPT

   A. Japanese investors buying U.S. Treasury securities
   B. U.S. investors buying Japanese securities
   C. increase in Japan's trade surplus over that of the United States
   D. general decrease in U.S. interest rates

3. Disintermediation is most likely to occur when

   A. money is tight
   B. interest rates remain low across all savings institutions and investments
   C. margin requirements are high
   D. the interest ceilings on certificates of deposit have been raised

4. To tighten credit during inflationary periods, the Federal Reserve Board may take any of the following actions EXCEPT

   A. raise reserve requirements
   B. change the amount of U.S. government debt held by major banks
   C. sell securities in the open market
   D. lower taxes

5. Which of the following is not part of M1?

   A. Traveler's checks
   B. Money market mutual funds
   C. Coins
   D. Consumer checking accounts

14. 4   TECHNICAL ANALYSIS

Both technical and fundamental analyses attempt to predict the supply and demand of markets and individual stocks. **Technical analysis** attempts to predict the direction of prices on the basis of historic price and trading volume patterns when laid out graphically on charts. **Fundamental analysts** concentrate on broad-based economic trends; current business conditions within an industry; and the quality of a particular corporation's business, finances, and management.

14. 4. 1   MARKET AVERAGES AND INDEXES

Stock prices tend to move, or **trend**, together, although some move in the opposite direction. The average stock, by definition, tends to rise in a bull market and decline in a bear market. Technical analysts chart the daily prices and volume movements of individual stocks and market indexes to discern patterns that allow them to predict the direction of market price movements.

14. 4. 1. 1 Trading Volume

Market trading volume substantially above normal signifies or confirms a pattern in the direction of prices. If overall volume has been listless for months and suddenly jumps significantly, a technical analyst views that as the beginning of a trend.

14. 4. 1. 2 Advances/Declines

The number of issues closing up or down on a specific day reflects **market breadth**. The number of advances and declines can be a significant indication of the market's relative strength. When declines outnumber advances by a large amount, the market is bearish even if it closed higher. In bull markets, advances substantially outnumber declines. Technical analysts plot daily advances and declines on a graph to produce an **advance/decline line** that gives them an indication of market breadth trends.

14. 4. 2 CHARTING STOCKS

In addition to studying the overall market, technical analysts attempt to identify patterns in the prices of individual stocks.

14. 4. 2. 1 Trendlines

Although a stock's price may spike up or down daily, over time its price tends to move in one direction. Technical analysts identify patterns in the trendlines of individual stocks from graphs as they do patterns in the overall market. They base their buy or sell recommendations on a stock's price trendline. An upward trendline is bullish; a downward one is bearish.

Upward and Downward Trendlines

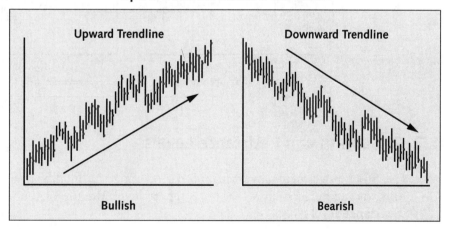

A trendline connects the lows in an uptrend and the highs in a downtrend. Three common patterns in stock price trendlines are consolidations, reversals, and support and resistance levels.

14. 4. 2. 1. 1 Consolidations

If a stock's price stays within a narrow range, it is said to be **consolidating**. When viewed on a graph, the trendline is horizontal and moves sideways, neither up nor down.

14. 4. 2. 1. 2 Reversals

A **reversal** indicates that an upward or a downward trendline has halted and the stock's price is moving in the opposite direction. Between the two trendlines, a period of consolidation occurs, and the stock price levels off. A genuine reversal pattern can be difficult to recognize because trends are composed of many rises and declines, which may occur at different rates and for different lengths of time.

Because of its gently curving shape, an easily identifiable reversal pattern is called a **saucer** (reversal of a downtrend) or an **inverted saucer** (reversal of an uptrend). A similar reversal pattern is the **head-and-shoulders** pattern, named for its resemblance to the human body.

The head and shoulders top pattern indicates the beginning of a bearish trend in the stock. First, the stock price rises, then it reaches a plateau at the neckline (left shoulder). A second advance pushes the price higher, but then the price falls back to the neckline (head). Finally, the stock price rises again, but falls back to the neckline (right shoulder) and continues downward, indicating a reversal of the upward trend.

When reversed, this pattern is called a **head-and-shoulders bottom**, or an **inverted head-and-shoulders**, and indicates a bullish reversal.

Head-and-Shoulders Top and Bottom Trendlines

14. 4. 2. 2 Support and Resistance Levels

Stock prices may move within a narrow range for months or even years. The bottom of this trading range is known as the **support level**; the top of the trading range is called the **resistance level**.

Support and Resistance Levels

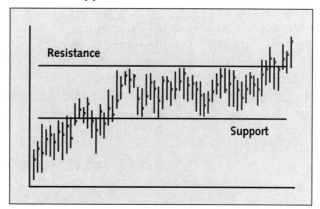

When a stock declines to its support level, the low price attracts buyers, whose buying supports the price and keeps it from declining farther. When a stock increases to its resistance level, the high price attracts sellers, whose selling hinders a further price rise. Stocks may fluctuate in trading ranges for months, testing their support and resistance levels. If a particular stock's price penetrates either the support or the resistance level, the change is considered significant.

A decline through the support level is called a **bearish breakout**; a rise through the resistance level is called a **bullish breakout**. Breakouts usually signal the beginning of a new upward or downward trend.

14. 4. 2. 3 Overbought and Oversold

If market indexes such as the S&P 500 and the Dow are declining, but the number of declining stocks relative to the number of advancing stocks is falling (fewer stocks declining), the market is said to be oversold and is likely to reverse itself.

Conversely, if market indexes are rising, but the number of declining stocks relative to the number of advancing stocks is rising (fewer stocks rising), the market is said to be overbought and is ready for a correction.

14. 4. 3 TECHNICAL MARKET THEORIES

Technical analysts follow various theories regarding market trends. Some of them are outlined below.

14. 4. 3. 1 Dow Theory

Analysts use the **Dow theory** to confirm the end of a major market trend. According to the theory, the three types of changes in stock prices are **primary trends** (one year or more), **secondary trends** (3–12 weeks), and **short-term fluctuations** (hours or days).

In a bull market, the primary trend is upward. However, stock prices may still drop in a secondary trend within the primary upward trend, even for as long as 12 weeks. The trough of the downward secondary trend should be higher than the trough of the previous downward trend. In a bear market, secondary upward trends may occur, but the highs reached during those secondary upward movements are successively lower.

According to the Dow theory, the primary trend in a bull market is a series of higher highs and higher lows. In a bear market, the primary trend is a series of lower highs and lower lows. Daily fluctuations are considered irrelevant.

A primary upward trend interrupted by secondary downward movements is shown in the following chart. The chart illustrates a series of successively higher highs and lows, conforming to the definition of a primary upward trend.

Any change in direction is considered deceptive unless the Dow Jones Industrial and Transportation Averages reflect the change. However, using this average lacks precision and is sometimes slow in confirming changes in market trends.

Dow Theory of Market Trends

14. 4. 3. 2 Odd-Lot Theory

Typically, small investors engage in **odd-lot trading**. Followers of the **odd-lot theory** believe that these small investors invariably buy and sell at the wrong times. When odd-lot traders buy, odd-lot analysts are bearish. When odd-lot traders sell, odd-lot analysts are bullish.

14. 4. 3. 3 Short Interest Theory

Short interest refers to the number of shares that have been sold short. Because short positions must be repurchased eventually, some analysts believe that short interest reflects mandatory demand, which creates a support level for stock prices. High short interest is a bullish indicator, and low short interest is a bearish indicator.

14. 4. 3. 4 Modern Portfolio Theory

Instead of emphasizing particular stocks, **modern portfolio theory (MPT)** focuses on the relationship of all the investments in a portfolio. The theory holds that analysts' ability to predict price movements is of no value. Adherents to MPT believe securities markets are efficient markets, meaning securities prices react so quickly to most investment information that no analyst is likely to outsmart the market as a whole. MPT portfolio managers select a general mix of investments weighted to emphasize economic trends.

14. 4. 3. 5 Random Walk and Efficient Market Theories

The **random walk theory** is an academic theory maintaining that the direction of stock or market prices is unpredictable. This hypothesis is based on the **efficient market theory**, which holds that the stock market is perfectly efficient, with prices reflecting all known information at any given time. It is impossible, therefore, to beat the market using fundamental or technical analysis (i.e., throwing darts at the stock listings is as good a method as any for selecting stocks for investment).

TEST TOPIC ALERT

Technical analysts are sometimes called **market timers**. They determine whether to buy or sell on the basis of such trends as market breadth, trading volume, and the market theories you have just read about. Be prepared to identify technical analysis tools versus fundamental analysis tools for test questions. Be aware of the following about market indexes.

- The Dow Jones Industrial Average (DJIA) is the oldest and most widely quoted index.

- The Dow Jones Composite includes 30 industrial, 20 transportation, and 15 utility issues.

- The Value Line Index includes 1,700 NYSE and OTC stocks.

- The Wilshire 5000 Index is the broadest market index and includes all NYSE listed stocks, as well as all Nasdaq listed stocks.

- The S&P 500 consists of 500 of the most widely held companies chosen with respect to market size, liquidity, and industrial sector.

QUICK QUIZ 14.C

1. When a technical analyst says that the market is consolidating, the trendline is moving

    A. upward
    B. downward
    C. sideways
    D. unpredictably

2. From a chartist's (technical analyst's) viewpoint, which of the following statements is TRUE?

    A. Once a trendline is established, the price movement of a stock usually follows the trendline.
    B. More odd-lot buying than selling is bullish.
    C. Heavy volume in a declining market is bullish.
    D. Light volume in an advancing market is bullish.

3. Proponents of which of the following technical theories assume that small investors are usually wrong?

    A. Breadth-of-market theory
    B. Short-interest theory
    C. Volume-of-trading theory
    D. Odd-lot theory

4. Which of the following is the narrowest measure of the market?
   A. NYSE Composite Index
   B. Value Line Index
   C. DJIA
   D. Standard & Poor's 500

14. 5 FUNDAMENTAL ANALYSIS

Fundamental analysis is the study of the business prospects of an individual company within the context of its industry and the overall economy.

14. 5. 1 INDUSTRY ANALYSIS

Because business cycle phases have different effects on different industries, fundamental analysts look for companies in industries that offer better-than-average opportunities in the context of the business cycle. It is useful to distinguish between the four types of industries and investments: defensive, cyclical, growth, and special situation.

14. 5. 1. 1 Defensive Industries

Defensive industries are least affected by normal business cycles. Companies in defensive industries generally produce nondurable consumer goods, such as food, pharmaceuticals, and tobacco. Public consumption of such goods remains fairly steady throughout the business cycle. During recessions and bear markets, stocks in defensive industries generally decline less than stocks in other industries, but during expansions and bull markets, defensive stocks may advance less. Investments in defensive industries tend to involve less risk and, consequently, lower investment returns.

14. 5. 1. 2 Cyclical Industries

Cyclical industries are highly sensitive to business cycles and inflation trends. Most cyclical industries produce durable goods, such as heavy machinery, and raw materials, such as steel and automobiles. During recessions, the demand for such products declines as manufacturers postpone investments in new capital goods and consumers postpone purchases of these goods, such as automobiles. **Counter-cyclical industries**, on the other hand, tend to turn down as the economy heats up and to rise when the economy turns down.

14. 5. 1. 3 Growth Industries

Every industry passes through four phases during its existence: introduction, growth, maturity, and decline. An industry is considered in its **growth phase** if the industry is growing faster than the economy as a whole because of technological changes, new products, or changing consumer tastes. Computers and bioengineering are current growth industries. Because many growth companies retain nearly all of their earnings to finance their business expansion, growth stocks usually pay little or no dividends.

14. 5. 1. 4 Special Situation Stocks

Special situation stocks are stocks of a company with unusual profit potential resulting from nonrecurring circumstances. These situations might include new management, the discovery of a valuable natural resource on corporate property, patents pending, or the introduction of a new product.

14. 6   CORPORATE ANALYSIS

After considering the state of the economy and the health of various industries, fundamental analysts study a company's position within its industry, prospects for growth and stability, and financial strength. Fundamental analysts look at a firm's quality of management and its historical earnings trends, compare the level and stability of its projected growth with that of its competitors, and examine the structure of a corporation's capitalization and use of working capital.

14. 6. 1   FINANCIAL STATEMENTS

A corporation's **financial statements** provide a fundamental analyst with the raw material needed to assess that corporation's profitability, financial strength, and operating efficiency. By examining how certain static numbers from the statement relate to one another and how the resulting ratios relate to the company's competitors, the analyst can determine how financially viable the company is.

Companies issue quarterly and annual financial reports that include a balance sheet and income statement to their stockholders.

14. 6. 1. 1 Balance Sheet

The **balance sheet** provides a snapshot of a company's financial position at a specific time. It identifies the value of the company's assets (what it owns) and its liabilities (what it owes). The difference between these two figures is the corporation's **equity**, or **net worth**.

A corporation can be compared to a homeowner who borrows money to buy a home. The homeowner's equity is the difference between the mortgage balance (liability) and the home's market value (asset value). A corporation can buy assets using borrowed money (liabilities) and equity raised by selling stock. The value of its assets must equal (balance with) the value of its liabilities and equity.

Although it is useful in determining a company's current value, the balance sheet cannot tell the analyst whether the company's business is improving or deteriorating.

The Balance Sheet Equation

	Liabilities Current liabilities Long-term liabilities
Assets Current assets Fixed assets Other assets	**Equity (net worth)** Preferred stock par value Common stock par value Additional paid-in capital Treasury stock Retained earnings

Assets = liabilities + shareholders' equity

14. 6. 1. 2   Balance Sheet Components

The balance sheet gets its name from the fact that its two sides must balance. The balance sheet equation mathematically expresses the relationship between the two sides of the balance sheet.

TAKE NOTE   Assets – liabilities = net worth

14. 6. 1. 2. 1 Assets

Assets appear on the balance sheet in order of **liquidity** (the ease with which they can be turned into cash). Those most readily convertible into cash are listed first, followed by less liquid assets. Balance sheets commonly identify three types of assets: **current assets** (cash and assets easily convertible into cash), **fixed assets** (physical assets that could eventually be sold), and **other assets** (usually intangible and only of value to the corporation owning them).

Current Assets. Current assets include all cash and other items expected to be converted into cash within the next 12 months and include the following:

- **Cash and equivalents**—cash and short-term safe investments (such as money market instruments) that can be sold readily, as well as other marketable securities
- **Accounts receivable**—amounts due from customers for goods delivered or services rendered, reduced by the allowance for bad debts
- **Inventory**—the cost of raw materials, work in process, and finished goods ready for sale
- **Prepaid expenses**—items a company has already paid for but has not yet benefited from (e.g., prepaid advertising, rents, taxes, and operating supplies)

Fixed Assets. Fixed assets are typically property, plant, and equipment. Unlike current assets, they are not easily converted into cash. Fixed assets, such as factories, have limited useful lives because wear and tear eventually reduce their value. For this reason, their cost can be **depreciated** over time—deducted from taxable income in annual installments to compensate for loss in value. Note that on the example balance sheet (see below), depreciation has reduced fixed assets by $10 million.

Other Assets. Intangible assets are nonphysical properties, such as formulas, contract rights, and trademarks. **Goodwill**, also an intangible asset, is a company's value over and above its book value. This extra sum is paid for the corporation's reputation and relationship with its clients. In the example, $5 million in other assets was reported, including intangible assets and goodwill.

14. 6. 1. 2. 2 Liabilities

Total liabilities on a balance sheet represent all financial claims by creditors against the corporation's assets. Balance sheets usually include two main types of liabilities: **current liabilities** (debts due within 12 months) and **long-term liabilities** (debts or bonds maturing in more than 12 months).

Current Liabilities. Current liabilities are corporate debt obligations due for payment within the next 12 months. In the example, these include:

- **accounts payable**—amounts owed to suppliers of materials and other business costs;
- **accrued wages payable**—unpaid wages, salaries, commissions, and interest; and
- **current long-term debt**—any portion of long-term debt due within 12 months.

A balance sheet might also include the following as current liabilities:

- **Notes payable**—the balance due on equipment purchased on credit or cash borrowed
- **Accrued taxes**—unpaid federal, state, and local taxes

Long-Term Liabilities. Long-term debts are financial obligations due for payment after 12 months. Examples of long-term debts are mortgages on real property, long-term promissory notes, and outstanding corporate bonds. **Funded debt** is any long-term debt payable in five years or more.

Example Balance Sheet

Balance Sheet Amalgamated Widget as of Dec. 31, (applicable year)			
ASSETS			
Current assets	Cash and equivalents	$ 5,000,000	
	Accounts receivable	15,000,000	
	Inventory	19,000,000	
	Prepaid expenses	1,000,000	
	Total current assets		$ 40,000,000
Fixed assets	Buildings, furniture, and fixtures (including $10 million depreciation)	$ 40,000,000	
	Land	15,000,000	
	Total fixed assets		$ 55,000,000
Other (intangibles, goodwill)			$ 5,000,000
Total assets			$100,000,000
LIABILITIES AND NET WORTH			
Current liabilities	Accounts payable	$ 5,000,000	
	Accrued wages payable	4,000,000	
	Current portion of long-term debt	1,000,000	
	Total current liabilities		$ 10,000,000
Long-term liabilities	8% 20-year convertible debentures		$ 50,000,000
Total liabilities			$ 60,000,000
Net worth	Preferred stock $100 par ($5 noncumula- tive convertible 200,000 shares issued)	$20,000,000	
	Common stock $1 par (1 million shares)	1,000,000	
	Capital in excess of par	4,000,000	
	Retained earnings	15,000,000	
Total net worth			$ 40,000,000
Total liabilities and net worth			$100,000,000

14. 6. 1. 3 Shareholders' Equity

Shareholders' equity, also called **net worth** or **owners' equity**, is the stockholders' claims on a company's assets after all of its creditors have been paid. Shareholders' equity equals total assets less total liabilities. On a balance sheet, three types of shareholders' equity are identified: capital stock at par, capital in excess of par, and retained earnings.

14. 6. 1. 3. 1 Capital Stock at Par

Capital stock includes preferred and common stock listed at par value. **Par value** is the total dollar value assigned to stock certificates when a corporation's owners (the stockholders) first contributed capital. Par value of common stock is an arbitrary value with no relationship to market price.

14. 6. 1. 3. 2 Capital in Excess of Par

Capital in excess of par, often called **additional paid-in capital** or **paid-in surplus**, is the amount of money over par value that a company received for selling stock.

14. 6. 1. 3. 3 Retained Earnings

Retained earnings, sometimes called **earned surplus**, are profits that have not been paid out in dividends. Retained earnings represent the total of all earnings held since the corporation was formed, less dividends paid to stockholders. Operating losses in any year reduce the retained earnings from prior years.

14. 6. 1. 3. 4 Capitalization

A company's **capitalization** is the combined sum of its long-term debt and equity accounts. The **capital structure** is the relative amounts of debt and equity that compose a company's capitalization. Some companies finance their business with a large proportion of borrowed funds; others finance growth with retained earnings from normal operations and little or no debt.

14. 6. 1. 3. 5 Liquidity

Working capital is the amount of capital or cash a company has available. Working capital is, therefore, a measure of a firm's liquidity—its ability to quickly turn assets into cash to meet its short-term obligations. The formula for working capital is:

$$\text{Current assets} - \text{current liabilities} = \text{working capital}$$

Liquidity is important because it is the measure of a company's ability to pay the expenses associated with running the business.

14. 6. 1. 4   Changes That Affect the Balance Sheet

14. 6. 1. 4. 1 Balancing the Balance Sheet

Balance sheets, by definition, must balance. Every financial change in a business requires two offsetting changes on the company books, known as **double-entry bookkeeping**.

14. 6. 1. 4. 2 Depreciating Assets

Because fixed assets, such as buildings, equipment, and machinery, wear out as they are used, they decline in value over time. This decline in value is called **depreciation**. A company's tax bills are reduced each year the company depreciates fixed assets used in the businesses.

Depreciation affects the company in two ways: accumulated depreciation reduces the value of fixed assets on the balance sheet, and the depreciation deduction reduces taxable income on the income statement.

Companies may elect either straight line or accelerated depreciation. Using the straight line method, a company depreciates fixed assets by a set amount each year over the asset's useful life. A piece of equipment costing $1 million with a 10-year useful life will generate a depreciation deduction of $100,000 per year.

Accelerated depreciation is a method that depreciates fixed assets more during the earlier years of their useful life and less during the later years.

TAKE NOTE

Compared with straight line, accelerated depreciation generates larger deductions (lower taxable income) during the early years and smaller deductions (higher taxable income) during the later years.

TAKE NOTE

The basic balance sheet equation can be expressed in two ways:

Assets – liabilities = net worth

Assets = liabilities + net worth

14. 6. 2   CAPITAL STRUCTURE

A corporation builds its capital structure with the following four elements:

- Long-term debt
- Capital stock (common and preferred)
- Capital in excess of par
- Retained earnings (earned surplus)

EXAMPLE

(See the table below for reference and explanation of the following terms.) The total capitalization on the sample balance is $90 million ($50 million in long-term debt, $20 million in preferred stock, and $20 million in common shareholders' equity). Remember, capital stock + capital in excess of par + retained earnings = shareholders' equity (net worth).

Total capitalization	$90 million
LT debt	$50 million
+ Pfd.	$20 million
+ Common	$1 million
+ Cap. surplus	$4 million
+ Ret. earnings	$15 million

If a company changes its capitalization by issuing stock or bonds, the effects will show up on the balance sheet.

14. 6. 2. 1 Inventory Valuation

Under the FIFO method (first in, first out), the oldest items in inventory are used to compute cost of sales. During inflationary periods, this method matches current sales with older, cheaper inventory and tends to inflate reported profits. The more recently purchased items remain, so inventory values are fairly stated.

Under the LIFO method (last in, first out), the most recently purchased items are matched against current sales. In inflationary periods, this matches costs with sales better. On the other hand, inventory values are understated.

Example Income Statement

Income Statement Amalgamated Widget Jan. 1–Dec. 31, (applicable year)		
Net sales		$60,000,000
Cost of goods sold	$10,000,000	
General operating expenses (including $2 million depreciation)	$30,000,000	$40,000,000
Operating income		$20,000,000
Interest expense		$ 4,000,000
Pretax income		$16,000,000
Taxes		$ 6,000,000
Net income after taxes		$10,000,000
Preferred dividends		$ 1,000,000
Earnings available to common		$ 9,000,000

14. 6. 2. 2 Issuing Securities

The example balance sheet indicates the company issued 1 million shares of $1 par common stock. If it issues another 1 million shares, the net worth (shareholders' equity) will increase by the additional capital raised, and the amount of cash on the asset side of the balance sheet will increase.

14. 6. 2. 3 Convertible Securities

When an investor converts a convertible bond into shares of common stock, the amount of liabilities will decrease and owners' equity increases. The changes are on the same side of the balance sheet, so there is no change to the assets.

14. 6. 2. 4 Bond Redemption

When bonds are redeemed, liabilities on the balance sheet are reduced. The offsetting change would be a decrease in cash on the asset side of the balance sheet. The company would have less debt outstanding, but it would also have less cash. The balance sheet balances.

14. 6. 2. 5 Dividends

When a cash dividend is declared, retained earnings are lowered and current liabilities are increased. The declaration of a cash dividend establishes a current liability until it is paid. Once paid, it reduces cash in current assets and also reduces current liabilities.

Distribution of stock dividends has no effect on corporate assets or liabilities, nor does it change the stockholders' proportionate equity in the corporation. The number of shares each stockholder owns increases, but each single share represents a smaller slice of ownership in the corporation.

14. 6. 2. 6 Stock Splits

Like a stock dividend, a **stock split** does not affect shareholders' equity. On the balance sheet, only the par value per share and number of shares outstanding change.

14. 6. 2. 7 Spin-offs

This is a type of corporate divestiture. It occurs when a new company is created by the sale of all shares of a subsidiary company or the distribution of new shares of an existing business or division by a parent company. Both sides of the balance sheet for the parent company will be affected to the extent of the equity and debt they have divested themselves of.

14. 6. 2. 8 Financial Leverage

Financial leverage is a company's ability to use long-term debt to increase its return on equity. A company with a high ratio of long-term debt to equity is said to be **highly leveraged**.

Stockholders benefit from leverage if the return on borrowed money exceeds the debt service costs. But leverage is risky because excessive increases in debt raise the possibility of default in a business downturn.

The Federal Reserve Board defines industrial companies with debt-to-equity ratios of 50% or more as highly leveraged. However, utilities, with their relatively stable earnings and cash flows, can be more highly leveraged without subjecting stockholders to undue risk. If highly leveraged, the company is also affected more by changes in interest rates.

TEST TOPIC ALERT   The Series 7 exam does not generally ask for calculations with balance sheet or income statement items. Make sure to recognize the main components of each of these financial statements. You may be asked about the impact of a certain transaction on the balance sheet.

1. Which of the following choices are affected when a corporation purchases a printing press for cash?

    A. Current assets
    B. Current liabilities
    C. Working capital
    D. Total assets
    E. Total liabilities
    F. Net worth

    Answer: A and **C**. A payment of cash reduces current assets. Whenever either current assets or current liabilities change, working capital is also affected. The new printing press increases the value of the fixed assets. Total assets, however, are unchanged because the decrease in current assets is offset by the increase in fixed assets.

2. Which are affected when a corporation declares a cash dividend?

    Answer: B, C, E, and **F**. The declaration (not payment) of a dividend creates a current liability on the books of the corporation. Because current liabilities are affected, working capital and total liabilities also change. The declaration of a dividend reduces the net worth because the dividend will be paid from retained earnings.

When the dividend is paid, current assets will decrease and current liabilities will decrease (this also decreases both total assets and total liabilities). Working capital does not change because both current assets and current liabilities decrease by the same amount.

If a corporation has a stock split, the balance sheet categories above are not affected. A stock split will increase the number of shares and reduce the value of each share, but the total par value as shown in the equity section of the balance sheet is not affected.

QUICK QUIZ 14.D

1. The difference between current assets and current liabilities is called
   A. net worth
   B. working capital
   C. cash flow
   D. quick assets

2. As a result of corporate transactions, a company's assets remain the same and its equity decreases. Which of the following statements is TRUE?
   A. Prepaid expenses decrease.
   B. Total liabilities increase.
   C. Accrued expenses decrease.
   D. Net worth increases.

3. Which of the following is NOT affected by the issuance of a bond?
   A. Assets
   B. Total liabilities
   C. Working capital
   D. Shareholders' equity

4. A company has been experiencing increased earnings but has kept its dividend payments constant. As a result solely of this, the company's balance sheet would reflect
   A. decreased net working capital
   B. decreased net worth
   C. decreased retained earnings
   D. increased shareholders' equity

14. 6. 2. 9 Private Equity

Private equity is equity capital invested in operating companies that are not traded publicly. Often, these companies may have issued equity securities that do trade publicly, like common and preferred shares. Regarding the private equity investments, they can be made by firms specializing in these types of investments, generally known as private equity firms, venture capital firms, funds that specialize in investing in non-public companies, and private investors. The majority of private equity is provided by institutional and accredited investors who are able to commit larger amounts of money for longer periods of time. The long holding periods often required for private equity commitments, in theory, allow the placed equity the time needed to accomplish the intended goal of the investment.

Private equity capital can be used to fund new technologies, make acquisitions, strengthen a company's cash position or balance sheet, turn around a distressed company, or even to take a publicly traded company private. In the latter example, private equity firms have been known to pool assets together in order to raise the large sums of money needed to buy back shares of a publicly traded company in order to take it private.

14. 6. 2. 9. 1 Business or Growth Development Company (BDC)

A Business (Growth) Development Company (BDC) is one that is created to help grow small companies while still in the initial stages of their development. While the targeted objective is similar to what venture capital funds do, there is one major difference. BDCs tend to allow smaller, nonaccredited investors the opportunity to invest in very speculative startup ventures. Understandably, BDCs have become a popular way to finance startup companies because they provide the needed capital to their managements by allowing the general public to invest in the BDC.

Many are set up like closed-end investment companies which can be listed and traded on exchanges. Others are nontraded. FINRA notes that nontraded BDCs can be particularly problematic in terms of suitability for retail investors. FINRA considers nontraded BDCs to be fairly illiquid and cautions that an investor's opportunity to exit the investment may be limited to periodic share repurchases by the BDC which typically come at high discounts to current market value.

14. 6. 3 INCOME STATEMENT

The **income statement** summarizes a corporation's revenues and expenses for a fiscal period, usually quarterly, year-to-date, or the full year. It compares revenue with costs and expenses during the period.

Fundamental analysts use the income statement to judge the efficiency of a company's operation and its profitability.

Income Statement Entries

Net Sales

−	Cost of goods sold (COGS)
−	Operating costs (including depreciation)
=	Operating profit
+	Nonoperating income
=	Operating income (earnings before interest and taxes)
−	Interest expenses
=	Taxable income (pre-tax income)
−	Taxes
=	Net income after taxes
−	Preferred dividends
=	Earnings available to common
−	Common dividends
=	Retained earnings

The various operating and nonoperating expenses on the income statement are discussed here.

14. 6. 3. 1 Operating Income or Earnings Before Interest and Taxes (EBIT)

Operating income, also called operating margin or earnings before interest and taxes (EBIT), is a company's profits from business operations. In other words, this is the amount of money a company has retained before paying taxes and interest on outstanding debt issues.

14. 6. 3. 1. 1 Earnings Before Taxes (EBT)

Earnings before taxes (EBT) is the amount of money retained by a company before deducting the money to be paid for taxes. It should be noted that EBT includes money to be paid in interest on a company's debt instruments. Therefore, it can be calculated by subtracting interest from earnings before interest and taxes (EBIT), also known as operating income found on the income statement.

14. 6. 3. 1. 2 Earnings Before Interest, Taxes, Depreciation, and Amortization (EBITDA)

Earnings before interest, taxes, depreciation, and amortization (EBITDA) is exactly as its title implies. It can be calculated by looking at an income statement and reversing out interest, taxes, depreciation, and amortization from net income.

It is a metric used by public investors to measures cash earnings that can be used to pay interest and repay principal on debt while eliminating the effects of paying interest and taxes, or the accounting effects of including depreciation and amortization. In theory, investors' use of EBITDA arises from the perception that accountants' measures of profits, using accrual accounting, can be manipulated, and therefore, a measure of cash earnings using EBITDA would be more reliable in assessing the health of a company's ability to repay debt obligations than stated profits.

14. 6. 3. 2 Interest Expense

Interest payments on a corporation's debt are not considered an operating expense. Interest payments reduce the corporation's taxable income. Pretax income (the amount of taxable income) is operating income less interest payment expenses.

14. 6. 3. 3 Net Income After Taxes

If dividends are paid to stockholders, they are paid out of net income after taxes have been paid. After preferred dividends have been paid, the remaining income is available to invest in the business or pay dividends to common stockholders.

Interest payments reduce a corporation's taxable income, whereas dividend payments to stockholders are paid with after-tax dollars. Because they are taxable as income to stockholders, dividends are taxed twice, but interest payments are taxed once as income to the recipient.

14. 6. 3. 4 Earnings Per Share (EPS)

Earnings per share is what remains after payment of interest, taxes, and preferred dividends. Dividing net income after taxes, interest, and payment of preferred dividends by the number of common shares outstanding determines earnings per share.

$$\frac{\text{Earnings available to common}}{\text{Number of shares outstanding}}$$

EXAMPLE   To determine EPS, divide earnings available to common by the number of shares outstanding. Amalgamated Widgets has 4.5 million shares outstanding. With its earnings available to common of $9 million, EPS is $2.

14. 6. 3. 5 Retained Earnings

Retained earnings (earned surplus) are earnings not paid out in dividends.

14. 6. 4 FOOTNOTES

Footnotes to a company's financial statements identify significant financial and management issues that may affect the company's overall performance. Footnotes, which can sometimes be lengthy and numerous, are generally found at the bottom of the financial statements and will address accounting methods used, pending litigation, and management philosophy, among other significant items.

14. 7   FINANCIAL RATIOS AND ANALYZING CORPORATE EQUITY

Figures from the balance sheet or income statement can be expressed as **ratios**. Financial ratios allow an analyst to compare a company's performance to its past performance and to the performances of other companies within its industry. Such comparisons provide a more thorough understanding of a company's financial strengths and weaknesses.

TEST TOPIC ALERT   As you review financial ratios, remember that the test asks very few questions on this section and usually tests concepts rather than math. Understanding what the ratios measure is more important than mastering the calculations.

14. 7. 1 CAPITALIZATION RATIOS

Analysts can assess the risk of a company going bankrupt by studying the amount of **leverage** (the proportionate amount of long-term debt) in its overall **capitalization** (long-term debt plus equity).

When assessing a company's capitalization, analysts use ratios that express the percentage of capitalization composed of long-term debt, common stock, and preferred stock. The following four ratios are commonly used to assess the stability of a corporation's capitalization:

Debt-to-equity ratio = total long-term debt ÷ total shareholders' equity
Bond ratio (debt ratio) = long-term liabilities ÷ total capitalization
Common stock ratio = common shareholders' equity ÷ total capitalization
Preferred stock ratio = preferred stock ÷ total capitalization

14. 7. 1. 1   Leverage

Leverage is the use of long-term debt financing to increase earnings. The **debt-to-equity ratio** provides a common measure of leverage.

More debt may lead to greater EPS but may also increase risk to the common stockholders. A company with a disproportionately high amount of debt may not be able to meet its interest obligations during a business downturn. Low debt-to-equity ratios are considered more conservative than high debt-to-equity ratios. The debt-to-equity ratio is similar to the **bond ratio**, which compares total long-term debt to total capitalization rather than to shareholders' equity.

The **bond ratio**, or **debt ratio**, measures the percentage of total capitalization provided by long-term debt financing. The **common stock ratio** measures the percentage of total capitalization contributed by common stockholders, including the stock's par value, amount paid for the stock in excess of par, and retained earnings. The **preferred stock ratio** measures the percentage of total capitalization from preferred stock.

TAKE NOTE   The capitalization of a company is calculated from its balance sheet. Add the long-term debt and the equity (net worth) to calculate a company's total capitalization. Highly leveraged companies have greater capital risk.

14. 7. 2   LIQUIDITY RATIOS

Liquidity ratios measure a firm's ability to meet its current financial obligations. **Working capital**, though not a ratio, is the amount of liquid assets available to pay for short-term obligations. It is calculated as follows:

$$\text{Working capital} = \text{current assets} - \text{current liabilities}$$

Because working capital is a dollar amount, it does not, by itself, allow analysts to compare companies. The **current ratio**, on the other hand, compares current assets with a company's current financial obligations, regardless of the company's size or business.

$$\text{Current ratio} = \frac{\text{current assets}}{\text{current liabilities}}$$

Another measure of liquidity is **quick assets**, which subtracts **unsold inventory**, a current asset, from other current assets because inventory is not as **liquid** (as quick to convert to cash) as cash or receivables. Analysts use quick assets instead of current assets to calculate the acid-test ratio. The **acid-test ratio**, also called the **quick ratio**, is a more stringent measure of a company's liquidity than its current ratio. The quick assets and acid-test ratio equations are as follows:

$$\text{Quick assets} = \text{current assets} - \text{inventory}$$

$$\text{Acid-test ratio} = \frac{\text{quick assets}}{\text{current liabilities}}$$

The **cash assets ratio** is the most stringent measure of a company's liquidity.

$$\text{Cash asset ratio} = \frac{\text{cash and equivalents}}{\text{current liabilities}}$$

14. 7. 2. 1 Debt Service Ratio

The **debt service ratio** reflects a company's ability to meet the principal and interest payments on its bonds.

$$\text{Debt service ratio} = \frac{\text{EBIT}}{\text{annual interest} + \text{principal payments}}$$

14. 7. 2. 1. 1 Asset Coverage Ratio

The asset coverage ratio measures the ability of a company to meet its outstanding debt obligations with its assets. The ratio factors both tangible and monetary assets against the outstanding debt. Generally, the higher the ratio, the better the picture of financial health is for that company. In this light, the ratio is an analytical tool that allows investors to predict future earnings and to assess if any insolvency risk might be present. One caution regarding use of the ratio is that it uses book value when valuing the assets, which may or may not be reflective of their actual worth if liquidated.

As with all ratios, the asset coverage ratio presents a picture that is a snapshot in time and is best utilized with other analytical ratios and tools in order to get a clearer picture of a company's financial strengths or weaknesses. Additionally, different industries have different acceptable norms as to what the ratio should be. For example, industrials tend to have higher asset coverage ratios than utilities.

14. 7. 2. 2 Book Value Per Share

In a **liquidation**, a company sells its tangible assets and uses the proceeds to pay creditors and stockholders. Potential investors want to know how the value of **tangible assets**, also known as **net tangible asset value**, compares to the size of the company's debt and equity.

The **book value** of a company's assets (the amount at which they are carried on the books) is determined by deducting all liabilities and preferred stock from the company's total tangible assets. Dividing this figure by the number of shares of common stock shows how much a company's assets are worth (assuming they are sold for their book value) per share.

$$\frac{\text{Assets} - \text{liabilities} - \text{intangibles} - \text{par value of preferred stock}}{\text{Shares of common stock outstanding}} = \begin{array}{c}\text{book value}\\\text{per share}\end{array}$$

14. 7. 3 VALUATION RATIOS

Valuation ratios are used by analysts to compare companies within an industry as well as in different industries.

14. 7. 3. 1 Earnings Per Share (EPS)

Among the most widely used statistics, EPS measures the value of a company's earnings for each common share.

$$\text{EPS} = \frac{\text{earnings available to common}}{\text{no. of common shares outstanding}}$$

Earnings available to common are the remaining earnings after the preferred dividend has been paid. Earnings per share relates to common stock only. Preferred stockholders have no claims to earnings beyond the stipulated preferred stock dividends.

14. 7. 3. 2 Earnings Per Share After Dilution

If a corporation has rights, warrants, convertible preferred stock, or convertible bonds outstanding, the EPS could be diluted by an increase in the number of shares of common outstanding. That is, if the same amount of earnings available to common stockholders were allocated to more shares of stock, earnings would be less for each share. EPS is sometimes called **primary earnings per share** or **basic earnings per share** to differentiate it from earnings after dilution.

EPS after dilution assumes that all convertible securities have been converted into the common. Because of tax adjustments, the calculations for figuring EPS after dilution can be complicated.

14. 7. 3. 3 Dividends Per Share

The **dividends per share** is simply the dollar amount of cash dividends paid on each common share during the year.

$$\text{Dividends per share} = \frac{\text{annual cash dividends}}{\text{no. of common shares outstanding}}$$

14. 7. 3. 4 Current Yield (Dividend Yield)

A common stock's **current yield**, like the current yield on bonds, expresses the annual dividend payout as a percentage of the current stock price.

$$\text{Current yield} = \frac{\text{annual dividends per common share}}{\text{market value per common share}}$$

14. 7. 3. 5 Dividend Payout and Dividend Retention Ratio

The **dividend payout ratio** measures the proportion of earnings paid to stockholders as dividends.

$$\text{Dividend payout ratio} = \frac{\text{annual dividends per common share}}{\text{earnings per share (EPS)}}$$

In general, older companies pay out larger percentages of earnings as dividends. Utilities as a group have an especially high payout ratio. Growth companies normally have the lowest ratios because they reinvest their earnings in the businesses. Companies on the way up hope to reward stockholders with gains in the stock value rather than with high dividend income.

The dividend retention ratio is the complement of the dividend payout ratio. That percentage of earnings that is not paid out in the form of dividends would be the remaining percentage of earnings retained by the company for future use.

14. 7. 3. 6 Price-to-Earnings Ratio

The widely used **price-to-earnings (PE) ratio** provides investors with a rough idea of the relationship between the prices of different common stocks compared with the earnings that accrue to one share of stock.

$$\text{PE ratio} = \frac{\text{current market price of common share}}{\text{earnings per share (EPS)}}$$

Growth companies usually have higher PE ratios than cyclical companies. Investors are willing to pay more per dollar of current earnings if a company's future earnings are expected to be dramatically higher than earnings for stocks that rise and fall with business cycles. Companies subject to cyclical fluctuations generally sell at lower PEs; declining industries sell at still lower PEs. Investors should beware of extremely high or extremely low PEs. Speculative stocks often sell at one extreme or the other.

If a stock's market price and PE ratio are known, the earnings per share can be calculated as follows:

$$\text{EPS} = \text{current market price of common stock} \div \text{PE ratio}$$

14. 7. 3. 7   Inventory Turnover Ratio

Inventory turnover ratio is a measure of efficiency regarding the management of inventory within a business or company. It is considered to be a relative measure within a particular industry where comparison between two companies in the same industry or business, or comparison of one company to an acceptable industry norm, would be a useful analytical tool. Comparing two companies in dissimilar industries would have no value.

In general, the higher the ratio value, the better the management of inventory is perceived to be; the lower the ratio value is, the more it indicates potential inefficiency in the handling of inventory. Consider that a lower inventory turnover ratio may be an indication of overstocking. This can increase inventory handling costs and increase risk that the inventory may become obsolete before it can be sold. However, a ratio that is too high by comparison could result in lost sales due to inventory shortages. Understandably, it would be expected that industries dealing in perishable goods will have higher inventory turnover ratios than those dealing in durable goods.

TEST TOPIC ALERT

A quick rundown of the most testable points about ratios follows.

- Low debt-equity ratios are considered more conservative than high debt-equity ratios.

- The acid-test ratio is a more stringent measurement of liquidity than the current ratio.

- Book value is the company's theoretical liquidation value expressed on a per share basis.

- Speculative companies typically have very high or very low PE ratios.

- Growth companies have higher PE ratios than cyclical companies.

- Earnings per share relates only to common stock; it assumes preferred dividends were paid.

QUICK QUIZ 14.E

Choose **T** (technical analysis) or **F** (fundamental analysis).

_____ 1. Concerned with the overall economy

_____ 2. Interested in corporate annual reports

_____ 3. Concerned with daily trading volumes on the NYSE

_____ 4. Studies support and resistance diagrams

_____ 5. May follow the odd-lot trading theory

_____ 6. Concerned with a company's financial strength within an industry

_____ 7. Concerned with structure and use of a company's capital

UNIT TEST

1. A fundamental analyst is concerned with all of the following EXCEPT

   A. historical earnings trends
   B. inflation rates
   C. capitalization
   D. trading volumes

2. Which of the following is a lagging economic indicator?

   A. S&P 500
   B. Housing permits issued
   C. Corporate profits
   D. Hours worked

3. Disintermediaton is a movement of funds which results when all of the following occurs EXCEPT

   A. the money supply tightens
   B. the FRB increases reserve requirements
   C. money market rates are higher than typical savings account rates
   D. the discount rate is decreased by FRB

4. All of the following ratios are measures of the liquidity of a corporation EXCEPT

   A. acid-test ratio
   B. debt-to-equity ratio
   C. current ratio
   D. quick ratio

5. The FOMC purchases T-bills in the open market. Which of the following scenarios are likely to occur?

   I. Secondary bond prices will rise.
   II. Secondary bond prices will fall.
   III. Interest rates will rise.
   IV. Interest rates will fall.

   A. I and III
   B. I and IV
   C. II and III
   D. II and IV

6. Which of the following statements regarding the economics of fixed-income securities are TRUE?

   I. Short-term rates are more volatile than long-term rates.
   II. Long-term rates are more volatile than short-term rates.
   III. Short-term bond prices react more than long-term bond prices given a change in interest rates.
   IV. Long-term bond prices react more than short-term bond prices given a change in interest rates.

   A. I and III
   B. I and IV
   C. II and III
   D. II and IV

7. Which of the following interest rates is considered the most volatile?

   A. Discount rate
   B. Federal funds rate
   C. Prime rate
   D. Broker call loan rate

8. To tighten credit during inflationary periods, the Federal Reserve Board can take any of the following actions EXCEPT

   A. raise reserve requirements
   B. increase the amount of U.S. government debt held by primary dealers
   C. sell securities in the open market
   D. lower taxes

9. Which of the following is a leading economic indicator?

   A. Stock market index
   B. Gross domestic product
   C. Duration of unemployment claims
   D. Industrial production

10. All of the following are used by the Federal Reserve to control the money supply EXCEPT

    A. open market operations
    B. setting reserve requirements for member banks
    C. setting the discount rate
    D. setting the federal funds rate

11. If the U.S. dollar depreciates in value, which of the following statements is NOT true?

    A. The same amount of yen would buy more dollars.
    B. The balance of payments deficit probably would be reduced.
    C. Foreign goods would become more expensive in the United States.
    D. Travel abroad would be less expensive for Americans.

12. Which organization or governmental unit sets fiscal policy?

    A. Federal Reserve Board (FRB)
    B. Government Economic Board
    C. Congress and the president
    D. Secretary of the Treasury

13. Which of the following economists is considered a supporter of demand-side economics?

    A. Adam Smith
    B. John Maynard Keynes
    C. Arthur Laffer
    D. Milton Friedman

14. ABC, with 3 million shares outstanding, reports after-tax earnings of $7.5 million. Annual cash dividends total $1 per share. The dividend payout ratio is

    A. 20%
    B. 25%
    C. 33%
    D. 40%

15. Which of the following stocks is regarded as a defensive stock?

    A. Aerospace stock
    B. Stock selling close to its support level
    C. Stock with a strong cash position and a low ratio of debt
    D. Electric utility stock

16. If XYZ Corporation sells an additional 1 million common stock with a par value of $1 for $10 per share, which of the following is TRUE?

    A. Its EPS will increase.
    B. Its paid-in surplus will increase.
    C. Its liquidity ratio will decrease.
    D. Current ratio will decrease.

17. Which of the following corporations is most likely a growth company?

	ABC	DEF	GHI	JKL
EPS	$1.10	$1.25	$1.50	$1.90
Div.	0	.25	.75	1.33

    A. ABC
    B. DEF
    C. GHI
    D. JKL

18. Stock market indexes such as the S&P 500 and the DJIA are declining daily, but the number of declining stocks relative to advancing stocks is falling. A technical analyst would conclude that the market is

    A. overbought
    B. oversold
    C. becoming volatile
    D. unstable

19. Profits that are not distributed to shareholders are called

    A. capital surplus
    B. dividends
    C. retained earnings
    D. interest

20. A support level is

    A. a point at which an upward trend is expected to stop
    B. a point at which a downward trend is expected to stop
    C. the point at which an investment banker purchases for his own account
    D. usually evidence of an overbought position

ANSWERS AND RATIONALES

1. **D.** A fundamental analyst is concerned with the economic climate, the inflation rate, how an industry is performing, a company's historical earnings trends, how it is capitalized, and its product lines, management, and balance sheet ratios. A technical analyst is concerned with trading volumes or market trends and prices.

2. **C.** Both the S&P 500 and housing permits are leading indicators. The measure of hours worked is also a leading indicator because it reflects changes in the average work week during the current period of time. Corporate profits are a lagging indicator.

3. **D.** Money flowing from banks and thrifts into money market instruments is known as disintermediation, which tends to occur when money is tight and rates are rising, making money funds more attractive than passbook savings rates. The FRB decreasing the discount rate would loosen its hold on the money supply.

4. **B.** Liquidity ratios measure a firm's ability to meet its current financial obligations and include the current ratio and acid-test (quick) ratio. However, the debt-to-equity ratio is a capitalization ratio and measures the amount of leverage, compared with equity, in a company's overall capital structure.

5. **B.** When the Federal Open Market Committee purchases T-bills in the open market, it pays for the transaction by increasing member banks' reserve accounts, the net effect of which increases the total money supply and signals a period of relatively easier credit conditions. Easier credit means interest rates will decline, and the price for existing or secondary bonds will therefore rise.

6. **B.** There are two separate issues in this question: the volatility of rates and volatility of bond prices. Short-term rates are more volatile than long-term rates and will move more quickly than long-term rates. The most volatile interest rate in the U.S. economy is the federal funds rate, which is an overnight rate of interest. Given a change in rates, long-term bond prices move more than short-term bond prices because of the compounding effect over a much longer period of time.

7. **B.** The federal funds rate is the interest rate that banks with excess reserves charge other banks that are associated with the Federal Reserve System and that need overnight loans to meet reserve requirements. Because the federal funds rate tends to fluctuate daily, it is the most sensitive indicator of interest rate direction.

8. **D.** To curb inflation, the Fed can sell securities in the open market, thus changing the amount of U.S. government debt institutions hold. It can also raise the reserve requirements, discount rate, or margin requirements. The Fed has no control over taxes, which are changed by Congress.

9. **A.** Stock market indexes are generally leading indicators. GDP and industrial production are coincident indicators; the duration of unemployment claims is a lagging indicator.

10. **D.** Open market operations, setting reserve requirements for member banks, and setting the discount rate are all tools used by the Federal Reserve Bank (FRB). Though the federal funds rate is a market rate of interest heavily influenced by the FRB, it is not set by them.

11. **D.** If the dollar is devalued, travel abroad for Americans will become more expensive. Because the dollar is worth less, it will buy fewer London theater tickets, Swiss watches, and French perfumes.

12. **C.** Congress and the president set fiscal policy, whereas the FRB sets monetary policy.

13. **B.** John Maynard Keynes was the first demand-side economist; he believed that by increasing the income available for spending and saving, a government could increase demand and improve the country's economic well-being. Higher taxes and higher government spending are key tenets of this theory.

14. **D.** First compute earnings per share by dividing $7.5 million by the 3 million shares outstanding to get $2.50. Then divide the $1 dividend by $2.50 to get a 40% dividend payout ratio. The corporation paid out 40% of earnings to its shareholders.

15. **D.** Analysts regard a defensive stock as one that is in an industry that is least affected by business cycles. Most defensive industries produce nondurable consumer goods (e.g., the food industry or the utility industry).

16. **B.** Paid-in surplus is a balance sheet entry that accounts for money raised from the issuance of stock in excess of par value. When more shares are sold, paid-in surplus will increase.

17. **A.** A growth company pays out very little in dividends and retains most of its earnings to fund future growth. ABC Corporation has the highest retained earnings ratio and is most likely to be a growth company.

18. **B.** The momentum of the market decline seems to be easing as the number of decliners to advancers is leveling out. It looks like the advance/decline line is moving in a direction away from decliners. A technical analyst would conclude that the market is oversold and is approaching a bottom.

19. **C.** When a corporation's board of directors determines how much of the net income to distribute as a dividend, the balance is retained by the company as retained earnings, sometimes called earned surplus.

20. **B.** Think of a support level as a floor—something to support you. Choice A describes a resistance level.

Q U I C K   Q U I Z   A N S W E R S

Quick Quiz 14.A

1. **LE**

2. **C**

3. **LA**

4. **C**

5. **LE**

6. **LE**

7. **LA**

Quick Quiz 14.B

1. **B.** When the FOMC buys T-bills in the open market, it pays for the transaction by increasing the reserve accounts of member banks, the net effect of which increases the total money supply and signals a period of relatively easier credit conditions. Easier credit means interest rates will decline and the price for existing bonds will rise.

2. **A.** Increased foreign investment in the United States would raise the U.S. dollar's relative value. A decrease in U.S. interest rates would chase money out of the United States and increase the foreign currency's relative value. In Choice B, the value of the yen should increase, meaning the dollar will fall in comparison. In Choice C, U.S. consumers are buying more Japanese goods than the Japanese are buying U.S. goods. Therefore, the value of the dollar should fall relative to the yen.

3. **A.** Disintermediation is the flow of deposits out of banks and savings and loans into alternative, higher-paying investments. It occurs when money is tight and interest rates are high because these alternative investments may then offer higher yields than S&Ls and banks.

4. **D.** To curb inflation, the Fed can sell securities in the open market, thus changing the amount of U.S. government debt institutions hold. It can also raise the reserve requirements, discount rate, or margin requirements. The Fed has no control over taxes, which are changed by Congress.

5. **B.** Although money market funds are highly liquid investments, they are considered time deposits and so are part of M2.

Quick Quiz 14.C

1. **C.** If a market is staying within a narrow price range, it is said to be consolidating.

2. **A.** A trendline connects the lows in an uptrend and the highs in a downtrend. Once established, trendlines are not easily halted or reversed.

3. **D.** Odd-lot trading typically is done by small investors. Followers of the odd-lot theory act on the belief that small investors invariably buy and sell at the wrong times.

4. **C.** The narrowest measure of the market is the Dow Jones Industrial Average, which charts the performance of 30 industrial stocks.

Quick Quiz 14.D

1. **B.** Working capital (or net working capital) is, by definition, the difference between current assets and current liabilities.

2. **B.** The formula for the balance sheet is: assets = liabilities + shareholders' equity. If assets stay the same and equity (net worth) decreases, liabilities must increase. Prepaid expenses are assets; accrued expenses are liabilities.

3. **D.** On the issuance of a bond, cash is received (thus increasing current assets) and long-term debt increases (increasing total liabilities). Because there is no corresponding increase in current liabilities, working capital will increase; it would have no effect on shareholders' equity.

4. **D.** If earnings increase, retained earnings also increase. If the increased retained earnings are not paid out as dividends, shareholders' equity increases.

Quick Quiz 14.E

1. **F.**

2. **F.**

3. **T.**

4. **T.**

5. **T.**

6. **F.**

7. **F.**

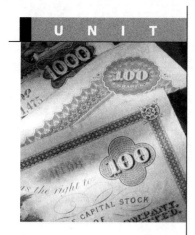

UNIT

15

Ethics, Recommendations, and Taxation

This Unit reviews the importance of strict ethical standards in the securities industry. When registered representatives deal with customers, providing suitable recommendations is a critical aspect of the relationship. To offer suitable investment recommendations, a representative must consider the customer's financial objectives, financial status, investment constraints, and tax situation.

Tax considerations will often be an important consideration in selecting an investment. Income-oriented investors, in particular, must be aware of the after-tax returns of investment alternatives. When securities are sold, the cost basis of the original investment must be calculated.

Expect to see 15–20 questions on ethics, recommendations, and taxation on the Series 7 exam. ■

When you have completed this Unit, you should be able to:

- **describe** a registered representative's ethical responsibility to the public;

- **describe** prohibited customer account practices;

- **identify** financial and nonfinancial criteria essential to customer recommendations;

- **define** the basic types of investment risks;

- **identify** various portfolio management strategies;

- **describe** the tax treatment of investment income and capital gains or losses;

- **calculate** the adjusted cost basis of bonds purchased at a premium or discount; and

- **contrast** progressive and regressive taxes and give examples of each.

15. 1   ETHICS IN THE SECURITIES INDUSTRY

The securities industry is governed by a very strict code of ethics. Unacceptable behavior is subject to sanctions ranging from fines and reprimands to expulsion from the industry and/or imprisonment.

15. 1. 1   ETHICAL BUSINESS PRACTICES

Our industry measures business behavior and practices against clear standards for fairness and equity.

Securities industry regulators work to prevent and detect unethical behavior. Investigators regularly examine activity at all levels—from large firms and investment advisers to registered representatives and individual investors. Even the most junior of broker-dealer employees is expected to adhere to high standards of business ethics in dealing with the public.

15. 1. 1. 1 Corporate Ethics and Responsibility

The rules that guide relationships between members of the securities industry and all other participants are set by the SEC, FINRA, and other regulatory bodies.

One aspect of corporate responsibility for ethical behavior involves a commitment to self-regulation. It is every broker-dealer's duty to supervise all of its associated persons. Each firm must have a written procedures manual and must designate one or more supervisors (principals) to be responsible for enforcing its rules.

EXAMPLE   A principal must review and approve all correspondence and keep a record of all securities transactions and correspondence.

EXAMPLE   Member firms must periodically review all branch office activities to detect and discipline any individuals who engage in unethical behavior.

15. 1. 1. 2 Customer Ethics and Responsibility

Practices (such as insider trading) that provide an unfair advantage to certain investors over the general public are strictly prohibited. The individual investor must abide by the regulations that guide customer ethics.

EXAMPLE   It is the customer's responsibility to provide full and honest disclosure to his registered representative or investment adviser.

The representative or adviser will base recommendations on information the customer provides. A customer's failure to provide accurate information could result in inappropriate recommendations.

Several points on ethical business practices follow.

- All broker-dealers are required to maintain written supervisory procedures.

- A principal is responsible for enforcing the rules of the broker-dealer.

- A broker-dealer may have its own house rules that can be more stringent than those of the self-regulatory organization (SRO), but these rules can never be less stringent.

- The **Conduct Rules** deal with ethical treatment of customers.

15. 1. 2 PROHIBITED BUSINESS PRACTICES

The following practices in customer dealings are prohibited at all times.

15. 1. 2. 1 Manipulative and Fraudulent Devices

FINRA member firms are strictly prohibited from using manipulative, deceptive, or other fraudulent tactics or methods to induce a security's sale or purchase. The statute of limitations under the Act of 1934 is three years from the alleged manipulation and within one year of discovering it. No dollar limit is placed on damages in lawsuits based on allegations of manipulation.

15. 1. 2. 2 Outside Business Activity

An associated person cannot work for any business other than his member firm (independent activity) without his employing broker-dealer's knowledge. If a registered person wants to be employed by or accept compensation from an entity other than the member firm, that person must provide prior written notice to the member. Note that the employing member's permission is not required. The firm, however, does have the right to reject or restrict any outside affiliation if they feel a conflict of interest exists. These affiliations would also include serving as an officer or director of a company or owning any interest in another financial services company.

A **passive investment**, such as the purchase of a limited partnership unit, is not considered an outside business activity. An associated person may make a passive investment for his own account without providing written notice to the employing broker-dealer.

15. 1. 2. 3 Private Securities Transactions

The Conduct Rules define a **private securities transaction** as any sale of securities outside an associated person's regular business and his employing member. Private securities transactions are also known as **selling away**.

15. 1. 2. 3. 1 Notification

If an associated person wishes to enter into a private securities transaction, that person must:

■ provide prior written notice to his employer;

■ describe in detail the proposed transaction;

■ describe in detail his proposed role in the transaction; and

■ disclose whether he has or may receive compensation for the transaction.

With Compensation. If the transaction involves compensation, the employing member may approve or disapprove the associated person's participation. If the member approves the participation, it must treat the transaction as if it is being done on its own behalf by entering the transaction on its own books and supervising the associated person during the transaction. If the member disapproves the transaction, the associated person may not participate in it.

Without Compensation. If the associated person has not received or will not receive compensation for the private securities transaction, the employing member must acknowledge that it has received written notification and may require the associated person to adhere to specified conditions during his participation.

Transactions that the associated person enters into on behalf of immediate family members and for which the associated person receives no compensation are excluded from the definition of private securities transactions.

15. 1. 2. 4 Recommendations

Investment recommendations must be consistent with customer needs, financial capability, objectives, and risk tolerance. Investment recommendations should be in a customer's best interest—not the registered representative's. Each investment (especially its risks) should be explained fully. At no time should customers own an investment that could put them at risk beyond their financial capacity.

15. 1. 2. 5 Paying for Referrals

FINRA prohibits members or any person associated with a member firm such as a registered representative, from paying cash or non-cash compensation to nonmembers for referrals of prospective or actual brokerage business. These prohibited referral payments, sometimes known as *finders-fees*, include payments made in connection with locating, introducing, or referring brokerage account customers to the member firm or registered representative.

EXAMPLE   A registered representative offers an attorney and an accountant two tickets to a professional sporting event each time one of them refers one of their clients to him. These tickets would be considered noncash compensation, and giving them in exchange for referrals would be prohibited.

15. 1. 3 FAIR DEALING

The Conduct Rules and the laws of most states require broker-dealers, registered representatives, and investment advisers to inquire into a customer's financial situation before making any recommendation to buy, sell, or exchange securities. This includes determining the client's other security holdings, income, net worth, and financial goals and objectives.

The following activities violate the fair dealing rules:

- Recommending any investment that is not suitable for the customer's financial situation and risk tolerance
- Short-term trading of mutual funds
- Setting up fictitious accounts to transact business that otherwise would be prohibited
- Making unauthorized transactions or use of funds
- Recommending purchases inconsistent with the customer's ability to pay
- Committing fraudulent acts, such as forgery and the omission or misstatement of material facts
- Guaranteeing customers against loss

15. 1. 3. 1 Excessive Trading (Churning)

Excessive trading in a customer's account to generate commissions rather than to help achieve the customer's stated investment objectives is an abuse of fiduciary responsibility known as **churning**. Excessive frequency or excessive size of transactions not in keeping with the client's trading history or financial ability are often signs that churning might be occurring.

To prevent such abuses, self-regulatory organizations require that a principal of the member firm review all accounts, especially those for which a registered representative or an investment adviser has discretionary authority.

EXAMPLE   A principal, while reviewing transactions done by the firm, notices that a client who had previously done a trade or two per quarter recently has been doing one or two per week. At a minimum, this should generate a red flag for churning. A discussion with the registered representative assigned to the account should occur to determine if any further monitoring or actions should take place.

15. 1. 3. 1. 1 Reverse Churning

According to the SEC, "reverse churning" is the specific practice of placing clients who trade infrequently in fee-based accounts. A fee-based account is one where one annual fee, usually a percentage of assets under management, covers all transactions rather than paying commissions on a per trade basis, as would typically occur in a commission-based account. If the annual fee paid would be appreciably greater than the annual commissions paid given the number of transactions the customer would normally do or could be reasonably expected to do, the fee-based account would not be appropriate. This would be noted as reverse churning.

15. 1. 3. 2 Influencing Employees of Other Firms

Broker-dealers may not distribute business-related compensation (cash or noncash gifts or gratuities) to the employees of other member firms. However, a broker-dealer may give other firms' employees gratuities without violating the rules, provided:

- the compensation is not conditional on sales or promises of sales;
- it has the employing member's prior approval;
- the compensation's total value does not exceed the annual limit set by the regulatory bodies (currently $100 per year); and
- the gift is in association with a life event such as bereavement, wedding, or the birth or adoption of a child.

TAKE NOTE   These rules permit occasional noncash expenditures that exceed the $100 limit, such as dinners, seminars, tickets to entertainment events, or reminder advertising. Vacations or season tickets are always violations.

15. 1. 3. 3 Employment Contracts

This rule does not apply to legitimate employment contracts in which an employee of one firm supplies or performs services for another firm. The leasing of another firm's employee is acceptable, provided that a written employment agreement specifies the employment duties and compensation and that the person's employer, the temporary employer, and the employee all give their written consent.

15. 1. 3. 4 Borrowing and Lending

Firms that permit lending arrangements between representatives and customers must have written procedures in place to monitor such activity. Registered persons who wish to borrow from or lend money to customers are, in most cases, required to provide prior written notice of the proposed arrangement to the firm, and the firm must approve the arrangement in writing. The Conduct rules permit the following five types of lending arrangements.

- There is an immediate family relationship between the representative and the customer (no notice or approval is needed).
- The customer is in the business of lending money (e.g., a bank; no approval is needed).
- The customer and the representatives are both registered persons with the same firm.
- The customer and the representative have a personal relationship outside the broker-customer relationship.
- The customer and the representative have a business relationship outside the broker-customer relationship.

TAKE NOTE   Generally, before borrowing from or lending to a customer, a representative must advise his firm in writing and receive written permission. However, notice and approval are not needed if the loan is between immediate family members, and approval is not needed if the customer is a lending institution and the loan is on standard commercial terms.

15. 1. 3. 5 Misrepresentations

Registered representatives and investment advisers may not misrepresent themselves or their services to clients or potential clients. Included in this prohibition are misrepresentations covering:

■ qualifications, experience, and education;

■ nature of services offered; and

■ fees to be charged.

It is a misrepresentation to inaccurately state or fail to state a material fact regarding any of these.

15. 1. 3. 6 Research Reports

An investment adviser or a broker-dealer is prohibited from presenting to a client research reports, analyses, or recommendations prepared by other persons or firms without disclosing the fact that the adviser did not prepare them. An adviser or a broker-dealer may base a recommendation on reports or analyses prepared by others as long as these reports are not represented as the adviser's or broker-dealer's own.

15. 1. 3. 6. 1 Soft Dollar Arrangements

Broker dealers often charge a commission rate that is commensurate with all of the bundled services they offer to their clients. Soft dollar arrangements generally arise when an adviser or someone acting in a fiduciary capacity receives brokerage products or services, typically research, from a broker-dealer in exchange for placing securities transactions with that broker-dealer. In order to receive the products or services, the adviser may be paying more than the lowest possible commission rate. Because the research or other services are being provided in exchange for client commission dollars, which in this context are known as *soft dollars* rather than being paid for directly with cash *hard dollars*, and because commissions are viewed as client assets, an adviser could be viewed as breaching its fiduciary duty to clients by using client assets (the commissions paid) for its own benefit. Under traditional fiduciary principles, a fiduciary cannot use assets entrusted by clients for its own benefit.

When a fiduciary places orders for execution with a broker-dealer in exchange for services such as research from the broker-dealer for the soft dollar commission payments, those transitions are generally referred to as directed transactions.

Safe Harbor Rule for Soft Dollar Arrangements. Although soft dollar arrangements have come under scrutiny for potential misuse of client assets and for potential conflicts of interest, the Securities Exchange Act of 1934 provides a safe harbor for advisers that enter into soft dollar arrangements, as long as certain conditions of the safe harbor rule within the 1934 Act are satisfied. The SEC describes this determination as a three step process:

■ Determining the eligibility of the research or service under the safe harbor regulations. Specific services, research for example, have specific eligibility requirements.

■ Determining whether the product or service provides lawful and appropriate assistance in investment decision making.

■ Determining reasonableness of commissions paid in light of the value of the services provided.

Lastly, the SEC requires that all soft dollar arrangements be disclosed by fiduciaries to their clients, and that their soft dollar policies and procedures be disclosed as well.

Following is a list of products or services that would likely qualify under the Safe Harbor section of the Securities Act of 1934 regarding soft dollar arrangements, as well as some that would not. These are not all-inclusive lists.

The following would likely qualify under the Safe Harbor Rule for soft dollar arrangements:

- Research reports
- Financial newsletters and trade journals
- Quantitative analytical securities software
- Seminars and conferences with appropriate content

The following would likely not qualify under the Safe Harbor Rule for soft dollar arrangements:

- Providing telephone lines
- Providing office furniture or equipment including computers
- Travel expenses to travel to seminars
- Rent for office space
- Software not directly related to the analysis of securities
- Internet services
- Training services

15. 1. 3. 7 Guarantees and Sharing in Customer Accounts

Broker-dealers, investment advisers, and registered representatives may not guarantee any customer against a loss or guarantee that he will achieve a gain. Members, advisers, and representatives are also prohibited from sharing in any profits or losses in a customer's account. An exception is made if a joint account has received the member firm's prior written approval and the registered representative shares in the profits and losses only to the extent of his proportionate contribution to the joint account.

If the member firm authorizes such a shared account, any such sharing must be directly proportionate to the financial contributions each party makes. If a member or an associated person shares an account with a member of that person's immediate family, directly proportionate sharing of profits and losses is not required.

Immediate family members include parents, siblings, spouses, in-laws, and children. It also includes any person who is financially dependent on the employee.

EXAMPLE A registered representative sets up a joint account for herself and her spouse.—PERMITTED

EXAMPLE A registered representative sets up a joint account for herself and a client, contributing half of the account proceeds. The account is approved by the firm.—PERMITTED

EXAMPLE　　　　A registered representative sets up a joint account for herself and a client, contributing her knowledge of the markets and securities they intend to buy and sell in the account.—NOT PERMITTED

15. 1. 3. 8 Misuse of Nonpublic Information

Every investment adviser must establish, maintain, and enforce written policies and procedures to prevent the use of nonpublic inside information.

15. 1. 3. 9 Abuse of Fiduciary Information

During the normal course of business, employees of member firms will have access to proprietary information regarding individual customers and securities issuers. Such information is to be treated with strict confidentiality.

15. 1. 3. 9. 1 Confidentiality of Customer Information

Broker-dealer and investment adviser employees may not divulge any personal information about customers without a customer's express permission. This includes security positions, personal and financial details, and trading intentions.

15. 1. 4 OTHER UNETHICAL TRADING PRACTICES

Transactions intended to portray an artificial market for a stock are prohibited.

15. 1. 4. 1 Painting the Tape

When one party sells stock to another with the understanding that the stock will be repurchased later in the day at virtually the same price, it is known as **painting the Tape**. The intent of such transactions is to make it appear that far more activity in a stock exists than actually does.

15. 1. 4. 2 Marking the Close

Effecting trades or falsely reporting trades to influence the closing price of a stock is called marking the close and is prohibited.

EXAMPLE　　　　A firm's proprietary trader is compensated by salary and bonuses based on profits in the firm's trading account each quarter. On the last day of trading in March (the fiscal quarter end), he enters numerous small buy orders at 3:55 pm ET in securities the account already holds long positions in. This could be an attempt to mark the close—push prices of these securities up one or two ticks just before the close of the day, and thus the quarter, inflating the paper profits the account will show for the end of the quarter to secure a larger bonus. Marking the close is a prohibited activity.

15. 1. 4. 3 Payments Designed to Influence Market Prices

FINRA member firms are prohibited from attempting to influence the market price of securities by paying for favorable reviews, articles, or other mentions in newspapers or other financial publications. This prohibition does not apply to paid advertisements placed in these publications and marked as such.

15. 1. 4. 4 Spreading False Information

Broker-dealers must not promote or disseminate false or misleading information.

15. 1. 4. 5 Front Running

If a firm or any associated person has nonpublic knowledge of an impending block order to buy or sell, that firm or person may not place an order in front of the block order. For purposes of this rule, a block order is an order for 10,000 shares or more.

EXAMPLE   Assume that a representative has nonpublic knowledge of an impending order to buy 100,000 shares of a Nasdaq stock. If the representative places an order to buy stock for his personal account in front of the order, the representative would likely benefit from a free ride because the stock would rise on the execution of a large block.

15. 1. 4. 6 Interpositioning

Interpositioning is the act of adding another broker-dealer to a transaction when there is no benefit to buyer or seller. The prohibited practice occurs when one BD inserts another into his own transactions simply to generate commissions or fees for the other BD. Violations of interpositioning have revealed that these prohibited practices are generally reciprocal arrangements between BDs.

TEST TOPIC ALERT   If a registered representative (RR) witnesses or believes unethical trading or business practices are occurring, a regulatory tip may be filed with FINRA via the Regulatory Tip Line in Washington, DC.

15. 2   INVESTMENT CONSIDERATIONS AND SUITABILITY

Given the numerous investment opportunities and products that exist for clients to choose from, considering your client's personal circumstances and situation is of the utmost importance when determining which investments may or may not be suitable.

15. 2. 1   KNOW YOUR CUSTOMER

FINRA and other SROs require brokers to know their customers. This implies understanding a customer's financial status (net worth and net income), investment objectives, and all facts essential in making suitable recommendations. It is a registered representative's responsibility to perform due diligence to determine the validity of a customer's information.

Based on that information, registered representatives must have a reasonable basis to believe that a recommended transaction or investment strategy involving a security or securities is suitable for the customer. The term "investment strategy" applies to recommendations to invest in, hold, or sell specific securities as well as suggestions pertaining to market sectors, day trading, or liquifying an asset or other investments to make funds available to purchase securities. The definition does not include non-security investments.

Regarding the term "customer," FINRA defines it to exclude other brokers and certain potential investors (someone who is not your client at the time the advice is given). Therefore, the rule would not apply if the recipient of the advice is not currently a client and neither the representative nor the firm receives direct or indirect compensation as a result of giving the advice.

15. 2. 1. 1   Nonfinancial Considerations

A customer's nonfinancial considerations are often as important as his financial concerns. Therefore, a registered representative or an investment adviser should know the:

- customer's age;
- customer's marital status;
- number and ages of customer's dependents;
- customer's employment status;
- employment of customer's family members; and
- customer's current and future financial needs.

15. 2. 1. 2   Risk Tolerance and Investment Goals

A customer's risk tolerance and investment goals are other important considerations that will shape his portfolio. To understand a customer's attitude about investment alternatives, the representative or adviser should ask the customer the following questions.

- What kind of risks can you afford to take?
- How liquid must your investments be?
- How important are tax considerations?
- Are you seeking long-term or short-term investments (investment time horizon)?
- What is your investment experience?
- What types of investments do you currently hold?

15. 2. 2   CUSTOMER INVESTMENT OUTLOOK

Typical financial objectives that customers often have are outlined here.

15. 2. 2. 1   Preservation of Capital

For many people, the most important investment objective is to preserve their capital. In general, when clients speak of safety, they usually mean preservation of capital.

TEST TOPIC ALERT   For preservation of capital and low risk tolerances, move toward government securities and away from corporate securities and equities, in particular.

15. 2. 2. 2   Current Income

Many investors, particularly those on fixed incomes, want to generate current income from their investments.

Corporate bonds, municipal bonds, government and agency securities, income-oriented mutual funds, some stocks (including utilities and REITs), money market funds, and annuities are among the investments that can contribute current income through dividend or interest payments.

TEST TOPIC ALERT   Remember that if current income on a monthly basis is the customer's investment objective, variable annuities or GNMAs should be considered first. The investor's profile and needs will determine which of the two is better.

The Investment Pyramid

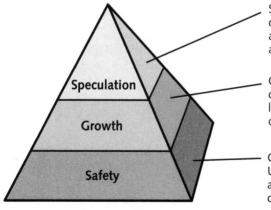

Speculative stocks and stock options, low-rated debt securities, precious metals, commodities and futures, speculative limited partnerships, and speculative mutual funds

Growth and small-capitalization stocks, stock options, nonbank-grade bonds, growth-oriented limited partnerships, growth stock mutual funds, commodities funds, and variable annuities

Cash, money market funds, certificates of deposit, US Treasury securities, bank-grade corporate and municipal bonds, blue-chip stocks, and blue-chip stock and bond mutual funds

15. 2. 2. 3   Capital Growth

Growth refers to an increase in an investment's value over time. This can come from increases in the security's value, the reinvestment of distributions, or both. The most common growth-oriented investments are common stock and common stock mutual funds.

15. 2. 2. 4   Tax Advantages

Investors often seek ways to reduce or defer taxes. Some vehicles, like **individual retirement accounts (IRAs)** and annuities, allow earnings to accumulate tax deferred (an investor pays no taxes until he withdraws money from his account). Other products, like municipal bonds, offer tax-free interest income.

15. 2. 2. 5   Portfolio Diversification

Investors with portfolios concentrated in one (single stock) or just a few securities or investments are exposed to much higher risks, and the value of the entire portfolio can be wiped out if one investment or industry performs poorly.

For these investors, **portfolio diversification** can be an important objective. These customers may be retirees with large profit-sharing distributions of one company's stock or investors with all of their money invested in certificates of deposit (CDs) or U.S. government bonds.

15. 2. 2. 6   Liquidity

Some people want immediate access to their money at all times. A product is **liquid** if a customer can sell it quickly at a fair market price.

Stock, for instance, has varying degrees of liquidity, whereas DPPs, annuities, and bank CDs generally are considered illiquid. Real estate is the classic example of an illiquid investment because of the time and money it takes to convert it into cash. Money market funds are highly liquid and are often used for this purpose.

15. 2. 2. 7   Speculation

A customer may want to **speculate**—that is, try to earn much higher-than-average returns in exchange for higher-than-average risks.

TEST TOPIC ALERT   You may see several questions about recommendations based on a customer's investment objectives. The following table is a quick guide of key words to help with these questions.

Investor Objective and Recommendation

Investor Objective	Recommendation
Preservation of capital; safety	Government securities or Ginnie Maes
Growth	Common stock or common stock mutual funds
Balanced or moderate growth	Blue-chip stocks
Aggressive growth/speculation	Technology stocks or sector funds
Income	Bonds—but not zero-coupons
Tax-free income	Municipal bonds or municipal bond funds
High-yield income	Corporate bonds or corporate bond funds
Form an income-oriented stock portfolio	Preferred stock and utility stocks
Liquidity	Money market funds (DPPs, real estate, and annuities are not considered liquid)
Keep pace with inflation	Stock portfolio

QUICK QUIZ 15.A

1. Which of the following characteristics best define(s) the term *growth*?

    A. Increase in the value of an investment over time
    B. Increase in principal and accumulating interest and dividends over time
    C. Investments that appreciate tax deferred
    D. All of the above

2. Which of the following investments is least appropriate for a client primarily concerned with liquidity?

    A. Preferred stock
    B. Municipal bond mutual funds
    C. Bank savings accounts
    D. Direct participation programs

3. Which of the following securities generates the greatest current income with moderate risk?

    A. Common stock of a new company
    B. Security convertible into the common stock of a company
    C. Fixed-income security
    D. Income bond

4. Which of the following investments is most suitable for an investor seeking monthly income?

    A. Zero-coupon bond
    B. Growth stock
    C. Mutual fund investing in small-cap issues
    D. GNMA mutual fund

Quick Quiz answers can be found at the end of the Unit.

15. 3   SUITABILITY: ANALYZING FINANCIAL RISKS AND REWARDS

Because all investments involve trade-offs, the investment adviser's or registered representative's task is to select securities that provide the right balance between investor constraints and investment capabilities. Registered representatives are expected to make suitable investment recommendations for the customer.

15. 3. 1   UNSUITABLE TRADES

Occasionally, a customer asks a registered representative to enter a trade that the representative believes is unsuitable. It is the representative's responsibility to explain why the trade might not be appropriate for the customer. If the customer insists on entering the transaction, the registered representative should consider having the customer sign a statement acknowledging that the representative advised against the trade, and the representative should mark the order ticket *Unsolicited.*

15. 3. 2   INVESTMENT RISKS

In general terms, the greater the risk an investor assumes, the greater the potential for reward. Several types of risk must be considered in determining the suitability of various investment types.

15. 3. 2. 1   Inflation Risk

Also known as **purchasing power risk,** inflation risk is the effect of continually rising prices on investment returns. If a bond's yield is lower than the inflation rate, the purchasing power of the client's money diminishes over time. A client who buys a bond or a fixed annuity is usually able to purchase far less with money distributed when the investment matures.

15. 3. 2. 2   Capital Risk

Capital risk is the potential for an investor to lose some or all of his money—his invested capital—under circumstances unrelated to an issuer's financial strength.

15. 3. 2. 3 Timing Risk

Even an investment in the strongest company with the most profit potential might do poorly simply because the investment was timed incorrectly. The risk to an investor of buying or selling at the wrong time and incurring losses or lower gains is known as **timing risk**.

15. 3. 2. 4 Interest Rate Risk

Interest rate risk is the sensitivity of an investment's value to fluctuations in interest rates. This risk is generally associated with bonds because bond prices correspond inversely with interest rate changes. Bonds with long-term maturities, low coupons, or deep discounts are most susceptible to interest rate risk.

15. 3. 2. 5 Reinvestment Risk

When interest rates decline, it is difficult to invest proceeds from redemptions, calls, or investment distributions to maintain the same level of income without increasing credit or market risks.

TEST TOPIC ALERT
The Series 7 exam expects you to know that mortgage-backed instruments are susceptible to reinvestment risk.

When interest rates fall, mortgage holders typically refinance at lower rates. This means that they pay off their mortgages early, which causes a prepayment of principal to holders of mortgage-backed securities. The early principal payments cannot be reinvested at a comparable return.

Sometimes the test asks which instruments are not subject to reinvestment risk. Of the ones listed, the best answer to choose is typically a zero-coupon bond. Because no interest is paid on a current basis, the investor has no reinvestment risk.

15. 3. 2. 6 Call Risk

Related to reinvestment risk, **call risk** is the risk that a bond might be called before maturity and an investor will be unable to reinvest the principal at a comparable rate of return. When interest rates are falling, bonds with higher coupon rates are most likely to be called. Investors concerned about call risk should look for **call protection**—a period during which a bond cannot be called. Most corporate and municipal issuers generally provide some years of call protection.

15. 3. 2. 7 Market Risk

Both stocks and bonds involve some degree of **market risk**—that is, the risk that investors may lose some of their principal as a result of price volatility in the overall market (**systematic risk**). Stock market momentum may affect stock prices independently of matters affecting a particular corporation. Bond prices fluctuate with changing interest rates, and an inverse relationship between bond prices and bond yields exists: as bond yields rise, bond prices decline, and vice versa.

Systematic risk, or the risk of a general market decline, cannot be diversified away. Nonsystematic risk, also known as selection risk, is the risk that a single investment will not perform. Diversifying a portfolio minimizes nonsystematic risk.

15. 3. 2. 8 Credit Risk

Credit risk, also called **financial risk** or **default risk,** is the danger of losing one's invested principal through an issuer's failure. Credit risk varies with the investment product. Bonds backed by the federal government or most municipalities have low credit risk. Long-term bonds involve more credit risk than short-term bonds because of the future's uncertainty.

15. 3. 2. 9 Liquidity (Marketability) Risk

The risk that a client might not be able to sell his investment quickly at a fair market price is known as **liquidity** or **marketability risk.** The marketability of the securities a registered representative recommends must be consistent with the client's liquidity needs.

Government bonds are sold easily, whereas DPPs are illiquid and extremely difficult to sell. Municipal securities have regional markets rather than a national market; therefore, they may be less marketable than more widely-held securities.

15. 3. 2. 10 Legislative Risk

Congress has the power to change laws affecting securities. The risk that such legal changes might affect an investment adversely is known as **legislative risk** or **political risk.** When recommending suitable investments, a registered representative should warn clients of any pending changes in the law that may affect those investments.

15. 3. 3   RISK MEASUREMENTS

In finance, **risk** is defined as the uncertainty that an investment will earn its expected rate of return.

15. 3. 3. 1 Alpha and Beta

Alpha is a measure of performance that adjusts for risk, relative to a known benchmark. The alpha for any investment type, a particular asset, or a portfolio is the abnormal rate of return on the investment in relation to what would normally be predicted by the benchmark. For example, if the normal rate of return for a portfolio was estimated or predicted by a pricing model to be 10%, but the portfolio actually had returns of 12%, it's alpha would be 2 (2% being the excess of 12% over the predicted 10%).

Alpha can also be negative, as would be the case for underperforming assets. So where a positive alpha of 1 indicates the asset has outperformed its benchmark by 1%, a negative alpha of 1 indicates that the asset has underperformed its benchmark by 1%.

A stock's **beta** is a measure of its volatility in relation to the overall market. Stocks with a beta of 1 move in line with the market; stocks with a beta greater than 1 are more volatile than the market; and stocks with a beta less than 1 move less than, or are less volatile than, the overall market.

EXAMPLE

If the S&P 500 rises or falls by 10%, a stock with a beta of 1 rises or falls by about 10%; a stock with a beta of 1.5 rises or falls by about 15%; and a stock with a beta of .75 rises or falls by about 7.5%.

Beta measures a security's **systemic** (or **systematic**) **risk**—the risk that can be associated with the market in general. The higher the beta, the more volatile the stock. High betas imply greater capital gains in a rising market and greater potential losses in declining markets. High beta stocks are usually considered aggressive, and low beta stocks are considered conservative. Risks specific to a stock, such as from competition, mismanagement, or product deficiencies, are independent of the general market. This is **nonsystematic risk**.

TAKE NOTE

Examples of high-beta stocks include technology and automobile companies. These stocks are quite volatile because their earnings fluctuate substantially. Low-beta stocks include utilities and drug companies. Because their earnings are more consistent from year to year, their prices generally move more slowly than the market overall.

QUICK QUIZ 15.B

Match each of the following items with the appropriate description below.

A. Market risk
B. Credit risk
C. Marketability risk
D. Purchasing power risk

_____ 1. Also known as liquidity risk, or the risk that a security cannot be sold quickly at a fair market price

_____ 2. Also known as inflation risk, or the risk of continually rising prices on investments

_____ 3. Also known as default risk, or the risk that principal may be lost as a result of issuer failure

_____ 4. Also known as systematic risk, or the risk that principal may be lost as a result of price volatility

5. A customer is pursuing an aggressive stock-buying strategy. Which of the following is most suitable for the customer's needs?

    A. ABC stock with a beta coefficient of 1.0
    B. DEF stock with a beta coefficient of 0.93
    C. GHI stock with a beta coefficient of 1.20
    D. Convertible bonds of a blue-chip company

6. An investor's portfolio has a beta coefficient of 1.1. If the overall market goes up 10%, the portfolio's value is likely to

    A. increase by 10%
    B. increase by 11%
    C. decrease by 10%
    D. decrease by 11%

15. 4   PORTFOLIO MANAGEMENT

A **portfolio** is an individual's combined investment holdings. A portfolio of securities offers investors diversification.

Many things influence a portfolio's makeup, including personal and market factors. A portfolio of securities that is appropriate for a 25-year-old unmarried man may not be appropriate for a 45-year-old married man with two children in college or a 65-year-old woman facing retirement.

Defensive investment strategies may have growth or income as an objective, but safety of principal tends to be the top priority. Such portfolios often are invested in blue-chip stocks with moderate or low volatility and AAA rated bonds.

Examples of defensive stock include food, utility, and drug companies. These stocks tend to hold their value during poor economic times.

Aggressive investment strategies attempt to maximize investment returns by assuming higher risks. Such strategies include:

■ selecting highly volatile stocks;

■ buying securities on margin; and

■ using put and call option strategies.

Most investors adopt a combination of aggressive and defensive strategies when making decisions about the securities in their portfolios. A **balanced**, or mixed, portfolio holds securities of many types.

15. 4. 1   MODERN PORTFOLIO THEORY AND RISK MANAGEMENT

Modern portfolio theory is an approach that attempts to quantify and control portfolio risk. It differs from traditional securities analysis in that it emphasizes determining the relationship between risk and reward in the total portfolio rather than analyzing specific securities. This is derived from the **capital asset pricing model (CAPM),** which states that the pricing of a stock must take into account two types of risk: systematic and nonsystematic.

Where investments are concerned, risk is normally associated with losing money. Investors use many techniques to reduce the potential for portfolio losses. Some of the most common are discussed here.

15. 4. 1. 1 Diversification

Diversification (i.e., buying different types of securities in various economic sectors) is a widely used investment strategy. A portfolio can be diversified in many ways, including:

- type of instrument (e.g., equity, debt, or packaged);
- industry;
- companies within an industry;
- length of maturity;
- investment rating; and
- geography.

By mixing industries and types of securities, investors attempt to spread their risk.

TAKE NOTE With regard to a domestic bond portfolio, diversification by geography is relevant if the portfolio consists of municipal bonds. However, if the portfolio consists of corporate bonds, geographic diversification is not relevant. For example, it does not matter whether IBM is based in New York or Illinois.

TEST TOPIC ALERT International equities and equity funds can add even more diversification to a portfolio if this is the objective, but remember that investments abroad generally carry more risk.

15. 4. 1. 2 Dollar Cost Averaging

Dollar cost averaging involves periodic purchases of a fixed dollar amount in one or more common stocks or mutual funds. In a fluctuating market, the average cost of the stock purchased in this manner is always less than the average market price. Dollar cost averaging does not guarantee against loss (it is fraudulent to imply so), but it does help control the cost of investing.

15. 4. 1. 3 Constant Ratio Plan

In a **constant ratio plan**, an investor buys or sells securities in a manner that keeps the portfolio balanced between equity and debt securities. The investor initially sets an equity-to-debt ratio, such as 60% equity and 40% debt, and buys or sells stocks and bonds to maintain the ratio.

15. 4. 1. 4 Constant Dollar Plan

The **constant dollar plan**'s primary goal is to buy and sell securities so that a set dollar amount remains invested at all times.

By using this technique, the client sells as prices rise and buys as prices fall, thus selling when the market rallies and buying when the market declines.

15. 4. 2 ASSET ALLOCATION

Asset allocation refers to the balancing of different asset classes, generally stocks, bonds, and cash, within an investment portfolio. In asset allocation, the mix of assets within a portfolio, rather than individual security selection, is the primary factor underlying portfolio performance.

15. 4. 2. 1 Strategic Asset Allocation

Strategic asset allocation refers to the proportion of various types of investments that should compose a long-term investment portfolio.

EXAMPLE   A standard asset allocation model suggests subtracting a person's age from 100 to determine the percentage of the portfolio that should be invested in stocks. Under this method, a 30-year-old would be 70% invested in stocks and 30% in bonds and cash; a 70-year-old would be invested 30% in stocks with the remainder in bonds and cash.

15. 4. 2. 2 Tactical Asset Allocation

Tactical asset allocation refers to short-term portfolio adjustments that adjust the portfolio mix between asset classes in consideration of current market conditions.

EXAMPLE   If the stock market is expected to do well over the near term, a portfolio manager may allocate greater portions of a portfolio to stocks. If the market is expected to decline, the portfolio manager may allocate greater portions of the portfolio to bonds and cash.

15. 4. 3 ACTIVE AND PASSIVE MANAGEMENT

An active portfolio manager uses a particular stock selection approach to buy and sell individual stocks. **Active management** relies on the manager's stock picking and market timing ability to outperform market indices.

EXAMPLE   An active portfolio manager may position the portfolio in stocks within a few market sectors, such as drugs and technology, frequently trading in and out of the stocks. An active manager may change his sector focus to capitalize on relative performance of different sectors during different stages of the business cycle.

A passive portfolio manager believes that no particular management style will consistently outperform market averages. Therefore, by constructing a portfolio that mirrors a market index, such as the S&P 500, passive portfolio management seeks a low-cost means of generating consistent, long-term returns with minimal turnover.

15. 4. 3. 1 Growth

Growth portfolio managers focus on stocks of companies whose earnings are growing faster than most other stocks and are expected to continue to do so. Because rapid growth in earnings is often priced into the stocks, growth investment managers are likely to buy stocks that are at the high end of their 52-week price range.

EXAMPLE

KLM Co., a 10-year-old company, is the dominant provider of routers used in telecommunications switching systems. Its earnings have grown in excess of 20% annually for the past seven years. It has $1.2 billion in annual sales, operating profit of 40% of sales, no debt, and it pays no dividend. The stock trades at 50 times annual earnings.

15. 4. 3. 2 Value

Value portfolio managers concentrate on undervalued or out-of-favor securities whose prices are low relative to the company's earnings or book value and whose earnings prospects are believed to be unattractive by investors and securities analysts. Value investment managers seek to buy undervalued securities before the company reports positive earnings. Value investment managers are more likely to buy stocks that are at the bottom of their 52-week price range.

EXAMPLE

ABC Co., established after World War II, is a metal processor for parts used in the automotive industry. The company has grown by 10% per year for the past 15 years but is highly susceptible to downturns in the economy. Twenty percent of its capitalization is in debt used to build a factory, and the stock has paid a quarterly dividend that has increased five times during the past 10 years. Conservatively managed, the company owns assets and cash that exceed the market value of its common stock.

QUICK QUIZ 15.C

1. Which of the following constitutes a constant dollar plan?

    A. 60% equities, 40% fixed income
    B. 40% equities, 60% fixed income investments
    C. Fixed amount in the portfolio regardless of market price
    D. Fixed amount in fixed-income investments regardless of market price

2. An investor who makes transactions once a month using dollar cost averaging would

    A. buy the same dollar amount of a stock
    B. buy the same number of shares of a stock
    C. put 70% of the money in a bond fund and buy stocks with the rest
    D. buy equal amounts of speculative and blue-chip securities

15. 5 FEDERAL AND STATE TAXATION

Taxes at both the federal and state level are labeled as either regressive or progressive.

15. 5. 1 REGRESSIVE TAXES

Regressive taxes, such as sales, excise, payroll, property, and gasoline taxes, are levied equally regardless of income, thus representing a smaller portion of income for wealthy taxpayers than for taxpayers with lower incomes. Because low-income families spend a larger percentage of their incomes than they save or invest, regressive taxes take a larger fraction of the income of economically disadvantaged people than of wealthy people.

EXAMPLE Income does not determine the amount of sales tax paid to purchase a computer. Each person purchasing the computer will pay the same percentage state sales tax in that state. As a regressive tax, sales taxes impact lower-income individuals more than those with higher incomes.

15. 5. 2 PROGRESSIVE TAXES

Progressive taxes, such as estate and income taxes, increase the tax rate as income increases. Progressive taxes affect people with high incomes more than people with low incomes.

EXAMPLE Two individuals earning different salaries in the same state will pay different amounts of income tax depending on their salaries. As a progressive tax, income taxes impact those with higher incomes more than those with lower incomes.

15. 5. 3 TYPES OF INCOME

Income can be either active or passive. Income derived exclusively from holding or trading securities is known as portfolio income.

15. 5. 3. 1 Earned (Active) Income

Earned income includes salary, bonuses, and income derived from active participation in a trade or business. Earned income is sometimes known as active income.

15. 5. 3. 2 Passive Income

Passive income and losses come from rental property, limited partnerships, and enterprises (regardless of business structure) in which an individual is not actively involved. For the general partner, income from a limited partnership is earned income; for the limited partner, such income is passive. Passive income is netted against passive losses to determine net taxable income. Passive losses may be used to offset passive income only.

15. 5. 3. 3 Portfolio Income

Portfolio income includes dividends, interest, and net capital gains derived from the sale of securities. No matter what the source of the income, it is taxed during the year in which it is received.

15. 5. 4 TAXATION AND INVESTMENT PORTFOLIOS

Investments may generate income, capital gains, or capital losses. Income and capital gains are taxed at different rates. Tax law separates capital gains (or losses) into short term and long term. Longer-term capital gains are eligible for lower tax rates.

TAKE NOTE   Short-term capital gains have a holding period of 12 months or less and are taxed as ordinary income. Long-term capital gains have a holding period of more than 12 months with a maximum tax rate as determined by the IRS tax code for long-term capital gains.

Capital losses may offset capital gains, but if capital losses exceed capital gains, a taxpayer may use only $3,000 of net capital losses to offset income. The taxpayer may carry unused capital losses forward indefinitely.

EXAMPLE   In the current year, an investor has capital losses of $12,000 and capital gains of $5,000. The investor has a net capital loss of $7,000. A total of $3,000 may be deducted from ordinary income. The remaining $4,000 is unused but may be carried forward to subsequent years.

15. 5. 4. 1 Interest Income

Interest paid on debt securities is income to the bondholder. It may or may not be taxable, depending on the type of security.

15. 5. 4. 1. 1 Taxable Interest Income

Corporate Bonds. Interest income from corporate bonds is taxable by federal, state, and some local governments.

U.S. Government Securities. Interest income on U.S. Treasury bills, notes, and bonds is exempt from state and local taxes but is federally taxable.

Agency Issues. The interest income on most federal agency debt, like that on Treasury securities, is taxable by the federal government but is exempt from state and local taxes. However, mortgage-backed securities issued by government agencies are taxable at all levels.

TAKE ✔ NOTE   Fannie Mae and Freddie Mac are corporations and are therefore taxable at all
                               levels.

Accrued Interest. Interest income includes **accrued interest** that an investor receives
when bonds are sold between interest payment dates. The trade confirmation discloses two
amounts: the amount received for the bond and the amount of accrued interest. The accrued
interest is taxable income to the seller. For tax reporting, the buyer deducts the amount of
accrued interest paid to the seller from the total interest received, to ensure that the buyer
pays tax only on the net amount.

15. 5. 4. 1. 2 Tax-Exempt Interest Income

Municipal Securities. Interest on municipal bonds is exempt from federal taxes. Furthermore, interest from municipal obligations of U.S. territories (Puerto Rico, Guam, and the
Virgin Islands) is exempt from federal, state, and local taxes. Interest on a municipal bond
or note normally is not taxable for residents of the state in which the bond or note is issued.

States or municipalities issue **private purpose bonds** (i.e., industrial revenue bonds) to
meet nonessential government functions. Although federally tax exempt for most taxpayers,
the interest on such municipal securities is a tax preference item for the alternative minimum
tax (AMT), discussed later. These bonds are issued by local or regional industrial development
authorities to provide jobs and to enhance the area's economic base. They are often used by
the private sector to finance shopping centers and manufacturing plants.

15. 5. 4. 2 Dividend Income

A dividend distribution is a share of a company's profits that is divided among shareholders. Investors who own stocks or mutual funds may receive dividends from those investments.
Dividends will be taxed as either nonqualified (ordinary) or qualified. In order to be taxed as
qualified dividends, the investment must have been held for more than 60 days (at least 61
days) during a 121-day period that begins 60 days before the ex-dividend date.

The maximum tax rate on qualified dividends is specified by current IRS tax code and will
depend on the investor's income tax rate. The higher the investor's income tax bracket the
higher the tax on qualified dividends will be, up to the maximum. Nonqualified or ordinary
dividends are taxed as ordinary income at the investor's ordinary income tax rate.

15. 5. 4. 2. 1 Dividend Income from Mutual Funds

Owners of mutual fund shares receive dividends that represent the pass-through of
dividends and interest earned on the underlying portfolio. Tax consequences depend on the
types of securities in the underlying portfolio.

- Municipal bond mutual funds and municipal unit investment trusts (UITs) distribute federally tax-free dividends to shareholders.
- Dividend distributions from corporate bond funds are taxable as ordinary income during
  the year an investor receives them.
- Dividend distributions from stock funds are taxed in accordance with current IRS tax code
  and not as ordinary income.

- Long-term capital gains distributions are taxed in accordance with current IRS tax code and not as ordinary income.
- Short-term capital gains distributions are taxed as ordinary income.

TAKE NOTE   Whether mutual fund distributions are taken in cash or reinvested into additional shares, they are taxable during the year of distribution.

15. 5. 4. 3 Foreign Securities

The interest and dividend income from a foreign investment, such as stock issued by a foreign corporation or bonds issued by a foreign government, is taxed by the country in which the investor is a citizen. A U.S. citizen who owns bonds or stock issued in another country is liable for federal and state taxes as well as local taxes if applicable (but not foreign taxes) on interest and dividend income received.

If foreign tax has been withheld on a distribution of dividends or interest from a foreign security, a U.S. citizen is eligible for an income tax credit for the amount withheld.

15. 5. 5 TAXABLE UPON RECEIPT

Interest and dividends are taxable only during the year they are received. Investors do not owe taxes on cash dividends or interest declared or accrued until they receive the money.

TAKE NOTE   Although cash dividends payable to shareholders are taxable, stock dividends or stock splits are not taxable. Instead, the shareholder has an increased number of shares with a reduced cost basis.

15. 5. 6 CAPITAL GAINS AND LOSSES

The sale of securities can result in a capital gain or a capital loss. **A capital gain** occurs when a security is sold for a price higher than the cost basis; if the selling price is lower than the cost basis, a **capital loss** occurs.

Remember, assets held one year or less qualify as short-term and short-term gains are taxed at ordinary income tax rates. Assets held for more than one year are considered long-term. Long-term gains are not taxed as ordinary income but instead are taxed in accordance with current IRS tax code. The long-term tax rate that applies depends on the investor's income tax bracket and will be higher for those in higher brackets up to the stated maximum long-term rate.

15. 5. 6. 1 Adjusting Cost Basis

An investment's cost basis is used to determine whether a taxable gain or a tax-deductible loss occurs when an asset is sold. Because many events affect an asset's cost basis, the IRS allows the cost basis to be adjusted for such occurrences as stock splits and stock dividends.

15. 5. 6. 1. 1 Capital Gains

A capital gain occurs when capital assets (securities, real estate, and tangible property) are sold at prices that exceed the adjusted cost basis. Usually, computing the capital gain or loss on an asset involves comparing the purchase price with the selling price.

EXAMPLE
A customer bought 100 shares of ABC at $90 plus commission of $100. The payment due was $9,100. The customer's cost basis was $91 per share. The customer sold the shares six months later at $96, less commission of $100. The customer's net proceeds were $9,500 ($9,600 − $100).

The customer's capital gain is calculated by comparing the cost basis to the sales proceeds as follows.

Cost basis	$9,100	or	$91 per share
...ds	$9,500	or	$95 per share
	$ 400	or	$4 per share

...d the shares after holding them for six months, the cus-
...gain taxable as ordinary income.

...are sold at prices that are lower than the adjusted

...sses

...first add all short-term capital gains and losses for
...rm capital gains and losses. Finally, the taxpayer
...l **gain or loss** for the year. If the result is a net
...d taxed.

...capital losses are deductible against earned income to a maximum of $3,000 per year. Any capital losses not deducted in a taxable year may be carried forward indefinitely to be used in future years.

15. 5. 6. 2 Determining Which Shares to Sell

An investor holding identical securities with different acquisition dates and cost basis must show to the IRS which shares are being sold for purposes of reporting gains and losses. This is achieved with the election of one of three accounting methods: **first in, first out (FIFO)**; **share identification**; or **average basis**. If the investor fails to choose, the IRS assumes that the investor liquidates shares on a FIFO basis.

An investor who chooses to identify shares sold must do so before the sale transaction settles. For stocks and mutual funds, this would typically mean trade date plus two business days (T+2). Share identification is the most flexible of the three methods. The investor keeps track of the cost of each share purchased and specifies which shares to sell based on his anticipated year-end tax needs. The average basis method is commonly used by mutual fund investors because it is the simplest with regards to fractional shares.

Lastly broker-dealers must report annually to their clients and the IRS via a statement showing both cost basis and sales proceeds when shares are sold.

15. 5. 6. 3   Wash Sales

An investor may not use capital losses to offset gains or income if the investor sells a security at a loss and purchases the same or a substantially identical security within 30 days before or after the trade date establishing the loss. The sale at a loss and the repurchase within this period is a **wash sale**.

Buying call options, rights, warrants, and convertible bonds of the same issuer is considered buying a substantially identical stock. Writing deep in the money puts on the stock sold, or to be sold, at a loss is also included in this definition.

If a loss is disallowed because of the wash sale rule, investors are permitted to adjust the cost basis of the reacquired position by the amount of the disallowed loss.

E X A M P L E

October 21, 2002	Buy 1,000 XYZ at 30
November 17, 2004	Sell 1,000 XYZ at 28
November 23, 2004	Buy 1,000 XYZ at 27

The $2,000 loss on the November 17, 2004, sale is disallowed because the investor bought back the security within 30 days of sale date. However, the investor can adjust the cost basis of the reacquired stock by the amount of the disallowed loss. Therefore, the cost basis of the stock bought on November 23, 2004, is 29 per share (27 + 2). In other words, the investor will eventually be able to take the loss when the reacquired stock is sold.

Similarly, the wash sale rule applies to short sales.

E X A M P L E

October 21, 2002	Sell short 1,000 ABC at 72
November 17, 2004	Buy back 1,000 ABC at 75
November 23, 2004	Sell short 1,000 ABC at 76

The $3,000 loss on the November 17, 2004, covering purchase is disallowed because the investor sold short the security within 30 days of covering date. The sale price of the reacquired position is adjusted by the amount of the disallowed loss (76 – 3 = 73).

The wash sale rule applies only to realized losses; it does not apply to realized gains.

T A K E   N O T E

Municipal tax swaps occur frequently at year-end. As a tax strategy, investors sell depreciated bonds to generate a deductible capital loss for the year. During a year when rates have risen (forcing bond prices down), investors, at year-end, often sell their bond positions for a loss and immediately use the proceeds of the sale to buy other bonds. The bonds purchased will provide a higher yield to the investor than the ones sold because rates have risen.

To avoid the wash sale rule, investors usually will buy bonds of a different issuer. Tax advisors generally recommend changing two of the following three characteristics to avoid the wash sale rule:

- Issuer
- Coupon
- Maturity

EXAMPLE

Changing the maturity and coupon or changing the maturity and issuer are acceptable to be in compliance with the wash sale rule.

Wash Sale

Trade date

30 days before   30 days after

April 15   May 15   June 14

TAKE NOTE

The wash sale rule will apply to an investor who, after selling for a loss, writes deep in the money puts on the same issuer.

QUICK QUIZ 15.D

1. An American citizen purchases a bond issued by the government of Sweden. The interest payments received are taxed at which of the following levels?

   I. Federal
   II. State
   III. Local

   A. I and II
   B. I and III
   C. II and III
   D. I, II and III

2. The income from all of the following securities is fully taxable at the federal, state, and local levels EXCEPT

   A. Ginnie Maes
   B. Treasury bonds
   C. reinvested mutual fund dividends
   D. corporate bonds

3. If each of the bonds under consideration has the same maturity, place the following bonds in order of their pretax yields, from highest to lowest.

I. U.S. government bonds
II. AAA municipal bonds
III. AA corporate bonds

A. I, II, III
B. II, I, III
C. III, I, II
D. III, II, I

15. 5. 7 ADJUSTING THE COST BASIS OF MUNICIPAL BONDS

If and how cost basis is adjusted for municipal bonds depends first on if the bond was purchased at a premium or a discount.

15. 5. 7. 1 Bonds Purchased at a Premium

The investor who buys a municipal bond at a premium, whether as a new issue or in the secondary market, must **amortize** the premium (**straight line**) over the remaining life of the bond.

EXAMPLE

A customer buys an 8% municipal bond with eight years to maturity at a dollar price of 108. The premium of eight points ($80) must be amortized over the remaining eight years to maturity. The annual amortization amount is one point, or $10 per bond. After one year, the cost basis is 107; after two years, 106; and so on. If held to maturity, there is no capital loss because the cost basis at that time has been reduced to par.

Amortization:

■ reduces cost basis; and
■ reduces reported interest income.

In the example, cost basis is reduced each year by $10 per bond. In addition, interest income of $80 per bond is reduced to $70 per bond (the amount of the annual amortization). Because interest income on municipal bonds is not taxed, its annual amortization has no tax effect.

If the bond is sold before maturity, gain or loss is the difference between sales price and adjusted cost basis. Take the following example. A customer buys a five-year municipal bond at 105. Two years later, the bond is sold at 104. What is the customer's gain or loss?

The premium of five points must be amortized over a five-year period, so the annual amortization is one point, or $10 per bond. After two years, the bond's cost basis is 103. Therefore, a sale at 104 creates a one-point capital gain per bond.

15. 5. 7. 2 Bonds Purchased at a Discount

If a municipal bond is bought at a discount, the discount is accreted. **Accretion** is the process of adjusting the cost basis back up to par. The actual tax effect of accretion depends on whether the bond was purchased as an **original issue discount (OID)** (i.e., a new issue being offered at a discount) or an issue purchased at a discount in the secondary market.

Accretion:

- increases cost basis; and
- increases reported interest income.

EXAMPLE

A customer buys a 5% municipal bond with 10 years to maturity at 90. The amount of the annual accretion is $10 per bond (10-point discount ÷ 10 years to maturity). Each year, the cost basis is adjusted upward by one point. At maturity, there is no reported capital gain.

If the bond was purchased as an OID, the reported interest income would be $60 per bond ($50 plus the annual accretion of $10). Because interest income on municipal bonds is tax free, the accretion has no tax effect. If, however, the bond was purchased at a discount in the secondary market, the annual accretion would be taxed as ordinary income.

TAKE NOTE

Assume a customer buys a 5% municipal bond with a 10-year maturity at 90 in the secondary market. Five years later, the customer sells the bond at 97. What are the tax consequences? The annual accretion of $10 per bond is taxable each year as ordinary income. The customer's cost basis at the time of sale is 95. When sold at 97, the customer has a capital gain of $20 per bond. Had the bond been purchased as an OID, the only tax consequence would be a capital gain of $20 per bond. The annual accretion for an OID is considered municipal interest income and is therefore not taxable.

TEST TOPIC ALERT

An investor buys a 5% bond at 94. The yield to maturity is 6%. If the bond is bought as an OID, the customer's effective after-tax yield is 6%. If the bond is bought in the secondary market, the customer's effective tax yield would be somewhere between 5 and 6% because the annual accretion is taxable as ordinary income.

A customer buys a 5% municipal bond with 10 years to maturity at 110. At that price, the basis (YTM) is 3.81%. After taking taxes into consideration, the customer's effective after-tax yield is

- A.   less than 3.81%
- B.   3.81%
- C.   between 3.81 and 5%
- D.   more than 5%

Answer: B. In almost all cases, the stated yield to maturity on municipal bonds is the effective after-tax yield. The only exception is for bonds purchased at a discount in the secondary market. For such bonds, the effective after-tax yield is somewhere between the stated yield to maturity and the coupon on the bond.

15. 5. 8 ADJUSTING THE COST BASIS OF CORPORATE BONDS

If a corporate bond is bought at a discount, either as an OID or in the secondary market, the annual accretion is taxable as ordinary income.

TAKE NOTE

Accretion increases reported interest income, which for corporate bonds, is fully taxable.

If, however, a corporate bond is purchased at a premium, either as a new issue or in the secondary market, the investor has the option to amortize or not. If the customer elects not to amortize and holds the bond until maturity, the investor will have a capital loss for tax purposes. If the customer elects to amortize, there will be no capital loss at maturity. However, each year the investor who elects to amortize will report lower interest income for tax purposes.

TEST TOPIC ALERT

- The discount on all bonds bought in the secondary market is taxed as interest income.

- For corporate bonds bought at a premium, the investor has the option to amortize.

EXAMPLE

A customer buys a corporate bond at 104, paying $30 of accrued interest per bond. The customer elects not to amortize. What is the customer's cost basis on this bond for tax purposes?

A. 100
B. 101
C. 104
D. 107

Answer: C. Because the customer elects not to amortize, the cost basis is 104. Accrued interest has no effect on cost basis.

15. 5. 9 OTHER TAX CONSIDERATIONS

In the following sections, we'll discuss some unique tax considerations.

15. 5. 9. 1 Donated and Inherited Securities

When securities are donated or inherited, different variables impact cost basis and other tax consequences.

15. 5. 9. 1. 1 Donations to Charity

When donations of appreciated property are made to charitable organizations, the donor receives a tax deduction equal to the market value on the date of the donation. The recipient's cost basis is equal to the higher current market value. There is no tax liability on the appreciation if the asset was held for more than one year before the donation. If the asset was held for one year or less, tax is due on the increase in value.

15. 5. 9. 1. 2 Donations to Others

When donations or gifts are made to family members or others, no deduction is available. The cost basis to the recipient is the original cost basis of the donor. Such gifts are subject to gift taxes.

15. 5. 9. 1. 3 Inherited Securities

When a person dies and leaves securities to heirs, the cost basis to the recipients is the fair market value on the date of the owner's death.

15. 5. 9. 2 Estate and Gift Taxes

Taxes can be levied upon the estate of a deceased person and upon those gifting securities to others. This section discusses these unique scenarios.

15. 5. 9. 2. 1 Donor Taxes

When a person dies, tax is due on the estate. This tax is payable by the estate, not by heirs who inherit the estate (although certain other taxes may apply to heirs). Likewise, if a person gives a gift, tax is due on the gift. Gift tax is payable by the donor, not the recipient. Estate and gift taxes are progressive taxes. For tax purposes, the valuation of the estate is the date of death; the valuation of a gift is the date it is given.

15. 5. 9. 2. 2 Gift Tax Exemption

Individuals may give gifts up to a maximum amount per year to any number of individuals without incurring gift tax. The amount of the exclusion is subject to change depending on current tax law. Interspousal gifts, no matter what the size, are not subject to tax. If a gift tax is due, it is paid by the donor.

15. 5. 9. 2. 3 Estate Tax Exclusion

The estate of a deceased person is allowed to exclude some of that person's estate from taxation. The amount of the exclusion is subject to change depending on current tax law.

TAKE NOTE   Estate and gift taxes are progressive taxes that increase with the size of the estate or the gift.

15. 5. 9. 2. 4 Unlimited Marital Deduction

Married couples are allowed to transfer their entire estate to the surviving spouse at death. This unlimited marital deduction results in taxes being owed at the death of the survivor.

15. 5. 9. 3 Margin Expenses

Margin interest is a tax-deductible expense. The one exception is interest expenses incurred in the purchase of municipal securities. Because municipal interest income is federally tax exempt, the IRS does not allow taxpayers to claim deductions for the margin interest expense on municipal securities. Investors can deduct interest expenses for other securities to the extent that they do not exceed their net investment income, which includes interest income, dividends, and all capital gains.

TAKE NOTE   If banks purchase bank-qualified municipal bonds (small GO issues of $10 million or less), the bank may deduct, for tax purposes, 80% of the costs incurred in financing the purchase.

15. 5. 9. 4 Shorting Against the Box

Selling **short against the box** is a strategy that has been used to lock in a capital gain that was to be deferred into a later tax period. Instead of selling shares a customer holds long, the customer borrows the same shares and sells them short. Because the borrowed shares were sold, there is no tax event. The customer instead is taxed at the point when the borrowed shares are replaced with the shares the customer owns.

A 5% margin requirement applies on the proceeds from selling short against the box. The firm may release 95% of the sales proceeds to the customer.

TAKE NOTE   The tax law revisions of 1997 greatly minimized the effectiveness of shorting against the box for tax deferral. The law now allows tax deferral only if the short position is closed within 30 days of year end and the customer stays long in the stock for an additional 60 days. Shorting against the box cannot be used to stretch a short-term gain into a long-term gain.

15. 5. 10 ALTERNATIVE MINIMUM TAX (AMT)

Congress enacted the **alternative minimum tax (AMT)** to make certain that high-income taxpayers do not escape paying taxes.

15. 5. 10. 1 Tax Preference Items

Certain items receive favorable tax treatment. These items must be added back into taxable income for the AMT. They include:

- accelerated depreciation on investment property;
- certain costs associated with DPPs, such as research and development costs and intangible drilling costs;
- local tax and interest on investments that do not generate income;

- tax-exempt interest on private purpose, nonessential government service municipal bonds; and

- incentive stock options exceeding their fair market value.

TAKE NOTE   The Internal Revenue Code (IRC) language says that taxpayers are required to add the excess of the AMT over the regular tax to their regular tax to determine their total tax liability.

---

15. 5. 11 CORPORATE TAXES

Corporations are major investors in securities. One tax provision affecting corporations as investors is the following.

15. 5. 11. 1 Dividend Exclusion Rule

Dividends paid from one corporation to another are 70% exempt from taxation. A corporation that receives dividends on stocks of other domestic corporations, therefore, pays taxes on only 30% of the dividends received. This provision encourages corporations to invest in common and preferred stock of other U.S. corporations.

QUICK QUIZ 15.E

1. An investor has purchased a number of municipal bonds on margin. The margin interest paid is

    A. fully deductible
    B. only deductible if the investor has investment income
    C. partially deductible
    D. not deductible

2. An investor has donated securities that have appreciated since purchased to her favorite charity. Wanting to use the donation as a tax deduction on her tax return, the investor will be allowed to deduct

    A. the original cost of the securities when purchased
    B. the market value of the securities on the date of the donation
    C. the amount by which the securities have appreciated
    D. no portion of the donation

3. A U.S. corporation purchases shares of stock in another U.S. corporation and, as a result, receives dividends. Taxes will be due on what percentage of the dividends received?

    A. 100% taxable
    B. 70% taxable
    C. 30% taxable
    D. 0% (tax free)

UNIT TEST

1. Income from which of the following investments is passive income?

I. Real estate DPP
II. Real estate investments
III. REITs
IV. CMOs

A. I and II
B. I and III
C. II and III
D. III and IV

2. Which of the following statements regarding gift taxes are TRUE?

I. Gifts of unlimited amounts per person per year can be given without a gift tax liability.
II. All gifts, regardless of dollar amount, are taxable to the donor.
III. The donor, not the recipient, is responsible for any tax liability.
IV. The tax rate increases with the size of the gift.

A. I and II
B. I and III
C. II and III
D. III and IV

3. If a customer buys a new issue municipal bond at a discount in the primary market, which of the following statements are TRUE?

I. The discount must be accreted.
II. The discount may not be accreted.
III. At maturity, there is a capital gain.
IV. At maturity, there is no capital gain.

A. I and III
B. I and IV
C. II and III
D. II and IV

4. A father makes a gift of securities to his 10-year-old daughter. Gift taxes would be based on

A. the cost of the securities
B. the market value of the securities at date of gift
C. the market value of the securities as of April 15 of the year during which the gift is made
D. the market value of the securities as of December 31 of the year in which the gift is made

5. Which of the following investments should a representative recommend to a corporate client whose objective is current income with moderate risk?

A. Preferred stock
B. Aggressive growth fund
C. Money market fund
D. High-yield bond fund

6. A person's investment decisions should be based primarily on his

I. risk tolerance
II. representative's recommendations
III. investment needs
IV. broker-dealer's available inventory

A. I and II
B. I and III
C. II and III
D. III and IV

7. Income from all of the following is partially exempt to a corporate investor EXCEPT

A. convertible bonds
B. common stock
C. preferred stock
D. preferred stock mutual funds

8. When determining whether a tax swap of municipal bonds will result in a wash sale, all of the following are considered EXCEPT

   A. maturity
   B. principal amount
   C. issuer
   D. coupon

9. A married couple sets up a JTWROS account with a balance of $1 million. If the wife dies, what is the husband's estate tax liability?

   A. He pays federal and state taxes on the entire balance.
   B. He pays federal and state taxes on $500,000.
   C. He pays federal taxes only on $500,000.
   D. He pays no estate tax.

10. Which of the following taxes are known as progressive taxes?

    I. Sales
    II. Cigarette
    III. Income
    IV. Estate

    A. I and II
    B. II and III
    C. II and IV
    D. III and IV

11. A municipal bond is purchased in the secondary market at 102½. The bond has 5 years to maturity. Two years later, the bond is sold for 102. The tax consequence to the investor is

    A. a capital loss of $5 per bond
    B. a capital gain of $5 per bond
    C. a capital loss of $20 per bond
    D. no capital gain or loss

12. A mother makes a gift of appreciated securities to her 10-year-old son. The son's cost basis in the stock is

    A. the original cost of the securities to the mother
    B. the market value of the securities on the date of the gift
    C. the market value of the securities on April 15 of the year when the gift is made
    D. the market value of the securities on December 31 of the year when the gift is made

13. A customer bought 100 ABC at 60 in January of 1998. In February 2000, the stock was worth $100 per share, and the customer donated it to charity. The consequences are

    I. $6,000 deduction
    II. $10,000 deduction
    III. no tax is due on appreciation
    IV. tax is due on appreciation

    A. I and III
    B. I and IV
    C. II and III
    D. II and IV

14. A customer has $12,000 of capital gains and $15,000 of capital losses. How much unused loss is carried forward to the following tax year?

    A. $0
    B. $3,000
    C. $12,000
    D. $15,000

15. A husband makes a gift of $100,000 to his wife. How much of the gift is subject to gift taxes?

    A. $0
    B. $50,000
    C. $90,000
    D. $100,000

ANSWERS AND RATIONALES

1. **A.** Passive income is income from DPPs and from direct investments in real estate. REITs and CMOs are securities, and income from securities is considered portfolio income.

2. **D.** In accordance with gift tax regulations, an individual may give a gift up to an allowable limit per person in one year with no gift tax liability. If the gift exceeds the allowable limit, it is the donor who is responsible for any tax due. The gift tax is a progressive tax, which means that as the size of the taxable gift increases, the percentage of tax that applies will also increase.

3. **B.** If a new issue municipal bond is bought at a discount in the primary market, the discount must be accreted. The accretion is considered interest income and, therefore, is not taxable.

4. **B.** If a gift tax is due, it is paid by the donor based upon the value of the gift on the date it is given.

5. **A.** Preferred stock generates current income in the form of dividends. Aggressive growth funds strive for capital appreciation rather than current income. Money market funds have low yields, not the high yields that an income investor wants. Although high-yield bonds provide current income, they entail a high degree of risk.

6. **B.** Investment objectives and understanding and acceptance of risk should determine an individual's investment decisions. Recommendations by a representative may merit possible actions, but the client must make a decision on the basis of whether the investment is suitable.

7. **A.** 70% of dividend income received from investments in common stock and preferred stock is excluded from taxation for a corporate investor. This exclusion applies to dividends from mutual funds in which all of the portfolio securities are preferred or common stock.

8. **B.** In judging whether bonds purchased are substantially identical to bonds sold for a loss, the tax code considers maturity, issuer, and coupon rate. If at least two of the three are different, a wash sale will generally not result. Principal amount is not a consideration.

9. **D.** Establishing a joint tenants with right of survivorship account allows for the transfer of assets to the survivor upon death. The surviving spouse is not taxed on assets transferred in this manner.

10. **D.** With a progressive tax, the tax percentage amount increases as the taxable amount increases. Income and estate taxes are progressive. Sales and cigarette taxes are regressive because all persons pay the same percentage tax regardless of their income.

11. **B.** Municipal bonds bought at a premium, either in the new issue or secondary market, must be amortized. Each year, the premium must be amortized so that, if held to maturity, there is no reported capital gain or loss. The amount of the premium is 2½ points, or $25. Because the bond has five years to maturity, the annual amortization amount is $5 per bond. After 2 years, the bond's basis has been amortized down to 101½. At that point, a sale at 102 generates a capital gain of $5 per bond.

12. **A.** When a gift of securities is made while the donor is alive, the original cost of the securities is the cost basis, not the value of the security on the date of the gift. Note that market value at date of gift is used to determine whether gift taxes are applicable.

13. **C.** When an investor donates appreciated securities to charity, the investor will receive a tax deduction based on the value as of the donation date. There will be no tax due on the amount of appreciation as long as the stock was held long term as of the date of the charitable donation.

14. **A.** After netting capital gain and losses, the customer has a net capital loss of $3,000. Since $3,000 of net losses can be deducted during any one tax year, there is no carry forward.

15. **A.** Interspousal gifts, regardless of amount, are not subject to gift taxes.

QUICK QUIZ ANSWERS

Quick Quiz 15.A

1. **A.** Growth refers to an increase in the value of an investment over time. This growth can come from increases in the value of the security, the reinvestment of distributions, or both.

2. **D.** Direct participation programs or limited partnerships are illiquid investments because there is no immediate market for them.

3. **C.** Of the answers offered, to generate the greatest return, a fixed-income security (a bond) is most suitable. Common stock is not suitable; convertibles (bonds or preferred) generally pay out a lower income rate than nonconvertibles because the investors receive benefit from the conversion feature; income bonds pay interest only if the corporation meets targeted earnings levels.

4. **D.** The GNMA mutual fund is the most suitable investment for an investor seeking monthly income. The other securities offer higher long-term growth potential, but they are not designed to provide monthly income.

Quick Quiz 15.B

1. **C.**

2. **D.**

3. **B.**

4. **A.**

5. **C.** Beta coefficients greater than 1 signify that the stock will fluctuate more than the market as a whole. In general, the higher the beta, the greater the risk. Such risk-taking is appropriate for investors who seek aggressive stock-buying strategies and have both the financial ability and the temperament to withstand downturns in the market.

6. **B.** A beta of 1.1 means the portfolio is considered to be 1.1 times more volatile than the overall market. Therefore, if the market is up 10%, the portfolio with a beta of 1.1 is likely to be up 11% ($1.1 \times 10\%$).

Quick Quiz 15.C

1. **C.** In a constant dollar plan, a fixed dollar amount is invested in the portfolio. If the market value rises, the excess is sold. If the market value falls, securities are purchased to restore the constant dollar position.

2. **A.** Because the dollar amount remains constant, the investor will automatically buy more shares when the price is low, thus reducing the average cost.

Quick Quiz 15.D

1. **D.** Interest income from foreign securities is fully taxable to U.S. citizens. If foreign tax is withheld in the country of origin (Sweden, in this case), the investor will receive a tax credit to offset the foreign tax liability.

2. **B.** Dividends (whether reinvested or not), Ginnie Maes, Fannie Maes, and corporate bonds are all fully taxable. U.S. government securities are exempt from state and local taxes.

3. **C.** Normally, the greater the risk, the higher the yield that must be offered to potential investors. Therefore, government securities yield less than corporate securities. In this problem, take into account the difference in taxable bonds (corporate and governments) versus tax-free bonds (municipals); this difference in taxation causes the pretax yield of municipals to be lower than that of corporate and government bonds.

Quick Quiz 15.E

1. **D.** Because interest received from municipal bonds is tax exempt, the government does not allow margin interest paid to purchase them to be used as a deduction on one's income tax return.

2. **B.** When an individual has donated appreciated securities to a charity, the amount of the allowable tax deduction is equal to the current market value of the securities on the day the donation was made.

3. **C.** When a U.S. corporation receives dividends from another U.S. corporation it has invested in, 70% of the dividends received are excluded from taxation. This means that the dividends received are 30% taxable.

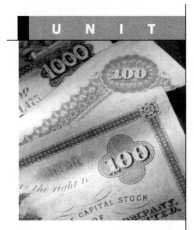

16

U.S. Government and State Rules and Regulations

The securities industry is heavily regulated. The stock market crash of 1929 caused significant government response to the functioning of the securities business. The government took an active interest in implementing legislation to protect the public and correct abusive practices by industry practitioners.

This Unit presents an overview of the major pieces of federal legislation and state securities law. It is important to know the general boundaries of these rules and regulations for success on the exam and as a representative.

On the Series 7 exam, you will encounter approximately 15–20 questions on these regulations. ∎

When you have completed this Unit, you should be able to identify and define the scope and boundaries of the following major securities legislation:

- Securities Act of 1933

- Securities Exchange Act of 1934

- Maloney Act

- Trust Indenture Act of 1939

- Investment Company Act of 1940

- Investment Advisers Act of 1940

- Securities Investor Protection Act of 1970

- Securities Acts Amendments of 1975

- Uniform Securities Act (USA)

- Insider Trading and Securities Fraud Enforcement Act of 1988

- Penny stock cold-calling rules

- Bank Secrecy Act

- Sarbanes-Oxley Act of 2002

- Uniform Securities Act

16. 1   OVERVIEW OF FEDERAL AND SECURITIES LEGISLATION

This section highlights the acts of 1933 and 1934 and discusses other legislation that expanded or amended these acts.

16. 1. 1   THE SECURITIES ACT OF 1933

The Act of 1933 was the federal government's first legislative response to the stock market crash of 1929. After investigating the conditions that led to the crash, it was determined that investors had little protection against fraud in the sale of new issues of securities. To correct this problem, the Act of 1933 requires full and fair disclosure of nonexempt issues. The following list encompasses the major aspects of the act.

■ Issuers of nonexempt securities must file registration statements with a regulatory body. The regulatory body referenced in the Act of 1933 was officially created shortly thereafter as the Securities Exchange Commission (SEC) in the Act of 1934.

■ Prospectuses must be provided to all purchasers of new, nonexempt issues for full and fair disclosure.

■ Fraudulent activity in connection with underwriting and issuing of all securities is prohibited.

16. 1. 2   THE SECURITIES EXCHANGE ACT OF 1934

The Act of 1934 was a further reaction to the crash of 1929. It picks up where the Act of 1933 finished, addressing fraudulent practices in the secondary marketplace.

The Act of 1934 is responsible for the:

■ creation of the SEC;

■ registration of all persons and firms that trade securities OTC and on exchanges for the public;

■ regulation of exchanges and the OTC market;

■ regulation of credit by the Federal Reserve Board;

■ regulation of trading activities;

■ regulation of insider transactions, short sales, and proxies;

■ regulation of client accounts;

■ customer protection rule;

■ net capital rule and financial responsibility for broker-dealers; and

■ reporting requirements for issuers (e.g., annual reports).

Key words help identify the Act of 1934 in test questions. The Act of 1934 is associated with:

- the secondary market;

- outstanding securities; and

- trading activities.

Consider the Act of 1934 as the **People Act**. It regulates all the persons involved in trading securities on behalf of customers.

Although certain securities are exempt from the registration requirements of the Act of 1933, no security is exempt from the antifraud provisions of the Act of 1934. This means that certain securities are exempt from registration and prospectus requirements, but fraud or market manipulation cannot be involved in the trading of any security, exempt or nonexempt.

16. 1. 2. 1 Tender Offers

If a company makes a cash tender offer for another company, the Act of 1934 states that shareholders of the target company may tender their shares only to the extent of their net long position.

E X A M P L E   Assume ABC makes a cash tender offer at $40 per share for any and all shares of XYZ. If a customer were long 500 shares of XYZ in his cash account and short 200 shares in his margin account, the customer could only tender 300 shares, his net long position.

The act also states that customers may not borrow stock in order to tender the borrowed shares.

16. 1. 2. 2 Maloney Act of 1938

The **Maloney Act** amended the Act of 1934 and enabled the SEC to create SROs, or **designated examining authorities (DEAs),** for monitoring brokers and dealers not affiliated with a stock exchange. SROs for brokers and dealers not affiliated with an exchange would be FINRA and the MSRB.

16. 1. 3 TRUST INDENTURE ACT OF 1939

The **Trust Indenture Act of 1939** applies to corporate bonds (nonexempt) with the following characteristics:

- Issue size of more than $50 million within 12 months
- Maturity of nine months or more
- Offered interstate

This act was passed to protect bondholders and requires that issuers of these bonds appoint a trustee to ensure that promises (covenants) between the issuer and trustee who acts solely for the benefit of the bondholders are carried out. The document is filed at the office of a custodian so that investors may review it if they choose.

TEST TOPIC ALERT   The test might ask about the definition of a trust indenture. The best answer defines the trust indenture as a series of promises between the issuer and the trustee for the benefit of the bondholders.

16. 1. 4 THE INVESTMENT COMPANY ACT OF 1940

The **Investment Company Act of 1940** defines and regulates investment companies, including mutual funds. It requires investment companies to:

- register with the SEC before selling shares publicly;
- clearly state their investment objectives in their registration statement and prospectus;
- have net worth of at least $100,000 before offering shares to the public;
- be owned by a minimum of 100 shareholders; and
- comply with standards on pricing, public sale, and reporting.

TAKE NOTE   The three classifications of investment companies—face-amount certificate companies (FACs), unit investment trusts (UITs), and management companies—are described in the *Investment Company Products* Unit.

16. 1. 5 THE INVESTMENT ADVISERS ACT OF 1940

The purpose of the **Investment Advisers Act of 1940** is to require anyone who, as part of their business, gives investment advice for compensation to register as investment advisers under the act. Broker-dealers who provide advice for a fee (e.g., a **wrap account**) are subject to registration under this act. Agents of investment advisers must register and pass the Series 65 exam or Series 66 exam (for representatives with a Series 7). Providing advice and not charging separately for it (i.e., acting as a registered representative) does not require registration as an adviser.

EXAMPLE   A registered representative who is registered under the Securities Act of 1934 and has been charging commissions for transactions now wants to charge separately for investment advice regardless of whether a transaction takes place or not. In order to do so, even though already registered under the Act of 1934, the RR would now need to register under the Investment Advisors Act of 1940 by passing the appropriate exam (Series 65 or 66).

16. 1. 6 THE SECURITIES INVESTOR PROTECTION ACT AND THE SIPC

After many brokerage firm defaults in the 1960s, the **Securities Investor Protection Act** was passed in 1970 to protect customers from broker-dealer failure or insolvency. This act intensified broker-dealer financial requirements and also created the **Securities Investor Protection Corporation (SIPC)**.

16. 1. 6. 1 Membership and Assessments

Though SIPC is an independent, government-sponsored corporation, it is not a government agency. SIPC collects annual assessments from broker-dealers. These assessments create a general insurance fund to be used for customer claims that may result if a broker-dealer fails.

All broker-dealers registered with the SEC must be SIPC members except for those handling only:

■ mutual funds or unit trusts; and

■ variable annuities or insurance.

However, investment advisers are not broker-dealers and are therefore not SIPC members. Firms that fail to pay their SIPC assessments may not engage in the brokerage business.

16. 1. 6. 1. 1 Violation of Net Capital

If a firm is suspected by the SEC or any SRO of a violation of its minimum net capital requirements, a notification is made to SIPC. If SIPC believes that a violation has occurred or that the firm is insolvent, it will petition a court to appoint a liquidating trustee, and the firm ceases doing business.

When a liquidation proceeding takes place, the order of events is as follows.

■ Securities held in customer name are delivered to registered owners.

■ Cash and street name securities are distributed on a pro rata basis.

■ SIPC funds are distributed to meet remaining claims up to the maximum allowed per customer.

■ Customers with excess claims become general creditors of the broker-dealer.

16. 1. 6. 2 SIPC Coverage

Under SIPC, accounts are covered to a maximum of $500,000, with cash claims not to exceed $250,000 of that total per separate customer. How an account is titled will determine if it represents a separate customer.

TAKE NOTE

In margin accounts, it is the equity in the account, not the long market value, that is considered the securities value for coverage purposes.

Examples of SIPC Customer Coverage Limits	
John Doe—cash account John Doe—margin account	1 customer = $500,000 coverage
John and Mary Doe— joint account	1 customer = $500,000 coverage
John Doe as custodian for Jane Doe	1 customer = $500,000 coverage

Commodities and commodities futures contracts are not covered by SIPC because they are not considered securities. Customers with claims in excess of SIPC limits become general creditors of the broker-dealer.

16. 1. 6. 3 Use of SIPC Membership in Advertising

Broker-dealers must include their SIPC membership on all advertising but may not imply that SIPC coverage is more than it actually is or that its benefits are unique to only that firm. The term *SIPC* may not appear larger than the firm's own name. Also, all member firms must post a sign that indicates SIPC membership.

In addition, SIPC members must provide written disclosure to customers that they may obtain information about SIPC, including the SIPC brochure, by contacting SIPC. This disclosure must be made to new customers at the time an account is opened and to all customers at least once each year thereafter.

TEST TOPIC ALERT

Cash and margin accounts are combined for SIPC coverage purposes.
Also know that the valuation date for customer securities claims is generally the same day the customer protection proceedings begin. This would be the same time the court is petitioned to appoint a SIPC trustee.

16. 1. 7 THE SECURITIES ACTS AMENDMENTS OF 1975

The **Securities Acts Amendments of 1975** established the **Municipal Securities Rulemaking Board (MSRB)**. The MSRB regulates the issuance and trading of municipal securities.

16. 1. 8 INSIDER TRADING AND SECURITIES FRAUD ENFORCEMENT ACT OF 1988

Although the Securities Act of 1934 prohibited the use of insider information in making trades, the Insider Trading and Securities Fraud Enforcement Act of 1988 amends its provisions and specifies penalties for insider trading and securities fraud.

16. 1. 8. 1 Insiders

An **insider** is any person who has access to nonpublic information about a company that would most likely influence the price of the company's stock. Inside information is any information that has not been disseminated to, or is not readily available to, the general public.

16. 1. 8. 2 Tippers and Tippees

The act prohibits insiders trading on or communicating nonpublic information. Both the **tipper** (the person who gives the tip) and the **tippee** (the person who receives the tip) are liable, as is anyone who trades on information that they know or should know is not public or who has control over the misuse of this information.

The key elements of tipper and tippee liability under insider trading rules are as follows.

- Is the information material and nonpublic?

- Does the tipper owe a fiduciary duty to a company or its stockholders? Has he breached it?

- Does the tipper meet the personal benefits test (even something as simple as enhancing a friendship or reputation)?

- Does the tippee know or should the tippee have known that the information was inside or confidential?

EXAMPLE   A building custodian finds papers in a waste paper basket indicating that the company is about to launch a takeover of another company within 30 days. The information is marked "release date not yet determined". He tells his spouse and his best friend. His best friend passes the information on to his brother, sister, and two neighbors. Within a week, some, but not all, of these persons have called their broker-dealers to put in buy orders for shares of the target company. Under the ACT of 1988, who, if any one of these individuals, is liable? All parties are liable under the Act of 1988. The definition of insider, essentially, is anyone who has or passes on information not yet known to the public.

16. 1. 8. 3 Written Supervisory Procedures

All broker-dealers must establish written supervisory procedures specifically prohibiting the misuse of inside information. Additionally, they must establish policies that restrict the passing of potentially material nonpublic information between a firm's departments. This barrier against the free flow of sensitive information is known as a **firewall,** or an **information barrier**.

EXAMPLE   Most firms establish procedures ensuring that information from their mergers and acquisitions department is not able to flow to their proprietary trading or retail trading departments. This ensures that the firm's own proprietary traders or the firm's retail customers will not know any merger or acquisition information until it is made public.

16. 1. 8. 3. 1 Penalties

The SEC can investigate any person, not just those with securities registration licenses, suspected of violating any of the provisions of the Insider Trading Act. If the SEC determines that a violation has occurred, civil penalties of up to three times profits made or losses avoided may be levied. A controlling person such as a registered representative or broker-dealer could be fined a dollar amount that has been linked to an inflation index (and therefore changes) or three times the profit made or loss avoided, whichever is greater.

Violators may also face criminal penalties of up to $5 million and up to 20 years in jail. If the violator is an employee of the broker-dealer, the firm (which is supposed to have procedures in place to prevent this) could be fined up to treble damages or $25 million, whichever is greater.

TAKE NOTE   *Treble* is a legal word often used in federal securities law; it means three times damages or losses avoided.

16. 1. 8. 4   Contemporaneous Traders

Persons who enter trades at or near the same time in the same security as a person who has inside information are known as **contemporaneous traders**. Contemporaneous traders may sue persons that have violated insider trading regulations, and suits may be initiated up to five years after the violation has occurred.

16. 1. 8. 4. 1 Informer Bounty

The Insider Trading Act specifically allowed for payment to informers. However, amended under the Dodd-Frank legislation, awards may now be paid in connection with original information concerning any violation of securities law, including insider trading. The information bounty or award can range from 10 to 30 percent of amounts recovered based on the information received.

TAKE NOTE   Simply giving someone inside information, although imprudent, is not a violation. When the information is used to trade for profit or to avoid a loss, a violation occurs. In this case, both the tipper and tippee are liable.

QUICK QUIZ 16.A

1. A client not covered by SIPC in a broker-dealer bankruptcy

   A. becomes a secured creditor

   B. becomes a general creditor

   C. becomes a preferred creditor

   D. loses his investment

2. A client has a cash account with stock valued at $460,000 and $40,000 in cash. The same client also has a joint account with a spouse that has a market value of $100,000 and $300,000 in cash. SIPC coverage is

    A. $460,000 for the cash account and $300,000 for the joint account
    B. $500,000 for the cash account and $350,000 for the joint account
    C. $500,000 for the cash account and $250,000 for the joint account
    D. a total of $1 million for both accounts

3. SIPC uses which of the following to determine the value of customer claims when a broker-dealer becomes insolvent?

    A. Market value on the date the broker-dealer becomes insolvent
    B. Market value on the date a federal court is petitioned to appoint a trustee
    C. Market value on the date the trustee pays the customers their balances
    D. Average market value from the time a trustee is appointed to the payment date

4. Which of the following statements regarding the civil penalties that may be imposed for insider trading violations under the Securities Exchange Act of 1934 is NOT true?

    A. A civil penalty may be imposed only on a person registered under a securities act.
    B. The violation for which the penalty may be imposed is defined as buying or selling securities while in possession of material, nonpublic information.
    C. The SEC may ask a court to impose a penalty of up to three times the loss avoided or profit gained on an illegal transaction.
    D. Improper supervision may cause a broker-dealer to be liable if one of its representatives commits an insider trading violation.

5. Under the Securities Exchange Act of 1934, insiders include

    I.   the attorney who writes an offering circular for a company
    II.   the bookkeeper in a company's accounting department
    III. the wife of a company's president
    IV.   the brother of a company's president

    A. I and II
    B. II and III
    C. III and IV
    D. I, II, III and IV

6. Which of the following acts requires corporations to issue annual reports?

    A. Securities Act of 1933
    B. Securities Exchange Act of 1934
    C. Trust Indenture Act of 1939
    D. Investment Company Act of 1940

7. Under the Securities Exchange Act of 1934, the SEC

   I.   regulates the securities exchanges
   II.   requires the registration of brokers and dealers
   III.   prohibits inequitable and unfair trade practices
   IV.   regulates the over-the-counter markets

   A.   I and II
   B.   I and IV
   C.   III and IV
   D.   I, II, III and IV

Quick Quiz answers can be found at the end of the Unit.

16. 1. 9 PENNY STOCK COLD-CALLING RULES

The SEC adopted the **penny stock cold-calling rules** to prevent certain abusive sales practices involving high-risk securities sold to unsophisticated investors. These rules involve the solicitation of non-Nasdaq equity securities traded in the OTC market for less than $5 per share. These equity securities are frequently referred to as **penny stocks** and are considered highly speculative.

These rules state that when a broker-dealer's representative contacts a potential customer to purchase penny stocks, the representative must first determine suitability on the basis of information about the buyer's financial situation and objectives. The customer must sign and date this suitability statement before the penny stock trades can be affected. In addition, the broker-dealer must disclose:

- the name of the penny stock;
- the number of shares to be purchased;
- a current quotation; and
- the amount of commission that the firm and the representative received.

Regardless of activity, if the account holds penny stocks, broker-dealers must provide a monthly statement of account to the customer. This must indicate the market value and number of shares for each penny stock held in the account as well as the issuer's name.

16. 1. 9. 1 Established Customers

Established customers are exempt from the suitability statement requirement but not from the disclosure requirements. An **established customer** is someone who:

- has held an account with the broker-dealer for at least one year (and has made a deposit of funds or securities); or
- has made at least three penny stock purchases of different issuers on different days.

TAKE NOTE   The provisions of the penny stock rules apply only to solicited transactions. Transactions not recommended by the broker-dealer are exempt.

16. 1. 10 BANK SECRECY ACT

The Bank Secrecy Act establishes the U.S. Treasury Department as the lead agency for developing regulations in connection with anti-money laundering programs. It also requires broker-dealers to establish internal compliance procedures to detect abuses. Before September 11, 2001, money laundering rules were concerned with the origin of the cash.

Under the act, regulators are more concerned with where the funds are going. The idea is to prevent "clean" money from being used for "dirty" purposes (such as funding terrorist activities).

The three basic stages of money laundering are as follows:

16. 1. 10. 0. 1   Placement

This first stage of laundering is when funds or assets are moved into the laundering system. This stage is recognized as the time when illegal funds are the most susceptible to detection.

16. 1. 10. 0. 2   Layering

The goal of money launderers during this stage is to conceal the source of the funds or assets. This is done through a series of layers of transactions that are generally numerous and can vary in form and complexity.

16. 1. 10. 0. 3   Integration

In the final stage, illegal funds are commingled with legitimate funds in what appear to be viable legitimate business concerns. This can be accomplished using front companies operating on a cash basis, import/export companies, and many other types of businesses.

TEST TOPIC ALERT   Current regulations require that broker-dealers file **suspicious activity reports (SARs)** on "financial behavior which is commercially illogical and serves no apparent purpose."

The threshold that triggers the filing of a suspicious activity report (SAR) is $5,000.

16. 1. 10. 1 Red Flags

There are signs of suspicious activity that suggest the possibility of money laundering. If a red flag is detected, report it to your manager immediately. Examples of red flags include:

- a customer exhibiting a lack of concern regarding risks, commissions, or other transaction costs;
- a customer attempting to make frequent or large deposits of currency or cashier's checks;
- a customer making a large number of wire transfers to unrelated third parties;
- a customer engaging in excessive journal entries between unrelated accounts; and
- a customer who designs currency deposits or withdrawals to fall under the $10,000 cash transaction report (CTR) filing threshold, a practice known as structuring.

EXAMPLE If a customer were to make 12 $1,000 deposits on settlement date for securities purchased, this should be recognized as an attempt to structure payments to fall beneath the $10,000 cash transaction report (CTR) limit. A SAR should be filed.

16. 1. 11 REGULATION NMS (NATIONAL MARKET SYSTEM)

Regulation NMS (National Market System) is a broad sweeping regulation that was enacted to bring trading and reporting uniformity to the various U.S. securities markets. Among the rules mandated by the SEC under Regulation NMS are the following:

- The Order Protection Rule—This rule prohibits a trade-through, which is a trade taking place for a customer order at a price that does not represent the best price available at that time or trading through a customer limit that represents the best price available in order to execute an order in another market.

EXAMPLE If a stock is being offered on the NYSE at 18.20, and a firm buys the stock in the third market for a customer at a price of 18.25, the firm traded through the best price that was available at the time of the transaction and in so doing did not execute at the best price available for their customer.

- Limit Up/Limit Down (LULD) is a rule designed to address sudden and severe price movements. It provides a marketwide limit up and limit down mechanism to prevent trades in NMS stocks from occurring outside of specified price bands. This is coupled with trading pauses in the event of more significant and prolonged price moves. The price bands are expressed as percentages up and down from a mean reference price such as the last sale. These percentages up and down (price bands) are specified depending on factors such as the current price of the stock. To account for increased volatility around market openings and closings, the percentage parameters are doubled during those times. Displays of bids above the upper price band and offers below the lower price band are prohibited.

- Minimum Increments Pricing Rule (sub-penny)—This rule establishes the minimum price increments allowed depending on the price of the security. For stocks priced at $1.00 per share or greater, the minimum increment is $.01. Sub-penny pricing is permitted for stocks under $1.00 per share.

16. 2   STATE SECURITIES REGULATIONS

In addition to federal securities regulations, each state has laws that pertain to the issuance and trading of securities. These state securities laws are known as **blue-sky laws** because of a statement made by a Kansas Supreme Court justice who referred to "speculative schemes that have no more basis than so many feet of blue sky."

16. 2. 1   THE UNIFORM SECURITIES ACT (USA)

The **Uniform Securities Act** provides a legal framework for the state registration of securities. It may be adopted by individual states and adapted to their needs. State registration requirements apply to broker-dealers, investment advisers, investment adviser representatives, and registered representatives. State securities administrators have the power to revoke any of these registrations if a violation of the state's law has occurred.

State laws require that broker-dealers with an office in the state, or those that direct calls into the state or receive calls from the state, be registered in that state. Registered representatives must register in a state if they are residents or if they solicit business in a state. Registrations must be renewed annually.

TAKE NOTE   Isolated unsolicited transactions are exempt from state registration requirements, so these transactions may be accepted by a registered representative not registered in that state.

16. 2. 1. 1   Registering Securities

States have three ways to register (or blue sky) securities: coordination, filing, and qualification.

Coordination. The issuer files with the state at the same time it files with the SEC. Registration is effective at the time the federal filing becomes effective. Coordination can only be used for IPOs (securities that have not been previously registered with the SEC).

Filing (Notification). If an issuer has met various financial criteria and has filed previously in a state, it may notify the state that it is about to sell securities. If the state does not reply, the registration is effective on the fifth business day after the filing.

Qualification. If registration cannot be accomplished by coordination or filing, it must be registered by qualification. In this situation, the issuer must respond to any requirement the state specifies. This type of registration is effective only when so ordered by the state securities administrator. It is the most difficult way of registering securities in a state.

QUICK QUIZ 16.B

Using the content throughout this unit, match the following securities legislation or acts to the appropriate description:

A.   Investment Company Act of 1940

B.   Trust Indenture Act of 1939

C.   Securities Act of 1934

D.   Securities Acts Amendments of 1975

E.   Bank Secrecy Act

F.   Regulation NMS (National Market System)

_____ 1.   Established the MSRB

_____ 2.   Regulates the trading of securities

_____ 3.   Established the U.S. Treasury as the lead agency for the development of regulations regarding anti-money laundering

_____ 4.   Established the order protection rule to prevent a customer order from being executed at a price that does not represent the best available at that time

_____ 5.   Protects bondholders of nonexempt corporate bonds

_____ 6.   Defined and regulates mutual funds

UNIT TEST

1. All of the following refer to blue-sky laws EXCEPT

   A. state laws designed to protect the public against fraud in securities sales within a state
   B. Securities Act of 1933 and Securities and Exchange Act of 1934
   C. forms requiring issuers selling securities in the state to comply with state securities laws
   D. state securities law that grants state securities Administrators the power to deny or revoke a broker-dealer or a registered representative's registration within its state

2. The Trust Indenture Act of 1939 applies to all of the following EXCEPT

   A. nonexempt debt securities
   B. interstate offerings
   C. offerings over $50 million
   D. offerings with maturities of less than 9 months

3. The Securities Exchange Act of 1934 contains sections that deal with

   A. regulation of investment companies
   B. trading activities such as short sales, stabilizing, and registering over-the-counter brokers and dealers
   C. form and content of the prospectus that must be given to all prospective purchasers of a security
   D. registration of persons engaged in the business of advising others about investment company transactions

4. In which of the following situations must a broker-dealer registered with the SEC under the Act of 1934 also be registered as an investment adviser under the Investment Advisers Act of 1940?

   A. Its registered representatives provide investment advice as part of its service.
   B. Its publications make purchase and sale recommendations without charge.
   C. It provides a financial planning service for a separate fee.
   D. No additional registration requirement applies.

5. The determination of a broker-dealer's financial failure is made under the provisions of

   A. the Securities Act of 1933
   B. the 1939 Trust Indenture Act
   C. the Securities Investor Protection Act of 1970
   D. the 1939 Maloney Act

6. Under SEC rules, a penny stock is defined as an unlisted, non-Nasdaq security trading at less than

   A. $1.00 per share only
   B. $2.00 per share only
   C. $2.50 per share only
   D. $5.00 per share only

7. Which of the following legislative acts exclusively regulates debt securities?

   A. Securities Act of 1933
   B. Securities Exchange Act of 1934
   C. Trust Indenture Act of 1939
   D. Investment Advisers Act of 1940

8. The antifraud provisions of the Securities Exchange Act of 1934 apply to all of the following EXCEPT

    A. municipal bonds
    B. National exchange-listed securities
    C. Nasdaq-listed securities
    D. fixed annuities

9. Which of the following customer accounts is(are) NOT SIPC insured?

    I. Customer margin account
    II. JTWROS account with spouse
    III. JTIC commodities account with son
    IV. JTIC account with business partner

    A. I only
    B. II and III
    C. II, III and IV
    D. III only

10. All of the following statements about SIPC are true EXCEPT

    A. it is a nonprofit membership corporation
    B. it is an agency of the U.S. government
    C. it is funded by broker-dealers
    D. coverage is limited to $500,000 per customer

11. Which of the following persons would NOT require state registration?

    A. In-state salesperson
    B. In-state broker-dealer
    C. Out-of-state salesperson doing business in that state
    D. Out-of-state broker-dealer doing no business in that state

12. Which of the following acts requires full disclosure of all material information about securities offered for the first time to the public?

    A. Securities Act of 1933
    B. Securities Exchange Act of 1934
    C. Trust Indenture Act of 1939
    D. Securities Investor Protection Act of 1970

13. The chairman of XYZ Corporation confides to a neighbor that his company will be announcing a major acquisition the following week. As a result of this conversation, the neighbor buys call options on the target company in his personal account. Who violated insider trading rules?

    A. The chairman
    B. The neighbor
    C. Both A and B
    D. Neither A nor B

14. The Securities Investor Protection Corporation will provide protection of up to $500,000 per separate account on customer claims for cash and securities in the event of the liquidation of a SIPC member. However, the amount of this coverage for cash left on deposit with a SIPC member is limited to a maximum of

    A. $250,000 per separate customer
    B. $500,000 per separate customer
    C. $500,000 per account
    D. $250,000 per account

15. Which of the following could be considered a structured transaction?

    A. Two unrelated customers transfer $8,000 and $9,000, respectively, to different accounts in New York and Ireland.
    B. A customer makes four cash deposits of $5,800 each, two on one day and two on the next day, to the same account.
    C. A husband and a wife each transfer $9,500 to the same account four weeks apart.
    D. On the same day, several unrelated customers wire different amounts to their own accounts at the same BD.

ANSWERS AND RATIONALES

1. **B.** Blue-sky laws are state securities laws. The Securities Act of 1933 and the Securities Exchange Act of 1934 are federal securities laws.

2. **D.** The Trust Indenture Act of 1939, as amended by the Jobs Act, applies to nonexempt issues of more than $50 million that are offered interstate within a 12-month period and have maturities of nine months or more.

3. **B.** The Securities Exchange Act of 1934, which has greater breadth than the Securities Act of 1933, addresses the creation of the SEC, the regulation of exchanges, the regulation of credit by the FRB, the registration of broker-dealers, the regulation of insider transactions, short sales and proxies, the regulation of trading activities, the regulation of client accounts, the customer protection rule, the regulation of the OTC market, and the net capital rule. The Investment Company Act of 1940 defines and regulates investment companies. The Securities Act of 1933 addresses registration and prospectus requirements. Persons who provide investment advice to others for a fee are subject to the Investment Advisers Act of 1940.

4. **C.** A broker-dealer who receives special compensation for providing investment advice (separate from any commissions, markups, or markdowns) must register as an investment adviser.

5. **C.** Determination of financial failure is made under the Securities Investor Protection Act of 1970.

6. **D.** SEC rules define penny stock as non-Nasdaq stock of less than $5 per share.

7. **C.** The Trust Indenture Act of 1939 protects investors in corporate bonds in the case of the default of the issuing company. Although the Acts of 1933 and 1934 both affect debt securities, the Trust Indenture Act of 1939 is the only act that regulates them exclusively.

8. **D.** All securities are subject to the antifraud provisions of federal securities law. However, fixed annuities are not securities.

9. **D.** SIPC coverage applies only to accounts holding securities; therefore, commodities accounts are not covered.

10. **B.** SIPC is a membership corporation formed to protect investors as of the Securities Investor Protection Act (SIPA) of 1970. It is not an agency of the U.S. government. Broker-dealers, other than mutual fund and variable annuity dealers, are required to pay membership assessments, which provide coverage of up to $500,000 per customer upon broker-dealer default.

11. **D.** Any broker-dealer or salesperson doing business in the state must be registered in that state. If a BD or salesperson is doing no business in a state, state registration in that state is not required.

12. **A.** The Securities Act of 1933 regulates new issues of corporate securities sold to the public.

13. **C.** Once inside information is used to trade for profit or to avoid a loss, both the tipper (the chairman) and the tippee (the neighbor) have violated insider trading rules.

14. **A.** There are two things to remember with this question. SIPC pays coverage only for each separate customer. That means that a client with a cash account, a margin account, and an options account with the firm would only be considered as one separate customer. In addition, only $250,000 of the $500,000 coverage is payable for losses of cash.

15. **B.** A structured transaction is one in which the parties involved engage in a series of currency deposits or withdrawals (transactions) that are an attempt to circumvent the $10,000 currency transaction reporting (CTR) requirement under the Bank Secrecy Act. Identifying attempts to avoid such reporting generally requires that a pattern of transactions is detected.

QUICK QUIZ ANSWERS

Quick Quiz 16.A

1. **B.** Any customer claims that SIPC does not cover result in the customer becoming a general (unsecured) creditor of the company.

2. **B.** SIPC coverage is $500,000 per separate customer account, with cash not to exceed $250,000. Thus, in the single-name account, SIPC provides full coverage, whereas in the joint account, SIPC covers the full $100,000 value of the securities but only $250,000 of the $300,000 in cash for total coverage of $350,000. The remaining $50,000 in uncovered cash becomes a general debt of the bankrupt broker-dealer.

3. **B.** Under SIPC rules, customer claims are valued on the day customer protection proceedings commence; this is the day a federal court is petitioned to appoint a trustee.

4. **A.** The penalty may be imposed on anyone who trades on inside information and not just persons registered under the act. Choice B defines insider trading; the penalty is up to 3 times profit gained or loss avoided; and an advisory firm may face a penalty for the actions of its representatives.

5. **D.** Although the Act of 1934 defines an insider as an officer, a director, or a 10% stockholder of a company, the courts have broadened the definition to include anyone who has inside information.

6. **B.** The Securities Exchange Act of 1934 mandates that companies file annual reports with the SEC.

7. **D.** The Securities Exchange Act of 1934, which has greater breadth than the Act of 1933, addresses the following: creation of the SEC, regulation of exchanges; regulation of credit by the FRB, registration of broker-dealers, regulation of insider transactions, short sales and proxies, regulation of trading activities, regulation of client accounts; the customer protection rule, regulation of the OTC market, and the net capital rule.

Quick Quiz 16.B

1. **D.**

2. **C.**

3. **E.**

4. **F.**

5. **B.**

6. **A.**

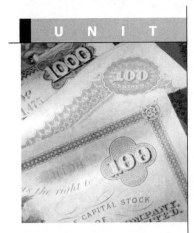

U N I T

17

Other SEC and SRO Rules and Regulations

The securities industry in the United States is among the most heavily regulated in the world. Firms and representatives must comply with SEC rules, the rules of the SROs, and house rules developed by the firm internally. The intent of these rules is to protect the public, and your career depends on your ability to follow the rules and regulations of the industry.

The SEC was created by the Securities Exchange Act of 1934 and is the primary regulatory body over the securities industry. SROs, acting under authority approved by the SEC, regulate the conduct of business. These include FINRA, MSRB, CBOE, and other U.S. exchanges. The type and location of a security transaction determines which SRO has jurisdiction. A substantial portion of the exam will be devoted to these and other industry rules.

The SEC and SRO rules presented in this Unit will account for approximately 15–20 questions on the Series 7 examination. ∎

When you have completed this Unit, you should be able to:

- **define** the role of the SEC in the securities industry;

- **explain** the relationship between the SEC and SROs;

- **describe** the function of the four largest SROs;

- **identify** the registration requirements for broker-dealers and associated persons;

- **identify** the rules and codes of FINRA;

- **compare** the Code of Procedure with the Code of Arbitration;

- **identify** unique rules of the NYSE Euronext trading floor;

- **describe** advertising and sales literature and applicable disclosure and filing rules; and

- **outline** compliance requirements of the Telephone Consumer Protection Act of 1991.

17. 1   REGISTRATION AND REGULATION OF BROKER-DEALERS

The securities industry is regulated. Registration is required, and members must abide by all industry rules and regulations.

17. 1. 1   THE SECURITIES AND EXCHANGE COMMISSION (SEC)

The **SEC** is the securities industry's primary regulatory body. Broker-dealers that transact securities business with customers or with other broker-dealers must apply and be approved for registration with the SEC.

Although a broker-dealer must register with the SEC, the broker-dealer may not claim that this registration in any way implies that the SEC has passed upon or approved the broker-dealer's financial standing, business, or conduct. Any such claim or statement is misrepresentation.

17. 1. 1. 1   Broker-Dealer Registration and Compliance

Broker-dealers must comply with SEC rules and regulations when conducting business. A broker-dealer that does not comply is subject to:

- censure;
- limits on activities, functions, or operations;
- suspension of its registration (or one of its associated person's license to do business);
- revocation of registration; or
- fine.

17. 1. 1. 1. 1 Associated Persons

An associated person may also be disciplined for violating SEC rules and regulations. If the SEC bars an associated person, no broker-dealer may allow that person to associate with it without the Commission's express permission. If a member firm suspends an associated person, the firm must report the suspension to the exchanges where the firm is a member.

17. 1. 1. 1. 2 Fingerprinting

Registered broker-dealers must have fingerprint records made for most of their employees, and all directors, officers, and partners must submit those fingerprint cards to the U.S. attorney general for identification and processing.

Exemptions. Certain broker-dealer employees (typically clerical) are exempt from the fingerprinting requirement if they:

- are not involved in securities sales;
- do not handle or have access to cash or securities or to the books and records of original entry relating to money and securities; and
- do not supervise other employees engaged in these activities.

TEST TOPIC ALERT

Just as the SEC does not approve the release of new issues of securities, it does not approve the way a firm or representative transacts business.

The SEC was created under the Securities Exchange Act of 1934, requires registration of all broker-dealers, and regulates all exchanges and trading markets.

Persons who must be fingerprinted are those involved in sales and those who handle cash or customer securities. Clerical persons (sometimes called ministerial persons) need not be fingerprinted.

17. 1. 2 SELF-REGULATORY ORGANIZATIONS (SROs)

SROs function under the SEC's oversight. Each SRO is accountable to the Commission for enforcing federal securities laws, as well as supervising securities practices within an assigned jurisdiction. The largest of these SROs and their jurisdictions follow.

17. 1. 2. 1 Financial Industry Regulatory Authority (FINRA)

Since the regulatory merger of NASD and NYSE Regulation, FINRA regulates all matters related to investment banking (securities underwriting), trading in the OTC market, trading in NYSE-listed securities, and the conduct of FINRA member firms and associated persons. FINRA also regulates investment companies and limited partnership transactions.

17. 1. 2. 2 Municipal Securities Rulemaking Board (MSRB)

The **MSRB** regulates all matters related to the underwriting and trading of state and municipal securities. The MSRB regulates but does not have enforcement powers—it depends on other SROs for the enforcement of its rules.

17. 1. 2. 3 Chicago Board Options Exchange (CBOE)

The **CBOE** regulates all matters related to trading standardized options and related contracts listed on that exchange.

17. 2 THE FINANCIAL INDUSTRY REGULATORY AUTHORITY (FINRA)

FINRA's purpose and objectives are to:

- promote the investment banking and securities business, standardize principles and practices, promote high standards of commercial honor, and encourage the observance of federal and state securities laws;

- provide a medium for communication among its members and between its members, the government, and other agencies;

- adopt, administer, and enforce rules designed to prevent fraudulent and manipulative practices as well as to promote just and equitable principles of trade; and

- promote self-discipline among members and investigate and resolve grievances between the public and members and between members.

17. 2. 1 CHARACTERISTICS OF FINRA

Like most membership organizations, FINRA member firms will pay dues to FINRA and be responsible for other assessments and charges.

17. 2. 1. 1 Dues, Assessments, and Other Charges

17. 2. 1. 1. 1 Assessments

FINRA is funded by assessments of member firms' registered representatives and applicants and by annual fees. The annual fee each member pays includes a(n):

- basic membership fee;
- assessment based on gross income;
- fee for each principal and registered representative; and
- charge for each branch office.

Failure to pay dues may result in suspension or revocation of membership.

17. 2. 1. 2 Use of the FINRA Corporate Name

Members may not use the FINRA name in a manner that would suggest that FINRA has endorsed a member firm. Members may use the phrase *Member of FINRA*, provided the firm places no undue emphasis on it.

17. 2. 2 THE FINRA MANUAL

FINRA describes four sets of rules and codes in their manual.

17. 2. 2. 1 Conduct Rules

The **Conduct Rules** set out fair and ethical trade practices that member firms and their representatives must follow when dealing with the public.

17. 2. 2. 2 Uniform Practice Code (UPC)

The **UPC** established the uniform trade practices, including settlement, good delivery, ex-dates, confirmations, don't know (DK) procedures, and other guidelines for broker-dealers to follow when they do business with other member firms.

17. 2. 2. 3 Code of Procedure

The **Code of Procedure** describes how member violations of the Conduct Rules will be heard and handled.

17. 2. 2. 4 Code of Arbitration Procedure

The **Code of Arbitration Procedure** governs the resolution of disagreements and claims between members, registered representatives, and the public; it addresses monetary claims.

17. 2. 3 FINRA MEMBERSHIP AND REGISTRATION

The **National Adjudicatory Council (NAC)** establishes rules, regulations, and membership eligibility standards. At present, the following membership standards and registration requirements are in place.

17. 2. 3. 1 Broker-Dealer Registration

Any broker-dealer registered with the SEC is eligible and may apply for membership to FINRA. Any person who affects transactions in securities as a broker, a dealer, or an investment banker also may register with FINRA, as may municipal bond firms. Application for FINRA membership carries the applying firm's specific agreement to:

- comply with the association's rules and regulations;
- comply with federal securities laws; and
- pay dues, assessments, and other charges in the manner and amounts fixed by the association.

A membership application is made to the FINRA district office in the district in which the applying firm has its home office. If a district committee passes on the firm's qualifications, the firm can be accepted into membership.

17. 2. 3. 1. 1 Home Offices

It is not unusual for a broker-dealer to allow registered representatives to operate out of their home residences, commonly referred to as working from a home office. In these instances, approval of the member firms self regulatory organization (SRO) is required as it would be for any office associated with the broker-dealer. All normal business activities including taking customer orders for the purchase and sale of securities would be permitted. Additionally, the home office address and telephone number may be advertised in any normal manner such as on business cards or through various media venues like newspapers and websites.

17. 2. 3. 2 Associated Person Registration

Any person associated with a member firm who intends to engage in the investment banking or securities business must be registered with FINRA as an associated person. Anyone applying for registration with FINRA as an associated person must be sponsored by a member firm.

17. 2. 3. 2. 1 Qualifications Investigated

Before submitting an application to enroll any person with FINRA as a registered representative, a member firm must ascertain the person's business reputation, character, education, qualifications, and experience. As part of the application process, the member firm must certify that it has made an investigation and that the candidate's credentials are in order.

17. 2. 3. 2. 2 Failure to Register Personnel

A member firm's failure to register an employee who performs any of the functions of a registered representative may lead to disciplinary action by FINRA.

17. 2. 4   POSTREGISTRATION RULES AND REGULATIONS

Beyond initial registration, firms and registered individuals are required to abide by rules and regulations on an ongoing basis.

17. 2. 4. 1   Continuing Education

Registered persons are required to participate in continuing education programs. The CE requirement has two components: a regulatory element and a firm element.

17. 2. 4. 1. 1 Regulatory Element

The **regulatory element** requires that all registered persons complete a computer-based training session within 120 days of the person's second registration anniversary and every three years thereafter (i.e., within 120 days of the person's 5th, 8th, 11th registration anniversary, and so on). The content of the regulatory element is determined by FINRA and is appropriate to either the registered representative or principal status of the person.

If a person fails to complete the regulatory element within the prescribed period, FINRA will inactivate that person's registration until the requirements of the program are met.

17. 2. 4. 1. 2 Firm Element

The **firm element** requires member firms to prepare an annual training plan taking into account such factors as recent regulatory developments, the scope of the member's business activities, the performance of its personnel in the regulatory element, and its supervisory needs. This annual in-house training must be given to all registered persons who have direct contact with the public.

17. 2. 4. 2   Annual Compliance Review

FINRA requires that each registered representative and principal receive compliance training on an annual basis. The purpose of the meeting is to discuss compliance matters relevant to the activities of the registered person. The meeting delivery method can be individually or in groups, regionally or at a central location, in person or by webcast, which can be either live or on-demand (recorded). FINRA requires certain safeguards to be in place. For instance, firms must be able to ensure that registered personnel attend the entire meeting and have an opportunity to ask questions or engage in dialogue with presenters either live or electronically.

17. 2. 4. 3   Registered Persons Changing Firms

FINRA registration is **nontransferable**. A registered person who leaves one member firm to join another firm must terminate registration at the first firm on a **U-5 form** and reapply for registration with the new employing member firm on a **U-4 form**. If a person terminates his registration with one firm, he must register with another firm within two years, or he will be required to requalify for his license.

17. 2. 4. 4 Continuing Commissions

A registered representative who leaves a member firm—upon retirement, for instance—may continue to receive commissions on business placed while employed. However, the representative must have a contract to this effect before leaving the firm. A deceased representative's heirs also may receive continuing commissions on business the representative placed if a contract exists.

17. 2. 4. 5 Notification of Disciplinary Action

A member firm must notify FINRA if any associated person in the firm's employment is subjected to disciplinary action by one of the following:

- National securities exchange or association
- Clearing corporation
- Commodity futures market regulatory agency
- Federal or state regulatory commission

The notification must include the individual's name and the nature of the action. A member firm must notify FINRA of disciplinary action the firm has taken against an associated person and the nature of the action.

17. 2. 4. 6 Terminations

Whenever any registered person's employment is terminated, the member firm must notify FINRA in writing within 30 calendar days.

17. 2. 4. 6. 1 Terminating Representatives Under Investigation

If a registered representative or another associated person is under investigation for federal securities law violations or has disciplinary action pending against him from FINRA or any other SRO, a member firm may not terminate its business relationship with the person until the investigation or disciplinary action has been resolved.

17. 2. 5 QUALIFICATIONS EXAMINATIONS

To become a registered representative or principal, an individual must pass the appropriate licensing examination(s).

17. 2. 5. 1 Registered Representatives

All associated persons engaged in the investment banking and securities business are considered **registered representatives**, including any:

- assistant officer who does not function as a principal;
- individual who supervises, solicits, or conducts business in securities; and
- individual who trains people to supervise, solicit, or conduct business in securities.

17. 2. 5. 1. 1 General Securities Representative License (Series 7)

After passing the Series 7 licensing exam and registration with FINRA has been completed, a registered representative qualifies as being able to solicit, purchase, and/or sell almost all securities products, including corporate securities, municipal securities, municipal fund securities, options, direct participation programs, investment company products, and variable contracts.

17. 2. 5. 2 Registered Principals

Anyone who manages or supervises any part of a member's investment banking or securities business must be registered as a **principal** with FINRA (including people involved solely in training associated persons). Unless the member firm is a sole proprietorship, it must employ at least two registered principals.

17. 2. 5. 2. 1 General Securities Principal License (Series 24)

Any person actively engaged in managing a member's securities or investment banking business, including supervising, soliciting, and conducting business, or in training persons associated with the member, must qualify by examination and register with FINRA as a general securities principal.

17. 2. 6 INELIGIBILITY AND DISQUALIFICATIONS

A person may not act as a registered representative or principal unless FINRA's eligibility standards regarding training, experience, and competence are met.

17. 2. 6. 1 Statutory Disqualification

Disciplinary sanctions by the SEC, another SRO, a foreign financial regulator, or a foreign equivalent of an SRO may be cause for statutory disqualification of FINRA membership.

An individual applying for registration as an associated person will be rejected if he:

- has been or is expelled or suspended from membership or participation in any other SRO or from the foreign equivalent of an SRO;
- is under an SEC order or an order of a foreign financial regulator denying, suspending, or revoking his registration or barring him from association with a broker-dealer; or
- has been found to be the cause of another broker-dealer or associated person being expelled or suspended by another SRO, the SEC, or a foreign equivalent of an SRO.

The following also can automatically disqualify an applicant for registration:

■ Misstatements willfully made in an application for membership or registration as an associated person

■ A felony conviction, either domestic or foreign, or a misdemeanor conviction involving securities or money within the past 10 years

■ Court injunctions prohibiting the individual from acting as an investment adviser, an underwriter, or a broker-dealer or in other capacities aligned with the securities and financial services industry

---

TAKE NOTE

The Central Registration Depository (CRD) maintains information on the disciplinary history of all persons currently registered. A customer can access this information toll free through the CRDs Broker Check. BrokerCheck is a public site maintained by FINRA containing basic information on currently registered representatives and those that have been registered within the past 10 years. Anyone can use BrokerCheck, found on FINRA's website, to research a registered representative's background and disciplinary history. Additionally, a hyperlink to BrokerCheck is required on all FINRA member firm's websites. The hyperlink needs to appear on:

■ the initial web page that the firm intends to be viewed by retail investors, and

■ any other web page that includes a professional profile of one or more registered persons who conduct business with retail investors.

---

17. 3 INVESTIGATION: CODE OF PROCEDURE AND CODE OF ARBITRATION PROCEDURE

In connection with any investigation, complaint, or examination by FINRA, the association may require a member firm or any person associated with a member to:

■ provide information orally, in writing, or electronically;
■ give testimony under oath; and
■ provide access to or copies of any books, records, or accounts.

If a member or associated person fails to comply, the National Adjudicatory Council (NAC), after providing 20 days' written notice, has the right to suspend the member and revoke the registration of any associated person.

The NAC is responsible for the development of regulatory and enforcement policy and rule changes relating to the business and sales practices of member firms. It is also responsible for the oversight of the Department of Enforcement, which has the authority to file complaints against member firms and their associated persons.

17. 3. 1 CODE OF PROCEDURE

The **Code of Procedure** deals with alleged violations of FINRA rules, MSRB rules, and federal securities laws. If, after an investigation or audit, FINRA believes a member and/or its associated persons has violated one or more rules or laws, the Department of Enforcement will issue a formal complaint. With the filing of a complaint, the department will name a hearing officer to preside over the disciplinary proceeding (hearing) and will appoint panelists to serve as a jury. All panelists in Code of Procedure hearings are from the industry.

The respondent has 25 days after receiving the complaint to file an answer with the hearing officer. Answers must specifically admit, deny, or state that the respondent does not have sufficient information to admit or deny.

FINRA requires that records of customer complaints be kept on file by a broker-dealer for four years.

TAKE NOTE   If a complaint is filed against a registered representative, it is not all that unusual for that person's designated supervisor (e.g., branch manager) to be charged as well for failure to supervise.

17. 3. 1. 1 Offer of Settlement

A respondent has the option of proposing a settlement. An **offer to settle** must be in writing and must:

■ describe the specific rule or law that the member or associated person is alleged to have violated;

■ describe the acts or practices that the member or associated person is alleged to have engaged in or omitted;

■ include a statement consenting to findings of fact and violations contained in the complaint; and

■ propose sanctions consistent with the association's sanction guidelines.

17. 3. 1. 1. 1 Uncontested Offer

By submitting an offer of settlement, the respondent waives the right to a hearing and the right to appeal. If the offer is accepted by the Department of Enforcement, it is then sent to the NAC for review. If uncontested by the NAC, the offer is accepted and final—case closed.

17. 3. 1. 1. 2 Contested Offer

If the Department of Enforcement opposes the offer, the offer is contested. At this point, the offer and the department's written opposition are submitted to the hearing officer. The hearing officer may order a settlement conference between the parties in an attempt to work out a compromise or may forward the offer and the department's opposition to the NAC. If the NAC rejects the offer (or compromise offer), the hearings begin. If accepted by the NAC, the offer (or compromise offer) is final. The good news is that if an offer of settlement is ultimately rejected, it may not be introduced as evidence at the hearing.

17. 3. 1. 1. 3 Acceptance, Waiver, and Consent (AWC)

If the respondent does not dispute the allegations, the Department of Enforcement may prepare and request that the respondent sign a letter accepting a finding of violation, consenting to the imposition of sanctions and waiving the right to a hearing and the right to appeal. If agreed to by the respondent, the letter is then sent to the NAC and becomes final if approved. If opposed by the NAC, the next stop is formal hearings. However, it is most likely that if the Department of Enforcement felt there was a chance of opposition from the NAC, it would not have offered AWC in the first place.

17. 3. 1. 1. 4 Minor Rule Violation (MRV)

If the complaint involves a minor violation and the respondent does not dispute the allegation, the Department of Enforcement may prepare and request that the respondent sign an **MRV letter**, accepting a finding of violation. **Minor rule violations** are failure to:

- have advertising or sales literature approved by a principal before use;
- maintain a file for advertising and sales literature;
- file advertising and sales literature with FINRA within the required time frame;
- file timely reports on short positions;
- file accurate counts for options position and exercise limits with OCC;
- keep books and records in accordance with SEC rules; or
- submit trading data if requested by FINRA.

Once the respondent signs an MRV letter, the settlement is final. The NAC, as a sanction, may impose a fine not to exceed $2,500.

17. 3. 1. 2 Hearing

At the **hearing**, which resembles a courtroom proceeding, the prosecution (Department of Enforcement) proceeds first. Cross-examination of witnesses is permitted. At the conclusion, panelists convene and, within 60 days, render a written decision reflecting the majority view.

17. 3. 1. 3 Sanctions

Sanctions against a member or associated person, if found guilty, are included with the written decision. Under Code of Procedure, sanctions could include:

- censure;
- fine;
- suspension of the membership of a member or suspension of the registration of an associated person for a definite period;
- expulsion of the member, canceling the membership of the member;
- barring an associated person from association with all members; and
- imposition of any other fitting sanction.

17. 3. 1. 3. 1 Suspension

If an associated person is **suspended**, that person may not remain associated with the member in any capacity, including a clerical or administrative capacity (during the suspension period, that person may not remain on the member's premises). Also, the member is prohibited from paying a salary, commission, or remuneration that the person might have earned during the suspension period.

TAKE NOTE   The suspended person could be paid monies earned before the suspension period.

17. 3. 1. 3. 2 Effective Date of Sanctions

Other than a bar or an expulsion, effective as of the decision date, sanctions imposed are effective on a date specified by the hearing officer, but no earlier than 30 days after the written decision is handed down.

17. 3. 1. 4 Appeals

If either side is displeased with the decision, an appeal may be made to the NAC. Any appeal must be made within 25 days of decision date; otherwise, the decision is final. If no satisfaction is received from the NAC, the appealing party may take the case to the SEC. Again, if turned down, the appealing party has the right to continue the appeal process by taking its case to the federal court system. Appealing a decision stays the effective date of any sanctions other than a bar or expulsion.

17. 3. 2 CODE OF ARBITRATION

The **Code of Arbitration** was originally established to mediate unresolved industry disputes. It was mandatory in controversies involving:

- a member against another member or registered clearing agency;
- a member against an associated person; and
- an associated person against another associated person.

Over time, customer complaints became subject to mandatory arbitration resulting in two codes: the "Customer Code" and the "Industry Code."

TAKE NOTE   In the absence of a signed arbitration agreement, a customer can still force a member to arbitration, but a member cannot force a customer to arbitration.

Today, virtually all new account forms contain a predispute arbitration clause that must be signed by customers before account opening. Thus, assuming the customer has signed the arbitration agreement or the new account form containing the predispute arbitration agreement, unresolved customer complaints must be mediated under the Code of Arbitration.

Class action claims are not subject to arbitration. In addition, claims alleging employment discrimination brought against a member firm by its own employees, including sexual harassment claims, are not required to be arbitrated unless the parties agree.

The advantages of arbitration over suits in state or federal courts are savings of time, money, and the fact that all decisions are final and binding; no appeals are allowed. One party may not like the result, but the dispute is settled.

If a customer requests to see the predispute arbitration agreement they have signed, a member firm must supply them with a copy within 10 business days of the request.

17. 3. 2. 1 Initiation of Proceedings

Any party to an unresolved dispute may initiate proceedings by filing a claim with the director of arbitration of FINRA. The **statement of claim** must describe in detail the controversy in dispute, include documentation in support of the claim, and state the remedy being sought (dollar amount). The claimant must also include a check for the required claim filing fee. The director will then send a copy of the claim to the other party (respondent).

The respondent then has 45 calendar days to respond to both the director and the claimant. The answer must specify all available defenses and any related counterclaim the respondent may have against the claimant. A respondent who fails to answer within 45 days may, at the sole discretion of the director, be barred from presenting any matter, arguments, or defenses at the hearing.

If the dispute involves irreparable injury to one of the parties, that party may seek an interim injunction or a permanent injunction. The party seeking relief must make a clear showing that its case is likely to succeed on its merits and that it will suffer permanent harm unless immediate relief is granted.

17. 3. 2. 2 Mediation

If both parties agree, before the opening of hearings, a meeting may be held in an attempt to work out a settlement. A mediator is selected to preside over the discussions and to assist the parties in reaching their own solution. If mediation is unsuccessful, then the problem goes on to the hearing.

A mediator is prohibited from serving on an arbitration panel regarding any matter in which that person served as mediator.

17. 3. 2. 3 Selection of Arbitrators

FINRA maintains a list of arbitrators divided into two categories: nonpublic and public. **Nonpublic arbitrators** are as follows:

■ Any persons who worked in the financial industry for any duration during their careers including persons associated with a mutual fund or a hedge fund, and persons associated with an investment adviser, will always be classified as nonpublic arbitrators.

■ Any financial industry professional who regularly represents or provides services to investor parties in disputes concerning investment accounts or transactions including attorneys, accountants, or other professionals whose firms earned significant revenue from representing individual and/or institutional investors relating to securities matters are classified as nonpublic arbitrators. However, for these individuals, waiting five years (cooling-off period) after ending the affiliation based on their own activities, or two years after ending an affiliation based on someone else's activities reclassifies and allows them to serve as public arbitrators.

TAKE NOTE There is no cooling-off period for anyone who has worked in the financial industry.

Public arbitrators are as follows:

■ Any persons who do not meet the definition of nonpublic arbitrator may serve as a public arbitrator.

17. 3. 2. 4 Arbitration Thresholds and Simplified Arbitration

For both the customer and the industry codes, the following threshold rules apply:

■ $50,000 or less—one arbitrator
■ Greater than $50,000 and up to and including $100,000—one arbitrator unless both parties agree to three
■ Greater than $100,000—three arbitrators unless both parties agree to one

Any dispute involving a dollar amount of $50,000 or less is eligible for simplified arbitration. In this instance, a single arbitrator reviews all of the evidence and renders a binding decision within 30 business days.

TAKE NOTE For arbitration disputes involving a customer in amounts greater than $100,000, the customer can request that all three arbitrators selected be from the public sector.

17. 3. 2. 5 Awards

All monetary awards must be paid within 30 days of the decision date. Any award not paid within this time will begin to accrue interest as of the decision date. In addition, all awards and details on the underlying arbitration claim are made publicly available by FINRA.

17. 3. 2. 6 Statute of Limitations

No claim is eligible for submission to arbitration if six years or more have elapsed from the time of the event giving rise to the claim.

QUICK QUIZ 17.A   True or False?

_____ 1. In the absence of a signed arbitration agreement, customers can still force member firms to arbitration, but member firms cannot force customers to arbitration.

_____ 2. In simplified arbitration, a panel of 3 arbitrators reviews all the evidence and renders a binding decision no matter what dollar amount the claim is for.

_____ 3. The statute of limitations for submission of a claim to arbitration is 6 years.

_____ 4. Monetary awards, if not paid immediately, begin accruing interest as of the decision date.

_____ 5. Under the Code of Arbitration, a respondent to a statement of claim must respond to the director of arbitration of FINRA and the claimant within 45 days.

Quick Quiz answers can be found at the end of the Unit.

17. 4   SROs: THE NYSE CONSTITUTION AND RULES

The NYSE is a corporation operated by a board of directors consisting of 10 Exchange members, 10 public representatives, and a chairperson. The board is responsible for setting policy, supervising Exchange and member activities, listing securities, overseeing the transfer of members' seats on the Exchange, and judging whether an applicant is qualified to be a specialist (Designated Market Maker).

17. 4. 1 NYSE MEMBERSHIP

The number of memberships (seats) on the NYSE is fixed. To become a member, one must buy a seat from the exchange or a member. A seat's price is negotiated between the buyer and seller. Membership can be transferred from one person to another only with the board of directors' approval.

Only individuals may own seats on the Exchange. Many seat ownerships, however, are sponsored and funded by firms, which is where the term *member firm* originates.

17. 4. 1. 1 Allied Members

Allied members are executive officers, directors, or holders of more than 5% of a member firm's voting stock. Though allied members are responsible for supervising their organizations, they are not allowed to trade on the Exchange floor. The number of allied memberships is unlimited, and they are not transferable.

17. 4. 2 REGISTRATION OF EMPLOYEES

Salespersons of NYSE member firms must be registered with FINRA through their firms. Registration may be denied to unacceptable applicants. Registered representatives must agree to abide by the rules and regulations.

17. 4. 2. 1 Training Program

The NYSE no longer imposes a formalized training period. However, once a broker-dealer receives an enrollment notification for an employee, the sponsored person has 120 days to successfully complete (pass) the Series 7 licensing exam. This is known as the testing window. Extensions to the 120 period are not granted easily. It is important to note that without registration, employees may not be paid commissions or any compensation that is trade based. Salary and bonuses are allowed.

17. 4. 2. 2 Compensation

A representative may receive compensation for securities transactions only from his employer. The registered representative may be paid a salary, commissions, or both.

17. 5   COMMUNICATIONS WITH THE PUBLIC

In accordance with FINRA, there are three categories of communications:

- Retail communications
- Correspondence
- Institutional communications

17. 5. 1   RETAIL, CORRESPONDENCE, AND INSTITUTIONAL COMMUNICATIONS

"Retail communication" means any written (including electronic) communication that is distributed or made available to more than 25 retail investors within any 30 calendar-day period. A retail investor is any person other than an institutional investor, regardless of whether the person has an account with the member.

"Correspondence" means any written (including electronic) communication that is distributed or made available to 25 or fewer retail investors within any 30 calendar-day period.

"Institutional communication" means any written (including electronic) communication that is distributed or made available only to institutional investors, but does not include a member's internal communications (e.g., internal memos). Examples of institutional investors are:

- another member firm or registered representative;
- bank;
- savings and loan (S&L);
- insurance company;
- registered investment company (mutual fund);
- employee benefit plan;
- governmental entity or subdivision;
- person acting solely on behalf of an institutional investor; and
- any entity with $50 million or more of total assets.

FINRA mandates that no member may treat a communication as having been distributed to an institutional investor if the member firm has reason to believe that the communication or any part of it will be forwarded or made available to any retail investor.

TAKE NOTE   If an entity does not fall under any of the designated categories for institutional investor then they must be considered and treated as a retail customer.

17. 5. 1. 1 Public Appearances

Public appearances include participation in a seminar, forum (including an interactive electronic forum such as a webcast), radio or TV interview, or other public appearance or public speaking activity. Since it is considered a form of communication with the public, principal supervision or approval of any materials or script used may be required.

17. 5. 2 APPROVAL AND FILING REQUIREMENTS

Retail communications must be approved by a registered principal of the member firm before first use or filing with FINRA's Advertising Regulation Department, whichever is earlier. Pre-approval would not be needed if:

- another member firm has filed it with FINRA and has received a letter stating that it is consistent with all applicable communications standards;

- the member is using it in reliance upon a FINRA letter already received and has not materially altered the communication and will not use it in a manner that is inconsistent with the conditions of FINRA's letter;

- the communication is posted on an online interactive electronic forum; or

- the communication does not make any financial or investment recommendations or promote a product or service.

Filing with FINRAs Advertising Regulation Department must take place 10 days prior to first use for any retail communications during a BD's first year of existence.

For certain products and under certain circumstances a BD must still observe the 10-day pre-filing rule for retail communications beyond the first year if the communication includes a performance ranking that is not one of the regularly published ones (i.e., Morningstar or Lipper) or it is one that an investment company has created itself. Those products are:

- investment companies (open or closed-end);

- variable products (annuities);

- exchange-traded funds (ETFs);

- unit investment trusts (UITs); or

- securities futures.

Finally, filing retail communications within 10 business days of first use or publication (not pre-filing) would apply to retail communications concerning:

- registered investment companies (including mutual funds, exchange-traded funds, variable insurance products, closed-end funds, and unit investment trusts);

- direct participation programs (DPPs);
- collateralized mortgage obligations (CMOs); and
- securities registered under the Securities Act and that are derived from or based on a single security, a basket of securities, an index, a commodity, a debt issuance, or a foreign currency.

Correspondence must be supervised and is subject to review requirements. This means that each member must establish written procedures that are appropriate to its business, size, structure, and customers for the review of incoming and outgoing correspondence with the public. This includes procedures to review incoming correspondence directed to registered representatives in order to properly identify and handle customer complaints and to ensure that customer funds and securities are handled in accordance with the member firm's procedures.

Review by a principal can take place before or after use in accordance with the firm's written procedures. However, if pre-use review is not required by the firm, the firm must have provisions for the education and training of associated persons regarding the firm's procedures. Evidence that these supervisory procedures have been implemented and carried out must be maintained and made available to FINRA upon request.

Filing correspondence with FINRA is not required.

Institutional communications, like correspondence, must be supervised and are subject to review.

Filing institutional communications with FINRA is not required.

17. 5. 2. 1   Investment Companies and DPPs

Filing requirements for Investment Company (open and closed end) retail communications are as follows:

- 10-day pre-filing for retail communications if the communication includes a performance ranking that is not one of the regularly published ones (e.g., Morningstar or Lipper) or it is one that the investment company has created itself
- Within 10 business days of first use or publication if the communication does not include a performance ranking as noted above

When the investment company retail communication is generic in nature and does not discuss the benefits of a specific fund or fund family, filing with FINRA is not required. An example of such communications may be those that simply describe different mutual fund types (e.g., balanced fund, growth and income fund) or the different share classes available.

FINRA reasons that this type of material is typically intended to educate the public about investment companies in general or the types of products that a firm offers. Therefore, this information does not present the same risks of including potentially misleading information as communications about specific funds or fund families and their benefits.

Filing requirements for Direct Participation Program retail communications are as follows:

- Within 10 business days of first use or publication

17. 5. 2. 2   Options

Ten-day prefiling is required for retail communications having to do with options.

17. 5. 2. 3 Spot Checks

Each member's written and electronic communications may be subject to a spot-check procedure. Upon written request from FINRA, each member must submit the material requested within the time frame specified by FINRA.

17. 5. 2. 4 Exceptions to Filing Requirements

As noted earlier, correspondence and institutional communications are exempt from filing with FINRA. Some specific types of retail communications are excluded entirely from filing with FINRA as well. Examples include:

- retail communications previously filed with FINRA that are to be used without material change;
- retail communications that do not make any financial or investment recommendation or otherwise promote a product or service of the member;
- communications that refer to types of investments solely as part of a listing of products or services offered by the member;
- retail communications that are posted on an online interactive electronic forum;
- prospectuses, preliminary prospectuses, fund profiles, offering circulars, and similar documents that have been filed with the SEC or any state; and
- press releases that are made available only to members of the media.

17. 5. 3 RULES CONCERNING PUBLIC COMMUNICATIONS

FINRA holds broker-dealers to certain general standards regarding all member firm communications. All member communications must be based on principles of fair dealing and good faith. Statements must be clear and not misleading within the context that they are made and must be fair and balanced regarding potential risks and benefits. Omission of material facts is not permitted, nor is making false, exaggerated, or misleading statements or claims. No communication should ever imply that past performance will be repeated. Finally, FINRA mandates that members must consider the nature of the audience to which the communication will be directed and should provide details and explanations appropriate to the audience.

17. 5. 3. 1 Identification of Source and Recordkeeping

All retail communications and correspondence must prominently disclose the name of the member and should disclose the name of the person or firm (if prepared by another member or firm outside the BD). To comply with all recordkeeping requirements, communications should be retained for at least a period of three years in a format and media that complies with regulations and for the first two years be in a readily accessible location.

17. 5. 3. 1. 1 Disclosure Requirements

Proposals and written presentations that include specific recommendations must have reasonable basis to support the recommendation, and the member firm must provide these in the proposal or other document or offer to furnish them upon request.

EXAMPLE   If a recommendation includes a stock purchase, the firm must provide the stock's current price.

References. When, in recommending a security to a customer, a firm uses material referring to the performance of past recommendations, it must reveal certain information, including:

- the price or price range of the recommended security at the date and time that the recommendation is made;
- the market's general direction;
- the availability of information supporting the recommendation;
- any recommendations made of similar securities within the past 12 months and the nature of the recommendations (buy, sell, or hold); and
- all recommendations (winners and losers) the firm made over the time in question.

17. 5. 3. 1. 2 Recommending Investment Company Products

When recommending mutual funds to clients as investments and when using advertisements or sales literature developed for those investments, a broker-dealer should:

- use charts or graphs showing a fund's performance over a period long enough to reflect variations in value under different market conditions—generally, at least 10 years;
- reveal the source of the graphics;
- separate dividends from capital gains when making statements about a fund's cash returns;
- not state that a mutual fund is similar to or safer than any other type of security;
- reveal a fund's highest sales charge, even if the client appears to qualify for a breakpoint; and
- not make fraudulent or misleading statements or omissions of facts.

Advertising Returns. An investor's total return from a mutual fund investment may include income distributions, gains distributions, and share appreciation, minus any sales charges and fees. However, average annual total return, as defined by the SEC, assumes reinvestment of all dividends and capital gains distributions and does not deduct any sales charges or management fees.

Advertisements that feature total return must also explain how the SEC calculates fund performance. If an advertisement includes any performance figures, the minimum information provided must be 1-, 5-, and 10-year or life-of-fund average annual total returns.

Similarly, the SEC requires that **current yield calculations** be based only on income distributions for the past 12 months divided by the current per-share price: annual dividend ÷ current price = current yield.

TEST TOPIC ALERT A typical question about mutual funds requires calculation of current yield.

NavCo mutual fund has a NAV of $9.50 and POP of $10. Over the past 12 months, it distributed dividends totaling $1 and capital gains totaling $.75. What is NavCo's current yield?

This question gives you excess information. The first point is that capital gains are not included in calculation of a mutual fund's current yield. You must also remember that the NAV is not involved. The calculation is:

$$\frac{\text{Annual dividend}}{\text{POP}}$$

NavCo's current yield is $1 ÷ $10 or 10%.

17. 5. 4 OTHER COMMUNICATION PROHIBITIONS

FINRA communications rules can be specific to certain scenarios or representations. Following are some that all members must be aware of.

17. 5. 4. 1 Claims and Opinions Couched as Facts and Conclusions

Passing off opinions, projections, and forecasts as guarantees of performance violates regulations. Any attempt of a representative to make a customer believe a claim or opinion is a fact is prohibited.

17. 5. 4. 2 Testimonials

FINRA requires that if any testimonial in a communication is used, the person making the testimonial must have the knowledge and experience to form a valid opinion. When retail communications or correspondence use testimonials regarding investment advice or investment performance of a member or its products, the communications piece must disclose:

- that the testimonial may not be representative of the experience of other customers;
- that the testimonial is no guarantee of future performance or success; and
- the fact that it is a paid testimonial if more than $100 in cash or value is paid.

17. 5. 4. 3 Offers of Free Service

Offers of free service may not include obligations of any kind. Reports, analyses, or other services offered to the public must be furnished entirely free and without condition or obligation.

TAKE NOTE Following are some additional rules regarding unprofessional practices.

- A communication must not state or imply that research facilities are more extensive than they actually are.

- Hedge clauses, caveats, and disclaimers must not be used if they are misleading or inconsistent with the material's content.

17. 5. 4. 4 Ambiguous References

Ambiguous references to FINRA or other SROs must not be made with the aim of leading people to believe that a broker-dealer acts with the endorsement and approval of the association or one of the other SROs. If FINRA's name or logo is used in a member's advertising, sales literature, or, for instance, on a member's website, it must not appear in a typeface larger or more prominent than the one used for the member's own name.

TEST TOPIC ALERT Regarding a FINRA member's website, there is no requirement to list or mention the FINRA membership. However, a hyperlink to BrokerCheck is required on all FINRA member websites.

17. 5. 4. 5 Use of Members' Names

FINRA also mandates to members how the member's name may or may not appear in communications with the public.

17. 5. 4. 5. 1 General Standards

A material fact may not be omitted if the omission causes the advertisement or literature to be misleading. As a result, all advertising and sales literature must:

- clearly and prominently disclose the FINRA member's name;
- clearly describe the relationship between the FINRA member and the named entities and products when multiple entities and products are being offered;
- clearly disclose the relationship of an individual and a FINRA member when an individual is named in the communication;
- not use or refer to nonexistent degrees or designations; and
- not use degrees or designations in a misleading manner.

17. 5. 4. 5. 2 Fictional Names

A **fictional name** or **doing business as (DBA)** designation is permitted if the name is filed with FINRA and the SEC on Form BD and is the name used to designate the member.

17. 5. 4. 5. 3 Generic Names

FINRA permits a member to use an altered version of a firm name as an umbrella identification for purposes of promoting name recognition. A **generic**, or **umbrella**, **name** may be used as long as:

- it is displayed with the FINRA member name also prominently displayed;
- its relationship with the member name is clear (i.e., the information describes the link or separation between the member and the generic name); and
- there is no implication that the generic or umbrella name is the broker-dealer.

17. 5. 4. 5. 4 *Other Designations*

A member may designate a portion of its business using such terms as *division of*, *service of*, or *securities offered through* only if a bona fide division exists. The member name must be clearly designated, and the division must be clearly identified as a division of the member.

For use by a nonmember firm, the nonmember must clearly and prominently display the member firm's name and its relationship to the member. Additionally, the securities function must be clearly identified as a function of the member, not as a nonmember function.

17. 5. 4. 6 Recruitment Advertising

Companies that advertise to attract new registered representatives are regulated by the same conduct rules that cover companies advertising investment products. The advertisements must be truthful, informative, and fair in representing the opportunities in the industry and must not contain exaggerated or unwarranted claims.

The advertisements may not emphasize the salaries of top-paid salespeople without revealing that the salaries are not representative, and they may not contain any other statements that may be misleading or fraudulent.

Broker-dealers are permitted, in this one instance of recruitment advertising, to run blind advertisements (advertisements that do not list a company's name).

17. 5. 4. 7 Social Media, Websites, and the use of Personal Devices for Business Communications

FINRA has offered guidance to broker-dealers and registered personnel in their notices to members (NTMs) regarding the use of different technologies and devices for the delivery of business communications. As the technology, communications platforms, and devices are ever-changing, so will be the guidance, and FINRA will continue to supply interpretive materials to assist in that respect. Currently, the use of email, instant messaging, and websites, including social networking sites such as Facebook or LinkedIn, chat rooms, blogs, bulletin boards, and tweets or tweeting are all included within FINRA's guidance.

While the challenge is generally to determine which category of public communication any piece falls under to determine its supervisory and filing requirements (retail, correspondence, or institutional), FINRA has said that it shall always be the content delivered that ultimately determines this, and not the technology, platform, or device used to deliver it. In this light, FINRA reminds members that compliance responsibilities when communicating via the internet or other electronic media are the same as in face-to-face discussions or in written communications with the public. Therefore, all existing FINRA rules and regulations applicable to communications with the public would also be applicable to communications delivered electronically by any technology or device if the content is business related. In addition, RRs must be aware of internal firm policies and procedures that may restrict or prohibit the use of certain electronic communications, and in those instances, FINRA directs that employees of the firm must abide by the firms internal policies.

QUICK QUIZ 17.B

1. A testimonial used by a member firm must state which of the following?

   A. Qualifications of the person giving the testimonial if a specialized or experienced opinion is implied
   B. Fact that past performance does not indicate future performance and that other investors may not obtain comparable results
   C. Fact that compensation above a specified threshold was paid to the person giving the testimonial if such is the case
   D. All of the above

2. Which of the following forms of written or electronic communication must be approved by a principal before its use?

   A. Letter to a customer confirming an annual account review appointment
   B. Letter sent to 50 customers offering advice about a stock
   C. Interoffice memorandum
   D. Preliminary prospectus

3. A written recommendation to purchase LMN stock by a registered representative to one of the firm's clients would be inappropriate if

   A. the stock's current price was included in the written recommendation
   B. the communication disclosed that the broker-dealer was a market maker in the stock in the communication
   C. the broker-dealer had recently issued a statement forecasting a downturn in the price of LMN stock
   D. there was an offer to provide supporting information or documentation if the client requested it

4. If AFM fund company uses performance charts and return-on-investment statistics in its sales literature, which of the following FINRA policy statements apply?

   I. Performance charts and similar financial information displays should cover a minimum of 10 years or the life of the fund, if shorter; periods exceeding 10 years may be reported in 5-year increments.
   II. All earnings and total return figures should disclose reinvestment of dividends and capital gains.
   III. In computing and reporting historical yields and return on investment, the fund should use the shares' maximum sales charge.
   IV. Current yield figures must be based on the fund's dividend distributions only.

   A. I and III
   B. II and IV
   C. III and IV
   D. I, II, III and IV

17. 5. 5 TELEPHONE COMMUNICATIONS WITH THE PUBLIC

The **Telephone Consumer Protection Act of 1991 (TCPA)**, administered by the **Federal Communications Commission (FCC)**, was enacted to protect consumers from unwanted telephone solicitations.

A **telephone solicitation** is defined as a telephone call initiated for the purpose of encouraging the purchase of or investment in property, goods, or services.

The act governs commercial calls, recorded solicitations from autodialers, and solicitations and advertisements to fax machines and modems.

The act requires an organization that does telemarketing (cold calling in particular) to:

- maintain a Do-Not-Call list of prospects who do not want to be called and keep a prospect's name on the list until they request it be removed;

- institute a written policy on maintenance procedures for the Do-Not-Call list;

- train representatives on using the list;

- ensure that representatives acknowledge and immediately record the names and telephone numbers of prospects who ask not to be called again;

- ensure that anyone making cold calls for the firm informs prospects of their name, the firm's name, and the firm's telephone number or address;

- ensure that telemarketers do not call a prospect from the time of their Do-Not-Call request; and

- ensure that solicitation occurs only between the hours of 8:00 am and 9:00 pm of the time zone where the prospect lives.

The act exempts calls:

- made to parties with whom the caller has an established business relationship or from whom the caller has prior express permission or invitation;

- made on behalf of a tax-exempt nonprofit organization;

- not made for a commercial purpose; and

- made for legitimate debt collection purposes.

TAKE NOTE   Asking a particular broker dealer to add your name to that broker dealer's do-not-call list is not the same as adding your name to the National Do Not Call Registry. These types of requests, known as "broker specific requests" are subject to the industry's five-year record retention requirements.

17. 6   OTHER FINRA REGULATIONS

FINRA regulations extend to every facet of a member firm's business and operations. All reasonably expected situations and scenarios are covered by the rules and regulations members must abide by.

17. 6. 1   BUSINESS CONTINUITY AND DISASTER RECOVERY PLAN

FINRA requires member firms to create and maintain a business continuity plan to deal with the possibility of a significant business disruption. The plan must address certain points having to do with the consequences of the event, including but not limited to the following:

- Data backup and recovery (hardcopy and electronic)
- Alternate communications between the firm and its customers

- Alternate communications between the firm and its employees
- Alternate physical location of employees
- Communications with regulators
- Prompt customer access to funds and securities in the event the firm is unable to continue its business

Firms must designate a member of senior management who is also a principal to approve, update, and conduct an annual review of the plan. Additionally, FINRA requires firms to provide them with the names of two emergency contact persons who may be contacted by FINRA, in the event of a significant business disruption. Each contact person must be a principal and a member of senior management, and firms must update this contact information promptly, in no case later than 30 days following any change.

Regarding communicating this information to customers, a firm must disclose to its customers how it will respond to significant events of varying scope. This disclosure must be made, in writing, to customers at the time of account opening, posted on the firm's website, and mailed to customers on request.

UNIT TEST

1. A registered representative's recommendations to a customer

   A. must be approved in advance by a principal and must be suitable based on the facts the customer discloses regarding other holdings and investment objectives

   B. must be suitable based on the facts the customer discloses regarding other holdings and investment objectives

   C. must be approved in advance by a principal

   D. are not covered by any industry rules

2. All of the following disputes may be resolved using arbitration under the Code of Arbitration EXCEPT

   A. a member against a person associated with a member

   B. a member against another member

   C. a member against a public customer with consent of the customer

   D. class action suits against a member

3. A registered representative who does not complete the regulatory element of continuing education within the prescribed time frame

   A. may continue to function as a representative with the written permission of a principal

   B. may not perform any of the functions of a representative until the CE requirement is met

   C. is limited to accepting unsolicited orders only until the CE requirement is met

   D. is required to take a 120-day leave of absence

4. A registered representative sends a sales piece by email to 16 existing clients. This piece is a

   A. retail communication

   B. institutional communication

   C. correspondence

   D. nonregulated electronic communication

5. A firm must disclose to its customers how it will respond to significant events such as a business disruption

   A. by mail upon request only

   B. on its website only

   C. in writing at the time of the account opening, on its website, and upon request

   D. in writing at the time of the account opening and on its website

6. To which of the following persons may a broker-dealer pay commissions under a continuing commission contract?

   I. Retired employee, for past business

   II. Widow of a former employee, for past business

   III. Retired employee who refers an old neighbor to the broker-dealer

   IV. Retired employee who, in the course of his travels, acquires new business for the broker-dealer

   A. I and II

   B. II and III

   C. II and IV

   D. III and IV

7. A customer buys 100 shares of RFTQ at $10 per share. Several months later, the stock is trading at 4.60–5, at which time the registered representative offers to buy back the stock from the customer for his own account at $9 per share. This action is

   A. permitted because it allows the customer to sell at a price higher than the current market

   B. prohibited because FINRA does not allow registered representatives to guarantee customers against loss

   C. permitted with the written permission of a principal

   D. prohibited because it violates the Uniform Practice Code

8. Which of the following statements regarding recruiting advertising by FINRA member firms are TRUE?

  I. It is not subject to FINRA filing.
  II. It may not contain exaggerated claims about opportunities in the securities business.
  III. It is not permitted.
  IV. They need not include the name of the member firm.

  A. I and II
  B. II and III
  C. II and IV
  D. III and IV

9. Which of the following statements is true if a registered representative is permitted by an employing broker-dealer to work from a home residence?

  A. The home address and telephone number may be advertised.
  B. No self regulatory organization (SRO) approval for the location is required.
  C. The broker-dealer is in violation to permit working from a home residence.
  D. Orders from customers for the purchase or sale of securities may never be taken at an office maintained in a home residence.

10. FINRA may take all of the following actions against members that violate the Conduct Rules EXCEPT

  A. expulsion
  B. suspension
  C. fine
  D. criminal penalty

11. Rulings under the Code of Arbitration

  A. are binding on members but not on customers
  B. are binding on all parties
  C. may be appealed to the National Adjudicatory Council
  D. may be appealed to the SEC

12. Which of the following need NOT be included in a testimonial made on behalf of a member firm and distributed to potential clients?

  A. Qualifications of the person giving the testimonial if a specialized or an expert opinion is implied
  B. Length of time the testimonial covers
  C. Fact that the returns and investment performance cited in the testimonial may not be easily duplicated
  D. Whether compensation was paid to the person giving the testimonial in cash or material value above a specified threshold

13. Which of the following is TRUE regarding institutional communications?

  A. Communications with institutional customers need not be supervised.
  B. Filing with FINRA is not required.
  C. Institutional communication does not include literature sent to other broker-dealers.
  D. Institutional communication does not include literature sent to a municipality.

14. A registered representative leaves the industry to accept a position as a professor. The representative must requalify by examination to return to the industry if he is unaffiliated with a broker-dealer for more than

  A. 2 years
  B. 3 years
  C. 5 years
  D. 10 years

15. The Code of Arbitration would handle

  A. settlement dates on securities
  B. disputes involving a member and the public if brought by the public customer
  C. trade practice complaints
  D. violations of the Uniform Practice Code

ANSWERS AND RATIONALES

1. **B.** Recommendations made to a customer must be suitable for that customer. Individual recommendations do not require advance principal approval.

2. **D.** The Code of Arbitration is mandatory in member-against-member disputes. In a dispute between a member and a public customer, the member cannot force the customer to arbitrate, but arbitration may be used at the customer's request. Arbitration is optional in claims of employment discrimination (including sexual harassment) by associated persons against broker-dealers. Class actions brought against member firms are not subject to arbitration.

3. **B.** If a registered person does not complete the regulatory element of CE within the prescribed time frame, the representative's license will be suspended by FINRA. Therefore, until the element is completed, the representative may not perform any of the functions of a registered representative. The regulatory element must be completed within 120 days of the representative's second registration anniversary and every 3 years thereafter.

4. **C.** Whether in writing or electronic, a sales piece sent to 25 or fewer retail customers is considered to be and regulated as correspondence.

5. **C.** In accordance with a firm's business continuity and disaster recovery plan, a firm must disclose to its customers how it will respond to significant events (such as a business disruption) in writing at the time of the account opening, on its website, and upon request.

6. **A.** A member firm may continue to pay commissions to either a retired employee or to a former employee's widow, provided that a prior written contract exists. Commissions may be paid only on business generated while employed.

7. **B.** A representative may never guarantee a customer against a loss. This is specified in the Conduct Rules, not the Uniform Practice Code.

8. **C.** Recruiting advertisements are allowed to be "blind" advertisements which exclude the firm's name. They may not contain exaggerated claims about brokerage business opportunities or compensation.

9. **A.** A broker-dealer violates no rules when it allows registered representatives to work from home residences. The home residence, like any other broker-dealer office location must be approved by the firm's self regulatory organization (SRO). All normal business activities such as taking orders from customers is allowed, and both the home address and telephone number may be advertised as with any other office location.

10. **D.** Members or employees of members found to have violated the conduct rules are subject to expulsion, censure, fine, and suspension. Criminal penalties, such as jail sentences, cannot be administered under FINRA's member conduct rules.

11. **B.** A customer who chooses to submit a claim or dispute to arbitration under the Code of Arbitration is bound by the arbitration decision.

12. **B.** When a member firm uses a testimonial, the testimonial must be accompanied by a statement that this person's experience does not necessarily represent those of other customers; disclosure of compensation paid in cash or material value if above a specified threshold; and the testimonial giver's qualifications, if an expert opinion is implied. While the specific length of time the testimonial covers would likely be mentioned, it is not required.

13. **B.** Although filing institutional communications with FINRA is not required, it must still be supervised by a principal. It includes literature sent to other broker-dealers, government entities such as municipalities, banks and S&Ls, and investment companies or any entity with $50 million or more in total assets.

14. **A.** All securities licenses become null and void once an individual is unaffiliated for more than 2 years.

15. **B.** Disputes between the public and a member firm can be handled via the arbitration process.

QUICK QUIZ ANSWERS

Quick Quiz 17.A

1. **T.** Customers can force members into arbitration, but without an arbitration agreement, a member cannot force a customer into arbitration. However, virtually all new account forms contain a predispute arbitration clause that must be signed by customers before opening an account; this way, unresolved customer complaints must be mediated under the Code of Arbitration.

2. **F.** In simplified arbitration, one arbitrator is assigned for disputes of $50,000 or less. Greater than $50,000 up to and including $100,000, one arbitrator is assigned unless both parties agree to three. Above $100,000, three are assigned unless both parties agree to one.

3. **T.**

4. **F.** Monetary awards resulting from arbitration must be paid within 30 days of the decision date. If not paid within 30 days, the award will begin accruing interest as of the decision date.

5. **T.**

Quick Quiz 17.B

1. **D.** Testimonials must state whether the testimonial giver was paid if over a specified threshold, that the giver's experience may not be experienced by others, and the giver's qualifications if a specialized or experienced opinion is implied.

2. **B.** A letter sent to more than 25 customers offering advice about a security would fall into the category of retail communications and would need to be approved by a principal before use.

3. **C.** Because this is a purchase, it would be inappropriate for a firm to recommend a stock if it projected a continued decline in the security's price. Each of the other statements would be appropriate because they are required disclosures.

4. **D.** Performance charts should cover enough years to allow prospective buyers to evaluate a mutual fund's performance during both good and bad times, which is why FINRA approves of 10-year performance histories. FINRA also believes that prospective buyers should be alerted as to whether a fund's performance is based on reinvestment of capital gains only or on reinvestment of capital gains and dividends. Furthermore, for purposes of both reporting fairness and statistical consistency, yield and total return figures should be based on the maximum sales charge during the period covered.

Common Abbreviations

ABS asset-backed security
ADR/ADS American depositary receipt (share)
AGC Assured Guaranty Corporation
AIR assumed interest rate
AMBAC AMBAC Indemnity Corporation
ARS auction rate security
BA banker's acceptance
BD broker-dealer
BDC business development (growth) company
CD certificate of deposit
CDO collateralized debt obligation
CEO chief executive officer
CMO collateralized mortgage obligation
CMV current market value
COP Code of Procedure
CPI Consumer Price Index
CQS Consolidated Quotation System
CY current yield
DBCC District Business Conduct Committee
DEA designated examining authority
DJIA Dow Jones Industrial Average
DMM Designated Market Maker
EE Series EE savings bonds
ELN equity linked note
EPS earnings per share
ERISA Employee Retirement Income Security Act of 1974
ETF exchange-traded fund
FAC face-amount certificate
Fed Federal Reserve System
FDIC Federal Deposit Insurance Corporation
FGIC Financial Guaranty Insurance Company
FIFO first in, first out
FINRA Financial Industry Regulatory Authority
FMV fair market value
FNMA Federal National Mortgage Association
FOMC Federal Open Market Committee
FRB Federal Reserve Board
GNMA Government National Mortgage Association
GDP gross domestic product
GO general obligation bond
HH Series HH savings bond
HSA health savings account
IDR/IDB industrial development revenue bond
IPO initial public offering
IRA individual retirement account
IRC Internal Revenue Code
IRS Internal Revenue Service

JTIC joint tenants in common
JTWROS joint tenants with right of survivorship
LIFO last in, first out
LOI letter of intent
MIG Moody's Investment Grade
MSRB Municipal Securities Rulemaking Board
NASAA North American Securities Administrators' Association
Nasdaq National Association of Securities Dealers Automated Quotation system
NAV net asset value
NHA New Housing Authority
NL no load
NMS National Market System
NYSE New York Stock Exchange
OSJ office of supervisory jurisdiction
OTC over the counter
PAC planned (programed) amortization class
PE price-to-earnings ratio
PHA Public Housing Authority
POP public offering price
PPN principal protected note
REIT real estate investment trust
RR registered representative
SAI statement of additional information
SEC Securities and Exchange Commission
SEP simplified employee pension plan
SIPC Securities Investor Protection Corporation
SLMA Student Loan Marketing Association
SRO self-regulatory organization
STRIPS Separate Trading of Registered Interest and Principal of Securities
T+2 trade date plus two business days settlement
TAC targeted amortization class
TCPA Telephone Consumer Protection Act
TSA tax-sheltered annuity
UGMA/UTMA Uniform Gift (Transfers) to Minors Act
UIT unit investment trust
UPC Uniform Practice Code
VIX volatility market index
VLI variable life insurance
VRDOS variable rate demand obligations
YLD yield
YTC yield to call
YTM yield to maturity
ZR zero-coupon

Calculations

To Calculate...	Use Formula...
Dividend yield	$\dfrac{\text{Annual dividend}}{\text{Current market price}}$
Current yield	$\dfrac{\text{Annual interest}}{\text{Current market price}}$
Number of shares for conversion	$\dfrac{\text{Par value}}{\text{Conversion price}}$
Parity	$\dfrac{\text{Bond market value}}{\text{Number of shares}}$
Tax-free equivalent yield	Corporate rate × (100% – tax bracket)
Tax-equivalent yield	$\dfrac{\text{Municipal rate}}{(100\% - \text{tax bracket})}$
NAV of mutual fund share	$\dfrac{\text{Fund NAV}}{\text{Number of shares outstanding}}$
Sales charge percentage	$\dfrac{\text{POP} - \text{NAV}}{\text{POP}}$
Public offering price (POP)	$\dfrac{\text{NAV per share}}{(100\% - \text{sales charge percentage})}$
Dollar cost average	$\dfrac{\text{Total dollars invested}}{\text{Number of shares purchased}}$
Average market price	$\dfrac{\text{Share price total}}{\text{Number of investments}}$
Number of outstanding shares	Issued shares – treasury shares
Shareholders' equity	Assets – liabilities

Glossary

A

ACATS *See* Automated Customer Account Transfer Service.

acceptance, waiver, and consent A process for settling a charge or complaint that is quicker and less formal than the regular complaint procedure. *Related item(s)*: Code of Procedure.

acceptance ratio *See* placement ratio.

account executive (AE) *See* registered representative.

accredited investor As defined in Rule 502 of Regulation D, any institution or individual meeting minimum net worth requirements for the purchase of securities qualifying under the Regulation D registration exemption.

An accredited investor is generally accepted to be one who:

■ has a net worth of $1 million or more not including net equity in a primary residence; or

■ has had an annual income of $200,000 or more during each of the two most recent years (or $300,000 jointly with a spouse) and who has a reasonable expectation of reaching the same income level during the current year.

accretion of bond discount An accounting process whereby the initial cost of a bond purchased at a discount is increased annually to reflect the basis of the bond as it approaches maturity.

accrual accounting A method of reporting income when earned and expenses when incurred, as opposed to reporting income when received and expenses when paid.

accrued interest The interest that has accumulated since the last interest payment up to, but not including, the settlement date and is added to a bond transaction's contract price.

There are two methods for calculating accrued interest: the 30-day-month (360-day-year) method for corporate and municipal bonds and the actual-calendar-days (365-day-year) method for government bonds. Income bonds, bonds in default and zero-coupon bonds trade without accrued interest (flat). *Related item(s)*: flat.

accumulation account An account established to hold securities pending their deposit into a municipal securities unit investment trust.

accumulation stage The period during which contributions are made to an annuity account. *Related item(s)*: accumulation unit; distribution stage.

accumulation unit An accounting measure used to determine an annuitant's proportionate interest in the insurer's separate account during an annuity's accumulation (deposit) stage. *Related item(s)*: accumulation stage; annuity unit; separate account.

acid-test ratio A measure of a corporation's liquidity, calculated by adding cash, cash equivalents, and accounts and notes receivable, and dividing the result by total current liabilities. It is a more stringent test of liquidity than current ratio. *Syn.* quick ratio. *Related item(s)*: cash assets ratio; current ratio.

ACT *See* Automated Confirmation Transaction service.

Act of 1933 *See* Securities Act of 1933.

Act of 1934 *See* Securities Exchange Act of 1934.

adjacent acreage Producing or nonproducing oil or gas leases located within the area of an existing well site. Adjacent acreage may prove valuable for continued development of the original oil or gas prospect.

adjusted basis The value attributed to an asset or security that reflects any deductions taken on, or capital improvements to, the asset or security. Adjusted basis is used to compute the gain or loss on the sale or other disposition of the asset or security.

adjusted gross income (AGI) Earned income plus net passive income, portfolio income, and capital gains. *Related item(s)*: tax liability.

administrator (1) A person authorized by a court of law to liquidate an intestate decedent's estate. (2) An official or agency that administers a state's securities laws.

ADR *See* American depositary receipt.

ad valorem tax A tax based on the value of real or personal property. Property taxes are the major source of revenues for local governing units. *Related item(s)*: assessed value.

advance/decline line A technical analysis tool representing the total of differences between advances and declines of security prices. The advance/decline line is considered the best indicator of market movement as a whole. *Related item(s)*: breadth-of-market theory.

advance refunding Refinancing an existing municipal bond issue before its maturity or call date by using money from the sale of a new bond issue. The proceeds of the new bond issue are used to purchase government securities, and the municipality puts the principal and interest received from these securities into an escrow account; it then uses these funds to pay off the original bond issue at the first call date. *Syn.* pre-refunding. *Related item(s)*: defeasance; refunding.

advertisement Any promotional material designed for use by newspapers, magazines, billboards, radio, television, telephone recording, or other public media where the firm has little control over the type of individuals exposed to the material. *Related item(s):* sales literature.

advisory board Under the Investment Company Act of 1940, a board that advises an investment company on matters concerning its investments in securities, but does not have the power to make investment decisions or take action itself. An advisory board must be composed of persons who have no other connection with, and serve no other function for, the investment company.

AE *See* registered representative.

affiliate (1) A person who directly or indirectly owns, controls or holds with power to vote 10% or more of the outstanding voting securities of a company. (2) With respect to a direct participation program, any person who controls, is controlled by, or is under common control with the program's sponsor and includes any person who beneficially owns 50% or more of the equity interest in the sponsor. (3) Under the Investment Company Act of 1940, a person who has any type of control over an investment company's operations, which includes anyone with 5% or more of the outstanding voting securities of the investment company or any corporation of which the investment company holds 5% or more of outstanding securities. *Related item(s):* control person; insider.

agency basis *See* agency transaction.

agency issue A debt security issued by an authorized agency of the federal government. Such an issue is backed by the issuing agency itself, not by the full faith and credit of the U.S. government (except GNMA and Federal Import Export Bank issues). *Related item(s):* government security.

agency transaction A transaction in which a broker-dealer acts for the accounts of others by buying or selling securities on behalf of customers. *Syn.* agency basis. *Related item(s):* agent; broker; principal transaction.

agent (1) An individual or a firm that effects securities transactions for the accounts of others. (2) A person licensed by a state as a life insurance agent. (3) A securities salesperson who represents a broker-dealer or an issuer when selling or trying to sell securities to the investing public; this individual is considered an agent whether he actually receives or simply solicits orders. *Related item(s):* broker; broker-dealer; dealer; principal.

aggressive investment strategy A method of portfolio allocation and management aimed at achieving maximum return. Aggressive investors place a high percentage of their investable assets in equity securities and a far lower percentage in safer debt securities and cash equivalents, and they pursue aggressive policies, including margin trading, arbitrage, and option trading. *Related item(s):* balanced investment strategy; defensive investment strategy.

AGI *See* adjusted gross income.

agreement among underwriters The agreement that sets forth the terms under which each member of an underwriting syndicate will participate in a new issue offering and states the duties and responsibilities of the underwriting manager. *Related item(s):* syndicate; underwriting manager.

agreement of limited partnership The contract that establishes guidelines for the operation of a direct participation program, including the roles of the general and limited partners.

AIR *See* assumed interest rate.

allied member A general partner of an NYSE member firm who is not an NYSE member, an owner of 5% or more of the outstanding voting stock of an NYSE member corporation, or a principal executive director or officer of a member corporation. Allied members do not own seats on the NYSE.

all-or-none order (AON) An order that instructs the firm to execute the entire order. Firm does not have to execute immediately.

all-or-none underwriting (AON) A form of best efforts underwriting in which the underwriter agrees that if it is unable to sell all the shares (or a prescribed minimum), the issuer will cancel the offering. This type of agreement may be used when the issuer requires a minimum amount of capital to be raised; if the minimum is not reached, the securities sold and the money raised are returned. Commissions are not paid unless the offering is completed. *Related item(s):* underwriting.

alternative minimum tax (AMT) An alternative tax computation that adds certain tax preference items back into adjusted gross income. If the AMT is higher than the regular tax liability for the year, the regular tax and the amount by which the AMT exceeds the regular tax are paid. *Related item(s):* tax preference item.

alternative order An order to execute either of two transactions—for example, placing a sell limit (above the market) and a sell stop (below the market) on the same stock. *Syn.* either/or order; one cancels other order.

AMBAC Indemnity Corporation (AMBAC) A corporation that offers insurance on the timely payment of interest and principal obligations of municipal securities. Nonrated insured bonds typically have a AAA implied rating.

American depositary receipt (ADR) A negotiable U.S. security certificate representing a given number of shares of stock in a foreign corporation. It is bought and sold in the American securities markets, just as stock is traded. *Syn.* American depositary share.

amortization (1) The paying off of debt in regular installments over a period of time. (2) The ratable deduction of certain capitalized expenditures over a specified period of time.

amortization of bond premium An accounting process whereby the initial cost of a bond purchased at a premium is decreased to reflect the basis of the bond as it approaches maturity. *Related item(s):* accretion of bond discount.

annual compliance review The annual meeting that all registered representatives and principals must attend, the purpose of which is to review compliance issues.

annual ROI The annual return on a bond investment, which equals the annual interest and either plus the prorated discount or minus the prorated premium.

annuitant A person who receives an annuity contract's distribution.

annuitize To change an annuity contract from the accumulation (pay-in) stage to the distribution (pay-out) stage.

annuity A contract between an insurance company and an individual, generally guaranteeing lifetime income to the individual on whose life the contract is based in return for either a lump-sum or a periodic payment to the insurance company. The contract holder's objective is usually retirement income. *Related item(s):* deferred annuity; fixed annuity; immediate annuity; variable annuity.

annuity unit An accounting measure used to determine the amount of each payment during an annuity's distribution stage. The calculation takes into account the value of each accumulation unit and such other factors as assumed interest rate and mortality risk. *Related item(s):* accumulation unit; annuity; distribution stage.

Anti-Money Laundering Programs developed under the Bank Secrecy Act to prevent and detect the act of "clean" money or money that has been laundered through legitimate businesses later being used for "dirty" purposes such as terrorist activities.

AON *See* all-or-none order; all-or-none underwriting.

AP *See* associated person of a member.

appreciation The increase in an asset's value.

approved plan *See* qualified retirement plan.

arbitrage The simultaneous purchase and sale of the same or related securities to take advantage of a market inefficiency.

arbitrageur One who engages in arbitrage.

arbitration The arrangement whereby FINRA or a designated arbitration association hears and settles disagreements between members, member organizations, their employees, and customers.

ascending triangle On a technical analyst's trading activity chart, a pattern indicating that the market has started to move back up; considered to be a bullish indicator. *Related item(s):* descending triangle.

ask An indication by a trader or a dealer of a willingness to sell a security or a commodity; the price at which an investor may buy from a broker-dealer. *Syn.* offer. *Related item(s):* bid; public offering price; quotation.

assessed value The value of a property as appraised by a taxing authority for the purpose of levying taxes. Assessed value may equal market value or a stipulated percentage of market value. *Related item(s):* ad valorem tax.

assessment An additional amount of capital that a participant in a direct participation program may be called upon to furnish beyond the subscription amount. Assessments may be mandatory or optional and must be called within 12 months.

asset (1) Anything that an individual or a corporation owns. (2) A balance sheet item expressing what a corporation owns.

asset allocation fund A mutual fund that splits its investment assets among stocks, bonds, and other vehicles in an attempt to provide a consistent return for the investor. *Related item(s):* mutual fund.

asset-backed security One whose value and income payments are backed by the expected cash flow from a specific pool of underlying assets. Pooling the assets into financial instruments allows them to be sold to investors more easily than selling them individually. This process is called securitization.

assignee A person who has acquired a beneficial interest in a limited partnership from a third party, but who is neither a substitute limited partner nor an assignee of record.

assignee of record A person who has acquired a beneficial interest in a limited partnership and whose interest has been recorded on the books of the partnership and is the subject of a written instrument of assignment.

assignment (1) A document accompanying or part of a stock certificate that is signed by the person named on the certificate for the purpose of transferring the certificate's title to another person's name. (2) The act of identifying and notifying an account holder that the option owner has exercised an option held short in that account. *Related item(s):* stock power.

associated person of a member (AP) Any employee, manager, director, officer, or partner of a member broker-dealer or another entity (e.g., issuer or bank) or any person controlling, controlled by, or in common control with that member. *Related item(s):* registered representative.

assumed interest rate (AIR) The net rate of investment return that must be credited to a variable life insurance policy to ensure that at all times the variable death benefit equals the amount of the death benefit. The AIR forms the basis for projecting payments, but it is not guaranteed.

at-the-close order *See* market-on-close order.

at the money The term used to describe an option when the underlying stock is trading precisely at the exercise price of the option. *Related item(s):* in the money; out of the money.

at-the-opening order An order that specifies it is to be executed at the opening of the market of trading in that security or else it is to be canceled. The order will be executed at the opening price. *Related item(s):* market-on-close order.

auction market A market in which buyers enter competitive bids and sellers enter competitive offers simultaneously. The NYSE is an auction market. *Syn.* double auction market.

auction rate securities (ARS) Issued by municipalities, nonprofit hospitals, utilities, housing finance agencies, and universities, auction rate securities are long-term variable rate bonds tied to short-term interest rates.

audited financial statement A financial statement of a program, a corporation, or an issuer (including the profit and loss statement, cash flow and source and application of revenues statement, and balance sheet) that has been examined and verified by an independent certified public accountant.

authorized stock The number of shares of stock that a corporation can issue. This number of shares is stipulated in the corporation's state-approved charter and may be changed by a vote of the corporation's stockholders.

authorizing resolution The document enabling a municipal or state government to issue securities. The resolution provides for the establishment of a revenue fund in which receipts or income is deposited.

Automated Confirmation Transaction (ACT) Service The post-execution, online transaction reporting and comparison system.

Automated Customer Account Transfer Service (ACATS) Automated service accommodating customer positions being transferred broker to broker. Via the service utilizing form ACAT, positions can be validated and transfered.

automatic exercise Unless other instructions have been given, contracts that are in the money by a specified amount at expiration will automatically be exercised. The amount, determined by OCC, applies to both customer and institutional accounts.

average A price at a midpoint among a number of prices. Technical analysts frequently use averages as market indicators. *Related item(s):* index.

average basis An accounting method used when an investor has made multiple purchases at different prices of the same security; the method averages the purchase prices to calculate an investor's cost basis in shares being liquidated. The difference between the average cost basis and the selling price determines the investor's tax liability. *Related item(s):* first in, first out; last in, first out; share identification.

average price A step in determining a bond's yield to maturity. A bond's average price is calculated by adding its face value to the price paid for it and dividing the result by two.

B

B Consolidated Tape market identifier for the Boston Stock Exchange.

BA *See* banker's acceptance.

BABs *See* Build America Bonds.

back away The failure of a market maker to honor a firm bid and asked price. This violates the Conduct Rules.

back-end load A commission or sales fee that is charged when mutual fund shares or variable annuity contracts are redeemed. It declines annually, decreasing to zero over an extended holding period—up to eight years—as described in the prospectus. *Syn.* contingent-deferred sales load. *Related item(s):* front-end load.

balanced fund A mutual fund whose stated investment policy is to have at all times some portion of its investment assets in bonds and preferred stock, as well as in common stock, in an attempt to provide both growth and income. *Related item(s):* mutual fund.

balanced investment strategy A method of portfolio allocation and management aimed at balancing risk and return. A balanced portfolio may combine stocks, bonds, packaged products, and cash equivalents.

balance of payments (BOP) An international accounting record of all transactions made by one particular country with others during a certain time period; it compares the amount of foreign currency the country has taken in with the amount of its own currency it has paid out. *Related item(s):* balance of trade.

balance of trade The largest component of a country's balance of payments; it concerns the export and import of merchandise (not services). Debit items include imports, foreign aid, domestic spending abroad, and domestic investments abroad. Credit items include exports, foreign spending in the domestic economy, and foreign investments in the domestic economy. *Related item(s):* balance of payments.

balance sheet A report of a corporation's financial condition at a specific time.

balance sheet equation A formula stating that a corporation's assets equal the sum of its liabilities plus shareholders' equity.

balloon maturity A repayment schedule for an issue of bonds wherein a large number of the bonds come due at a prescribed time (normally at the final maturity date); a type of serial maturity. *Related item(s):* maturity date.

BAN *See* bond anticipation note.

banker's acceptance (BA) A money market instrument used to finance international and domestic trade. A banker's acceptance is a check drawn on a bank by an importer or exporter of goods and represents the bank's conditional promise to pay the face amount of the note at maturity (normally less than three months).

bank guarantee letter The document supplied by a commercial bank in which the bank certifies that a put writer has sufficient funds on deposit at the bank to equal the aggregate exercise price of the put; this releases the option writer from the option margin requirement.

banking act *See* Glass-Steagall Act of 1933.

Bank Secrecy Act The act establishing the U.S. Treasury Department as the lead agency for developing regulation in connection with anti-money laundering programs, which require broker-dealers to establish internal compliance procedures to detect abuses.

bar chart A tool used by technical analysts to track the price movements of a commodity over several consecutive time periods. *Related item(s):* moving average chart; point-and-figure chart.

basis point A measure of a bond's yield, equal to $1/_{100}$ of 1% of yield. A bond whose yield increases from 5.0 to 5.5% is said to increase by 50 basis points. *Related item(s):* point.

basis quote The price of a security quoted in terms of the yield that the purchaser may expect to receive.

BD *See* broker-dealer.

bear An investor who acts on the belief that a security or the market is falling or will fall. *Related item(s):* bull.

bearer bond *See* coupon bond.

bear market A market in which prices of a certain group of securities are falling or are expected to fall. *See* bull market.

best efforts underwriting A new issue securities underwriting in which the underwriter acts as an agent for the issuer and puts forth its best efforts to sell as many shares as possible. The underwriter has no liability for unsold shares, unlike in a firm commitment underwriting. *Related item(s):* underwriting.

beta coefficient A means of measuring the volatility of a security or a portfolio of securities in comparison to the market as a whole. A beta of 1 indicates that the security's price will move with the market. A beta greater than 1 indicates that the security's price will be more volatile than the market. A beta less than 1 means that the security's price will be less volatile than the market.

bid An indication by an investor, a trader, or a dealer of a willingness to buy a security; the price at which an investor may sell to a broker-dealer. *Related item(s):* offer; public offering price; quotation.

bid form The form submitted by underwriters in a competitive bid on a new issue of municipal securities. The underwriter states the interest rate, price bid, and net interest cost to the issuer.

blind pool A direct participation program that does not state in advance all of the specific properties in which the general partners will invest the partnership's money. At least 25% of the proceeds of the offering are kept in reserve for the purchase of nonspecified properties. *Syn.* nonspecified property program.

block trade In general, 10,000 shares of stock would be considered a block trade.

blue-chip stock The equity issues of financially stable, well-established companies that have demonstrated their ability to pay dividends in both good and bad times.

blue sky To register a securities offering in a particular state. *Related item(s):* blue-sky laws; registration by coordination; registration by filing; registration by qualification.

blue-sky laws The nickname for state regulations governing the securities industry. The term was coined in the early 1900s by a Kansas Supreme Court justice who wanted regulation to protect against "speculative schemes that have no more basis than so many feet of blue sky." *Related item(s):* Series 63; Uniform Securities Act.

board of directors (1) Individuals elected by stockholders to establish corporate management policies. A board of directors decides, among other issues, if and when dividends will be paid to stockholders. (2) The body that governs the NYSE. It is composed of 20 members elected by the NYSE general membership for a term of two years.

bona fide quote An offer from a broker-dealer to buy or sell securities. It indicates a willingness to execute a trade under the terms and conditions accompanying the quote. *Related item(s):* firm quote; nominal quote.

bond An issuing company's or government's legal obligation to repay the principal of a loan to bond investors at a specified future date. Bonds are usually issued with par, or face, values of $1,000, representing the amount of money borrowed. The issuer promises to pay a percentage of the par value as interest on the borrowed funds. The interest payment is stated on the face of the bond at issue.

bond anticipation note (BAN) A short-term municipal debt security to be paid from the proceeds of long-term debt when it is issued.

bond attorney *See* bond counsel.

Bond Buyer indexes Indexes of yield levels of municipal bonds published daily by *The Bond Buyer*. The indexes are indicators of yields that would be offered on AA and A rated general obligation bonds with 20-year maturities and revenue bonds with 30-year maturities.

bond counsel An attorney retained by a municipal issuer to give an opinion concerning the legality and tax-exempt status of a municipal issue. *Syn.* bond attorney. *Related item(s)*: legal opinion of counsel.

bond fund A mutual fund whose investment objective is to provide stable income with minimal capital risk. It invests in income-producing instruments, which may include corporate, government, or municipal bonds. *Related item(s)*: mutual fund.

bond interest coverage ratio An indication of the safety of a corporate bond. It measures the number of times by which earnings before interest and taxes exceeds annual interest on outstanding bonds. *Syn.* fixed charge coverage ratio; times fixed charges earned ratio; times interest earned ratio.

bond laddering A fixed income investment strategy which involves purchasing several smaller bonds each with a different maturity date spread over months or years rather than one larger bond maturing on a single date.

bond quote One of a number of quotations listed in the financial press and most daily newspapers that provide representative bid prices from the previous day's bond market. Quotes for corporate and government bonds are percentages of the bonds' face values (usually $1,000). Corporate bonds are quoted in increments of $1/8$, where a quote of $99^1/_8$ represents 99.125% of par ($1,000), or $991.25. Government bonds are quoted in 32nds. Municipal bonds may be quoted on a dollar basis or on a yield-to-maturity basis. *Related item(s)*: quotation; stock quote.

bond rating An evaluation of the possibility of a bond issuer's default, based on an analysis of the issuer's financial condition and profit potential. Standard & Poor's, Moody's Investors Service, and Fitch Investors Service, among others, provide bond rating services.

bond ratio One of several tools used by bond analysts to assess the degree of safety offered by a corporation's bonds. It measures the percentage of the corporation's capitalization that is provided by long-term debt financing, calculated by dividing the total face value of the outstanding bonds by the total capitalization. *Syn.* debt ratio.

bond swap The sale of a bond and the simultaneous purchase of a different bond in a like amount. The technique is used to control tax liability, extend maturity, or update investment objectives. *Syn.* tax swap. *Related item(s)*: wash sale.

bond yield The annual rate of return on a bond investment. Types of yield include nominal yield, current yield, yield to maturity, and yield to call. Their relationships vary according to whether the bond in question is at a discount, a premium, or at par. *Related item(s)*: current yield; nominal yield.

book-entry security A security sold without delivery of a certificate. Evidence of ownership is maintained on records kept by a central agency; for example, the Treasury keeps records of Treasury bill purchasers. Transfer of ownership is recorded by entering the change on the books or electronic files. *Related item(s)*: coupon bond; registered; registered as to principal only.

book value per share A measure of the net worth of each share of common stock. It is calculated by subtracting intangible assets and preferred stock from total net worth, then dividing the result by the number of shares of common outstanding. *Syn.* net tangible assets per share.

branch office Any location identified by any means to the public as a place where a registered broker-dealer conducts business.

breadth-of-market theory A technical analysis theory that predicts the strength of the market according to the number of issues that advance or decline in a particular trading day. *Related item(s)*: advance/decline line.

breakeven point The point at which gains equal losses.

breakout In technical analysis, the movement of a security's price through an established support or resistance level. *Related item(s)*: resistance level; support level.

breakpoint The schedule of sales charge discounts a mutual fund offers for lump-sum or cumulative investments.

breakpoint sale The sale of mutual fund shares in an amount just below the level at which the purchaser would qualify for reduced sales charges. This violates the Conduct Rules.

broad-based index An index designed to reflect the movement of the market as a whole. Examples include the S&P 100, the S&P 500, the Major Market Index, and the Value Line Composite Index. *Related item(s)*: index.

broker (1) An individual or a firm that charges a fee or commission for executing buy and sell orders submitted by another individual or firm. (2) The role of a firm when it acts as an agent for a customer and charges the customer a commission for its services. *Related item(s):* agent; broker-dealer; dealer.

broker-dealer (BD) A person or firm in the business of buying and selling securities. A firm may act as both broker (agent) and dealer (principal), but not in the same transaction. Broker-dealers normally must register with the SEC, the appropriate SROs, and any state in which they do business. *Related item(s):* agent; broker; dealer; principal.

broker fail *See* fail to deliver.

broker's broker (1) A specialist (DMM) executing orders for a commission house broker or another brokerage firm. (2) A floor broker on an exchange or a broker-dealer in the over-the-counter market executing a trade as an agent for another broker.

broker's loan Money loaned to a brokerage firm by a commercial bank or other lending institution for financing customers' margin account debit balances. *Related item(s):* call loan; rehypothecation.

bucketing Accepting customer orders without executing them immediately.

Build America Bonds Issued by municipalities under the Economic Recovery and Reinvestment Act of 2009, Build America Bonds (BABs) make interest payments that are taxable to bondholders. Some types of BABs offer tax credits to the issuer (Direct Payment BABs) and others offer tax credits to the bondholder (Tax Credit or Issuer BABs).

bull An investor who acts on the belief that a security or the market is rising or will rise. *Related item(s):* bear.

bulletin board *See* OTC Bulletin Board.

bull market A market in which prices of a certain group of securities are rising or will rise. *Related item(s):* bear market.

business cycle A predictable long-term pattern of alternating periods of economic growth and decline. The cycle passes through four stages: expansion, peak, contraction, and trough.

business day A day on which financial markets are open for trading. Saturdays, Sundays, and legal holidays are not considered business days.

business development company A business development company (BDC) is one that is created to help grow small companies while still in the initial stages of their development. Also referred to as growth development companies, these allow smaller nonaccredited investors the opportunity to invest in startup companies.

buyer's option A settlement contract that calls for delivery and payment according to a number of days specified by the buyer. *Related item(s):* regular way; seller's option.

buy-in The procedure that the buyer of a security follows when the seller fails to complete the contract by delivering the security. The buyer closes the contract by buying the security in the open market and charging the account of the seller for transaction fees and any loss caused by changes in the markets. *Related item(s):* sell-out.

buying power The amount of fully margined securities that a margin client may purchase using only the cash, securities, and special memorandum account balance and without depositing additional equity.

buy stop order An order to buy a security that is entered at a price above the current offering price and that is triggered when the market price touches or goes through the buy stop price.

C

C Consolidated Tape market identifier for the Cincinnati Stock Exchange.

calendar spread *See* horizontal spread.

call (1) An option contract giving the owner the right to buy a specified amount of an underlying security at a specified price within a specified time. (2) The act of exercising a call option. *Related item(s):* put.

callable bond A type of bond issued with a provision allowing the issuer to redeem the bond before maturity at a predetermined price. *Related item(s):* call price.

callable preferred stock A type of preferred stock issued with a provision allowing the corporation to call in the stock at a certain price and retire it. *Related item(s):* call price; preferred stock.

call buyer An investor who pays a premium for an option contract and receives, for a specified time, the right to buy the underlying security at a specified price. *Related item(s):* call writer; put buyer; put writer.

call date The date, specified in the prospectus of every callable security, after which the security's issuer has the option to redeem the issue at par or at par plus a premium.

call feature *See* call provision.

call loan A collateralized loan of a brokerage firm having no maturity date that may be called (terminated) at any time. The loan has a fluctuating interest rate that is recomputed daily. Generally, the loan is payable on demand the day after it is contracted. If not called, the loan is automatically renewed for another day. *Related item(s):* broker's loan.

call loan rate The rate of interest a brokerage firm charges its margin account clients on their debit balances.

call price The price, usually a premium over the issue's par value, at which preferred stocks or bonds may be redeemed before an issue's maturity.

call protection A provision in a bond indenture stating that the issue is noncallable for a certain period of time (e.g., 5 years or 10 years) after the original issue date. *Related item(s):* call provision.

call provision The written agreement between an issuing corporation and its bondholders or preferred stockholders giving the corporation the option to redeem its senior securities at a specified price before maturity and under certain conditions. *Syn.* call feature.

call risk The potential for a bond to be called before maturity, leaving the investor without the bond's current income. Because this is more likely to occur during times of falling interest rates, the investor may not be able to reinvest the principal at a comparable rate of return.

call spread An option investor's position in which the investor buys a call on a security and writes a call on the same security but with a different expiration date, exercise price, or both.

call writer An investor who receives a premium and takes on, for a specified time, the obligation to sell the underlying security at a specified price at the call buyer's discretion. *Related item(s):* call buyer; put buyer; put writer.

capital Accumulated money or goods available for use in producing more money or goods.

capital appreciation A rise in an asset's market price.

capital asset All tangible property, including securities, real estate, and other property, held for the long term.

capital contribution The amount of a participant's investment in a direct participation program, not including units purchased by the sponsors.

capital gain The profit realized when a capital asset is sold for a higher price than the purchase price. *Related item(s):* capital loss; long-term gain.

capitalization The sum of a corporation's long-term debt, stock, and surpluses. *Syn.* invested capital. *Related item(s):* capital structure.

capitalization ratio A measure of an issuer's financial status that calculates the value of its bonds, preferred stock, or common stock as a percentage of its total capitalization.

capital loss The loss incurred when a capital asset is sold for a lower price than the purchase price. *Related item(s):* capital gain; long-term loss.

capital market The segment of the securities market that deals in instruments with more than one year to maturity—that is, long-term debt and equity securities.

capital risk The potential for an investor to lose all money invested owing to circumstances unrelated to an issuer's financial strength. For example, derivative instruments such as options carry risk independent of the underlying securities' changing value. *Related item(s):* derivative.

capital stock All of a corporation's outstanding preferred stock and common stock listed at par value.

capital structure The composition of long-term funds (equity and debt) a corporation has as a source for financing. *Related item(s):* capitalization.

capital surplus The money a corporation receives in excess of the stated value of stock at the time of first sale. *Syn.* paid-in capital; paid-in surplus. *Related item(s):* par.

capped index option A type of index option issued with a capped price at a set interval above the strike price (for a call) or below the strike price (for a put). The option is automatically exercised once the underlying index reaches the capped price. *Related item(s):* index option.

capping Placing selling pressure on a stock in an attempt to keep its price low or to move its price lower; this violates the Conduct Rules.

carried interest A sharing arrangement in an oil and gas direct participation program whereby the general partner shares the tangible drilling costs with the limited partners but pays no part of the intangible drilling costs. *Related item(s):* sharing arrangement.

cash account An account in which the customer is required by the SEC's Regulation T to pay in full for securities purchased not later than two days after the standard payment period set by the Uniform Practice Code. *Syn.* special cash account.

cash assets ratio The most stringent test of liquidity, calculated by dividing the sum of cash and cash equivalents by total current liabilities. *Related item(s):* acid-test ratio; current ratio.

cash dividend Money paid to a corporation's stockholders out of the corporation's current earnings or accumulated profits. The board of directors must declare all dividends.

cash equivalent A security that may be readily converted into cash. Examples include Treasury bills, certificates of deposit, and money market instruments and funds.

cash flow The money received by a business minus the money paid out. Cash flow is also equal to net income plus depreciation or depletion.

cashiering department The department within a brokerage firm that delivers securities and money to and receives securities and money from other firms and clients of the brokerage firm. *Syn.* security cage.

cash market Transactions between buyers and sellers of commodities that entail immediate delivery of and payment for a physical commodity. *Syn.* cash-and-carry market; spot market.

cash trade *See* cash transaction.

cash transaction A settlement contract that calls for delivery and payment on the same day the trade is executed. Payment is due by 2:30 pm ET or within 30 minutes of the trade if it occurs after 2:00 pm ET. *Syn.* cash trade. *Related item(s):* regular way; settlement date.

catastrophe call The redemption of a bond by an issuer owing to disaster (e.g., a power plant that has been built with proceeds from an issue burns to the ground).

CATS *See* Certificate of Accrual on Treasury Securities.

CBOE *See* Chicago Board Options Exchange.

CD *See* negotiable certificate of deposit.

certificates of accrual on Treasury securities (CATS) One of several types of zero-coupon bonds issued by brokerage firms and collateralized by Treasury securities. *Related item(s):* Treasury receipt.

certificate of deposit (CD) *See* negotiable certificate of deposit.

change (1) For an index or average, the difference between the current value and the previous day's market close. (2) For a stock or bond quote, the difference between the current price and the last trade of the previous day.

chartist A securities analyst who uses charts and graphs of the past price movements of a security to predict its future movements. *Syn.* technician. *Related item(s):* technical analysis.

CHB *See* commission house broker.

Chicago Board Options Exchange (CBOE) The self-regulatory organization with jurisdiction over all writing and trading of standardized options and related contracts listed on that exchange. Also, the first national securities exchange for the trading of listed options.

Chicago Stock Exchange (CHX) Regional exchange that provides a listed market for smaller businesses and new enterprises. In 1949, the exchange merged with the St. Louis, Cleveland, and Minneapolis/St. Paul exchanges to form the Midwest Stock Exchange, but in 1993, the original name was reinstated. *Related item(s):* regional exchange.

churning Excessive trading in a customer's account by a registered representative who ignores the customer's interests and seeks only to increase commissions. This violates the Conduct Rules. *Syn.* overtrading.

class Options of the same type (i.e., all calls or all puts) on the same underlying security. *Related item(s):* series; type.

Class A share A class of mutual fund share issued with a front-end sales load. A mutual fund offers different classes of shares to allow investors to choose the type of sales charge they will pay. *Related item(s):* Class B share; Class C share; Class D share; front-end load.

Class B share A class of mutual fund share issued with a back-end load. A mutual fund offers different classes of shares to allow investors to choose the type of sales charge they will pay. *Related item(s):* back-end load; Class A share; Class C share; Class D share.

Class C share A class of mutual fund share issued with a level load. A mutual fund offers different classes of shares to allow investors to choose the type of sales charge they will pay. *Related item(s):* Class A share; Class B share; Class D share; level load.

Class D share A class of mutual fund share issued with both a level load and a back-end load. A mutual fund offers different classes of shares to allow investors to choose the type of sales charge they will pay. *Related item(s):* back-end load; Class A share; Class B share; Class C share; level load.

classical economics The theory that maximum economic benefit will be achieved if government does not attempt to influence the economy (i.e., if businesses are allowed to seek profitable opportunities as they see fit).

clearing agency An intermediary between the buy and sell sides in a securities transaction that receives and delivers payments and securities. Any organization that fills this function, including a securities depository but not including a Federal Reserve Bank, is considered a clearing agency.

clearing broker-dealer A broker-dealer that clears its own trades as well as those of introducing brokers. A clearing broker-dealer may hold customers' securities and cash. *Syn.* carrying broker.

CLN *See* construction loan note.

close The price of the last transaction for a particular security on a particular day.

closed-end covenant A provision of a bond issue's trust indenture stating that any additional bonds secured by the same assets must have a subordinated claim to those assets. *Related item(s):* junior lien debt; open-end covenant.

closed-end investment company An investment company that issues a fixed number of shares in an actively managed portfolio of securities. The shares may be of several classes; they are traded in the secondary marketplace, either on an exchange or over the counter. The market price of the shares is determined by supply and demand and not by net asset value. *Syn.* publicly traded fund. *Related item(s):* dual-purpose fund; mutual fund.

closed-end management company An investment company that issues a fixed number of shares in an actively managed portfolio of securities. The shares may be of several classes; they are traded in the secondary marketplace, either on an exchange or over the counter. The shares' market price is determined by supply and demand, not by net asset value. *Syn.* publicly traded fund. *Related item(s):* dual-purpose fund.

closing date The date designated by the general partners in a direct participation program as the date when sales of units in the program cease; typically the offering period extends for one year.

closing purchase An options transaction in which the seller buys back an option in the same series; the two transactions effectively cancel each other out, and the position is liquidated. *Related item(s):* closing sale; opening purchase.

closing range The relatively narrow range of prices at which transactions take place during the final minutes of the trading day. *Related item(s):* close.

closing sale An options transaction in which the buyer sells an option in the same series; the two transactions effectively cancel each other out, and the position is liquidated. *Related item(s):* closing purchase; opening sale.

CMO *See* collateralized mortgage obligation.

CMV *See* current market value.

COD *See* delivery vs. payment.

Code of Arbitration Procedure The formal method of handling securities-related disputes or clearing controversies between members, public customers, clearing corporations, or clearing banks. Any claim, dispute or controversy between member firms or associated persons must be submitted to arbitration.

Code of Procedure (COP) The formal procedure for handling trade practice complaints involving violations of the Conduct Rules. The Department of Enforcement (DOE) is the first body to hear and judge complaints. The National Adjudicatory Council handles appeals and review of DOE decisions.

coincident indicator A measurable economic factor that varies directly and simultaneously with the business cycle, thus indicating the current state of the economy. Examples include nonagricultural employment, personal income, and industrial production. *Related item(s):* lagging indicator; leading indicator.

collateral Certain assets set aside and pledged to a lender for the duration of a loan. If the borrower fails to meet obligations to pay principal or interest, the lender has claim to the assets.

collateralized mortgage obligation (CMO) A mortgage-backed corporate security. Unlike pass-through obligations issued by FNMA and GNMA, its yield is not guaranteed, and it does not have the federal government's backing. These issues attempt to return interest and principal at a predetermined rate.

collateral trust bond A secured bond backed by stocks or bonds of another issuer. The collateral is held by a trustee for safekeeping. *Syn.* collateral trust certificate.

collateral trust certificate *See* collateral trust bond.

collection ratio (1) For corporations, a rough measure of the length of time accounts receivable have been outstanding. It is calculated by multiplying the receivables by 360 and dividing the result by net sales. (2) For municipal bonds, a means of detecting deteriorating credit conditions; it is calculated by dividing taxes collected by taxes assessed.

collect on delivery (COD) *See* delivery vs. payment.

combination An option position that represents a put and a call on the same stock at different strike prices, expirations, or both.

combination fund An equity mutual fund that attempts to combine the objectives of growth and current yield by dividing its portfolio between companies that show long-term growth potential and companies that pay high dividends. *Related item(s):* mutual fund.

combination privilege A benefit offered by a mutual fund whereby the investor may qualify for a sales charge breakpoint by combining separate investments in two or more mutual funds under the same management.

combined account A customer account that has cash and long and short margin positions in different securities. *Syn.* mixed account.

combined distribution *See* split offering.

commercial bank An institution that is in the business of accepting deposits and making business loans. Commercial banks may not underwrite corporate securities or most municipal bonds. *Related item(s):* investment banker.

commercial paper An unsecured, short-term promissory note issued by a corporation for financing accounts receivable and inventories. It is usually issued at a discount reflecting prevailing market interest rates. Maturities range up to 270 days.

commingling (1) The combining by a brokerage firm of one customer's securities with another customer's securities and pledging them as joint collateral for a bank loan; unless authorized by the customers, this violates SEC Rule 15c2-1. (2) The combining by a brokerage firm of customer securities with firm securities and pledging them as joint collateral for a bank loan; this practice is prohibited.

commission A service charge an agent assesses in return for arranging a security's purchase or sale. A commission must be fair and reasonable, considering all the relevant factors of the transaction. *Syn.* sales charge. *Related item(s):* markup.

commissioner The state official with jurisdiction over insurance transactions.

commission house broker (CHB) A member of an exchange who is eligible to execute orders for customers of a member firm on the floor of the exchange. *Syn.* floor broker.

Committee on Uniform Securities Identification Procedures (CUSIP) A committee that assigns identification numbers and codes to all securities, to be used when recording all buy and sell orders.

common stock A security that represents ownership in a corporation. Holders of common stock exercise control by electing a board of directors and voting on corporate policy. *Related item(s):* equity; preferred stock.

common stock ratio One of several tools used by bond analysts to assess the degree of safety offered by a corporation's bonds. It measures the percentage of the corporation's total capitalization that is contributed by the common stockholders and is calculated by adding the par value, the capital in excess of par, and the retained earnings and then dividing the result by the total capitalization. *Related item(s):* bond ratio.

communications with the public FINRA categorizes public communications into three categories: retail, institutional, and correspondence. *See* retail communications, institutional communications and correspondence.

competitive bid underwriting A form of firm commitment underwriting in which rival syndicates submit sealed bids for underwriting the issue. *Related item(s):* negotiated underwriting.

compliance department The department within a brokerage firm that oversees the firm's trading and market-making activities. It ensures that the firm's employees and officers abide by the rules and regulations of the SEC, exchanges, and SROs.

Composite Average *See* Dow Jones Composite Average.

concession The profit per bond or share that an underwriter allows the seller of new issue securities. The selling group broker-dealer purchases the securities from the syndicate member at the public offering price minus the concession. *Syn.* reallowance.

Conduct Rules Regulations designed to ensure that FINRA member firms and their representatives follow fair and ethical trade practices when dealing with the public. The rules complement and broaden the Securities Act of 1933, the Securities Exchange Act of 1934, and the Investment Company Act of 1940.

conduit theory A means for an investment company to avoid taxation on net investment income distributed to shareholders. If a mutual fund acts as a conduit for the distribution of net investment income, it may qualify as a regulated investment company and be taxed only on the income the fund retains. *Syn.* pipeline theory.

confidence theory A technical analysis theory that measures the willingness of investors to take risks by comparing the yields on high-grade bonds to the yields on lower rated bonds.

confirmation A printed document that states the trade date, settlement date, and money due from or owed to a customer. It is sent or given to the customer on or before the settlement date. *Related item(s):* duplicate confirmation.

congestion A technical analysis term used to indicate that the range within which a commodity's price trades for an extended period of time is narrow.

Consolidated Quotation System (CQS) A quotation and last-sale reporting service for members that are active market makers of listed securities in the third market. It is used by market makers willing to stand ready to buy and sell securities for their own accounts on a continuous basis but that do not wish to do so through an exchange.

Consolidated Tape (CT) A New York Stock Exchange service that delivers real-time reports of securities transactions to subscribers as they occur on the various exchanges.

The Tape distributes reports to subscribers over two different networks that the subscribers can tap into through either the high-speed electronic lines or the low-speed ticker lines. Network A reports transactions in NYSE-listed securities. Network B reports regional exchange transactions.

consolidation The technical analysis term for a narrowing of the trading range for a commodity or security, considered an indication that a strong price move is imminent.

constant dollar plan A defensive investment strategy in which the total sum of money invested is kept constant, regardless of any price fluctuation in the portfolio. As a result, the investor sells when the market is high and buys when it is low.

constant ratio plan An investment strategy in which the investor maintains an appropriate ratio of debt to equity securities by making purchases and sales to maintain the desired balance.

construction loan note (CLN) A short-term municipal debt security that provides interim financing for new projects.

constructive receipt The date on which the Internal Revenue Service considers that a taxpayer receives dividends or other income.

Consumer Price Index (CPI) A measure of price changes in consumer goods and services used to identify periods of inflation or deflation.

consumption A term used by Keynesian economists to refer to the purchase by household units of newly produced goods and services.

contemporaneous trader A person who enters a trade at or near the same time and in the same security as a person who has inside information. The contemporaneous trader may bring suit against the inside trader. *Related item(s):* Insider Trading and Securities Fraud Enforcement Act of 1988.

contingent deferred sales load *See* back-end load.

contingent order An order that is conditional upon the execution of a previous order and that will be executed only after the first order is filled.

contra broker The broker on the buy side of a sell order or on the sell side of a buy order.

contraction A period of general economic decline, one of the business cycle's four stages. *Related item(s):* business cycle.

contractionary policy A monetary policy that decreases the money supply, usually with the intention of raising interest rates and combating inflation.

control (controlling, controlled by, under common control with) The power to direct or affect the direction of a company's management and policies, whether through the ownership of voting securities, by contract, or otherwise. Control is presumed to exist if a person, directly or indirectly, owns, controls, holds with the power to vote, or holds proxies representing at least 10% of a company's voting securities.

control person (1) A director, an officer, or another affiliate of an issuer. (2) A stockholder who owns at least 10% of any class of a corporation's outstanding securities. *Related item(s):* affiliate; insider.

control security Any security owned by a director, an officer, or another affiliate of the issuer or by a stockholder who owns at least 10% of any class of a corporation's outstanding securities. Who owns a security, not the security itself, determines whether it is a control security.

conversion parity Two securities, one of which may be converted into the other, of equal dollar value. A convertible security holder can calculate parity to help decide whether converting would lead to gain or loss.

conversion price The dollar amount of a convertible security's par value that is exchangeable for one share of common stock.

conversion privilege A feature the issuer adds to a security that allows the holder to change the security into shares of common stock. This makes the security attractive to investors and, therefore, more marketable. *Related item(s):* convertible bond; convertible preferred stock.

conversion rate *See* conversion ratio.

conversion ratio The number of shares of common stock per par value amount that the holder would receive for converting a convertible bond or preferred share. *Syn.* conversion rate.

conversion value The total market value of common stock into which a senior security is convertible.

convertible bond A debt security, usually in the form of a debenture, that may be exchanged for equity securities of the issuing corporation at specified prices or rates. *Related item(s):* debenture.

convertible preferred stock An equity security that may be exchanged for common stock at specified prices or rates. Dividends may be cumulative or noncumulative. *Related item(s):* cumulative preferred stock; noncumulative preferred stock; preferred stock.

cooling-off period The period (a minimum of 20 days) between a registration statement's filing date and the registration's effective date. In practice, the period varies in length.

COP *See* Code of Procedure.

corporate account An account held in a corporation's name. The corporate agreement, signed when the account is opened, specifies which officers are authorized to trade in the account. In addition to standard margin account documents, a corporation must provide a copy of its charter and bylaws authorizing a margin account.

corporate bond A debt security issued by a corporation. A corporate bond typically has a par value of $1,000, is taxable, has a term maturity, and is traded on a major exchange.

corporation The most common form of business organization, in which the organization's total worth is divided into shares of stock, each share representing a unit of ownership. A corporation is characterized by a continuous life span and its owners' limited liability.

correspondence FINRA defines this category of communications with the public as any written (including electronic) communication that is distributed or made available to 25 or fewer retail investors within any 30 calendar-day period.

cost basis The price paid for an asset, including any commissions or fees, used to calculate capital gains or losses when the asset is sold.

cost depletion A method of calculating tax deductions for investments in mineral, oil, or gas resources. The cost of the mineral-, oil- or gas-producing property is returned to the investor over the property's life by an annual deduction, which takes into account the number of known recoverable units of mineral, oil, or gas to arrive at a cost-per-unit figure. The tax deduction is determined by multiplying the cost-per-unit figure by the number of units sold each year.

coterminous A term used to describe municipal entities that share the same boundaries. For example, a municipality's school district and fire district may issue debt separately although the debt is backed by revenues from the same taxpayers. *Related item(s):* overlapping debt.

coupon bond A debt obligation with attached coupons representing semiannual interest payments. The holder submits the coupons to the trustee to receive the interest payments. The issuer keeps no record of the purchaser, and the purchaser's name is not printed on the certificate. *Syn.* bearer bond. *Related item(s):* book-entry security; registered; registered as to principal only.

coupon yield *See* nominal yield.

covenant A component of a debt issue's trust indenture that identifies bondholders' rights and other provisions. Examples include rate covenants that establish a minimum revenue coverage for a bond; insurance covenants that require insurance on a project; and maintenance covenants that require maintenance on a facility constructed by the proceeds of a bond issue.

coverage ratio A measure of the safety of a bond issue, based on how many times earnings will cover debt service plus operating and maintenance expenses for a specific time period.

covered call writer An investor who sells a call option while owning the underlying security or some other asset that guarantees the ability to deliver if the call is exercised.

covered put writer An investor who sells a put option while owning an asset that guarantees the ability to pay if the put is exercised (e.g., cash in the account).

CPI *See* Consumer Price Index.

CQS *See* Consolidated Quotation System.

CR *See* credit balance.

credit agreement A component of a customer's margin account agreement, outlining the conditions of the credit arrangement between broker and customer.

credit balance (CR) The amount of money remaining in a customer's account after all commitments have been paid in full. *Syn.* credit record; credit register. *Related item(s):* debit balance.

credit department *See* margin department.

creditor Any broker or dealer, member of a national securities exchange, or person associated with a broker-dealer involved in extending credit to customers.

credit risk The degree of probability that a bond's issuer will default in the payment of either principal or interest. *Syn.* default risk; financial risk.

credit spread A position established when the premium received for the option sold exceeds the premium paid for the option bought. *Related item(s):* debit spread.

crossed market The situation created when one market maker bids for a stock at a price higher than another market maker is asking for the same stock, or when one market maker enters an ask price to sell a stock at a price lower than another market maker's bid price to buy the same stock. This violates the Conduct Rules. *Related item(s):* locked market.

crossover point The point at which a limited partnership begins to show a negative cash flow with a taxable income. *Related item(s):* phantom income.

CTR *See* currency transaction report.

cum rights A term describing stock trading with rights. *Related item(s):* ex-rights.

cumulative preferred stock An equity security that offers the holder any unpaid dividends in arrears. These dividends accumulate and must be paid to the cumulative preferred stockholder before any dividends may be paid to the common stockholders. *Related item(s):* convertible preferred stock; noncumulative preferred stock; preferred stock.

cumulative voting A voting procedure that permits stockholders either to cast all of their votes for any one candidate or to cast their total number of votes in any proportion they choose. This results in greater representation for minority stockholders. *Related item(s):* statutory voting.

currency transaction report (CTR) A report filed by financial institutions to the IRS for deposits of any currency on a single day of more than $10,000.

current assets Cash and other assets that are expected to be converted into cash within the next 12 months. Examples include such liquid items as cash and equivalents, accounts receivable, inventory, and prepaid expenses.

current liabilities A corporation's debt obligations due for payment within the next 12 months. Examples include accounts payable, accrued wages payable, and current long-term debt.

current market value (CMV) The worth of the securities in an account. The market value of listed securities is based on the closing prices on the previous business day. *Syn.* long market value. *Related item(s):* market value.

current price *See* public offering price.

current ratio A measure of a corporation's liquidity; that is, its ability to transfer assets into cash to meet current short-term obligations. It is calculated by dividing total current assets by total current liabilities. *Syn.* working capital ratio.

current yield The annual rate of return on a security, calculated by dividing the interest or dividends paid by the security's current market price. *Related item(s):* bond yield.

CUSIP *See* Committee on Uniform Securities Identification Procedures.

custodial account An account in which a custodian enters trades on behalf of the beneficial owner, often a minor. *Related item(s):* custodian.

custodian An institution or a person responsible for making all investment, management, and distribution decisions in an account maintained in the best interests of another. Mutual funds have custodians responsible for safeguarding certificates and performing clerical duties. *Related item(s):* mutual fund custodian.

customer Any person who opens a trading account with a broker-dealer. A customer may be classified in terms of account ownership, trading authorization, payment method, or types of securities traded.

customer agreement A document that a customer must sign when opening a margin account with a broker-dealer; it allows the firm to liquidate all or a portion of the account if the customer fails to meet a margin call.

customer ledger The accounting record that lists separately all customer cash and margin accounts carried by a firm.

customer statement A document showing a customer's trading activity, positions, and account balance. The SEC requires that customer statements be sent quarterly, but customers generally receive them monthly.

cyclical industry A fundamental analysis term for an industry that is sensitive to the business cycle and price changes. Most cyclical industries produce durable goods, such as raw materials and heavy equipment.

D

dated date The date on which interest on a new bond issue begins to accrue.

day order An order that is valid only until the close of trading on the day it is entered; if it is not executed by the close of trading, it is canceled.

day trader A trader in securities who opens all positions after the opening of the market and offsets or closes out all positions before the close of the market on the same day.

dealer (1) An individual or a firm engaged in the business of buying and selling securities for its own account, either directly or through a broker. (2) The role of a firm when it acts as a principal and charges the customer a markup or markdown. *Syn.* principal. *Related item(s):* broker; broker-dealer.

dealer paper Short-term, unsecured promissory notes that the issuer sells through a dealer rather than directly to the public.

debenture A debt obligation backed by the issuing corporation's general credit. *Syn.* unsecured bond.

debit balance (DR) The amount of money a customer owes a brokerage firm. *Syn.* debit record; debit register. *Related item(s):* credit balance.

debit register *See* debit balance.

debit spread An options position established when the premium paid for the option bought exceeds the premium received for the option sold. *Related item(s):* credit spread.

debt financing Raising money for working capital or for capital expenditures by selling bonds, bills, or notes to individual or institutional investors. In return for the money lent, the investors become creditors and receive the issuer's promise to repay principal and interest on the debt. *Related item(s):* equity financing.

debt per capita *See* net debt per capita.

debt ratio *See* bond ratio.

debt security A security representing an investor's loan to an issuer such as a corporation, a municipality, the federal government, or a federal agency. In return for the loan, the issuer promises to repay the debt on a specified date and to pay interest. *Related item(s):* equity security.

debt service The schedule for repayment of interest and principal (or the scheduled sinking fund contribution) on an outstanding debt. *Related item(s):* sinking fund.

debt service ratio An indication of the ability of an issuer to meet principal and interest payments on bonds.

debt service reserve fund The account that holds enough money to pay one year's debt service on a municipal revenue bond. *Related item(s):* flow of funds.

debt-to-equity ratio The ratio of total long-term debt to total stockholders' equity; it is used to measure leverage.

declaration date The date on which a corporation announces an upcoming dividend's amount, payment date, and record date.

decreasing debt service A schedule for debt repayment whereby the issuer repays principal in installments of equal size over the life of the issue. The amount of interest due therefore decreases, and the amount of each payment becomes smaller over time. *Related item(s):* level debt service.

deduction An item or expenditure subtracted from adjusted gross income to reduce the amount of income subject to tax.

default The failure to pay interest or principal promptly when due.

default risk *See* credit risk.

defeasance The termination of a debt obligation. A corporation or municipality removes debt from its balance sheet by issuing a new debt issue or creating a trust that generates enough cash flow to provide for the payment of interest and principal. *Related item(s):* advance refunding.

defensive industry A fundamental analysis term for an industry that is relatively unaffected by the business cycle. Most defensive industries produce nondurable goods for which demand remains steady throughout the business cycle; examples include the food industry and utilities.

defensive investment strategy A method of portfolio allocation and management aimed at minimizing the risk of losing principal. Defensive investors place a high percentage of their investable assets in bonds, cash equivalents, and stocks that are less volatile than average.

deferred annuity An annuity contract that delays payment of income, installments, or a lump sum until the investor elects to receive it. *Related item(s):* annuity.

deferred compensation plan A nonqualified retirement plan whereby the employee defers receiving current compensation in favor of a larger payout at retirement (or in the case of disability or death).

deficiency letter The SEC's notification of additions or corrections that a prospective issuer must make to a registration statement before the SEC will clear the offering for distribution. *Syn.* bedbug letter.

defined benefit plan A qualified retirement plan that specifies the total amount of money that the employee will receive at retirement.

defined contribution plan A qualified retirement plan that specifies the amount of money that the employer will contribute annually to the plan.

deflation A persistent and measurable fall in the general level of prices. *Related item(s):* inflation.

delivery The change in ownership or in control of a security in exchange for cash. Delivery takes place on the settlement date.

delivery vs. payment (DVP) A transaction settlement procedure in which securities are delivered to the buying institution's bank in exchange for payment of the amount due. *Syn.* collect on delivery (COD).

demand A consumer's desire and willingness to pay for a good or service. *Related item(s):* supply.

demand deposit A sum of money left with a bank (or borrowed from a bank and left on deposit) that the depositing customer has the right to withdraw immediately. *Related item(s):* time deposit.

demand-pull An excessive money supply that increases the demand for a limited supply of goods that is believed to result in inflation.

depletion A tax deduction that compensates a business for the decreasing supply of the natural resource that provides its income (oil, gas, coal, gold, or other nonrenewable resource). There are two ways to calculate depletion: cost depletion and percentage depletion. *Related item(s):* cost depletion; percentage depletion.

depreciation (1) A tax deduction that compensates a business for the cost of certain tangible assets. (2) A decrease in the value of a particular currency relative to other currencies.

depreciation expense A bookkeeping entry of a noncash expense charged against earnings to recover the cost of an asset over its useful life.

depression A prolonged period of general economic decline.

derivative An investment vehicle, the value of which is based on another security's value. Futures contracts, forward contracts, and options are among the most common types of derivatives. Institutional investors generally use derivatives to increase overall portfolio return or to hedge portfolio risk.

descending triangle On a technical analyst's trading activity chart, a pattern indicating that the market has started to fall; considered to be a bearish indicator. *Related item(s):* ascending triangle.

designated market maker (DMM) Previously known as specialists, they are exchange members who are assigned to securities on the trading floor and are charged with keeping a fair and orderly market in those securities while providing liquidity to the market place.

designated order In a municipal bond underwriting, a customer order that is submitted by one syndicate member but that specifies more than one member to receive a percentage of the takedown. The size of the order establishes its priority for subscription to an issue. *Related item(s):* group net order; member-at-the-takedown order; presale order.

devaluation A substantial fall in a currency's value, compared with the value of gold or to the value of another country's currency.

developmental drilling program A limited partnership that drills for oil, gas, or minerals in areas of proven reserves or near existing fields. *Related item(s):* exploratory drilling program; income program; step-out well.

diagonal spread An option position established by the simultaneous purchase and sale of options of the same class but with different exercise prices and expiration dates. *Related item(s):* spread.

dilution A reduction in earnings per share of common stock. Dilution occurs through the issuance of additional shares of common stock and the conversion of convertible securities.

direct debt The total of a municipality's general obligation bonds, short-term notes, and revenue debt.

direct paper Commercial paper sold directly to the public without the use of a dealer.

direct participation program (DPP) A business organized so as to pass all income, gains, losses, and tax benefits to its owners, the investors; the business is usually structured as a limited partnership. Examples include oil and gas programs, real estate programs, agricultural programs, cattle programs, condominium securities, and Subchapter S corporate offerings. *Syn.* program.

discount The difference between the lower price paid for a security and the security's face amount at issue.

discount bond A bond that sells at a lower price than its face value. *Related item(s):* par.

discount rate The interest rate charged by the 12 Federal Reserve Banks for short-term loans made to member banks.

discretion The authority given to someone other than an account's beneficial owner to make investment decisions for the account concerning the security, the number of shares or units, and whether to buy or sell. The authority to decide only timing or price does not constitute discretion. *Related item(s):* limited power of attorney.

discretionary account An account in which the customer has given the registered representative authority to enter transactions at the representative's discretion.

disintermediation The flow of money from low-yielding accounts in traditional savings institutions to higher yielding investments. Typically, this occurs when the Fed tightens the money supply and interest rates rise.

disposable income (DI) The sum that people divide between spending and personal savings. *Related item(s):* personal income.

disproportionate sharing A sharing arrangement whereby the sponsor in an oil and gas direct participation program pays a portion of the program's costs but receives a disproportionately higher percentage of its revenues. *Related item(s):* sharing arrangement.

distribution Any cash or other property distributed to shareholders or general partners that arises from their interests in the business, investment company, or partnership.

distribution stage The period during which an individual receives distributions from an annuity account. *Syn.* payout stage. *Related item(s):* accumulation stage; accumulation unit.

diversification A risk management technique that mixes a wide variety of investments within a portfolio, thus minimizing the impact of any one security on overall portfolio performance.

diversified common stock fund A mutual fund that invests its assets in a wide range of common stocks. The fund's objectives may be growth, income, or a combination of both. *Related item(s):* growth fund; mutual fund.

diversified investment company As defined by the Investment Company Act of 1940, an investment company that meets certain standards as to the percentage of assets invested. These companies use diversification to manage risk. *Related item(s):* management company; nondiversified investment company; 75-5-10 test.

diversified management company As defined by the Investment Company Act of 1940, a management company that meets certain standards for percentage of assets invested. These companies use diversification to manage risk. *Related item(s):* management company; 75-5-10 test.

divided account *See* Western account.

dividend A distribution of a corporation's earnings. Dividends may be in the form of cash, stock, or property. The board of directors must declare all dividends. *Syn.* stock dividend. *Related item(s):* cash dividend; dividend yield; property dividend.

dividend department The department within a brokerage firm that is responsible for crediting client accounts with dividends and interest payments on client securities held in the firm's name.

dividend disbursing agent (DDA) The person responsible for making the required dividend distributions to the broker-dealer's dividend department.

dividend exclusion rule An IRS provision that permits a corporation to exclude from its taxable income 70% of dividends received from domestic preferred and common stocks. The Tax Reform Act of 1986 repealed the dividend exclusion for individual investors.

dividend payout ratio A measure of a corporation's policy of paying cash dividends, calculated by dividing the dividends paid on common stock by the net income available for common stockholders. The ratio is the complement of the retained earnings ratio.

dividends per share The dollar amount of cash dividends paid on each common share during one year.

dividend yield The annual rate of return on a common or preferred stock investment. The yield is calculated by dividing the annual dividend by the stock's purchase price. *Related item(s):* current yield; dividend.

DJIA *See* Dow Jones Industrial Average.

DK *See* don't know.

DNR *See* do not reduce order.

doctrine of mutual reciprocity The agreement that established the federal tax exemption for municipal bond interest. States and municipalities do not tax federal securities or properties, and the federal government reciprocates by exempting local government securities and properties from federal taxation. *Syn.* mutual exclusion doctrine; reciprocal immunity.

dollar bonds Municipal revenue bonds that are quoted and traded on a basis of dollars rather than yield to maturity. Term bonds, tax-exempt notes, and New Housing Authority bonds are dollar bonds.

dollar cost averaging A system of buying mutual fund shares in fixed dollar amounts at regular fixed intervals, regardless of the share's price. The investor purchases more shares when prices are low and fewer shares when prices are high, thus lowering the average cost per share over time.

donor A person who makes a gift of money or securities to another. Once the gift is donated, the donor gives up all rights to it. Gifts of securities to minors under the Uniform Gifts to Minors Act provide tax advantages to the donor. *Related item(s):* Uniform Gifts to Minors Act.

do not reduce order (DNR) An order that stipulates that the limit or stop price should not be reduced in response to the declaration of a cash dividend.

don't know (DK) A response to a confirmation received from a broker-dealer indicating a lack of information about, or record of, the transaction.

double-barreled bond A municipal security backed by the full faith and credit of the issuing municipality as well as by pledged revenues. *Related item(s):* general obligation bond; revenue bond.

Dow Jones averages The most widely quoted and oldest measures of change in stock prices. Each of the four averages is based on the prices of a limited number of stocks in a particular category. *Related item(s):* average; Dow Jones Industrial Average.

Dow Jones Composite Average (DJCA) A market indicator composed of the 65 stocks that make up the Dow Jones Industrial, Transportation, and Utilities Averages. *Related item(s):* average; Dow Jones Industrial Average; Dow Jones Transportation Average; Dow Jones Utilities Average.

Dow Jones Industrial Average (DJIA) The most widely used market indicator, composed of 30 large, actively traded issues of industrial stocks. *Related item(s):* average.

Dow Jones Transportation Average (DJTA) A market indicator composed of 20 transportation stocks. *Related item(s):* average; Dow Jones Composite Average; Dow Jones Industrial Average; Dow Jones Utilities Average.

Dow Jones Utilities Average (DJUA) A market indicator composed of 15 utilities stocks. *Related item(s):* average; Dow Jones Composite Average; Dow Jones Industrial Average; Dow Jones Transportation Average.

Dow theory A technical market theory that long-term trends in the stock market may be confirmed by analyzing the movements of the Dow Jones Industrial Average and the Dow Jones Transportation Average.

down tick *See* minus tick.

DPP *See* direct participation program.

DR *See* debit balance.

dry hole A well that is plugged and abandoned without being completed or that is abandoned for any reason without having produced commercially for 60 days. *Related item(s):* productive well.

dual-purpose fund A closed-end investment company that offers two classes of stock: income shares and capital shares. Income shares entitle the holder to share in the net dividends and interest paid to the fund. Capital shares entitle the holder to profit from the capital appreciation of all securities the fund holds. *Related item(s):* closed-end management company.

due bill A printed statement showing the obligation of a seller to deliver securities or rights to the purchaser. A due bill is also used as a pledge to deliver dividends when the transaction occurs after the record date.

due diligence The careful investigation by the underwriters that is necessary to ensure that all material information pertinent to an issue has been disclosed to prospective investors.

due diligence meeting A meeting at which an issuing corporation's officials and representatives of the underwriting group present information on and answer questions about a pending issue of securities. The meeting is held for the benefit of brokers, securities analysts, and institutional investors.

duplicate confirmation A copy of a customer's confirmation that a brokerage firm sends to an agent or an attorney if the customer requests it in writing. In addition, if the customer is an employee of another broker-dealer, SRO regulations may require a duplicate confirmation to be sent to the employing broker-dealer. *Related item(s):* confirmation.

DVP *See* delivery vs. payment.

E

earned income Income derived from active participation in a trade or business, including wages, salary, tips, commissions, and bonuses. *Related item(s):* portfolio income; unearned income.

earned surplus *See* retained earnings.

earnings per share (EPS) A corporation's net income available for common stock divided by its number of shares of common stock outstanding. *Syn.* primary earnings per share.

earnings per share fully diluted A corporation's earnings per share calculated by assuming that all convertible securities have been converted. *Related item(s):* earnings per share.

Eastern account A securities underwriting in which the agreement among underwriters states that each syndicate member will be responsible for its own allocation as well as for a proportionate share of any securities remaining unsold. *Syn.* undivided account. *Related item(s):* syndicate; Western account.

economic risk The potential for international developments and domestic events to trigger losses in securities investments.

EE savings bond *See* Series EE bond.

effective date The date the registration of an issue of securities becomes effective, allowing the underwriters to sell the newly issued securities to the public and confirm sales to investors who have given indications of interest.

efficient market theory A theory based on the premise that the stock market processes information efficiently. The theory postulates that, as new information becomes known, it is reflected immediately in the price of stock and, therefore, stock prices represent fair prices.

Employee Retirement Income Security Act of 1974 (ERISA) The law that governs the operation of most corporate pension and benefit plans. The law eased pension eligibility rules, set up the Pension Benefit Guaranty Corporation, and established guidelines for the management of pension funds. Corporate retirement plans established under ERISA qualify for favorable tax treatment for employers and participants. *Syn.* Pension Reform Act.

endorsement The signature on the back of a stock or bond certificate by the person named on the certificate as the owner. An owner must endorse certificates when transferring them to another person. *Related item(s):* assignment.

EPS *See* earnings per share.

EQ *See* equity.

equipment bond *See* equipment trust certificate.

equipment-leasing limited partnership A direct participation program that purchases equipment for leasing to other businesses on a long-term basis. Tax-sheltered income is the primary objective of such a partnership.

equipment trust certificate A debt obligation backed by equipment. The title to the equipment is held by an independent trustee (usually a bank), not the issuing company. Equipment trust certificates are generally issued by transportation companies such as railroads. *Syn.* equipment bond; equipment note.

equity (EQ) Common and preferred stockholders' ownership interests in a corporation. *Related item(s):* common stock; preferred stock.

equity financing Raising money for working capital or for capital expenditures by selling common or preferred stock to individual or institutional investors. In return for the money paid, the investors receive ownership interests in the corporation. *Related item(s):* debt financing.

equity option A security representing the right to buy or sell common stock at a specified price within a specified time. *Related item(s):* option.

equity security A security representing ownership in a corporation or another enterprise. Examples of equity securities include:

- common and preferred stock; and
- put and call options on equity securities.

ERISA *See* Employee Retirement Income Security Act of 1974.

escrow agreement The certificate provided by an approved bank that guarantees that the indicated securities are on deposit at that bank. An investor who writes a call option and can present an escrow agreement is considered covered and does not need to meet margin requirements.

eurobond A long-term debt instrument of a government or corporation that is denominated in the currency of the issuer's country but is issued and sold in a different country.

eurodollar U.S. currency held in banks outside the United States.

excess equity (EE) The value of money or securities in a margin account that is in excess of the federal requirement. *Syn.* margin excess; Regulation T excess.

excess margin securities The securities in a margin account that are in excess of 140% of the account's debit balance. Such securities are available to the broker-dealer for debit balance financing purposes, but they must be segregated and earmarked as the customer's property.

exchange Any organization, association, or group of persons that maintains or provides a marketplace in which securities may be bought and sold. An exchange need not be a physical place, and several strictly electronic exchanges do business around the world.

Exchange Act *See* Securities Exchange Act of 1934.

exchange-listed security A security that has met certain requirements and has been admitted to full trading privileges on an exchange. The NYSE and regional exchanges set listing requirements for volume of shares outstanding, corporate earnings, and other characteristics. Exchange-listed securities may also be traded in the third market, the market for institutional investors.

exchange market All of the exchanges on which listed securities are traded.

exchange privilege A feature offered by a mutual fund allowing an individual to transfer an investment in one fund to another fund under the same sponsor without incurring an additional sales charge.

exchange rate *See* foreign exchange rate.

exchange-traded fund (ETF) An investment company legally classified as an open-end company or Unit Investment Trust (UIT), but differing from traditional open-end companies (mutual funds) and UITs. An ETF issues shares in large blocks that are known as Creation Units. Those who purchase Creation Units are frequently large institutional traders or investors. The Creation Units can then be split up and sold as individual shares in the secondary markets allowing individual investors to purchase shares.

ex-date The first date on which a security is traded that the buyer is not entitled to receive distributions previously declared. *Syn.* ex-dividend date.

ex-dividend date *See* ex-date.

executor A person given fiduciary authorization to manage the affairs of a decedent's estate. An executor's authority is established by the decedent's last will.

exempt security A security exempt from the registration requirements (although not from the antifraud requirements) of the Securities Act of 1933. Examples include U.S. government securities and municipal securities.

exempt transaction A transaction that does not trigger a state's registration and advertising requirements under the Uniform Securities Act. Examples of exempt transactions include:

- nonissuer transactions in outstanding securities (normal market trading);
- transactions with financial institutions;
- unsolicited transactions; and
- private placement transactions.

No transaction is exempt from the Uniform Securities Act's antifraud provisions.

exercise To effect the transaction offered by an option, a right, or a warrant. For example, an equity call holder exercises a call by buying 100 shares of the underlying stock at the agreed-upon price within the agreed-upon time period.

exercise price The cost per share at which an option or a warrant holder may buy or sell the underlying security. *Syn.* strike price.

ex-legal A municipal issue that trades without a written legal opinion of counsel from a bond attorney. An ex-legal issue must be designated as such at the time of the trade. *Related item(s):* legal opinion of counsel.

expansion A period of increased business activity throughout an economy; one of the four stages of the business cycle. *Syn.* recovery. *Related item(s):* business cycle.

expansionary policy A monetary policy that increases the money supply, usually with the intention of lowering interest rates and combating deflation.

expense ratio A ratio for comparing a mutual fund's efficiency by dividing the fund's expenses by its net assets.

expiration cycle A set of four expiration months for a class of listed options. An option may have expiration dates of January, April, July, and October (JAJO); February, May, August, and November (FMAN); or March, June, September, and December (MJSD).

expiration date The specified date on which an option buyer no longer has the rights specified in the option contract.

exploratory drilling program A limited partnership that aims to locate and recover undiscovered reserves of oil, gas, or minerals. These programs are considered highly risky investments. *Syn.* wildcatting. *Related item(s):* developmental drilling program; income program.

exploratory well A well drilled either in search of an undiscovered pool of oil or gas or with the hope of substantially extending the limits of an existing pool of oil or gas.

ex-rights Stock trading without rights. *Related item(s):* cum rights.

ex-rights date The date on or after which stocks will be traded without subscription rights previously declared.

F

FAC *See* face-amount certificate company.

face-amount certificate company (FAC) An investment company that issues certificates obligating it to pay an investor a stated amount of money (the face amount) on a specific future date. The investor pays into the certificate in periodic payments or in a lump sum.

face value *See* par.

fail to deliver A situation where the broker-dealer on the sell side of a transaction or contract does not deliver the specified securities to the broker-dealer on the buy side. *Syn.* broker fail; fails; fails to deliver; failure to deliver.

fail to receive A situation where the broker-dealer on the buy side of a transaction or contract does not receive the specified securities from the broker-dealer on the sell side. *Syn.* fails; fails to receive; failure to receive.

Fannie Mae *See* Federal National Mortgage Association.

Farm Credit Administration (FCA) The government agency that coordinates the activities of the banks in the Farm Credit System. *Related item(s):* Farm Credit System.

Farm Credit System (FCS) An organization of 37 privately owned banks that provide credit services to farmers and mortgages on farm property. Included in the system are the Federal Land Banks, Federal Intermediate Credit Banks, and Banks for Cooperatives. *Related item(s):* Federal Intermediate Credit Bank.

FCA *See* Farm Credit Administration.

FCO *See* foreign currency option.

FCS *See* Farm Credit System.

FDIC *See* Federal Deposit Insurance Corporation.

Fed *See* Federal Reserve System.

Fed call *See* margin call.

federal call *See* margin call.

Federal Deposit Insurance Corporation (FDIC) The government agency that provides deposit insurance for member banks and prevents bank and thrift failures.

federal funds The reserves of banks and certain other institutions greater than the reserve requirements or excess reserves. These funds are available immediately.

federal funds rate The interest rate charged by one institution lending federal funds to another.

Federal Home Loan Bank (FHLB) A government-regulated organization that operates a credit reserve system for the nation's savings and loan associations.

Federal Home Loan Mortgage Corporation (FHLMC) A publicly traded corporation that promotes the nationwide secondary market in mortgages by issuing mortgage-backed pass-through debt certificates. *Syn.* Freddie Mac.

Federal Intermediate Credit Bank (FICB) One of 12 banks that provide short-term financing to farmers as part of the Farm Credit System.

Federal National Mortgage Association (FNMA) A publicly held corporation that purchases conventional mortgages and mortgages from government agencies, including the Federal Housing Administration, Department of Veterans Affairs, and Farmers Home Administration. *Syn.* Fannie Mae.

Federal Open Market Committee (FOMC) A committee that makes decisions concerning the Fed's operations to control the money supply.

Federal Reserve Board (FRB) A seven-member group that directs the operations of the Federal Reserve System. The President appoints board members, subject to Congressional approval.

Federal Reserve System The central bank system of the United States. Its primary responsibility is to regulate the flow of money and credit.

FHLB *See* Federal Home Loan Bank.

FHLMC *See* Federal Home Loan Mortgage Corporation.

FICB *See* Federal Intermediate Credit Bank.

fictitious quotation A bid or an offer published before being identified by source and verified as legitimate. A fictitious quote may create the appearance of trading activity where none exists; this violates the Conduct Rules.

fidelity bond Insurance coverage required by the self-regulatory organizations for all employees, officers, and partners of member firms to protect clients against acts of lost securities, fraudulent trading, and check forgery. *Syn.* surety bond.

fiduciary A person legally appointed and authorized to hold assets in trust for another person and manage those assets for that person's benefit.

filing *See* registration by filing.

filing date The day on which an issuer submits to the SEC the registration statement for a new securities issue.

fill-or-kill order (FOK) An order that instructs the floor broker to fill the entire order immediately; if the entire order cannot be executed immediately, it is canceled.

final prospectus The legal document that states a new issue security's price, delivery date, and underwriting spread as well as other material information. It must be given to every investor who purchases a new issue of registered securities. *Syn.* prospectus.

Financial Guaranty Insurance Corporation (FGIC) An insurance company that offers insurance on the timely payment of interest and principal on municipal issues and unit investment trusts.

financial risk *See* credit risk.

firewall A descriptive name also referred to as an information barrier for the division within a brokerage firm that prevents insider information from passing from corporate advisers to investment traders, who could make use of the information to reap illicit profits. *Related item(s):* Insider Trading and Securities Fraud Enforcement Act of 1988.

firm commitment underwriting A type of underwriting commitment in which the underwriter agrees to sell an entire new issue of securities. The underwriter acts as a dealer, pays the issuer a lump sum for the securities, and assumes all financial responsibility for any unsold shares. *Related item(s):* underwriting.

firm quote The actual price at which a trading unit of a security (such as 100 shares of stock or five bonds) may be bought or sold. All quotes are firm quotes unless otherwise indicated. *Related item(s):* bona fide quote; nominal quote.

first in, first out (FIFO) An accounting method used to assess a company's inventory, in which it is assumed that the first goods acquired are the first to be sold. The same method is used by the IRS to determine cost basis for tax purposes. *Related item(s):* average basis; last in, first out; share identification.

fiscal policy The federal tax and spending policies set by Congress or the President. These policies affect tax rates, interest rates, and government spending in an effort to control the economy. *Related item(s):* monetary policy.

5% markup policy The guideline for the percentage markups, markdowns, and commissions on securities transactions. The policy is intended to ensure fair and reasonable treatment of the investing public.

fixed annuity An insurance contract in which the insurance company makes fixed dollar payments to the annuitant for the term of the contract, usually until the annuitant dies. The insurance company guarantees both earnings and principal. *Syn.* fixed dollar annuity; guaranteed dollar annuity. *Related item(s):* annuity; variable annuity.

fixed asset A tangible, physical property used in the course of a corporation's everyday operations; it includes buildings, equipment, and land.

fixed charge coverage ratio *See* bond interest coverage ratio.

fixed dollar annuity *See* fixed annuity.

fixed unit investment trust An investment company that invests in a portfolio of securities in which no changes are permissible.

flat A term used to describe bonds traded without accrued interest. They are traded at the agreed-upon market price only. *Related item(s):* accrued interest.

flat yield curve A chart showing the yields of bonds with short maturities as equal to the yields of bonds with long maturities. *Syn.* even yield curve. *Related item(s):* inverted yield curve; normal yield curve; yield curve.

floor broker *See* commission house broker.

floor trader An exchange member who executes transactions from the floor of the exchange only for his own account. *Syn.* local.

flow of funds The schedule of payments disbursed from the proceeds of a facility financed by a revenue bond. The flow of funds determines the order in which the operating expenses, debt service, and other expenses are paid. Typically, the priority is (1) operations and maintenance, (2) debt service, (3) debt service reserve, (4) reserve maintenance, (5) renewal and replacement, (6) surplus. *Related item(s):* debt service reserve fund.

flow-through A term that describes the way income, deductions, and credits resulting from the activities of a business are applied to individual taxes and expenses as though each incurred the income and deductions directly. *Related item(s):* limited partnership.

FNMA *See* Federal National Mortgage Association.

FOK *See* fill-or-kill order.

FOMC *See* Federal Open Market Committee.

forced conversion Market conditions created by a corporation to encourage convertible bondholders to exercise their conversion options. Often conversion is forced by calling the bonds when the market value of the stock is higher than the redemption price offered by the corporation. *Related item(s):* redemption.

forced sell-out The action taken when a customer fails to meet the deadline for paying for securities and no extension has been granted: the broker-dealer must liquidate enough securities to pay for the transaction.

foreign currency Money issued by a country other than the one in which the investor resides. Options and futures contracts on numerous foreign currencies are traded on U.S. exchanges.

foreign currency option (FCO) A security representing the right to buy or sell a specified amount of a foreign currency. *Related item(s):* option.

foreign exchange rate The price of one country's currency in terms of another currency. *Syn.* exchange rate.

foreign fund *See* specialized fund.

Form 10K An annual audited report that covers essentially all the information contained in an issuing company's original registration statement. A Form 10K is due within 90 days of year end.

Form 10Q A quarterly report containing a corporation's unaudited financial data. Certain nonrecurring events that arise during the quarterly period, such as significant litigation, must be reported. A Form 10Q is due 45 days after the end of each of the first three fiscal quarters.

forward pricing The valuation process for mutual fund shares, whereby an order to purchase or redeem shares is executed at the price determined by the portfolio valuation calculated after the order is received. Portfolio valuations occur at least once per business day.

401(k) plan A tax-deferred defined contribution retirement plan offered by an employer.

403(b) plan A tax-deferred annuity retirement plan available to employees of public schools and certain nonprofit organizations.

fourth market The exchange where securities are traded directly from one institutional investor to another without a brokerage firm's services, primarily through ECNs.

fractional share A portion of a whole share of stock. Mutual fund shares are frequently issued in fractional amounts. Fractional shares used to be generated when corporations declared stock dividends, merged, or voted to split stock, but today it is more common for corporations to issue the cash equivalent of fractional shares.

fraud The deliberate concealment, misrepresentation, or omission of material information or the truth to deceive or manipulate another party for unlawful or unfair gain.

FRB *See* Federal Reserve Board.

Freddie Mac *See* Federal Home Loan Mortgage Corporation.

free credit balance The cash funds in customer accounts. Broker-dealers must notify customers of their free credit balances at least quarterly.

freeriding Buying and immediately selling securities without making payment. This practice violates the SEC's Regulation T.

freeriding and withholding The failure of a member participating in the distribution of a hot issue to make a bona fide public offering at the public offering price. This practice violates the Conduct Rules. *Related item(s):* hot issue.

front-end fee The expenses paid for services rendered during a direct participation program's organization or acquisition phase, including front-end organization and offering expenses, acquisition fees and expenses, and any other similar fees designated by the sponsor.

front-end load (1) A mutual fund commission or sales fee that is charged at the time shares are purchased. The load is added to the share's net asset value when calculating the public offering price. *Related item(s):* back-end load.

frozen account An account requiring cash in advance before a buy order is executed and securities in hand before a sell order is executed. An account holder under such restrictions has violated the SEC's Regulation T.

Full Disclosure Act *See* Securities Act of 1933.

full power of attorney A written authorization for someone other than an account's beneficial owner to make deposits and withdrawals and to execute trades in the account. *Related item(s):* limited power of attorney.

full trading authorization An authorization, usually provided by a full power of attorney, for someone other than the customer to have full trading privileges in an account. *Related item(s):* limited trading authorization.

fully registered bond A debt issue that prints the bond-holder's name on the certificate. The issuer's transfer agent maintains the records and sends principal and interest payments directly to the investor. *Related item(s):* registered; registered as to principal only.

functional allocation A sharing arrangement whereby the investors in an oil and gas direct participation program are responsible for intangible costs and the sponsor is responsible for tangible costs; revenues are shared. *Related item(s):* sharing arrangement.

fundamental analysis A method of evaluating securities by attempting to measure the intrinsic value of a particular stock. Fundamental analysts study the overall economy, industry conditions, and the financial condition and management of particular companies. *Related item(s):* technical analysis.

funded debt All long-term debt financing of a corporation.

funding An ERISA guideline stipulating that retirement plan assets must be segregated from other corporate assets.

fund manager *See* portfolio manager.

funds statement The part of a corporation's annual report that analyzes why working capital increased or decreased.

fungible Interchangeable, owing to identical characteristics or value. A security is fungible if it can be substituted or exchanged for another security.

G

GAN *See* grant anticipation note.

GDP *See* gross domestic product.

general account The account that holds all of an insurer's assets other than those in separate accounts. The general account holds the contributions paid for traditional life insurance contracts. *Related item(s):* separate account.

general obligation bond (GO) A municipal debt issue backed by the full faith, credit, and taxing power of the issuer for payment of interest and principal. *Syn.* full faith and credit bond. *Related item(s):* double-barreled bond; revenue bond.

general partner (GP) An active investor in a direct participation program who is personally liable for all debts of the program and who manages the business of the program. The GP's duties include: making decisions that bind the partnership; buying and selling property; managing property and money; supervising all aspects of the business; and maintaining a 1% financial interest in the partnership. *Related item(s):* limited partner.

general partnership (GP) An association of two or more entities formed to conduct a business jointly. The partnership does not require documents for formation, and the general partners are jointly and severally liable for the partnership's liabilities. *Related item(s):* limited partnership.

General Securities Principal *See* Series 24.

General Securities Representative *See* Series 7.

generic advertising Communications with the public that promote securities as investments but that do not refer to particular securities. *Syn.* institutional advertising.

Ginnie Mae *See* Government National Mortgage Association.

Glass-Steagall Act of 1933 Federal legislation that forbids commercial banks to underwrite securities and forbids investment bankers to open deposit accounts or make commercial loans. *Syn.* banking act.

GNMA *See* Government National Mortgage Association.

GNP *See* gross domestic product.

GO *See* general obligation bond.

good delivery A term describing a security that is negotiable, in compliance with the contract of the sale, and ready to be transferred from seller to purchaser.

good faith deposit A deposit contributed by each syndicate involved in a competitive bid underwriting for a municipal issue. The deposit ensures performance by the low bidder. The amount required to be deposited is stipulated in the official notice of sale sent to prospective underwriters; it is usually 2% of the par value.

good til canceled order (GTC) An order that is left on the order book until it is either executed or canceled. *Syn.* open order.

goodwill An intangible asset that represents the value that a firm's business reputation adds to its book value.

Government National Mortgage Association (GNMA) A wholly government-owned corporation that issues pass-through mortgage debt certificates backed by the full faith and credit of the U.S. government. *Syn.* Ginnie Mae.

government security A debt obligation of the U.S. government, backed by its full faith, credit, and taxing power, and regarded as having no risk of default. The government issues short-term Treasury bills, medium-term Treasury notes, and long-term Treasury bonds. *Related item(s):* agency issue.

GP *See* general partner; general partnership.

grant anticipation notes (GANs) Short-term municipal revenue notes issued with the expectation of receiving grant money from the federal government.

green shoe option A provision of an issue's registration statement that allows an underwriter to buy extra shares from the issuer (thus increasing the size of the offering) if public demand proves exceptionally strong. The term derives from the Green Shoe Manufacturing Company, which first used the technique.

gross domestic product (GDP) The total value of goods and services produced in a country during one year. It includes consumption, government purchases, investments, and exports minus imports.

gross income All income of a taxpayer, from whatever source derived.

gross proceeds The total of the initial invested capital in a direct participation program contributed by all of the original and additional limited partners.

gross revenue pledge The flow of funds arrangement in a municipal revenue bond issue indicating that debt service is the first payment to be made from revenues received. The pledge is contained in the trust indenture. *Related item(s):* net revenue pledge.

gross revenues All money received by a business from its operations. The term typically does not include interest income or income from the sale, refinancing, or other disposition of properties.

group net order In a municipal bond underwriting, an order received by a syndicate member that is credited to the entire syndicate. Takedowns on these orders are paid to members according to their participation in the syndicate. *Related item(s):* designated order; member-at-the-takedown order; presale order.

growth development company *See* business development company (BDC).

growth fund A diversified common stock fund that has capital appreciation as its primary goal. It invests in companies that reinvest most of their earnings for expansion, research or development. *Related item(s):* diversified common stock fund; mutual fund.

growth industry An industry that is growing faster than the economy as a whole as a result of technological changes, new products, or changing consumer tastes.

growth stock A relatively speculative issue that is believed to offer significant potential for capital gains. It often pays low dividends and sells at a high price/earnings ratio.

GTC *See* good till canceled order.

guaranteed bond A debt obligation issued with a promise from a corporation other than the issuing corporation to maintain payments of principal and interest.

guaranteed dollar annuity *See* fixed annuity.

guaranteed stock An equity security, generally a preferred stock, issued with a promise from a corporation other than the issuing corporation to maintain dividend payments. The stock still represents ownership in the issuing corporation, but it is considered a dual security.

guardian A fiduciary who manages the assets of a minor or an incompetent for that person's benefit. *Related item(s):* fiduciary.

H

HALT A message on the Consolidated Tape indicating that trading in a particular security has been stopped. *Related item(s):* trading halt.

head and shoulders On a technical analyst's trading chart, a pattern that has three peaks resembling a head and two shoulders. The stock price moves up to its first peak (the left shoulder), drops back, then moves to a higher peak (the top of the head), drops again, but recovers to another, lower peak (the right shoulder). A head and shoulders top typically forms after a substantial rise and indicates a market reversal. A head and shoulders bottom (an inverted head and shoulders) indicates a market advance.

hedge An investment made to reduce the risk of adverse price movements in a security. Normally, a hedge consists of a protecting position in a related security. *Related item(s):* long hedge.

HH savings bond *See* Series HH bond.

high The highest price a security reaches during a specified period of time. *Related item(s):* low.

holder The owner of a security. *Related item(s):* long.

holding company A company organized to invest in and manage other corporations.

holding period A time period signifying how long the owner possesses a security. It starts the day after a purchase and ends on the day of the sale.

hold in street name A securities transaction settlement and delivery procedure whereby a customer's securities are transferred into the broker-dealer's name and held by the broker-dealer. Although the broker-dealer is the nominal owner, the customer is the beneficial owner. *Related item(s):* transfer and hold in safekeeping; transfer and ship.

horizontal spread The purchase and sale of two options on the same underlying security and with the same exercise price but different expiration dates. *Syn.* calendar spread; time spread. *Related item(s):* spread.

hot issue A new issue that sells or is anticipated to sell at a premium over the public offering price. *Related item(s):* freeriding and withholding.

house maintenance call *See* margin maintenance call.

house maintenance requirement *See* margin maintenance requirement.

Housing Authority bond *See* New Housing Authority bond.

HR-10 plan *See* Keogh plan.

hypothecation Pledging to a broker-dealer securities bought on margin as collateral for the margin loan. *Related item(s):* rehypothecation.

I

IDB *See* industrial development bond.

IDC *See* intangible drilling cost.

identified security The particular security designated for sale by an investor holding identical securities with different acquisition dates and cost bases. This allows the investor to control the amount of capital gain or loss incurred through the sale.

IDR *See* industrial development bond.

immediate annuity An insurance contract purchased for a single premium that starts to pay the annuitant immediately following its purchase. *Related item(s):* annuity.

immediate family A parent, mother- or father-in-law, husband or wife, child, sibling, or other relative supported financially by a person associated with the securities industry.

immediate-or-cancel order (IOC) An order that instructs the floor broker to execute it immediately, in full or in part. Any portion of the order that remains unexecuted is canceled.

income bond A debt obligation that promises to repay principal in full at maturity. Interest is paid only if the corporation's earnings are sufficient to meet the interest payment and if the board of directors declares the interest payment. Income bonds are usually traded flat. *Syn.* adjustment bond. *Related item(s):* flat.

income fund A mutual fund that seeks to provide stable current income by investing in securities that pay interest or dividends. *Related item(s):* mutual fund.

income program A limited partnership that buys and markets proven reserves of oil and gas: it buys the value of the oil in the ground. *Related item(s):* developmental drilling program; exploratory drilling program.

income statement The summary of a corporation's revenues and expenses for a specific fiscal period.

index A comparison of current prices to some baseline, such as prices on a particular date. Indexes are frequently used in technical analysis. *Related item(s):* average.

index option A security representing the right to receive in cash the difference between the underlying value of a market index and the strike price of the option. The investor speculates on the direction, degree, and timing of the change in the numerical value of the index. *Related item(s):* capped index option.

indication of interest (IOI) An investor's expression of conditional interest in buying an upcoming securities issue after the investor has reviewed a preliminary prospectus. An indication of interest is not a commitment to buy.

individual retirement account (IRA) A retirement investing tool for employed individuals that allows an annual contribution of 100% of earned income up to a maximum annual allowable limit. Some or all of the contribution may be deductible from current taxes, depending on the individual's adjusted gross income and coverage by employer-sponsored qualified retirement plans. *Related item(s):* Keogh plan; nonqualified retirement plan; qualified retirement plan; simplified employee pension plan.

industrial development bond (IDB) A debt security issued by a municipal authority, which uses the proceeds to finance the construction or purchase of facilities to be leased or purchased by a private company. The bonds are backed by the credit of the private company, which is ultimately responsible for principal and interest payments. *Syn.* industrial revenue bond.

industrial revenue bond (IRB) *See* industrial development bond.

industry fund *See* sector fund.

inflation A persistent and measurable rise in the general level of prices. *Related item(s):* deflation.

inflation risk *See* purchasing power risk.

information barrier A descriptive name also referred to as a "firewall" for the division within a brokerage firm that prevents insider information from passing from corporate advisers to investment traders, who could make use of the information to reap illicit profits. *Related item(s):* Insider Trading and Securities Fraud Enforcement Act of 1988.

informer bounty (award) An award paid in connection for original information concerning any violation of securities law. Under Dodd-Frank legislation, awards may range from 10 to 30 percent of amounts recovered.

initial margin requirement The amount of equity a customer must deposit when making a new purchase in a margin account. The SEC's Regulation T requirement for equity securities is currently 50% of the purchase price. The initial minimum requirement is a deposit of $2,000 but not more than 100% of the purchase price. *Related item(s):* margin; margin call.

initial public offering (IPO) A corporation's first sale of common stock to the public. *Related item(s):* new issue market; public offering.

in-part call The redemption of a certain portion of a bond issue at the request of the issuer. *Related item(s):* in-whole call.

inside information Material information that has not been disseminated to, or is not readily available to, the general public.

inside market The best (highest) bid price at which an OTC stock may be sold, and the best (lowest) ask price at which the same stock may be bought in the interdealer market. *Related item(s)*: affiliate; control person.

insider Any person who possesses or has access to material nonpublic information about a corporation. Insiders include directors, officers, and stockholders who own at least 10% of any class of equity security of a corporation.

Insider Trading Act *See* Insider Trading and Securities Fraud Enforcement Act of 1988.

Insider Trading and Securities Fraud Enforcement Act of 1988 Legislation that defines what constitutes the illicit use of nonpublic information in making securities trades and the liabilities and penalties that apply. *Syn.* Insider Trading Act. *Related item(s)*: Chinese wall; insider.

institutional account An account held for the benefit of others. Examples of institutional accounts include banks, trusts, pension and profit-sharing plans, mutual funds, and insurance companies.

institutional communication FINRA defines this category of communications with the public as any written (including electronic) communication that is distributed or made available only to institutional investors, but does not include a member's internal communications (i.e., internal memos).

institutional investor A person or organization that trades securities in large enough share quantities or dollar amounts that it qualifies for preferential treatment such as lower commissions. Institutional investors are covered by fewer protective regulations because it is assumed that they are more knowledgeable and better able to protect themselves. Examples would include another member firm, bank or savings and loan, insurance company, registered investment company, government entity, or any entity with $50 million or more in total assets.

insurance covenant A provision of a municipal revenue bond's trust indenture that helps ensure the safety of the issue by promising to insure the facilities built. *Related item(s)*: maintenance covenant; rate covenant.

intangible asset A property owned that is not physical, such as a formula, a copyright, or goodwill. *Related item(s)*: goodwill.

intangible drilling cost (IDC) In an oil and gas limited partnership, a tax-deductible cost; usually this is for a nonphysical asset, such as labor or fuel, which does not depreciate. The cost may be expensed in the year incurred, or deductions may be amortized over the life of the well. *Syn.* intangible drilling development expense.

intangible drilling development expense *See* intangible drilling cost.

interbank market An unregulated, decentralized, international market in which the various major currencies of the world are traded.

interest The charge for the privilege of borrowing money, usually expressed as an annual percentage rate.

interest coverage ratio *See* bond interest coverage ratio.

interest rate option A security representing the right to buy or sell government debt securities. The federal deficit has created a large market in securities that are sensitive to changes in interest rates; the investor can profit from fluctuations in interest rates and can hedge the risks created by the fluctuations.

interest rate risk The risk associated with investments relating to the sensitivity of price or value to fluctuation in the current level of interest rates; also, the risk that involves the competitive cost of money. This term is generally associated with bond prices, but it applies to all investments. In bonds, prices carry interest risk because, if bond prices rise, outstanding bonds will not remain competitive unless their yields and prices adjust to reflect the current market.

Internal Revenue Code (IRC) The legislation that defines tax liabilities and deductions for U.S. taxpayers.

Internal Revenue Service (IRS) The U.S. government agency responsible for collecting most federal taxes and for administering tax rules and regulations.

interstate offering An issue of securities registered with the SEC sold to residents of states other than the state in which the issuer does business.

in the money The term used to describe an option that has intrinsic value, such as a call option when the stock is selling above the exercise price or a put option when the stock is selling below the exercise price. *Related item(s)*: at the money; intrinsic value; out of the money.

intrastate offering An issue of securities exempt from SEC registration, available to companies that do business in one state and sell their securities only to residents of that same state. *Related item(s)*: Rule 147.

intrinsic value The potential profit to be made from exercising an option. A call option is said to have intrinsic value when the underlying stock is trading above the exercise price. *Related item(s)*: time value.

inverted yield curve A chart showing long-term debt instruments having lower yields than short-term debt instruments. *Syn.* negative yield curve. *Related item(s)*: flat yield curve; normal yield curve.

invested capital *See* capitalization.

investment adviser (1) Any person who makes investment recommendations in return for a flat fee or a percentage of assets managed. (2) For an investment company, the individual who bears the day-to-day responsibility of investing the cash and securities held in the fund's portfolio in accordance with objectives stated in the fund's prospectus.

Investment Advisers Act of 1940 Legislation governing who must register with the SEC as an investment adviser. *Related item(s):* investment adviser.

investment banker An institution in the business of raising capital for corporations and municipalities. An investment banker may not accept deposits or make commercial loans. *Syn.* investment bank.

investment banking business A broker, dealer, or municipal or government securities dealer that underwrites or distributes new issues of securities as a dealer or that buys and sells securities for the accounts of others as a broker. *Syn.* investment securities business.

investment company A company engaged in the business of pooling investors' money and trading in securities for them. Examples include face-amount certificate companies, unit investment trusts, and management companies.

Investment Company Act of 1940 Congressional legislation regulating companies that invest and reinvest in securities. The act requires an investment company engaged in interstate commerce to register with the SEC.

investment grade security A security to which the rating services (e.g., Standard & Poor's and Moody's) have assigned a rating of BBB/Baa or above.

investment objective Any goal a client hopes to achieve through investing. Examples include current income, capital growth, and preservation of capital.

investment pyramid A portfolio strategy that allocates investable assets according to an investment's relative safety. The pyramid base is composed of low-risk investments, the middle portion is composed of growth investments, and the pyramid top is composed of speculative investments.

investment value The market price at which a convertible security (usually a debenture) would sell if it were not converted into common stock. *Related item(s):* conversion value; convertible bond; debenture.

investor The purchaser of an asset or security with the intent of profiting from the transaction.

invitation for bids A notice to securities underwriters soliciting bids for the issuing of a bond issue. These notices are published in *The Bond Buyer*, newspapers, and journals.

in-whole call The redemption of a bond issue in its entirety at the option of the issuer, as opposed to its redemption based on a lottery held by an independent trustee. *Related item(s):* in-part call.

IOC *See* immediate-or-cancel order.

IOI *See* indication of interest.

IPO *See* initial public offering.

IRA *See* individual retirement account.

IRA rollover The reinvestment of assets that an individual receives as a distribution from a qualified tax-deferred retirement plan into an individual retirement account within 60 days of receiving the distribution. The individual may reinvest either the entire sum or a portion of the sum, although any portion not reinvested is taxed as ordinary income. *Related item(s):* individual retirement account; IRA transfer.

IRA transfer The direct reinvestment of retirement assets from one qualified tax-deferred retirement plan to an individual retirement account. The account owner never takes possession of the assets, but directs that they be transferred directly from the existing plan custodian to the new plan custodian. *Related item(s):* individual retirement account; IRA rollover.

IRC *See* Internal Revenue Code.

irrevocable stock power *See* stock power.

issued stock Equity securities authorized by the issuer's registration statement and distributed to the public. *Related item(s):* outstanding stock; treasury stock.

issuer The entity, such as a corporation or municipality, that offers or proposes to offer its securities for sale.

J

joint account An account in which two or more individuals possess some form of control over the account and may transact business in the account. The account must be designated as either tenants in common or joint tenants with right of survivorship. *Related item(s):* tenants in common; joint tenants with right of survivorship.

joint life with last survivor An annuity payout option that covers two or more people, with annuity payments continuing as long as one of the annuitants remains alive.

joint tenants with right of survivorship (JTWROS) A form of joint ownership of an account whereby a deceased tenant's fractional interest in the account passes to the surviving tenant(s). It is used almost exclusively by husbands and wives. *Related item(s):* tenants in common.

joint venture The cooperation of two or more individuals or enterprises in a specific business enterprise rather than in a continuing relationship—as in a partnership.

JTWROS *See* joint tenants with right of survivorship.

junior lien debt A bond backed by the same collateral backing a previous issue and having a subordinate claim to the collateral in the event of default. *Related item(s):* closed-end covenant; open-end covenant.

K

Keogh plan A qualified tax-deferred retirement plan for persons who are self-employed and unincorporated or who earn extra income through personal services aside from their regular employment. *Syn.* HR-10 plan. *Related item(s):* individual retirement account; nonqualified retirement plan; qualified retirement plan.

Keynesian economics The theory that active government intervention in the marketplace is the best method of ensuring economic growth and stability.

know your customer rule *See* Rule 405.

L

lagging indicator A measurable economic factor that changes after the economy has started to follow a particular pattern or trend. Lagging indicators are believed to confirm long-term trends. Examples include average duration of unemployment, corporate profits, and labor cost per unit of output. *Related item(s):* coincident indicator; leading indicator.

last in, first out (LIFO) An accounting method used to assess a corporation's inventory in which it is assumed that the last goods acquired are the first to be sold. The method is used to determine cost basis for tax purposes; the IRS designates last in, first out as the order in which sales or withdrawals from an investment are made. *Related item(s):* average basis; first in, first out; share identification.

leading indicator A measurable economic factor that changes before the economy starts to follow a particular pattern or trend. Leading indicators are believed to predict changes in the economy. Examples include new orders for durable goods, slowdowns in deliveries by vendors, and numbers of building permits issued. *Related item(s):* coincident indicator; lagging indicator.

LEAPS *See* long-term equity option.

lease rental bond A debt security issued by a municipal authority to raise funds for new construction with the understanding that the finished structure will be rented to the authority and that the rental payments will finance the bond payments.

legal list The selection of securities that a state agency (usually a state banking or insurance commission) determines to be appropriate investments for fiduciary accounts, such as mutual savings banks, pension funds, and insurance companies.

legal opinion of counsel The statement of a bond attorney affirming that an issue is a municipal issue and that interest is exempt from federal taxation. Each municipal bond certificate must be accompanied by a legal opinion of counsel. *Related item(s):* ex-legal; qualified legal opinion; unqualified legal opinion.

legislative risk The potential for an investor to be adversely affected by changes in investment or tax laws.

letter of intent (LOI) A signed agreement allowing an investor to buy mutual fund shares at a lower overall sales charge, based on the total dollar amount of the intended investment. A letter of intent is valid only if the investor completes the terms of the agreement within 13 months of signing the agreement. A letter of intent may be backdated 90 days. *Syn.* statement of intention.

level debt service A schedule for debt repayment whereby principal and interest payments remain essentially constant from year to year over the life of the issue. *Related item(s):* decreasing debt service.

level load A mutual fund sales fee charged annually based on the net asset value of a share. A 12b-1 asset-based fee is an example of a level load. *Related item(s):* back-end load; Class C share; Class D share; front-end load.

Level One The basic level of Nasdaq service; through a desktop quotation machine, it provides registered representatives with up-to-the-minute inside bid and ask quotations on hundreds of over-the-counter stocks. *Related item(s):* National Association of Securities Dealers Automated Quotation System.

Level Three The highest level of Nasdaq service; through a desktop quotation machine, it provides up-to-the-minute inside bid and ask quotations, supplies the bids and askeds of each market maker for a security, and allows each market maker to enter changes in those quotations. *Related item(s):* National Association of Securities Dealers Automated Quotation System.

Level Two The second level of Nasdaq service; through a desktop quotation machine, it provides up-to-the-minute inside bid and ask quotations and the bids and askeds of each market maker for a security. *Related item(s):* National Association of Securities Dealers Automated Quotation System.

leverage Using borrowed capital to increase investment return. *Syn.* trading on the equity.

liability A legal obligation to pay a debt owed. Current liabilities are debts payable within 12 months. Long-term liabilities are debts payable over a period of more than 12 months.

LIBOR *See* London Interbank Offered Rate.

life annuity/straight life An annuity payout option that pays a monthly check over the annuitant's lifetime.

life annuity with period certain An annuity payout option that guarantees the annuitant a monthly check for a certain period and thereafter until the annuitant's death. If the annuitant dies before the period expires, the payments go to the annuitant's named beneficiary.

life contingency An annuity payout option that provides a death benefit during the accumulation stage. If the annuitant dies during this period, a full contribution is made to the account, which is paid to the annuitant's named beneficiary.

LIFO *See* last in, first out.

limited liability An investor's right to limit potential losses to no more than the amount invested. Equity shareholders, such as corporate stockholders and limited partners, have limited liability.

limited partner (LP) An investor in a direct participation program who does not participate in the management or control of the program and whose liability for partnership debts is limited to the amount invested in the program. *Related item(s):* general partner; participant; passive investor.

limited partnership (LP) An association of two or more partners formed to conduct a business jointly and in which one or more of the partners is liable only to the extent of the amount of money invested. Limited partners do not receive dividends but enjoy direct flow-through of income and expenses. *Related item(s):* flow-through; general partnership.

limited partnership agreement The contract between a partnership's limited and general partners that provides the guidelines for partnership operation and states the rights and responsibilities of each partner.

limited power of attorney A written authorization for someone other than an account's beneficial owner to make certain investment decisions regarding transactions in the account. *Related item(s):* discretion; full power of attorney.

limited tax bond A general obligation municipal debt security issued by a municipality whose taxing power is limited to a specified maximum rate.

limited trading authorization An authorization, usually provided by a limited power of attorney, for someone other than the customer to have trading privileges in an account. These privileges are limited to purchases and sales; withdrawal of assets is not authorized. *Related item(s):* full trading authorization.

limit order An order that instructs the floor broker to buy a specified security below a certain price or to sell a specified security above a certain price. *Syn.* or better order. *Related item(s):* stop limit order; stop order.

limit order book *See* specialist's book.

liquidation priority In the case of a corporation's liquidation, the order that is strictly followed for paying off creditors and stockholders:

1. Unpaid wages
2. Taxes
3. Secured claims (mortgages)
4. Secured liabilities (bonds)
5. Unsecured liabilities (debentures) and general creditors
6. Subordinated debt
7. Preferred stockholders
8. Common stockholders

liquidity The ease with which an asset may be converted to cash in the marketplace. A large number of buyers and sellers and a high volume of trading activity provide high liquidity.

liquidity ratio A measure of a corporation's ability to meet its current obligations. The ratio compares current assets to current liabilities. *Related item(s):* acid-test ratio; current ratio.

liquidity risk The potential that an investor might not be able to sell an investment as and when desired. *Syn.* marketability risk.

listed option An option contract that may be bought and sold on a national securities exchange in a continuous secondary market. Listed options carry standardized strike prices and expiration dates. *Syn.* standardized option. *Related item(s):* OTC option.

listed security A stock, a bond, or another security that satisfies certain minimum requirements and is traded on a regional or national securities exchange such as the New York Stock Exchange.

LMV *See* current market value.

loan consent agreement An optional contract between a brokerage firm and a margin customer that permits the firm to lend the margined securities to other brokers; the contract is part of the margin agreement. *Syn.* consent to lend agreement.

locked market The situation created when there is no spread between the bid and the ask on the same security; that is, one market maker bids for a stock at the same price that another market maker quotes its ask price. This violates the Conduct Rules. *Related item(s):* crossed market.

LOI *See* letter of intent.

London Interbank Offered Rate (LIBOR) The average of the interbank-offered interest rates for dollar deposits in the London market, based on the quotations at five major banks.

long The term used to describe the owning of a security, contract, or commodity. For example, a common stock owner is said to have a long position in the stock. *Related item(s):* short.

long hedge Buying puts as protection against a decline in the value of a long securities or actuals position. *Related item(s):* hedge.

long market value (LMV) *See* current market value.

long straddle An option investor's position that results from buying a call and a put on the same stock with the same exercise price and expiration month. *Related item(s):* short straddle; spread; straddle.

long-term equity option An option contract that has a longer expiration than traditional equity option contracts. The most common long-term equity option is the CBOE's long-term equity anticipation security (LEAPS).

long-term gain The profit earned on the sale of a capital asset that has been owned for more than 12 months. *Related item(s):* capital gain; capital loss; long-term loss.

long-term loss The loss realized on the sale of a capital asset that has been owned for more than 12 months. *Related item(s):* capital gain; capital loss; long-term gain.

loss carryover A capital loss incurred during one tax year that is carried over to the next year or later years for use as a capital loss deduction. *Related item(s):* capital loss.

low The lowest price a security or commodity reaches during a specified period. *Related item(s):* high.

LP *See* limited partner; limited partnership.

M

M1 A category of the money supply that includes all coins, currency, and demand deposits (i.e., checking accounts and NOW accounts). *Related item(s):* M2; M3; money supply.

M2 A category of the money supply that includes M1 in addition to all time deposits, savings deposits, and non-institutional money market funds. *Related item(s):* M1; M3; money supply.

M3 A category of the money supply that includes M2 in addition to all large time deposits, institutional money market funds, short-term repurchase agreements, and certain other large liquid assets. *Related item(s):* M1; M2; money supply.

maintenance call *See* margin maintenance call.

maintenance covenant A provision of a municipal revenue bond's trust indenture that helps ensure the safety of the issue by promising to keep the facility and equipment in good working order. *Related item(s):* insurance covenant; rate covenant.

maintenance requirement *See* margin maintenance requirement.

Major Market Index (MMI) A market indicator designed to track the Dow Jones industrials. It is composed of 15 of the 30 Dow Jones industrials and five other large NYSE-listed stocks. *Related item(s):* index.

make a market To stand ready to buy or sell a particular security as a dealer for its own account. A market maker accepts the risk of holding the position in the security. *Related item(s):* market maker.

managed underwriting An arrangement between the issuer of a security and an investment banker in which the banker agrees to form an underwriting syndicate to bring the security to the public. The syndicate manager then directs the entire underwriting process.

management company An investment company that trades various types of securities in a portfolio in accordance with specific objectives stated in the prospectus. *Related item(s):* closed-end management company; diversified management company; mutual fund; nondiversified management company.

management fee The payment to the sponsor of a direct participation program for managing and administering the program. The fee is capped at about 5% of the program's gross revenues.

manager of the syndicate *See* underwriting manager.

managing partner The general partner of a direct participation program that selects the investments and operates the partnership.

managing underwriter *See* underwriting manager.

mandatory call The redemption of a bond by an issuer authorized in the trust indenture and based on a predetermined schedule or event. *Related item(s):* catastrophe call; partial call.

margin The amount of equity contributed by a customer as a percentage of the current market value of the securities held in a margin account. *Related item(s):* equity; initial margin requirement; margin call; Regulation T.

margin account A customer account in which a brokerage firm lends the customer part of the purchase price of securities. *Related item(s):* cash account; Regulation T.

margin call The Federal Reserve Board's demand that a customer deposit a specified amount of money or securities when a purchase is made in a margin account; the amount is expressed as a percentage of the market value of the securities at the time of purchase. The deposit must be made within one payment period. *Syn.* Fed call; federal call; federal margin; Reg T call; T call. *Related item(s):* initial margin requirement; margin.

margin deficiency *See* margin maintenance requirement.

margin department The department within a brokerage firm that computes the amount of money clients must deposit in margin and cash accounts. *Syn.* credit department.

margin excess *See* excess equity.

margin maintenance call A demand that a margin customer deposit money or securities when the customer's equity falls below the margin maintenance requirement set by the broker-dealer or the SRO the broker dealer reports to. *Syn.* house maintenance call; maintenance call; FINRA maintenance call.

margin maintenance requirement The minimum equity that must be held in a margin account, determined by the broker-dealer and by the SRO the broker-dealer reports to. The amount of equity required varies with the type of security bought on margin, and the broker-dealer's house requirement is usually higher than that set by the SRO. *Syn.* house maintenance requirement; maintenance requirement; FINRA maintenance requirement.

margin risk The potential that a margin customer will be required to deposit additional cash if his security positions are subject to adverse price movements.

margin security A security that is eligible for purchase on margin, including any registered security, OTC margin stock or bond, or Nasdaq Global Select or Global Market security. A firm is permitted to lend money to help customers purchase these securities and may accept these securities as collateral for margin purchases. *Syn.* eligible security. *Related item(s):* nonmargin security; OTC margin security.

markdown The difference between the highest current bid price among dealers and the lower price that a dealer pays to a customer.

marketability The ease with which a security may be bought or sold; having a readily available market for trading.

market letter A publication that comments on securities, investing, the economy, or other related topics and is distributed to an organization's clients or to the public. *Related item(s):* sales literature.

market maker A dealer willing to accept the risk of holding a particular security in its own account to facilitate trading in that security. *Related item(s):* make a market.

market NH *See* not held order.

market not held order *See* not held order.

market-on-close order An order that specifies it is to be executed at the close. The order will be executed at the closing price. *Syn.* at-the-close order. *Related item(s):* at-the-opening order.

market order An order to be executed immediately at the best available price. A market order is the only order that guarantees execution. *Syn.* unrestricted order.

market-out clause The standard provision of a firm commitment underwriting agreement that relieves the underwriter of its obligation to underwrite the issue under circumstances that impair the investment quality of the securities.

market risk The potential for an investor to experience losses owing to day-to-day fluctuations in the prices at which securities may be bought or sold. *Related item(s):* systemic risk.

market value The price at which investors buy or sell a share of common stock or a bond at a given time. Market value is determined by buyers' and sellers' interaction. *Related item(s):* current market value.

mark to market To adjust the value of the securities in an account to the current market value of those securities; used to calculate the market value and equity in a margin account.

markup The difference between the lowest current offering price among dealers and the higher price a dealer charges a customer.

markup policy A guideline for reasonable markups, markdowns, and commissions for secondary transactions. According to the policy, all commissions on broker transactions and all markups or markdowns on principal transactions should be fair and reasonable for a particular transaction.

married put The simultaneous purchase of a stock and a put on that stock specifically identified as a hedge.

material information Any fact that could affect an investor's decision to trade a security.

maturity date The date on which a bond's principal is repaid to the investor and interest payments cease. *Related item(s):* par; principal.

maximum loan value The percentage of market value a broker-dealer is permitted to lend a margin customer for the purchase of securities. Loan value is equal to the complement of the Regulation T requirement: if Reg T were 65%, the maximum loan value would be 35%. *Syn.* loan value.

maximum market value The market value to which a short sale position may advance before a margin maintenance call is issued. Maximum market value is set by the SRO the broker-dealer reports to and currently equals the credit balance divided by 130%. *Syn.* maximum short market value.

member-at-the-takedown order In a municipal bond underwriting, a customer order submitted by one syndicate member who will receive the entire takedown. Member-at-the-takedown orders receive the lowest priority when the securities of the issue are allocated. *Syn.* member order. *Related item(s):* designated order; group net order; presale order.

member firm A broker-dealer in which at least one of the principal officers is a member of an exchange, a self-regulatory organization or a clearing corporation.

member order *See* member-at-the takedown order.

mini-max underwriting A form of best efforts underwriting in which the issuer sets a floor and a ceiling on the amount of securities to be sold. *Related item(s):* underwriting.

mini-options Option contracts that overlay only 10 shares of the underlying security instead of 100 shares as is the case for standard options contracts.

minimum increment price rule Under SEC Regulation NMS, this rule sets the minimum price increments for stocks depending on their current price. *Related item(s):* sub-penny price.

minimum margin requirement *See* margin maintenance requirement.

minor rule violation (MRV) In instances where the Department of Enforcement considers a violation minor and the respondent does not dispute the allegation, the Department of Enforcement may prepare and request that the respondent sign an MRV letter, accepting a finding of violation. Once the respondent signs an MRV letter, the settlement is final.

minus tick A security transaction's execution price that is below the previous execution price, by a minimum amount. *Syn.* down tick. *Related item(s):* plus tick; tick; zero-minus tick.

modern portfolio theory (MPT) A method of choosing investments that focuses on the importance of the relationships among all of the investments in a portfolio rather than the individual merits of each investment. The method allows investors to quantify and control the amount of risk they accept and return they achieve.

monetarist theory An economic theory holding that the money supply is the major determinant of price levels and that, therefore, a well-controlled money supply will have the most beneficial impact on the economy.

monetary policy The Federal Reserve Board's actions that determine the size and rate of the money supply's growth, which, in turn, affect interest rates. *Related item(s):* fiscal policy.

money laundering The act of cleaning money gotten from illegitimate businesses through three stages known as placement, layering, and integration for the purpose of hiding its origin in anticipation of its later use for both legitimate and illegitimate purposes.

money market The securities market that deals in short-term debt. Money market instruments are liquid forms of debt that mature in less than one year. Treasury bills make up the bulk of money market instruments.

money market fund A mutual fund that invests in short-term debt instruments. The fund's objective is to earn interest while maintaining a stable net asset value of $1 per share. Generally sold with no load, the fund may also offer draft-writing privileges and low opening investments. *Related item(s):* mutual fund.

money supply The total stock of bills, coins, loans, credit, and other liquid instruments in the economy. It is divided into four categories—L, M1, M2, and M3—according to the type of account in which the instrument is kept. *Related item(s):* M1; M2; M3.

Moody's Investors Service One of the best known investment rating agencies in the United States. A subsidiary of Dun & Bradstreet, Moody's rates bonds, commercial paper, preferred and common stocks, and municipal short-term issues. *Related item(s):* bond rating; Standard & Poor's Corporation.

moral obligation bond A municipal revenue bond for which a state legislature has the authority, but no legal obligation, to appropriate money in the event the issuer defaults.

mortgage bond A debt obligation secured by a property pledge. It represents a lien or mortgage against the issuing corporation's properties and real estate assets.

moving average chart A tool used by technical analysts to track the price movements of a commodity. It plots average daily settlement prices over a defined period (e.g., over three days for a three-day moving average). *Related item(s):* bar chart; point-and-figure chart.

MSRB *See* Municipal Securities Rulemaking Board.

multiplier effect The expansion of the money supply that results from a Federal Reserve System member bank's being able to lend more money than it takes in. A small increase in bank deposits generates a far larger increase in available credit.

municipal bond A debt security issued by a state, a municipality, or another subdivision (such as a school, a park, or a sanitation or other local taxing district) to finance its capital expenditures. Such expenditures might include the construction of highways, public works, or school buildings. *Syn.* municipal security.

municipal bond fund A mutual fund that invests in municipal bonds and operates either as a unit investment trust or as an open-end fund. The fund's objective is to maximize federally tax-exempt income. *Related item(s):* mutual fund; unit investment trust.

municipal note A short-term municipal security issued in anticipation of funds from another source. *Related item(s):* municipal security.

Municipal Securities Rulemaking Board (MSRB) A self-regulatory organization that regulates the issuance and trading of municipal securities. The Board functions under the Securities and Exchange Commission's supervision; it has no enforcement powers. *Related item(s):* Securities Acts Amendments of 1975.

municipal security *See* municipal bond.

mutual fund An investment company that continuously offers new equity shares in an actively managed portfolio of securities. All shareholders participate in the fund's gains or losses. The shares are redeemable on any business day at the net asset value. Each mutual fund's portfolio is invested to match the objective stated in the prospectus. *Syn.* open-end investment company; open-end management company. *Related item(s):* asset allocation fund; balanced fund; net asset value.

mutual fund custodian A national bank, a stock exchange member firm, a trust company, or another qualified institution that physically safeguards the securities a mutual fund holds. It does not manage the fund's investments; its function is solely clerical.

N

naked The position of an option investor who writes a call or a put on a security he does not own. *Syn.* uncovered.

naked call writer An investor who writes a call option without owning the underlying stock or other related assets that would enable the investor to deliver the stock should the option be exercised. *Syn.* uncovered call writer. *Related item(s):* naked put writer.

naked put writer An investor who writes a put option without owning the underlying stock or other related assets that would enable the investor to purchase the stock should the option be exercised. *Syn.* uncovered put writer. *Related item(s):* naked call writer.

narrow-based index An index that is designed to reflect the movement of a market segment, such as a group of stocks in one industry or a specific type of investment. Examples include the Technology Index and the Gold/Silver Index. *Related item(s):* broad-based index; index.

Nasdaq *See* National Association of Securities Dealers Automated Quotation system.

Nasdaq Capital Market (formerly the Nasdaq SmallCap Market) The new name better reflects the capitalization of the issuers included in this market tier. Of the three Nasdaq market tiers, this market has the least stringent listing requirements.

Nasdaq Global Market (formerly the Nasdaq National Market) The largest of the three Nasdaq market tiers was renamed to better reflect the global nature of the securities included. These OTC stocks have high interest and appeal.

Nasdaq Global Select Market This market tier, the newest for Nasdaq, has initial listing standards, both financial and with regard to liquidity, that are among the highest of any other market.

Nasdaq 100 An index of the largest 100 nonfinancial stocks on Nasdaq, weighted according to capitalization.

National Association of Securities Dealers Automated Quotation system (Nasdaq) The nationwide electronic quotation system for up-to-the-minute bid and asked quotations on approximately 5,500 over-the-counter stocks.

National Market System (Regulation NMS) A broad sweeping SEC regulation designed to bring trading and reporting uniformity to U.S. securities markets. *Related item(s):* order protection rule; minimum increment price rule.

National Public Finance Guarantee A public corporation offering insurance as to the timely payment of principal and interest on qualified municipal issues (formerly Municipal Bond Investors Assurance Corp.—MBIA). Nonrated issues with insurance are implied to be rated AAA.

National Securities Clearing Corporation (NSCC) An organization that acts as a medium through which member brokerage firms and exchanges reconcile accounts with each other.

NAV *See* net asset value.

NAV of fund The net total of a mutual fund's assets and liabilities; used to calculate the price of new fund shares.

NAV per share The value of a mutual fund share, calculated by dividing the fund's total net asset value by the number of shares outstanding.

negotiability A characteristic of a security that permits the owner to assign, give, transfer, or sell it to another person without a third party's permission.

negotiable certificate of deposit (CD) An unsecured promissory note issued with a minimum face value of $100,000. It evidences a time deposit of funds with the issuing bank and is guaranteed by the bank.

negotiated underwriting A form of underwriting agreement in which a brokerage firm consults with the issuer to determine the most suitable price and timing of a forthcoming securities offering. *Related item(s):* competitive bid underwriting.

net asset value (NAV) A mutual fund share's value, calculated once a day, based on the closing market price for each security in the fund's portfolio. It is computed by deducting the fund's liabilities from the portfolio's total assets and dividing this amount by the number of shares outstanding. *Related item(s):* mutual fund.

net change The difference between a security's closing price on the trading day reported and the previous day's closing price. In over-the-counter transactions, the term refers to the difference between the closing bids.

net current asset value per share The calculation of book value per share that excludes all fixed assets. *Related item(s):* book value per share.

net debt per capita A measure of the ability of a municipality to meet its debt obligations; it compares the debt issued by the municipality to its property values.

net debt to assessed valuation A measure of the financial condition of a municipality; it compares the municipality's debt obligations to the assessed value of its property. *Related item(s):* net debt to estimated valuation.

net debt to estimated valuation A measure of the financial condition of a municipality; it compares the municipality's debt obligations to the estimated value of its property. *Related item(s):* net debt to assessed valuation.

net direct debt The amount of debt obligations of a municipality, including general obligation bonds and notes and short-term notes. Self-supported debt from revenue bond issues is not included in the calculation.

net domestic product A measure of the annual economic output of a nation adjusted to account for depreciation. It is calculated by subtracting the amount of depreciation from the gross domestic product. *Related item(s):* gross domestic product.

net fixed assets per bond A measure of a bond's safety; it is a conservative measure because it excludes intangible assets, working capital, and accumulated depreciation.

net income to net sales *See* net profit ratio.

net interest cost (NIC) A means of evaluating the competitive bids of prospective bond underwriting syndicates. It calculates the coupon interest to be paid by the issuer over the life of the bond. *Related item(s):* true interest cost.

net investment income The source of an investment company's dividend payments. It is calculated by subtracting the company's operating expenses from the total dividends and interest the company receives from the securities in its portfolio.

net investment return The rate of return from a variable life insurance separate account. The cumulative return for all years is applied to the benefit base when calculating the death benefit.

net operating profits interest A sharing arrangement in an oil and gas direct participation program whereby the general partner bears none of the program's costs but is entitled to a percentage of profits after all royalties and operating expenses have been paid. *Related item(s):* sharing arrangement.

net proceeds The amount of money received from a direct participation program offering less expenses incurred, such as selling commissions, syndicate fees, and organizational costs.

net profit margin *See* net profit ratio.

net profit ratio A measure of a corporation's relative profitability. It is calculated by dividing aftertax income by net sales. *Syn.* net income to net sales; net profit margin; net profits to sales; profit after taxes; profit ratio.

net profits to sales *See* net profit ratio.

net revenue pledge The flow of funds arrangement in a municipal revenue bond issue pledging that operating and maintenance expenses will be paid before debt service. The pledge is contained in the trust indenture. *Related item(s):* gross revenue pledge.

net tangible assets per share *See* book value per share.

net total debt The sum of the debt obligations of a municipality, calculated by adding the municipality's net direct debt to its overlapping debt. *Related item(s):* net direct debt; overlapping debt.

Network A A Consolidated Tape reporting system that provides subscribers with information on transactions in NYSE-listed securities. *Related item(s):* Consolidated Tape.

Network B A Consolidated Tape reporting system that provides subscribers with information on transactions in regional exchange-listed securities. *Related item(s):* Consolidated Tape.

net worth The amount by which assets exceed liabilities. *Syn.* owners' equity; shareholders' equity; stockholders' equity.

new account form The form that must be filled out for each new account opened with a brokerage firm. The form specifies, at a minimum, the account owner, trading authorization, payment method, and types of securities appropriate for the customer.

new construction program A real estate direct participation program that aims to provide capital appreciation from building new property.

New Housing Authority bond (NHA) A municipal special revenue bond backed by the U.S. government and issued by a local public housing authority to develop and improve low-income housing. *Syn.* Housing Authority bond; Public Housing Authority bond.

new issue market The securities market for shares in privately owned businesses that are raising capital by selling common stock to the public for the first time. *Syn.* primary market. *Related item(s):* initial public offering; secondary market.

New Issues Act *See* Securities Act of 1933.

New York Stock Exchange (NYSE) The largest stock exchange in the United States.

New York Stock Exchange Composite Index Index of common stocks listed on the NYSE, based on the price of each stock weighted by its total value of shares outstanding. *Syn.* NYSE Index.

NH *See* not held order.

NHA *See* New Housing Authority bond.

NIC *See* net interest cost.

no-load fund A mutual fund whose shares are sold without a commission or sales charge. The investment company distributes the shares directly. *Related item(s):* mutual fund; net asset value; sales load.

nominal owner The person in whose name securities are registered if that person is other than the beneficial owner. This is a brokerage firm's role when customer securities are registered in street name.

nominal quote A quotation on an inactively traded security that does not represent an actual offer to buy or sell, but is given for informational purposes only. *Related item(s):* bona fide quote; firm quote.

nominal yield The interest rate stated on the face of a bond that represents the percentage of interest the issuer pays on the bond's face value. *Syn.* coupon rate; stated yield. *Related item(s):* bond yield.

nonaccredited investor An investor not meeting the net worth requirements of Regulation D. Nonaccredited investors are counted for purposes of the 35-investor limitation for Regulation D private placements. *Related item(s):* accredited investor; private placement; Regulation D.

nonaffiliate A buyer of an unregistered public offering security who has no management or major ownership interest in the company being acquired. Nonaffiliates may sell this stock only after a specified holding period.

noncompetitive bid An order placed for Treasury bills in which the investor agrees to pay stop out price and, in return, is guaranteed that the order will be filled.

noncumulative preferred stock An equity security that does not have to pay any dividends in arrears to the holder. *Related item(s):* convertible preferred stock; cumulative preferred stock; preferred stock.

nondiscrimination In a qualified retirement plan, a formula for calculating contributions and benefits that must be applied uniformly so as to ensure that all employees receive fair and equitable treatment. *Related item(s):* qualified retirement plan.

nondiversified investment company A management company that does not meet the diversification requirements of the Investment Company Act of 1940. These companies are not restricted in the choice of securities or by the concentration of interest they have in those securities. *Related item(s)*: diversified investment company; management company; mutual fund.

nonequity option A security representing the right to buy or sell an investment instrument other than a common stock at a specified price within a specified period. Examples of such investment instruments include foreign currencies, indexes, and interest rates. *Related item(s)*: equity option; foreign currency option; index option; interest rate option; option.

nonmargin security A security that must be purchased in a cash account, that must be paid for in full, and that may not be used as collateral for a loan. Examples include put and call options, rights, insurance contracts, and new issues. *Related item(s)*: margin security.

nonqualified retirement plan A corporate retirement plan that does not meet the standards set by the Employee Retirement Income Security Act of 1974. Contributions to a nonqualified plan are not tax deductible. *Related item(s)*: qualified retirement plan.

nonrecourse financing Debt incurred for the purchase of an asset that pledges the asset as security for the debt but that does not hold the borrower personally liable. *Related item(s)*: recourse financing.

nonsystematic risk Company-specific risk.

normal yield curve A chart showing long-term debt instruments having higher yields than short-term debt instruments. *Syn.* positive yield curve. *Related item(s)*: flat yield curve; inverted yield curve; yield curve.

note A short-term debt security, usually maturing in five years or less. *Related item(s)*: Treasury note.

not held order (NH) An order that gives the floor broker discretion as to the price and timing of the order's execution. Not held orders are often entered for large amounts of a security. *Syn.* market NH; market not held order.

notification *See* registration by filing.

NSCC *See* National Securities Clearing Corporation.

numbered account An account titled with something other than the customer's name. The title might be a number, symbol, or special title. The customer must sign a form designating account ownership.

NYSE *See* New York Stock Exchange.

NYSE Composite Index *See* New York Stock Exchange Composite Index.

NYSE maintenance call *See* margin maintenance call.

NYSE maintenance requirement *See* margin maintenance requirement.

O

OBO *See* order book official.

OCC *See* Options Clearing Corporation.

OCC Disclosure Document *See* options disclosure document.

odd lot An amount of a security that is less than the normal unit of trading for that security. Generally, an odd lot is fewer than 100 shares of stock or five bonds. *Related item(s)*: round lot.

odd-lot theory A technical analysis theory based on the assumption that the small investor is always wrong. Therefore, if odd-lot sales are up—that is, small investors are selling stock—it is probably a good time to buy.

offer Under the Uniform Securities Act, any attempt to solicit a purchase or sale in a security for value. *Related item(s)*: bid; public offering price; quotation, ask.

offering circular An abbreviated prospectus used by corporations issuing less than $5 million of stock. The SEC's Regulation A allows these offerings an exemption from the full registration requirements of the 1933 Act. *Related item(s)*: Regulation A.

official notice of sale The invitation to bid on a municipal bond issue; the invitation is sent to prospective underwriters and specifies, among other things, the date, time and place of sale, description of the issue, maturities, call provisions, and amount of good faith deposit required.

official statement (OS) A document concerning a municipal issue that must be provided to every buyer. The document is prepared by the underwriter from information provided by the issuer; typically included are the offering terms, descriptions of the bonds and the issuer, the underwriting spread, fees received by brokers, initial offering price, and tax status.

OID *See* original issue discount bond.

oil and gas direct participation program A direct participation program formed to locate new oil and gas reserves, develop existing reserves, or generate income from producing wells. A high return is the primary objective of such a program. *Syn.* oil and gas limited partnership.

oil depletion allowance An accounting procedure that reduces the taxable portion of revenues from the sale of oil to compensate for the decreased supply of oil in the ground. Depletion is the natural resource counterpart of depreciation.

omnibus account An account opened in the name of an investment adviser or a broker-dealer for the benefit of its customers. The firm carrying the account does not receive disclosure of the individual customers' names or holdings and does not maintain records for the individual customers. *Syn.* special omnibus account.

open-end covenant A provision of a bond's trust indenture allowing the issuer to use the same collateral backing a bond as collateral for future bond issues. As a result, new creditors have the same claim on the collateral as existing creditors. *Related item(s):* closed-end covenant; junior lien debt.

open-end investment company *See* mutual fund.

opening purchase Entering the options market by buying calls or puts. *Related item(s):* closing sale; opening sale.

opening sale Entering the options market by selling calls or puts. *Related item(s):* closing purchase; opening purchase.

open-market operations The buying and selling of securities (primarily government or agency debt) by the Federal Open Market Committee to effect control of the money supply. These transactions increase or decrease the level of bank reserves available for lending.

open order *See* good till canceled order.

operating expenses (1) The day-to-day costs incurred in running a business. (2) In an oil and gas program, any production or leasehold expense incurred in the operation of a producing lease, including district expense; direct out-of-pocket expenses for labor, materials, and supplies; and those shares of taxes and transportation charges not borne by overriding royalty interests.

operating income The profit realized from one year of operation of a business.

operating ratio The ratio of operating expenses to net sales; the complement to the margin of profit ratio.

operations and maintenance fund The account from which are paid current operating and maintenance expenses on a facility financed by a municipal revenue bond. *Related item(s):* flow of funds.

operator The person who supervises and manages the exploration, drilling, mining, production, and leasehold operations of an oil and gas or mining direct participation program.

option A security that represents the right to buy or sell a specified amount of an underlying security—such as a stock, bond, or futures contract—at a specified price within a specified time. The purchaser acquires a right, and the seller assumes an obligation.

option agreement The document a customer must sign within 15 days of being approved for options trading. In it, the customer agrees to abide by the rules of the options exchanges and not to exceed position or exercise limits.

option contract adjustment An adjustment made automatically to the terms of an option on the ex-dividend date when a stock pays a stock dividend or if there is a stock split or a reverse split.

options account A customer account in which the customer has received approval to trade options.

Options Clearing Corporation (OCC) The organization that issues options, standardizes option contracts, and guarantees their performance. The OCC made secondary trading possible by creating fungible option contracts.

options disclosure document A publication of the Options Clearing Corporation that outlines the risks and rewards of investing in options. The document must be given to each customer at the time of opening an options account and must accompany any options sales literature sent to a customer. *Syn.* OCC Disclosure Document.

order book official (OBO) The title given to a specialist or market maker employed on the Pacific, Philadelphia, and Chicago Board Options exchanges.

order department The department within a brokerage firm that transmits orders to the proper market for execution and returns confirmations to the appropriate representative. *Syn.* order room; wire room.

order memorandum The form completed by a registered representative that contains customer instructions regarding an order's placement. The memorandum contains such information as the customer's name and account number, a description of the security, the type of transaction (e.g., buy, sell, or sell short), and any special instructions (such as time or price limits). *Syn.* order ticket.

order protection rule Under SEC Regulation NMS, this rule prohibits a trade-through.

order room *See* order department.

order ticket *See* order memorandum.

ordinary income Earnings other than capital gain.

organization and offering expense The cost of preparing a direct participation program for registration and subsequently offering and distributing it to the public; the cost includes sales commissions paid to broker-dealers.

original issue discount bond (OID) A corporate or municipal debt security issued at a discount from face value. The bond may or may not pay interest. The discount on a corporate OID bond is taxed as if accrued annually as ordinary income. The discount on a municipal OID bond is exempt from annual taxation; however, the discount is accrued for the purpose of calculating cost basis. *Related item(s):* zero-coupon bond.

OTC Bulletin Board An electronic quotation system for equity securities that are not listed on a national exchange or included in the Nasdaq system.

OTC margin security A security that is not traded on a national exchange but that has been designated by the Federal Reserve Board as eligible for trading on margin. The Fed publishes a list of such securities. *Related item(s):* margin security.

OTC market The security exchange system in which broker-dealers negotiate directly with one another rather than through an auction on an exchange floor. The trading takes place over computer and telephone networks that link brokers and dealers around the world. Both listed and OTC securities, as well as municipal and U.S. government securities, trade in the OTC market.

OTC Market Group, Inc. The publisher of compiled quotes from market makers in over-the-counter stocks and bonds.

OTC option An option contract that is not listed on an exchange. All contract terms are negotiated between buyer and seller. *Syn.* nonstandard option. *Related item(s):* listed option.

out of the money The term used to describe an option that has no intrinsic value, such as a call option when the stock is selling below the exercise price or a put option when the stock is selling above the exercise price. *Related item(s):* at the money; in the money; intrinsic value.

outstanding stock Equity securities issued by a corporation and in the hands of the public; issued stock that the issuer has not reacquired. *Related item(s):* treasury stock.

overbought A technical analysis term for a market in which more and stronger buying has occurred than the fundamentals justify. *Related item(s):* oversold.

overlapping debt A condition resulting when property in a municipality is subject to multiple taxing authorities or tax districts, each having tax collection powers and recourse to the residents of that municipality. *Related item(s):* coterminous.

overriding royalty interest A sharing arrangement whereby a person with a royalty interest in an oil and gas direct participation program takes no risks but receives a share of the revenues; the share is carved out of the working interest without liability for any costs of extraction. *Related item(s):* sharing arrangement.

oversold A technical analysis term for a market in which more and stronger selling has occurred than the fundamentals justify. *Related item(s):* overbought.

P

paid-in capital *See* capital surplus.

paid-in surplus *See* capital surplus.

par The dollar amount the issuer assigns to a security. For an equity security, par is usually a small dollar amount that bears no relationship to the security's market price. For a debt security, par is the amount repaid to the investor when the bond matures, usually $1,000. *Syn.* face value; principal; stated value. *Related item(s):* capital surplus; maturity date.

parity In an exchange market, a situation in which all brokers bidding have equal standing and the winning bid is awarded by a random drawing. *Related item(s):* precedence; priority.

parity price of common The dollar amount at which a common stock is equal in value to its corresponding convertible security. It is calculated by dividing the convertible security's market value by its conversion ratio.

parity price of convertible The dollar amount at which a convertible security is equal in value to its corresponding common stock. It is calculated by multiplying the market price of the common stock by its conversion ratio.

partial call The redemption by an issuer of a portion of an outstanding bond issue before the maturity date. *Related item(s):* catastrophe call; mandatory call.

participant (1) A person who advises stockholders in a proxy contest. (2) The holder of an interest in a direct participation program. *Related item(s):* limited partner.

participating preferred stock An equity security that offers the holder a share of corporate earnings remaining after all senior securities have been paid a fixed dividend. The payment is made in addition to the fixed dividend stated on the certificate and may be cumulative or noncumulative. *Related item(s):* convertible preferred stock; cumulative preferred stock; noncumulative preferred stock; preferred stock.

participation The provision of the Employee Retirement Income Security Act of 1974 requiring that all employees in a qualified retirement plan be covered within a reasonable time of their dates of hire.

partnership A form of business organization in which two or more individuals manage the business and are equally and personally liable for its debts.

partnership account An account that empowers the individual members of a partnership to act on the behalf of the partnership as a whole.

partnership management fee The amount payable to the general partners of a limited partnership or to other persons for managing the day-to-day partnership operations. *Syn.* program management fee; property management fee.

par value The dollar amount assigned to a security by the issuer. For an equity security, par value is usually a small dollar amount that bears no relationship to the security's market price. For a debt security, par value is the amount repaid to the investor when the bond matures, usually $1,000. *Syn.* face value; principal; stated value. *Related item(s):* capital surplus; discount bond; premium bond.

passive income Earnings derived from a rental property, limited partnership, or other enterprise in which the individual is not actively involved. Passive income, therefore, does not include earnings from wages or active business participation, nor does it include income from dividends, interest, and capital gains. *Related item(s)*: passive loss; unearned income.

passive investor *See* limited partner.

passive loss A loss incurred through a rental property, limited partnership, or other enterprise in which the individual is not actively involved. Passive losses may be used to offset passive income only, not wage or portfolio income. *Related item(s)*: passive income.

pass-through certificate A security representing an interest in a pool of conventional, VA, Farmers Home Administration, or other agency mortgages. The pool receives the principal and interest payments, which it passes through to each certificate holder. Payments may or may not be guaranteed. *Related item(s)*: Federal National Mortgage Association; Government National Mortgage Association.

pattern A repetitive series of price movements on a chart used by a technical analyst to predict future movements of the market.

payment date The day on which a declared dividend is paid to all stockholders owning shares on the record date.

payment period As defined by the Federal Reserve Board's Regulation T, the period corresponding to the regular way settlement period.

payout stage *See* distribution stage.

payroll deduction plan A retirement plan whereby an employee authorizes a deduction from his check on a regular basis. The plan may be qualified, such as a 401(k) plan, or nonqualified.

P/E *See* price-to-earnings ratio.

peak The end of a period of increasing business activity throughout the economy, one of the four stages of the business cycle. *Syn.* prosperity. *Related item(s)*: business cycle.

pension plan A contract between an individual and an employer, a labor union, a government entity, or another institution that provides for the distribution of pension benefits at retirement.

P/E ratio *See* price-to-earnings ratio.

percentage depletion A method of tax accounting for a direct participation program whereby a statutory percentage of gross income from the sale of a mineral resource is allowed as a tax-deductible expense. Percentage depletion is available to small producers only and not to purchasers of producing interests.

person As defined in securities law, an individual, a corporation, a partnership, an association, a fund, a joint stock company, an unincorporated organization, a trust, a government, or a political subdivision of a government.

personal income (PI) An individual's total earnings derived from wages, passive business enterprises, and investments. *Related item(s)*: disposable income.

phantom income In a limited partnership, taxable income that is not backed by a positive cash flow. *Related item(s)*: crossover point.

Pink—OTC Pink A weekly electronic publication compiled by the OTC Market Group, Inc. and containing interdealer wholesale quotations for over-the-counter stocks.

pipeline theory *See* conduit theory.

placement ratio A ratio compiled by *The Bond Buyer* indicating the number of new municipal issues that have sold within the last week. *Syn.* acceptance ratio.

plan custodian An institution retained by an investment company to perform clerical duties. The custodian's responsibilities include safeguarding plan assets, sending out customer confirmations, and issuing shares. *Related item(s)*: custodian; mutual fund custodian.

plus tick A security transaction's execution price that is above the previous execution price by a minimum amount. *Syn.* up tick. *Related item(s)*: minus tick; tick; zero-plus tick.

point A measure of a bond's price; $10 or 1% of the par value of $1,000. *Related item(s)*: basis point.

point-and-figure chart A tool used by technical analysts to track the effects of price reversals, or changes in the direction of prices, of a commodity over time. *Related item(s)*: bar chart; moving average chart.

POP *See* public offering price.

portfolio income Earnings from interest, dividends, and all nonbusiness investments. *Related item(s)*: earned income; passive income; unearned income.

portfolio manager The entity responsible for investing a mutual fund's assets, implementing its investment strategy, and managing day-to-day portfolio trading. *Syn.* fund manager.

position The amount of a security either owned (a long position) or owed (a short position) by an individual or a dealer. Dealers take long positions in specific securities to maintain inventories and thereby facilitate trading.

position limit The rule established by options exchanges that prohibits an investor from having a net long or short position of more than a specific number of contracts on the same side of the market.

positive yield curve *See* normal yield curve.

power of substitution *See* stock power.

precedence In an exchange market, the ranking of bids and offers according to the number of shares involved. *Related item(s):* parity; priority.

preemptive right A stockholder's legal right to maintain her proportionate ownership by purchasing newly issued shares before the new stock is offered to the public. *Related item(s):* right.

preferred dividend coverage ratio An indication of the safety of a corporation's preferred dividend payments. It is computed by dividing preferred dividends by net income.

preferred stock An equity security that represents ownership in a corporation. It is issued with a stated dividend, which must be paid before dividends are paid to common stockholders. It generally carries no voting rights. *Related item(s):* callable preferred stock; convertible preferred stock; cumulative preferred stock.

preferred stock fund A mutual fund whose investment objective is to provide stable income with minimal capital risk. It invests in income-producing instruments such as preferred stock. *Related item(s):* bond fund.

preliminary prospectus An abbreviated prospectus that is distributed while the SEC is reviewing an issuer's registration statement. It contains all of the essential facts about the forthcoming offering except the underwriting spread, final public offering price, and date on which the shares will be delivered. *Syn.* red herring.

premium (1) The amount of cash that an option buyer pays to an option seller. (2) The difference between the higher price paid for a security and the security's face amount at issue. *Related item(s):* discount.

premium bond A bond that sells at a higher price than its face value. *Related item(s):* discount bond; par value.

pre-refunding *See* advance refunding.

presale order An order communicated to a syndicate manager before formation of the underwriting bid of a new municipal bond issue. If the syndicate wins the bid, the order takes the highest priority when orders are filled. *Related item(s):* designated order; group net order; member-at-the-takedown order.

price-to-earnings ratio (P/E) A tool for comparing the prices of different common stocks by assessing how much the market is willing to pay for a share of each corporation's earnings. It is calculated by dividing the current market price of a stock by the earnings per share.

price risk The potential that the value of a currency or commodity will change between the signing of a delivery contract and the time delivery is made. The futures markets serve to manage price risk.

price spread *See* vertical spread.

primary distribution *See* primary offering.

primary earnings per share *See* earnings per share.

primary market *See* new issue market.

primary dealer Large bank or brokerage firm designated by the Federal Reserve Board to bid at Treasury auctions.

primary offering An offering in which the proceeds of the underwriting go to the issuing corporation, agency, or municipality. The issuer seeks to increase its capitalization either by selling shares of stock, representing ownership, or by selling bonds, representing loans to the issuer. *Syn.* primary distribution.

prime rate The interest rate that commercial banks charge their prime or most creditworthy customers, generally large corporations.

principal A person who trades for his own account in the primary or secondary market. Also, a dealer.

principal transaction A transaction in which a broker-dealer either buys securities from customers and takes them into its own inventory or sells securities to customers from its inventory. *Related item(s):* agency transaction; agent; broker; dealer; principal.

priority In an exchange market, the ranking of bids and offers according to the first person to bid or offer at a given price. Therefore, only one individual or firm can have priority. *Related item(s):* parity; precedence.

prior lien bond A secured bond that takes precedence over other bonds secured by the same assets. *Related item(s):* mortgage bond.

private label CMO Collateralized mortgage obligations issued by investment banks or their subsidiaries, financial institutions, or home builders.

private placement An offering of new issue securities that complies with Regulation D of the Securities Act of 1933. According to Regulation D, a security generally is not required to be registered with the SEC if it is offered to no more than 35 nonaccredited investors or to an unlimited number of accredited investors. *Related item(s):* Regulation D.

productive well An oil or gas well that produces mineral resources that may be marketed commercially. *Related item(s):* dry hole.

profitability The ability to generate a level of income and gain in excess of expenses.

profit ratio *See* net profit ratio.

profit-sharing plan An employee benefit plan established and maintained by an employer whereby the employees receive a share of the business's profits. The money may be paid directly to the employees or deferred until retirement. A combination of both approaches is also possible.

progressive tax A tax that takes a larger percentage of the income of high-income earners than that of low-income earners. An example is the graduated income tax. *Related item(s):* regressive tax.

property dividend A distribution made by a corporation to its stockholders of securities it owns in other corporations or of its products. *Related item(s):* dividend.

prospectus *See* final prospectus.

Prospectus Act *See* Securities Act of 1933.

proxy A limited power of attorney from a stockholder authorizing another person to vote on stockholder issues according to the first stockholder's instructions. To vote on corporate matters, a stockholder must either attend the annual meeting or vote by proxy.

proxy department The department within a brokerage firm that is responsible for sending proxy statements to customers whose securities are held in the firm's name, and for mailing financial reports received from issuers to their stockholders.

prudent investor rule A legal maxim that restricts discretion in a fiduciary account to only those investments that a reasonable and prudent person might make.

Public Housing Authority bond (PHA) *See* New Housing Authority bond.

publicly traded fund *See* closed-end investment company.

public offering The sale of an issue of common stock, either by a corporation going public or by an offering of additional shares. *Related item(s):* initial public offering.

public offering price (POP) (1) The price of new shares that is established in the issuing corporation's prospectus. (2) The price to investors for mutual fund shares, equal to the net asset value plus the sales charge. *Related item(s):* ask; bid; mutual fund; net asset value.

public purpose bond A municipal bond that is exempt from federal income tax as long as no more than 10% of the proceeds benefit private entities.

Public Securities Association (PSA) An organization of banks and broker-dealers that conduct business in mortgage-backed securities, money market securities, and securities issued by the U.S. government, government agencies, and municipalities.

purchasing power risk The potential that, because of inflation, a certain amount of money will not purchase as much in the future as it does today. *Syn.* inflation risk.

put (1) An option contract giving the owner the right to sell a certain amount of an underlying security at a specified price within a specified time. (2) The act of exercising a put option. *Related item(s):* call.

put bond A debt security requiring the issuer to purchase the security at the holder's discretion or within a prescribed time. *Syn.* tender bond.

put buyer An investor who pays a premium for an option contract and receives, for a specified time, the right to sell the underlying security at a specified price. *Related item(s):* call buyer; call writer; put writer.

put spread An option investor's position in which the investor buys a put on a particular security and writes a put on the same security but with a different expiration date, exercise price, or both.

put writer An investor who receives a premium and takes on, for a specified time, the obligation to buy the underlying security at a specified price at the put buyer's discretion. *Related item(s):* call buyer; call writer; put buyer.

pyramiding A speculative strategy whereby an investor uses unrealized profits from a position held to increase the size of the position continuously but by ever-smaller amounts.

Q

qualification *See* registration by qualification.

qualified legal opinion The statement of a bond attorney affirming the validity of a new municipal bond issue but expressing reservations about its quality. *Related item(s):* legal opinion of counsel; unqualified legal opinion.

qualified retirement plan A corporate retirement plan that meets the standards set by the Employee Retirement Income Security Act of 1974. Contributions to a qualified plan are tax deductible. *Syn.* approved plan. *Related item(s):* individual retirement account; Keogh plan; nonqualified retirement plan.

quick assets A measure of a corporation's liquidity that takes into account the size of the unsold inventory. It is calculated by subtracting inventory from current assets, and it is used in the acid-test ratio. *Related item(s):* acid-test ratio.

quick ratio *See* acid-test ratio.

quotation The price or bid a market maker or broker-dealer offers for a particular security. *Syn.* quote. *Related item(s):* ask; bid; bond quote; stock quote.

quote *See* quotation.

R

RAN *See* revenue anticipation note.

random walk theory A market analysis theory that the past movement or direction of the price of a stock or market cannot be used to predict its future movement or direction.

range A security's low price and high price for a particular trading period, such as the close of a day's trading, the opening of a day's trading, or a day, month, or year. *Syn.* opening range.

rate covenant A provision of a municipal revenue bond's trust indenture that helps ensure the safety of the issue by specifying the rates to be charged the user of the facility. *Related item(s):* insurance covenant; maintenance covenant.

rating An evaluation of a corporate or municipal bond's relative safety, according to the issuer's ability to repay principal and make interest payments. Bonds are rated by various organizations, such as Standard & Poor's and Moody's. Ratings range from AAA or Aaa (the highest) to C or D, which represents a company in default.

rating service A company, such as Moody's or Standard & Poor's, that rates various debt and preferred stock issues for safety of payment of principal, interest, or dividends. The issuing company or municipality pays a fee for the rating. *Related item(s):* bond rating; rating.

ratio writing An option hedge position in which the investor writes more than one call option for every 100 shares of underlying stock that the investor owns. As a result, the investor has a partly covered position and a partly naked position.

raw land program A real estate direct participation program that aims to provide capital appreciation by investing in undeveloped land.

real estate investment trust (REIT) A corporation or trust that uses the pooled capital of many investors to invest in direct ownership of either income property or mortgage loans. These investments offer tax benefits in addition to interest and capital gains distributions.

real estate limited partnership A direct participation program formed to build new structures, generate income from existing property, or profit from the capital appreciation of undeveloped land. Growth potential, income distributions, and tax shelter are the most important benefits of such a program.

realized gain The amount a taxpayer earns when he sells an asset. *Related item(s):* unrealized gain.

reallowance A portion of the concession available to firms that sell shares in an offering but are not syndicate or selling group members.

recapitalization Changing the capital structure of a corporation by issuing, converting, or redeeming securities.

recapture The taxation as ordinary income of previously earned deductions or credits. Circumstances that may cause the IRS to require this tax to be paid include excess depreciation, premature sale of an asset, or disallowing of a previous tax benefit.

recession A general economic decline lasting from 6 to 18 months.

reciprocal immunity *See* doctrine of mutual reciprocity.

reclamation The right of the seller of a security to recover any loss incurred in a securities transaction owing to bad delivery or other irregularity in the settlement process.

reclassification The exchange by a corporation of one class of its securities for another class of its securities. This shifts ownership control among the stockholders and therefore falls under the purview of the SEC's Rule 145. *Related item(s):* Rule 145.

record date The date a corporation's board of directors establishes that determines which of its stockholders are entitled to receive dividends or rights distributions.

recourse financing Debt incurred for the purchase of an asset and that holds the borrower personally liable for the debt. *Related item(s):* nonrecourse financing.

recovery *See* expansion.

redeemable security A security that the issuer redeems upon the holder's request. Examples include shares in an open-end investment company and Treasury notes.

redemption The return of an investor's principal in a security, such as a bond, preferred stock, or mutual fund shares. By law, redemption of mutual fund shares must occur within seven days of receiving the investor's request for redemption.

redemption notice A published announcement that a corporation or municipality is calling a certain issue of its bonds.

red herring *See* preliminary prospectus.

refinancing Issuing equity, the proceeds of which are used to retire debt.

refunding Retiring an outstanding bond issue at maturity using money from the sale of a new offering. *Related item(s):* advance refunding.

regional exchange A stock exchange that serves the financial community in a particular region of the country. These exchanges tend to focus on securities issued within their regions, but also offer trading in NYSE-listed securities.

regional fund *See* sector fund.

registered Describes a security that prints the owner's name on the certificate. The owner's name is stored in records kept by the issuer or a transfer agent.

registered as to principal only The term describing a bond that prints the owner's name on the certificate, but that has unregistered coupons payable to the bearer. *Syn.* partially registered. *Related item(s):* coupon bond; fully registered bond; registered.

Registered Options Principal (ROP) The officer or partner of a brokerage firm who approves, in writing, accounts in which options transactions are permitted.

registered principal An associated person of a member firm who manages or supervises the firm's investment banking or securities business. This includes any individual who trains associated persons and who solicits business.

Unless the member firm is a sole proprietorship, it must employ at least two registered principals, one of whom must be registered as a general securities principal and one of whom must be registered as a financial and operations principal. If the firm does options business with the public, it must employ at least one registered options principal.

registered representative (RR) An associated person engaged in the investment banking or securities business. This includes any individual who supervises, solicits, or conducts business in securities or who trains people to supervise, solicit, or conduct business in securities.

Anyone employed by a brokerage firm who is not a principal and who is not engaged in clerical or brokerage administration is subject to registration and exam licensing as a registered representative. *Syn.* account executive; stockbroker. *Related item(s):* associated person of a member.

registrar The independent organization or part of a corporation responsible for accounting for all of the issuer's outstanding stock and certifying that its bonds constitute legal debt.

registration by coordination A process that allows a security to be sold in a state. It is available to an issuer that files for the security's registration under the Securities Act of 1933 and files duplicates of the registration documents with the state administrator. The state registration becomes effective at the same time the federal registration statement becomes effective.

registration by filing A process that allows a security to be sold in a state. Previously referred to as *registration by notification*, it is available to an issuer who files for the security's registration under the Securities Act of 1933, meets minimum net worth and certain other requirements, and notifies the state of this eligibility by filing certain documents with the state administrator. The state registration becomes effective at the same time the federal registration statement becomes effective.

registration by notification *See* registration by filing.

registration by qualification A process that allows a security to be sold in a state. It is available to an issuer who files for the security's registration with the state administrator; meets minimum net worth, disclosure, and other requirements; and files appropriate registration fees. The state registration becomes effective when the legal document that discloses all pertinent information concerning an offering of a security and its issuer is filed. It is submitted to the SEC in accordance with the requirements of the Securities Act of 1933, and it forms the basis of the final prospectus distributed to investors.

regressive tax A tax that takes a larger percentage of the income of low-income earners than that of high-income earners. Examples include gasoline tax and cigarette tax. *Related item(s):* progressive tax.

Reg T *See* Regulation T.

Reg T call *See* margin call.

regular way A settlement contract that calls for delivery and payment within a standard payment period from the date of the trade. The Uniform Practice Code sets the standard payment period. The type of security being traded determines the amount of time allowed for regular way settlement. *Related item(s):* cash transaction; settlement date.

regulated investment company An investment company to which Subchapter M of the Internal Revenue Code grants special status that allows the flow-through of tax consequences on a distribution to shareholders. If 90% of its income is passed through to the shareholders, the company is not subject to tax on this income.

Regulation A The provision of the Securities Act of 1933 that exempts from registration small public offerings valued at no more than $5 million worth of securities issued during a 12-month period.

Regulation D The provision of the Securities Act of 1933 that exempts from registration offerings sold to a maximum of 35 nonaccredited investors during a 12-month period. *Related item(s):* private placement.

Regulation NMS (National Market System) A broad sweeping SEC regulation designed to bring trading and reporting uniformity to U.S. securities markets. *Related item(s):* order protection rule; minimum increments rule.

Regulation SP Regulation enacted by the SEC to protect the privacy of customer information, particularly nonpublic personal information. Your firm must provide a privacy notice describing its privacy policies to customers whenever a new account is opened and annually thereafter. The notice must provide customers a reasonable means to opt out of the disclosure of the customer's nonpublic personal information to unaffiliated third parties.

Regulation T The Federal Reserve Board regulation that governs customer cash accounts and the amount of credit that brokerage firms and dealers may extend to customers for the purchase of securities. Regulation T currently sets the loan value of marginable securities at 50% and the payment deadline at two days beyond regular way settlement. *Syn.* Reg T. *Related item(s):* Regulation U.

Regulation U The Federal Reserve Board regulation that governs loans by banks for the purchase of securities. Call loans are exempt from Regulation U. *Related item(s):* broker's loan; call loan; Regulation T.

rehypothecation The pledging of a client's securities as collateral for a bank loan. Brokerage firms may rehypothecate up to 140% of the value of their customers' securities to finance margin loans to customers. *Related item(s):* hypothecation.

reinstatement privilege A benefit offered by some mutual funds, allowing an investor to withdraw money from a fund account and then redeposit the money without paying a second sales charge.

REIT *See* real estate investment trust.

rejection The right of the buyer of a security to refuse to accept delivery in completion of a trade because the security does not meet the requirements of good delivery.

renewal and replacement fund The account that is used to fund major renewal projects and equipment replacements financed by a municipal revenue bond issue. *Related item(s):* flow of funds.

reoffering price The price or yield at which a municipal security is sold to the public by the underwriters.

reorganization department The department within a brokerage firm that handles transactions that represent a change in the securities outstanding, such as trades relating to tender offers, bond calls, preferred stock redemptions, and mergers and acquisitions.

repo *See* repurchase agreement.

repurchase agreement A sale of securities with an attendant agreement to repurchase them at a higher price on an agreed-upon future date; the difference between the sale price and the repurchase price represents the interest earned by the investor. Repos are considered money market instruments and are used to raise short-term capital and as instruments of monetary policy. *Syn.* repo. *Related item(s):* reverse repurchase agreement.

reserve maintenance fund The account that holds funds that supplement the general maintenance fund of a municipal revenue bond issue. *Related item(s):* flow of funds.

reserve requirement The percentage of depositors' money that the Federal Reserve Board requires a commercial bank to keep on deposit in the form of cash or in its vault. *Syn.* reserves.

residual claim The right of a common stockholder to corporate assets in the event that the corporation ceases to exist. A common stockholder may claim assets only after the claims of all creditors and other security holders have been satisfied.

resistance level A technical analysis term describing the top of a stock's historical trading range. *Related item(s):* breakout; support level.

restricted account A margin account in which the equity is less than the Regulation T initial requirement. *Related item(s):* equity; initial margin requirement; margin account; retention requirement.

restricted security An unregistered, nonexempt security acquired either directly or indirectly from the issuer, or an affiliate of the issuer, in a transaction that does not involve a public offering. *Related item(s):* holding period; Rule 144.

retail communications FINRA defines this category of communications with the public as any written (including electronic) communication that is distributed or made available to more than 25 retail investors within any 30 calendar-day period. A retail investor is any person other than an institutional investor, regardless of whether the person has an account with the member firm or not.

retained earnings The amount of a corporation's net income that remains after all dividends have been paid to preferred and common stockholders. *Syn.* earned surplus; reinvested earnings.

retention requirement The provision of Regulation T that applies to the withdrawal of securities from a restricted account. The customer must deposit an amount equal to the unpaid portion of the securities being withdrawn, in order to reduce the debit balance. The retention requirement is the reciprocal of the initial margin requirement. *Related item(s):* restricted account.

retirement account A customer account established to provide retirement funds.

retiring bonds Ending an issuer's debt obligation by calling the outstanding bonds, by purchasing bonds in the open market, or by repaying bondholders the principal amount at maturity.

return on common equity A measure of a corporation's profitability, calculated by dividing aftertax income by common shareholders' equity.

return on equity A measure of a corporation's profitability, specifically its return on assets, calculated by dividing aftertax income by tangible assets.

return on investment (ROI) The profit or loss resulting from a security transaction, often expressed as an annual percentage rate.

revenue anticipation note (RAN) A short-term municipal debt security issued in anticipation of revenue to be received.

revenue bond A municipal debt issue whose interest and principal are payable only from the specific earnings of an income-producing public project. *Related item(s):* double-barreled bond; general obligation bond; municipal bond; special revenue bond.

reverse churning The unsuitable practice of placing a client who trades infrequently in a fee-based account rather than a commission based account that would be more appropriate. *Related item:* churning

reverse repo *See* reverse repurchase agreement.

reverse repurchase agreement A purchase of securities with an attendant agreement to resell them at a higher price on an agreed-upon future date; the difference between the purchase price and the resale price represents the interest earned by the investor. The purchaser initiates the deal. *Syn.* reverse repo. *Related item(s):* repurchase agreement.

reverse split A reduction in the number of a corporation's shares outstanding that increases the par value of its stock or its earnings per share. The market value of the total number of shares remains the same. *Related item(s):* stock split.

reversionary working interest A sharing arrangement whereby the general partner of a direct participation program bears none of the program's costs and does not share in revenues until the limited partners receive payment plus a predetermined rate of return. *Syn.* subordinated interest; subordinated reversionary working interest. *Related item(s):* sharing arrangement.

right A security representing a stockholder's entitlement to the first opportunity to purchase new shares issued by the corporation at a predetermined price (normally less than the current market price) in proportion to the number of shares already owned. Rights are issued for a short time only, after which they expire. *Syn.* subscription right; subscription right certificate. *Related item(s):* preemptive right; rights offering.

right of accumulation A benefit offered by a mutual fund that allows the investor to qualify for reduced sales loads on additional purchases according to the fund account's total dollar value.

rights agent An issuing corporation's agent who is responsible for maintaining current records of the names of rights certificate owners.

rights offering An issue of new shares of stock accompanied by the opportunity for each stockholder to maintain a proportionate ownership by purchasing additional shares in the corporation before the shares are offered to the public. *Related item(s):* right.

risk arbitrage The purchase of stock in a company that is being acquired and the short sale of stock in the acquiring company to profit from the anticipated increase in the acquired corporation's shares and decrease in the acquiring corporation's shares.

riskless and simultaneous transaction The buying or selling by a broker-dealer of a security for its own account to fill an order previously received from a customer. Although the firm is technically acting as a principal in the trade, the transaction is relatively riskless because the purchase and sale are consummated almost simultaneously. *Syn.* riskless transaction.

ROI *See* return on investment.

rollover The transfer of funds from one qualified retirement plan to another qualified retirement plan. If this is not done within a specified time period, the funds are taxed as ordinary income.

ROP *See* Registered Options Principal.

round lot A security's normal unit of trading, which is generally 100 shares of stock or five bonds. *Related item(s):* odd lot.

royalty interest The right of a mineral rights owner to receive a share in the revenues generated by the resource if and when production begins. The royalty interest retained is free from production costs.

Rule 144 SEC rule requiring that persons who hold control or restricted securities sell them only in limited quantities, and that all sales of restricted stock by control persons must be reported to the SEC by filing a Form 144, "Notice of Proposed Sale of Securities." *Related item(s):* control security; restricted security.

Rule 145 SEC rule requiring that, whenever the stockholders of a publicly owned corporation are solicited to vote on or consent to a plan for reorganizing the corporation, full disclosure of all material facts must be made in a proxy statement or prospectus that must be in the hands of the stockholders before the announced voting date. *Related item(s):* reclassification.

Rule 147 SEC rule that provides exemption from the registration statement and prospectus requirements of the 1933 Act for securities offered and sold exclusively intrastate.

Rule 15c2-1 SEC rule governing the safekeeping of securities in customer margin accounts. It prohibits broker-dealers from (1) using a customer's securities in excess of the customer's aggregate indebtedness as collateral to secure a loan without written permission from the customer, and (2) commingling a customer's securities without written permission from the customer. *Related item(s):* rehypothecation.

Rule 405 NYSE rule requiring that each member organization exercise due diligence to learn the essential facts about every customer. *Syn.* know your customer rule.

Rule 415 SEC rule governing shelf offerings. The rule allows an issuer to sell limited portions of a new issue over a three-year period. *Related item(s):* shelf offering.

Rule 504 SEC rule providing that an offering of less than $1 million during any 12-month period may be exempt from full registration. The rule does not restrict the number of accredited or nonaccredited purchasers.

Rule 505 SEC rule providing that an offering of $1 million to $5 million during any 12-month period may be exempt from full registration. The rule restricts the number of nonaccredited purchasers to 35 but does not restrict the number of accredited purchasers.

Rule 506 SEC rule providing that an offering of more than $5 million during any 12-month period may be exempt from full registration. The rule restricts the number of nonaccredited purchasers to 35 but does not restrict the number of accredited purchasers.

Rule G-1 MSRB rule that classifies as municipal securities dealers any separately identifiable departments of banks that engage in activities related to the municipal securities business. *Related item(s):* separately identifiable department or division.

Rule G-2 MSRB rule that sets professional qualification standards.

Rule G-3 MSRB rule governing the classification of municipal securities principals and representatives.

Rule G-6 MSRB rule governing the fidelity bond requirements for member broker-dealers.

Rule G-7 MSRB rule governing the documentation that must be kept on each associated person.

Rule G-10 MSRB rule requiring that an investor brochure be delivered in response to a customer complaint.

Rule G-11 MSRB rule governing the priority given to orders received for new issue municipal securities.

Rule G-12 MSRB rule governing the uniform practices for settling transactions between municipal securities firms.

Rule G-13 MSRB rule requiring broker-dealers to publish only bona fide quotations for municipal securities unless the quotations are identified as informational.

Rule G-15 MSRB rule governing the confirmation, clearance, and settlement of customer municipal securities transactions.

Rule G-16 MSRB rule requiring inspections to be conducted every 24 months to verify compliance.

Rule G-17 MSRB rule that sets ethical standards for conducting municipal securities business.

Rule G-18 MSRB rule requiring firms to make an effort to obtain the best price when executing municipal securities transactions for customers.

Rule G-19 MSRB rule governing discretionary accounts and the suitability of municipal securities recommendations and transactions.

Rule G-20 MSRB rule that sets a limit on the value of gifts and gratuities given by municipal securities firms.

Rule G-21 MSRB rule governing the advertising of municipal securities.

Rule G-22 MSRB rule requiring disclosures to customers of control relationships between municipal firms and issuers.

Rule G-23 MSRB rule that seeks to minimize conflicts of interest arising out of the activities of financial advisers that also act as municipal underwriters to the same issuer.

Rule G-24 MSRB rule prohibiting the misuse of confidential information about customers obtained by municipal securities firms acting in fiduciary capacities.

Rule G-25 MSRB rule prohibiting the improper use of assets by municipal securities firms and their representatives.

Rule G-27 MSRB rule requiring each municipal securities firm to designate a principal to supervise its municipal securities representatives.

Rule G-28 MSRB rule governing employee accounts held at other municipal securities firms.

Rule G-29 MSRB rule governing the availability of MSRB regulations.

Rule G-30 MSRB rule requiring that prices and commissions charged by municipal securities firms be fair and reasonable.

Rule G-31 MSRB rule prohibiting a municipal securities professional from soliciting business from an investment company portfolio in return for sales of that fund to its customers.

Rule G-32 MSRB rule requiring that customers receive a copy of the preliminary or final official statement when purchasing a new municipal issue.

Rule G-33 MSRB rule governing the calculation of accrued interest on municipal bonds using a 360-day year.

Rule G-37 MSRB rule prohibiting municipal securities dealers from underwriting securities issued under the authority of a public official to whom an associated person of the dealer has contributed money.

Rule G-39 MSRB rule requiring telemarketers calling on behalf of a firm to limit calls to between 8:00 am and 9:00 pm in the called person's time zone. The caller must disclose his name, the firm's name, the firm's telephone number or address, and the fact that he is calling to solicit the purchase of municipal bonds or investment services. The rule does not apply if the person called is an established customer.

Rule G-41 MSRB rule requiring municipal securities dealers to establish and implement an anti-money laundering compliance program designed to achieve and monitor ongoing compliance with the requirements of the Bank Secrecy Act.

S

SAR *See* suspicious activity report.

sale *See* sell.

sales charge *See* commission.

sales literature Any written material a firm distributes to customers or the public in a controlled manner. Examples include circulars, research reports, form letters, market letters, performance reports, and text used for seminars. *Related item(s):* advertisement; market letter.

sales load The amount added to a mutual fund share's net asset value to arrive at the offering price. *Related item(s):* mutual fund; net asset value; no-load fund.

Sallie Mae *See* Student Loan Marketing Association.

S&P *See* Standard & Poor's Corporation.

S&P 100 *See* Standard & Poor's 100 Stock Index.

S&P 500 *See* Standard & Poor's Composite Index of 500 Stocks.

savings bond A government debt security that is not negotiable or transferable and that may not be used as collateral. *Related item(s):* Series EE bond; Series HH bond.

scale A list of each of the scheduled maturities in a new serial bond issue. The list outlines the number of bonds, maturity dates, coupon rates, and yields. *Related item(s):* writing a scale.

SEC *See* Securities and Exchange Commission.

secondary distribution (1) A distribution, with a prospectus, that involves securities owned by major stockholders (typically founders or principal owners of a corporation). The sale proceeds go to the sellers of the stock, not to the issuer. *Syn.* registered secondary distribution. (2) A procedure for trading very large blocks of shares of stock whereby the trade is executed off the floor of an exchange after the market closes.

secondary market The market in which securities are bought and sold subsequent to their being sold to the public for the first time. *Related item(s):* new issue market.

secondary offering A sale of securities in which one or more major stockholders in a company sell all or a large portion of their holdings; the underwriting proceeds are paid to the stockholders rather than to the corporation. Typically, such an offering occurs when the founder of a business (and perhaps some of the original financial backers) determines that there is more to be gained by going public than by staying private. The offering does not increase the number of shares of stock outstanding. *Related item(s):* secondary distribution.

sector fund A mutual fund whose investment objective is to capitalize on the return potential provided by investing primarily in a particular industry or sector of the economy. *Syn.* industry fund; specialized fund.

secured bond A debt security backed by identifiable assets set aside as collateral. In the event that the issuer defaults on payment, the bondholders may lay claim to the collateral. *Related item(s):* debenture.

Securities Act of 1933 Federal legislation requiring the full and fair disclosure of all material information about the issuance of new securities. *Syn.* Act of 1933; Full Disclosure Act; New Issues Act; Prospectus Act; Trust in Securities Act; Truth in Securities Act.

Securities Acts Amendments of 1975 Federal legislation that established the Municipal Securities Rulemaking Board. *Related item(s):* Municipal Securities Rulemaking Board.

Securities and Exchange Commission (SEC) Commission created by Congress to regulate the securities markets and protect investors. It is composed of five commissioners appointed by the President of the United States and approved by the Senate. The SEC enforces, among other acts, the Securities Act of 1933, the Securities Exchange Act of 1934, the Trust Indenture Act of 1939, the Investment Company Act of 1940, and the Investment Advisers Act of 1940.

Securities Exchange Act of 1934 Federal legislation that established the Securities and Exchange Commission. The act aims to protect investors by regulating the exchanges, the over-the-counter market, the extension of credit by the Federal Reserve Board, broker-dealers, insider transactions, trading activities, client accounts, and net capital. *Syn.* Act of 1934; Exchange Act.

Securities Investor Protection Corporation (SIPC) A nonprofit membership corporation created by an act of Congress to protect clients of brokerage firms that are forced into bankruptcy. Membership is composed of all brokers and dealers registered under the Securities Exchange Act of 1934. SIPC provides brokerage firm customers up to $500,000 coverage for cash and securities held by the firms (although cash coverage is limited to $250,000).

securitization Pooling assets that may be smaller or less liquid into financial instruments, allowing them to be sold more easily to investors.

security Other than an insurance policy or a fixed annuity, any piece of securitized paper that can be traded for value. Under the Act of 1934, this includes any note, stock, bond, investment contract, debenture, certificate of interest in a profit-sharing or partnership agreement, certificate of deposit, collateral trust certificate, preorganization certificate, option on a security, or other instrument of investment commonly known as a *security*.

segregation Holding customer-owned securities separate from securities owned by other customers and securities owned by the brokerage firm. *Related item(s):* commingling.

selection risk The potential for loss on an investment owing to the particular security chosen performing poorly in spite of good overall market or industry performance.

self-regulatory organization (SRO) One of eight organizations accountable to the SEC for the enforcement of federal securities laws and the supervision of securities practices within an assigned field of jurisdiction. For example, the Financial Industry Regulatory Authority regulates trading on the NYSE and the over-the-counter market; the Municipal Securities Rulemaking Board supervises state and municipal securities; and certain exchanges, such as the Chicago Board Options Exchange, act as self-regulatory bodies to promote ethical conduct and standard trading practices.

sell To convey ownership of a security or another asset for money or value. This includes giving or delivering a security with or as a bonus for a purchase of securities, a gift of assessable stock, and selling or offering a warrant or right to purchase or subscribe to another security. Not included in the definition is a bona fide pledge or loan or a stock dividend if nothing of value is given by the stockholders for the dividend. *Syn.* sale.

seller *See* writer.

seller's option A settlement contract that calls for delivery and payment according to a number of days specified by the seller. *Related item(s):* buyer's option.

selling away An associated person engaging in private securities transactions without the employing broker-dealer's knowledge and consent. This violates the Conduct Rules.

selling concession *See* concession.

selling dividends (1) Inducing customers to buy mutual fund shares by implying that an upcoming distribution will benefit them. This practice is illegal. (2) Combining dividend and gains distributions when calculating current yield.

selling group Brokerage firms that help distribute securities in an offering but that are not members of the syndicate.

sell out The procedure that the seller of a security follows when the buyer fails to complete the contract by accepting delivery of the security. The seller closes the contract by selling the security in the open market and charging the account of the buyer for transaction fees and any loss caused by changes in the market. *Related item(s)*: buy-in.

sell stop order An order to sell a security that is entered at a price below the current market price and that is triggered when the market price touches or goes through the sell stop price.

senior lien debt A bond issue that shares the same collateral as is backing other issues but that has a prior claim to the collateral in the event of default.

senior security A security that grants its holder a prior claim to the issuer's assets over the claims of another security's holders. For example, a bond is a senior security over common stock.

SEP *See* simplified employee pension plan.

separate account The account that holds funds paid by variable annuity contract holders. The funds are kept separate from the insurer's general account and are invested in a portfolio of securities that match the contract holders' objectives. *Related item(s)*: accumulation unit; annuity; general account.

separately identifiable department or division A department of a bank that engages in the business of buying or selling municipal securities under the direct supervision of an officer of the bank. Such a department is classified by the Municipal Securities Rulemaking Board as a municipal securities dealer and must comply with MSRB regulations. *Related item(s)*: Rule G-1.

Separate Trading of Registered Interest and Principal of Securities (STRIPS) A zero-coupon bond issued and backed by the Treasury Department. *Related item(s)*: zero-coupon bond.

SEP-IRA *See* simplified employee pension plan.

serial bond A debt security issued with a maturity schedule in which parts of the outstanding issue mature at intervals until the entire balance has been repaid. Most municipal bonds are serial bonds. *Related item(s)*: maturity date; series bond.

series Options of the same class that have the same exercise price and the same expiration date. *Related item(s)*: class; type.

series bond A debt security issued in a series of public offerings spread over an extended time period. All the bonds in the series have the same priority claim against assets. *Related item(s)*: serial bond.

Series EE bond A nonmarketable, interest-bearing U.S. government savings bond issued at face value. Interest on Series EE bonds is exempt from state and local taxes. *Related item(s)*: savings bond; Series HH bond.

Series HH bond A nonmarketable, interest-bearing U.S. government savings bond issued at par and purchased only by trading in Series EE bonds at maturity. Interest on Series HH bonds is exempt from state and local taxes. *Related item(s)*: savings bond; Series EE bond.

Series 6 The investment company/variable contract products limited representative license, which entitles the holder to sell mutual funds and variable annuities and is used by many firms that sell primarily insurance-related products. The Series 6 can serve as the prerequisite for the Series 26 license.

Series 63 The uniform securities agent state law exam, which entitles the successful candidate to sell securities and give investment advice in those states that require Series 63 registration. *Related item(s)*: blue-sky laws; Uniform Securities Act.

Series 7 The general securities registered representative license, which entitles the holder to sell all types of securities products, with the exception of commodities futures (which requires a Series 3 license). The Series 7 is the most comprehensive of the FINRA representative licenses and serves as a prerequisite for most of the principals examinations.

Series 24 The General Securities Principal License, which entitles the holder to supervise the business of a broker-dealer. A Series 7 or a Series 62 qualification is a prerequisite for this license.

settlement The completion of a trade through the delivery of a security or commodity and the payment of cash or other consideration.

settlement date The date on which ownership changes between buyer and seller. The Uniform Practice Code standardizes settlement provisions. *Related item(s)*: cash transaction; regular way.

75-5-10 test The standard for judging whether an investment company qualifies as diversified under the Investment Company Act of 1940. Under this act, a diversified investment company must invest at least 75% of its total assets in cash, receivables, or invested securities and no more than 5% of its total assets in any one company's voting securities. In addition, no single investment may represent ownership of more than 10% of any one company's outstanding voting securities. *Related item(s)*: diversified management company.

share identification An accounting method that identifies the specific shares selected for liquidation in the event that an investor wishes to liquidate shares. The difference between the buying and selling prices determines the investor's tax liability.

sharing arrangement A method of allocating the responsibility for expenses and the right to share in revenues among the sponsor and limited partners in a direct participation program. *Related item(s):* carried interest; disproportionate sharing; functional allocation; net operating profits interest; overriding royalty interest; reversionary working interest.

shelf offering An SEC provision allowing an issuer to register a new issue security without selling the entire issue at once. The issuer may sell limited portions of the issuer over a three-year period without reregistering the security or incurring penalties. *Related item(s):* Rule 415.

short The term used to describe the selling of a security, contract, or commodity that the seller does not own. For example, an investor who borrows shares of stock from a broker-dealer and sells them on the open market is said to have a *short position* in the stock. *Related item(s):* long.

short against the box The term used to describe the selling of a security, contract, or commodity that the seller owns but prefers not to deliver; frequently, this is done to defer taxation.

short-interest theory A technical analysis theory that examines the ratio of short sales to volume in a stock. Because the underlying stock must be purchased to close out the short positions, a high ratio is considered bullish.

short sale The sale of a security that the seller does not own, or any sale consummated by the delivery of a security borrowed by or for the account of the seller.

short straddle An option investor's position that results from selling a call and a put on the same stock with the same exercise price and expiration month. *Related item(s):* long straddle; spread; straddle.

short-term capital gain The profit realized on the sale of an asset that has been owned for 12 months or less. *Related item(s):* capital gain; capital loss; short-term capital loss.

short-term capital loss The loss incurred on the sale of a capital asset that has been owned for 12 months or less. *Related item(s):* capital gain; capital loss; short-term capital gain.

simplified arbitration An expedient method of settling disputes involving claims not exceeding $50,000, whereby a panel of arbitrators reviews the evidence and renders a decision. All awards are made within 30 business days. *Related item(s):* arbitration.

simplified employee pension plan (SEP) A qualified retirement plan designed for employers with 25 or fewer employees. Contributions made to each employee's individual retirement account grow tax deferred until retirement. *Related item(s):* individual retirement account.

single account An account in which only one individual has control over the investments and may transact business.

sinking fund An account established by an issuing corporation or municipality into which money is deposited regularly so that the issuer has the funds to redeem its bonds, debentures, or preferred stock.

SIPC *See* Securities Investor Protection Corporation.

SLD A message on the Consolidated Tape indicating that the sale being reported was not reported on time and is therefore out of sequence.

SLMA *See* Student Loan Marketing Association.

SMA *See* special memorandum account.

solvency The ability of a corporation both to meet its long-term fixed expenses and to have adequate money for long-term expansion and growth.

special assessment bond A municipal revenue bond funded by assessments only on property owners who benefit from the services or improvements provided by the proceeds of the bond issue. *Related item(s):* revenue bond.

specialist *See* Designated Market Maker

specialist's book A journal in which a specialist (designated market maker) records the limit and stop orders that he holds for execution. The contents of the journal are confidential. *Syn.* limit order book. *Related item(s):* specialist.

specialized fund *See* sector fund.

special memorandum account (SMA) A notation on a customer's general or margin account indicating that funds are credited to the account on a memo basis; the account is used much like a line of credit with a bank. An SMA preserves the customer's right to use excess equity. *Syn.* special miscellaneous account.

special revenue bond A municipal revenue bond issued to finance a specific project. Examples include industrial development bonds, lease rental bonds, special tax bonds, and New Housing Authority bonds. *Related item(s):* revenue bond.

special situation fund A mutual fund whose objective is to capitalize on the profit potential of corporations in nonrecurring circumstances, such as those undergoing reorganizations or being considered as takeover candidates.

special tax bond A municipal revenue bond payable only from the proceeds of a tax on certain items, rather than an ad valorem tax. *Related item(s):* revenue bond.

speculation Trading a commodity or security with a higher-than-average risk in return for a higher-than-average profit potential. The trade is effected solely for the purpose of profiting from it and not as a means of hedging or protecting other positions.

speculator One who trades a commodity or security with a higher than average risk in return for a higher than average profit potential. *Related item(s):* speculation.

spin-off A type of divestiture where a parent company sells all of the shares of a subsidiary or distributes new shares of a company or division it owns to create a new company.

split offering A public offering of securities that combines aspects of both a primary and a secondary offering. A portion of the issue is a primary offering, the proceeds of which go to the issuing corporation; the remainder of the issue is a secondary offering, the proceeds of which go to the selling stockholders. *Syn.* combined distribution. *Related item(s):* primary offering; secondary offering.

sponsor A person who is instrumental in organizing, selling, or managing a limited partnership.

spousal account A separate individual retirement account established for a nonworking spouse. Contributions to the account made by the working spouse grow tax deferred until withdrawal. *Related item(s):* individual retirement account.

spread In a quotation, the difference between a security's bid and ask prices.

spread order A customer order specifying two option contracts on the same underlying security and a price difference between them.

SRO *See* self-regulatory organization.

$\frac{s}{s}$ A symbol on the Consolidated Tape indicating that the stock in question sold in 10-share units.

stabilizing Bidding at or below the public offering price of a new issue security. Underwriting managers may enter stabilizing bids during the offering period to prevent the price from dropping sharply.

stagflation A period of high unemployment in the economy accompanied by a general rise in prices. *Related item(s):* deflation; inflation.

Standard & Poor's Composite Index of 500 Stocks (S&P 500) A value-weighted index that offers broad coverage of the securities market. It is composed of 400 industrial stocks, 40 financial stocks, 40 public utility stocks, and 20 transportation stocks. The index is owned and compiled by Standard & Poor's Corporation. *Related item(s):* index; Standard & Poor's Corporation; Standard & Poor's 100 Stock Index.

Standard & Poor's Corporation (S&P) A company that rates stocks and corporate and municipal bonds according to risk profiles and that produces and tracks the S&P indexes. The company also publishes a variety of financial and investment reports. *Related item(s):* bond rating; Moody's Investors Service; rating; Standard & Poor's 100 Stock Index; Standard & Poor's Composite Index of 500 Stocks.

Standard & Poor's 100 Stock Index (S&P 100) A value-weighted index composed of 100 blue-chip stocks. The index is owned and compiled by Standard & Poor's Corporation. *Related item(s):* index; Standard & Poor's Corporation; Standard & Poor's Composite Index of 500 Stocks.

standby underwriter An investment banker that agrees to purchase any part of an issue that has not been purchased by current stockholders through a rights offering. The firm exercises the remaining rights, maintains a trading market in the rights, and offers the stock acquired to the public. *Related item(s):* rights offering.

stated yield *See* nominal yield.

statutory disqualification Prohibiting a person from associating with a self-regulatory organization because the person has been expelled, barred, or suspended from association with a member of an SRO; has had his registration suspended, denied or revoked by the SEC; has been the cause of someone else being suspended, barred, or having their license revoked; has been convicted of certain crimes; or has falsified an application or a report that he must file with or on behalf of a membership organization.

statutory voting A voting procedure that permits stockholders to cast one vote per share owned for each position. The procedure tends to benefit majority stockholders. *Related item(s):* cumulative voting.

step-out well An oil or gas well or prospect adjacent to a field of proven reserves. *Related item(s):* developmental drilling program.

stock ahead The term used to describe the inability to fill a limit order at a specific price because other orders at the same price were entered previously.

stockbroker *See* registered representative.

stock certificate Written evidence of ownership in a corporation.

stock dividend *See* dividend.

stock loan agreement The document that an institutional customer must sign when the broker-dealer borrows stock from the customer's account; the document specifies the terms of the loan and the rights of both parties.

stock power A standard form that duplicates the back of a stock certificate and is used for transferring the stock to the new owner's name. A separate stock power is used if a security's registered owner does not have the certificate available for signature endorsement. *Syn.* irrevocable stock power; power of substitution. *Related item(s):* assignment.

stock quote A list of representative prices bid and asked for a stock during a particular trading day. Stocks are quoted in points, where one point equals $1. Stock quotes are listed in the financial press and most daily newspapers. *Related item(s):* bond quote.

stock split An increase in the number of a corporation's outstanding shares, which decreases its stock's par value. The market value of the total number of shares remains the same. The proportional reductions in orders held on the books for a split stock are calculated by dividing the stock's market price by the fraction that represents the split.

stop limit order A customer order that becomes a limit order when the market price of the security reaches or passes a specific price. *Related item(s):* limit order; stop order.

stop order (1) A directive from the SEC that suspends the sale of new issue securities to the public when fraud is suspected or filing materials are deficient. (2) A customer order that becomes a market order when the market price of the security reaches or passes a specific price. *Related item(s):* limit order; market order; stop limit order.

straddle An option investor's position that results from buying a call and a put or selling a call and a put on the same security with the same exercise price and expiration month. *Related item(s):* long straddle; short straddle; spread.

straight-line depreciation An accounting method used to recover the cost of a qualifying depreciable asset, whereby the owner writes off the cost of the asset in equal amounts each year over the asset's useful life.

strike price *See* exercise price.

striking price *See* exercise price.

stripped bond A debt obligation that has been stripped of its interest coupons by a brokerage firm, repackaged, and sold at a deep discount. It pays no interest but may be redeemed at maturity for the full face value. *Related item(s):* zero-coupon bond.

stripper well An oil well that produces fewer than 10 barrels per day.

STRIPS *See* Separate Trading of Registered Interest and Principal of Securities.

Student Loan Marketing Association (SLMA) A publicly owned corporation that purchases student loans from financial institutions and packages them for sale in the secondary market, thereby increasing the availability of money for educational loans. *Syn.* Sallie Mae.

subject quote A securities quotation that does not represent an actual offer to buy or sell but is tentative, subject to reconfirmation by the broker-dealer. *Related item(s):* bona fide quote; firm quote; nominal quote; workout quote.

subordinated debenture A debt obligation backed by the general credit of the issuing corporation that has claims to interest and principal subordinated to ordinary debentures and all other liabilities. *Related item(s):* debenture.

subordinated debt financing A form of long-term capitalization used by broker-dealers in which the claims of lenders are subordinated to the claims of other creditors. Subordinated financing is considered part of the broker-dealer's capital structure and is added to net worth when computing its net capital.

subordinated interest *See* reversionary working interest.

subordinated loan A loan to a broker-dealer in which the lender agrees to subordinate its claim to the claims of the firm's other creditors.

subordinated reversionary working interest *See* reversionary working interest.

sub-penny pricing Pricing increments of less than $.01 for stocks priced less than $1 as allowed under the minimum increment pricing rule under Regulation NMS. *Related item(s):* minimum increment pricing; Regulation NMS.

subscription agreement A statement signed by an investor indicating an offer to buy an interest in a direct participation program. In the statement, the investor agrees to grant power of attorney to the general partner and to abide by the limited partnership agreement. The sale is finalized when the subscription agreement is signed by the general partner.

subscription amount The total dollar amount that a participant in a direct participation program has invested.

subscription right *See* right.

suitability A determination made by a registered representative as to whether a particular security matches a customer's objectives and financial capability. The representative must have enough information about the customer to make this judgment. *Related item(s):* Rule 405.

Super Display Book (SDBK) The electronic order entry and processing system used by the New York Stock Exchange.

supplemental liquidity provider (SLP) An off-floor market maker who trades only for his proprietary account and may compete with the on-floor Designated Market Maker in a stock listed on the NYSE. The SLP must maintain a bid or an offer in an assigned stock at least 10% of the trading day.

supply The total amount of a good or service available for purchase by consumers. *Related item(s):* demand.

supply-side theory An economic theory holding that bolstering an economy's ability to supply more goods is the most effective way to stimulate economic growth. Supply-side theorists advocate income tax reduction insofar as this increases private investment in corporations, facilities, and equipment.

support level A technical analysis term describing the bottom of a stock's historical trading range. *Related item(s):* breakout; resistance level.

suspicious activity report (SAR) A report filed by broker-dealers and financial institutions when investor behavior is detected that is commercially illogical and serves no apparent purpose. The filing threshold for a SAR is $5,000.

syndicate A group of investment bankers formed to handle the distribution and sale of a security on behalf of the issuer. Each syndicate member is responsible for the sale and distribution of a portion of the issue. *Syn.* underwriting syndicate. *Related item(s):* Eastern account; Western account.

syndicate manager *See* underwriting manager.

systematic risk The potential for a security to decrease in value owing to its inherent tendency to move together with all securities of the same type. Neither diversification nor any other investment strategy can eliminate this risk. *Related item(s):* market risk.

T

T Consolidated Tape market identifier for trades of exchange-listed securities executed over the counter.

takedown The discount from the public offering price at which a syndicate member buys new issue securities from the syndicate for sale to the public. *Related item(s):* concession.

TAN *See* tax anticipation note.

Tape *See* Consolidated Tape.

taxability The risk of the erosion of investment income through taxation.

taxable gain The portion of a sale or distribution of mutual fund shares subject to taxation.

tax and revenue anticipation note (TRAN) A short-term municipal debt security to be paid off from future tax receipts and revenues.

tax anticipation note (TAN) A short-term municipal or government debt security to be paid off from future tax receipts.

tax basis The amount that a limited partner has invested in a partnership.

tax credit An amount that can be subtracted from a tax liability, often in connection with real estate development, energy conservation, and research and development programs. Every dollar of tax credit reduces the amount of tax due, dollar for dollar. *Related item(s):* deduction.

tax-deferred annuity *See* tax-sheltered annuity.

tax-equivalent yield The rate of return a taxable bond must earn before taxes in order to equal the tax-exempt earnings on a municipal bond. This number varies with the investor's tax bracket.

taxes per capita *See* taxes per person.

taxes per person A measure of the tax burden of a municipality's population, calculated by dividing the municipality's tax receipts by its population. *Syn.* taxes per capita.

tax-exempt bond fund A mutual fund whose investment objective is to provide maximum tax-free income. It invests primarily in municipal bonds and short-term debt. *Syn.* tax-free bond fund.

tax-free bond fund *See* tax-exempt bond fund.

tax liability The amount of tax payable on earnings, usually calculated by subtracting standard and itemized deductions and personal exemptions from adjusted gross income, then multiplying by the tax rate. *Related item(s):* adjusted gross income.

tax preference item An element of income that receives favorable tax treatment. The item must be added to taxable income when computing alternative minimum tax. Tax preference items include accelerated depreciation on property, research and development costs, intangible drilling costs, tax-exempt interest on municipal private purpose bonds, and certain incentive stock options. *Related item(s):* alternative minimum tax.

tax-sheltered annuity (TSA) An insurance contract that entitles the holder to exclude all contributions from gross income in the year they are made. Tax payable on the earnings is deferred until the holder withdraws funds at retirement. TSAs are available to employees of public schools, church organizations, and other tax-exempt organizations. *Syn.* tax-deferred annuity.

T-bill *See* Treasury bill.

T-bond *See* Treasury bond.

T-call *See* margin call.

TDA *See* tax-sheltered annuity.

technical analysis A method of evaluating securities by analyzing statistics generated by market activity, such as past prices and volume. Technical analysts do not attempt to measure a security's intrinsic value. *Related item(s):* chartist; fundamental analysis.

technician *See* chartist.

Telephone Consumer Protection Act of 1991 (TCPA) Federal legislation restricting the use of telephone lines for solicitation purposes. A company soliciting sales via telephone, facsimile, or email must disclose its name and address to the called party and must not call any person who has requested not to be called.

tenants in common (TIC) A form of joint ownership of an account whereby a deceased tenant's fractional interest in the account is retained by his estate. *Related item(s)*: joint tenants with right of survivorship.

tender offer An offer to buy securities for cash or for cash plus securities.

term bond *See* term maturity.

term maturity A repayment schedule for a bond issue in which the entire issue comes due on a single date. *Syn.* term bond. *Related item(s)*: maturity date.

testimonial An endorsement of an investment or service by a celebrity or public opinion influencer. The use of testimonials in public communications is regulated by FINRA.

third market The exchange where listed securities are traded in the over-the-counter market.

third-party account (1) A customer account for which the owner has given power of attorney to a third party. (2) A customer account opened by an adult naming a minor as beneficial owner. (3) A customer account opened for another adult. This type of account is prohibited.

30-day visible supply *See* visible supply.

thomson A municipal wire service offering Thomson Muni News and Thomson Muni Market Monitor (formerly *Munifacts*)

tick A minimum upward or downward movement in the price of a security. *Related item(s)*: minus tick; plus tick.

Ticker Tape *See* Consolidated Tape.

TIGR *See* Treasury Investors Growth Receipt.

time deposit A sum of money left with a bank (or borrowed from a bank and left on deposit) that the depositing customer has agreed not to withdraw for a specified time period or without a specified amount of notice. *Related item(s)*: demand deposit.

time spread *See* horizontal spread.

time value The amount an investor pays for an option above its intrinsic value; it reflects the amount of time left until expiration. The amount is calculated by subtracting the intrinsic value from the premium paid. *Related item(s)*: intrinsic value.

timing risk The potential for an investor to incur a loss as a result of buying or selling a particular security at an unfavorable time.

T-note *See* Treasury note.

tombstone A printed advertisement that solicits indications of interest in a securities offering. The text is limited to basic information about the offering, such as the name of the issuer, type of security, names of the underwriters, and where a prospectus is available.

total capitalization The sum of a corporation's long-term debt, stock accounts, and capital in excess of par.

TRACE (Trade Reporting and Compliance Engine) FINRA-approved trade reporting system for corporate debt securities, asset-backed securities (ABS), Treasury securities, and collateralized mortgage obligations (CMOs) in the OTC secondary market.

trade confirmation A printed document that contains details of a transaction, including the settlement date and amount of money due from or owed to a customer. It must be sent to the customer on or before the settlement date.

trade date The date on which a securities transaction is executed.

Trade Reporting and Compliance Engine (TRACE) FINRA-approved trade reporting system for corporate bonds trading in the OTC secondary market.

trade-through Generally, any time an order is executed through the price limit of another order that would have represented a better execution. Trade-throughs are prohibited under the order protection rule of Regulation NMS.

trading authorization *See* full trading authorization; limited trading authorization.

trading halt A pause in the trading of a particular security on one or more exchanges, usually in anticipation of a news announcement or to correct an order imbalance. During a trading halt, open orders may be canceled and options may be exercised.

TRAN *See* tax and revenue anticipation note.

tranche One of the classes of securities that form an issue of collateralized mortgage obligations. Each tranche is characterized by its interest rate, average maturity, risk level, and sensitivity to mortgage prepayments. Neither the rate of return nor the maturity date of a CMO tranche is guaranteed. *Related item(s)*: collateralized mortgage obligation.

transfer agent A person or corporation responsible for recording the names and holdings of registered security owners, seeing that certificates are signed by the appropriate corporate officers, affixing the corporate seal, and delivering securities to the new owners.

transfer and hold in safekeeping A securities buy order settlement and delivery procedure whereby the securities bought are transferred to the customer's name but are held by the broker-dealer. *Related item(s)*: hold in street name; transfer and ship.

transfer and ship A securities buy order settlement and delivery procedure whereby the securities bought are transferred to the customer's name and sent to the customer. *Related item(s)*: hold in street name; transfer and hold in safekeeping.

Transportation Average *See* Dow Jones Transportation Average.

Treasury bill A marketable U.S. government debt security with a maturity of less than one year. Treasury bills are issued through a competitive bidding process at a discount from par; they have no fixed interest rate. *Syn.* T bill.

Treasury bond A marketable, fixed-interest U.S. government debt security with a maturity of more than 10 years. *Syn.* T bond.

Treasury Bond Receipt (TBR) One of several types of zero-coupon bonds issued by brokerage firms and collateralized by Treasury securities. *Related item(s):* Treasury receipt.

Treasury Investors Growth Receipt (TIGR) One of several types of zero-coupon bonds issued by brokerage firms and collateralized by Treasury securities. *Related item(s):* Treasury receipt.

Treasury note A marketable, fixed-interest U.S. government debt security with a maturity of between two and 10 years. *Syn.* T note.

Treasury receipt The generic term for a zero-coupon bond issued by a brokerage firm and collateralized by the Treasury securities a custodian holds in escrow for the investor.

treasury stock Equity securities that the issuing corporation has issued and repurchased from the public at the current market price. *Related item(s):* issued stock; outstanding stock.

trendline A tool used by technical analysts to trace a security's movement by connecting the reaction lows in an upward trend or the rally highs in a downward trend.

triangle On a technical analyst's trading activity chart, a pattern that shows a narrowing of the price range in which a security is trading. The left side of the triangle typically shows the widest range, and the right side narrows to a point. *Syn.* pennant. *Related item(s):* ascending triangle; descending triangle.

trough The end of a period of declining business activity throughout the economy, one of the four stages of the business cycle. *Related item(s):* business cycle.

true interest cost (TIC) A means of evaluating the competitive bids of prospective bond underwriting syndicates. Each syndicate provides a calculation of the coupon interest to be paid by the issuer over the life of the bond, taking into account the time value of money. *Related item(s):* net interest cost.

trust agreement *See* trust indenture.

trustee A person legally appointed to act on a beneficiary's behalf.

trust indenture A legal contract between a corporation and a trustee that represents its bondholders that details the terms of a debt issue. The terms include the rate of interest, maturity date, means of payment, and collateral. *Syn.* deed of trust; trust agreement.

Trust Indenture Act of 1939 The legislation requiring that certain publicly offered, nonexempt debt securities be registered under the Securities Act of 1933 and be issued under a trust indenture that protects the bondholders.

Trust in Securities Act *See* Securities Act of 1933.

Truth in Securities Act *See* Securities Act of 1933.

TSA *See* tax-sheltered annuity.

12b-1 asset-based fees An Investment Company Act of 1940 provision that allows a mutual fund to collect a fee for the promotion or sale of or another activity connected with the distribution of its shares. The fee must be reasonable (typically .25% to 1% of net assets managed).

two-dollar broker An exchange member that executes orders for other member firms when their floor brokers are especially busy. Two-dollar brokers charge a commission for their services; the amount of the commission is negotiated.

type A term that classifies an option as a call or a put. *Related item(s):* class; series.

U

UGMA *See* Uniform Gift to Minors Act.

UIT *See* unit investment trust.

uncovered *See* naked.

uncovered call writer *See* naked call writer.

uncovered put writer *See* naked put writer.

underlying securities The securities that are bought or sold when an option, right, or warrant is exercised.

underwriter An investment banker that works with an issuer to help bring a security to the market and sell it to the public.

underwriting The procedure by which investment bankers channel investment capital from investors to corporations and municipalities that are issuing securities.

underwriting compensation The amount paid to a broker-dealer firm for its involvement in offering and selling securities.

underwriting discount *See* underwriting spread.

underwriting manager The brokerage firm responsible for organizing a syndicate, preparing the issue, negotiating with the issuer and underwriters, and allocating stock to the selling group. *Syn.* manager of the syndicate; managing underwriter; syndicate manager. *Related item(s):* agreement among underwriters; syndicate.

underwriting spread The difference in price between the public offering price and the price an underwriter pays to the issuing corporation. The difference represents the profit available to the syndicate or selling group. *Syn.* underwriting discount; underwriting split.

underwriting syndicate *See* syndicate.

undivided account *See* Eastern account.

unearned income Income derived from investments and other sources not related to employment services. Examples of unearned income include interest from a savings account, bond interest, and dividends from stock. *Related item(s):* earned income; passive income; portfolio income.

Uniform Gift to Minors Act (UGMA) Legislation that permits a gift of money or securities to be given to a minor and held in a custodial account that an adult manages for the minor's benefit. Income and capital gains transferred to a minor's name are taxed at a lower rate. *Related item(s):* Uniform Transfers to Minors Act.

Uniform Securities Act (USA) Model legislation for securities industry regulation at the state level. Each state may adopt the legislation in its entirety or it may adapt it (within limits) to suit its needs. *Related item(s):* blue-sky laws; Series 63.

Uniform Transfers to Minors Act (UTMA) Legislation adopted in some states that permits a gift of money or securities to be given to a minor and held in a custodial account that an adult manages for the minor's benefit until the minor reaches a certain age (not necessarily the age of majority). *Related item(s):* Uniform Gifts to Minors Act.

unit A share in the ownership of a direct participation program that entitles the investor to an interest in the program's net income, net loss, and distributions.

unit investment trust (UIT) An investment company that sells redeemable shares in a professionally selected portfolio of securities. It is organized under a trust indenture, not a corporate charter. *Related item(s):* fixed unit investment trust; unit of beneficial interest.

unit of beneficial interest A redeemable share in a unit investment trust, representing ownership of an undivided interest in the underlying portfolio. *Syn.* share of beneficial interest. *Related item(s):* unit investment trust.

unit refund annuity An insurance contract in which the insurance company makes monthly payments to the annuitant over the annuitant's lifetime. If the annuitant dies before receiving an amount equal to the account's value, the money remaining in the account goes to the annuitant's named beneficiary.

unqualified legal opinion The statement of a bond counsel affirming the compliance of a new municipal bond issue with municipal statutes and tax regulations and expressing no reservations about its validity. *Related item(s):* legal opinion of counsel; qualified legal opinion.

unrealized gain The amount by which a security appreciates in value before it is sold. Until it is sold, the investor does not actually possess the sale proceeds. *Related item(s):* realized gain.

unsecured bond *See* debenture.

uptick *See* plus tick.

USA *See* Uniform Securities Act.

U.S. government and agency bond fund A mutual fund whose investment objective is to provide current income while preserving safety of capital through investing in securities backed by the U.S. Treasury or issued by a government agency.

Utilities Average *See* Dow Jones Utilities Average.

UTMA *See* Uniform Transfers to Minors Act.

V

Value Line An investment advisory service that rates hundreds of stocks as to safety, timeliness, and projected price performance. *Related item(s):* Value Line Composite Index.

Value Line Composite Index A market index composed of 1,700 exchange and over-the-counter stocks. *Related item(s):* index; Value Line.

variable annuity An insurance contract in which, at the end of the accumulation stage, the insurance company guarantees a minimum total payment to the annuitant. The performance of a separate account, generally invested in equity securities, determines the amount of this total payment. *Related item(s):* accumulation stage; annuity; fixed annuity; separate account.

variable-rate demand note *See* variable-rate municipal note.

variable-rate demand obligation Municipal bonds issued with variable, or floating, rates of interest. These securities offer interest payments tied to the movements of another specified interest rate.

variable-rate municipal note A short-term municipal debt security issued when either general interest rates are expected to change or the length of time before permanent funding is received is uncertain. *Syn.* variable-rate demand note.

vertical spread The purchase and sale of two options on the same underlying security and with the same expiration date but with different exercise prices. *Syn.* money spread; price spread. *Related item(s):* spread.

vesting (1) An ERISA guideline stipulating that an employee must be entitled to his entire retirement benefits within a certain period of time even if he no longer works for the employer. (2) The amount of time that an employee must work before retirement or before benefit plan contributions made by the employer become the employee's property without penalty. The IRS and the Employee Retirement Income Security Act of 1974 set minimum requirements for vesting in a qualified plan.

visible supply (1) The disclosure, published in *The Bond Buyer,* of the total dollar amount of municipal securities known to be coming to market within the next 30 days. (2) All supplies of goods and commodities that are readily deliverable.

VIX The volatility market index, known as the fear index, that measures investor expectation of implied volatility in the S&P 500.

volatility The magnitude and frequency of changes in the price of a security or commodity within a given time period.

volume of trading theory A technical analysis theory holding that the ratio of the number of shares traded to total outstanding shares indicates whether a market is strong or weak.

voluntary accumulation plan A mutual fund account into which the investor commits to depositing amounts on a regular basis in addition to the initial sum invested.

voting right A stockholder's right to vote for members of the board of directors and on matters of corporate policy—particularly the issuance of senior securities, stock splits and substantial changes in the corporation's business. A variation of this right is extended to variable annuity contract holders and mutual fund shareholders, who may vote on material policy issues.

W

warrant A security that gives the holder the right to purchase securities from the warrant issuer at a stipulated subscription price. Warrants are usually long-term instruments with expiration dates years in the future.

wash sale Selling a security at a loss for tax purposes and, within 30 days before or after, purchasing the same or a substantially identical security. The IRS disallows the claimed loss. *Related item(s):* bond swap.

Western account A securities underwriting in which the agreement among underwriters states that each syndicate member will be liable only for the sale of the portion of the issue allocated to it. *Syn.* divided account. *Related item(s):* Eastern account; syndicate.

when-, as-, and if-issued security *See* when issued security.

when-issued contract A trade agreement regarding a security that has been authorized but is not yet physically available for delivery. The seller agrees to make delivery as soon as the security is ready, and the contract includes provisions for marking the price to the market and for calculating accrued interest.

when-issued security (WI) A securities issue that has been authorized and is sold to investors before the certificates are ready for delivery. Typically, such securities include new issue municipal bonds, stock splits, and Treasury securities. *Syn.* when-, as-, and if-issued security.

WI *See* when-issued security.

wildcatting *See* exploratory drilling program.

Wilshire 5,000 Equity Index A value-weighted market indicator composed of 5,000 exchange-listed and over-the-counter common stocks. It is the broadest measure of the market. *Related item(s):* index.

wire room *See* order department.

workable indication The price at which a municipal securities dealer is willing to purchase securities from another municipal dealer. The price may be revised if market conditions change.

working capital A measure of a corporation's liquidity; that is, its ability to transfer assets into cash to meet current short-term obligations. It is calculated by subtracting total current liabilities from total current assets.

working capital ratio *See* current ratio.

working interest An operating interest in a mineral-bearing property entitling the holder to a share of income from production and carrying the obligation to bear a corresponding share of all production costs.

workout quote A qualified quotation whereby a broker-dealer estimates the price on a trade that will require special handling owing to its size or to market conditions. *Related item(s):* bona fide quote; firm quote; nominal quote; subject quote.

writer The seller of an option contract. An option writer takes on the obligation to buy or sell the underlying security if and when the option buyer exercises the option. *Syn.* seller.

writing a scale The process by which a syndicate establishes the yield for each maturity in a new serial bond issue in order to arrive at its competitive bid. *Related item(s):* scale.

Y

yield The rate of return on an investment, usually expressed as an annual percentage rate. *Related item(s):* current yield; dividend yield; nominal yield.

yield-based option A security representing the right to receive, in cash, the difference between the current yield of an underlying U.S. government security and the strike price of the option. A yield-based option is used to speculate on or hedge against the risk associated with fluctuating interest rates; its strike price represents the anticipated yield of the underlying debt security.

yield curve A graphic representation of the actual or projected yields of fixed-income securities in relation to their maturities. *Related item(s):* flat yield curve; inverted yield curve.

yield to call (YTC) The rate of return on a bond that accounts for the difference between the bond's acquisition cost and its proceeds, including interest income, calculated to the earliest date that the bond may be called by the issuing corporation. *Related item(s):* bond yield.

yield to maturity (YTM) The rate of return on a bond that accounts for the difference between the bond's acquisition cost and its maturity proceeds, including interest income. *Related item(s):* bond yield.

YTC *See* yield to call.

YTM *See* yield to maturity.

Z

zero-coupon bond A corporate or municipal debt security traded at a deep discount from face value. The bond pays no interest; rather, it may be redeemed at maturity for its full face value. It may be issued at a discount, or it may be stripped of its coupons and repackaged.

zero-minus tick A security transaction's execution price that is equal to the price of the last sale but lower than the last different price. *Related item(s):* minus tick; plus tick; zero-plus tick.

zero-plus tick A security transaction's execution price that is equal to the price of the last sale but higher than the last different price. *Related item(s):* minus tick; plus tick; zero-minus tick.

Index

Notes

Notes

Notes

Notes

Notes

Notes